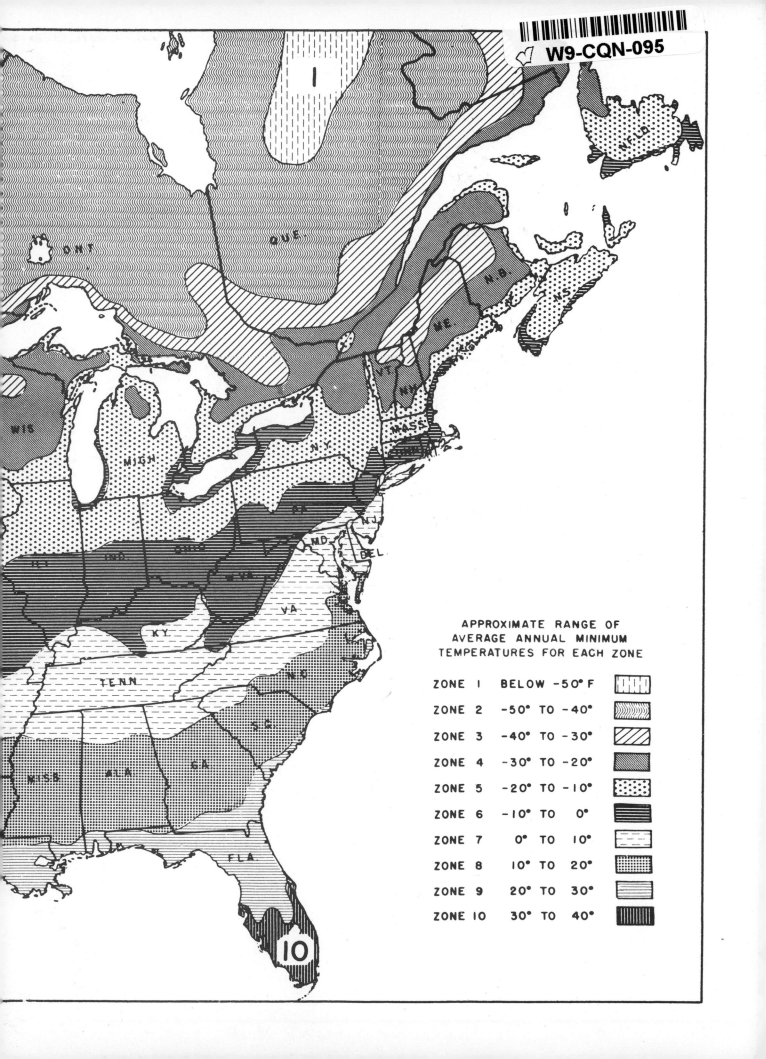

APPROXIMATE RANGE OF
AVERAGE ANNUAL MINIMUM
TEMPERATURES FOR EACH ZONE

ZONE 1   BELOW −50° F
ZONE 2   −50° TO −40°
ZONE 3   −40° TO −30°
ZONE 4   −30° TO −20°
ZONE 5   −20° TO −10°
ZONE 6   −10° TO   0°
ZONE 7   0° TO 10°
ZONE 8   10° TO 20°
ZONE 9   20° TO 30°
ZONE 10   30° TO 40°

Flowering Shrubs

Welcome! This is my front door with *Cornus kousa*, the Japanese dogwood, in full bloom beside it.

Flowering Shrubs

Isabel Zucker

Director, National Garden Bureau

Black and white photographs by MYRON ZUCKER
Color photographs by the author

D. Van Nostrand Company, Inc.

Princeton, New Jersey   Toronto   New York   London

D. VAN NOSTRAND COMPANY, INC.
120 Alexander St., Princeton, New Jersey (*Principal office*)
24 West 40 Street, New York 18, New York

D. VAN NOSTRAND COMPANY, LTD.
358, Kensington High Street, London, W.14, England

D. VAN NOSTRAND COMPANY (Canada), LTD.
25 Hollinger Road, Toronto 16, Canada

Published simultaneously in Canada by
D. VAN NOSTRAND COMPANY (Canada), LTD.

Library of Congress Catalog Card No. 66-16912

For 2 Zuckers, 6 Clarks, and 1 Mason

ABOUT THE BOOK

Somehow, despite early acquaintance with the strawberry bush, snowball, weigela, and lilacs in the garden of my childhood; courses in woody plants in college; and planning the plantings of countless shrubs in gardens I have designed, I never really appreciated shrubs until the spring our daughter was nearly three and our son was born.

In addition to caring for husband, household, and children, I was in the midst of redesigning and replanting the grounds around six school buildings. That season all our perennial borders went untended, the annuals never were planted and only the shrubs carried on, giving their usual bloom without any attention whatsoever.

Appreciation of shrubs grew as they helped me over various hurdles. For instance, there was the time when the PTA called for 25 corsages to be ready within three hours. Clearly visible from the telephone, through a window across the room, were two large Father Hugo's roses and two Chinese lilacs, all in full bloom. Even as I said I would make the corsages, I knew where the flowers for them would come from.

When the neighborhood in which we lived gradually became commercial, and we were looking elsewhere for a home, I wanted more land. My husband protested that I didn't have time to take care of the half-acre garden I already possessed. But, I told him, the next garden would depend largely on shrubs and flowering trees which wouldn't require the same care as perennials. Nor would *I* have to give that care—others could do it since shrubs are larger than perennials and more readily seen. Furthermore, I was going to buy and grow all the shrubs that could be grown in our area and put together a picture book of shrubs.

Now, almost fourteen years since this six-acre garden was started, the shorter and fewer perennial borders still go unweeded some years, but the garden is not dependent on them for design, color or bloom. Shrubs provide all these things.

In pursuit of knowledge about shrubs I have walked the rows of hundreds of nurseries in the United States, Canada and abroad, visited almost all of the major botanical gardens in the world, and grown hundreds of the shrubs in the garden.

Purpose

There are two reasons for writing this book. The first is to give the interested gardener a profusely illustrated book of shrubs available for purchase that will cut his upkeep while beautifying his garden and providing flowers galore for use in the house.

The second is to furnish nurserymen, landscape architects and garden center operators with the book they have told me they need and want—one which pictures hundreds of shrubs so that they can show their customers and clients what the flowers and fruits look like, which provides up-to-date information on numerous aspects of gardening with shrubs and which uses currently correct botanical names.

If I have accomplished both of these objectives, to interest the home gardener and assist the professional, then the work of assembling the book will have been worth while.

Scope

Since it is obvious that all of the shrubs hardy in the United States and Canada cannot be grown in a single garden, so that they can be photographed as they flower and fruit, I decided to include in this book only shrubs and small trees hardy in Zones 6 through 1 of the United States Department of Agriculture's "Plant Hardiness Zone Map", Miscellaneous Publication #814, copies of which are available for 15 cents from the Government Printing Office, Washington, D. C. 20025.

This map was prepared by a Commission of the American Horticultural Council (now merged with the American Horticultural Society under the latter name) chairmanned by Dr. Henry Skinner, director of the National Arboretum.

The shrubs and small trees included in this book are those readily available for purchase since they are listed in catalogs or lists of nurserymen in either the United States or Canada, most of them located in the plant hardiness zones given above. The nurserymens' associations in both countries have cooperated by furnishing me lists of their members. I circularized them, and from the catalogs of those who replied, compiled the lists of shrubs and small trees included in this book—and also the sources. Sufficient description is given of each plant in Chapters 14 and 15 so that you can choose those that fulfill your requirements.

Nomenclature

Quite early in the work of assembling this book I realized that, as far as nomenclature was concerned, the nursery catalogs and lists left much to be desired. If I used the names as given in them, I would often have to list the same plant under several to many variations of the same botanical name (many retail and most wholesale nursery catalogs list plants under their botanical names). So I had to decide whether to use what I knew to be sometimes botanically invalid and other times incorrect names or straighten out the nursery catalogs, giving their incorrect names as synonyms for the currently correct botanical names. Though the latter course meant checking and rechecking botanical names in one reference after another, this is the course I chose to follow.

Because there is no one up-to-date botanical authority, the following authorities have been checked:

Hortus II by Liberty Hyde Bailey and Ethel Zoe Bailey (1941)
The Standard Cyclopedia of Horticulture by Liberty Hyde Bailey (1935)
Manual of Cultivated Plants by Liberty Hyde Bailey (1949)
Manuscript for "Hortus III", being compiled by the staff of the Bailey Hortorium, Cornell University, Ithaca, N. Y.
Manual of Cultivated Trees and Shrubs Hardy in North America, Second Edition, by Alfred Rehder (1940)
Bibliography of Cultivated Trees and Shrubs by Alfred Rehder (1949)
Gray's Manual of Botany, 8th edition, largely rewritten and expanded by Merritt Lyndon Fernald (1950)

Trees and Shrubs of the Upper Midwest by Carl O. Rosendahl (1955)

A Checklist of Woody Ornamental Plants of California by Mildred E. Mathias and Elizabeth McClintock (California Agricultural Experiment Station Extension Service Manual #32) (April, 1963)

An article titled "Are Our Labels Right or Wrong?" by Floyd Swink, Vol. CXIX, No. 8, *American Nurseryman* (April 15, 1964)

I also have consulted the following monographs or similar references:

"Cultivars in the Genus Chaenomeles" by Claude Weber, Vol. 23, number 3 of *Arnoldia,* published by the Arnold Arboretum, Jamaica Plain, Mass. (April 5, 1963)

"Registration Lists of Cultivar Names in Cornus L." by Richard A. Howard, Vol. 21, Number 2 of *Arnoldia* (January 27, 1961)

"Registration Lists of Cultivar Names in the Genus Pieris D. Don" by Burdette L. Wagenknecht, Vol. 21, Number 8 of *Arnoldia* (April 28, 1961)

Various other articles in issues of *Arnoldia*

"Maples Cultivated in the United States and Canada" by Brian O. Mulligan (August, 1958)

After Mr. Swink's article appeared in the *American Nurseryman,* I thought that he might be the perfect taxonomist to ask to make a final check of the botanical names for the book for he had used the catalogs of 50 nurseries in compiling the names in the article and only a taxonomist accustomed to nursery catalogs could render me real assistance. In the course of this final check he has used these additional publications:

Nederlandse Dendrologie by B. K. Boom, Wageningen, Holland (1959)

Handbuch der Laubegeholze by Gerd Krussmann of the Botanic Garden at Dortmund, Germany (1960)

Various articles in the *Journal of the Arnold Arboretum* including a monograph of the genus Philadelphus by Dr. Shiu-Ying Hu which appeared in the issues of October 1954, January 1955 and January 1956

The *Kew Bulletin* of the Royal Botanic Gardens, Kew in England

A monograph by H. L. J. Rhodes of the genus Potentilla in *Baileya,* publication of the Bailey Hortorium, Ithaca, N. Y.

The *Journal of the Royal Horticultural Society,* Vincent Square, London, S. W. 1, England

In reviewing all of these botanical references we have found that occasionally botanists disagree regarding the correct name of a particular shrub. In these cases Mr. Swink has given me "the score" of botanists for and against and I have decided which botanist or botanists to follow.

Anyone wishing to know why we have used a particular name in preference to another is invited to write to Mr. Floyd Swink, taxonomist, Morton Arboretum, Lisle, Illinois. He volunteered to explain our choices and decisions.

Following the advice of Dr. George H. M. Lawrence, director of the Hunt Botanical Library, Carnegie Institute of Technology, Pittsburgh, Pa. and Dr. Harold W. Rickett, recently retired from the New York Botanical Garden, Bronx, New York City, I have dropped capitalization of species names but retained the spellings of names which end in ii.

Descriptions of Shrubs

Despite my insistence on the correct botanical names for the trees and shrubs in this book, the descriptions are not given in botanical terminology, but in the simplest possible English. Thus, an "inflorescence" becomes either a cluster or a spike, depending on its form, and a leaf is not "pubescent," it is hairy. This book, obviously, is not written for botanists. I happen to be a horticulturist and I write for gardeners.

Color

The color authority for this book is the Nickerson Color Fan, the brain child of Miss Dorothy Nickerson of the United States Department of Agriculture. The fan is the outcome of the work of a Commission of the American Horticultural Council (now merged with the American Horticultural Society) headed by R. Milton Carleton, research director of Vaughan Seed Co. It is obtainable from the American Horticultural Society, 1600 Bladensburg Road, N. E., Washington, D. C.

The fan, which is pictured on page 145 is published by the Munsell Color Co., Inc. of Baltimore, Maryland. It measures a mere 7¾ by 1¾ inches so is easily handled in the garden. It consists of 40 leaves, each of which "displays samples of a single hue, ranging from dark samples at the bottom to light samples at the top." All that is necessary for a gardener to do is hold the fan to a flower and move the fan until the matching sample is reached. Sometimes a flower color does not precisely match any sample on the fan. It may lie between two of the hues, in which case it may be described by giving the numbers of both. In a few cases there is no sample on the fan that even nearly matches the flower color. In this case the color may be given as "nearest to" and then the number of the sample. This is what I have done in trying to give you accurate descriptions of numerous flower and some foliage colors in this book.

Since a detailed explanation of the fan is included with it, none is attempted here.

It is amazing, as one compares the colors of flowers with those on the fan (there are 262 color samples on it), how many flower colors precisely match one of the samples and also how many are not exactly what we think they are or what we call them. Most people refer to the flower color of a double-flowering almond as "pink." The color fan describes it as "deep purplish pink" and it matches color sample 7.5 RP 6/12 of the fan.

You will find the fan extremely useful if you are interested in flower colors. One reason it was selected as the authority for this book is that it is inexpensive, so that many gardeners can afford a copy.

Pictures

While the hundreds of pictures of shrubs have been taken primarily for identification, an attempt has been made to make them attractive at the same time. Those of entire branches are staged to show not only leaves; flowers, twigs, and fruits, but also their abundance, their relative size and positions.

Most of the pictures have been taken from the direction from which one would ordinarily see the branch on a growing shrub. However, if this position hides some important feature or detail, then the branch has been arranged in a position to reveal the desired point. Sometimes an additional picture has been added to show the gardener what he misses if he does not look "behind the scenes."

Great pains have been taken to show the relative color of the flowers and gradations of green of the leaves. When the leaves look light green in the photograph you can expect the leaves of the plants also to be light shades of that color.

The lighting was chosen and arranged to aid these tonal effects; was sometimes directed to show important details (such as the "cork" of cork-barked euonymus). Hence the lighting will not always seem as it does out-doors because it was not; this work could be done only under "studio" (our music room) conditions.

The closeups which accompany many pictures of whole branches were taken to show either beauty or interesting detail but also, in many cases, may be used for identification. The "aftermaths" of the flowers pictured, which sometimes remain on the plant all winter, also may be used for identification, especially for the gardener who buys a new house during the season of no bloom.

The black and white pictures in Chapters 14 and 15 were taken almost entirely by my husband, Myron Zucker, an electrical engineer by profession, using an Ilex #3 Universal view camera or, on rare occasions a Speed Graphic. The black and white pictures in the other chapters are mine, using sometimes a 4″ x 5″ Speed Graphic but more often a Rolleiflex. The frontis-piece is of our front door, photographed by my husband. The color pictures in Chapter 14 are my work and I have used one or the other of my two Argus C-44's or, occasionally, an old Eastman Bantam special. They have been supplemented by 5 subjects photographed by our daughter, Judith Zucker Clark.

We have tried to photograph each shrub when the plant was at its height of bloom. My job has been to walk our half-mile of shrub borders early each evening during the blooming season to select and cut specimen branches of shrubs not previously photographed (unless the specimens were better than previous ones, in which case we rephotographed). After arranging the branch or branches and making certain that my husband's "picture" on the ground glass showed the features you would be interested in seeing, I retired to allow him to take the picture, then reappeared to arrange the next "setup." This has gone on, sometimes for months, every night in the week and until the wee, small hours. Since my husband manages his business dur-ing the daytime hours and I direct the National Garden Bureau, all pho-tography has been "extra-curricular," and has required a period of five years.

The other aspects of the book are explained in the chapters to which they apply.

Thank you

Professor Clarence Lewis, professor in horticulture, Michigan State University and Mr. Arthur R. Buckley, horticulturist, Ornamental Plant Section, Central Experimental Farm, Canada Department of Agriculture, for reading and commenting upon the manuscript of this book.

Mr. Lewis Lipp, horticulturist at the Holden Arboretum and formerly propagator at the Arnold Arboretum for reading Chapter 13, "Other Ways of Acquiring Shrubs: Propagation." David W. Clark, my son-in-law, for reading the same chapter from your viewpoint of an interested amateur.

Messrs. W. H. Wheeler, Assistant Director, Plant Quarantine Division, Agricultural Research Service, United States Department of Agriculture and H. G. Carmody, Regulations Enforcement Officer, Plant Protection Division, Production and Marketing Branch, Canada Department of Agriculture, for reading Chapter 12, "How to Import Shrubs," to make certain it was correct.

Messrs. G. H. Large, Surveyor for H. Beardmore, collector of Customs and Excise, National Revenue, Canada and L. P. Johnson, Assistant Deputy Commissioner, Entry and Value, Bureau of Customs, United States Treasury Department, for checking parts of the same chapter, which discuss customs regulations of the two countries.

Dr. Cynthia Westcott, *The Plant Doctor*, for reading and commenting upon the original version of Chapter 9, "Shrub Troubles." You are not, of course, in any way responsible for the present version or my attitude towards shrub pests.

Mr. Ray Brush, secretary of the American Association of Nurserymen, for reading Chapters 10 and 11, "How to Buy Plants" and "Where to Buy Plants" and for furnishing me with up-to-date copies of several of the association's publications.

Dr. L. C. Snyder and Mr. Albert G. Johnson, Department of Horticulture, University of Minnesota, for checking the list of shrubs in this book and indicating those hardy at the Minnesota Landscape Arboretum in plant hardiness Zone 4. Mr. Buckley for supplying me with copies of your "Arboretum Notes" which provided a second list of shrubs known to be hardy in Zone 4.

Dr. Harold Moore, director, and others on the staff of the Bailey Hortorium for help in determining correct nomenclature of plants in this book. Mr. Floyd Swink, taxonomist, Morton Arboretum, for many hours spent in the final checking of botanical names. Dr. George H. M. Lawrence, director, Hunt Botanical Library, and Dr. Harold W. Rickett, senior botanist, New

York Botanical Garden, for advice on certain treatments of botanical nomenclature.

Mr. H. L. R. Rhodes, formerly with the Canada Department of Agriculture, for information about botanical names of Potentillas not included in your monograph in "Baileya." Dr. John Fogg, director, Morris Arboretum, for advice on nomenclature of Magnolias. Dr. Elizabeth McClintock, Associate Curator in Botany, California Academy of Sciences, for a frank statement of your policy of not disturbing long-established generic names.

Dr. Richard P. White, former executive vice-president of the American Association of Nurserymen and Mr. Henry Kohankie, former owner of one of the finest nurseries in the United States, for your good advice when this book was just an idea.

Dr. R. Milton Carleton, compiler of "Index to Common Names of Herbaceous Plants," for lending me your card file of common names of woody plants for inclusion in this book.

Carroll Welch and Charlene and Jack Ferris for your prompt processing of shrub pictures for three years and two years respectively and for realizing that many a shrub remains in bloom for such a short time that a photographer must know immediately whether his pictures have turned out well. Carroll Welch and James McGarrigle for the final printing of the pictures and Jim for taking the snapshot of me which adorns (?) the jacket. This was "snapped" after we had worked all morning photographing tulips and needs only three or four pencils sticking from my hair to be a perfect likeness.

Nurserymen of many countries, particularly the United States, Canada and Great Britain, all the hundreds of you that I have visited, for escorting me around your nurseries and answering my questions. Most particularly the nurserymen who supplied the catalogs for the "Buyer's Guide Chart" and Mr. John Light of Richland, Michigan, for allowing the Zuckers to roam your nursery and cut specimen branches at will.

My family. How is it possible to thank you adequately, Myron, for your uncounted hours behind the camera and your unfailing interest in the manuscript of this book? Or you, Judy, for all the trips here and the many hours you spent assembling the first version of the "Buyer's Guide Chart" as well as the idea for and the execution of the original "Bloom Time Chart"? Or Jack for the innumerable morning and night drop offs to and pick ups from the processors of our photographs and for helping Judy?

This is, I think, the best way to show my appreciation to all the people who have helped me.

Gratefully yours,
ISABEL ZUCKER

CONTENTS

List of Illustrations

COLOR ILLUSTRATIONS
Between Pages 148 and 149

BLACK AND WHITE PHOTOGRAPHS

LINE DRAWINGS

PART I: USING SHRUBS

Chapter 1

SHRUBS ARE FOR EVERY GARDEN

Plant for plant, dollar for dollar, and backache for backache, you'll get more satisfaction from flowering shrubs than you will from any other class of plants you can grow in your garden.

That's a broad statement, but it's true.

A shrub is planted but once, unless you're the sort of person who is perpetually moving plants. It will last a lifetime or more in that one place, if carefully planted then given reasonable care. There are two shrubs in the garden at Mt. Vernon which verbal tradition says were given to George Washington by Lafayette during his 1784 visit. One is a calycanthus or strawberry shrub, the other an oak-leaved hydrangea. Think how many human lifetimes these two shrubs have survived!

Shrubs are easy to grow. Most of them require no constant care—just good planting—to thrive and produce a wealth of bloom. Most shrubs need no fertilization, very little pruning, little or no spraying for pest control. Thus your upkeep of a garden of shrubs is little compared with a garden composed of any other type of plants.

Shrubs really produce what you want most, if you're an average gardener—they produce flowers by the armful. Even the shrubs that can be accommodated in a small back-yard garden will give the household more blooms than it can use. Cutting sprays of bloom is an easy way of pruning shrubs, while at the same time making use of the prunings for indoor decoration.

In addition to these advantages, shrubs have another: they are available in a wide, wide variety of heights, shapes, foliage colors, foliage textures and forms, flower colors, flower forms, fruit shapes and colors. There is at least one shrub in bloom practically every month of the year; during the five months of heavy shrub bloom there are so many in flower that one garden cannot possibly accommodate them all.

Thus, regardless of where you live, the garden color scheme you decide upon, the height or shape or anything else you desire, you'll find that there's a shrub available which will precisely fill your need and desire. In fact, there probably will be several shrubs to fill the bill, so that you'll have a choice.

Shrubs have something else to give a garden. They give it a lightness that no evergreen, not even a graceful hemlock, can give it. If you ever have first walked through a garden solely of evergreens and then into one which features shrubs, you know precisely what I mean. They give a garden variety in form, height and foliage texture, such as no other type of plants give. If you plan well, shrubs also will give your garden a constantly renewed, constantly changing focus of attention, which shifts from place to place according to the season of the year—thus adding a kind of interest much harder to obtain from other categories of plants.

Shrubs are indeed for every garden—and every garden needs at least a few of them.

1

Chapter 2

GETTING ACQUAINTED WITH SHRUBS

What are these woody plants that we call shrubs? And how can one distinguish them from the other woody plants we call trees? There are several definitions and comparisons that will help.

The first is a comparison of the form in which trees and shrubs grow. A tree is a plant that grows with one stem (trunk) from the ground. A shrub, on the other hand, usually grows with several to many stems emerging from the earth.

These definitions, however, are not always accurate because a tree that has been cut back or injured often grows again with several stems whereas a weak shrub or one especially trained may have only one stem. Furthermore, there are times when a normal tree will sprout more than one stem or trunk and a normal shrub will grow sparsely with but a single stem. Thus, these definitions and this comparison are applicable only in a broad sense.

A second way of distinguishing a shrub from a tree is by its new growth. This is usually at the tips of existing branches if the plant is a tree, while a shrub also may grow by sending up new shoots or stems from the ground.

Even if both of these definitions of a shrub are kept in mind when viewing a woody plant, it still is not always easy to say "this is a shrub" or "this is a tree" and that is why botanical descriptions often read "shrub or small tree." This way of describing a plant at least allows for normal variations in the growth of the plant.

For the purposes of this book, plants growing usually with several stems will be considered shrubs and those normally achieving only one main stem or trunk will be considered trees.

Getting to Know Them

The shrub most people know best is the lilac. It is such a long-lived shrub that many still exist next to old foundations where once houses stood. While the houses are long since gone, the lilacs still thrive.

To get acquainted with lilacs (if you aren't already) and with other shrubs, take a walk around any residential neighborhood near you that has older houses and gardens. The better the neighborhood, the more shrubs and the more different kinds of shrubs you are apt to see. For, as I already said, a garden is a mighty poor one if it doesn't include at least some shrubs.

April, May, and June are the months of "big bloom" for shrubs, so take your walk, if possible, during these months. You'll see some of the owners of the gardens out working in them. Ask them the names of the shrubs you see in their gardens. Chances are very good that they'll know.

Never think that you are bothering these people or taking up their time unduly. Every good gardener delights in sharing his garden and whatever knowledge he has of plants and gardening.

Thus, in your own neighborhood or one nearby, you can learn about the shrubs that grow well there. However, this walk around a few blocks serves merely to whet your appetite for shrubs and their flowers. You will find that, regardless of the state in which you live, there are other neighborhoods and more distant places where many more shrubs will show off for your edification. The colleges in your state have beautifully planted campuses, where shrubs are used in great quantity and usually in great variety. There may be a botanical garden or arboretum or two for you to visit. Or perhaps finely landscaped gardens are open to you when garden tours or pilgrimages take place in your town.

In addition to these, the commercial nurseries have rows of shrubs. There are nurseries in every state—in every province.

Shrubs used with evergreen in an imposing landscape—the rock garden in Hamilton, Ontario. Acer palmatum 'Dissectum' in foreground.

Specimen of Viburnum carlcephalum with Viburnum opulus 'Nanum' on lower right. Photographed in the rock garden, Hamilton, Ontario.

Caragana pygmaea trained to "tree" form—photographed outside the Oakes gardens, Niagara Falls, Ontario.

Pleasing planting of shrubs and trees at Planting Fields, Oyster Bay, Long Island, New York—taken to show bare tree trunk used as focal point of planting.

Visiting the neighbors, the university campus, the botanic garden, the arboretum, may be done during weekends, as part of your family's recreation program. Visiting local flower and garden

3

shows adds to the places and things you can include in this program. Garden pilgrimages or planned visits usually include weekends, since more people can attend then. But visiting nurseries is another thing.

Nursery Visits

If you know exactly what you want to buy and are going to the nursery in order to buy it, consider yourself welcome at any time. If, however, you are visiting a nursery in order to learn about shrubs, in order to ask questions of the nurseryman, then confine your visiting days to Monday and Tuesday, the slowest days of the week for the nurseryman, therefore those on which he has the most time to spend with you.

There is no possible substitute for seeing shrubs if you wish to become better acquainted with them in order to choose those you like best to grow in your garden. However, there are people who cannot possibly see shrubs in the ways suggested, and there are many others who need further guidance, including a memory jogger to help them remember the shrubs they have seen, to "interpret" their notes from places visited. That's where this book becomes useful.

Pictures

In Chapter 14 you will find not only verbal descriptions of the shrubs in commerce but also pictures of their flowers, fruits, and any other characteristic of interest. My husband, who is the chief photographer, and I feel that the berry, fruit or whatever other "aftermath" of the bloom there happens to be is almost as important as the flower, for it gives the shrub continued interest even into winter. Furthermore, it helps identify the shrub in winter; particularly important to the gardener who has bought property at that time of the year. Therefore, we have pictured both flower and "aftermath" where it seemed desirable.

Shrub Listings

In getting acquainted with shrubs, sooner or later, in this case sooner, you are going to meet botanical names. In this book, in Chapter 14, the shrubs are listed alphabetically according to their botanical names because these are their only valid names. These botanical names are in the index and there also you'll find the various common names of the same shrub, so if you know only a common name, look it up in the index and it will lead you to the botanical name, the description of the shrub and, usually, a picture or two.

Some people will not like the listing of shrubs in this way because the botanical name happens to be either Latin or Latinized. They will feel that the botanical names are too hard to pronounce or to remember, that it is too much "bother" to use them, or that people who use them are all snobs. Actually, the person using a botanical name is not snobbish but sensible, for this is the only name known all over the world for that particular plant and the only one by which it surely can be bought. It doesn't make much difference whether or not you pronounce botanical names correctly, just so you can spell the one belonging to the plant you want. The nurseryman will recognize it, and maybe he doesn't know the correct pronunciation either.

As to its being a "bother" to learn botanical names or too hard to do so, let me ask you a question. Do you have a hobby? If so, didn't you have to learn a new terminology or "language" in order to talk to others about that hobby? For instance, in stamp collecting the word "mint" means "unused." To the general public it doesn't mean that at all.

Another example of specialized language: the first time we exhibited an Irish setter at a dog show, I discovered, much to my astonishment, that "bitch" was a respectable word in dog show circles!

And so it is with every new hobby. There's a new language to learn. So why balk at learning a little botanical Latin, since this happens to be the language of shrubs and shrub identification?

Certainly some of the words are long and are tongue twisters. But what did you do when you were in about the 4th grade and one of your classmates told you, with great glee, that the longest word in the English language is antidisestablishmentarianism? Did you avoid this word? Of course not. You learned it immediately, so you could show it off to a less informed classmate.

This doesn't mean that everyone who learns the Latin names of plants is doing so to show them off to people not in the know (though some of them, being only human, certainly learn a few names for this very reason). Most people learn a Latin name so they can buy the precise plant they have in mind and not have another plant foisted upon them.

Here are two true stories of what happens when you want to buy a specific shrub but don't know (or won't learn) the botanical name.

The first concerns a reader who wrote me to ask the name of a small shrub which had beautiful purple berries in early autumn. It seemed to her that it would fit exactly a certain corner in her small yard. This shrub, I told her, is callicarpa, or beauty berry, and there are several species of this genus available, all of them effective at that time of year. I warned her to take the name of the shrub with her to the nursery when she went to buy it, since callicarpas are not found in every sales lot.

She must have failed to do this. Result: next autumn I got another letter from her complaining that the shrub she had purchased, which had borne beautiful pink flowers in great masses in May, didn't bear a single berry that fall!

This doesn't seem like much of a story, does it? But to me it meant that she had been sold beauty bush rather than beauty berry and, instead of a small shrub with insignificant flowers but handsome purple berries in fall, she'd bought a shrub that will grow 12 feet high and stretch 12 feet across, which has abundant and lovely pink flowers in May, bears no berries at all, but has attractive greyish seed heads after the flowers fade. In her small garden, the ultimate size of that beauty bush, lovely as it is, will be a problem!

The other story concerns my aunt. She told me, when her garden was quite new, that she wanted to buy an old-fashioned fragrant mock orange. I wrote down its Latin name for her—*Philadelphus coronarius*. She scoffed at the thought of a Latin name.

So, a couple of years later, she told me about her mock orange, which had intensely fragrant blooms, but double, not single like the ones she wanted. She had, quite evidently, been sold *Philadelphus virginalis*, instead of *Philadelphus coronarius*. To make a long story short, she finally owned eight mock oranges, some with fragrant blooms, some not, and not one of them was the old-fashioned species she wanted! While she steadily refused to "bother with the Latin name," she kept bemoaning the lack of that old-fashioned mock orange every time we met!

So, as you see, it doesn't pay not to know botanical names. But, on the other hand, does it pay to know them? It certainly does, not only on the nursery sales lot, but also if and when you travel. Here's one short true story to illustrate:

My husband and I were at the Taj Mahal, not in the beautiful park around the building, which every tourist sees, but in the "working" garden where the plants for the park are grown. Many were in pots set on the concrete paths which border the garden. Some I knew on sight. Others I wasn't certain I knew. About one of these I said to my husband (who certainly wouldn't know the answer, but was the only person around to address, since the guide obviously was bored to tears with me), "I wonder if that's ——?" giving the botanical name I thought might belong to the plant in question.

You could have knocked me down with half a feather when, from behind me, came the botanical name. The man who uttered it was certainly the most ragged looking specimen of East Indian I ever have seen. He was one of the gardeners, knew the botanical name of every plant in the garden, and we spent a happy half hour "Latin naming" each other to my edification. I didn't speak his language, nor he mine, but in the universal language of botany we were both at home.

Botanical Names

After all those stories, perhaps a short explanation of botanical names is in order. The first thing to keep in mind about them is that they are given to plants, shrubs included, by taxonomic botanists who are seeking to *classify* plants, not by horticulturists who want only to *describe* plants so that it is possible to tell one from the other.

The second fact you need to know about botanical names is that they are not necessarily static. Botanists disagree about some of them, particularly, at the moment, about varieties and cultivars (see below) and occasionally change one or more names. This usually is because, in searching botanical records, they find that a plant has been given another name previously (and, according to the International Code of Botanical Nomenclature, a plant must bear the *first* name assigned to it) but sometimes for another reason. In making these changes in botanical names, botanists quite generally ignore the effects on the nursery business or on gardeners.

Despite the fact that botanists give the names to provide a means of reference, a botanical name, in many cases, *does* describe a plant, at least to some extent. And, whether you like botanical names or not, they just happen to be the only ones that really identify a plant to a horticulturist as well as to a botanist.

Most plants have botanical names consisting of two words. The first is the genus or generic name; the second the species or specific name. Both the genus and the species are groups of plants; the genus usually the larger of the two.

Although two taxonomic botanists discussing in my presence the definition of a species agreed that "a species is what a good botanist thinks a species is," I am going to step in where angels fear to tread and define a species. It is a unit or group of individual plants which bear a close resemblance to one another—so much so that this particular group will not be mistaken for another group combined with it in the same genus. The individuals in this group called a species will vary only slightly from one another, perhaps in such relatively minor details as precise shape of leaf, flower color or something similar.

When several species resemble each other to a fair degree, so that some physical feature, such as a leaf or flower form, is the same as that in other species, and these species may be considered to have some common ancestry, they are grouped into a genus. Thus, as previously stated, the genus is a group of plants and the species also is a group of plants, but the plants in a species more closely resemble one another than those in a genus.

The minor details indicated two paragraphs above, where they exist, are cared for by a third name—the varietal name. This makes clear the further way in which a particular plant differs from others in the same species. When a variety has been developed in cultivation, rather than found in the wild, it is called a "cultivar," a coined word. Cultivars are not natural hybrids such as occur in the wild but most are hybrids often deliberately perpetuated. The specific names of the parents must be omitted in designating hybrid cultivars because the cultivar name cannot favor either parent. Cultivars which are seedlings or bud sports may have both generic and specific names before the cultivar name to indicate their parentage.

Cultivar names usually are in English rather than Latin, and are set off by single quotation marks. The cultivar names that are in Latin usually are names which have been in existence longer; often names of species or varieties now found by botanists to be cultivars instead.

This may sound complicated, so let's try one botanical name to see how the nomenclature system works. *Cercis* (pronounced Ser-siss in English, though in Latin it would be Ker-kiss), is the botanical name for redbud, a small tree or large shrub that blooms in early spring. One species is called *canadensis* because it was found growing in an area which was at that time part of Canada; another is *chinensis*, for an equally obvious reason. The two species differ in habit of growth, in their ability to stand winter cold, and slightly in flower color—reasons why they are separate species.

Cercis canadensis has red-violet flowers. To distinguish the wild, white-flowered form from this species, a varietal name has been added and the white-flowered form is called *Cercis canadensis alba, alba* being the Latin word for white.

There also are several cultivars or horticultural varieties of *Cercis canadensis*, one of which is named 'Withers' Pink Charm', Withers being the name of the man who found it. It also has flowers in the red-violet range, like the species *canadensis*, but a different shade, much more pinkish-violet than red-violet. The proper name of this plant is *Cercis canadensis* 'Withers' Pink Charm'. The cultivar name, in this case, indicates the difference in flower color, just as does the varietal name *alba*.

In the example above, the cultivar 'Withers' Pink Charm' was not a hybrid and had only one parent, the species *Cercis canadensis*. When a cultivated variety (cultivar) *is* a hybrid and thus has *two* parents, the rules of nomenclature require that neither parent be favored. This means that the specific name of neither can precede the cultivar designation. Thus, for these hybrid cultivars there is a different designation. The generic or genus name is given first, followed by the cultivar name. *Philadelphus* 'Enchantment' is an example of such a listing.

What Latin Names Can Tell You

The following exposition of botanical (Latin) names is intended to bring a little interest, meaning and fun to this usually dull subject. These names, chosen for each plant, usually at the discretion of the discoverer, can be either useful in describing or identifying the plant or may be merely interesting.

The "interesting" names are those that indicate the place of origin of the shrub (e.g. americana, amurensis, koreana, orientalis, persica, virginicus) or that are the name of a person (baileyi, fortunei, kolkwitzia, schlippenbachii, wilsonii).

Both baffling and helpful are the names that describe something about the plant, distinguishing it from others in the same group. Many of these descriptive terms are used over and over again in different plant genera, so once you know what they mean your knowledge carries over. To understand these terms, it helps to know what features they are describing. A few examples are given here:

Some names apply to the general shape of the plant: arborescens—tree-like; compactus—compact-growing; nanus—dwarf.

Others tell about the plant's habitat: alpinus—growing in the mountains; maritimus—a seashore plant; and some about the season of bloom: praecox—very early; autumnale—autumnal.

When "flora" or some modification of this word is a part of the botanical name, you can expect some information about the flowers. This may be about quantity or size of bloom: floribunda—free-blooming; grandiflora—large-flowered; or form of flower cluster: paniculata—a "panicle" type of cluster, or racemosa—flowers formed in a "raceme," simplex—single, plenoflora or floreplena—double. Or it may tell about the flower color: alba—white, aureus—golden, lutea—yellow, rosea—pink, rubra—red, purpureus—purple, or perhaps about the odor: fragrans—pleasant smell, foetida—fetid.

Another important category of descriptive words is those including some form of the words "folia" or "phyllum" meaning "leaf." For instance, when each leaf grows from the branch at a different level from another leaf, this is "alternifolia." A shrub with small leaves may be called "microphyllum," which is the word meaning small-leaved.

The shape of the leaf may be indicated by names such as "acerifolia"—like a maple (the genus *Acer*) or "trifoliata"—with three leaflets. Sometimes the leaf characteristic is indicated by such descriptive words as "incisa"—deeply-cut or "laciniata"—slashed. Or leaf shape may be the important characteristic and be indicated by such names as "rotundifolia"—round-leaved, "angustifolia"—narrow-leaved, or "prunifolia"—leaf shaped like that of a member of the genus *Prunus* (which includes plums, cherries, peaches, apricots and nectarines, as well as almonds).

At other times the botanical name describes the leaf *tip*, with such terms as "apiculata"—tipped with a point, or "mucronata"—tipped with a very short point. Or, perhaps the *edge* or *margin* of the leaf is important in identification as with "dentata" —having big teeth or "serrata"—having small teeth. Even the leaf *texture* may be denoted by such terms as "crispa"—curled or "rugosa"—wrinkled. A roughly-fuzzed leaf *surface* may give the name "incana" to a shrub and finally, leaf *color* may be included in the plant's name as "variegata"—mottled or patterned, "marginata"—an edge or rim color different from that of the remainder of the leaf, usually lighter; or "polifolia"—white leaved.

So, the botanical or Latin names, once understood, may be helpful to you in many ways because they indicate the characteristics which the person naming the shrub considered most important to distinguish it from others that are similar.

The reader who knows any Latin and who scans the botanical names in these chapters will note immediately that the genders of modifying adjectives quite often do not agree with the nouns which they modify. Apparently, even though there have been attempts to bring proper relationships between nouns and adjectives (e.g. *Rosa multiflora*), there have been so many shifts and modifications of names over the years that often the words in a given botanical name have differing endings. For instance, *Euonymus alata*. So, as long as the meaning is understood without precise Latin, pay no attention to the fact that the word endings often are not correct.

Common Names

After the Latin or botanical name of each shrub, which is the one currently correct for that shrub, you'll find in this book the so-called "common" or "vulgar" or "folk" name or names of the shrub. If you wonder how a shrub can have two or more common names, while it has only one correct Latin name, you have hit on the weakness of common names. They vary too, too much. It's as simple as that.

Different people in different parts of the world gave shrubs and other plants their common names. Thus common names vary from country to country, from state to state and even from community to community! For example, down in Kentucky a certain shrub is known as "hearts abustin' with love". More widely over the United States it is called strawberry bush, though it has other local names. Its botanical name is *Euonymus americana*—all over the world. Thus the gardener who knows the Latin names of plants can converse easily with nurserymen, botanists and plantsmen the world over, even if he speaks only English.

Changing Shrub Names

As previously stated, botanists give plants their botanical names and occasionally find reasons for changing a few of them. Also, as already explained, one reason for their so doing is that a previously published name is found and the International Code of Botanical Nomenclature decrees a change to it.

It seems to me that in addition to this Code botanists need a statute of limitations, so that a botanical name which has been valid for, let's say 50 years, cannot be changed. It certainly seems ridiculous that *Paeonia albiflora*, named in 1788, should now be changed to *Paeonia lactiflora* merely because a botanist found that *lactiflora* was assigned to the species about 12 years before *albiflora*. After all, the two names were given the plant by the same man and how, almost 200 years later, can any botanist know that the man didn't simply change his mind?

All would be well for the gardener despite these changes in botanical names if only every nurseryman would change the listings in his catalog accordingly. But nurserymen are busy growing plants and selling them. A few try to keep up with botanical changes and succeed. Most do not try.

So, while I am expressing my thoughts about

changes in botanical nomenclature, I feel that just as botanists need a statute of limitations, nurserymen need some central agency to keep their catalogs correct botanically. After all, they no longer are using methods in vogue half a century ago, so why should they continue to refer to *Cornus racemosa* as *Cornus paniculata*, when this change in nomenclature was made about 50 years ago?

In general, the generic or genus name is correct in the catalogs, except for a few cases when a plant was known for many, many years by one name, later changed by the botanists for valid scientific reasons which may be obscure to the gardener, and the nurseryman didn't see fit to change. Thus, in numerous catalogs you'll find the Japanese flowering quince listed as *Cydonia japonica*, which was its correct name for years and years. Botanists then shifted it to the genus *Chaenomeles*. Thus, the old name, *Cydonia japonica* is synonymous with *Chaenomeles lagenaria* or the newer *Chaenomeles speciosa* and the same plant is meant by all three names.

When it comes to species, variety, and cultivar names, there is much confusion in the catalogs. There is a too-common practice, by nurserymen and others, of using a varietal name as a substitute for a specific name. Thus, *Caragana arborescens* 'Lorbergii', the beautiful fine-leaved form of Siberian pea tree, often is listed merely as *Caragana lorbergi* without the capital letter which, according to the Code, is mandatory at the beginning of an English word used as a cultivar name. As you see, in the last case, the species name is left out entirely.

All of these discrepancies between catalog names and correct botanical names have been resolved, to the best of my ability, in the five years of work on this manuscript. It would have been much simpler and infinitely easier to use the botanical names found in most catalogs, but then one plant would have been listed by several to many botanical names, and the book would have been of little use to nurserymen, who really need to correct their listings. Furthermore, my German ancestors would never have permitted me to allow the incorrect names to stand.

Since there obviously must be some authority for plant names, and most of the authorities are out-of-date, having been published many years ago, it has been necessary for me to work from the oldest to the newest of the various publications listing botanical names. All of the authorities consulted

are listed in "About the Book." In some cases it has been necessary to choose which name I would use because authorities disagreed. In this case I have tried to choose the name given by the most recent authority.

I hope all this checking of botanical names will make it possible for you to avoid buying the self-same plant under three different botanical names from three different nurseries. Also, for this same reason, all synonyms found *in the catalogs,* as well as those in botanical literature, are given in parentheses after the presently correct botanical name of the shrub.

If you are wondering why I place so much emphasis on the nursery listings, consider this: Who grows the plants offered for sale? Nurserymen. Who ought to know which plants will grow in a given area? The nurseryman who grows them year in and year out. Then what better place to find a listing of plants that grow from plant hardiness Zone 6 northward in the United States and Canada (the area included in this book) than the catalogs and lists of nurserymen in these zones in the two countries?

A nursery sales lot operator may buy his plants from any zone at all—and the same applies to the garden center operator unless he is the nurseryman. I have seen many plants that would winter perfectly in Virginia and similar climates sold on lots here in Michigan where they are certain to die, long before the winter cold becomes severe. Many nursery sales lot operators neither know nor care about the ability of a plant to grow in a given climate. Nurserymen ought to care—if they expect to stay in business.

In addition to providing a listing of shrubs grown in Zones 6, 5, 4, 3, and 2, the nursery catalogs provide sources for those plants. What good would it do for you to know about a shrub, drool over the description, and want to buy it—if it isn't available? Many a description has been given in an article or book of a plant in a botanical garden, an arboretum, or some similar place, for which there is no commercial source. I learned the hard way, during my many years as garden editor of a large metropolitan newspaper, never to mention a plant for which I did not know at least one source, for, just as surely as I did, some reader wanted to buy it. So, the nursery catalogs, tabulated in Chapter 11, not only furnish me with a list of available shrubs but furnish you with a list of sources for them.

Chapter 3

USING SHRUBS IN THE GARDEN

You notice that the title of this chapter is not "Landscaping With Shrubs": I am not going to talk about any of the landscaping principles, as these are available in plenty of good books. Instead, I'm going to try to show you how to use shrubs to fill the various needs of your garden.

Garden Problems

Every garden has problems, even if they're as simple to solve as finding a very low-growing, low-staying plant to use under a large picture window where the foundation looks bare. If you'll look at the lists which comprise most of this chapter, you'll see that there's a wide choice of low shrubs available to solve this particular problem, even though the lists cover only the shrubs in this book and therefore are not complete.

What are the problems in your garden? It would be an excellent plan for you to make a list of them. Nothing fancy, mind you—just jot down the places you're not sure what to plant and why you aren't sure. Add a dimension or two—height available, if it's restricted (as by an overhanging roof); width available, also only if it's restricted; depth available, ditto. From then on the lists and descriptions are your chief guides.

It seems to me that the very best way I can help you to use the lists would be for us, you and me, to go through the solutions of several problems together. So, please be my guest for a few minutes and let's meet outside our front gate.

Steep Bank

Here, before we even started building our house, the county decided to widen our road 4 inches on each side for use as a detour while a nearby main road was being widened from a two-lane to four-lane highway. In order to widen our road 4 inches on each side, the county sliced away several feet of the 4-foot-high bank which is the front of our acreage, removing all topsoil and most of the wild plums and other shrubs and trees which had been growing there, and exposing a good portion of the roots of an enormous hickory and an equally enormous butternut.

Of course I phoned the county road commission and read the engineer who answered a lecture on conservation of soil and trees, but much good that did. I was faced with planting a steep 4-foot-high bank with something that wouldn't cost too much, (we own 220 feet of frontage on that road), would grow in practically clear yellow clay subsoil, would eventually cover most of the bank, and would also hold the soil in place. At the same time the plants used must need little or no maintenance which, because of the steepness of the bank left by the county, would be hard to give.

You will agree that I had a problem? The solution proved to be not too hard, because it required only the planting of 11 *Forsythia suspensa* (weeping forsythia) and 11 plants of *F. suspensa sieboldii* which is a variety with slightly darker yellow flowers. I thought as long as I was planting that many weeping forsythias, I might as well take advantage of the variation in flower color. These forsythias were planted at the top of the bank. Eventually, as their drooping branches touch the ground (and some already do), they'll root where they touch and new branches will grow upward from these points, to in turn arch over and root, etc.

To hold the rest of the bank in the meantime, while the forsythias grew, we dug excess tall-bearded iris plants and our daughter and a girl friend planted them along the most exposed parts of the bank. Later we added excess plants of Siberian iris, and common wild daylily. I also scattered seeds of calliopsis, which now seeds itself. As a result, the bank blooms during a good part of the year and doesn't look too badly. The forsythias

9

grow larger yearly, encouraging me to look forward to the day when they'll have taken over completely.

If you look at the list headed "These Shrubs May Be Used To Hold Banks" you'll find *Forsythia suspensa* there and it might solve your problem too.

Now, will you step inside the front gate with me? You are facing north and looking along a 350-foot-long driveway which runs only a few feet from the east property line. This is placed where it is because years before we bought the land, someone had started to construct a gravel driveway and the foundation was there, all ready to use. Along the right (or east) side of the driveway there are arborvitae, selected because both our driveway and that of our neighbor drain into the narrow area in which these evergreens grow. Since arborvitae grow naturally in swamps they were an obvious choice. As the driveway slopes gradually upward toward the house, the evergreens lining its east side change to Hick's yews for these will accommodate themselves to the shade of huge old poplars which were there when we bought the place and which furnish welcome height as well as shade. Both arborvitae and yews hide the cyclone fence desired by our neighbors but abhorred by me.

Unlikely Soil

Just in front of the yews, where the property line curves gradually eastward away from the driveway, is a planting of shrub roses—old timers which dote on poor soil. Believe me they have it, for where they are planted is a part of the old gravel driveway foundation and we had to use a pick to dig every planting hole. If you read the requirements of shrub roses in Chapter 14, you can see readily why these were selected. They get sun only from the west; require no fertilizer, no upkeep except pruning out any dead branches in spring, and no spraying. Austrian Copper is here. It undoubtedly *ought* to be sprayed as it defoliates every summer because of blackspot, but I don't pay any attention to that. This is a tough rose and it will have plenty of leaves and flowers again the next spring. Other roses that thrive in this place, in case you have a similar problem spot, are Father Hugo's rose (*R. hugonis*), Scotch briar rose (*R. pimpinellifolia*), Harison's Yellow (*R. harisonii*), two *R. rugosa* hybrids, 'F. G. Grootendorst' and 'Pink Grootendorst,' the red-leaved rose (*R. glauca*), a few moss roses, including Old Pink Moss, and a few more given me by friends. Since they didn't know the rose names, I don't either, as they're not varieties I

recognize. There also are three or four plants of a modern rose—'Betty Prior," one of the most satisfactory of modern roses.

From the time *hugonis* blooms with the tulips, to the time frost comes, when there still will be a few blooms on 'Betty Prior' and perhaps on one or both of the Grootendorsts, there are some flowers in that area, just about every day. What more could one ask from an old gravel driveway foundation?

Narrow Space

But, you may be thinking, I don't have a steep bank to plant nor an old gravel driveway to think about, so what good do these solutions do me? I also have had problems which may be nearer to your own. For instance, the narrow planting space on one side of the front door—it is only 2 feet wide and 15 feet long—underneath the east windows of my end of the office. Many, many properties have a similar area. Added to the problem of the space was that of sun—I needed a sun shade during the summer only, for both those east-facing and 3 south-facing windows. The solution is as follows: in the corner next to the front door, in front of the only solid wall of any height, I planted a wisteria which has been trained above east and south windows to form a sunshade. As you know, even a large vine like wisteria takes up little ground space. The remainder of that narrow area was planted to glossy abelias (*Abelia grandiflora*), partly because I am fond of that shrub, partly because it is not reliably hardy in this climate and the office wing protects the plants from the prevailing wind while the house wall must temper the cold somewhat, and also because the climate never will permit the plants to grow higher than the 3-foot-high wall under the windows.

Certainly by now you are following the train of thought—most areas present some problem; solutions are easy to find among shrubs, and those chosen should fulfill not only the requirements of the particular area, but also satisfy your own tastes.

Northeast Exposure

The area behind the house, on the northeast side, presented quite a different aspect. There was virtually unlimited space and no problems involved but keeping the planting clear of the windows. Since the north or northeast sides of a building are as perfect places as can be found for broad-leaved evergreens, these were what I chose to use.

Narrow beds were made next to the house (narrow so they could be weeded without stepping into them) and the shrubs were planted in groups of several of a genus. Thus the eastwing bed contains leucothoës and azaleas, with old-fashioned goutweed as a ground cover beneath the shrubs. The middle bed, under the huge picture window of the music room, is planted with mahonias with Baltic ivy and pachysandra as ground covers. The corner between this wing and the west wing, since it is partly shaded, is occupied by several plants of pieris with more mahonias in the foreground. Here a rock garden plant, a sedum (*Sedum acre*) carpets the ground. The westwing bed is filled with laurel, mountain and bog, (*Kalmia latifolia* and *K. polifolia*), *Mahonia bealii* and azaleas, one of them evergreen. *Pachistima canbyi* is the soil-covering plant in this bed. None of these shrubs ever will grow high enough, in this climate, to obscure the view from any of the windows.

Outward from the house and these beds there is a 20-foot-wide gravel terrace, extending the full length of the house, 65 feet. In line with the huge window in the music room and the almost equally large one in the dining room one floor above (the house is built into a hillside), is a pool planted with water lilies. This we look out to from the music room, down upon from the dining room. The shrub grouping I now wish to describe is that behind the pool.

All Season Bloom

As I said previously, space was no problem, so it was merely a question of deciding what I wanted to plant there. The first thing I wanted was something behind the pool to furnish a background of green all year. So here we set three pyracanthas, which not only fulfill my requirement, but furnish white flowers and, in the occasional autumn when the warblers don't eat them all, bright orange berries.

I decided that I also would like to have on either side of the pyracanthas low-growing shrubs that would give us flowers to look at all during the growing season. Now we have the following shrubs in the grouping: for April bloom, two dwarf flowering quinces (*Chaenomeles japonica alpina*) and, to bloom with them, one plant of flowering almond, not with pink blossoms, but with white. For May flowers we have both the double-flowered kerria in the background and the shorter-growing single-flowered *Kerria japonica* 'Picta' with variegated green and white leaves in the foreground. By June *Deutzia rosea* 'Pink Pompon' is in flower and four potentillas put on their show of yellow or white flowers. *Spirea bumalda* 'Anthony Waterer' and *S. bumalda* 'Crispa' flower in July; in August *Hypericum* 'Sun Gold' is in bloom and the potentillas still

Buxus sempervirens 'Welleri' hedge curved to outline part of our north terrace—shrub planting in background is part of grouping behind our small lily pool.

are flowering. And, finally, in September, in addition to the orange berries which may be left us by the warblers on the pyracanthas, both *Caryopteris clandonensis* 'Blue Mist' and *Elsholtzia stauntonii* bloom.

Perhaps these last two examples of using shrubs in the garden are more helpful to you in your garden than the first two which present greater problems, but the important thing is that you follow the thinking and planning involved, since these are the two requisites to a successful planting of your own garden.

How To Solve *Your* Garden Problems

I often have wished that it was possible to pass on one's knowledge of a subject with the same ease that an outgoing chairman passes on a gavel to the incoming chairman. But, since that is not possible, the next best thing certainly must be to point out the places in the garden where shrubs are most likely to be used and indicate how to plan these areas.

Most people who buy a new home or start renovating the planting of an older one start with the planting around the house—a logical place to begin. If you will drive down almost any suburban street you will notice that these house plantings are almost entirely of narrow-leaved (needled) evergreens, and also that most of these plantings are deadly dull. Livelier and far more interesting plantings are achieved by using needled, broad-leaved and deciduous plants together. Look for yourself and you'll find that this is so.

Doorway planting which combines small tree (red-leaved plum), evergreen (yew) hedge, and shrubs. Potentilla fruticosa (foreground). Euonymus alata 'Compacta', rear.

Cotoneaster horizontalis, combined with yew clipped to ball form, makes a corner planting.

You will notice that, in the paragraph above, I used the words "house planting." The term used to be "foundation planting" but, since houses nowadays are not built with ugly foundations that need to be hidden with planting or with ungainly high foundations that mean the house must be "tied to the ground" by use of plants, there seems to be little sense in continuing to use the old terminology.

House Planting

The most important point to remember in planning the planting around *your* house is that you are endeavoring to enhance the house, not smother it. The house is the important object, not the planting. On the house walls the openings are the most important features. And, of doors and windows, the doors are more important. So, look first at the doors, front, side, back, in that order. Are they so beautiful or so unique in appearance that no plants will help accent or enhance them? If so, leave well enough alone and use only a ground cover near the doorways. If not, what do the doorways need? If they are too narrow, adding a fairly wide shrub, preferably one with horizontal branches, on either side will make for a wider appearance. A too-wide doorway, however, will not be made to appear narrower by using a tall, narrow shrub on either side. It is better to balance the too-wide doorway with a wide shrub somewhere else, perhaps at a house corner.

Since a few shrubs around the house are sufficient to enhance its architecture, plant the doorways first and then look to see what other plants are needed.

The other openings—windows—may also need to be enhanced or accented. Full length windows, of course, are treated the same as doors except when on the same wall as a door, in which case the door planting still should be considered first and more important. Picture windows usually are enhanced by low plantings under them. Sometimes a ground cover is sufficient planting, at other times shrubs that when mature will reach to the bottom of the window will look better.

High windows may or may not need plantings under them—much depends on the house architecture and on your personal opinion. One thing, however, is certain: windows never were placed in a house wall to be obscured by planting of any kind, so select plants for your windows with due consideration of the footage between ground and sill.

It is possible that a house corner needs accenting. A high, narrow shrub will do this. Or it may need softening, in which case a tall-growing, fairly small-leaved and many-branched shrub may be the solution.

There are times when whoever planned the house did not do a perfect job, so that it seems unbalanced. For instance, a wing at one end may look far too heavy for the rest of the building. Try planting a large, visually heavy shrub or small tree at the other end of the building and watch the visual weight of the wing diminish.

Sometimes a huge chimney dominates the house. A shrub such as a pyracantha, espaliered against the chimney, its branches trained to any pattern that pleases you, will break up the mass of the chimney into smaller masses which are not so dominant.

So much for solving problems of house plantings. But bear in mind three things when you select the shrubs for this important location: (1) choose those that thrive in the exposure in which they are to be planted—in other words don't choose a shade-loving shrub for the south side of the house—you might just as well throw your money out of the window; (2) choose only shrubs that are absolutely hardy in your climate (if you want to try some that may or may not be hardy, plant them elsewhere than around the house), so that you don't have to build a burlap screen around a choice boxwood and look at burlap all winter through your picture window; (3) think of the appearance of the shrubs you choose at *all* times of year and *before* you buy eliminate any from your plan that do not

A single Korean dogwood makes a handsome specimen, even in winter when viewed through a window.

look well at *every* season. This does not mean that only broad-leaved evergreen shrubs should be planted. Cork-barked euonymus (*Euonymus alata*), for example, is just as interesting and attractive in winter, with its odd corky wings and definite branching habit, as it is at any other time of year.

Screening, Delineating

After their use in the house planting, shrubs are most frequently used for screening or delineating and both may be accomplished with the same shrubs in the same planting. Screening may be of the outdoor living area, of an unsightly view or of the neighboring property. In any one of these cases, the same shrub planting also may delineate the property line. While a single line of shrubs may be and often is planted as a screen, several lines or rows of shrubs are more frequently found in border plantings.

If you wish to plant only a single line of shrubs, why not consider a hedge of one kind of shrub or, if height is a factor, one kind of small tree? It is not necessary that this hedge be kept clipped since there are many shrubs which present an attractive appearance without this additional care. But, especially if only a short screen planting is required, it will look far more homogeneous and therefore attractive if only one kind of plant is used. The columnar form of buckthorn (*Rhamnus*), for instance, makes a handsome sheared or unsheared

A single viburnum used as a specimen against a house wall. English ivy ground cover in foreground.

hedge. If, however, a shrub with showier flowers is desired, beauty bush (*Kolkwitzia*) will grow to a comparable height. This is best left unclipped and is only for a tall, *wide* screen, whereas the buck-thorn, while it will grow tall, also will stay narrow. If you will look at the list of hedge shrubs on page 22 of this chapter you will find that there is a wide choice of heights, widths, and kinds available. As a matter of fact, *any* shrub may be used for a hedge, but some are more satisfactory than others.

A long screen planting permits a wider variety of shrubs. If your property requires such a plant-ing, look first to see what the neighboring property possesses that can be turned to your advantage. Evergreen or deciduous trees on the other side of the property line may lend the necessary height to *your* border without your waiting for small plants set on your side of the line to grow tall. Bright yel-low-flowering forsythias on the other side of the line might be "faced down" with lavender-flower-ing azaleas (*Rhododendron mucronulatum*) on your side, thus furnishing you with a beautiful, early-spring combination of flowers without the necessity of buying the forsythias.

If there is no neighboring planting, then of course you have to do all of it. But remember that shrubs grow wider as well as taller and buy either only as many as will fill the entire space eventually or as will fill half the space immediately. Then later, as they grow, you can move half the plants to fill the other half of the space. If there is a rea-son why you need an immediate effect in one part of a shrub border, this "doubling up" of the num-ber of plants and moving half of them later is a satisfactory solution, even though it entails extra work.

Planning Shrub Borders

How to design a shrub border? The easiest way is to take a sheet of cross section paper (available at any stationery store) and select a scale for your design—perhaps you wish to have one square on the paper equal one foot on the ground, but it is easier, considering the size of cross section sheets, to select a figure like 5 or 6 feet for the equivalent of each square. After measuring or pacing off the length the border will be, count squares according to the scale you have selected and mark the length of the border on the paper. Mark also the ultimate width you wish the border to be. If it has to be narrow yet tall, and you do not wish a hedge planting yet you will be limited to a single line of shrubs, select only sufficient kinds of shrubs of the desired ultimate height so that there will be two or three of each kind next to one another in the line. One successful way to design such a single-line border is select for bloom each month of the flowering season one shrub that grows to the chosen

From the outside, looking in. A single row of shrubs screens a small terrace. Each shrub is a different kind. Appearance would have been improved if all shrubs had been of one, or possibly two, kinds.

From the inside, looking out. Even with a single row shrub screen, terrace privacy is complete.

height and width, so that there always will be one group of shrubs coming into bloom as flowers on another group are fading.

After choosing the shrubs, with the help of the height lists on pages 19 to 23 of this chapter and the Bloom Time Chart at the end of the chapter, read the descriptions of the shrubs in Chapter 14 or of small trees in Chapter 15. When you are certain of your choice, make a circle in the appropriate square on the cross section paper to indicate where the center of the first shrub will be when you dig the hole in which to plant it. The distance between these centers should be equal to half the sum of the ultimate width of adjacent shrubs. Label each circle with a number, then make a list of shrubs indicating on it the name of the shrub that number represents. Thus number 1 might mean a plant of *Spiraea vanhouttei* and there might be three of these in a row, each circle numbered 1. Number 2 will indicate another plant. This list becomes your "buying" list when you go to a nursery: your diagram with its circled numbers will show how many of each kind of shrub you need to buy.

If more depth is available for your border, it may have two rows of shrubs. The easiest way to place these is in zig-zag fashion with one lower-growing shrub in the front row (the row toward your property) in between each of the taller-growing shrubs in the back row. While this is the easiest way, it does not, by any means, give the best appearance as the plants grow. It is more satisfactory, for instance, to line up three shrubs of one kind in the back row, then a single shrub with particularly beautiful foliage, form or bloom, and in front of that single shrub group five or six very low-growing shrubs, with perhaps only one medium-high shrub in front of the group of three.

Always remember that even lower-growing shrubs will extend both up and sideways and allow sufficient space for them to do so.

The three-shrub-deep border allows for zig-zag planting of back and middle rows if desired, and group planting of the front row. It also allows for a far greater variety of shrubs. But one shrub of each kind in such a planting makes it a collection of shrubs rather than a border, while groups of several shrubs of each kind in each row results in a more attractive and more harmonious planting. The shrub border is the place to try that doubtfully-hardy shrub for if it fails to live its loss will not be too noticeable and it can be replaced with a hardier shrub the following planting season.

The choice of shrubs for a border depends on

Shrub border with Spiraea vanhouttei in full bloom.

how frequently you will look at those shrubs. If the border is close to the house, perhaps around the outdoor living area or as a background for some garden feature to be seen from a window, do as you did for the house planting: select only shrubs that will look well all year (most certainly those in the row nearest the house). Try to select one group of shrubs to bloom in early spring and another to color or fruit in autumn, but choose them in relation to the border as a whole. In the same way, consider the border as a whole when you decide on the flower colors of the shrubs.

This does not mean that all the shrubs must have flowers of the same color or colors, but it does mean that you should not be spacing forsythias evenly throughout the border every 10 feet so that when they bloom you will have dots of yellow here and there. It is far better to design one group of shrubs with, for example, forsythias in the background and Korean abelia leaf (*Abeliophyllum distichum*) in the foreground, to bloom at forsythia time and concentrate your forsythias in that area or in two areas, perhaps at opposite ends of the border and with another kind of shrub in the foreground of the second grouping. Not only does color grouping give a more pleasing effect than color dotting, but clashing colors can be avoided by planning groups that bloom at one time, of colors that contrast or blend. It is to help you do this that the Bloom Time Chart is included in this book.

In a long shrub border it is the mark of an expert designer to use, just once or twice in the length of the border, a single outstanding shrub or small tree which, even though it may grow high and wide, is set either near the front of the border or in the foreground—against the border but out from it.

It is not easy in a shrub border to mix shrubs that require acid soil with those that do not. It is far better for the shrubs and easier for the gardener to plant acid-lovers together in one area. Keep in mind that there also are shrubs which may be killed by acidifiers added to soil nearby. Shade-loving shrubs should, of course, be reserved for shaded areas and sun lovers set in sunny places. The same applies to shrubs which delight in moist soil and those which abhor it.

In a long border it is important that there be some blending and also some contrasting foliage textures. A bold-textured, large-leaved shrub may well be placed in the foreground of several fine-foliaged shrubs. Select each shrub to harmonize with its neighbors on either side but also keep constantly in mind the appearance of the border as a whole, so that there are not too many bold contrasts nor too long stretches of small-foliaged shrubs.

Consider also the winter appearance of the border against the sky. There should be some variation in height if it is to be interesting, even if it means greater border width for a taller, wider plant in some places or cutting down on the number of rows of plants in those areas to accommodate the taller, wider plant.

Spiraea thunbergii with its fine, feathery foliage is an excellent foil for split cedar sapling fence and rock.

Shrubs with distorted shapes do not belong in the border: save them for use as specimens.

Specimens

Planting a shrub for a specimen does not mean digging a hole in the middle of a lawn and planting it there. That is the poorest possible use of a shrub as a specimen. Usually it distorts the entire landscape.

A specimen shrub, one planted to show off its perfect or unusual form, foliage, coloring or bloom, may be used, as indicated in the discussion of shrub borders above, in the foreground of a border; or it also might be used to draw the eye to a certain spot in the garden (in landscape parlance this is called using the shrub as a "focal point"). Other possible uses are by a gate or other entrance to the garden or next to the place where one part of the garden (perhaps the outdoor living area) opens onto another part (perhaps a lawn area). Still another possible place for a specimen shrub is any place where you want to draw the eye of the beholder—for instance to the point where a path leads off a lawn into a wooded area.

Only a very large property will need more than one or two shrubs placed as specimens. Beware: too many competing beauties produce a feeling of restlessness.

Windbreaks

There are times when it is desirable to plant a windbreak of shrubs. In such cases shrubs should be selected first for their absolute hardiness in your area and second for their twigginess, for only plants with many branches and twigs really break the force of the wind. A windbreak planting of shrubs must be not only tall, but also "thick" so the wind's force is spent by the time it goes through the shrubs. Plenty of width must be allowed for such a planting, which should be at least three rows deep and better four.

Barriers or Obstructions

When you wish to keep people and/or animals in or out of specific areas or from cutting across them, shrubs and small trees can furnish useful barriers or obstructions. For this use, the most satisfactory choice usually is a tree or shrub with thorns.

Among the very best for this purpose are hawthorns, small trees which may be allowed to grow unclipped to full height or kept clipped to medium height and formal shape. They make a more formidable barrier when clipped, for then they grow so dense and their thorns are so sharp that a planting is virtually impenetrable.

There are, however, other trees and shrubs which can serve this same purpose. You will find a list of them on page 23. Use them with discretion and you'll avoid lawsuits.

Other Uses

You will find among the lists at the end of this chapter one of shrubs useful for ground cover planting where it is desired to use something other than grass or a deciduous or evergreen perennial and also a list of shrubs to use for planting on banks to hold soil in place (and to cover the ground). Indicated in the shrub descriptions in Chapter 14 are shrubs which may be planted in rock gardens and on tops of walls. Really shrubs are a wonderful group of plants, available in sufficient variety and versatile enough to solve many a garden problem.

Using Shrubs In *Your* Garden

The procedure of planning the shrubs for use in your garden is, as you now know, the same in all

Problem: narrow space between walk and house plus narrow space between windows. Solution: one plant of firethorn (pyracantha) pruned so top is vinelike against the house and bottom grows as a low shrub.

Shrubs on either side of a grass path. Our lilac lane about five years after planting. Leaning hickory on right has since been removed.

cases. Select the area you wish to plant. Take sufficient measurements so you can make sensible decisions on the basis of ultimate height or spread of the plants. Look long and carefully at the area until you have an idea of the shapes of the plants you want to use there. Also try to recognize any problems that exist in the area or if, within the space limits, you are free to choose any shrub you wish.

If there is a problem, state it either to yourself or your spouse or a neighbor, as much to clarify it to yourself as for the purpose of talking it over (the old "saw" about two heads being better than one still holds good). Then use the lists at the end of this chapter and the descriptions of plants in Chapters 14 and 15 to help you decide which shrub or tree you want to use.

Remember, in choosing, that good-looking foliage all season is more important than beautiful flowers for two weeks and that, where the plant is prominent in winter, an interesting silhouette becomes of prime importance. Also, that the smaller the garden, the more important each individual plant becomes.

If you need to use several different kinds of shrubs in one group, as in a border, look in the Bloom Time Chart in this chapter to see which shrubs bloom together, before you read their descriptions and, once again, make your choice according to which kinds appeal to you.

No one else can choose for you. The best landscape architect will only suggest and recommend plants. It is of course far better if you see the actual shrubs before choosing which to plant, and this you may be able to do in one of the places suggested in Chapter 2.

Above all, have fun, for shrubs are plants that can delight the owner without snowing him under with upkeep. Also, they are cheap enough so that you can take a chance on moving them elsewhere or discard them and buy anew, in case you make a horrible mistake either in placement or choice of your plants.

SHRUBS THAT EVENTUALLY GROW TALLER THAN 10 FEET

Amelanchier alnifolia
Amorpha fruticosa
Aralia spinosa
Buddleia alternifolia
Buxus sempervirens
Caragana arborescens
      " frutex
Cephalanthus occidentalis
Cornus sanguinea
Corylus avellana
Cotinus coggygria
      " " 'Purpureus'
Cotoneaster acutifolia
Cyrilla racemiflora
Elaeagnus commutata
Euonymus yedoensis
Fontanesia fortunei
Hamamelis japonica
      " mollis
      " virginiana
Holodiscus discolor
Hydrangea paniculata
      " " 'Grandiflora'
Ilex opaca
 " pedunculata
 " verticillata
Kolkwitzia amabilis
Ligustrum amurense
      " ovalifolium
      " vulgare
Lindera benzoin
Lonicera korolkowii
      " maackii
Parrotia persica
Prunus triloba
Pyracantha coccinea
      " " 'Lalandei'
Rhamnus cathartica
      " frangula
      " " 'Columnaris'
Rhododendron arborescens
      " maximum
      " schlippenbachii
Rhus typhina
Rosa multiflora
 " setigera
Salix discolor
Sambucus canadensis
      " racemosa
Shepherdia argentea
Sorbus tianshanica
Staphylea trifolia
Stewartia ovata
Syringa chinensis
      " " 'Saugeana'
      " josikaea
      " reflexa
      " vulgaris
Tamarix gallica
      " parviflora
      " pentandra
Viburnum americanum
      " cassinoides
      " dentatum
      " lantana
      " molle
      " opulus
      " " 'Roseum'
      " prunifolium
      " sargentii
      " setigerum
      " sieboldii
      " trilobum
plus all the small trees described in Chapter 15.

SHRUBS WHICH RANGE IN HEIGHT FROM 6 TO 10 FEET AT MATURITY

Acanthopanax sieboldianus
Aesculus parviflora
Berberis mentorensis
      " thunbergii
Buddleia davidii and cultivars
Buxus sempervirens
      " " 'Suffruticosa'
Caragana arborescens 'Lorbergii'
Cephalanthus occidentalis
Clethra alnifolia
Colutea arborescens
Cornus alba
      " 'Argenteo-marginata'
      " 'Sibirica'
      " amomum
      " racemosa
      " stolonifera
      " " baileyi
Corylus americana
Cotoneaster divaricata
      " foveolata
      " multiflora
      " " calocarpa
      " racemiflora soongorica
Deutzia scabra
      " " plena
      " " 'Pride of Rochester'
Diervilla sessilifolia
Elaeagnus multiflora
      " umbellata
Enkianthus campanulatus
Euonymus alata
      " kiautschovica
      " sachalinensis
Exochorda giraldii wilsonii
      " racemosa
Forsythia 'Beatrix Farrand'
      " intermedia
      " " 'Spectabilis'
      " ovata
      " suspensa
      " " fortunei
      " viridissima
Fothergilla major
Halimodendron halodendron
Hamamelis vernalis
Hibiscus syriacus
Hydrangea arborescens
      " quercifolia
Ilex glabra
 " serrata
Lespedeza bicolor
Ligustrum ibolium
      " obtusifolium
Lonicera bella 'Candida'
      " fragrantissima
      " maackii podocarpa
      " morrowii
      " tatarica and varieties
Magnolia liliflora 'Nigra'
Malus sargentii
Myrica pensylvanica
Philadelphus coronarius
      " grandiflorus
Physocarpus opulifolius
      " " 'Luteus'
Prunus besseyi
      " cistena
      " tomentosa
Rhamnus utilis
Rhododendron arborescens
Rhododendron calendulaceum
      " catawbiense

Rhododendron grandavense
      " kaempferi
      " mucronatum
      " obtusum arnoldianum
      " vaseyi
      " viscosum
Rhus glabra
Ribes odoratum
Rosa alba
 " eglanteria
 " foetida
      " " 'Persian Yellow'
 " glauca
 " harisonii
 " moyesii
 " rugosa
 " virginiana
Rubus odoratus
Salix gracilistyla
 " purpurea
Sorbaria aitchisonii
Spiraea billiardii
      " macrothyrsa
      " prunifolia
      " trichocarpa
      " vanhouttei
Stephanandra incisa
Symplocos paniculata
Syringa laciniata
      " microphylla
      " persica
      " " 'Alba'
      " prestoniae
      " pubescens
      " swegiflexa
      " villosa
Tamarix odessana
Vaccinium corymbosum
Viburnum acerifolium
      " bitchiuense
      " bodnantense
      " burkwoodii
      " " 'Chenault'
      " carlcephalum
      " dilatatum
      " fragrans
      " judii
      " plicatum
      " " tomentosum
      " rhytidophylloides
      " rhytidophyllum
      " wrightii
Weigela floribunda
      " florida
      " 'Vanicek'

SHRUBS THAT GROW 3 TO 6 FEET IN HEIGHT WHEN MATURE

Abelia grandiflora
Abeliophyllum distichum
Aronia arbutifolia
      " 'Brilliantissima'
Berberis julianae
      " koreana
      " thunbergii 'Atropurpurea'
      " " 'Erecta'
      " verruculosa
Buddleia farquhari
Buxus microphylla
      " " koreana
Callicarpa dichotoma
      " japonica
Calycanthus floridus
Caryopteris incana
Chaenomeles japonica

Clethra alnifolia
      " 'Rosea'
Comptonia peregrina
Coronilla eremurus
Cornus stolonifera coloradensis
      " 'Flaviramea'
Cotoneaster apiculata
      " bullata floribunda
      " dielsiana
      " divaricata
      " integerrima
Cytisus praecox
      " scoparius
Daphne 'Somerset'
Deutzia gracilis
      " lemoinei
      " rosea
      " " 'Pink Pompon'
Elsholtzia stauntonii
Euonymus alata 'Compacta'
      " americana
      " fortunei 'Vegeta'
      " nana turkestanica
Exochorda macrantha 'The Bride'
Forsythia suspensa sieboldii
Fothergilla monticola
Hypericum frondosum
      " prolificum
Kalmia latifolia
Kerria japonica
      " " 'Pleniflora'
Lespedeza bicolor
      " thunbergii
Leucothoë fontanesiana
Ligustrum obtusifolium regelianum
Lonicera xylosteoides 'Clavey's Dwarf'
      " korolkowii 'Zabelii'
Mahonia aquifolium
Paeonia suffruticosa
Philadelphus coronarius 'Aureus'
      " lemoinei
      " virginalis
Photinia villosa
Physocarpus monogynus
      " opulifolius 'Nanus'
Pieris floribunda
Potentilla fruticosa
      " parvifolia
Prinsepia sinensis
Prunus besseyi
Prunus glandulosa and varieties
      " laurocerasus 'Schipkaensis'
      " maritima
      " tenella
Rhododendron carolianum
      " " album
      " kosterianum
      " molle
      " mucronulatum
      " nudiflorum
      " obtusum 'Amoenum'
      " roseum
      " yedoense
Rhodotypos scandens
Rhus copallina
      " trilobata
Ribes alpinum
      " aureum
      " diacanthum
Rosa blanda
      " hugonis
      " pimpinellifolia
Salix purpurea 'Gracilis'
Sorbaria sorbifolia

Spiraea arguta
      " bumalda 'Froebelii'
      " gemmata

Spiraea japonica 'Atrosanguinea'
"   multiflora
"   thunbergii
"   tomentosa
"   trilobata
Symphoricarpos albus laevigatus
"   orbiculatus
Syringa velutina
Tamarix hispida
Viburnum carlesii
Vitex agnus-castus 'Latifolia'
Weigela florida 'Alba'
"   "   'Variegata'
Zenobia pulverulenta

SHRUBS WHICH REACH 3 FEET OR LESS OF HEIGHT AT MATURITY

Amelanchier stolonifera
Aronia melanocarpa
Berberis candidula
"   julianae 'Nana'
"   thunbergii 'Atropurpurea Nana'
"   "   minor
Buxus microphylla 'Compacta'
"   sempervirens 'Grand Rapids'
"   "   'Inglis'
"   "   'Suffruticosa'
"   "   'Vardar Valley'
"   "   'Welleri'
Calluna vulgaris
Caragana pygmaea
Caryopteris clandonensis
Ceanothus americanus
Chaenomeles japonica alpina
Chamaedaphne calyculata
Cornus stolonifera 'Kelsey'
Corylopsis pauciflora
Cotoneaster adpressa
"   "   praecox
"   dammeri
"   horizontalis
"   "   perpusilla
"   microphylla
Cytisus battandieri
Daphne cneorum
"   genkwa
"   mezereum
Deutzia kalmiaeflora
"   lemoinei 'Compacta'
Diervilla lonicera
Erica carnea
"   vagans
Euonymus alata 'Gracilis'
Forsythia intermedia 'Arnold Dwarf'
"   viridissima 'Bronxensis'
Genista tinctoria
Hydrangea arborescens grandiflora
"   macrophylla and cultivars
Hypericum calycinum
"   kalmianum
"   moserianum
Ilex crenata 'Compacta'
"   "   'Convexa'
"   "   'Helleri'
"   "   'Hetzi'
"   "   'Microphylla'
"   "   'Repandens'
"   "   'Stokes'
"   glabra 'Compacta'
Kerria japonica 'Picta'
Lavandula officinalis
Leucothoë fontanesiana
"   "   'Girard's Rainbow'
Ligustrum vicaryi
Mahonia bealii
"   repens
Pachistima canbyi

Pieris japonica 'Compacta'
"   "   'Variegata'
Potentilla davurica
"   "   'Veitchii'
"   parvifolia 'Farreri'
Rhododendron canadense
"   yedoense poukhanense
Rosa nitida
"   . wichuraiana
Spiraea albiflora
"   arguta compacta
"   bumalda 'Anthony Waterer'
"   "   'Crispa'
Stephanandra incisa 'Crispa'
Symphoricarpos chenaultii
"   "   'Hancock'
Viburnum carlesii 'Compactum'
"   opulus 'Nanum'
Xanthorhiza simplicissima

THE FOLLOWING SHRUBS HAVE BRANCHES GROWING FIRST UPRIGHT, THEN ARCHING OR DROOPING

Buddleia alternifolia
Caragana arborescens 'Pendula'
"   "   'Lorbergii'
"   pygmaea
Cornus florida 'Pendula'
Cotoneaster dielsiana
"   divaricata
"   multiflora
"   "   calocarpa
"   racemiflora soongorica
Deutzia kalmiaeflora
Euonymus alata 'Gracilis'
Forsythia suspensa
"   "   fortunei
"   "   sieboldii
"   viridissima
Holodiscus discolor
Lespedeza bicolor
"   thunbergii
Leucothoë fontanesiana
Pieris japonica
Rosa multiflora
"   setigera
Spiraea arguta
"   thunbergii
"   trilobata
"   vanhouttei
Stephanandra incisa
Symphoricarpos albus laevigatus
Syringa microphylla
Weigela florida

THESE SHRUBS OR SMALL TREES BRANCH HORIZONTALLY

Cotoneaster horizontalis
Euonymus alata
"   "   'Compacta'
Crataegus (many)
Ligustrum obtusifolium regelianum
Prunus laurocerasus 'Schipkaensis'
Viburnum plicatum 'Mariesir'
"   "   tomentosum
"   prunifolium

THESE SHRUBS HAVE LEAVES VARIEGATED OR COLORED OTHER THAN GREEN

YELLOW

Corylus 'avellana 'Aurea'
Ligustrum vicaryi
Philadelphus coronarius 'Aureus'
Physocarpus opulifolius 'Luteus'
Sambucus canadensis 'Aurea'
"   racemosa 'Plumosa' aurea
Xanthorhiza simplicissima

PURPLISH-RED

Acer palmatum 'Atropurpureum'
Berberis thunbergii 'Atropurpurea'
"   "   'Atropurpurea Nana'
Corylus avellana 'Fusco-rubra'
"   maxima 'Purpurea'
Cotinus coggygria 'Purpureus'
Erica carnea 'Vivellii'
Prunus cistena (also some of the Prunus' in Chapter 15)
Rosa glauca

GRAY OR GRAY-GREEN

Amorpha fruticosa
Buddleia alternifolia
Caryopteris clandonensis
Cotoneaster racemiflora soongorica
Cytisus battandieri
Daphne cneorum
Elaeagnus angustifolia
"   commutata
"   multiflora
"   umbellata
Holodiscus discolor
Lavandula officinalis
Lonicera bella 'Candida'
Myrica pensylvanica
Shepherdia argentea
Viburnum lantana
Vitex (several species)

BLUE-GREEN

Lonicera korolkowii
"   "   'Zabelii'
Mahonia bealii
"   repens
Tamarix gallica
"   hispida
Viburnum bitchiuense

RED TURNING GREEN OR GREENISH

Acer palmatum 'Ornatum'

VARIEGATED GREEN AND WHITE

Cornus alba 'Argenteo-marginata'
Kerria japonica 'Picta'
Pieris japonica 'Variegata'

VARIEGATED GREEN AND YELLOW

Cornus alba 'Spaethii'
Weigela florida 'Variegata'

VARIEGATED GREEN, WHITE AND PINK

Cornus alba 'Gouchaultii'
Cornus florida 'Welchii'
Leucothoë fontanesiana 'Girard's Rainbow'

THESE SHRUBS HAVE COLORED BARK OR TWIGS OR STEMS FOR WINTER INTEREST

GRAY

Acanthopanax sieboldianus
Buddleia alternifolia
Clethra alnifolia
Cornus racemosa
Ilex verticillata
Lonicera morrowii
"   tatarica

Viburnum opulus
"   sargentii
"   trilobum

YELLOW

Cornus stolonifera 'Flaviramea'

GREEN

Cytisus scoparius
Forsythia viridissima
Kerria japonica

PURPLE

Cornus alba 'Kesselringii'

RED

Acer palmatum
Cornus alba
"   "   'Sibirica'
"   amomum
"   florida
"   sanguinea
"   stolonifera
"   "   baileyi
"   "   coloradensis
"   "   'Kelsey'
Rosa nitida
"   virginiana

SHRUBS AND SMALL TREES THAT HAVE BEAUTIFUL AUTUMN FOLIAGE COLORS

PURPLE OR PURPLISH

Berberis verruculosa
Cornus amomum
"   racemosa
Cotoneaster apiculata
"   horizontalis
Forsythia intermedia
"   viridissima
Hydrangea quercifolia
Ligustrum obtusifolium
"   "   regelianum
Mahonia aquifolium
"   repens
Pachistima canbyi
Physocarpus monogynus
Prunus maritima
Rhododendron roseum
Stewartia pseudocamellia
Rhododendron yedoense
Symphoricarpus chenaultii
Viburnum acerifolium
"   carlesii
"   dilatatum
"   lentago
"   molle
"   plicatum

PINK, RED, SCARLET OR CRIMSON

Acer ginnala
"   palmatum
Aralia spinosa
Aronia arbutifolia
"   "   'Brilliantissima'
"   melanocarpa
Berberis koreana
"   mentorensis
"   thunbergii
"   "   'Erecta'
"   "   minor

Chaenomeles speciosa
Cornus alba
" " 'Sibirica'
" amomum
" florida
" kousa
" mas
" sanguinea
" stolonifera
" " baileyi
Cotinus coggygria
Cotoneaster adpressa
" dielsiana
" divaricata
" foveolata
" horizontalis
Crataegus crus-galli
" lavallei
" oxyacantha
" " 'Paul's Scarlet'
" phaenopyrum
Diervilla lonicera
" sessilifolia
Enkianthus campanulatus
Euonymus alata
" " 'Compacta'
" atropurpurea
" europaea
" yedoensis
Oxydendrum arboreum
Photinia villosa
Rhododendron arborescens
" mucronulatum
" schlippenbachii
" vaseyi
Rhus aromatica
" copallina
" glabra
" typhina
Ribes alpinum
" aureum
" odoratum
Rosa nitida
" setigera
Rubus odoratus
Spiraea prunifolia
Stephanandra incisa
Syringa microphylla
Vaccinium corymbosum
Viburnum bitchiuense
" burkwoodii
" carlcephalum
" cassinoides
" dentatum
" fragrans
" lantana
" opulus
" plicatum tomentosum
" prunifolium
" trilobum
" wrightii

YELLOW AND/OR ORANGE

Acanthopanax sieboldianus
Aesculus parviflora
Amelanchiers (various)
Callicarpa japonica (and others)
Cercis canadensis
" chinensis
Chionanthus retusus
" virginicus
Clethra alnifolia
" " 'Rosea'
Fothergilla (all species)
Halesia carolina
Hamamelis mollis
" vernalis
" virginiana

Hypericum calycinum and other species
Kerria japonica
Koelreuteria paniculata
Lindera benzoin
Physocarpus opulifolius
Prinsepia sinensis
Rhododendron calendulaceum
Sambucus canadensis
Spiraea thunbergii
Stewartia ovata

BRONZE

Abelia grandiflora
Buxus microphylla koreana
Euonymus nana turkestanica
Leucothoë fontanesiana

RED AND YELLOW

Berberis mentorensis
Cotinus coggygria
Franklinia alatamaha
Parrotia persica
Rosa rugosa
" virginiana
Viburnum setigerum

SHRUBS THAT WILL GROW IN SHADY PLACES (but not necessarily deep shade)

Full (or complete) shade — that found under low-branching trees or under evergreens. Practically no shrubs will grow in this type of shade.

Dense (or deep) shade — that found in fairly dense woods where spring wildflowers bloom but there is little but foliage covering the ground during summer.

Semi- (or half) shade — that found in shade of buildings, trees, or large shrubs which cast a shadow for about half the day, allowing full exposure to sun the rest of the day. Because of half-time sun and half-time shade, it is difficult to find shrubs to grow in this type of shade.

Light shade — that found under high-branched trees which allow filtered sunlight to reach plants. The perfect type of shade for shade-loving shrubs and trees.

Abelia grandiflora
Acanthopanax sieboldianus
Amelanchier species
Aronia arbutifolia and other species
Berberis julianae
" thunbergii
" verruculosa
Buxus (most species)
Calycanthus floridus
Ceanothus americanus
Cephalanthus occidentalis
Cercis canadensis
" chinensis
Chionanthus virginicus
Clethra alnifolia
" " 'Rosea'
Comptonia peregrina
Cornus alba
" amomum
" mas
" racemosa
" stolonifera
Corylus americana and other species
Cyrilla racemiflora

Daphne mezereum
Diervilla lonicera
Diervilla sessilifolia
Enkianthus campanulatus
Euonymus americana
" kiautschovicus
Fothergilla (all species)
Hamamelis virginiana
*Hydrangea quercifolia
Hypericum calycinum
" frondosum
" prolificum
Ilex glabra
" verticillata
Kalmia latifolia
Leucothoë fontanesiana
*Ligustrum obtusifolium regelianum
Ligustrum vulgare
Lonicera (many species
Mahonia aquifolium
" bealii
" repens
Pachistima canbyi
Philadelphus coronarius
Physocarpus opulifolius
Pieris floribunda
" japonica
Rhamnus cathartica
Rhododendron (many species and cultivars)
particularly those below
Rhodendron calendulaceum
" catawbiense
" gandavense
" kaempferi
" maximum
" nudiflorum
Rhodotypos scandens
Ribes alpinum
" odoratum
Rubus odoratus
Sorbaria sorbifolia
Staphylea trifolia
Stephanandra incisa
" " 'Crispa'
Styrax species
Symphoricarpos albus laevigatus
" orbiculatus
Vaccinium species
Viburnum acerifolium
" cassinoides
" dentatum
" lantana
" lentago
" plicatum tomentosum
" prunifolium
" sieboldii
Weigela (most)
Xanthorhiza simplicissima
Zenobia pulverulenta

*will grow in deep shade -- if you cannot grow these, no shrub will grow

SHRUBS THAT WILL THRIVE IN A MOIST SITUATION

Amelanchier species
Aronia arbutifolia
Calycanthus floridus
Cephalanthus occidentalis
Chamaedaphne calyculata
Clethra alnifolia
" " 'Rosea'
Comptonia peregrina
Cornus alba
" amomum
" sanguinea
" stolonifera
" " baileyi

Hamamelis, many species
Hippophaë rhamnoides
Ilex glabra
" verticillata
Kalmia latifolia
Leucothoë fontanesiana
Lindera benzoin
Pachistima canbyi
Rhododendron arborescens
" canadense
" nudiflorum
" vaseyi
" viscosum
Salix caprea
" discolor and other willows
Sambucus canadensis
Spiraea tomentosa
Staphylea trifolia
Vaccinium corymbosum
Viburnum acerifolium
" cassinoides
" dentatum
" lentago
" opulus
" sieboldii
" trilobum
Zenobia pulverulenta

SHRUBS AND SMALL TREES THAT WILL THRIVE IN A VERY DRY SITUATION AND/OR IN SANDY SOIL

Acanthopanax sieboldianus
Acer ginnala
Amelanchier stolonifera
Amorpha fruticosa
Aralia spinosa
Berberis mentorensis
" thunbergii
Buddleia alternifolia
Caragana arborescens
" frutex
Ceanothus americanus
Chaenomeles speciosa
Colutea arborescens
Cornus racemosa
Coronilla eremurus
Cotinus coggygria
Cytisus species
Deutzia scabra
Diervilla lonicera
" sessilifolia
Elaeagnus angustifolia
" commutata
" multiflora
Genista species
Kolkwitzia amabilis
Lavandula species
Lespedeza bicolor
Ligustrum obtusifolium regelianum and other privets
Lonicera morrowii
Myrica pensylvanica
Philadelphus coronarius
Physocarpus opulifolius
Potentilla fruticosa
Prunus besseyi
" maritima
Ribes alpinum
" odoratum
Rhamnus cathartica
" frangula
Rhodotypos scandens
Rhus aromatica
" copallina
" glabra
" trilobata
" typhina

Robinia hispida
Rosa multiflora
" nitida
" rugosa
" setigera
" pimpinellifolia
" virginiana
Shepherdia argentea
Symphoricarpos species
Tamarix gallica
" parviflora
Viburnum lantana
" lentago
Vitex agnus-castus 'Latifolia'

THESE SHRUBS AND SMALL TREES SUCCEED PARTICULARLY WELL UNDER SEASHORE CONDITIONS

Aronia arbutifolia
Calluna vulgaris
Clethra alnifolia
" " 'Rosea'
Comptonia peregrina
Cornus stolonifera
" " baileyi
Cotoneaster acutifolia
" adpressa
" apiculata
" dielsiana
" divaricata
" foveolata
" multiflora
Cytisus scoparius
Elaeagnus angustifolia
Halimodendron halodendron
Hibiscus syriacus
Hippophaë rhamnoides
Hydrangea (all species)
Ilex glabra
Lavandula (all species)
Ligustrum amurense
" ovalifolium
Lonicera morrowii
" tatarica
Myrica pensylvanica
Potentilla fruticosa
Prunus maritima
Rhamnus cathartica
Ribes (many species)
Rosa blanda
" eglanteria
" multiflora
" pimpinellifolia
" rugosa
" virginiana
Sambucus canadensis
Spiraea (many species)
Syringa vulgaris
Tamarix (all species)
Vaccinium corymbosum
Viburnum cassinoides
" dentatum

THE FOLLOWING SHRUBS AND SMALL TREES DO WELL UNDER CITY CONDITIONS

Acanthopanax sieboldianus
Acer ginnala
Aesculus parviflora
Amelanchier laevis
Amorpha fruticosa
Aralia spinosa
Aronia arbutifolia
Berberis thunbergii
Buxus microphylla koreana

Caragana arborescens
Cercis canadensis
Chaenomeles japonica
Chionanthus virginicus
Cornus alba 'Sibirica'
" amomum
" mas
" officinalis
" racemosa
" sanguinea
" stolonifera 'Flaviramea'
Cotinus coggygria
Cotoneaster acutifolia
Crataegus crus-galli
" intricata
" mollis
" oxyacantha
" phaenopyrum
Deutzia scabra
Elaeagnus angustifolia
" umbellata
Eyonymus alata
" " 'Compacta'
" europaea
Forsythia intermedia 'Spectabilis'
" ovata
" suspensa
" " fortunei
Hamamelis (several species)
Hibiscus syriacus
Hippophaë rhamnoides
Hydrangea arborescens
" paniculata
Hypericum frondosum
Ilex crenata
Kalmia latifolia
Kerria japonica
Leucothoë fontanesiana
Ligustrum amurense
" obtusifolium regelianum
" vulgare
Lonicera fragrantissima
" tatarica
Magnolia soulangeana
" stellata
Mahonia aquifolium
Malus sargentii
Myrica pensylvanica
Philadelphus coronarius
" virginalis
Physocarpus opulifolius
Pieris japonica
Potentilla fruticosa
Prunus tomentosa
" subhirtella
Pyracantha coccinea 'Lalandei'
Rhamnus cathartica
" frangula
Rhododendron calendulaceum
" carolinianum
" catawbiense
" mucronulatum
" obtusum 'Amoenum'
Rhodotypos scandens
Rhus aromatica
" glabra
" typhina
Ribes alpinum
" odoratum
Rosa multiflora
" rugosa
" wichuraiana
Sambucus canadensis
Spiraea bumalda 'Anthony Waterer'
" vanhouttei
Symphoricarpos chenaultii
Syringa amurensis japonica
" villosa
" vulgaris
Tamarix parviflora

Viburnum burkwoodii
" carlesii
" dentatum
" lantana
" lentago
" opulus
" plicatum
" " tomentosum
" prunifolium
" trilobum
Vitex agnus-castus 'Latifolia'
Weigela florida

THESE SHRUBS MAY BE USED FOR HEDGES. ALL MAY BE LEFT UNCLIPPED, THOSE MARKED * WILL TOLERATE CLIPPING

*Abelia grandiflora
*Acanthopanax sieboldianus
*Acer ginnala
*Berberis (several-see text)
Calycanthus floridus
Caragana arborescens
*Chaenomeles japonica
* speciosa
*Cornus mas
* " racemosa
" stolonifera 'Kelsey'
Corylus avellana
*Cotoneaster acutifolia
* " apiculata
*Crataegus (many, see text)
*Deutzia gracilis
* " lemoinei
* " rosea
*Elaeagnus angustifolia
*Euonymus alata
* " " 'Compacta'
* " europaea
* " fortunei 'Vegeta'
* " kiautchovica
*Fontanesia fortunei
*Forsythia intermedia
Hamamelis mollis
" virginiana
*Hibiscus syriacus
Hydrangea arborescens grandiflora
" paniculata
*Ilex (several, see text)
Kolkwitzia amabilis
*Lavandula officinalis
*Ligustrum (many, see text)
*Lonicera (many, see text)
*Malus sargentii
*Myrica pensylvanica
Philadelphus (several, see text)
*Physocarpus monogynus
* " opulifolius
*Prinsepia sinensis
*Prunus tomentosa
*Rhamnus cathartica
* " frangula
* " " 'Columnaris'
*Rhodotypos scandens
*Ribes alpinum
* " diacanthum
* " odoratum
Rosa blanda
" harisonii
* " hugonis
* " rugosa
" virginiana
Salix purpurea 'Gracilis'
*Spiraea arguta
* " compacta
" bumalda 'Anthony Waterer'
" " 'Froebelii'

*Spiraea prunifolium
" thunbergii
" vanhouttei
*Symphoricarpos (several, see text)
*Syringa chinensis
* " prestoniae
" pubescens
* " villosa
* " vulgaris
Tamarix pentandra
Vaccinium corymbosum
Viburnum cassinoides
" dilatatum
" lantana
" opulus
" " 'Nanum'
" plicatum tomentosum
" prunifolium
" sieboldii

FOR A THORNY HEDGE CHOOSE:

Acanthopanax sieboldianus
Berberis species
Chaenomeles species
Crataegus species
Elaeagnus multiflora
Prinsepia sinensis

Or one of the roses under Rosa

THESE SHRUBS MAY BE USED TO HOLD BANKS

Amelanchier stolonifera
Ceanothus americanus
Clethra alnifolia
" " 'Rosea'
Comptonia peregrina
Cornus alba
" amomum
" stolonifera
Cotoneaster horizontalis
Cytisus scoparius
Diervilla lonicera
" sessilifolia
Forsythia intermedia 'Arnold Dwarf'
" suspensa
" " sieboldii
Holodiscus discolor
Hypericum calycinum
Rhus aromatica
" copallina
Robinia hispida
Rosa multiflora
" rugosa
" setigera
" virginiana
" wichuraiana
Rubus odoratus
Symphoricarpos, several
Xanthorhiza simplicissima

THESE SHRUBS MAKE GOOD GROUND COVERS

Aronia melanocarpa
Calluna vulgaris
Cotoneaster adpressa
" praecox
" horizontalis
" microphylla
Forsythia intermedia 'Arnold Dwarf'
Hypericum calycinum
Pachistima canbyi
Rhus aromatica
Stephanandra incisa 'Crispa'
Xanthorhiza simplicissima

22

THESE SHRUBS ARE THE BEST FOR ESPALIERING OR TRAINING AGAINST A FENCE OR WALL

Chaenomeles japonica
Cotoneaster horizontalis
" " perpusilla
Forsythia suspensa
" " sieboldii
Pyracantha coccinea 'Lalandei'

FRUITS OF THE FOLLOWING GENERA AND SPECIES ARE RELISHED BY BIRDS

Amelanchier
Aralia spinosa
Aronia
Berberis
Chionanthus
Cornus
Cotoneaster
Crataegus
Elaeagnus
Euonymus fortunei 'Vegeta'
Hippophaë
Ilex
Ligustrum
Lonicera
Malus
Myrica
Photinia
Prunus
Pyracantha
Rhamnus
Rhus
Ribes
Rosa
Rubus
Sambucus
Sorbus
Symplocos
Vaccinium
Viburnum

FRUITS ARE FORMED ON THE FOLLOWING GENERA ONLY IF PLANTS WITH BLOOMS OF BOTH SEXES ARE PRESENT

Comptonia
Cotinus
Hippophaë
Ilex

Lindera
Maclura
Myrica
Rhus
Ribes
Shepherdia

THE FOLLOWING SHRUBS ARE BEST MOVED IN SPRING

Buddleia
Calycanthus
Colutea
Cornus florida, its varieties and cultivars
Crataegus
Hibiscus syriacus and its cultivars
Kalmia latifolia
Lindera
Magnolia
Rhododendron (including azalea)
Rhus
Stephanandra
Tamárix

THE FOLLOWING GENERA AND SPECIES OF SHRUBS MUST HAVE ACID SOIL TO THRIVE

Amelanchier
Calluna
Clethra
Cyrilla racemiflora
Cytisus
Enkianthus
Erica
Fothergilla
Ilex
Kalmia
Leucothoë
Magnolia virginiana
Myrica pensylvanica
Rhododendron (including most Azaleas)
Vaccinium
Xanthorhiza simplicissima
Zenobia pulverulenta

THE FOLLOWING SHRUBS ARE THORNY, SO MAKE EXCELLENT BARRIERS

Acanthopanax sieboldianus
Berberis, all species

Chaenomeles japonica
" speciosa
Crataegus, all species
Malus sargentii
Prinsepia sinensis
Rhamnus cathartica
Rosa, all species
Rubus, all species

SHRUBS FOR EASY MAINTENANCE: MINIMUM CARE NEEDED

Acanthopanax sieboldianus
Aronia arbutifolia
Berberis thunbergii
Clethra alnifolia*
" " 'Rosea'*
Comptonia asplenifolia
Corylus americana
Deutzia gracilis
" rosea
Diervilla (all species)
Elaeagnus angustifolia
" commutata
" multiflora
Forsythia intermedia
" suspensa fortunei
Hamamelis (all species)
Hypericum frondosum
" prolificum
Ilex glabra*
" verticillata*
Kalmia latifolia*
Ligustrum vulgare
Lindera benzoin
Lonicera (all species)
Myrica pensylvanica*
Potentilla fruticosa
Rhododendron calendulaceum*
" canadense*
" carolinianum*
" kaempferi*
" maximum*
" nudiflorum*
" vaseyi*
" viscosum
Rhus (all species)
Ribes (all species)
Robinia hispida
Rosa blanda
" glauca
" nitida
" virginiana

Viburnum acerifolium
" cassinoides
" dentatum
" lantana
" lentago
" molle
" prunifolium

*Assuming soil is acid or is made acid.

SHRUBS FOR EASY MAINTENANCE: FEW OR NO PESTS

Acanthopanax sieboldianus
Amorpha fruticosa
Buxus sempervirens
Calluna vulgaris
Clethra alnifolia
" " 'Rosea'
Colutea arborescens
Coronilla eremurus
Corylus avellana
Diervilla (all species)
Elaeagnus angustifolia
Enkianthus campanulatus
Forsythia (all species)
Fothergilla (all species)
Hamamelis (all species)
Hypericum (all species)
Ilex crenata
" glabra
" verticillata
Kalmia latifolia
Kerria japonica
Koelreuteria paniculata
Ligustrum vulgare
Lonicera fragrantissima
" korolkowii
" maackii
" morrowii
" tatarica
Magnolia stellata
Philadelphus (all species)
Physocarpus (all species)
Pieris (all species)
Rhododendron (many)
Rhodotypos scandens
Rhus (all species)
Spiraea (all species)
Tamarix (all species)
Viburnum (all species) except V. opulus 'Roseum'
Xanthorhiza simplicissima

BLOOM TIME CHART

LISTED BELOW ARE ULTIMATE HEIGHT, FLOWER COLOR, BLOOM TIME, FRUIT COLOR AND FRUIT TIME OF SHRUBS IN THIS BOOK HAVING SHOWY FLOWERS.

TIMES OF MONTHS INDICATED ARE FOR BLOOM IN ZONE 5B. PLANTS WILL FLOWER EARLIER IN THE SOUTH AND LATER IN THE NORTH, BUT THE SEQUENCE WILL BE THE SAME.

L	M	H	Name	Mar E	Mar M	Mar L	Apr E	Apr M	Apr L	May E	May M	May L	Jun E	Jun M	Jun L	Jul E	Jul M	Jul L	Aug E	Aug M	Aug L	Sep E	Sep M	Sep L
		x	Hamamelis vernalis	Y----																				
x	x	x	Salix species & cv.	G------------																				
x	x	x	Corylus species	BR-------																				
	x		Forsythia ovata		Y-------																			
		x	Hamamelis japonica		Y-------																			
		x	" flavo-purpurascens		R-------																			
		x	" mollis		Y-------																			
		x	Cornus mas & cv.				Y-----									Fr/R-------------								
		x	" officinalis				Y----									Fr/S-----------								
x			Erica carnea	RO-PR																				
x			" 'Vivellii'	PR																				
		x	Viburnum fragrans				P									Fr/R to B----------								
	x		Abeliophyllum distichum					W-----																
	x	x	Corylopsis species					Y																
x			Daphne mezereum					P-PR								Fr/R								
x			" 'Alba'					W								Fr/Y								
x	x	x	Forsythia species, vars. & cvs.					Y-----																
		x	Lindera benzoin					Y----											Fr/R---					
		x	Lonicera fragrantissima					C-W-				Fr/R												
		x	Magnolia stellata					W-----										Fr/GR to T&R					
		x	" rosea					P-----										Fr/GR to T&R					
		x	" rubra					PR-P										Fr/GR to T&R					
		x	" 'Waterlily'					P----										Fr/GR to T&R					
		x	Pieris japonica & cv.					W-----																
	x		" taiwanensis					W-----																
		x	Amelanchier laevis						W					Fr/BL-B										
x			Chaenomeles japonica, var. & cv.						O-R------											Fr/GR to Y-----				
	x		" speciosa						S--------											Fr/GR to Y----				
	x		" cvs.						Num.											Fr/GR to Y----				
x			Chamaedaphne calyculata						W---															
x			Daphne genkwa						L-------															
	x		Halesia carolina						W-------															
	x		Magnolia kobus						W-------										Fr/GR to T&R					
	x		Pieris floribunda						W-------															
	x		Prunus cerasifera cvs.						P, W											Fr/Y to R				
	x		" persica cvs.						P, R, W									Fr/R or Y						
	x		" subhirtella & cvs.						P--------								Fr/B							
x			" tenella						RO--------									Fr/R						
	x		" tomentosa						W---					Fr/R---										
	x		" triloba						P---															
	x		Rhododendron molle						Y-----															
x			" mucronulatum						L--------															
	x		Viburnum bodnantense						P--------										Fr/B					
	x		Amelanchier grandiflora							W--								Fr/R to B					
x			" stolonifera							W--								Fr/B					
		x	Chionanthus virginicus							W--											Fr/B--------		
		x	Exochorda giraldii wilsonii							W--													
x			" macrantha 'The Bride'							W-													
		x	Halesia monticola							W--													
		x	Magnolia soulangiana & cvs.							W--								Fr/GR to T&R------------					
x	x		Mahonia species							Y----				Fr/B					or	Fr/Bl-B		
	x		Prunus blireiana							P----											Fr/R-PR		
	x		" glandulosa & cvs.							P or W								Fr/R					
x			" 'Hally Jolivette'							W-----													
x			" maritima							W-----									Fr/PR			
	x		" serrulata & cvs.							W or P					Fr/B							
x			Rhododendron canadense							R-PR--													
x	x		" Shammarello hybrids							P, R and W													
x			Rhus aromatica							Y----				Fr/R								
	x		Ribes species							Y--											Fr/PR or B		
		x	Sambucus racemosa and cv.							W--					Fr/S-------------							
x			Spiraea arguta & var.							W--													
x			" thunbergii							W--													

CODE

Dashes and spacing of code letters show duration of bloom.

L = Low (to 3' in height)	P = Pink	W = White	PR = Purple
M = Medium-high (3' to 6')	Y = Yellow	R = Red	T = Tan
H = High (over 6')	RO = Rose	B = Black	BL = Blue
xx or xxx means growing to these 2 or 3 heights	V = Violet	S = Scarlet	L = Lavender
(see text for which)	BR = Brown	O = Orange	C = Cream
	G = Gray	GR = Green	CR = Crimson
* calls attention to the fact that the true flower	Num. = numerous or various		
is yellow; the bracts, for which the shrub is	cv. = cultivar	var. = variety	These terms include only those shrubs in this book.
grown, are a different color.	cvs. = cultivars	vars. = varieties	

HEIGHT				MAY	JUNE	JULY	AUGUST	SEPTEMBER	OCTOBER
L	M	H		E M L	E M L	E M L	E M L	E M L	E M L
		x	Viburnum bitchiuense	P---		Fr/B			
	x		carlesii & cv.	P to W		Fr/B			
	x		juddii	P to W		Fr/B			
		x	Amelanchier alnifolia	W--		Fr/BL-B			
x			Berberis candidula	Y--				Fr/PR	
	x		julianae	Y--				Fr/BL-B	
	x		koreana	Y--				Fr/S-R	
		x	mentorensis	Y--				Fr/R	
		x	thunbergii, var. & cv.	Y--				Fr/S-R thru winter	
	x		triacanthophora	W & R				Fr/BL-B	
	x		Calycanthus floridus	R-BR					
x		x	Caragana species & cv.	Y--					
		x	Cercis canadensis & cv.	R-PR					
		x	" 'Alba'	W--					
		x	chinensis	R-PR					
		x	Chionanthus retusus	W		Fr/T------------	---	Fr/B---	
		x	Colutea arborescens	Y--					---
		x	Cornus florida & cvs.	*W (Y)				Fr/R----------	
		x	'Cherokee Chief'	*RO (Y)				Fr/R----------	
		x	rubra & cv.	*P-RO (Y)				Fr/R----------	
		x	xanthocarpa	*W (Y)				Fr/Y----------	
		x	Crataegus mollis	W-----			Fr/S---------------		
	x		Cytisus praecox 'Hollandica'	Y & R					
x			purgans	Y-----					
	x		scoparius	Y-----					
	x		" 'Andreanus'	Y & R					
x			Daphne cneorum	P------------					
		x	Enkianthus campanulatus	Y to O					
		x	Exochorda racemosa	W-----					
	x		Fothergilla major	W-----					
		x	monticola	W-----					
x	x		Kerria japonica & cvs.	Y------------					
	x		Magnolia liliflora 'Nigra'	PR------------		Fr/GR to T & R---------------------------	---		
		x	soulangiana 'Rubra'	RO-PR		Fr/GR to T & R---------------------------	---		
	x		Malus sargentii	W-----			Fr/R-------------------		
	x		Prunus besseyi	W-----				Fr/PR-B	
	x		cistena	W or P				Fr/B-PR	
x			Rhododendron yedoense	R-PR					
	x		" poukhanense	R-PR					
		x	Syringa vulgaris	L-PR--------					
		x	" 'Alba'	W------------					
		x	" hybrids	Num.-----					
		x	Viburnum burkwoodii	P to W			Fr/B		
	x		carlcephalum	P to W					
		x	opulus 'Roseum'	GR-W--------					
		x	plicatum tomentosum & cv.	W------------		Fr/R to B			
	x		Weigela florida 'Venusta'	RO-P					
		x	Acer ginnala		Y-------- Fr/R---------------------------------				
	x	x	Aesculus pavia		RO--------				
	x		Aronia arbutifolia & cv.		W--------			Fr/R----thru winter	
x			melanocarpa		W--------			Fr/PR-BL---------	
	x		Berberis verruculosa		Y--------			Fr/PR-BL	
		x	Buddleia alternifolia		L---------				
		x	Cornus alba & cvs.		C-W----------		Fr/BL-W		
		x	alternifolia		W----------		Fr/BL-B		
		x	sanguinea		W----------			Fr/PR-B	
	x	x	stolonifera		W----------				Fr/W------
		x	" baileyi		W----------		Fr/W--------		
	x		" coloradensis		W----------			Fr/BL-W---------	
	x		" 'Flaviramea'		W----------	Fr/W--------			
x			" 'Kelsey'		W----------				
	x		Coronilla eremurus		Y---				
		x	Cotoneaster acutifolia		P-W			Fr/B---------------	
x	x		adpressa & var.		P----------			Fr/R-------------	
	x		apiculata		PR-P--------			Fr/R-------------	
	x		bullata floribunda		P----------			Fr/S-------------	

CODE
Dashes and spacing of code letters show duration of bloom.

L = Low (to 3' in height)
M = Medium-high (3' to 6')
H = High (over 6')
xx or xxx means growing to these 2 or 3 heights
   (see text for which)

* calls attention to the fact that the true flower
  is yellow; the bracts, for which the shrub is
  grown, are a different color.

P = Pink	W = White	PR = Purple
Y = Yellow	R = Red	T = Tan
RO = Rose	B = Black	BL = Blue
V = Violet	S = Scarlet	L = Lavender
BR = Brown	O = Orange	C = Cream
G = Gray	GR = Green	CR = Crimson
Num. = numerous or various		
cv. = cultivar	var. = variety	
cvs. = cultivars	vars. = varieties	These terms include only those shrubs in this book.

BLOOM TIME CHART (cont'd)

L	M	H	Plant	May	June	July	August	September	October
x			Cotoneaster dammeri	W———				Fr/R———	
	x		divaricata	PR–P———					Fr/R———
		x	foveolata	W———				Fr/B———	
	x		integerrima	P———			Fr/R———		
		x	lucida	P———				Fr/B———	
	x		multiflora & var.	W———			Fr/R———		
	x	x	racemiflora & var.	W———				Fr/R———	
		x	Crataegus species except those below	W———				Fr/R or S———	
		x	lavallei	W———					Fr/R–thru winter
		x	mordenensis 'Toba'	P———					Fr/R———
		x	oxyacantha 'Paul's Scarlet'	S———					
		x	" 'Rosea Plena'	RO———					
		x	viridis ('Winter King')	W———					Fr/R–thru winter
	x		Cytisus praecox	Y———					
	x		" 'Albus'	W———					
	x		Daphne burkwoodii 'Somerset'	P———					
x			Deutzia gracilis	W———					
x			kalmiaeflora	P———					
x	x		lemoinei & cv.	W———					
	x		rosea	W———					
		x	Laburnum species & cv.	Y———					
x	x	x	Lonicera species, vars. and cvs.	W, P, RO, PR		Fr/R or O			
		x	Magnolia soulangiana 'Lennei'	RO/PR			Fr/GR to T & R———		
		x	virginiana	W———————————			Fr/GR to T & R———		
	x		Paeonia suffruticosa	Num.					
	x		Photinia villosa	W———				Fr/R———	
		x	Prunus virginiana	W———			Fr/R———		
	x		Rhododendron carolinianum	PR–P———					
	x		" album	W———					
x	x		Exbury hybrids	Num.———					
x	x	x	Gable hybrids	Num.———					
	x	x	gandavense (Ghent hybrids)	Num.———					
	x		kaempferi	RO———					
	x		" hybrids	Num.———					
x	x		Knap Hill hybrids	Num.———					
	x		kosterianum (Mollis hybrids)	Num.———					
	x		nudiflorum	P or W					
x	x		P.J.M. hybrids	Num.———					
	x		roseum	P———					
x			Robinia hispida	PR–P———		Fr/R			
	x		Rosa blanda	RO–P———				Fr/R———	
	x		hugonis	Y———				Fr/S to R———	
	x	x	pimpinellifolia hybrids	Num.———					
		x	Sambucus nigra & cvs.	W———			Fr/B———		
		x	Sorbus species	W———			Fr/O–R———		
x			Spiraea japonica alpina	P———					
x			lemoinei alpestris	P———					
	x		media sericea	W———					
	x		multiflora	W———					
	x		pikoviensis	W———					
	x		prunifolia	W———					
	x		trilobata	W———					
	x		vanhouttei	W———					
		x	Symplocos paniculata	W———				Fr/BL	
		x	Syringa chinensis	L–PR———					
		x	" 'Saugeana'	R–PR———					
	x		laciniata	L———					
	x		microphylla	L———					
	x		" 'Superba'	P———					
	x		persica	L———					
	x		" 'Alba'	W———					
		x	Tamarix parviflora	P———					
	x		Vaccinium corymbosum & hybrids	W———			Fr/BL———		
	x		Viburnum acerifolium	W———				Fr/C to B	
	x		burkwoodii 'Chenault'	P to W			Fr/B———		
		x	dilatatum	C–W				Fr/S———	

CODE

Dashes and spacing of code letters show duration of bloom.

L = Low (to 3' in height)
M = Medium-high (3' to 6')
H = High (over 6')
xx or xxx means growing to these 2 or 3 heights
(see text for which)

* calls attention to the fact that the true flower is yellow; the bracts, for which the shrub is grown, are a different color.

P = Pink
Y = Yellow
RO = Rose
V = Violet
BR = Brown
G = Gray
Num. = numerous or various
cv. = cultivar
cvs. = cultivars

W = White
R = Red
B = Black
S = Scarlet
O = Orange
GR = Green

var. = variety
vars. = varieties

PR = Purple
T = Tan
BL = Blue
L = Lavender
C = Cream
CR = Crimson

These terms include only those shrubs in this book.

HEIGHT L	M	H	Plant	MAY	JUNE	JULY	AUGUST	SEPTEMBER	OCTOBER
		x	Viburnum dilatatum xanthocarpum	C–W				Fr/Y———	
		x	lantana	C–W				Fr/R to B	
		x	lantanaphyllum	C–W				Fr/R to B	
		x	lentago	W———				Fr/BL–B to winter	
		x	molle	C–W			Fr/BL–B		
		x	opulus & cv.	C–W					Fr/R thru winter
		x	" xanthocarpum	C–W					Fr/Y———
		x	plicatum & cvs.	W———		Fr/R to B			
		x	prunifolium	W———					Fr/BL–B
	x		rhytidophylloides	C–W					Fr/R to B
		x	rhytidophyllum	C–W					Fr/R to B
		x	sargentii	C–W					Fr/R to winter
		x	sieboldii	C–W			Fr/Y, R, BL, B		
		x	trilobum	C–W				Fr/R thru winter	
		x	wrightii	C–W			Fr/S———		
		x	Xanthoceras sorbifolium	W———				Fr/GR————BR	
x			Zenobia pulverulenta	W————					
		x	Cornus kousa, var. & cv.		*W (Y) ———			Fr/RO	
		x	Cotinus coggygria	P to G———————————————————Fr/G———————					
		x	" 'Purpureus'	P to PR——————————————————Fr/G———————					
x			Deutzia rosea 'Pink Pompon'	L–P———					
x			Genista tinctoria	Y———					
		x	Kolkwitzia amabilis	P———					
	x		Leucothoë fontanesiana & cv.	W———					
	x	x	Philadelphus species, vars. & cvs.	W———					
	x	x	Physocarpus species, var. & cv.	W or P				Fr/R or T————————	
		x	Rhododendron 'America'	R———					
		x	calendulaceum	Y, S, or C					
		x	catawbiense	R–PR					
	x		laetevirens	P to PR					
		x	Rosa foetida 'Bicolor' (Austrian Copper)	Y & R				Fr/R———	
		x	" 'Persian Yellow'	Y———					
		x	glauca	P———				Fr/R–O	
	x		harisonii	Y———				Fr/B	
x			pimpinellifolia	W———				Fr/B or BR	
	x		" 'Altaica'	C–W				FR/R–BR	
	x		rugosa	PR–P———————————————————Fr/O–R———————————					
	x		" 'Alba'	W———————————————————Fr/O–R———————————					
	x		" hybrids	Num.					
	x		Styrax species	W———					
	x		Syringa josikaea	L–PR———					
	x		reflexa	P–L					
	x		swegiflexa	P———					
	x		velutina	PR–P					
	x		Viburnum dentatum	C–W———				Fr/BL———	
	x		setigerum	C–W				Fr/RO———	
x	x	x	Weigela species, vars. & cvs.	W, P, RO or PR–R					
		x	Cornus amomum		W———		Fr/B		
	x		Cotoneaster dielsiana		P———				Fr/S———
x			horizontalis & var.		P———			Fr/R———————————	
x			microphylla		W———			Fr/S thru winter	
		x	Crataegus phaenopyrum		W———			Fr/R———————————	
		x	Deutzia scabra 'Pride of Rochester'		W———				
x			Hypericum patulum 'Hidcote'		Y————————————————————————				
	x		Kalmia latifolia		P———				
x	x		Potentilla species, vars. & cvs.		Y or W———————————————————————————				
	x		parviflora 'Tangerine'		O to Y———————————————————————				
	x		Pyracantha coccinea & cvs.		W———			Fr/O–R———————thru winter	
		x	Rhododendron 'Catawbiense Album'		W———				
		x	'English Roseum'		RO———				
		x	'Lee's Dark Purple'		PR———				
		x	'Purpureum Elegans'		B–L				
	x		'Roseum Elegans'		RO———				
		x	'Roseum Superbum'		PR–RO				
x			Rosa centifolia 'Muscosa' (moss roses)		Num.				
	x		eglanteria		RO–PR				Fr/O to S———

CODE

Dashes and spacing of code letters show duration of bloom.

L = Low (to 3' in height)
M = Medium-high (3' to 6')
H = High (over 6')
xx or xxx means growing to these 2 or 3 heights
   (see text for which)

* calls attention to the fact that the true flower
  is yellow; the bracts, for which the shrub is
  grown, are a different color.

P = Pink
Y = Yellow
RO = Rose
V = Violet
BR = Brown
G = Gray
Num. = numerous or various
cv. = cultivar
cvs. = cultivars

W = White
R = Red
B = Black
S = Scarlet
O = Orange
GR = Green

var. = variety
vars. = varieties

PR = Purple
T = Tan
BL = Blue
L = Lavender
C = Cream
CR = Crimson

These terms include only those shrubs in this book.

27

BLOOM TIME CHART (cont'd)

L	M	H		MAY	JUNE	JULY	AUGUST	SEPTEMBER	OCTOBER
x			Rosa moschata (musk) hybrids		Various				
x			" 'Robin Hood'		Ro–R————————————————————				
		x	moyesii		R—————			Fr/O–R———————————	
		x	" hybrids		Num.				
		x	multiflora		W————				Fr/R thru winter
	x		virginiana		P—————				Fr/R thru winter
	x		Spiraea sanssouciana		PR–P——				
	x		trichocarpa		W———				
x	x		Stephanandra incisa & var.		W———				
		x	Syringa amurensis japonica		W—————				
		x	prestonae		Num.				
		x	villosa & hybrids		Num.				
	x		Viburnum cassinoides		W———		Fr/P, BL, B		
x			Abelia grandiflora, vars. & cvs.		P—————————————————————————————				
x			Ceanothus americanus		W———————————————————		Fr/R——————		
		x	Cornus racemosa		W——————			Fr/W——————	
		x	Deutzia scabra		W———				
		x	" 'Plena'		W———				
	x		Diervilla species		Y———				
		x	Hydrangea arborescens		W————————				
		x	" 'Annabelle'		W———————————————————				
x			Hypericum moserianum		Y———————				
x			Lavandula officinalis & cv.		L————————				
		x	Rhododendron 'Album Elegans'		L–W to W				
		x	arborescens		W———				
		x	'Caractacus'		PR–R				
		x	maximum		RO————————				
x			Rosa nitida		RO————————		Fr/R		
x			'The Fairy'		P—————————————————————————				
		x	Sambucus canadensis & cv.		W——————		Fr/BL–B———		
	x		Sorbaria sorbifolia		W————————————————				
	x		Spiraea billiardii		PR–P———————————				
x			bumalda, var. & cv.		PR–P———————————				
x			japonica 'Atrosanguinea'		PR–P—————————				
	x		macrothyrsa		PR–P———————————				
x			nipponica tosaensis		W———				
	x		tomentosa		RO to RO–PR———————————				
		x	Amorpha fruticosa			V–PR———			
x			Callicarpa dichotoma			P————		Fr/L–PR	
x			japonica			P————		Fr/PR	
		x	Cyrilla racemiflora			W—————			
		x	Holodiscus discolor			W—————			
x			Hydrangea arborescens grandiflora			W————————————			
	x		heteromalla			W—————			
x			Hypericum kalmianum			Y————————————			
x			patulum henryi			Y———————————————			
	x		Rhododendron viscosum			W——————			
	x		Rosa setigera			P——————		Fr/R	
	x		Rubus odoratus			RO–P———		Fr/R——————	
x			Spiraea albiflora			W—————			
		x	Stewartia species			W—————			
	x		Tamarix pentandra 'Rubra' (Summer Glow)			P———————————			
x			Teucrium chamaedrys			P—————————————			
	x		Buddleia farquhari			L—————			
	x		Hydrangea quercifolia			W—————			
x			Hypericum frondosum			Y—————			
		x	Koelreuteria paniculata			Y———————————————Fr/GR to T			
	x		Nandina domestica			W—————		Fr/R thru winter	
x			Rosa wichuraiana			W—————		Fr/R—————	
	x		Tamarix odessana			P———			
		x	pentandra			P———			
		x	Aesculus parviflora				W——————	Fr/T——————————	
		x	Buddleia davidii cvs.				Num.———————————————————		
x			Calluna vulgaris				Ro–PR		
x			" 'Alba'				W————————		
	x		" 'Alba Erecta'				W————————		

CODE

Dashes and spacing of code letters show duration of bloom.

L = Low (to 3' in height)
M = Medium-high (3' to 6')
H = High (over 6')
xx or xxx means growing to these 2 or 3 heights
    (see text for which)

* calls attention to the fact that the true flower
is yellow; the bracts, for which the shrub is
grown, are a different color.

P = Pink
Y = Yellow
RO = Rose
V = Violet
BR = Brown
G = Gray
Num. = numerous or various
cv. = cultivar
cvs. = cultivars

W = White
R = Red
B = Black
S = Scarlet
O = Orange
GR = Green

var. = variety
vars. = varieties

PR = Purple
T = Tan
BL = Blue
L = Lavender
C = Cream
CR = Crimson

These terms include only those shrubs in this book.

HEIGHT				JUNE–NOVEMBER Bloom
L	M	H		
		x	Cephalanthus occidentalis	W-------------
	x		Clethra alnifolia	W-------------
x			Hydrangea macrophylla & cvs.	B or P-----------------------
x			Hypericum calycinum	Y--------------------------------
x			prolificum	Y------
x			'Sungold'	Y---------------------------
		x	Oxydendrum arboreum	W---------------------------
		x	Sorbaria aitchisonii	W-----------
		x	Tamarix gallica	RO–P---------
	x		pentandra 'Pink Cascade'	P--------------------
		x	Aralia spinosa	W----- Fr/B---
	x		Clethra alnifolia 'Rosea'	P------
x			Cytisus battandieri	Y------
		x	Hydrangea paniculata	W-------------------to P-------------------
		x	" 'Grandiflora'	W-------------------to P-------------------
	x		Vitex agnus-castus 'Latifolia'	L------------------
x			Elscholtzia stauntonii	L-----------------
x			Erica vagans	PR–P------------------------
x			" 'Alba'	W---------------------
		x	Hibiscus syriacus	Num.-----------------
	x		Lespedeza bicolor	PR–R---------------
	x		Tamarix hispida	P-----------------
	x		Caryopteris incana	V–Bl---------
x			Caryopteris clandonensis & cvs.	BL---------
		x	Franklinia alatamaha	W-----------------
		x	Hamamelis virginiana	Y------------------------------
x			Erica darleyensis	L–P thru March

Month header across top: JUNE (E M L) JULY (E M L) AUGUST (E M L) SEPTEMBER (E M L) OCTOBER (E M L) NOVEMBER (E M L)

CODE

Dashes and spacing of code letters show duration of bloom.

L = Low (to 3' in height)
M = Medium-high (3' to 6')
H = High (over 6')
xx or xxx means growing to these 2 or 3 heights
    (see text for which)

* calls attention to the fact that the true flower
is yellow; the bracts, for which the shrub is
grown, are a different color.

P = Pink	W = White	PR = Purple
Y = Yellow	R = Red	T = Tan
RO = Rose	B = Black	BL = Blue
V = Violet	S = Scarlet	L = Lavender
BR = Brown	O = Orange	C = Cream
G = Gray	GR = Green	CR = Crimson
Num. = numerous or various		
cv. = cultivar	var. = variety	
cvs. = cultivars	vars. = varieties	These terms include only those shrubs in this book.

29

Chapter 4

USING SHRUBS IN THE HOUSE

There are two ways in which you can use shrubs in the house—as growing plants and as cut branches.

Growing Plants

As you know, there are various commonly grown "house plants" which are shrubs. You doubtless have bought or received as gifts one or more of the following: azalea, gardenia, camellia and, perhaps, pittosporum, oleander or plumbago. These are just a few of the shrubs that may be grown in the home. They are grown in much the same manner as your other house plants.

There is, however, another way in which shrubs are grown in the house and that is as bonsai, dwarfed in the same manner as trees and shrubs are dwarfed by the Japanese. The shrubs we saw most frequently used in this manner, while we were in Japan, were:

1. azaleas
2. cotoneasters
3. Japanese maples

However, any of the following may be used:

1. Azaleas (already mentioned; choose small-leaved, low-growing varieties)

Japanese maples in bonsai form, photographed in Japan.

2. Warty barberry (*Berberis verruculosa*)
3. Korean barberry (*Berberis koreana*)
4. Rockspray (*Cotoneaster horizontalis*) and other Cotoneasters
5. European spindle-tree (*Euonymus europaea*)
6. Japanese apricot (*Prunus mume*)
7. Flowering quinces (use *Chaenomeles japonica* or *japonica alpina*, NOT *C. speciosa* or varieties)
8. Common privet (*Ligustrum vulgare*)
9. Sargent crabapple (*Malus sargentii*)
10. Scarlet firethorn (*Pyracantha coccinea*)

The idea of bonsai is to prevent the plant from growing to its normal size by restricting the roots, and by reducing nourishment to a minimum; and to shape it as fancy dictates, by continuous pruning and, if necessary, using wire to hold a branch in the desired manner. The aim is to make the miniature as much as possible like a mature, full-size tree of the same kind.

If the idea of using shrubs as bonsai appeals to you, the following books and pamphlets are available and all have directions for training bonsai:

Bonsai—Miniature Trees by Claude Chidamian, published by D. Van Nostrand Co., Inc.

The Art of Growing Miniature Trees, Plants and Landscapes by Tatsuo Ishimoto, published by Crown Publishers, Inc.

"Dwarf Potted Trees—The Bonsai of Japan," a special printing of Vol. 9, No. 3 of *Plants and Gardens*, August, 1959 available for $1 from the Brooklyn Botanic Garden, 1000 Washington Ave., Brooklyn 25, N. Y.

"Dwarf Potted Trees" by Ann Kimball Pipe and "Physiological Factors Involved in Dwarfing Trees" by Frits W. Went, in Vol. XLIX, No. 8 (Oct. 1961) of the *Missouri Botanic Garden Bulletin* (2315 Tower Grove Ave., St. Louis 10, Mo.).

Cut Branches

The time when cut branches of shrubs are probably most welcome in the house is in late winter.

By late January of every year the days already have grown noticeably longer and more of them are bright and sunny. It is on these crisp, clear days that the gardener who longs for spring goes out into the garden and "brings spring indoors."

Forcing

Forcing is accomplished simply by cutting branches or shoots of any one of the naturally early-flowering shrubs (or trees) and bringing them into the house to "force" into bloom.

Actually, there isn't much "force" necessary, for the buds on these branches are plump and full of life, just waiting for moisture and warmth to induce them to open blossoms. The moisture and warmth are what you supply in the forcing process.

The method which brings the branches into flower most quickly is this: Place cut branches in the bathtub, weighting them down with a brick or similar object, then run in sufficient lukewarm water to cover them. Leave them there overnight, then place cut ends in deep vases filled with lukewarm water and put these in a sunny place. It is possible to hasten flowering even more by spilling out half the water in the vase each day and replacing it with warm water (the mixture thus becoming lukewarm). Some people spray the tops of the branches each day during the forcing period, but I never have found this necessary.

Which shrubs you will force will depend, of course, on which ones are available to you, either in your own yard or those of friends, or in nearby woods. First-class shrubs for forcing purposes are: pussy willows, both wild and tame; flowering almonds, both pink and white; witch hazels, winter hazels, February daphne, pieris, fragrant honeysuckle, Cornelian cherry, forsythias, and flowering quinces. The flower colors of all of these shrubs will be paler when they open indoors than when they unfold outdoors.

Should you wish leaves instead of flowers, the red-osier dogwood will give them within just a few days. Alders and hazels will open their catkins indoors for your edification if you enjoy these more than conventional flowers.

And, of course, you can always add branches of flowering plums or magnolias or of other trees to your forcing project.

Preparing Shrub Branches for Arrangements

Later in the season, when shrubs bloom outdoors, they provide armfuls of flowers for household decoration.

The people who like to arrange flowers but who

Autumn arrangement of Osage oranges (Maclura pomifera fruits) and flowering quinces (similar fruits are borne on Chaenomeles speciosa or C. japonica). Coloring is soft yellow of quinces against dull green of Osage oranges.

shun shrubs because the branches must have a little preparation to keep well are missing a great deal. The long lines that shrubs have to give, and the wealth of bloom for only a few minutes spent in picking, are reasons enough for using them in arrangements.

It doesn't make any particular difference what time of day you cut shrub branches, but after they have been cut, the basal ends of the stems should be slit upwards, if at all possible, and the bark near

Black privet berries are used in the house during late autumn and early winter.

those ends all the way around the branches, should be pounded with a hammer to bruise it. These two types of wounding make it possible for the branches to absorb more water so that they last longer off the shrubs.

As soon as the wounding is accomplished, branches should be set in deep water. The leaves and some flowers even may be covered with water without any ill effects. After two or three hours in a cool, draft-free place, the branches are ready to arrange as you wish.

If you admire the long, beautiful sweep of a huge shrub branch, invest in one or two large, tall vases and find a place or two in your house where these may be set on the floor. Perhaps you have room by the side of the fireplace or in a corner of an entrance hall where, in former days, an umbrella stand would have sat. If you happen to be fortunate enough to own such a stand, it's a ready-made container for tall branches from shrubs.

Smaller containers, of course, call for the side shoots of many shrub branches rather than the entire branch. In this case do not wound the base of the large branch, but remove the side shoots after cutting the branch, and wound the basal ends of these.

The spring-flowering shrubs look beautiful used with flowers from the early bulbs—witch hazel, for instance, used with daffodils; a branch of flowering crabapple with white or pale pink flowers as a background for rose colored tulips.

In autumn, sprays of pyracantha with its orange berries or of cotoneaster with red berries may be accented with a few dahlias. Even in winter, the interesting branches of cork-barked euonymus may be used with a few begonia leaves at the base of the arrangement, or the branches of bayberry will make an unusual arrangement.

In fact, all year long, you can make interesting arrangements of shrub branches alone or with flowers or leaves of other types of plants. If you try using shrub branches, you'll soon find that they are so useful in providing indoor decorations that you'll wonder how you ever did without them.

PART II: GROWING SHRUBS

Chapter 5

HOW TO PLANT SHRUBS

The first requisite in planting is forethought, so that it will not be necessary to plant twice. So, before you plant, think. Is this the right shrub for the place you intend to plant it? If it isn't, you are either going to have to move the plant or else be sorry for years to come.

By the "right" shrub I mean the shrub that (1) will grow well in the particular location; (2) will thrive and bloom with the amount of light available; (3) will not outgrow its allotted space, and (4) will enhance the place in every way.

Selection

The lists in Chapter 3 will tell you which shrubs will tolerate damp soil, which will grow well in semi-shade, and so on. In Chapter 14, in the more detailed description of the shrubs, you will find the approximate ultimate height and/or spread. Consult these lists and figures BEFORE you BUY and doublecheck them BEFORE you PLANT. It will pay you to do so for you will thus avoid making mistakes. It will pay you also to use common sense in interpreting the height-width figures. If the soil in which you are planting is high in organic matter, the plant may grow a little taller or wider than others of the same species or variety set in poor soil. If space is limited, therefore, select a shrub that will grow a bit narrower or a bit lower than the available space rather than one that will grow certainly to its limits and may exceed them when planted in excellent soil or given plenty of fertilizer and water.

Handling Before Planting

Assuming your selection made and that you have bought the right shrub for the situation, the handling of the shrub from time of acquisition to time of planting becomes the important matter. Shrubs are living things and transplanting is a major operation in their lives. Recognize this in your treatment of them. Under no circumstances allow shrub roots to dry or shrub tops to be exposed to full sun while the shrub is out of the ground. The best thing to do, of course, is to plant within a few hours after the shrub is acquired. But sometimes this is not possible.

If you must wait to plant, set the shrub in a shady place. If the plant has an earth ball around its roots, check to make sure the ball is damp. Water it if necessary. If the shrub came to you with bare roots, open the package to allow air to reach the *tops,* but either keep it closed around the roots or open it, moisten the packing material around the roots if necessary, and repack around this area. Then put the shrub in a cool, shaded, airy place.

Should it be absolutely necessary for a bare root shrub to be held longer than one or two days before planting it, "heel it in" by inserting its roots into a v-shaped trench, the shrub lying supported against one side of the v. Cover roots with soil; shade tops with burlap. Water the roots and resolve to plant the shrub as soon as you can.

Balled and burlapped shrubs, watered when necessary, can wait a week or so before planting. If they cannot be planted by that time, heap peat, wood chips or a similar material around and between the earth balls to help prevent drying out until you can plant.

Digging

When you are ready to plant, remember that under normal circumstances, you are going to plant this shrub only once, so you may as well do a good job while you are about it. This means first digging a good, big hole, large enough to hold the roots of the plant when they are spread out in their natural positions—and then a bit larger, especially in poor soil. This extra-large hole permits an additional amount of loosened soil around the roots of the shrub, thus making it easier for these roots to re-establish themselves and grow outward for years.

As you dig, lay the top soil carefully on burlap or a tarpaulin at one side of the hole, subsoil on burlap or tarp at the other side. If you have brought the shrub along with you, be sure to keep it well protected from the drying effects of sun and wind, with damp burlap or sphagnum moss over both roots and tops. Keep it covered at all times.

Planting A Bare Root Shrub

Actual planting varies only slightly depending on whether the shrub is "B & B" (balled and burlapped) or bare root. Unwrap the bare root shrub, cut off any broken roots and branches and hold it in the hole so that the stems are about an inch below the level at which they grew before. You can see the former soil line on the stems if you look closely. Check the width and depth of the hole to make sure roots can spread out as they normally would.

If not, lay the shrub aside, covering it once more while digging the hole larger or wider or, if required, filling in a little with some of the topsoil from the pile. When the size is just right, hold the shrub in place once more so that it is vertical and in the center of the hole (unless all of its roots grow to one side, in which case you place the stems nearer the other side of the hole).

At this stage it is necessary to look over the shrub for its "front" or best side. There usually is one part which is far more shapely, more fully clothed with branches to the base, than any other. This is the side to set facing in the direction from which you most often will see the shrub.

Holding the shrub in this position, pull topsoil into the hole with your other hand, placing it under and around each root, as the root lies in normal position, and firming the soil to the roots by pressing with finger tips.

Once you have filled around the roots with topsoil, it makes little difference if you use subsoil to fill the rest of the hole. The roots will not be growing in it. If you are short of topsoil, use compost (if you have a compost pile), buy additional topsoil, or mix granulated peat moss with what topsoil you have, up to half peat and half soil. This peat should not be the extremely acid kind unless the shrub you are planting requires acid soil (see the section of this chapter headed "Acid-Soil Loving Plants"). Instead it should be either "neutral" or slightly acid. The reason for using peat to eke out your supply of topsoil is that peat improves soil texture as well as furnishing additional planting material. If your soil is sandy, and therefore drains too readily, peat mixed with it will help it hold water. If your soil is clay and therefore too retentive of water, peat mixed with it will help to lighten its texture so that it drains better.

When the planting hole is filled level with the tops of the roots, water thoroughly or soak with a solution of a wilt-reducing, root-growth-promoting plant hormone, like Transplantone. This comes in powder form and is not too easy to mix with water. If you will put the required amount of powder in a small container like a cup, add a little water and mix to a paste, then add more water until the paste is pourable, pour it into a pail or other container into which you first have put the correct amount of water, you will find it mixes readily. One 2½-gallon scrub- or household-pail full of this solution is sufficient to moisten roots of all but very large shrubs and small ones need only half a pailful.

The use of this solution is incomparably better than using water alone. Water certainly will settle the soil and help prevent wilting if the shrub has leaves. But the hormone solution does both of these, does a far better job in preventing wilting, and in addition stimulates root growth.

We plant dozens, sometimes hundreds of shrubs in a season, often in just a few days—and we have found that the transplanting solution pays its way, especially in late spring when shrubs are starting to leaf out or in early fall when we frequently move them with leaves still on. Shrubs in full leaf, like broad-leaved evergreens or deciduous shrubs that, for some reason or other, you need to move with the leaves on, are greatly benefitted by this treatment.

We are so sold on the use of the hormone treatment that, even when bare root shrubs arrive in early spring with leaves still unfolded, we put a metal bushel basket on a wheel barrow, fill it with the hormone solution, and set the shrubs with their roots in the solution. We move them to wherever we intend to plant them in this container, so that the roots have been treated with the hormone before planting. Then we use plain water to settle the soil and firm the plants in place. This saves carrying pails of the solution to places not readily accessible to water, even though we still may have to carry the water alone.

We have been known to follow the same system with B & B shrubs, especially when they arrived in wilted condition. In this case we set the balls in the bushel basket of solution and leave them there for two to three hours to soak it up.

After you have soaked the soil around the shrub's roots with either the hormone solution or water, fill in almost all of the rest of the hole with topsoil or subsoil, firming it as you near the top by tramping on it with your feet. This tramping definitely will not hurt the shrub unless you step on the tops, which will only happen if you forget to gather and hold the branches in your hands.

Leave the soil "cupped" at the top of the hole for ease in future watering. Lay the hose in this depression and let water dribble into the hole until you are satisfied that the soil in the hole is thoroughly soaked.

If, because of the contour of the land, it is not possible to leave a "cup" near the top of the hole, then build a "dike" of soil on the downhill side of the hole, well above the surrounding soil surface, so water will be held. Leave cup or dike in place during the first growing season after the shrub is planted for if you plant in spring, you will have to soak the shrub's roots with water from the hose once every single week, unless there is a soaking rain. If you plant in fall, you need water artificially only until fall rains begin.

It is a good idea to check, a week after planting, to see if the shrub still is in a vertical position. Sometimes beginning gardeners leave soil around the shrub too loose and the shrub settles so that it stands at an angle. Sometimes it stands straight, but has settled so it is too deep in the hole. If this has happened, loosen the soil around the outside of the hole with a shovel and, grasping all the shrub's tops in both hands, pull gently but steadily. Usually you can pull the shrub upwards the necessary inch or two so that it sits at the correct level. If the shrub is no longer vertical, loosen soil on the opposite side from the one it is slanting toward and pull it gently back. It may be necessary to drive a stake on that side of the shrub, from two to six feet away from it, distance depending on the height of the shrub, and "guy" the plant by tying a soft cord around the main branch or branches and tying the other end to the stake which has been hammered into the ground at an angle, so the top is further from the shrub than the bottom.

Planting B & B Shrubs

Planting shrubs that come with balls of earth and burlap around their roots follows the same general procedure as that described for bare root shrubs. A generous hole is dug. The ball of the shrub is held in the hole to make certain that the hole is sufficiently deep and wide, and topsoil is thrown into the hole so that the top of the ball will set level with the top of the soil. This soil is firmed. The ball is set on top of it and the plant inspected from several angles for verticality of tops and evenness of ball with soil surface, as well as for "best" side in the right direction. Necessary corrections are made.

Then comes the question that bothers most beginners—what to do with the burlap? The easiest way to handle this problem is to leave the burlap in place. As you water the shrub the burlap gradually will rot and disintegrate so it doesn't really make much difference whether or not it is removed. However, some gardeners become worried about leaving burlap in place. These people can make themselves feel better (and perhaps allow the shrub to grow new roots a tiny bit more rapidly) by loosening the burlap at the top, laying it back and doubling it outward so that the burlap is left only under the ball and a short distance up the sides. Only if you are CERTAIN that the earth ball will not break, will not even crack, should you remove all of the burlap. Occasionally, when the shrub has been growing in very heavy clay, the ball will be so solid that there is no chance of its breaking or cracking. Then, if you insist, the burlap may be taken off and the uncovered ball lowered onto the soil you have placed in the bottom of the hole.

As with a bare root shrub, topsoil is thrown in, this time to cover three quarters of the depth of the ball, and firmed as it is placed. Then sufficient hormone solution (or water) is poured in to soak the earth in the ball and around it. Subsoil may be used to fill over the topsoil, but the hole should not be entirely filled. The usual cup-shaped depression should be left to hold water and the earth fill should be tramped. Once again, all soil in hole and ball should be settled by a slow trickle of water from the hose.

Since the tops of broad-leaved evergreen shrubs, those usually purchased B & B, are in full leaf, it is only sensible to reduce water loss through the leaves while the plants are reestablishing their roots. To do this, spray the tops with any of the plastic coatings sold for the purpose. Be sure to spray both upper and lower surfaces of the leaves, for most of the stomata, the openings in the leaves through which water is lost, are in the lower surfaces.

The same spray materials may be used on bare-root shrubs should they have leaves on them.

Simply follow the directions on the package for dilution with water, then spray lightly but thoroughly. In due course of time the weather will cause the coating to disintegrate. Meanwhile it is practically invisible if you don't overspray.

Acid Soil-Loving Plants

Should the plant that is B & B be one of those that thrive only in acid soil (an azalea, a rhododendron, a mountain laurel or a similar plant) then you obviously must see to it that the soil in which it is planted is acid. This poses no problem for people who live where most soils are naturally acid; but for the people in areas with neutral or alkaline soils it may mean replacement of soil.

If you are in doubt as to whether or not your soil is acid, you can test it yourself by buying a soil testing kit (available at garden supply stores or by mail) and following directions that come with it to determine soil reaction. Or you can send a soil sample to your county agricultural agent or some other agency that tests soil. A phone call to your agricultural agent (listed under your *county* name) will get you the address of the nearest agency and the fee (if any) for such a test. To take a sample, dig a hole a foot deep and large enough for you to square off two sides with a spade. Put a piece of waxed paper in the bottom of the hole. Using the spade, cut down one of the squared sides, just as you would slice a cake, from top to bottom. Let the "slice" of soil fall on the paper, pick it up, mix it well and put a cupful of it in any glass container. Cover the container. Label it with your name and address, the name of the plant or plants you wish to grow in this soil and add a request for a test of the acidity of the soil. For accurate results take several such samples from various parts of the area where you wish to grow acid-soil plants. Such tests are well worth while because, should your soil already be sufficiently acid, you will avoid both the work and the expense of modifying it.

You may be disconcerted when you receive an answer from the soil testing agency for it may be given in terms with which you are unfamiliar. Chances are it will tell you that the pH of your soil is—and a figure will follow. This figure is easy to interpret and you needn't know any more about pH than how to interpret it. The figure 7, following the pH sign, means that your soil is neither acid nor alkaline ("sour" or "sweet"): it is "neutral." Any figure above 7 means that your soil is alkaline; any figure below 7 means that it is acid. The only other necessary fact you need is that the pH scale is logarithmic, so that pH 4 is ten times as acid as pH 5 and so on, on either side of the neutral point. (Most plants grow best when the soil reaction is between pH 6 and pH 6.5, slightly acid. No plants succeed in a very acid soil nor in an alkaline soil.)

The plants that need acid soil grow best in a pH of 4.5 to 5.5 so that is the figure at which you aim in treating or replacing your present soil, if it is alkaline or neutral.

The easiest, though not necessarily the best, way to acidify your soil is to mix an acidifying chemical with it. Aluminum sulphate has been recommended for this purpose but it should not be used as, sooner or later, free aluminum will be left in the soil and this is far from good for the plants growing in it. Better acidifiers, with no deleterious effects, are ferrous sulphate or sulphur. The amounts of these to mix with your soil will vary according to pH as shown by soil tests.

The difficulty is that only a small amount of either of these chemicals can be added at one time, so that the acidity can be increased only slowly. Time between applications should be at least a month. For instance a pound of sulphur may be applied at one time over 100 square feet of soil. Since ¾ pounds will lower the pH one point if the soil is sandy, this may be plenty if you have sandy soil. But if it is a medium-heavy loam, two or three times that much sulphur is needed and in heavy clay, far more than that, so much more that replacement of soil is far more feasible.

Replacing Soil

In this case dig out the existing soil to a depth of 18 inches. Make certain that drainage below this depth is good. Then mix acid peat with either existing soil or topsoil you have purchased, in proportions which may range from 50-50 to 75-25, the higher percentage being the acid peat. German and Swedish peats are acid and some Canadian and American peats are also. Their pH may range from 4 to 5.5 and the percentage of peat to use to soil will depend on this figure, usually stated on the bag or bale.

Any of the acidifying chemicals will work better and keep the soil properly acid for a longer time if the physical condition of the soil is good, as in the mixture suggested above where plenty of organic matter has been added in form of peat. Should you not need to replace your soil, because it is sufficiently acid, you should work in compost, acid peat, rotted leaves or even sawdust (plus 1 pound of ammonium sulphate to each bushel of sawdust) to improve its physical condition, if this is necessary. Of course if you have the ideal acid, woods soil, nothing need be added to it.

Many people make special beds for acid-soil plants, raising the beds above the existing ground level, especially if in a region of non-acid soil, so that the soil reaction can be completely controlled. Drainage must be provided if the natural soil is clay. The soil mixture previously suggested for a replacement for existing soil may be used, plus an acidifying chemical if necessary. However, it is not absolutely necessary to make special beds for acid-soil plants. If plants are set where drainage is good, it is sufficient to replace the soil around the earth ball to twice the width of the ball and to 18 inches in depth, including the depth of the earth ball.

It is most important, especially in regions where soil is not naturally acid, to buy acid-soil plants with earth balls around their roots. This is because some of the fungi present in the soil where these plants grow well, live in and on the roots of the plants. These fungi are called mycorrhiza and they are thought to perform the same role that root hairs do for other plants: that is, absorb nutrients in solution in the soil water. Apparently the mycorrhiza must have a soil high in organic matter to survive. And, equally apparently, acid-soil plants must have mycorrhiza to survive. Some are undoubtedly present in the soil of the earth ball around the roots. Planting the shrubs in a mixture with plenty of organic matter, will help keep these fungi growing and keeping the plants mulched will gradually increase the organic matter in the soil. (See "Mulching" in Chapter 6.)

Once soil is in good physical condition, with plenty of organic matter worked in, and is also acid in reaction, it should be tested once in six months or a year to make certain it stays acid in reaction. The water you give the plants from the hose, which comes from a well or a city water supply, may be sufficiently alkaline to gradually change the acidity of the soil. There are other possible factors which may do the same thing. So test at regular intervals to make certain of the soil reaction.

The foregoing paragraphs assume that your soil is alkaline or neutral and that you want to change it to have an acid reaction. But some soils are too acid to grow acid-loving plants and these need to be changed to have a less acid reaction. In this case add hydrated lime. Since you should not add any large amount at one time, start with 1 pound per 100 square feet, then test your soil in a month and, depending on the results of the test, add more. It is possible to add 5 pounds of lime per 100 square feet at one time, but never more, and even this will be deleterious to the plants growing in the soil.

Sandy soil always needs less lime than medium-heavy loam. Heavy soil needs most of any, which is the chief reason for replacing rather than attempting to change its reaction.

Is it worth while to try to grow acid-soil plants in a region where the soil is neutral or only slightly acid? I think it is. The picture of my little slope of rhododendrons shown on Color Page IV will show you why. And the rhododendrons are only a few of the acid-soil plants I grow. Azaleas number over 40, mountain laurels about a dozen, pieris about half a dozen, blueberries about a dozen, and so on through the roster of these plants.

We have a system for handling these plants that works well for us and might work for you under similar conditions. Since we live on a hilltop and gravel underlies the soil, drainage is no problem. Our topsoil is a clay loam, but not too heavy, testing pH 6.5. For all acid-soil plants but the heathers, we mix the existing soil and acid peat, in equal parts, add a handful of sulphur for each bushel of soil, and plant in this mixture. Heathers bloom best when soil is poor, so we mix acid peat and sand in equal proportions for these, adding the usual sulphur.

Once plants are settled they get special care just twice a year. In spring I make the circuit with a bag of fertilizer especially mixed for acid-soil plants and give each plant a bit, the amount depending on the size of the plant. Precise amounts are given on the bag. In autumn I duplicate the run, spreading a handful or two of cottonseed meal over the soil around each plant. This is a slow-acting organic fertilizer which has an acid effect on the soil.

Pruning Tops

In all this discussion of planting shrubs you may have noticed that there has been no mention of pruning the shrub tops. This is because, given the dual treatment of hormone solution on the roots plus plastic spray on the tops, such pruning is unnecessary.

The reason for pruning the tops of newly set shrubs is supposedly to reduce the size of the tops in proportion to the inevitable root loss because of transplanting, so that the remaining roots are sufficient to nourish the tops left after pruning. Thus there would be a minimum of wilting because of insufficient water getting to the tops.

When tops are sprayed to reduce transpiration (that is, water loss) to a great degree, roots are stimulated to grow rapidly and make up for any loss in moving, and plants are thoroughly watered once a week, pruning tops becomes merely a bad habit left over from the dark ages. The only top pruning necessary is the removal of any broken branches or twigs, which obviously no longer are doing the shrub any good.

Spring vs. Fall Planting

In spring the soil usually is very wet, digging is hard, and the weather uncertain. In fall the soil is mellow, easily worked, the weather likely to be clear and cool. So, plant in fall if you possibly can, unless you are planting shrubs purchased from considerably further south than where you live, shrubs of doubtful hardiness in your area or shrubs that prefer to be moved in spring (see list on page 23). Fall-planted shrubs almost certainly will bloom the following season; spring-planted shrubs may or may not flower the first season—usually they do not. This may be because they haven't strength to form flower buds or because these form but die.

Summer Planting

Shrubs that are purchased growing in containers can be planted all summer long and will thrive if planted carefully: watered regularly and thoroughly.

If you are moving and wish to take a shrub with you, you can do so even if it is in full leaf if you follow the directions given for use of hormone solution and plastic spray. Soak with the hormone solution the night before you expect to move the plant. Spray it with the plastic the day before moving. Dig with as large an earth ball as possible and burlap it carefully. Repeat the hormone solution soaking after replanting, and then water regularly and well.

Chapter 6

SHRUB MAINTENANCE

In writing this chapter, the assumptions have been made that you have (1) selected your shrubs with due regard to your climate; (2) planted them carefully in a place suitable to their hardiness and their ultimate size, at the right depth and with plenty of good soil around their roots; and (3) not crowded your shrubs so they have room to grow naturally and normally.

If you have considered and acted on all these factors, maintenance should be relatively simple, especially when compared with that necessary for many plants other than shrubs.

Watering Newly Planted Shrubs

Perhaps most important in maintaining newly planted (or transplanted) shrubs is watering them, because they simply cannot survive without water. Hang up a big calendar, one that hits you in the eye so you can't forget it, and mark on it the dates it has rained heavily. Any week in which there is a day-long or night-long soaking rain (which does not follow several weeks of no rain) is a week in which you can skip artificial watering.

Any week during which there is no such rain, is a week in which you MUST WATER. Mark the dates you soaked the roots of your newly set shrubs on the calendar too, so you don't have to trust to memory as to when you need water next.

Sprinkling water over the soil surface around shrubs does them more harm than good so don't let the word "sprinkle" enter your vocabulary. The only word permitted is "soak."

If, like us, you often set out several hundred shrubs in a single season, weekly watering can become a terrific chore. I know because I'm the person who does it in our garden. In this situation, it is easiest to divide the garden into sections and soak the shrubs in one section each day in the week. This gets all shrubs soaked once a week without devoting too much time to watering each day and without too many backaches.

I find that perforated hoses, arranged around and between shrubs that are close together, do a good soaking job when water is allowed to run through them for half a day. When you water a single shrub setting by itself, take off the hose nozzle, turn the faucet on only a little so the water dribbles into the depression you left around the base of the shrub. Let the water do this for several hours.

When shrubs are set out in fall, after their leaves have fallen, they need be watered only until late fall rains set in, in the parts of the country where these occur. Winter snows (which melt and therefore moisten soil), where these occur, and rains will take care of watering for the next few months and by spring the shrubs' roots will be sufficiently established so water will be needed only when there is a drought. Planting at this time of year saves so much watering that *fall* planting is my recommendation for hardiness zones 5 and 6 wherever there are rains at that season and snow or rain in winter. In zones north of these, spring planting is more satisfactory.

Shrubs set out in spring need weekly watering until late fall rains start. If you must plant shrubs in spring, water regularly and deeply. Even in Zones 5 and 6, spring planting is best for a shrub bought from one or two hardiness zones south because it has the whole growing season in which to become acclimated. Such doubtfully hardy shrubs should be moved ONLY in spring and should be given protection the first winter.

After shrubs have been in your garden a season, they should need little or no watering unless your soil is practically pure sand (in which case water weekly, unless there is a soaking rain, and improve the texture of your soil so it holds water) or there is a drought.

Drought

Shrubs past their first year in your garden can go without water for about ten days to two weeks before they are in trouble, because their roots grow deep enough so they can use water from lower soil layers even when the top few inches are dry. This does not apply to shallow-rooted shrubs like rhododendrons and this is the precise reason why such shrubs should be kept always under a mulch because, among other advantages, the mulch conserves moisture in the soil.

When the soil actually does dry out deeper than the top few inches, the first signs you'll see on your shrubs will be wilting leaves. Hydrangeas need a lot of water; leaves wilt and revive easily. Therefore the hydrangea is a good "indicator" of soil conditions. When hydrangea leaves droop, water hydrangeas, all rare shrubs and all others that wilt easily, like lespedezas. When viburnum leaves wilt, water all the shrubs in the garden.

Mulching

Mulching, that is covering over the soil surface with some porous material that admits water, not only helps keep the soil moist under the mulch but also cuts down on weeding (since the mulch smothers all but stubborn weeds) and improves the soil.

When a mulch is applied, the soil bacteria start to work on the lower layer of it, decomposing the leaves, straw, sawdust or whatever you have used for mulch. This decomposed organic material contains nutrients that plants need for good growth. So, as this becomes incorporated in the soil, you will notice a marked difference in the growth of the shrubs which are mulched over those that are not.

Mulch materials are many. For shrubs (though not necessarily for all the other plants you are growing), leaves, straw, hay, sawdust, wood chips, grass clippings and weeds (before seeds form on them) are all good. There are other mulch materials, good ones too, but why spend money on mulches for shrubs when you ought to be able to get those listed above either free or for the price of hauling them?

Leaves are available from your own trees or from those of your neighbors. Don't let anyone in the neighborhood burn leaves in the fall—haul them home and use them either as a mulch or on the compost pile. If they tend to blow away in high winds, hold them down with evergreen branches or chicken wire laid flat over the mulched area. They're much too valuable to be allowed to go up in smoke.

If you live in the right community, the city will be glad to dump loads of leaves collected from streets and parks right in your yard free of charge.

Just let city hall (usually the department of public works) know you want leaves.

Straw sometimes is available for the hauling from new building sites where it is used to cushion bricks and protect newly laid concrete. People who live near the coast often can cut and haul salt marsh hay which is exceptionally good because the seeds in it are those of aquatic plants which will not grow in the dryer soil of a garden.

Sawdust is usually available free for hauling from a sawmill. If there is one near you, investigate it as a source. When sawdust is used for a mulch, add 2 pounds of ammonium sulphate (a nitrogenous fertilizer) to each bushel of sawdust, to nourish the soil bacteria that will start to decompose it. If plenty of nitrogen is not available, these bacteria may use what is in the soil in which the shrubs are growing, to the detriment of the shrubs.

Let your local power company, phone company or city forestry department know that you want wood chips and when they are removing and "chipping" the overhanging tree branches in your neighborhood, they'll be pleased to use your yard for dumping their loads. Add 1/2 pound of ammonium sulphate to each bushel of wood chips.

Grass clippings are free as long as you have a lawn to cut. Catch them in a catcher attached to the mower or use a lawn sweeper after cutting the grass and dump the clippings over the soil around the shrubs.

I have not mentioned using manure for a mulch (though it is a good one despite the weed seeds in it) because most people cannot buy it at all or must pay a high price for it. Should it be available near you at a reasonable price, use it, though not on shrubs that like acid soil. Perhaps even better than manure, because it has been sterilized so contains no live weed seeds, is spent mushroom soil. If you live near a mushroom growing section, you often can have this soil free to haul home when they are changing soil in the mushroom houses, which they do once a year.

I also have not mentioned peat moss, so often recommended as a mulch. This is because I do not consider peat moss a satisfactory mulch, whether it comes from a bale or is granulated. While it is excellent when added to soil to improve texture and water-holding capacity, this ability to hold a great deal of water makes it a poor topping over soil. Rain or artificial water first must penetrate the peat before it reaches the soil and benefits the shrub roots. It cannot do this until the peat is saturated, which takes a very heavy rain or hours of watering.

Always soak the soil thoroughly before applying any type of mulch. It will take a bit of time to apply, but the mulch will save you sufficient time in the future to more than make up for that spent in application.

Fertilizing

When you add ammonium sulphate to a mulch as you apply it, or scatter it over a mulch after you have applied it (which should be done once a year, for the reason explained previously) you are fertilizing the shrubs in the area as well as nourishing soil bacteria, because ammonium sulphate contains nitrogen, one of the chemical elements needed for plant growth.

There are a number of these; nitrogen, phosphorus and potash being the most important ones. Nobody knows exactly how one element reacts with the others for plant growth, but the three named, plus others in smaller quantities, all are necessary for good growth of plants.

Any "complete" commercial fertilizer contains the three elements already named. You will find the percentages of these in a given fertilizer on the package as a series of numbers as, for instance, 5-10-5. These figures mean 5 percent nitrogen, 10 percent phosphoric acid and 5 percent potash. The three figures always are given in the same order—nitrogen first, phosphoric acid next and potash last. The rest of the fertilizer package contains material that makes it possible to spread these chemicals evenly and easily.

Thus, when you use a complete fertilizer on your shrubs, you are adding the three elements they most need to the soil around them.

The "trace" elements, needed only in small quantities by plants, are present in most soils in sufficient amounts for shrubs. Some of them are contained in chemical fertilizers as "impurities." Therefore, in most cases, you need not worry about them.

If your soil is even reasonably good, most shrubs will grow in it, even thrive in it, without really needing fertilizer (just as long as they are not mulched). Of course there are some shrubs that do best in poor, sandy soil (see list, page 21) and these should never be given fertilizer.

Since all shrubs have an ultimate height and spread beyond which they will not grow, even if fertilized, about all that fertilizer does is make them reach these limits sooner than they would without it. If you are in a rush for shrubs as large as they ever will grow, fertilize. If not, use the fertilizer for plants that need it a great deal more than do shrubs.

There are, however, four situations in which shrubs do need fertilizer. 1. A shrub has not leafed out, though it has been planted for several months.

It is obviously alive because a twig bends without breaking and when you scratch at the bark you see green tissue underneath. In this case use a liquid fertilizer, mixing it with water according to directions on the package given under the heading "foliar feeding." Even if the shrub has no leaves, it can absorb nutrients through its bark. The solution for foliar feeding is weaker than that for fertilizing through the roots.

If the shrub is small enough, mix up a pailful of the solution and simply dump it right over the shrub. This is quick and easy and works well. If the shrub is large, so large you canot dump several pails of solution over various sections of it, then spray the liquid fertilizer on the shrub.

Fertilizing through bark or leaves is an effective way to give a plant a boost since the plant can use the nutrients in the solution very quickly, sometimes in a matter of hours from the time they are applied. "Foliar" feeding is more expensive than the ordinary way of fertilizing a plant through the roots and the effects are nowhere near as long-lasting. Therefore, fertilizing through bark or leaves is no substitute for fertilizing through the roots.

It is possible to fertilize through bark or leaves daily if you wish to do so, with no harm to the plant. Even weekly application will help the plant while not exhausting the gardener.

2. A shrub shows obvious signs of lacking some chemical so it is time to try to determine the chemical needed (this is easier said than done) and supply it. Because of studies made on other types of plants, it is known that signs of lack of iron, manganese, calcium, and boron appear first on young leaves. Lack of sufficient nitrogen, phosphorus, potassium, and magnesium usually shows first on the lower leaves.

However, results of attacks by red spider mites, which are too tiny to be seen with the naked eye, often resemble nutrient deficiencies, so it is wise not to jump to conclusions too fast. To find out if red spider mites are causing the difficulty, hold a sheet of shiny white paper under a branch in the area which seems affected. With the other hand, hit the branch sharply, meanwhile watching the paper. If minute dark dots appear on the paper and, when carefully watched, they move, these are the mites. Spray with a miticide like Aramite, Dimite Ovotran, or Malathion to control them.

41

How can you tell which chemical is lacking in a shrub's nutrition? Very little work has been done on this subject except with azaleas and there is no reason to believe that all shrubs would similarly show their lacks. Best thing to do, when a shrub's growth is not as vigorous as it was or when yellowing or mottling of leaves indicate possible lack of nutrients is to use a complete fertilizer of a 10-6-4 formula at the rate of 1 pound to 100 square feet of area. If you are using a high-grade fertilizer, the chances are good that the manufacturer has added sufficient trace elements so the shrub will get these along with nitrogen, phosphorus, and potash.

Apply this fertilizer to DRY soil only, scattering it as evenly as possible around under the shrub and as far out from the center as the spread of the branches. SOAK the soil with water immediately after fertilizing.

Shrubs should not, under ordinary circumstances, be fertilized after July 1, because soft, new growth thus encouraged may be killed by winter cold. The best time to fertilize is in very early spring, but if a shrub later shows signs of deficiency of some chemical, try using a liquid fertilizer which contains the trace elements.

If the shrub does not lose the signs of malnutrition which caused you to use the complete fertilizer or the liquid fertilizer, try fritted trace elements sold as FTE, or a special fertilizer which contains all trace elements. This might be applied in late fall or in early spring.

Acid-Soil Plants

Acid-soil plants, the class to which rhododendrons and azaleas belong, sometimes show by the yellowing of their leaf blades, while veins remain green, that iron is lacking in their diet. The iron may be present in the soil, but in soils insufficiently acid it often is in a chemical form that is insoluble and therefore the plant cannot use it. As you know, plant root hairs take up chemicals dissolved in the soil water.

Iron may be supplied to the plant quickly by spraying its leaves with a solution of Sequestrene, or more slowly, by applying the same product to the soil.

Remember that signs of iron deficiency also call for acidifying the soil further for, if it were sufficiently acid for the acid-soil plants, the iron in it would be in soluble form that the plant could use. So, at the same time as you use Sequestrene or a similar product to relieve the deficiency, add a soil acidifier like sulphur to make the soil more acid.

Occasionally it may be necessary to apply lime to soil in which azaleas or other acid-soil plants are growing. This happens only when the soil becomes too acid, below pH 4.5. This subject is more fully discussed in Chapter 5.

3. A shrub has been in your garden for several years and has not yet flowered; so it is time to try to help it to bloom. An application in spring and again in fall of superphosphate, which contains phosphorus, the chemical most closely associated with flowering of plants, often helps the plant to produce blooms.

4. You may wish certain small shrubs or rare shrubs to grow a bit better. If so, use a 10-6-4 fertilizer at the rate of ½ pound per shrub in early spring and again before warm weather starts. Scatter it around under the shrub, over the soil. If the shrub is mulched, remove the mulch before you apply the fertilizer, replacing the mulch afterwards.

Special Fertilizers

There are numerous special formula fertilizers available, some of them highly touted for various types of plants, including shrubs and especially roses. Shrubs, however, will react just as well to a standard 10-6-4 fertilizer as to any of the special ones, with the exception of acid-soil shrubs. For these you can either mix a fertilizer which will have an acid reaction or you can buy one ready-mixed. Unless you expect to use large quantities, it is simpler and cheaper to buy it ready-mixed.

Pruning

There ought to be a law against allowing anyone, particularly a person of the male sex, to touch a pruning shears unless familiar with the natural form of the plant to be pruned. More crimes are committed against plants in the name of pruning than in any other way.

For pruning is not to be confused with "hacking." Pruning is done for a purpose and, lacking the purpose, there should be no pruning. Furthermore, regardless of the purpose, the form of the shrub should be carefully retained. The "butch cut" seen on too many shrubs is a confession of ignorance. The person who cut the top of a shrub off straight across obviously knows nothing about how a shrub renews itself, cares less, and in addition, has very poor taste.

Ignorance, too, is the reason for constant pruning of a plant. If it is necessary to prune a shrub that is not part of a hedge two or three times a season, then that shrub is in the wrong place. Move it to another place where it can grow as high and as wide as it should and replace it with a shrub which naturally grows in a shape that will fit the first place. The descriptions of the shrubs in Chapter 14 tell you their ultimate heights or widths.

Routine Pruning

Routine pruning, which should be done every two or three years, consists of removing: (1) dead parts of the shrub; (2) pieces that stick out too far and thus spoil the natural shape of the shrub; (3) parts that are injured or diseased or attacked by scale insects so that their removal will aid shrub health; (4) branches that are rubbing against one another so that, in time, one will rub the bark off the other, creating a place where disease may enter the plant; (5) suckers from the base of a grafted or budded plant which are not, of course, parts of the variety you wish to grow. In any of these "purposes" for pruning, the part to be pruned is better off the shrub than on.

Routine pruning also includes rejuvenation. Most shrubs that send up numerous stems from the ground will profit by having a few of the older, thicker ones cut off at ground level each year, thus allowing more room for the younger stems to develop. Shrubs that will profit from such pruning annually include weigelas, mock oranges, deutzias and spireas.

How to Do Routine Pruning

First of all the tools you use for pruning, shears and saws of various types and sizes, should be kept clean and sharp. If a badly diseased part of a shrub must be removed, the tool used should be disinfected after use by dipping it in a household disinfectant, then wiping it dry.

The first use of these tools should be to remove dead wood. This should be cut back to live growth. Scrape away a tiny bit of outer bark, if necessary, to find the green layer just underneath which shows that part of the shrub is alive. Make the cut just above the highest bud in the live wood.

Next, scrutinize the shrub with a view to its form and remove, only as far back as necessary, any branches that spoil it. Then remove any injured branches, cutting each one back far enough to remove all injury (or diseased areas, or scale-infested areas). In both of these cases make the cut just above the topmost bud that is pointing in the direction you wish a new branch or branchlet to grow. A bud that is heading towards the center of a "bushy" shrub is obviously not the one above which to prune. An outward pointing bud, even if lower on the branch, is preferable. The same

Lilac bent to the ground under the weight of the snow may require pruning in spring.

sort of bud choice must be made when one of two rubbing branches is removed from a shrub.

Always keep in mind when pruning that when live wood is removed from a plant, some of the growth energy and substance is removed at the same time. If only a small branch is removed, this makes little difference, but if pruning is drastic, it will affect the plant's root system and some of the roots will die. The plant soon adjusts to the new state of affairs, and new growth will start from the top bud which is left on the pruned branch, or, if the branch has been removed entirely, then new growth will start in the buds closest to the cut. The more wood that is pruned off a plant, the greater the tendency of the plant to make new growth WHERE THE PLANT WAS PRUNED. Growth always will be on the side where the plant has been pruned—never on the opposite side.

Any shoots growing from the base of a plant known to have been budded or grafted, or any shoots growing from the base of a plant which have leaves on them differing from those of the rest of the plant should be removed as soon as you notice them. Trace the shoots back to the point of origin which may be below the soil line, and cut the shoots off the plant at that point.

Other Types of Pruning

Pruning when Planting or Transplanting: Though broken roots or branches always should be removed at planting time, for obvious reasons, it is common practice to reduce the tops of newly set deciduous shrubs in about the same proportion as you GUESS their roots have been reduced in the transplanting process. I do not agree with this practice. If I buy and pay for a 3- to 4-foot shrub, why should I reduce it to a 2- to 3-foot shrub to make up for probable root loss? I might, then, just as well have saved money by buying the smaller size shrub to begin with.

If you will read, in Chapter 5, the thoughts about using root-growth-inducing, wilt-decreasing hormone powder in solution on shrub roots and plastic coating on shrub tops, you will understand why I consider pruning tops unnecessary. If plenty of water is given a shrub regularly after it is transplanted and has been treated as outlined above, the existing roots can support the existing tops with no difficulty.

On rare occasions, if an enormous, ancient shrub is to be moved from one place to another, it is advisable to prune the tops, but then they should be cut to within 6 inches of the ground. If the remaining root system is well cared for, new tops will grow in due course of time.

Pruning for Renewal: This same type of drastic pruning, to within a few inches of the ground, is necessary when an old shrub or hedge of shrubs looks so unsightly that no ordinary pruning will do any good. Old or untidy shrubs like lilacs, or hedges of privet or hedges of California privet which has winterkilled in a cold climate, all respond to such renewal pruning.

Ordinarily pruning for renewal is not so drastic. When a shrub becomes "leggy" and bears leaves only at the tops of long branches, first make sure it is getting sufficient light. If it is, then it may be rejuvenated by removing one or two of the older branches at ground level. One third of the branches should be removed each year for three years. Thus the plant's growth will not be upset by drastic pruning, but new shoots will have a chance to grow. I have found a keyhole saw ideal for the removal of these old branches because it is small enough to use between old and new branches without scraping bark off the new shoots when removing the old growth.

Pruning for Color: The newest wood is always the brightest on such red- and yellow-branched shrubs as certain dogwoods. If you depend on these shrubs for winter color in your garden, be sure to prune a little each year to keep the new wood growing. Some gardeners cut these shrubs to the ground every third year so that bright, new shoots will grow to make the winter garden gay.

Pruning to Increase Density: People plant hedges for privacy or to form divisions between various areas in the garden. Therefore, a good hedge is a dense one. The theory behind the frequent pruning of hedges to make them dense is that more than one shoot will grow in the place from which one shoot is pruned, therefore the more often the pruning, the more shoots that will grow and the denser the hedge.

Always prune any type of hedge so that it is broader at the base and tapers towards the top, so that air and light can reach the lower branches. If you prune the opposite way, wide at the top and narrow at the bottom, the lower branches soon die and the hedge no longer serves its purpose. As previously explained, a poorly shaped, old hedge of deciduous shrubs can be cut to the grounds to rejuvenate it. Do this in late winter or early spring, fertilize the plants then, and watch the new hedge grow.

Recently, while visiting a large chemical company, I saw the tests on a new chemical which restricts branch growth. It will be possible, in a few years, to prune a hedge only once in spring to the desired shape, spray with this material, and forget pruning for the remainder of the growing season.

Pruning to Increase Bloom: Some shrubs tend to form flower buds after their normal blooming time is past if they are pruned directly after their flowers fade. Stems which flowered should be cut back for this type of pruning, and strong new shoots should be shortened. Shrubs that profit from this pruning include Anthony Waterer spirea, *Spiraea japonica* and its varieties, weigelas and buddleias.

Pruning to Train: When gardeners wish to grow lilacs or roses-of-sharon or some other shrub in "standard" or "tree" form (that is, with only one trunk) special pruning is required. One straight branch is selected to be the trunk. This is tied to a stake to keep it growing straight. All side branches are cut from it and all remaining branches are removed from the shrub and not allowed to grow. When the trunk is sufficiently high to suit the trainer, the buds near the top of it are allowed to grow and these will form branches which may be permitted to grow naturally with little or no pruning or may be clipped to any desired shape.

When a shrub of formal shape is desired, shrubs which lend themselves to formal pruning, like boxwoods, barberries, or privets, should be chosen. These may be trained to globe shape or other shapes by careful pruning, even though no "trunk" is desired.

Pruning Dead Flowers: Pruning also includes removal of dead flowers before the seeds form, so that food manufactured by the plant is not used in seed production when the seed will not be used. There are conflicting ideas as to whether or not such flower removal does any real good other than to make the shrub look neater. I have proved to my own satisfaction, by careful, controlled tests on my own plants, that removal of dead flowers results in more bloom the following year. So I feel that it pays to prune off faded flowers on pieris, lilac, rhododendron, azalea, kalmia, magnolia and hibiscus.

When to Prune

Routine pruning actually can be done at any time of year. But for the sake of appearances, try not to prune shrubs in winter, for the white scars left by pruning show and make the shrub look mangy. Any branches that have to be cut back stick out like sore thumbs until the leaves appear to hide the wounds. If you can stand such unsightliness, go right ahead and prune.

Any pruning other than that for sanitation should, if possible, be done at times most propitious for the particular plants being pruned.

DECIDUOUS SHRUBS

In general all of those that flower on the wood of the previous year's growth should be pruned when they finish flowering, for many start forming next year's flower buds a month or two after blooming. When you prune an early-spring-flowering shrub like forsythia in late fall or in spring before it flowers, you prune off the flower buds.

Exceptions to pruning after flowering are the shrubs which are going to bear decorative fruits in fall. These may be pruned lightly in late fall, lightly in very early spring, or, if necessary, a little bit at both of these times of year.

Shrubs that flower on wood of the current season's growth, all may be pruned in very early spring. These shrubs include: *Abelia grandiflora, Acanthopanax, Berberis, Callicarpa, Clethra, Hibiscus syriacus, Hypericum, Hydrangea arborescens*

Pieris japonica in April. Plant in bloom (right) had seed pods removed the previous year as soon as they formed. Plant on left has no blooms, only old seed pods. Moral: It pays to remove seeds, not only on Pieris but also on Rhododendrons, Azaleas and Lilacs.

and *H. paniculata* and varieties of both of these, *Kerria, Ligustrum, Lonicera* (but not *L. fragrantissima*), *Neillia, Philadelphus, Rhus, Rosa, Spiraea, Staphylea, Stephanandra* and *Tamarix* (but not *T. parviflora*).

The "die-back" shrubs, those which have roots that are winter-hardy, but tops that are not, should be pruned as early in spring as possible. If the winter has been mild, they may need comparatively little dead wood removed, but if it has been severe, they will have died back and should be cut to the ground. These shrubs include: *Abelia grandiflora, Amorpha, Buddleia* (except *B. alternifolia* which freezes back only occasionally), *Callicarpa, Caryopteris, Ceanothus, Colutea* (sometimes freezes back), *Elscholtzia stauntonii, Lespedeza, Sorbaria, Tamarix* (sometimes freezes back) and *Vitex*.

A few deciduous shrubs that are not ordinarily die-back shrubs will have many more flowers if severely pruned right after flowering. The following may have about half of their branches cut back to two or three buds from the ground, cutting just above a bud: *Buddleia alternifolia, Deutzia, For-*

sythia, *Hydrangea arborescens* and *H. paniculata*, *Philadelphus*, early-blooming spireas, *Spiraea bumalda* 'Anthony Waterer' and *S. bumalda* 'Froebelii', *Tamarix* (but not *T. parviflora*) and *Weigela*.

These need very little pruning. Cut back the occasional dead branch and the occasional branch that spoils the shape; and prune off dead flowers. Removal of branches may be done at any time, but is best attempted in early spring so that new growth will hide pruning scars.

Shrubs which Require Little or No Pruning

After reading about all the shrubs that should be pruned, either every spring or occasionally, it comes as a relief to know that some shrubs should be pruned as seldom as possible, except to remove dead wood. These include *Amelanchier, Aronia, Azalea, Calycanthus, Caragana, Cercis, Chionanthus, Cotoneaster, Cytisus* (in cold climates), *Halesia, Kalmia, Laburnum, Prunus glandulosa, Magnolia, Mahonia, Pieris, Rhododendron, Ribes* and spring-flowering *Viburnums*. If you select from these shrubs, pruning in your garden will be kept to a minimum.

Winter Protection

The only protection most deciduous shrubs need, if they have been carefully chosen for hardiness, is protection from animals which eat off twigs, buds, and bark. Against rabbits either ring shrubs with chicken wire or hardware cloth high enough so that deep snow does not allow rabbits to eat over the tops of the wires, or spray with rabbit repellents. You will find rabbit repellents available in your garden supply store; chicken wire and hardware cloth at the hardware store.

There are several deer repellents on the market but, since we have no trouble from deer, I do not personally know how effective they may be.

Field mice may be kept from gnawing shrubs by sinking guard wires 2 inches into the soil or by setting out one of the various poison baits available.

Shrubs planted in very late fall sometimes heave out of the soil during the freezing and thawing in late winter. A mulch of any convenient material will prevent this.

Winter burn, or browning of leaves, is quite common on broad-leaved evergreens when the plants are placed so that they are exposed to the wind or where late winter sun touches them. This may be prevented by spraying the leaves of the plants in late fall, before freezing temperatures arrive, with one of the anti-dessicant sprays.

These substances reduce water loss from the leaves, thus reducing the ratio between the amount of water the plant loses through leaves (or, in the case of deciduous shrubs, through branches) and the amount the roots are able to take up from the soil. This will be little or none when the soil is frozen. Both wind and sun increase the amount of water lost, but, as long as the soil is frozen, there can be no increase in water intake.

Rhododendrons survive winter better when heavily mulched, preferably with oak leaves. Azaleas are less likely to mature their wood properly when mulched in late autumn; removal of the mulch for several weeks at that time of year will help them do so.

All woody plants survive winter best when the cold weather approaches gradually. When there is a long, warm autumn and suddenly the weather changes abruptly, the thermometer dropping 20 or 25 degrees in a single night, there is certain to be plant injury, regardless of hardiness. Sometimes woody stems split open. Some plants that ordinarily survive winter with ease are killed to the ground, but usually grow again from the roots in spring. All sorts of unusual injury may occur when the weather changes suddenly and there is little the gardener can do to prevent it.

There also is little he can do to counteract a sudden drop in temperature in spring when buds already are unfolding and bloom may be lost because they are nipped by a cold snap.

But these two freaks of nature are part of the hazards of gardening and happen only rarely.

Chapter 7

WHEN SHRUBS CHANGE

When a gardener buys a shrub, grows it, and sees its leaves and flowers add their beauty to the garden, he expects both foliage and bloom to continue in the same manner year after year. When a change occurs either in leaf or flower, it startles and alarms him. This results in letters like these to the local garden editor:

1. "One part of my lilac is blooming beautifully, but the rest of the bush isn't bloming at all and the leaves look different. They look like those on my neighbor's hedge."

Or 2. "Something is wrong with my lilac. Some of the leaves at the tips of the lower branches are all sort of scalloped at the edges and a different shape from the rest."

Or 3. "My snowball bush has different flowers from those it used to have. They used to be like little snowballs and now they are wider and flatter."

Or 4. "My daughter planted a beautiful red-flowered Blaze climbing rose; this year there is a white bridal wreath where the rose was."

Or 5. "Would you please tell me how it is possible for my rosebush to have buds that look all the same, but when the flowers open they may be pink or rose color or even white or yellow?"

Or 6. "My son gave my mother and me each a blue hydrangea for Mother's Day last year. We planted them outdoors later in the season. This year both are flowering, but the flowers on mine are pink while those on hers are blue. How can this be?"

Each one of these six gardeners is troubled because of a change either in the leaves or flowers of a shrub. And there are four entirely different reasons for the changes described in these six letters.

The first "reason" (letters 1, 3, and 4) is reversion.

The second reason (letter 2) is injury by the weed-killing chemical known as 2, 4-D.

The third reason (letter 5) is "sporting" by the plant.

The fourth reason (letter 6) is response to soil reaction.

Reversion

Let's go back to the first reason and see just how a plant "reverts." My dictionary gives the following as the "biological" definition of the word "revert": "to return to or toward or show some of the characteristics of an ancestral, primitive or earlier form." This is a good definition, because that's what plants sometimes do.

They may "return to" the original form of the plant if they are selections from or hybrids of that plant. Suppose you have a small-flowered polyantha rose which bears, ordinarily, orange flowers. One day you find, to your surprise, that one flower or flower cluster is red, rather than orange. The orange-flowered rose was bred from the red, so when it bears a few red flowers it may be said to be "reverting."

Sometimes a double-flowered shrub will have one branch which bears single flowers. This happens occasionally with double-flowered mock oranges. This, too, is reversion.

There is another more common occurrence with shrubs; also called reversion, but which is really quite different and should be called by a different name. This pseudo-reversion happens when a shrub is made up of parts of two different plants.

Sometimes these are of the same plant group, as roses or viburnums. Sometimes these are of different plant groups, as lilac on privet. In either case a strong-growing genus or variety is deliberately chosen to be the understock or rootstock of the new plant. Onto this rootstock is budded or grafted the more desirable (often a cultivar) top. Thus the plant you buy is composed of parts of two different plants.

Rose reversion. Rootstock on which Betty Prior rose was budded is starting to grow (see long, straight stem in center of plant and note that it starts below the soil line). If not removed, such shoots will, in time, outgrow the Betty Prior top.

Let us suppose that this plant is a lilac, as in letter number 1. When lilacs are not grown on their own roots, as they really always should be, they usually are budded onto a rootstock of privet. Privet is very strong growing and sometimes outgrows the lilac top. If the owner of a lilac does not realize what is happening and keep the privet shoots cut off below the ground surface, next thing he knows he'll have a nice, cheap privet bush instead of a nice, expensive lilac.

Now, let's consider letter number 3. The plant in this case is a snowball, known more accurately as a viburnum. In this case a fine-flowering variety, such as *Viburnum carlesii,* was budded onto a strong, fast-growing variety, as *Viburnum lantana.* The *lantana* has outgrown the *carlesii* or perhaps the *carlesii* has been unknowingly pruned off or has been injured, leaving only the lantana to grow. If you will look at the illustration on the right you

will see a dual-shrub. The *lantana* rootstock has outgrown the *carlesii,* which still survives.

Letter number 4 concerns a rose—a climbing rose, so a vine rather than a shrub. (However, the same thing happens with shrub roses.) The reason I have used this particular letter is that it tells an impossible story: presumes that a climbing rose has changed into a spirea (bridalwreath is the common name of several species of spirea).

What actually has happened in this case is that a fast-growing, strong-rooted species, *Rosa multiflora,* has been used for a rootstock. A bud of the red-flowered, named variety rose, Blaze, has been inserted into a multiflora cane and thus we have the two-parted rose which was purchased. It is obvious that somehow the Blaze top was lost. Perhaps it was killed by a too-cold winter. Or it was pruned off or injured. Or it just died. At any rate, the white non-"bridalwreath" blooms are those of the multiflora rose understock. See the illustration on the left.

These last three cases are all commonly called

Viburnum carlesii (lower left) was grafted on understock of Viburnum lantana (upper part of shrub) and the lantana rootstock sent up shoots which threaten to outgrow the more desirable carlesii.

"reversion" and, of course, in a sense they are reversion, but different types than that of the dictionary definition (the actual growth of a plant in the manner of one or another of its ancestors).

It isn't really necessary for you to endure this type of reversion. By insisting on being supplied with "own root" plants when you are buying them, you avoid a two-part plant. The nurseryman usually need not produce a dual plant because the variety used as the top doesn't root well—he grafts or buds almost always to get a saleable size plant sooner. True, this quick-grown plant will cost you less, but isn't it worth more to you to have a plant grow on its own roots?

Chemical Injury

The second reason for a change in the form of a plant, or rather the form of its leaves, is chemical injury. When gardeners spray lawns with 2, 4-D weed killers or run over them a fertilizer spreader filled with a dry formulation of the same weed-killing chemical, leaf injury and change in leaf form may result.

The gardener need not have been careless in applying the chemical. He may have been very careful. In fact, the gardener next door may be the one who, all unknowingly, caused the change. For the minute amount of chemical which may be carried by the wind to nearby shrubs is enough to make leaves look different if it drifts on them. This is the cause of the trouble described in letter 2.

There is little a gardener can do in this case but wait and pray. 2, 4-D does not differentiate between desirable and undesirable broad-leaved plants. It kills shrubs as well as weeds. If the injury has been slight, normal leaves will grow above the injured ones and, by another year, all leaves will be normal. In case of severe injury, the entire shrub may be lost.

Sporting

The change in the flower color of a plant, as described in letter number 5, is due to a bud mutation commonly called a "sport." The change itself is known as "sporting."

The way in which a plant sports was a matter of conjecture for generations. Recent developments have made it possible to know accurately how sporting occurs. An intensely interesting article titled "Nature of Plant Sports," by Haig Dermen, cytologist, U. S. Department of Agriculture Research Service, gives detailed evidence. It is written for the layman and appears in the July, 1960, issue of *The American Horticultural Magazine,* published by the American Horticultural Society, Inc. Sporting "is closely tied to the development of the *growing point* of the *shoot*" and is "brought about principally by a genetic change (mutation, sporting) in one or more genes or chromosomal changes occurring originally in the nucleus of a single cell at the very center of a growing point of a bud or shoot."

To explain the paragraph above, the nucleus is the central, denser part of a cell (and all living things are made up of cells). The nucleus is composed of chromosomes which are thread-like objects which bear the genes. *The genes determine the heredity of a plant or animal.* Thus, when there are changes in the genes or chromosomes these are inherited by the new plant part. For when there is new growth (caused by cell division) the chromosomes contract by coiling, first gather together near the center of the cell, then split lengthwise, and then half of each moves to the opposite ends of the cell. After that a new cell wall forms between the two groups of chromosomes and the single cell has become two cells. Thus each new cell inherits the changes in the genes or chromosomes that were in the single cell from which the new ones formed.

The paragraph above is, of course, an oversimplification of a complicated process. However, it is all the explanation that I feel is needed to explain to a gardener what happens when a plant "sports." Anyone who wishes to know more can obtain a copy of the article cited.

Now you see how it happens that a rose bud may open into a bloom of a color different from those on the rest of the plant. Or, a rose shoot may suddenly grow much, much taller than those on the rest of the plant, so that it is a "climbing" shoot.

Some plants seem to be especially prone to sport. Chrysanthemums often have some shoots which bear flowers of a different color than those on the rest of the plant. Some roses, like the old variety Ophelia, are quite likely to have white, pale pink, and deep rose flowers on a plant all at the same time.

Plant breeders use these sports to produce new varieties. By taking off the tip of the "climbing" shoot of a rose, and rooting it, a climbing type of the parent rose variety may be produced. Variegated-leaved varieties of shrubs and vines often are produced by propagating shoots that have "sported" with variegated rather than plain green leaves. New rose varieties also may be grown from sports.

So if you see any unusual variation on a shrub,

49

don't be too upset by it. Perhaps it means that you, too, will have a chance to produce a new variety.

Soil Reaction

Letter number 6 is just one example of thousands of letters written each year telling about an unaccountable (to the average amateur gardener) change in flower color of a hydrangea.

This change is due to the chemical reaction of the soil. When the soil in which a hydrangea is growing is acid in reaction, the flowers on that plant will be blue. When the soil reaction is alkaline, pink flowers are produced.

Not only that, but since soil reaction changes, there may come a year when a hydrangea will produce blue flowers on one side of the plant, pink on the other. Or the plant may have blue blooms for a few years, then pink for two or three, then shift to blue again.

Since soil and its reactions are covered in Chapter 5, "How to Plant Shrubs," no further details will be given here. If your hydrangea blooms blue and you want it to bloom pink, add a handful of lime to the soil around it. If it blooms pink and you want blue flowers, give the plant a handful of garden sulphur in the fall. Simply sprinkle either chemical on top of the soil around the plant, mix it into the top inch or two and water thoroughly.

White hydrangeas do not change flower color. You cannot make them have pink or blue flowers.

Minor Variations

Minor variations in color of flower often occur because of variations in soil. Your neighbor's weigela may be a shade pinker than yours, even though one was grown from a cutting taken from the other. These little variations are no cause for excitement.

There also are minor variations in foliage color, usually due to exposure to sun. Thus, if you enjoy arranging foliage indoors, and you admire the corkbark euonymus (*Euonymus alata*), AND if you have room for two plants, be sure to set one in full sun and the other in semi-shade. The fall color of the leaves of the one in sun will be brighter and redder; while the leaf color of the one in shade will be deeper and more purplish. The two shadings form an interesting contrast.

If you haven't room in your garden for two such large shrubs as *E. alata,* grow instead the dwarf form, *E. alata* 'Compacta.' It has the same corky bark, so pleasing for winter interest, the same handsome fall foliage coloration, but will take up far less room in your garden.

Chapter 8

HARDINESS

If we are going to talk about hardiness, the first thing to do is to decide what hardiness is. It is the ability of the plant to thrive in the climate in which it is growing. All plants have a set of growing conditions that they prefer. When one or several of these are changed, the plant cannot be expected to grow as well; in fact, it even may die.

Plants growing wild are growing under the best conditions for them or they would not be growing in that area. The more closely the conditions in your garden approximate those under which the plant normally grows, the more hardy the plant will be with you and the better it will grow for you.

Hardiness of a particular plant in a particular area depends on a number of factors: the lowest temperature in winter, the amount of water it has received during the growing season and receives during winter, the humidity of the air around it, the type of soil it is in and the drainage conditions surrounding it, the degree of protection from drying winds and the amount of sun it receives during the year.

Microclimates

In considering these factors, microclimates must be taken into account. Even though your garden is in a certain hardiness zone (see the map inside the covers) the lowest temperature in winter may be higher than those given for that zone because your garden may be protected by your house and garage, by nearby houses, or by evergreens in a windbreak more than others in the area. Or, if you are near the center of a city, it may be warmer by a degree or two in your garden than in the suburban gardens outside the city. Even within your own garden, there are always varying degrees of temperature and of protection that may make it quite possible for you to grow plants that people gardening only a block away cannot grow.

Minimum Temperature

Minimum temperature in winter determines where it is too cold for a given plant to grow and also where it is too warm for a given plant to grow. Many gardeners do not realize that some plants cannot thrive where winter temperatures are too high, just as others die where winter temperatures are too low. Peonies cannot be grown in New Orleans because winters are not sufficiently cold to give them the rest period they need.

To guide you in your choice of plants hardy in your area, as far as minimum winter temperature is concerned, the northernmost zone in which the plant grows well is given in the plant descriptions in Chapter 14. If your garden is sheltered, or you have sheltered areas in it, as described above, then you may be able to grow plants recommended for one zone south of you. There is little doubt that you can grow plants recommended for at least one and possibly two zones north of you. A glance at the number of shrubs carried by nurserymen in almost all the states and provinces listed in the Buyer's Guide Chart will show you how universally grown some of them are.

Water

The amount of water a plant has received during the growing season determines the state of its health about as much as any other factor. Shrubs that have grown well during the season are more likely to be hardy in your garden. Broad-leaved evergreen shrubs need copious watering in late fall because their leaves will be on them all winter and it is better for wet soil than dry soil to freeze around their roots. Deciduous shrubs do not need special watering in fall unless they were transplanted then. After their leaves have fallen their need for water decreases markedly.

Air

Some shrubs grow naturally where air is damp. They will not thrive under other conditions, so don't attempt to grow them unless your garden is in an area where such conditions prevail.

Drainage

Most shallow-rooted plants winter best when they are in well-drained positions. Only the plants that naturally grow along the banks of streams or lakes will come through the winter unscathed under those conditions. A few of the moist-soil-loving shrubs, like *Ilex verticillata,* will adapt themselves to drier soils, but they never grow quite as tall or quite as robust as in damper ones.

Soil

As is explained in Chapter 5 "How to Plant Shrubs," some plants must have acid soil, while most plants grow best in soil that is slightly acid to slightly alkaline. The plant that is growing in suitable soil is more likely to winter well than the one that is not.

No matter where you live, there are shrubs that will be hardy in your climate or in the microclimates which you either have in your garden or can create if you wish. If you have but little time for gardening, but want a garden anyway, choose your shrubs carefully, both for hardiness and minimum care, and you'll have a garden you can sit back and enjoy.

Chapter 9

SHRUB TROUBLES

Like all other living things, shrubs have their troubles. For most shrubs these troubles are so minor that the gardener need pay no attention to them. For other shrubs, troubles are, for all practical purposes, non-existent. Since these two groups of shrubs comprise the vast majority, there are left comparatively few shrubs which need a little of the gardener's time to control whatever the trouble may be.

In ALMOST every case, however, controlled or uncontrolled, the shrub will survive the trouble. This statement is the premise on which this chapter rests—for if shrubs weren't tough and practically without troubles, I never would have specialized in woody plants, I wouldn't be growing shrubs in quantity and, therefore, I certainly wouldn't be writing this book.

Should anyone ask me what has been the worst trouble MY shrubs have had during the many years I've been growing them, I can answer in a single word—"rabbits." Some gardeners undoubtedly would substitute mice or deer for rabbits, but the eating habits of certain animals, which can consume an entire large shrub during several months of a severe winter, so that only stubs are left, are certainly the most devastating shrub trouble.

Even when we lived in a city of 50,000 inhabitants, rabbits came into the yard and ruined shrubs. In our present 6-acre garden, despite the fact that hundreds of shrubs are ringed with fine-mesh chicken wire or hardware cloth, rabbits take their toll. We somehow, unknowingly leave unprotected each fall a few shrubs, such as flowering quince, that rabbits dote on; and, when the winter is snowy, drifts pile up so high that rabbits eat over the tops of the 2-foot-high wires. Furthermore, while nothing will convince me that rabbits cannot read the price tag on a shrub, by wire-guarding the new and expensive ones and those known to appeal to rabbits, the creatures merely are encouraged to eat other shrubs that they do not like quite so well.

Thus, in a "hard" winter, when snow is on the ground from mid-December to late March, getting deeper and deeper as the season progresses, rabbits will eat even barberries and buds from young lilacs, shrubs they do not ordinarily touch.

A man who lives down the road from us told me that, in one such hard winter, 20-year-old forsythias in his garden were eaten clear to the ground by rabbits. I have had what was a 5-foot-high *Prunus tomentosa* in the fall reduced to a 3-inch stub by spring.

Short of a campaign to trap and transport elsewhere all the rabbits or other shrub-loving animals that visit your yard, or systematic destruction of them, all you can do is put wires around favorite plants each fall—the animals' favorites as well as yours. Then you can spray the unguarded plants with one of several repellents on the market and hope for the best. The only bright spot in this dark picture is that, even when eaten to the ground, most shrubs will grow again from the roots. Shrubs are REALLY tough.

If the gardener's time is considered, it is relatively easier to control the shrub troubles caused by insects and diseases than by predators. Many troubles from these causes can be avoided.

Avoiding Shrub Troubles

If you have no desire to control shrub pests, you can avoid the work simply by not planting shrubs known to be highly susceptible to certain diseases or extremely attractive to certain insects.

For instance, anyone who has grown lilacs can practically guarantee to you that they will be attacked by scale insects at least once or twice in their lives. If they are, the scales will suck juices from the stems to which they have attached themselves and these stems will die an untimely death unless you spray once very early in spring to kill the scales. If this once-a-year or every other year spraying is too

Rabbit injury to flowering quince.

much trouble, don't plant any lilacs and you won't have to do it. (Of course, only the scale-infested stems will die—the rest of the shrub will go on growing well until the scales move to other stems. It will be years before you lose the lilac, but the plant probably won't bloom as much or perhaps won't bloom at all during certain of those years.)

Just as some shrubs are favorites of certain insects, some shrubs and small trees are prone to attack by certain plant diseases. For instance, some species of hawthorn (*Crataegus*) and some species of flowering crabapples (*Malus*) may be "alternate hosts" for certain "rusts." Rusts are diseases which make the leaves look "rusty," usually in distinct spots.

The two rusts referred to above—cedar apple rust and hawthorn rust—pass part of their lives on a member of the apple family, to which both hawthorns and crabapples belong, and the other part usually on red cedar (*Juniperus virginiana*) and its varieties. Both alternate hosts are absolutely necessary for the rust to complete its life cycle.

If you yearn for hawthorns or crabapples, then, you can either: (1) make certain that red cedars are not growing in your neighborhood and avoid planting them in your yard; (2) plant only varieties of hawthorns or crabapples that are resistant to rusts; (3) suppress your yearnings: don't plant hawthorns or crabapples; or (4) plant whichever varieties of the two you like best and prepare to spray the plants should rust attack. (It may never do so and the plants will live even if it does.)

When Troubles Are Slight

The gardener who does not make it a practice to look over his shrubs periodically never sees the minor troubles that his shrubs have and they flourish despite these troubles. As an example, lilacs often get mildew in the fall, especially if the weather is damp. Since the leaves will drop shortly because of the lateness of the season, the lilacs are not really bothered by this disease. Most gardeners never notice it, though it can be unsightly when the white coating gets heavy on the leaves. Unless your lilac is placed where it is conspicuous and the appearance of mildew annoys you, this is a shrub trouble to ignore.

Obviously, if you don't see insects on your shrubs, you won't know about them. For instance, caterpillars may feed on leaves of one branch of a shrub and, since they stop in due course of time (though you cannot tell in advance just how many branches they will defoliate before they stop) you may never notice their depredations. In a small garden, where the appearance of each shrub is important, it would be sensible to spray or dust that small part of the shrub on which caterpillars first are seen to prevent its disfigurement, provided you see the caterpillars.

In a large garden like mine, I am more likely to hold a paper bag under the branch and cut it off. At the end of each tour of the garden the bag, with whatever pest is in it, goes into the burner and usually that marks the end of the pest.

In precisely the same way, aphids, if seen when just starting to attack the tips of shrub branches, can be controlled by "dunking" those tips in a pail of nicotine sulphate (Black Leaf 40) solution or, if you can't reach the branches, spraying with the same insecticide. A few aphids may be washed off with water from a hose. Or, if no hose is within easy reach, the cut-and-burn method is effective.

When first observed, the troubles described above usually are minor. Control them then and they are not likely to become serious. But, regardless of whether or not the troubles are controlled the shrubs still will be with you for many years.

It would, of course, be ridiculous for me to pass off shrub troubles from insects or diseases as all minor or all needing little or no attention on the part of the gardener. Yet, before I go on to tell you about the commonest troubles that you are likely to encounter sooner or later if you grow shrubs, I would like to tell you a few plain facts:

1. We owned our former garden for 21 years. About 100 shrubs were included in its plant-

ings. In all those years the only spraying for a specific pest was to control scale on lilacs, and a few times branches of various shrubs were "dunked" to kill aphids on them.

2. Our present garden is 14 years old now. Some of the shrubs in it were moved, full size, from our previous garden. They never have been sprayed or dusted in this garden any more than in our previous one.

3. We now have over 1000 shrubs in this garden. During the past 14 years I have sprayed 3 times for lilac scale—that is, I have looked over the 63 lilacs to see whether or not scale insects were attacking and have sprayed the branches that had scales on them. A few times I have seen aphids on the tips of branches of an assortment of shrubs and have cut off and burned those tips. We have no such thing as a general spray program, in fact we simply leave the shrubs alone to grow big and produce the quantities of flowers for which I grow them.

4. Sometimes I know I should spray, but can't. For instance the big American holly outside the window my typewriter faces has been attacked by leaf miner for the last three years, but I have not done anything to control it because in the first place it is growing so well that no insect is going to stop it and in the second, how can I spray when at the proper time for doing so the silliest, flightiest female I ever have known, a female cardinal, builds her nest in it? A soil drench of Cygon would control the miners and the material is in the house, but I just haven't gotten around to using it.

I know also that I should have sprayed several springs ago the three pyracanthas back of the lily pool which we see below the dining room window because they have scab which coats stems and berries with black soot. But I seem never to be home at the correct time for spraying and, furthermore, even if the disease overlays the berries with unsightly soot, it makes little difference. I'm not going to enjoy them anyway, for the warblers stop at our garden on their southern migration just when the berries turn orange and they strip off every berry, then move to the huge female yew under the south windows of my office and do the same.

Post script: We forgot to protect these pyracanthas with wire last winter so the rabbits ate them to the ground. Of course they grew again from the roots and were soon as large as ever but there were *no signs of soot* this year on either *leaves or berries.* So even rabbits have silver linings!

If you have gathered from the above that my attitude toward insects and diseases is to leave well enough alone, you have gathered correctly. Usually I am far more interested in seeing whether or not a shrub will survive an attack than I am in controlling it. After all, should a shrub die from insect or disease attacks (and none ever has in all these years) I could always buy another one.

From the thousands of letters I have received from readers, I am convinced that people do more harm to their shrubs by coddling them and fussing about every little pest that comes along, than they do good. If your attitude and feelings about shrub troubles differ from mine, and you wish to know what they are and what to do about them, here are the commonest of the shrub troubles:

Common Shrub Troubles: From Insects

Aphids (plant lice)

When you see colonies of tiny insects concentrated at the tips of new shoots with succulent leaves, these are aphids. They come in several colors and many species. They injure a plant by sucking its juices, thereby reducing vigor and sometimes causing malformations. They secrete a substance called honeydew which in turn attracts a black sooty mold and this makes a plant unsightly. Aphids also act as carriers of virus diseases. Ants use aphids much as humans use cows, placing them on plants to feed and then, themselves feeding on the excretions of the aphids. Thus ant control contributes to aphid control.

To control aphids use nicotine sulphate (Black Leaf 40) in soapy water (the soap serving as a spreader and sticker), or rotenone, pyrethrum or Malathion. Lindane is particularly good to control wooly and gall aphids. There are also root aphids. Chlordane, which controls both the root aphids and the ants that carry them, is effective against these.

DDT also controls aphids but is not sensible to use as DDT also kills beneficial insects such as aphid lions and lady beetles which feed on aphids and thus keep the population under control. In fact, because of this, I have put DDT on the "don't use unless nothing else will do" list.

Bagworms

These are not found on shrubs as often as they are on evergreens, but since they are the homes of caterpillars, they should be cut off and burned when seen. If this cannot be done, spray the foliage where the caterpillars are feeding with any stomach poison, such as lead arsenate.

Beetles

While Japanese beetles have not yet spread to some parts of the United States, other areas have had to live with them for years. They are chewing insects, attack many plants and do enormous damage. These beetles are half an inch long, coppery green in color with tufts of white hair extending out from under the wing covers. They appear about the end of June and are not to be confused with rose chafers, which they resemble.

Since the grub stage in the life cycle of Japanese beetles is passed in the soil, where they feed on grass roots, one good way to control them is to treat lawn areas with Chlordane, Dieldrin, or lead arsenate to kill the grubs. Milky disease spore dust which carries a disease fatal to Japanese beetles also may be used to control them.

Beetles feeding on leaves and flowers may be controlled by spraying with Sevin, lead arsenate, Methoxychlor, Lindane or other substances. Sprays must be regular and frequent, for it is almost impossible to control beetles feeding on flowers which have opened between sprays.

Borers

These are one of three classes of insects that most gardeners never see. Borer signs are 1—holes in the stems or branches of shrubs, 2—little piles of "frass" hanging onto the riddled stem or lying on the ground underneath and close to the stem or 3—sap or "gum" exuding from the surface of a branch.

Borers attack particularly lilacs, rhododendrons, and roses among the shrubs. Borers may be controlled by several means: 1—poking a piece of wire up the borer hole and then attempting to spear the borer. 2—squirting carbon bisulphide up the borer hole and then plugging the hole with putty or childrens' modeling clay. 3—using Bor-tox or Borerkil which are pastes containing Lindane. Both come in tubes with applicator tips. A bit of paste is inserted into the hole which then is plugged. 4—spraying or painting the trunks or branches with DDT in spring or spraying the same parts with Borgo whenever borers are found.

Borers are most likely to attack shrubs in poor or weakened condition, so growing conditions should be made and kept as favorable as possible. Bark wounds always should be treated with tree wound paint or the aerosol spray made for that purpose, as, left untreated, they can open the way to borer attack.

Bugs

When rhododendrons are grown in full sun, lace bugs are almost sure to attack. These suck the undersides of the leaves, which become flecked with brown. Then the topsides become stippled in yellow as a result of the attack. To control these spray lower leaf surfaces with Lindane in late May or early June depending on how far north you live) for the first brood and in July for the second. Watch to see when the nymphs hatch and spray then.

There also is an azalea lace bug which has more broods per year than the rhododendron lace bug so more frequent spraying is needed to control them. Lindane or Malathion may be used.

Andromeda lace bug is a similar species and the same materials applied in early June when the young hatch will control them,

Sometimes the hawthorn lace bug works on cotoneasters, pyracanthas, and hawthorns.

Caterpillars

Innumerable species appear on various shrubs, some of them tying leaves together and feeding protected by these leaves, as sometimes happens on hydrangeas; others eat holes in the leaves. If they seem to be doing a large amount of damage, spray leaves with lead arsenate and let the caterpillars eat themselves to death.

Tent caterpillars occasionally select shrubs for their homes. If possible, cut off the piece of branch holding the nest, and burn the whole thing. If this is not possible, don't burn the nest while it is on the shrub as burning may injure the shrub. Instead put newspaper on the ground under the nest, then, using more newspaper in your hand, remove the nest. Any escaping caterpillars will fall on the paper already on the ground. You can then pick it up and burn both lots of paper.

Leaf Miners

Although there are times when adult forms may be seen clearly, leaf miners are the second of the "invisible" insects because most gardeners never see anything but the results of their attack. These manifest themselves as blisters on the leaves or blotches that outline the tunnels made inside the leaves by these pests (see illustration, below). Leaf miners feed between the upper and lower leaf surfaces. They are the larvae of beetles or moths, flies or sawflies and, since they spend most of their lives inside the plants they attack and therefore are well protected, they are not easy to control. Timing of the sprays is all-important since different broods hatch on different plants at different times.

Boxwood miner may be controlled with nicotine sulphate sprayed on the nymphs or Malathion or Lindane sprayed on the leaves to control the adult miners inside them. Mid-May is the proper time to spray in Southern Ohio, early June in Michigan and time in your area will depend on where you live.

Holly leaf miners usually have only 1 brood a year. Dieldrin or Lindane used during the month of mid-May to mid-June will control the adult flies in the leaves.

Or, for either of these miners, try a systemic poison which may be sprayed on the foliage at one dilution, applied around the roots as a soil drench in another dilution or, in granular form, sprinkled on the soil.

Mites

Most gardeners do not realize that these pests are at work until they see leaves turning color or see the tiny cobwebs which are the sure sign of mite attack. If you think the injury may be mites or may be something else, hold a piece of glazed white paper under an affected branch with one hand and hit the branch sharply with your other hand meanwhile looking at the paper. If minute specks drop on the paper and you see them moving, they're mites.

Tedion, aramite, sevin or dimite will control mites. The use of DDT or Malathion will increase the mite population as either one kills the insects which normally prey on mites.

Scales

While these really are easy to see if you know what to look for, they qualify as the third "invisible" insect because most people see first a plant that does not thrive. If they look further, they find numerous tiny bumps along the stems and these are the scale insects. Admittedly they don't look like most other insects. They belong to the class of sucking insects and the females are more deadly than the males. Females are wingless and, after

Tunnels of holly leaf miner.

57

Euonymus plant badly infested with euonymus scale.

a short period during which they are able to crawl, they stick their beaks into plant tissues and remain in those places, sucking plant juices through their beaks for the rest of their lives.

Gradually skins that have been molted, combined with special secretions, form a hard covering in the types of scale insects known as "armored" scales. The "soft" scales never form this armor. One of the soft scales familiar to almost every gardener is mealy bug, which has a covering that looks like fluffy wax.

There are numerous kinds of scales, but the oyster shell scale and the euonymus scale probably are the two most commonly seen on shrubs.

Oyster shell scale has the shape its name implies. It attacks a great number of deciduous trees and shrubs; may cause death of the plant if the attack is sufficiently severe. Euonymus scale attacks both shrub and vine forms of euonymus and both deciduous and evergreen species. It also sometimes is found on pachysandra. A badly infested plant, such as is shown in the illustration above, is a horrible sight.

Scale insects may be controlled in the crawling stage or in the fixed stage. Each different kind of scale crawls at a different time of year and crawlers of many kinds may be killed if sprayed with Malathion (either 50 percent wettable powder or 50 percent emulsion) at that time. Oyster shell scale should be sprayed about the middle of June. Spraying for the crawling stage of euonymus scale is effective about the first week in July and in early September in my area. Your county agricultural agent or local nurseryman should be able to tell you approximate dates for your area.

If you do not happen to see scale insects when they are crawling, the scales may be controlled by spraying with either a miscible oil or lime sulphur during late fall or early spring *while shrubs are dormant.* Spray when temperature is above 50 degrees and likely to stay there long enough for spray material to dry. Follow manufacturer's directions carefully, especially with miscible oils, as too strong a solution can injure even dormant shrubs, but especially unfolding buds or new growth. Do not use oil sprays on magnolias or Japanese maples.

If you use lime sulphur and buy the liquid form (it also comes as a powder) store it in a glass container as it corrodes metal. Since lime sulphur may discolor paint, don't use it on shrubs against buildings.

Thrips

These minute insects are mentioned here because they often attack privet hedges in Eastern United States making them look dust covered. They are sucking insects and may be controlled with contact insecticides, like nicotine sulphate, rotenone, or pyrethrum.

Wasps

The wasp known as giant hornet sometimes makes its appearance near lilacs in late summer. It can damage these shrubs badly in short order for it tears off the bark and shreds this material to make very large, paper-like nests in sheltered spots. Should you see signs of this wasp, immediately spray trunks and branches of lilacs with a strong DDT solution.

Common Shrub Troubles: From Diseases

Blights

Sudden death of branches, flowers, leaves or entire plants are the characteristics of blights which are actually invasions of plant tissues by fungi or bacteria.

Fire blight, which is a bacterial disease attacking fruit trees and ornamentals belonging to the rose family (hawthorns and pyracanthas among them), makes the affected plant part look as if blackened by fire. Prompt removal of the entire part, to half a foot below the blight, often arrests spread of this trouble.

Terramycin and streptomycin are used to control fire blight in fruit trees; may also be useful if this disease attacks ornamentals.

Azalea petal blight (also called flower blight and flower spot) was considered a disease of southern azaleas but seems to be working its way northward and has been found in New Jersey. This disease starts as a white spot on a colored azalea petal or a brown spot on a white azalea petal of a flower low down on the plant. Within a day the whole flower turns slimy and all flowers on a plant may be a mess in short order. This is a frightfully disfiguring disease. It now may be controlled by spraying 3 times weekly with Zineb (Parzate) or Nabam (Dithane Z-78) beginning as soon as so-called "mid-season" blooming azaleas start to show color in the buds.

Northern gardeners should take certain precautions in buying azalea plants from the south—they should buy only bare root plants and if they buy these in spring, should remove all flower buds showing color either just before or just after setting out the plants.

There also is a camellia flower blight, which is not discussed here because camellias are found largely in states in more southerly zones than are covered in this book.

Cankers

Caused by fungi, cankers are found on woody stems, sometimes as lesions, sometimes completely girdling a stem. An area turns brown, later the tissue shrinks and the area sinks and finally it cracks.

While some canker fungi invade a plant through tissue that is unbroken, many others invade through injured tissue, so avoid wounding trees and shrubs with lawn mowers and keep pruning wounds properly painted. Also keep mulch materials which hold moisture away from stems, so that stems are not kept moist.

Sometimes cankers, if sufficiently localized, can be removed by cutting them out. However, when cankers girdle a stem, interfering with water conduction in the plant, the plant part will die. Sometimes cankers involve the food-carrying layer of the bark and cause partial or complete starvation. In these latter cases, the entire stem will be lost to the plant.

Galls

These are swellings or enlargements of some plant part due to irritation of the tissue by insects, bacteria, fungi or sometimes viruses. Among shrubs there may be leaf galls (as on roses and euonymus), stem galls (as on euonymus) and root galls (on many plants).

The best way to handle leaf galls is to cut off the affected part and burn it, then watch the plant to make sure there is no other part affected.

Crown galls are found at the part of the plant where tops meet roots—usually at or below the soil line. They are caused by bacteria.

Often crown gall enters your garden on a new plant. To avoid bringing in such an infection, examine carefully crowns of newly purchased plants, especially of roses, euony-

59

59

Gall on stem of Euonymus.

mus and the bramble fruits. If you find a crown gall, cut it out and burn it if possible. If impossible, it is best to dig out and burn the plant, disinfect any tools you have used for pruning it, and disinfect the soil in which it grew.

Crown gall sometimes is found on stems of euonymus (see illustration up above) in which case it is easy to cut off the affected stem and burn it.

DO NOT *propagate plants which are infected with crown gall* as the infection will be spread by these new plants to other parts of the garden.

Root galls usually are caused by nematodes, but just seeing swellings on plant roots is not necessarily a cause for alarm. These may be beneficial nodules, common on plants of the legume family, which includes such shrub genera as *Caragana, Amorpha,* and *Indigofera.* Or they may be nodules on the roots of non-leguminous plants such as Russian olives (*Elaeagnus angustifolia*) and sweet ferns (*Comptonia peregrina*), which often have such swellings but for some unknown reason. However, they are *not* root galls.

It is difficult for an amateur to decide whether swellings on plant roots are beneficial nodules or harmful galls. When in doubt, expert advice should be sought. If the swellings are caused by nematodes, the best thing to do is to dig and burn the plant, then disinfect the soil.

Leaf Spots

Leaf spot diseases are present when discolored spots of dead tissue appear on leaves. They may be small or large, may have centers of one color, margins of another, but are quite well defined in extent, which is what differentiates them from anthracnose, blights, or blotches because these are indefinite in form. Leaf spots are worst in damp weather.

There are innumerable types of leaf spots, most caused by fungi. Some of them appear on various shrubs and cause little trouble so may be ignored. A few of them, like the one called "black spot" which appears on roses, are serious troubles. Black spot can cause all the leaves on the plant to drop, thus weakening the plant for future years.

As you already know, the only roses included in this book are those commonly called "shrub" roses. Most of them are tough; though they may be attacked by black spot and even completely defoliated by it, they will grow new leaves later in the season and will continue to survive such attacks year after year.

A shrub rose which can be guaranteed to get black spot in every year that weather conditions are favorable for the disease is *Rosa foetida* 'Bicolor,' the Austrian Copper rose. Its flowers are so beautiful that you may wish to grow it despite its propensity for this disease, but, if you do, plant it apart from other shrub roses so the disease does not spread from it to other nearby plants.

As previously indicated, you do not need to spray or dust shrub roses because they happen to be attacked by black spot. You can ignore the trouble and the plants will survive. If, however, you wish to control it, use Phaltan, starting when the leaves unfold and continuing every 10 days through the growing season. Phaltan will control powdery mildew at the same time that it controls black spot.

Rose spot anthracnose might be included here under leaf spots. This disease, however, is more common on climbing than on bush roses. It shows on leaves as round brown or blackish spots which turn grayish with a dark red border. Sometimes the quarter-inch spots merge into larger discolored areas. If they appear on canes, spots may be either spindle shaped or round, purplish or brownish but characterized by sunken centers which are gray. Ferbam is the usual control.

Mountain laurel, when it is planted in a damp or too-shaded place, especially where moisture from trees drips on the plants, is subject to a leaf spot which is hard to control. The best thing to do is to move the plant to a drier or less shaded spot, though spraying with Ferbam when new leaves are appearing, and repeating the spray two or three times at two-week intervals, will help control it.

If you feel you must control leaf spots on other shrubs, try first a copper fungicide like the old Bordeaux mixture which has the advantage of being widely available in garden supply stores. If this does not help, then try Ferbam or Captan. Since the fungi which cause most leaf spots are of various kinds, the type of fungicide that controls one fungus may not control another. A mixture of several types of fungicides may be your best bet.

Mildews

There are two distinct types of mildews: powdery and downy. Powdery appears on plants as a whitish coating that looks like felt, covering buds or stems or leaves, especially young ones. Downy mildew appears as white, gray, or sometimes purplish "down," usually on the under sides of leaves.

Powdery mildews grow best when the air is damp and the weather humid (but do not grow during rain). Poor air circulation, plants set too close together and warm days followed by cool nights all predispose plants to attack by powdery mildew. Mildex, Karathane, Phaltan, copper fungicides and sulphur all control this trouble which attacks many, many plants.

Downy mildews grow best in wet weather. Bordeaux mixture or Zineb will control them.

As has already been noted, powdery mildew often attacks lilacs in late summer and, while it may be unsightly, doesn't do any harm, so may be ignored. The same remark applies to the same mildew which sometimes appears on privets, viburnums, blueberries, azaleas, and euonymus at the same time of year.

Powdery mildew on roses may be controlled with Phaltan, Mildex, Karathane or sulphur or, as previously explained, when it attacks shrub roses (as differentiated from hybrid teas, floribundas, etc.) may be ignored.

Rots

When the tissue disintegrates into either a hard, dry mass or a soft, wet mass, the term used for the trouble is "rot." Since rots are most common in plants set in low, damp areas, avoid planting shrubs unadapted to such areas in these places.

The most devastating rot in shrubs is blueberry mummy berry (also called brown rot) caused by a fungus which invades tips of shoots and the flowers when they appear in spring and later affects the young berries. These turn color, usually tan or cream, and fall off. Thus the crop is materially reduced. Best control is to cut off and burn the affected parts when seen. Or, spread paper under the berry bushes so you can clean up rotting berries as they drop, before they can overwinter and allow the disease spores to reproduce in spring.

Rusts

The term "rust" is not necessarily properly applied to every rusty-appearing area on a plant. Such areas may or may not be true rusts which are microscopic fungi and damage many plants. Some of these are important crop plants, and one of these (black stem rust of wheat) has as its alternate host *Berberis vulgaris*, the common barberry. Alternate hosts were explained earlier in this chapter under "Avoiding Shrub Troubles," therefore, it is necessary to note here only that it is illegal in many wheat-growing states to grow *Berberis vulgaris* (an attractive shrub) and that it is illegal to import this shrub into these states or into the United States (see Chapter 12).

The Japanese barberry, (*Berberis thunbergii*) and its varieties and other barberries commonly grown in gardens are considered resistant varieties so may be grown in any state.

Cedar-apple rust, as previously explained, alternates during its life cycle between red cedar (*Juniperus virginiana*) and its varieties (and sometimes other junipers as *Juniperus horizontalis* and *Juniperus scopulorum*) and members of the apple family, notably the native crabapples and particularly Bechtel's crab. Best control is elimination of one or the other alternate host from your garden and those of your near neighbors. The next best control is to examine any of the susceptible junipers in early spring, particularly if weather is wet, and to take off and burn the galls which then are formed but have not yet grown horns or discharged spores.

Other possible controls are spraying junipers in early spring with wettable sulphur, spraying alternate hosts in the apple family with Actidione or sulphur mixed with Ferbam two or three times beginning in early spring and extending into early summer.

The same remarks apply to control measures for hawthorn rust and quince rust. Hawthorn rust galls on junipers usually are dark reddish and smaller than those of cedar-apple rust and those of quince rust usually are mere swellings on branches and twigs (which often die completely). Alternate host for hawthorn rust is usually hawthorns, but mountain ashes and flowering crabapples as well as crabapples grown for fruit, apples, and pears may also act as hosts, and buds, twigs and fruits may be distorted; leaves caused to drop prematurely. Quince rust may have as its alternate hosts, apples, crabapples, pears, quinces, mountain ashes, chokeberries, and amelanchiers, as well as hawthorns. This disease is especially noticeable on English hawthorn. Fruits may become covered with clusters of bright orange spores which are surrounded by white projections.

Currants (*Ribes* species) are alternate hosts of white pine blister rust. The European black currant is considered most susceptible and it is illegal to grow these fruits in many states and to import them into the United States and Canada. However, the ornamental currants commonly grown in gardens, as well as the red currants grown for fruit, are not considered susceptible, so may be grown anywhere.

There are other rusts of minor importance to shrubs but most of them may be ignored except if they mar the appearance of an important specimen. In this case try either sulphur or Ferbam or Zineb. A badly infected plant is, perhaps, better dug up and burned, though this is hardly likely to be necessary.

Wilts

When foliage of a plant becomes limp and "wilts" it is probably because the plant hasn't had enough water and the soil is dry. Try a thorough soaking of the soil around the plant before you jump to the conclusion that a disease is troubling it. If the plant responds you know what caused the trouble.

Wilting also may be due to water loss from plant tissues because of too much fertilizer. Do you remember from your high school course in biology an experiment demonstrating the process called "osmosis"? This showed the movement of liquids as it occurs within a plant and from soil to plant and vice versa. The conclusion was that there is movement of fluids both in and out of a plant cell, through the cell wall, but that the *greater* movement always is from the less dense liquid to the more dense. Normally, the cell sap is more dense than the soil water. However, when a plant is over-fertilized, the soil water becomes more dense with chemicals from the fertilizer than the cell sap and thus the normal movement of liquid from soil to plant is reversed, more fluid moves from plant to soil instead and the plant wilts.

This type of wilting usually can be corrected by soaking the soil with water so that excess fertilizer is washed out of the soil. When a plant wilts shortly after being fertilized, suspect this reverse movement of liquids rather than a disease, and act accordingly.

When a specific organism, like a fungus, clogs some of the cells in the conducting vessels or destroys them, obviously the plant wilts. If wilt occurs in just one branch, cutting it off below the infection may stop the trouble, but sometimes the entire plant wilts because of soil-borne fungi. Saving that particular plant is hopeless and soil sterilization outdoors often impractical, especially if other plants are growing nearby. Better sacrifice the one affected plant.

There is, of course, one precaution you can take and that is to grow "wilt-resistant" cultivars of plants subject to a wilt disease.

First Aid To Shrubs

It must be obvious to all but the most inexperienced gardener that this one short chapter just "hits the high spots" of possible shrub troubles. However, it is quite possible that you'll never need more information about them than this chapter gives, for all of them are not going to appear in your garden at one time, most of the attacks will be slight and easily dealt with, and, to repeat once more, most shrubs are not affected by troubles.

If one of your shrubs has symptoms of a disease

or is attacked by an insect for which you find no description here, you need either the services of an expert, in which case turn to your country agricultural agent or the plant pathology or entomology department of your state university, or you need a book devoted to plant troubles. Below are the names of those I own and have found useful in dealing with readers' questions over many years:

Pirone, Dodge & Rickett, *Diseases and Pests of Ornamental Plants,* Third Edition (1960). The Ronald Press Co., 15 East 26th St., New York 10, N. Y.

Cynthia Westcott, *Plant Disease Handbook,* new revised second edition (1960). D. Van Nostrand Company, Inc. 120 Alexander St., Princeton, N. J. and 25 Hollinger Rd., Toronto 16, Ontario, Canada.

Cynthia Westcott, *The Gardener's Bug Book,* 3rd Edition (1964). Doubleday & Co., Inc. Garden City, N. Y.

There are in addition to the above, which I use all the time, two books which may be well suited for use by most gardeners. They are:

A. W. Dimock, *The Gardener's ABC of Pest and Disease,* (1953). M. Barrows & Co., 425 Fourth Ave. New York 16, N. Y.; and T. H. Everett, *The Illustrated Book of Garden Pests and Diseases,* (1960). Hawthorn Books, Inc., 70 Fifth Ave., New York 11, N. Y.

If I were you and were going to invest in such a book (or books) I would first go to the largest library in the largest city near me and look them over to see which best suited me.

Horse Sense

If you had answered all the letters I have answered from people whose plants (not necessarily shrubs) were troubled by some pest, you'd know that most people go off half cocked at the first sign of trouble. This is not the way to react.

It doesn't make any sense at all to grab a sprayer or duster, fill it with the material closest at hand and cover the shrub with that material. This probably won't do any good and may do incalculable harm.

Instead, first examine the extent of the trouble. If it is slight and is in form of an insect, try washing it off with water from the hose or a pail. Watch the shrub and if the insect does not reappear, forget it. If trouble is slight and seems to be from a disease and the shape of the shrub won't be ruined if you remove the affected part, cut it off, burn it and maybe you can forget it.

If the trouble is greater in extent, take a good

look at it from all sides of the leaves, stems or whatever part is affected. If it seems to be from an insect, what is the insect doing? Eating holes in leaves? Then it's a chewing insect and any stomach poison, such as old reliable lead arsenate, sprayed on the leaves will cause it to commit suicide as it eats. Are there no visible holes, but signs of wilting leaves? If it isn't drought then it's a sucking insect and any insecticide that comes in contact with its body and either clogs the pores or burns it, like nicotine sulphate, will kill it. And so on.

If the trouble is definitely not from an insect, look through the common diseases in this chapter and see if what is attacking the plant fits one of those descriptions. If so, get one of the remedies advised then: READ THE DIRECTIONS ON THE LABEL and then FOLLOW THEM PRECISELY. No precise quantities are given in this chapter because manufacturers sometimes change formulas. If they do, they also will change directions on the package.

KEEP FIRMLY IN MIND that an INSECTICIDE will NOT control DISEASES and that a FUNGICIDE will NOT control insects. You need a specific kind of chemical for a specific kind of pest (and the chemicals are getting more specific all the time). TIMING is extremely important in control of some pests and even the right spray applied at the wrong time may be ineffective and therefore a waste of time and money. Since almost all pesticides are poisons, take ALL PRECAUTIONS printed on the label. Never disregard them thinking "it can't happen to me." I could tell you stories of things that have happened to nurserymen!!!

NEVER use a sprayer or duster in which a weed killer has been used for anything but weed killers. Keep one sprayer for pesticides, one for weed killers and MARK EACH CLEARLY with a tag on the handle *and* a sign painted on the side of the container, so that no one can possibly use the wrong one.

While it is true that a sprayer or duster may be cleaned so that little or no weed killer remains in it, the process is so lengthy that it is hardly practical. Furthermore, even if thoroughly cleaned, *and then stored for some time,* the next use *still may* prove lethal to the plant involved.

Trouble From Weed Killers

Even if you never accidentally spray a shrub with a weed killer, the use of one of these chemicals on your grounds, near shrubs or quite far from them, or even the use of one by your neighbor, still may show up as trouble on your shrubs. I remember the year the lilacs along our lilac lane had some leaves with scalloped edges. This turned out to be injury from 2, 4-D which had been used in granular form on the grass of the path between the lilacs the previous fall. Fortunately only a few leaves were affected on each plant and all plants survived. Sometimes shrubs are not so fortunate. A breeze blowing from a weed killer being sprayed on a lawn nearby can transport sufficient weed killer to injure and, sometimes kill, a valuable shrub. So use weed killers with greatest caution all times and in all places. Remember the chemicals cannot differentiate between a broad-leaved weed and a valuable ornamental shrub.

Looking Forward

New chemicals for control of plant troubles appear on the market each season. Some of them fall by the wayside. Some of them soon replace older ones. And still others offer a new approach to the control of pests. Such a one is Cygon, a brand name for Dimethoate. This is the first "systemic" insecticide available to the home gardener. Other systemics are so highly poisonous that their use has been confined to commercial plantings. Cygon, while still poisonous, is less so than others.

Cygon is used as a spray on leaves or as a soil drench and is absorbed by the plant either through its leaves or its roots. It enters the plant's system (hence the name "systemic") and stays there in the sap. When certain types of insects attack the plant they get a dose of the poison and die.

When used as a soil drench, Cygon usually has to be applied about once in eight weeks. Foliage applications must be repeated every two or three weeks to be effective. As is evident, Cygon is available in liquid form only. It is said to control such plant troubles as euonymus scale, boxwood and holly leaf miner and other sucking and burrowing insects.

Other systemics are in process of development, against plant diseases as well as insects. At a European chemical company I saw some work being done on a systemic against mildew of roses. The man with whom I was touring the plant said that this material was then ready for marketing. That was four years ago and so far I have not seen any signs of it on the market in the United States, nor have I been back in that particular country in Europe long enough to investigate the market there.

Meanwhile, in the United States, development of dry or granular forms of new systemic insecticides make possible one-application control of the sucking, boring or mining insects which hatch only one brood a season. Lessened numbers of applications are possible to control insects of similar kinds which have several broods a year. For instance, scientists at the University of Maryland have found that a single application of a granular systemic insecticide will control azalea lace bug for the season.

These granular chemicals are applied to the soil to be taken up by plant roots and translocated or moved within the plant to other parts, to be ready for the insects when they attack. They are easier to use than soil drenches or foliage applications and, furthermore, said to be safer than the former systemics.

They have been tried against and reported to control aphids (including snowball aphid) holly, boxwood and azalea leaf miners and other insects. As an example of their ease of use, a single treatment in early April is recommended for all-season control of the snowball aphid which is an annual visitor to the snowball (*Viburnum opulus* 'Roseum') and also frequently attacks the American cranberry bush (*V. trilobum*).

The three brand names of the new granular form of systemic insecticide are Vaughan's Systemic insecticide, Scope and (for southern states only) Greenlite.

The development of systemic insecticides presages more complete control of certain pests with considerably less work. However, it must be borne in mind that while systemic insecticides will be effective against any insects that suck plant sap (like aphids), or burrow or tunnel within the plant (like scale insects or leaf miners), and therefore *come into contact with the sap within the plant,* they will not control insects that feed on the layers of leaf tissue (epidermis) because the systemics are carried in the sap, not in the tissues.

PART III: ACQUIRING SHRUBS

Chapter 10

HOW TO BUY SHRUBS

Have you ever visited a nursery sales lot on a fine, sunny Sunday afternoon in May and listened to a family buying nursery stock to plant around the house? If you have, you must know that few families come to the nursery adequately prepared. If you haven't, follow an actual family of four—Mother, Father and two children and observe, as I did, what they buy and why they buy it.

Remember that the month is May and in the nursery sales lot there are hundreds of plants of azaleas in full bloom. Mother promptly selects several with flower colors a rosy-lavender. These she thinks may fit under the picture window at the front of the house even if it is rather close to the ground.

Father makes a beeline for the spruces because they look so sturdy, and decides he'll buy two of them, one for each side of the front door, close to the 3-foot-wide path from the sidewalk to the house.

The kids think the red-leaved barberry is such a pretty color and want their parents to buy some plants to place under the picture window at the front of the house—the same picture window for which Mother has selected the azaleas. So a compromise is reached and the family decides to buy some azaleas and some red-leaved barberries, both for under the same window.

This is a true example of what one family did and if it seems to you that they did a good job, consider the following: Since Mother lives in the Detroit area, the chances are better than even that the soil around her house is alkaline or circumneutral. Azaleas, with certain notable exceptions, must have acid soil to survive. She doesn't know this, so probably won't own the azaleas very long. Furthermore, she has not considered whether or not azaleas will tolerate the exposure at the front of the house, where she intends to plant them. In the hot summers of the climate in which Mother lives, azaleas

grow best on the north or east side of a building. If the picture window which she bought them to plant under faces south—this exposure would be another reason why she probably will not own the azaleas for long. And, of course, she has not armed herself with the exact measurement of the distance between that picture window and the ground.

Father's spruces, selected for their sturdiness, are sturdy indeed. They are forest trees which will grow so high that they will dominate any but a very tall house (and the one Father lives in is one story high) and will spread so wide that both the 3-foot-wide front path and the front doorway soon will be obscured and unusable.

The foliage color of the red-leaved barberries, though beautiful with the azaleas while they are clothed only with foliage, will clash with the flower color when they sport blooms and, if the house against which they are placed happens to be red brick, both red foliage and rosy-lavender flowers will battle the house color. Furthermore, barberries are poor plants to use in a house planting for this usually is the planting that the family wants to see best kept. The barberry thorns will make weeding between the plants an unpopular chore, which will not add to the chances of the house planting looking neat at all times.

This family, visiting the nursery without adequate measurements, also bought too many plants for the space they have unless their house is 100 feet long, and I'm willing to bet they also planted what they bought too close to the house wall. How do I know all this? I've made a practice of standing to one side and watching and listening to what goes on in nurseries (and other sales places for horticultural and allied products). It's an excellent way for a garden writer to get ideas for articles.

This family, of course, furnished a perfect example of the *wrong* way to buy woody plants, shrubs included.

The Right Way

Then what is the *right* way to go about such an enjoyable task as selecting plants for your own grounds? Stated briefly, to be elaborated upon further; you should: (1) first know the area for which you want to buy and (2) if the space is limited, as it usually is, have measurements with you which will help you to buy only as many plants as are needed of correct ultimate heights and spreads to fit your space.

(3) You should have some idea of how you wish this area to look and which shapes of plants will best assist the architectural lines of your house to look their best or, if they are not pleasing, to conceal them.

(4) Next, you should have some background knowledge of how the nurseryman sells shrubs, and (5) of course you should know something about the plants you are considering buying. If you know nothing about the plants, you'd better (6) know something about your nurseryman.

1 & 2: Observing and Measuring

Going back to points 1 & 2 above—it is easy to measure the footage you cover in one pace as you walk. You can use this figure to pace off the important distances in your yard. Putting these down on paper needn't be a chore either: cross-section paper, available at any stationery store, makes it simple. Depending on the size of the paper and the size of the squares, assign a foot to a square, or more, or less, and after that just count squares.

House measurements should be accurate—use a steel tape, or lacking that, a yardstick or a tape measure. Be sure to measure the distance from ground to windows as well as the wall space between windows and doors, and between these features and the house corners.

3: Picturing

If you own a camera, take pictures of your house from various angles. These are extremely helpful when planning the landscaping. If you have an enlargement made of a snapshot, ask that it be printed faintly, so you can draw right on it, if you wish. Or, you can draw on a piece of thin paper placed over it, if the picture is printed a normal darkness.

What to draw? Just the shapes of plants that will be most suitable to the type of architecture of your house or to the areas you wish to plant. For any shape and height you draw, there's surely a choice of plants that will meet your requirements. Just doodle a bit and see how you can make your house and lot look their best. For instance, suppose one wing of your house is higher than another and dominates the scene. A horizontally branched tree or large shrub planted at that end of the house will visually lower its height. A tall, slender plant of any type will accent the height.

Walk back and forth across the street from your house, looking at it as you do so, and you'll be much better able to judge the ultimate heights and the shapes of the plants you should acquire to enhance the picture.

After you have a good idea, not only of the shapes of the plants you wish to buy, but also the sizes to which they should ultimately grow to fill the areas in those sketches, these, together with the measurements you have taken, will help you and the nurseryman determine which kinds of plants and how many plants you actually need to buy.

It will help, at this stage of planning, if you will write down your positive likes and dislikes. If you detest plants with yellow or red foliage, write it down. If both husband and wife are concerned with the planning, it is just as well to avoid plants disliked by one or the other.

If you do not wish to do this planning yourself, you may want to have a nursery send a person, preferably one trained in landscape design and architecture, to your home to draw a simple plan, including the specification of the plants to be used. Usually, if you buy the plants from that nursery, there is no charge for the plan. However, there is a moral obligation implied, and you lay yourself open to the possibility of getting a stereotyped plan or else one that is drawn up to suit the convenience or the stock of the particular nursery.

When you do the planning yourself, you are free to visit several nurseries and buy plants where you see fit. Furthermore, if you do not wish to visit nurseries, you can buy from a mail order source.

Before you go further in planning, figure precisely how much money you can afford to spend for the planting. Decide whether you will do it all in one year or spread the cost over several years. Will you set out the plants yourself or have the nursery do it? If the nursery does the planting, there will be a charge for it. If you do it yourself you must include in your price estimate the cost of the necessary shovel and garden hose (unless you already own them) and the cost of peat moss or some other type of organic matter to improve the texture of your soil, which hardly is likely to be perfect. Fertilizer cost need not be included since no fertilizer should be used at planting time.

Should you decide to have the nurseryman plant, decide also whether or not you wish the plants guaranteed to live. Then ask the nurseryman how much he charges for this guarantee that the plant will live a year or the nursery will replace it at no charge.

Now you are ready to think about buying plants, including shrubs, either from a local nursery or a mail order concern. So, now you need some background knowledge about the nursery business.

4: Background Knowledge

Sizes And Price

a—Plants are available in many sizes. In general, the smaller the size, the cheaper the plant. However, this rule does not apply to certain dwarf plants. In these cases you are paying a higher price for a plant that grows slowly, takes more time to reach a saleable size, and never will outgrow the space you plan for it.

If you will remember that plants grow—an obvious fact, but one that isn't always recognized—just look at all the houses overgrown by plants—you will know that you can buy the smaller sizes if you haven't enough money to buy the larger ones and that the plants will eventually grow to the size you can't afford to buy at the start.

Spacing

This leads us to the matter of spacing. Plants should be set out sufficiently far from the house wall (at least 2 feet for a small plant, at least 3 feet for a medium-sized one and more for one that will grow very large) to allow for the ultimate spread of the plant. Thus the side of the plant towards the house will grow as full and beautiful as the side away from the house. Plants also should be set sufficiently far apart to allow for their spread, whether they're to be placed near the house or away from it in a shrub border.

There is no specific rule for spacing plants according to their ultimate size, so I'll tell you a general principle I've found useful. If the plant will ultimately grow 10 feet high, allow the same footage for the ultimate width. If it will ultimately grow from 5 to 10 feet high, allow three quarters of the ultimate height for the width. If the plant will some day be from 2 to 5 feet high, allow 3 feet for the ultimate spread. Plants lower than 2 feet often grow as wide as or wider than their heights, so the distance to plant them apart depends on the individual plants.

Hedge planting is another matter. Plants always

are set so they are closer together than in other plantings and thus will form a tight screen as they grow.

The reason you should inform yourself about spacing of plants is so that you avoid overbuying. This also is the reason you should plan first and keep in mind that plants grow.

Home Nursery

Realizing that plants grow offers the possibility of planting a home nursery of plants you cannot buy or cannot afford to buy in large sizes. Mail order firms often offer plants that your local nurseries do not carry, but mail order sizes usually are small because shipping charges are lower when plants weigh less.

The canny gardener makes a nursery bed somewhere on his lot and plants small plants before he builds a house, while the house is being built, or whenever he can buy the plants he desires. In this way, in just a few years, he has plants the sizes he wants, can move them into his landscaped area, and has saved the money he otherwise would have had to pay for a larger size of the same plant.

Packaging

b—Woody plants may be purchased with their roots bare of soil, sometimes packed in damp sphagnum moss or excelsior (or some other material that, moistened, will keep the roots damp) and sometimes not. These are known in the nursery trade as "bare root" plants.

Woody plants also may be purchased with their roots encased in the ball of earth in which they grew, this ball wrapped in burlap, pegged with nails or wound about with twine to hold it in place. Such plants the nurseryman calls "B & B," meaning balled and burlapped.

Most deciduous shrubs, those that drop their leaves in winter, are sold "bare root." Some nurseries plant these bare root shrubs in early spring in tar paper or other similar pots or cans, so that you can buy them, if you want, long after the regular planting season is over. If when you plant them, you slip them gently out of the containers and into prepared holes, their roots will not be disturbed and they will continue to grow. Shrubs available in containers are referred to as "container stock" or sometimes as "potted shrubs." The former name also is used, and more properly belongs, to plants grown in containers from the time they were rooted cuttings. When you see the term "container-grown stock," it refers to these plants grown with roots confined for easy transplanting.

The shrubs (and trees and evergreens) sold B & B are those of varieties that do not move well bare root, or are too large to move with bare roots. Nurserymen have had years of experience with plants, so they know which kinds tolerate transplanting with roots first bared of earth and which will not.

Because of labor charges, container stock costs more than bare root stock and B & B stock usually costs more than either of the other two.

Small sizes of shrubs (and other woody plants) sometimes are sold in little containers under such trade names as "Redi-potted" or "Peppy plants." Some nurseries specialize in these plants. If you have a home nursery, you might like to investigate these.

Mail order nurserymen usually ship bare root shrubs with moist wrappings around the roots. This is satisfactory for the purchaser since mail order sizes are not large. Mail order nurserymen also offer small sizes of evergreens, both broad and narrow-leaved, with small balls of earth around the roots, or in small containers in which the plants have been grown in sphagnum moss rather than soil. Shipping charges are a little higher for these plants, but by no means excessive.

Sizing Standards

c—Sizing of bare root, deciduous shrubs or B & B, broad-leaved evergreen shrubs is reasonably standardized. The sizes are expressed in terms of feet and/or inches of height if the shrub grows higher than wide. If it grows wider than high, the same terms of feet and/or inches refer to the spread rather than the height.

Smaller sizes of shrubs, up to 24" in height, usually are sized in 3" steps, as 12"-15" or 15"-18". Shrubs larger than 24" are sized by half-foot steps, as 2' to 2½', 2½' to 3'. Still larger shrubs are sorted according to one-foot steps, for instance, 4' to 5', 5' to 6'. Shrubs which are more than 6' high are sold in sizes which vary from one another by 2'. For example, 8'-10', 10'-12'.

The American Association of Nurserymen has published a leaflet for its members which sets forth in explicit detail size standards for woody plants. Since these have been approved by the American Standards Association, Inc., they are likely to remain unchanged for some years.

With regard to shrubs the standards state the minimum number of canes of a minimum height which a shrub of a given size (height or spread) and a certain type (seven types of deciduous, five of broad-leaved evergreens are delineated, with examples given of each) should have to be acceptable in the trade. All of these size standards are subject to certain grading tolerances.

Such further pertinent information also is included in the leaflet as recommended widths and depths of earth balls considered satisfactory for balled and burlapped stock, whether nursery grown or "collected."

Collected Plants

d—Plants offered for sale in nurseries, nursery sales lots and some catalogs are not always nursery grown. Some are "collected" which means that they are dug from the woods or fields where they grow wild. Because their roots usually spread wider and deeper than any reasonably sized earth ball can encompass and because they have not been repeatedly root pruned as are plants grown in nurseries, such plants are harder to reestablish in your garden. Additional care is needed in order that collected plants survive.

The extra work involved and the lessened chances of survival should be taken into account and weighed against the probable lower price of collected stock when you are considering such a purchase.

e—It is not usually worth while to collect plants yourself. Unless they are very small and you can dig them with an extra-large ball of earth around their roots, they are not likely to survive transplanting for the reasons given in the paragraphs above. Should you be considering collecting plants, make certain that you collect them from land you own or have permission from the owner of the land from which you dig them. Check also with your state department of agriculture to find out if an inspection certificate is required before transporting plants.

Handling

f—Nursery stock that is dug while you wait at the nursery, or has just been dug, or plants that have been properly packaged and refrigerated, are worth far more than the same size plants of the same kind that have been handled improperly or allowed to dry out after being dug. Carefully handled plants reestablish their roots more readily, grow better and grow larger in a shorter time.

Buying From Farther South

g—Another bit of background knowledge that you should have is that plants *normally hardy* in your climate may be purchased from nurseries in other climates and will thrive in your garden IF ONLY you give them a reasonable chance to do so.

For instance, a shrub grown in a nursery two hardiness zones south of where you garden is not likely to stand the shock of being moved to a much colder climate in late autumn. There will either be a dead shrub or one with far smaller tops when spring rolls around.

On the other hand, if you buy that same shrub in early spring (having ordered it the previous fall, specifying the earliest date on which you can plant it immediately or heel it into a large pile of peat or compost until weather permits planting), it has a long growing season ahead of it. During this it can reestablish its roots and, as the weather gradually cools, its wood will harden. While it might be sensible to protect a shrub spring-moved from the south the first winter after planting, it certainly should not be necessary to do so during any successive winter if, as I said above, the shrub is of a kind normally hardy in the hardiness zone in which you live.

I am speaking from experience in this matter (as in so many others) and I realize that what I am telling you is the opposite of what garden experts have been preaching for years—never to buy from farther south than one hardiness zone. This, I think, is silly, and I have umpteen shrubs in the garden to prove it.

Bargains?

h—Low priced plants are bargains only when they come from a good grower and have been carefully handled. It sometimes happens that such an establishment is overstocked on one kind of plant and can, therefore, offer it at reduced prices. These plants *are* bargains, but plants left over at the end of the season at an ordinary sales lot are worth precisely what you pay for them and no more.

An example that comes to my mind whenever bargain plants are mentioned is that of a now defunct (bankrupt, and no wonder) plant sales lot —not a nursery—that followed the interesting practice of laying bare root rose plants on the roof of a shed. These were invisible to a person standing on the ground in the sales lot, but clearly visible if one were driving on a nearby elevated expressway. When more bare root roses were needed to supply customers' demands, someone simply used a ladder to reach a supply of the poor plants, which then had their dried out roots wrapped in damp sphagnum moss and were packaged in water-proof paper before being sold. At the end of the season these plants were offered at a very special (and widely advertised) sale for only 25 cents each. By that time they weren't worth even a quarter.

5: Knowing About Shrubs

Way back at the beginning of this chapter I suggested that there were five different types of knowledge that you should have in order to buy shrubs intelligently. Point 5 was knowing something about the plants you consider buying. Since the greater portion of this book is devoted to descriptions of the shrubs available to you in the nurseries of the United States and Canada, you have only to read and look at the pictures in order to gain a modicum of knowledge about the shrubs you may wish to purchase. However, I do not consider such knowledge a substitute for actually seeing the plants. Places where you may go to see them are described in Chapter 2. Perhaps you'd like to read that once more?

6: Knowing Your Nurseryman

How does one go about knowing one's nurseryman? From hard experience gained through walking nursery rows several months of every year for many years, and visiting what by now must be thousands of nurseries and their garden centers, here are the points I look for when I judge a nursery and, therefore, its owner. First of all, I try always to look over the sales lot and part of the nursery before I meet the owner. As I walk, I ask myself the following questions:

Does the place look clean and well kept? I don't mean that the nursery must be weedless, because sometimes when weather is extremely hot and dry, it is better to leave weeds in place for a mulch. But it usually is easy to tell whether the proper work has been done around the nursery rows. Plants in the sales lot should definitely be weed free, well watered and generally well kept.

Are the plants well spaced? I don't like to buy plants that have been growing crowded together because too many roots usually are lost when digging one plant, because of the need for saving the roots of the ones on either side.

Are many plants in the nursery overgrown? If so, I always wonder why they weren't sold long ago. Of course every nursery has a few very large plants. That is normal, but too many are too many.

In reverse, are there too few holes visible from which plants have been dug? If so, I always wonder if the prices of the stock have been set so high that sales are few.

How about signs of insect pests? Or plant diseases? One thing a good nurseryman always does is keep his plants well sprayed to control these pests.

Are the rows labeled? Now I realize that it is next to impossible to keep labels in place over the entire nursery (I have seen children and even adult customers take labels out of the ground) but certainly most of the labels should be in place and legible. If a label is missing, a good nurseryman should not show signs of worry, because he should have a "map" of his nursery, with each kind of plant indicated on it. The plants in the sales lot certainly should be labeled and the more information on the labels, the better the nursery is likely to be.

Is the nursery growing only the commonest kinds of plants? Perhaps I should not include this point because you may be a new gardener, quite uninterested in any but the most common plants. However, this is an important point for me to notice, since I am interested in buying only the unusual shrubs I don't already own (and it gets harder to find these every year). But I do think that a nursery growing only the commonest plants is not progressive.

After all this walking and looking I have a fair idea of what is being grown in the nursery and an overall impression of it. So will you if you walk and ask yourself the same questions that I do. Now it's time to go to the office, but first, if there is a garden center, I walk through it and look around. Is it neat? Is the stock well displayed with instructive signs and prices? Are there interesting items as well as the usual pesticides and fertilizers? Is there literature to help the customer (this does not necessarily mean free literature)?

Now it's time to meet the nurseryman.

Perhaps it is not fair for me to tell you what I look for in a nurseryman, for I've been in some phase of the plant business since age 13, I've met many, many nurserymen and count some of them among my best friends. But the first and most important thing I look for in a nurseryman is knowledge of the plants he grows. If he doesn't know his plants, how they grow and why he is growing them the way he is, then he is not a person I trust and therefore I do not wish to deal with him.

It is not necessary that he be able to "out-Latin-name" me—this is hard to do. He needn't know more about every plant he owns than I do, though he certainly does about many of them, but he *should* have a good general knowledge of plants and not be flabbergasted by a botanical name.

A great many nurserymen, of course, are as plant crazy as I am and we have a wonderful time together, discussing plants. Most of the people who deal in plants *have* to be plant crazy or they'd never be in a business that deals with living things which require such a great deal of time, effort and care to help them survive and grow.

If, about now, you are asking yourself what difference it makes whether or not you know your nurseryman, let me try to tell you. He can give you the benefit of his years of experience as to which plants will thrive in your particular climate and soil. He can tell you the sizes to which these plants will eventually grow and their idiosyncracies if any. He can tell you how to modify your soil to suit the plants you buy, if this is necessary, and how to plant and care for them. That is, if he is a reliable nurseryman.

Because I know how much a reliable nurseryman can do for you, especially if you are an inexperienced gardener, I feel that, when you figure the price of the plants you buy, you ought to take into account the advice you get from your nurseryman, or from the nursery catalog in which you find the plants you desire. Assistance of this kind is not forthcoming when you buy low-price plants from a fly-by-night operator of a seasonal sales lot.

This professional advice is one of the most important things a nurseryman or cataloger has to offer. He wants to keep you as a customer, so that the prime ingredient of his sale to you is YOUR success with the plant you have bought from HIM.

Finally—if you feel that knowing how to buy woody plants is just too much bother—consider this. The cost of landscaping a building is generally considered to be approximately 20 percent of the cost of the building. Thus the cost of the planting around your house—whether you put in your own time or pay for that of the nurseryman—is a big part of your investment. This means (or should mean) that any time you spend learning how to buy plants and how to select plants is well justified if only to protect the investment in money and in planting time that you are about to make.

Chapter 11

WHERE TO BUY SHRUBS

Sources for all shrubs described in Chapter 14 and small trees described in Chapter 15 are listed in the Buyer's Guide Chart which takes up most of the pages of this chapter. This chart has been prepared entirely from nursery catalogs. One thousand and eighty members of the American Association of Nurserymen and 123 members of the Canadian Association of Nurserymen, whose places of business are located in the plant hardiness zones from Zone 7 northward, received a letter from me. This told a bit about this book and asked for copies of their catalogs or lists for use in the book.

Through the courtesy and cooperation of the American Association of Nurserymen, short items about this book appeared in two issues of the "Newsletter" of the Association. Each of these "reminders" to their members brought me more catalogs. The offerings of more than 200 nurseries from two countries comprise the Buyer's Guide Chart. (Frankly, after listing all the shrubs offered and typewriting the chart, I am relieved that no more nurseries responded.)

The reasons for the inclusion of some nurseries in Zone 7, in a book that covers only woody plants hardy in Zone 6 and northward are two: the first is that some of these nurseries are near the large cities on the eastern seaboard, the second is that some of them are large wholesale nurseries from which retailers all over the country can buy. Among these nurseries in Zone 7 are two with the longest lists of offerings in the United States.

Explaining the Chart

Near the center of each page of the chart you will find listed, by their botanical names, the shrubs and small flowering trees in commerce. (Common names are given in the descriptions of the shrubs and trees in Chapters 14 and 15 and you will find them also in the index beginning on page 367 so you can look in either of these places if you know only the common name).

To the right and left of this central column, at the top of each page, are the names of the states and provinces entirely or mostly located in Hardiness Zone 6 or northward. The west coast states are not included; nor are states in which Zone 6 is only on mountain tops or where there are no members of the AAN or states from which no nurseryman sent catalogs.

Under the state and province groupings and on the same lines as the names of the shrubs the nurseries list, are the code symbols for names of nurseries. Code *letters*, followed by the full name and address of each *retail* nursery, are listed alphabetically beginning on page 110. Names of *wholesale* nurseries are *not* listed; instead, next to the code *numbers* designating wholesale nurseries, are the names they furnished of several retail sources.

How to Use the Chart

First you must know the botanical name of the shrub you wish to buy. Next, locate it in the shrub listing. This list is alphabetical by genera.

Thus, if you want to find a source for a hardy boxwood called Vardar Valley, you will find from the index that the botanical name of boxwood is Buxus. Therefore you will look for it on the chart under the genus Buxus and find Vardar Valley listed as a cultivar under the species sempervirens.

To locate sources for this shrub, keep one finger on the name, Buxus sempervirens 'Vardar Valley' in the central column. Look across the top of the chart to find the group of states or provinces that includes yours, and trace down the chart from that point with your other hand until you reach the level of the shrub name. There you will find the code designations for nurseries in your state or province (or in one nearby) which list the shrub. Copy these abbreviations on a piece of paper and then turn to the nursery list beginning on page 110 to find nursery names and addresses.

If none of the nurseries in your state or province list the shrub, you may want to get it by mail order (many of the nurseries will ship plants), or you may want to go get it yourself. If you want to order by mail, check the nursery list to be sure the words "DOES NOT SHIP" do not follow the nursery name. Nurseries known not to ship are so indicated.

If you want to go get the shrub yourself, be sure first to find out the formalities of bringing in plants from other states or another country. Read Chapter 12, if you wish to import from another country and check with your state or province department of agriculture before you go to buy the shrub from another state or province. There may be no laws governing movement of shrubs into your area; there may be only an inspection tag to obtain from the nursery from which you buy; or it is possible that entry of the shrub is prohibited by your state or province.

When the name of the shrub genus, as listed in the Buyer's Guide Chart, is on a separate line with no specific name following it, the nursery or nurseries listed on the same line as this genus are specialists or have, in my opinion, especially good coverage of the genus. This identification is given so that people interested in collecting lilacs, for example, can look up *Syringa*, the botanical name of lilacs, and find the names of nurseries which have many species and varieties of lilacs for sale.

When the code letters or number of a nursery are underlined, it means that the nursery has a particularly good list of whatever shrub group appears on the same line. Thus, when a nursery has an especially good or long list of the so-called "French" hybrid lilacs, actually hybrids of *Syringa vulgaris*, the common lilac, its code letters are underlined as they appear on the same line as "Syringa vulgaris hybrids."

In some cases where there are far too many cultivars available to list all of them separately, you will find group listings included in the chart—for example, "Hibiscus syriacus cultivars." Nurseries designated as offering these may offer only one cultivar or many.

The Buyer's Guide Chart does not list all of the shrubs and small trees available. Many nurseries, some members and some non-members of the two associations, list and sell shrubs not on the chart. But this list provides a fair sampling of shrubs and trees in commerce. Many nurseries I asked for catalogs chose not to send them, so they are not listed. However, you'll find here 696 (counting a hybrid group or cultivar group as one) of the shrubs and small flowering trees commonly in commerce, enough to make almost any gardener happy.

About The Catalogs

Some of the catalogs, regardless of the size of the company publishing them, are models of correct botanical names and careful alphabetical listing. These listings were easy to transfer to the chart. Others sometimes list shrubs by botanical names, sometimes by common names—and in any order at all. These were not easy to unravel for entry on the chart. As long as the botanical names were those currently correct, we used them. When they were incorrect, we substituted the currently correct name for the name used in the catalog. The outmoded or incorrect name, if commonly used, is also shown in the index and in the descriptive section.

As an example, whenever *Cydonia japonica* is the name used in a catalog for "flowering quince," it appears as Chaenomeles speciosa on the chart, since botanists long since changed the genus *Cydonia* to *Chaenomeles*.

The hardest catalogs to organize, however, were those which did not use botanical names at all but merely common names. When descriptions followed these common names, I often could deduce which shrub was intended; but when they did not, I had to draw on my imagination or do general guess work or not list the shrub at all.

For instance, when a catalog lists "Pussy willow" described as having extra-large catkins, we have entered the shrub under Salix caprea. If there is no description of catkin size, we have considered it to be Salix discolor, since this is the pussy willow most commonly carried by nurseries. When the description is of rose-gold catkins, the shrub is shown on the chart as Salix gracilistyla. When identification in the catalog was not sufficient to determine which species or variety was meant, we have omitted the source.

When the name given was obviously incorrect according to the description which followed, the shrub is listed on the chart under its correct name, regardless of what the catalog calls it. Thus, often when the catalog has listed a lilac as *Syringa persica*, the Persian lilac, the description is that of the *Syringa chinensis*, the Rouen lilac. In this case, we have listed the plant on the chart as S. chinensis. When a nursery has listed both *persica* and *chinensis*, both are included on the chart.

Misspellings "due to typographical errors" in the catalogs have been corrected. And we have had many a laugh over the way some names turn out—for instance, the error that converts Moraine locust into "More Rain locust." This is a non-controversial example, since this locust, being a large tree, is not described in this book.

About The Nurseries

The fact that the nurseries listed on the chart are members of the nurserymen's organizations in their respective countries speaks for itself. I have dealt with a good many of them and found them reliable. Of course I can offer no guarantees, nor even guides as to quality, trueness to name, packing, etc.: this book gives information only.

You will understand, also, that there is a normal flow of shrubs in and out of a nursery, due to demand and supply, just as there is of models and colors of cars at your auto dealer. It is, therefore, impossible for a nursery always to have on hand in a saleable size every shrub it lists. Some nurseries will propagate a shrub if you ask them to and you then can buy it in a year or so. Other nurseries periodically add promising new items and stop propagating certain other shrubs when they find it unprofitable. Their lists change a little each year.

For Nurserymen Only

If you are interested in some of the offerings of the wholesale nurseries in the Buyer's Guide Chart or if some of your customers are interested, you can obtain a list of the code numbers of these nurseries and their names and addresses by writing to me in care of the publisher of this book, D. Van Nostrand & Co., Inc., 120 Alexander St., Princeton, N.J. I have prepared a mimeographed list and will be glad to send it to any *nurseryman writing on his letterhead stationery and enclosing a stamped, self-addressed envelope. It will not be sent to anyone else.*

Some of the shrubs and trees offered are finished stock, but others are liners or rooted cuttings. Better inquire before you order.

Why You Can't Find That Shrub

As has been said previously in this chapter, the Buyer's Guide Chart lists 696 different shrubs and flowering trees. Some of these, as you can see from the chart, are available from most nurseries; others from a single nursery only. Because the chart is, of necessity, limited in scope the shrub of your dreams may be sufficiently rare in commerce so that it is not among those on even this long list.

Now I know that when you've read an article that describes a shrub in such glowing terms that you'd like to buy it, or when you've seen a shrub in full flower or fruit and would like to buy it, nothing is more frustrating than not being able to find a source for it.

There are several possible reasons why, with the best of intentions, you are unable to do so. Consider these:

1. The name you attach to the shrub is incorrect. This can happen easily. Last spring the supermarket in which I shop had the usual bedding plants displayed outdoors in front of the building. After parking, I walked toward the door meanwhile eying the plants. Some were labeled and one name caught my eye. It read "Aramis."

"What on earth is aramis?", I said to myself, and went over to investigate. The plants it indicated were armerias!! Some clerk, knowing nothing of plants, must have misread a listing on a bill of lading and so coined a new Latin name which no one ever heard of before. Had you copied that name and then tried to find a plant to fit it you would have searched for years without success.

All last season, in a nursery sales lot which I pass frequently, there was a sign reading "Ilex roundifolia"—meaning *Ilex crenata rotundifolia* but who could guess that? You would look long and hard for this little holly under such an incorrect name, especially since it is now *Ilex crenata* 'Latifolia.'

2. Only part of a name has been given you, and because of this you are looking for the plant under the wrong letter.

This can happen when a nursery incorrectly leaves out a species epithet and gives only the variety. An example is the frequent listing of *Kerria japonica* 'Pleniflora' (globe flower) merely as *Kerria pleniflora* or, as many catalogs incorrectly list it, *Kerria floreplena*. If you have found Kerria under K and are looking for japonica under "j," it is not likely that you will look for the plant under "p."

3. If you have merely heard the name of the plant and spelled it phonetically, you may have a name that is unknown in horticultural literature.

This may happen when you write down the name yourself; or a person writing an article may mislead you by having done the same thing and then neglected to check with a botanical reference for the correct spelling.

Some years ago, while in Bellingrath Gardens near Mobile, Alabama I saw a plant with beautiful leaves. The gardener nearby said it was called "Fasha" and I wrote down just what he said. He also explained that it was the Chinese rice paper plant and it was this explanation rather than the name that enabled me to find it.

No such name as "Fasha" appeared in the encyclopedia. So I started looking through the F's and reading the descriptions of the plants. In one description I found first the words "rice paper" and later the word "Chinese" and knew I had found the correct plant. Its name is *Fatsia papyrifera.*

On another occasion I recall searching through the P's for "Polonia" which is the way it sounded when I was told the name of a beautiful tree in Virginia. This turned out to be *Paulonia.*

4. It is possible that you are searching for the shrub in the wrong kind of catalog. Many people, especially new gardeners, do not realize the differences between catalogs of seed firms and those of nurseries. Of course many seed catalogs also list nursery stock, perhaps just a few items, but often a good many. Nursery catalogs sometimes list seeds, but usually not those of herbaceous plants. If you cannot find the plant listed in one catalog, don't stop there. Look in a few more catalogs of different types.

If the shrub you wish to buy is so rare that it is not in the hundreds of catalogs abstracted in this Buyer's Guide Chart, then it still might be listed in a book titled *Plant Buyer's Guide* which lists some nurseries not included in this book and a number of nurseries in foreign countries. Published by the Massachusetts Horticultural Society, this book is available from the society, 300 Massachusetts Ave., Boston, Massachusetts. Or a copy may be in your local library.

Should that wanted shrub not be listed in this book or in *Plant Buyer's Guide,* you are really going to have a hunt for it. Institutions like horticultural societies and college libraries which own collections of catalogs are your only hope, and searching those catalogs is your only way of finding a commercial source.

The Bailey Hortorium, Cornell University, Ithaca, New York has a card file made up from an outstanding collection of catalogs, and is, therefore, often able to name a source. But you may find, as I did in searching for my currently "wanted" shrub, *Campyloptropis macrocarpa,* that the Rochester, New York, Park Department is the only source in this country. Of course the shrub may be available in a foreign catalog. If you find it in one, turn to Chapter 12 for directions for importing shrubs.

6. The plant may not be in commerce.

I hate to say this, being a garden writer myself, but some people who write garden columns have been known to either rewrite plant descriptions in garden encyclopedias or rave about some plant seen in a botanical garden or similar place possibly in a far-off country. This causes nothing but trouble for the reader and, consequently, sooner or later for the garden writer. It is my firm belief that there are sufficient plants in cultivation *and* in commerce to afford any garden writer subjects aplenty without naming plants for which a source is unknown. I learned this the hard way and I am not likely to forget the lesson.

7. One way of bringing your wants to the attention of numerous people who might know sources is to write to the various horticultural magazines giving the name of the shrub you want. Most of them have departments for readers' questions or list plants desired by readers. Both the American Horticultural Society and the Royal Horticultural Society in England list plants desired *by members* in their respective publications.

If you have considered and acted upon all seven of these possibilities and still cannot find a place to buy that shrub, start a "want list" in a notebook small enough to carry with you. Whenever you happen to be at a nursery or garden supply center, get it out and ask for the plants on it. It is amazing how many times it is possible to locate a plant, even after it has been on the want list for years. Good luck!

American redbud (Cercis canadensis) in bloom. Although
it looks as if the flowers grew directly from the branches,
they really are borne on tiny stems.

BUYER'S GUIDE

CANADA – ALBERTA, BRITISH COLUMBIA, MANITOBA, PRINCE EDWARD'S ISLAND, QUEBEC, SASKATCHEWAN	CANADA – ONTARIO	NORTH DAKOTA, SOUTH DAKOTA, WISCONSIN, MINNESOTA	IDAHO, COLORADO	MICHIGAN	SHRUBS AND TREES AVAILABLE FOR YOUR GARDEN
ED				WR, LI, FB	ABELIA 'Edward Goucher' grandiflora
					" 'Prostrata'
					" U.S.D.A. 210092
ED	SA			LI	ABELIOPHYLLUM distichum ACANTHOPANAX sieboldianus
LC, BT, AT, ED, PN, BB, GT, LS, PT. LW, GH, SM	RO, SH, HB, SD, PH, HA, CA, ME, 3, HD	CH, GU, LD, MK, WT, WG, 64, RH, 65, SA, GE, SW, PK	NL, WM, CG, GB, KB	BE, 62, LI, FB	ACER ginnala
ED					palmatum
ED, WX, PN, LW	RO, WE, SH, PH, WP, MC, HB, MD, NI, CA, VN, ME, 3, BA, MA		NL, GB	BE, WR, 62, LI, FB, WC	" 'Atropurpureum'
	SH, NI			LI	" 'Dissectum'
	SH, NI, CA			LI	" 'Ornatum'
BB					AESCULUS parviflora pavia
					ALTHEA (see HIBISCUS)
ED·	SH	LD, 65		LI	AMELANCHIER alnifolia grandiflora
				LI	laevis stolonifera
LC, GT, GH, SM	SD	LD			AMORPHA fruticosa
	SH	LD			ARALIA spinosa
		LD, MK			ARONIA arbutifolia
	SH	LD, GE, PK		BE, LI	" 'Brilliantissima'
	SA	NZ	62		melanocarpa
					AZALEA (see RHODODENDRON)
					BENZOIN aestivalis (see LINDERA benzoin)
ED			NL, WM, GB	62,	BERBERIS candidula julianae
					" 'Nana'
					" 'Pyramidalis'
PT, LW, GH, SM	SD, WP, HA	SA		LI	koreana
ED, BB	SH, PH, HA	GU, LD	NL, WM, NZ, GB, KB	BE, 62, LI	mentorensis
WX, DD, PN, BB, GT, LW, GH	HD, RO, WE, SH, SD, PH, WP, MC, MD, NI, HA, CA, VN, ME, 3, WV, HD, MA	CH, DV, GU, LD, MK, WJ, JG, WG, 64, RH, 65, GE, SW, PK	NL, WM, NZ, RB, KB	BE, 59, 60, EM, WR, LI	thunbergii
LC, AT, WX, DD, PN, BB, GT, LW	HD, RO, WE, SH, SD, PH, WP, MC, MD, NI, HA, CA, VN, ME, 3, BA, WV, HD, MA	CH, DV, GU, WD, LD, MK, WT, JG, WG, 64, RH, 65, SA, GE, SW, PK	NL, WM, CG, AL, NZ, GB, RB, KB	BE, 60, EM, WR, LI	" 'Atropurpurea'
PN	CA, RO, WE, SH, WP, NI, ME, WV, HD, MA	GU, WD, LD, WT, 65, GE, SW	WM, KB	BE, EM, WR, 61, LI, FB	" 'Atropurpurea Nana'
PN, BB	HA, CA, 3	SA, GE	CG, GB		" 'Erecta'
				LI	" 'Minor'
BT, PN, GT	SH, SD, PH, NI				" 'Sheridan Red'
		MK, 65, SA, PK			" 'Thornless'
ED				LI	triacanthophora
ED			NL	LI	verruculosa
BB	RO, SH			60	BUDDLEIA alternifolia
ED, WX, DD, BB	RO, WE, SH, PH, WP, MC, NI, CA, VN, ME, 3, BA, WV, HD, MA	GU, MK, JG, 65	NL, WM, CG, GB, KB	60, EM, WR, FB, BU	davidii cultivars

CHART

Note: Nurseries listed below as offering cultivars may offer only one or may offer many.

MISSOURI, KANSAS, NEBRASKA, IOWA	CONNECTICUT, MASSACHUSETTS, VERMONT	NEW YORK, NEW JERSEY (Note: Long Island and southern New Jersey nurseries are in Zone 7)	MARYLAND, VIRGINIA, DELAWARE Note: These states are in Zone 7.	WEST VIRGINIA, PENNSYLVANIA, OHIO, INDIANA, ILLINOIS	KENTUCKY, TENNESSEE Note: southern Kentucky and most of Tennessee are in Zone 7.
CV, HU, NO. 57, SB, PL, SK, HL	WF VP, AD, BC, HC, CS	BK, PR, LA, RD, ST, WJ, BL, 7, 12, TU, 68	ES, 14, 19, 20, WH, WB, IP SE, ES, BF, 14, 18, 19, 20, WH, 22, ML, WB, 5	EL, 27 DK, EN, EL, 27, DB, SQ, UP, SP, 35, 38, HB, 49, 67, AB, 23, HE	52, 55, HW BN, HM, 50, 51, 52, 53, 54, 55, 56, HW
			20, IP CR, 14, 5	HE	
HU, LE, HR	WF, GS AE, WF, VP, BI, LT, BC, CS	LA, 7	14	27, CE, DB, 33, 23 25, EL, SQ, 33, HB, 42, FC, 47	BN, HM, HW
CV, HU, PL, CM, FR, LE, HR, IA, HL	WF, BI, LT, CS	2, WJ, 7	ES, 14, KG, 5	EL, 33, NA, MM, HB, HN, LG, 44, 45, CD, FC, 46, 67, HE	
CV, PL, SK, HR	CS AE, CB, WY, WF, BI, LT, AD, CP, HT, BC, HC, 10, CS	BK, RD, MS, BL, TU, 68 BK, KE, PR, LA, RD, SR, WJ, 7	14 SE, CR, ES, 14, 19, 20, WH, WB, KG, IP, 5	27, DB, GR, FC BK, EN, MF, EL, 27, DB, SQ, UB, 31, 32, GR, 34, 37, NA, MM, HB, KR, HN, 42, 43, FC, 46, 67, 23, HE	BN, HM, 50, HW
SK	WF	BG, LA, RD, MS, BL, 7, 68 68	SE, 20, ML, IP	BK, HB, 67, 23	BN
CV	WF, 10 WF, HT	BK, SR, MS, 68	CR, 14, ML, 5	27, DB, FC, 67	
NO, 57, PL, HR			14, KG	67	50, 51, 53, 54, HW
HR	GS WF WF, HT, GS, CS		CR, 14 14, KG	FC LG HB, FC 45, FC, 47	
PL HR HU	HT HT AE, VP, LT, HC	PR, LA, BL, TU	14, ML SE, ES	FC UB, FC, 67, HE 33, CY, 39, KR, 41, CD, AB, FC, HE	56 HM
	AE, CB, WF, BI, CP, HT, 10, CS	RD, 7, 12	14, WB	EL, 27, DB, 33, CY, HB, FC, 47	BN, HM, HW
		7, TU		EL, 33, 41, CD, FC	
57, PL, SK	WF, LT, HC, CS	BK, PR, LA, RD, BL, 7, 12, 68	KG, IP SE, ES, 14, 18, 19, 20, WH, 22, ML, WB, KG, 5	25, EL, SQ, UB, 37, HB, 43, 49, 67, AB, HE	BN, 50, 52, 53, HW
	CB		14, 19, 20, 5 14, KG	27, DB	52
LE, HR			14	45, FC	
CV, HU, SB, PL, SK, WA, 58, HR, HL	WF, VP, LT, AD, BC, CS		SE, 14, 21	27, DB, 31, 33, 35, 38, MM, HB, HN, 41, LG, 42, 43, 45, FC, 47, 67, 23	HM, 50, 55, HW
57, SB, PL, CM, PF, SK, 58, FR, LE, HR, MY	AE, FM, CB, WY, WF, VP, BI, LT, AD, CP, PY, 10, CS, WL	BK, LA, MS, RD, ST, WJ, SC, 26, BL, 7, TU, 68	ES, 20, WH, WB, KG	DK, EN, MF, 25, EL, 27, DB, 28, SQ, UB, SP, 31, 33, 38, 39, NA, HB, KR, HN, KH, 41, LG, 42, 43, 44, 45, CD, FC, 46, 67, HE	BN, HM, 50, 51, 54, 56
CV, FA, NO, 57, SB, PL, CM, SK, WA, 58, FR, FE, LE, HR, MY, IA, HL	AE, FM, CB, WY, WF, VP, BI, LT, AD, CP, PY, BC, HC, CS, WL	BK, KE, LA, 5, MS, RD, ST, SR, WJ, SC, 26, BL, 7, TU, 68	ES, 14, 18, 20, WH, WB, 5	DK, EN, MF, 25, EL, 27, DB, 28, SQ, UB, SP, GR, 33, 35, 36, 37, 38, CY, NA, MM, HB, KR, HN, KH, 41, LG, 42, 43, 44, 45, CO, FC, 46, 67, HE	BN, HM, 50, 51, 54, 55, 56, HW
SB, CM, FR, FE, LE, HR, IA, HL	FM, WF, BI	BK, KE, LA, ST, 26, 68	SE, CR, 14, ML	25, SP, 32, 33, 35, 36, MM, HB, KH, LG, 42, FC, 46, 67, 23, HE	BN, HM
SB, PL	VP		14	EL, 33, LG, FC 25	
HR				FC, 67	
		BK, 7	19, 21, ML, IP	AB, HE	BN
	BI, LT	BK, PR, LA, RD, BL, 7, 68	SE, 14, 19, 20, ML, WB, KG, IP	27, DB, UB, FC, 67, AB	BN
	AE, WF, HT, BC		ML, KG	UB, FC, 23	
CV, NO, SB, CM, SK, WA, 58, FR, FE, LE, IA, HL	AE, CB, WF, VP, BI, LT, AD, HT, HC, CS	BK, KE, PR, LA, RD, ST, SR, WJ, SC, 26, BL, 7	SE, ES, 14, 20, ML, WB, 5	DK, EL, 27, DB, SQ, UB, SP, 31, 36, 38, CY, HB, KR, HN, 41, LG, 43, FC, 47, 23, HE	BN, HM, 50, 51, 56, HW

CANADA – ALBERTA, BRITISH COLUMBIA, MANITOBA, PRINCE EDWARD'S ISLAND, QUEBEC, SASKATCHEWAN	CANADA – ONTARIO	NORTH DAKOTA, SOUTH DAKOTA, WISCONSIN, MINNESOTA	IDAHO, COLORADO	MICHIGAN	SHRUBS AND TREES AVAILABLE FOR YOUR GARDEN
	RO				BUDDLEIA davidii magnifica
					farquhari
DD	RO, SH, PH, WP, WE, NI, HA, VN, ME, 3, WV, MA, CA	GU, LD, GE	GB	62, LI, FB	BUXUS microphylla
					'' 'Compacta'
					'' koreana
BB	SH, CA			LI	'' '' 'Wintergreen'
					sempervirens
				LI	'' 'Grand Rapids'
				LI	'' 'Inglis'
					'' 'Newport Blue'
	WV		NL	LI	'' 'Suffruticosa'
				EM, WR, 61, 63	'' 'Vardar Valley'
			NZ	LI	'' 'Welleri'
					CALLICARPA dichotoma
					japonica
					'' 'Leucocarpa'
				FB	CALLUNA vulgaris
					'' 'Alba'
					'' 'Alba Erecta'
BB					'' 'Atrorubens'
					'' 'Aurea'
BB					'' cultivars other than those listed
					'' 'Cuprea'
	RO			EM, LI, FB, BU	CALYCANTHUS floridus
BT, AT, PN, BB, LS, SM	RO, SH, SD, WP, WV, MA	DV, GU, LD, WT, 64, 65, SW, PK			CARAGANA arborescens
LC, BT, AT, PN, LS, PT, LW, GH, SM	RO, SH, SD, VN				'' 'Lorbergii'
LC, ED, DD, PN, PT, SM	SD, PH, SH, NI, VN, HD				'' 'Pendula'
LC, PN, GT, MT, PT, GH, ED	RO, SH, SD	CH, DV, SW			'' frutex
WX	RO, SH, PH, WP, NI, CA, 3, MA	DV, GU, WT, JG, WG, 64, 65	NL, WM, CG, AL, NZ, GB, RB, KB	BE, 60, EM, WR, LI, FB	'' pygmaea
					CARYOPTERIS clandonensis
					'' cultivars
		PK			incana
					CEANOTHUS americanus
					CEPHALANTHUS occidentalis
	SH, NI, CA, WV	GU, LD, MK	NL, NZ, GB	BE, EM, WR, 62, LI, FB, BU	CERCIS canadensis
				LI	CERCIS '' alba
				LI	'' 'Withers' Pink Charm'
					chinensis
ED, BB, LW, PN, WX	SH, PH, CA, VN, 3, HD, MA, WP, WV	LD, WD, 65, JG	WM, NL, KB, CG, GB, NZ, AL, RB	LI, FR, 60	CHAENOMELES japonica
		GU, LD, 64, 65		LI	'' alpina
DD	PH, SH				'Maulei'
DD, BB, ED	WE, SH, MC, RO, NI, BA, CA, WV	GU, WD, LD, MK, JG, 64, 65	CG, GB, KB	60, WR, LI	speciosa
ED, BB	SH, PH, NI, CA, VN, MC, WE, HA, WV		<u>NL</u>	BE, 60, WR, LI, FB, 62, EM, FR	'' cultivars
					CHAMAEDAPHNE calyculata
					CHIONANTHUS retusus

MISSOURI, KANSAS, NEBRASKA, IOWA	CONNECTICUT, MASSACHUSETTS, VERMONT	NEW YORK, NEW JERSEY (Note: Long Island and southern New Jersey nurseries are in Zone 7)	MARYLAND, VIRGINIA, DELAWARE Note: These states are in Zone 7.	WEST VIRGINIA, PENNSYLVANIA, OHIO, INDIANA, ILLINOIS	KENTUCKY, TENNESSEE Note: Southern Kentucky and most of Tennessee are in Zone 7.
	VP				50
CV				43	
			SE, ML, KG	HE	HM
			14, ML, KG, 5, ES	UB	
SB, CM, LE, IA	HT EA, WF, VP, HT, GS		ES, 14, ML, KG	27, DB, SP, 31, 32, GR, 33, 34, 35, 37, MM, HB, HN, CK, FC, 46, 47, 67, 23, HE	54
				35	
CV, 57, SK, HL	WF, VP, LT, HT, HC, CS	BL, 7	SE, ES, 14, 18, 19, 20, WH, ML, UB, IP, 5 ES, WH	EL, GR, 39, 67, HE	BN, HM, 50, 52, 54, HW
	CB, VP, CS HT	RD, LA, 7, 9, TK 68	SE, ES, 14, 19, 20, WH, ML, WB, KG, IP, 5 14, KG KG	27, DB, UB, KR, AB 25, 34	
CV, NO, 57, SK, 58, HL	CB FM, WF, BC VP, LT, HT EA EA, WF, VP, HT CB EA, WF, VP EA, CB, WF, VP, HT	BL, 7	ES, WB, 5 14	EL, 27, DB, UB, 23 23 23	BN, HM, HW
	EA, HT, VP, WF, CB	BK	CR, 14 CR	23	
CV, HU, NO, HR, HL	EA, WF AE, FM, CB, WF, VP, BI, LT, HT, PY, BC	BK, KE, PR, LA, MS, RD, ST, WJ, 26, BL, 7	14 CR, ES, 14, 20, WH, 5	DK, EN, MF, EL, 27, DB, SQ, SP, 33, 35, 36, 38, CY, 39, NA, HB, KR, HN, 43, FC, 47, AB, 23, HE	BN, HM, 50, 51, 53, 54, 56
	AE, WY, VP, BI, HT	LA, 5, 68 68	KG KG	EL, HB, 41, 43, 44, 45, CK, FC, 46 23 FC	56 BN
CV, FA, NO, 57, SB, PL, CM, PF, SK, WA, 58, FR, FE, LE, HR, IA, HL HU	CB, WF, BI, HT, PY, CS VP CS	BL KE, LA, RD, ST BK, 7	CR, ML, WB, KG, 5 SE, ES, WH	EL, 27, DB, SQ, SP, GR, 36, HB, HN, KH, LG, 43, 44, FC, 47, 23 FC FC	BN, 50
CV, IIU, NO, 57, SD, PL, CM, SK, WA, 58, FR, LE, HR, HL	AE, WF, VP, BI, AD, HT, BC, CS	BK, KE, PR, LA, RD, ST, WJ, SC, 7, TU, 68	SE, 14, 18, 19, 20, WH, WB, KG, IP, 5	EN, MF, 25, EL, 27, DB, 28, SQ, UB, SP, 33, 35, 38, CY, NA, MM, HB, KR, HN, KH, 41, 43, 44, 45, CD, FC, 46, 47, 67, AB, HE	BN, HM, 50, 51, 52, 54, 56, HW
HU, SK, WA, 58, HR	WF, CS	7	SE, CR, 14, KG, 5 SE, CR, 14, KG, 5	EL, UB, 32, NA, MM, HB, FC 23	BN
HU, NO, 57	WF, AD, BC	BL, 7, 68	CR, ES, 14, 20, WH, ML, KG, 5	27, DB, 23, HE	51, 53, 56
HU, LE, CV, 57, HL, SK, WA, GU, MY	VP, BI, LT, HC, WL, AE, BC	PR, LA, MS, 26, BK, KE, SC, BL, TU, 7	ES, 14, 19, 20, 21, KG, WB	DK, EL, 27, DB, SQ, UB, 35, 36, 38, MM, 41, 43, 44, AB, CY, EN, 67, 48 SQ, UB, NA FC	51, 53
CV, NO, 57, CM, SK, WX, 58, FR, FE, MY, HL	WY, WF, AD, HT, PY, BC, HC, 10, CS, WL, AE, CB, CP, LT, HM	RD, ST, WJ, SC, PR, 7, TU, BL	SE, WH, ML, WB, 5	33, KR, CY, FC, 46, 47, MF, HB, AB, 58	BN, 50, 51, 53, 54, 56, HW
NO, SK, 58, LE, HR, IA, FR, FE, CM	AE, FM, CB, WF, BI, LT, HT, BC, 10, HC, WY, PY, CP	BK, 7, RD	ES, 14, WH, 22, WB, KG, 5, ML, 19 14, KG 14, KG	33, KH, LG, 42, 45, CD, CF, HN, 27, DB, NA, MM, HB, 67, 23, FE, HE, 44, SQ, MF, 36, 38, CO, SP, 46 HE	HM, 52, 53, 54, BN, 50, 51, HW, 55, 56

CANADA – ALBERTA, BRITISH COLUMBIA, MANITOBA, PRINCE EDWARD'S ISLAND, QUEBEC, SASKATCHEWAN	CANADA – ONTARIO	NORTH DAKOTA, SOUTH DAKOTA, WISCONSIN, MINNESOTA	IDAHO, COLORADO	MICHIGAN	SHRUBS AND TREES AVAILABLE FOR YOUR GARDEN
ED	SH	LD		LI	CHIONANTHUS virginicus
BB	SH			LI	CLETHRA alnifolia
ED				LI, FB	" 'Rosea'
					barbinervis
	RO				COLUTEA arborescens
					COMPTONIA peregrina
PN, BB					CORNUS alba
LC, BT, ED, WX, DD, PN, BB, GT, LW, GH	MC, WP, PH, SD, SH, WE, RO, MD, NI, HA, CA, VN, ME, DO, 3, BA, WV, HD	CH, GU, LD, WT, JG, WG, 64, RH, 65, SA, GE, SW, PK	CG, NZ	BE, 60, WR, LI	" 'Argenteo-marginata'
PN, BB, GT, LW	SD, NI, CA, VN, WV, HD			60	" 'Gouchaultii'
				60	" 'Kesselringii'
LC, AT, DD, BB, GT, MT, LW, GH	SD, SH, RO, CA, 3, WV, MA	GU, MK, RH, 65, PK		60, LI	" 'Sibirica'
BB	WP, SH				" 'Spaethii'
		LD, MK, SA, PK			alternifolia
		LD, PK			amomum
ED, WX, BB, LW	PH, SH, NI, CA		NL	59, EM, WR, 62, LI, FB	florida
			NL	EM, WR, LI, FB	" 'Cherokee Chief'
			NL	FB	" 'Cherokee Princess'
				EM, 62	" 'Cloud 9'
					" 'Pendula'
					" 'Pluribracteata'
					" 'Prosser Red'
ED, BB	SH, NI, CA		NL	EM, WR, 62, LI, FB	" rubra
					" 'Salicifolia'
			NL		" 'Welchii'
					" xanthocarpa
BB	SH, NI			62, LI, FB	kousa
ED				LI	" chinensis
ED, DD, BB	SH	LD		60, LI	mas
					officinalis
	SH	LD, MK		LI	racemosa
BT		LD			sanguinea
LS, GH, SM	WP, SD	WD, LD, MK, WT, JG, WG, GE		BE, 60, WR, FB	stolonifera
PT		CH, DV, LD, MK, 64, 65, SW	NL, NZ		" baileyi
			WM, CG, KB		" coloradensis
BT, ED, DD, PN, BB, GT, GH	WP, SD, SH, RO, CA, 3, WV, MA	WD, LD, MK, WT, JG, 64, RH, 65, GE, PK	WM, CG, NZ, GB, KB	60, FB	" 'Flaviramea'
PT		WT	NZ		" 'Kelsei'
	SH				CORONILLA eremurus
ED					CORYLOPSIS glabrescens
					pauciflora
ED					sinensis
					spicata
		CH, LD, MK, SW	NL	EM	CORYLUS americana
				BU	avellana
	3				" 'Aurea'
	PH			BE, 62, LI, FB	" 'Contorta'
PN	SH, 3		NL	LI	" 'Fusco-rubra'
ED	MC, VN	LD		FB	maxima 'Purpurea'
DD, BB, LW	SH, WE, RO, MD, NI, CA, 3, HD,	GU, LD		59, WR, LI	COTINUS coggygria

MISSOURI, KANSAS, NEBRASKA, IOWA	CONNECTICUT, MASSACHUSETTS, VERMONT	NEW YORK, NEW JERSEY (Note: Long Island and southern New Jersey nurseries are in Zone 7)	MARYLAND, VIRGINIA, DELAWARE Note: These states are in Zone 7.	WEST VIRGINIA, PENNSYLVANIA, OHIO, INDIANA, ILLINOIS	KENTUCKY, TENNESSEE Note: Southern Kentucky and most of Tennessee are in Zone 7.
HU, 57, PL, SK, LE, HR	AE, FM, WY, VP, BI, HT, BC, CS, WL	BK, LA, RD, WJ, BL, 7	SE, 14, 18, ML, WB, KG, 5	EL, 27, DB, SQ, UB, 33, CY, NA, HN, LG, 44, CF, 46, 47, 23, HE	BN, HM, 50, 54, HW
HU, LE	AE, FM, CB, WY, WF, VP, CP, HT, PY, BC, CS, WL	BK, PR, LA, RD, WJ, BL, 7, 12, TU	SE, CR, ES, 14, KG, 5	EL, 27, DB, SQ, UB, 33, 37, FC, HE	
NO	CB, WY, WF, VP, BI, CP, HT, GS, WL	BK, KE, ST, 7	CR, 14, KG, 5	27, DB, 33, 23	BN
	HT		14, KG		
HR		2	14		HW
CV, SB, CM, PF, SK, FR, LE, MY	AE, FM, WF, VP, BI, BC, CS	KE, ST, SC	CR, KG	25, SP, GR, 33, 35, 36, 37, 38, KR, HN, KH, 42, 44, CK, FC, 47	BN
CV, FR, HR	AE, CB, WF, VP, BI, LT, CP, BC	7	SE	25, EL, SQ, 33, 38, CY, NA, HB, HN, KH, 41, LG, 42, 43, 44, 45, FC, 47 36	HM, 50, 53
HR	WY, HT	WJ, 7	14, KG	EL, 41, 45, CD, FC, 46 44, 45, FC, 47	
CV, HU, NO, 57, SB, PL, SK, HR, HL	AE, FM, CB, WY, WF, VP, BI, LT, AD, CP, HT, BC, HC, 10, CS, WL	BK, BG, KE, 2, PR, LA, RD, WJ, SC, BL, 7, 12, TU, 68	SE, ES, BF, 14, 18, 19, 20, WH, 22, ML, WB, KG, 5	DK, EN, MF, 25, EL, 27, DB, 28, SQ, UB, 30, SP, GR, SO, 33, 34, 36, 37, 38, CY, 39, NA, MM, HB, HN, KH, 43, CD, FC, 46, 47, HE, 23, 67, 49	BN, HM, 50, 51, 52, 53, 54, 55, HW
CV, FA, NO, SK	CB, WY, CP, BC, CS	KE	CR, BF, 22	25, CE, SP, 38, HB, KH, 67, HE	BN, HM, 52, 53, 55, 56
CV	WF, BC		CR, BF, 19, 22	KR, 67	52, 53, 55
CV, NO, SK	VP	G, 68	KG	UB	BN
	WF, 10	BG, LA, RD, 6, 12, 68 6	CR, 14, ML, KG	27, DB, GR 27, DB, GR, FC	BN, 50, 52, 55
CV, HU, NO, SB, SK, HR, IA, HL	AE, FM, CB, WY, WF, VP, BI, LT, AD, CP, HT, BC, HC, 10, CS, WL	BK, BG, KE, PR, LA, RD, ST, WJ, BL, 6, 7, 12, TU, 68	SE, CR, ES, BF, 14, 18, 19, 20, WH, 22, ML, WB, KG	DK, 16, EN, MF, 25, EL, 27, DB, 28, SQ, UB, 30, SP, GR, 33, 37, 38, CY, NA, MM, HB, KR, HN, 43, FC, 46, 47, 67, 23, HE	BN, HM, 50, 51, 52, 54, 55, 56, HW
	WF, VP, CS	BG, 6, 68	14, KG CR, KG 14	EL, 27, DB	BN
HU	CB, WF, LT, AD, CP, BC, HC, 10, CS, WL	BK, BG, PR, LA, RD, BL, 7, TU, 68	SE, ES, 14, 20, WH, ML, KG, IP	EL, 27, DB, UB, CY, FC, 46, HE	BN
HU	FM, WF, VP, BI, HT	BK, 6, 12, 68	CR, 14, ML, KG, 5	GR, KR, 23	55
	CB, WY, WF, LT, CP, HT, CS, WL	2, LA, RD, WJ, BL, 7, 68	CR, 14, 20, WB, KG	25, EL, 27, DB, SQ, 33, 35, CY, MM, 41, LG, 43, 44, 45, FC, 46, 47, 67, HE	BN, HM
FA, LE			14, ML	SP, 33, HB, 23	
HR	AB, CB, WF, LT	WJ, 7	KG	EL, 33, 41, 43, 45, CD, FC, 47, HE	53
58	WF, HC	BK, 7	20	FC, 46, 47, 67	53
PL, SK, 58, MY	LT, PY	BK, 2, PR, LA, WJ, 7	ES, 14, ML, WB	44, 45, CF, 47	50, 51, 53, 54, 56
CM, PF, LE	10			SP, 35, 44, CD, FC	
KB, IA					
PL, CM, PF, SK, 58, LE, MY	AE, WF, VP, BI, LT, BC, HC	BK, LA, 7	SE, 20, ML	25, EL, SQ, 33, 35, HN, KH, 41, LG, 42, 43, 44, 45, CD, DF, 46, 47	50
CM, 58, LE, KB	WP, GS		14 14 KG 14, ML, KG 14, ML, KG 14, KG	HN, LG, FC, 46, 47 27, DB, UB 27, DB 27, UB	
		7			
HL	VP	MS, 7	WB	EL, 33, NA, HB, 45, CD, FC	50, 51, 54, 56
		BL	14 14		
CV	CS	BK, 7	14	27, SP, HB, CD, AB, 23 27, DB, CD, FC	BN
	VP	BK	14		
FA, 57, PL, SK, 58, LE, HR, HL	AE, WY, WF, VP, BI, LT, AD, HT, PY, BC	PR, LA, WJ, SC, 26, BL, 7, TU	14, KG	MF, 25, EL, 27, DB, SP, 38, CY, HB, KR, HN, KH, 41, 43, CD, FC, 46, 47	BN, HM, 50, 51, 52, 53, 54, HW

CANADA – ALBERTA, BRITISH COLUMBIA, MANITOBA, PRINCE EDWARD'S ISLAND, QUEBEC, SASKATCHEWAN	CANADA – ONTARIO	NORTH DAKOTA, SOUTH DAKOTA, WISCONSIN, MINNESOTA	IDAHO, COLORADO	MICHIGAN	SHRUBS AND TREES AVAILABLE FOR YOUR GARDEN
ED, WX, BB, LW	SA, RO, MD, HA, CA, VN, WV, MA	LD	NL, WM	59, EM, FB, BU	COTINUS coggygria 'Purpureus'
ED, BB	MC, SH, NI, 3, BA, WV	SA, PK	NZ	60, WR, LI, FB	" 'Royal Purple'
LC, BT, AT, DD, PN, BB, GT, LS, MT, PT, LW, GH, SM	MC, WP, SD, SH, WE, RO, MD, CA, VN, 3, BA, HD, MA	CH, DV, GU, WD, LD, MK, WT, 64, RH, 65, SA, GE, SW, PK	WM, AL, NZ, GB, RB, KB	62	COTONEASTER acutifolia
ED, DD	SH, RO, HD				adpressa
ED, DD, PN	SH, WE, HA, CA, VN, WV, HD, MA			BE, 62, LI, FB	" praecox
		LD, SA, GE	NL	WR, 62, LI, FB, WC	apiculata
ED	PA, SH, CA				dammeri
ED					dielsiana
ED, BB	RO, CA	LD, MK, 65, SA, GE, PK	NL, WM, CG, NZ, KB	BE, EM, WR, LI, FB, WC	divaricata
		LD		LI	foveolata
ED, BB, LW	RO, SH, CA, MA		NL, WM, GB, RB	BE, 61, 62, LI	horizontalis
SM				BE	" perpusilla
LS, MT, SM			NL		integerrima
ED					microphylla
	RO, SH	LD, MK, WT, SA	NL	LI	multiflora
				LI	" calocarpa
				LI	racemiflora soongorica
		LD			CRATAEGUS
ED			NL	BE, 62, LI	'Autumn Glory'
	SH	LD, MK, 65	KB	59, LI	crus-galli
		LD, MK		LI	intricata
ED, BB, PN	SH	LD	NL	BE, 62	lavallei
		WD, LD		LI	mollis
BB		LD			monogyna
ED	SH				" 'Stricta'
LC, BY, ED, PN, BB, GT, LS, PT, GH, SM	SH, WP, MC, SD, CA, ME, HB	GE	NL	LI, FB	mordenensis 'Toba'
					nitida
		LD			oxyacantha
AT, ED, WX, PN, BB, PT, LW	SH, WP, NI, CA, VN, ME, WV, HD, MA	WD, MK, WT	NL, WM, GB	BE, 60, EM, WR, 62, LI, FB	" 'Paul's Scarlet'
ED	BA				" 'Rosea Plena'
	SH, CA	LD, MK	WM, GB, RB, KB	BE, 59, EM, WR, 62, LI, FB	phaenopyrum
					viridis ('Winter King')
					CYDONIA (see CHAENOMELES)
					CYRILLA racemiflora
ED					CYTISUS battandieri
ED, BB	WE, SH, NI			LI	praecox
ED					" 'Albus'
ED, BB	WE			FB	" 'Hollandia'
	WE, SH, NI, CA				purgans
					scoparius
					" 'Andreanus'
ED, DD	RO, ME, SH, PH, NI, CA, MA		NL		DAPHNE burkwoodii 'Somerset'
ED, SM	RO, SH, 3, CA		NL	EM, WR, LI, FB, WC	cneorum

MISSOURI, KANSAS, NEBRASKA, IOWA	CONNECTICUT, MASSACHUSETTS, VERMONT	NEW YORK, NEW JERSEY (Note: Long Island and southern New Jersey nurseries are in Zone 7)	MARYLAND, VIRGINIA, DELAWARE Note: These states are in Zone 7.	WEST VIRGINIA, PENNSYLVANIA, OHIO, INDIANA, ILLINOIS	KENTUCKY, TENNESSEE Note: Southern Kentucky and most of Tennessee are in Zone 7.
CV, NO, CM, WA, FR	WF, WY, LT, HT, PY	KE, ST, WJ, 7	SE, WH, ML, KG	25, NA, HB, KR, HN, LG	HM, 50, 53
SB, SK, FR, FE, LE, HR, IA	VP, BI, GS, BC, CS	BK, RD	CR	EL, 27, DB, SP, 33; 36, 38, CY, KH, 41, 43, FC, 46, 47	HM
PL, CM, PF, WA, 58, FR, LE, HR, MY	AE, BI, GS, WL	MS, SC	14	EL, 33, 39, NA, HB, KH, 41, LG, 42, 43, 44, 45, CD, FC, 46, 47	50
	EA, WF, CP	LA	KG	DK, FC, AB	
CV, HR	CB, WY, WF, VP, LT, CP, HT, BC, CS	RD, 7, TU, 68	CR, 14, 19, KG, 5	25, SQ, HN, KH, LG, CD, FC, 46, 67, 23	
	AE, FM, WF, BI, LT, CP	2, LA, RD, MS, BL, 12, 68	ML, KG, 5	DK, 25, EL, DB, 33, 35, 37, 39, NA, MM, HB, HN, KH, LG, 42, FC, 46, 47, 67, 23	BN
	WF, HT, HC	7	14, ML, KG, 5	27, DB, HE	
	LT	WJ		31, 39, FC, AB, 23	
CV, HU, 57, PL, CM, SK, 58, LE, HR, HL	FM, CB, WY, WF, VP, BI, LT, AD, CP, HT, HC, 10, CS, WL	BK, KE, PR, LA, RD, WJ, SC, 7, 12	SE, ES, 14, KG	DK, EL, 27, DB, SQ, 30, 31, 33, 34, 35, CY, 39, NA, MM, HB, HN, KH, 41, LG, 42, 44, 45, CD, FC, 46, 47, 67, HE, 23	BN, HM, HW
				FC	
HU, CM, SK	EA, CY, WY, WF, VP, BI, LT, AD, CP, HT, PY, BC, HC, 10, CS, WL	BK, 2, PR, LA, RD, WJ, BL, 7, 12, 68	14, 19, 20, ML, KG, IP, 5	EL, 27, SQ, UB, 30, 32, GR, 37, 43, FC, 49, AB, HE	50
	EA, WF	68	KG	EL, HE	
		LA, 7	14, WB, KG	35, FC	
	VP			37, KH, 41, 45, CD, FC	
FE	WF, HT		KG	LG	
				EL	
	AE, WF, BI, CS			EL, 27, DB, 67, 23	52
LE, HR	WF, 10, CS, WL	LA, RD, 7, 68	14, 19, WB	EL, SQ, 33, 35, MM, HB, HN, KH, 41, 43, 44, 45, CD, FC, 46, 47, HE	
				33, 41, 43, 44, 45, CD, FC	
	WF, CS	BK	14	EL, 33, 35, MM, HB, LG, CD, FC, 67	BN
HR	WF, HC	BK, BL, 7, 12	ML	35, HN, LG, CD, FC, 46	50
	HT		14	HE	
			14, ML	EL, 33, CD, 23, HE	
HU	WF, CS		SE, 14	31, NA, KH, CD, FC	
				FC, 41, 45, 47, HN	
	AE, CP, CS		14, WH, KG	33, 41, 43, 45, FC, 46, 47	50
WA	AE, WY, WF, VP, BI, LT, AD, HT, BC, HC, 10, CS	BK, KE, PR, LA, ST, WJ, SC, BL, 7, TU	14, 19, WB, KG	MF, 25, EL, 27, DB, 28, UB, 31, GR, 33, 38, CY, KR, KH, 41, 43, FC, 47, 67, 23, HE	52
	AE, WF, VP, BI, HT			EL, CD, 67	
CV, HU, PL, CM, SK, WA, 58, FR, LE, HR, HL	AE, FM, CB, WY, WF, VP, BI, LT, AD, CP, BC, HC, 10, CS, WL	BK, BG, 2, PR, LA, MS, RD, 5, WJ, SC, BL, 7, 12, TU, 68	SE, 14, 19, ML, WB, KG	DK, 25, EL, 27, DB, SQ, UB, SP, 33, CY, NA, 35, MM, HB, HN, KH, 41, LG, 43, 44, 45, CD, FC, 46, 47, 49, 67, HE	BN, HM, 50, 52, 53, HW
			14, ML	33, 35, NA, 40, MM, HB, KH, 46	HM
			14, ML, KG	UB	
				27, DB, 23, HE	
CV	EA, CB, WF, VP, BT, LT, BC	BK, RD, 7	CR, 14, ML, KG, IP	33, 23	BN
	HT		14		
	VP				
	EA		KG		
	EA, VP, HT, BC	LA	ES, 14, 20, WB, KG, IP	27, DB, SP, FC	51, 53, 54, 56
	EA, WF, VP, CS		KG		
				23	
HR	AE, CB, WY, WF, BI, LT, CP, HT, PY, GS, CS, WL	LA, SR	CR	DK, EL, 36, 23, HE	

83

CANADA – ALBERTA, BRITISH COLUMBIA, MANITOBA, PRINCE EDWARD'S ISLAND, QUEBEC, SASKATCHEWAN	CANADA – ONTARIO	NORTH DAKOTA, SOUTH DAKOTA, WISCONSIN, MINNESOTA	IDAHO, COLORADO	MICHIGAN	SHRUBS AND TREES AVAILABLE FOR YOUR GARDEN
PN, BB, LW	RO, NI, VN		NL	LI	DAPHNE genkwa
	RO			LI	mezereum
					" 'Alba'
					DAVIDIA involucrata
					DESMODIUM penduliflora
					(see LESPEDEZA thunbergii)
ED, BB, LW	RO, WE, SH, PH, HA, CA, 3, WV, HD, MA	LD, SA		BE, 60, WR, LI, FB	DEUTZIA gracilis
BB	SH			BE, 60	kalmiaeflora
PN	RO, CA, VN, 3, WV	LD, MK, GE			lemoinei
	SH, MA				" 'Compacta'
	3				rosea
		LD			" 'Pink Pom Pom'
					scabra
BB	SH, MA				" 'Plena'
ED, BB	PH, SH, RO, HA, ME, WV			60	" 'Pride of Rochester
		MK			DIERVILLA lonicera
					sessilifolia
ED, PN, GT, LS, MT, PT, LW, GH	PH, SD, SH, WE, RO, WX, WP, NI, 3, WV, HD	CH, DV, GU, LD, MK, WT, JG, WG, 64, RH, SA, GE, SW, PK	WM, CG, AL, NZ, GB, RB, KB	BE, 60, WR, 62, LI, FB	ELAEAGNUS angustifolia
LC, PN, BB	VN, WV, MA	SA			commutata
		LD		LI	multiflora
		LD, SA			umbellata
BB					ELSHOLTZIA stauntonii
				LI	ENKIANTHUS campanulatus
WX				63	ERICA carnea
					" 'Vivellii'
					darleyensis
					vagans
					" 'Alba'
ED, WX, DD, PN, BB, GT, GH	SD, SH, WE, RO, NI, HA, CA, VN, 3, WV, HD, MA	DV, WD, LD, MK, WT, WG, RH, 65, SA, GE, PK	NL, WM, CG, GB, KB	BE, 60, WR, 61, 62, LI, FB, WC	EUONYMUS alata
LC, BY, DD, PN, PT, SM	MC, PH, SH, WE, RO, NI, 3, BA	DV, GU, WD, LD, MK, WT, JG, 64, 65, SA, GE, PK	NL, WM, CG, NZ, GB, RB, KB	BE, 60, EM, WR, 62, LI, FB, WC	" 'Compacta'
		LD		LI	" 'Gracilis'
					americana
DD, BB	MA	LD, MK, WT, GE	NL, CG, GB, KB		atropurpurea
ED, WX, PN	PH, SH, RO, NI, CA	LD, MK, SW, PK	NL, WM, CG	BE, 62, LI	europaea
	MA		NL, AL		" 'Aldenhamensis'
	PA, SH, WV			60, 62, LI	fortunei
			NZ		" 'Carrierei'
					" 'Colorata',
					erect form
BB	WP, PA, SH, WE, VN, ME, 3, MA, CA				fortunei, Emerald (or Corliss)
	CA		NL	62, BE, LI	selections
					fortunei, erect form
		GU	NL		" radicans, erect form
ED	WP, PA, SH, WE, HA, ME, BA, WY, CA	LD	NL, WM, CG, NZ	BE, 60, WR, 61, 62, LI, 63, FB	fortunei 'Sarcoxie'
	SH, PA, SA, RO, PH, HA, VN, MC, 3, WV, HD, MA	LD, MK	NL, WM, CG	BE, 60, WR, 61, 62, LI, FB, WC	" 'Vegeta'

MISSOURI, KANSAS, NEBRASKA, IOWA	CONNECTICUT, MASSACHUSETTS, VERMONT	NEW YORK, NEW JERSEY (Note: Long Island and southern New Jersey nurseries are in Zone 7)	MARYLAND, VIRGINIA, DELAWARE Note: These states are in Zone 7.	WEST VIRGINIA, PENNSYLVANIA, OHIO, INDIANA, ILLINOIS	KENTUCKY, TENNESSEE Note: Southern Kentucky and most of Tennessee are in Zone 7.
	VP, HT	BK	CR, 14, ML, KG, 5	UB, 23, HE	
	WF, VP, HT		KG	EL, FC	
		7		FC	
			14, 20, KG, IP	27, DB, UB	
CV, HU, NO, SB, CM, SK, FR, FE, HL	AE, FM, CB, WY, WF, VP, BI, LT, AD, CP, HT, BC, HC, 10, CS, WL	BK, KE, PR, LA, RD, ST, WJ, SC, 26, BL, 7, TU	SE, CR, ES, 14, 19, 20, WH, ML, WB, KG, 5	25, EL, 27, DB, SQ, UB, SP, 31, GR, 33, 36, 38, MM, HB, HN, KH, LG, 43, 45, FC, 47, 49, 67, AB, 23, HE	BN, HM, 50, HW
	BC			23	
HU, SK, LE, HR	AE, CB, WF, VP, BI, LT, CS	PR, LA, ST, 7, TU	SE, CR, 5	25, EL, SQ, UB, CY, 43, 44, FC, 47, 67, 23, HE	BN, HM, HW
IA				35, LG	
CV, SB	WF, VP, HT, WL	KE, RD, ST, 7	CR, 14, 19, WB, KG, 5	36, 43, 67	HW
	WF	KE	CR	25, DB, 33, 23	
HU, WA		PR, TU	WB	38, FC, 46, 47, AB	50, 53, 54
			5	25	
58	AE, WF, VP, AD, HT, CS	LA, MS, 26, 7, TU	SE, 20, WB	DK, EL, SQ, SP, 38, HB, 43, 45, CF, 46, HE	HM, 50, 51, 53, 54, 56, HW
	FM, 66			45, FC	
				67, HE	
CV, NO, 57, CM, PF, SK, WA, 58, LE, HR, HL	FM, CB, WY, WF, VP, BI, LT, CS	LA, RD, ST, WJ, SC, 7	14, 20, WH, ML, WB	EL, 27, 33, 34, 35, HB, HN, KH, 41, LG, 42, 43, 44, 45, CD, FC, 46, 47, AB, HE	BN, HM, 50, 51, 56
			14	FC	
	AE, VP	7	14	UB, LG, FC, HE	
	WF, VP, CS	BK, 7	14, ML	MF, FC, 46	HW
	HT	7		23, HE	BN
	AE, FM, CB, WY, WF, VP, BI, LT, HT, HC, 10, CS	BK, BG, PR, LA, RD, 7, TU	14, ML, KG	DK, MF, 25, EL, 27, DB, UB, HB, FC, HE	BN
	EA, HT, CS	SR,	CR, 14	23	
	HT		14	23	
	EA	KE	14		
	HT		14		
	HT		CR		
HU, PF, LE, HR, MY	AE, EA, FM, CB, WY, WF, VP, BI, LT, AD, CP, HT, PY, BC, HC, CS, WL	BK, 2, PR, LA, RD, ST, WJ, SC, 26, BL, 7, TU	SE, CR, 14, WB, 5	DK, 25, EL, DB, SQ, SP, 33, 35, 37, CY, NA, MM, HB, HN, KH, 41, LG, 43, 44, 45, CD, FC, 46, 47, 67, HE	BN, HM, HW
CV, HU, FA, NO, 57, SB, CM, PF, SK, WA, 58, FR, FE, LE, HR, IA, HL	AE, EA, FM, CB, WY, WF, VP, BI, LT, AD, CP, HT, BC, HC, CS, WL	KE, 2, PR, LA, RD, 26, SR, WJ, SC, BL, 7, TU	14, 19, WH, ML, WB, 5	DK, 25, EL, 27, DB, SQ, UB, 31, GR, 33, 35, 36, 37, CY, 39, NA, MM, HB, KR, HN, KH, 41, LG, 42, 43, 44, 45, CD, FC, 46, 47, 67, AB, 23, HE, BS	BN, HM, 50, 55
				33, 37	55
				41, 45, FC	53
HR			14	EL, 43, 44, 45, FC	
HU, LE	AE, CB, PY, CS			EL, SQ, MM, KH, 41, 42, 43, 45, CD, FC	
HR	WF			33, LG, 47, 23	
58, FR	BC				
	HT, CS	68	21	25, SQ, CY, FC, 67	55
				NA, FC, KA, 44, CD	55
FE	AE, CB	2, PR		MM	52
				FC, 46, 47, DK, 25, 31, 37, SP, 33, HB	55
HR		SC		41, HN	
CV, HU, 57, SB, CM, SK, 58, FR, LE, HR, IA	WF, BI, CP, BC, 10, CS	LA, MS, 68	19	25, EL, SP, 31, 32, GR, 33, 34, 35, 36, 37, 39, HE, NA, MM, HB, KR, HN, 42, 43, 44, FC, 46, 47, 67	HM, 50, 52, 55
SB, LE, HR, IA	EA, FM, CB, WY, WF, VP, BI, AD, CP, HT, PY, BC, HC, 10, CS, WL	BK, KE, 2, LA, ST, SR, 7, 68	SE, 19, WH	25, EL, 27, DB, UB, 3, 32, GR, 33, 34, 37, CY, HE, BS, 39, NA, MM, HB, KR, HN, KH, 43, 44, CD, FC, 46, 47	HM

CANADA – ALBERTA, BRITISH COLUMBIA, MANITOBA, PRINCE EDWARD'S ISLAND, QUEBEC, SASKATCHEWAN	CANADA – ONTARIO	NORTH DAKOTA, SOUTH DAKOTA, WISCONSIN, MINNESOTA	IDAHO, COLORADO	MICHIGAN	SHRUBS AND TREES AVAILABLE FOR YOUR GARDEN
	RO		WM, GB, RB	61, 62, LI	EUONYMUS kiautschovica
			NL	61	" 'Dupont'
			GB, WM	62	" 'Manhattan'
			WM	60	" 'Newport'
LS, MT, GH, SM	SD, PT	DV, LD, PK	WM		nana turkestanica
ED					sachalinensis
BB		LD, MK	GB	BE, WR, LI	yedoensis
			NL	LI, FB	EXOCHORDA giraldii wilsonii
	PH, SH, CA				macrantha 'The Bride'
BB	SH				racemosa
		SA			FONTANESIA fortunei
ED, BB	SH, PH, MC, CA, ME	LD, MK, WT, GE	NL	60, EM, 62, LI, FB, WC	FORSYTHIA 'Beatrix Farrand'
		LD, MK	CG		intermedia
	SH, WE, CA	LD, WT, GE		60, 61	" 'Arnold Dwarf'
					" 'Arnold Giant'
ED, BB, LW	WE, SH, PH, WP, NI, CA, ME, 3, BA, MA	GU, LD, MK, WT, 64, RH	NL, WM	60, EM, WR, 62, LI, FB	FORSYTHIA intermedia 'Lynwood'
					" 'Primulina'
ED, BB	WP, WE, RO, SH, NI, HA, CA, VN, WV, HD, MA	WD, LD, 64, 65, PK	NL, NZ, GB, RB, KB	BE, 60, LI	" 'Spectabilis'
BB	SH, NI				" "
					Tree form
ED, DD, LW	SH, PH, VN	WD, LD, MK, WT, 64, SA, SW	NL, CG	WR, 61, LI, FB	intermedia 'Spring Glory'
	SH	DV, GU, GE			'Karl Sax'
WX, DD, PN, BB, PT, GH, SM	HB, SH, RO, MD	LD, MK, JG, WG, 65			ovata
DD, PN	RO, SH	LD, MK		WR, LI	suspensa
ED, BB		LD	CG, KB		" fortunei
					" sieboldii
		LD		62	viridissima
	SH				" 'Bronxensis'
BB				LI	FOTHERGILLA major
					monticola
					FRANKLINIA alatamaha
ED, PN, BB	RO, HB				GENISTA tinctoria
	SH				HALESIA carolina
PT, LW				FB	monticola
				LI	HALIMODENDRON halodendron
ED	SH, NI				HAMAMELIS japonica
					" flavo-purpurascens
					mollis
					" 'Brevipetala'
		LD		62, LI	vernalis
		MK		LI	virginiana
ED	WE, SH, PH, WP, MC, NI, HA, CA, VN, 3, BA, WV, MA	MK, GU	NL, WM, NZ, GB, RB, KB	BE, EM, WR, LI, FB, BU	HIBISCUS syriacus cultivars
				BE, EM	" Tree form
LC, WX, LS, MT, GH, MC	SH, SD	SA			HIPPOPHAË rhamnoides
					HOLLY (see ILEX)
					HOLODISCUS discolor
DD, BB	RO, NI, 3				HYDRANGEA arborescens
					" 'Annabelle'

MISSOURI, KANSAS, NEBRASKA, IOWA	CONNECTICUT, MASSACHUSETTS, VERMONT	NEW YORK, NEW JERSEY (Note: Long Island and southern New Jersey nurseries are in Zone 7)	MARYLAND, VIRGINIA, DELAWARE Note: These states are in Zone 7.	WEST VIRGINIA, PENNSYLVANIA, OHIO, INDIANA, ILLINOIS	KENTUCKY, TENNESSEE Note: Southern Kentucky and most of Tennessee are in Zone 7.
SB, PL, CM, SK, 58, HL	CS	LA, ST, BL, 7, TU	SE, ES, 14, 18, 20, 22, 5	27, DB, SQ, NA, KH, 43, FC, 49, 23, HE / MM, FC	BN, HM, 50, 52, 55
57, 58					
CV, 57, SK, 58, HL, IA / 57					
LE, HR, IA	GS			EL, NA, HB, 67	
FR, FE	AE, WF, VP, BI, LT / HT		14 / 14	FC, 23 / EL, SP, CY, LG, 44, FC	HM
				23	
HU, 58	AE, WF, VP, HT / CS	BL, 7	ES, 14, WH	FC, 47, AB, HE / 67	HM, HW
CV, 57, CM, 58, FR, FE, LE	AE, FM, WY, WF, BI, CP, HT, BC, HC, CS	BK, KE, 7	ES, 14, 22, WB, IP, 5	25, EL, 27, CE, DB, SP, 31, GR, 33, 35, 36, 37, 38, KR, HN, LG, 43, 44, CD, FC, 67, 23	BN, 55
SB, MY	CS, WL		KG	41, 43, 44, 45, CD, FC, 46	50, 56
57, HR	FM, WF, BI, HT	WJ, 12	KG	DB, 31, 33, 35, LG, 44, 45, 46, HE	
	WF, HT			25, FC	
CV, HU, NO, 57, CM, SK, WA, 58, FR, FE, IA, HL	AE, CB, WY, WF, BI, LT, AD, CP, HT, PY, BC, HC, 10, CS	KE, LA, RD, ST, SR, WJ, 26, BL, 7, TU, 68	SE, ES, 14, 19, 20, WH, 22, WB, KG, 5	DK, 25, EL, 27, DB, SQ, SP, 31, 33, 35, 36, 37, 38, CY, 39, MM, HB, HN, 41, LG, 43, 44, CD, FC, 47, 67, AB, 23, HE	BN, HM, 50, 51, 52, 53, 54, 56
				43, 67	
HU, NO, 57, SB, 58, FE	WY, HT / AE, CB, WY, WF, VP, LT, CP, HT, PY, BC, HC, CS, WL	BK, 2, LA, RD, WJ, SC, 26, BL, 7, TU, 68	ES, 14, WH, ML, KG, 5	DK, EN, EL, 27, DB, 28, SQ, UB, SP, 33, CY, NA, HB, KH, 43, 44, 45, FC, 46, 47, 67, AB, HE	HU, NO, 57, SB, 58, FE
HU, 57, CM, SK, 58, HR	AE, CB, WF, VP, BI, LT, AD, CP, HT, HC	BK, KE, RD, ST, WJ, 26, BL, 7, 12, TU	SE, ES, 14, 20, WH, KG, 5	DK, MF, 25, EL, DB, SQ, 33, 34, 35, 36, 37, 38, CY, 39, MM, HB, KR, HN, 42, 43, 44, 45, CD, FC, 47, AB, 23	BN, HM, 50, 51, 53, 54, 56
SB, HR, IA	AE, WF, HT		14 / KG	33, MM / 44, FC	
	AE, WF, BI, LT, PY, HC, CS, WL	LA, 7, 5	20, WB, KG	DK, EL, SQ, 33, 35, CY, 43, 45, FC, 46, 47	
SB	WF, HT, HC	DK		43, 45, FC	50, 56
	WF	WJ			
58		LA		45, FC	
	WF, HT / FM	RD, 7	14, ML, KG / KG, IP	31, 33, 35, 37, HB / 27, UB	BN
	WF, HC	LA, RD, 7, 68	CR, 14, WH, 22, ML, WB, KG, IP	DK, EL, 27, DB, UB, SQ, HB, 46, HE	
HU, HR / LE	AE, CS, LT / HT	BK, LA, 7 / 7	14, ML, KG / 14, ML, KG / 14	EL, 33, HB, FC, 67, HE / 27, DB, SQ, 67, 23	BN, 50
	WF / HT	BL, 7	14, KG, IP / 14, KG	27, DB, FC / 27, DB	
	WF, BI, HT, CS / WF,	BK, LA, 67, 68	CR, 14, ML, KG, 5 / 14, KG	27, UB, 33, FC / GR	
LE, HR	AE, WY, WF, VP, LT, HT, CS	LA, RD, 7	14, KG	33, 35, CY, HB, HN, LG, 45, FC	HM, 50, 53
HU, LE, HR	AE, WF, HT, CS, WL	BK, PR, LA, RD, 7	14, 18, KG	EL, 27, DB, 28, SQ, GR, 33, 36, CY, NA, HB, HN, KH, 41, LG, 45, CD, FC	BN, HM, 50, 53, 54
CV, FA, NO, 57, SB, PL, CM, SK, WA, 58, FR, FE, LE, HR, IA, HL	AE, FM, CB, WY, WF, VP, BI, LT, AD, CP, HT, BC, HC, CS	BK, KE, PR, LA, RD, ST, SR, WJ, SC, 26, BL, 7, TU	SE, CR, WH, ML, WB, 5	DK, 25, EL, 27, CE, DB, SP, 33, 35, 38, CY, HB, KR, HN, KH, 41, LG, 42, 43, 44, FC, 46, 47, AB, 23, HE	BN, HM, 50, 51, 53, 54, 56, HW
				44, 47	BN
	HT	BK	ML	23	
				FC	
HU	FM	PR			
LE, IA					

87

CANADA – ALBERTA, BRITISH COLUMBIA, MANITOBA, PRINCE EDWARD'S ISLAND, QUEBEC, SASKATCHEWAN	CANADA – ONTARIO	NORTH DAKOTA, SOUTH DAKOTA, WISCONSIN, MINNESOTA	IDAHO, COLORADO	MICHIGAN	SHRUBS AND TREES AVAILABLE FOR YOUR GARDEN
ED, PN, LW, GH	WE, SH, SD, PH, WP, MC, MD, CA, VN, ME, BA, WV, HD, MA	CH, DV, GU, WD, LD, MK, WT, JG, WG, 64, RH, 65, SA, GE, SW, PK	GB, KB	WR, LI, FB	HYDRANGEA arborescens grandiflora
BB	RO				heteromalla
WX					macrophylla
ED, BB	SH, PH, WP, MC, VN, ME, BA	WT, WG	NL	EM, WR, FB	'' cultivars
ED, WX, DD, PN, BB, LW	RO, WE, SH, SD, PH, WP, MC, MD, NI, HA, CA, VN, ME, 3, BA, WV, HD, MA	DV, GU, WD, LD, MK, WT, JG, WG, 64, RH, 65, SA, GE, SW, PK	NL, WM, NZ, KB	LI / 60, EM, WR, LI, FB, BU	paniculata / '' 'Grandiflora'
ED, DD, PN, BB	WE, SH, PH, WP, MC, NI, CA, VN, ME, DO, 3, BA, MA	WD, MK	NL	EM, LI, BU	'' '' Tree form
ED				FB	quercifolia
	CA				HYPERICUM calycinum / frondosum
LW		GU, GE		LI	kalmianum
ED					moserianum
ED			NL, NZ	LI / 60, EM, WR, LI, FB	patulum henryi / 'Hidcote'
			NL		prolificum / 'Sun gold'
					ILEX
					ILEX crenata
BB	HA				'' 'Compacta'
ED, BB	SH, 3, WV		NL	EM, 62, LI, FB	'' 'Convexa'
			NL	LI	'' 'Glass' / '' 'Green Island'
				LI	'' 'Helleri'
ED	CA			WR, 61, LI, FB	'' 'Hetzi'
ED				EM, 61, LI	'' 'Latifolia'
				LI	'' 'Microphylla'
				LI	'' 'Repandens'
				BE, LI	'' 'Stokes'
				LI	glabra
				LI	'' 'Compacta'
		GU		BE, EM, WR, LI, BU, WC	opaca
					'' cultivars
					'' xanthocarpa
				LI	pedunculosa
				BE	serrata

MISSOURI, KANSAS, NEBRASKA, IOWA	CONNECTICUT, MASSACHUSETTS, VERMONT	NEW YORK, NEW JERSEY (Note: Long Island and southern New Jersey nurseries are in Zone 7)	MARYLAND, VIRGINIA, DELAWARE Note: These states are in Zone 7.	WEST VIRGINIA, PENNSYLVANIA, OHIO, INDIANA, ILLINOIS	KENTUCKY, TENNESSEE Note: Southern Kentucky and most of Tennessee are in Zone 7.
CV, NO, 57, SB, CM, PF, SK, WA, 58, FR, FE, LE, HR, IA, HL	AE, CB, WY, WF, BI, LT, HT, PY, BC, HC	KE, ST, SR, WJ, SC, 26, 7	ES, 20, WB	25, EL, 27, DB, 33, 35, 38, MM, HB, KR, HN, KH, 41, LG, 43, 44, 45, CD, FC, 46, 47	BN, HM
CV, HR, HL / FA, NO, 57, SB, SK, WA, 58, FE, IA	WF / FM, WF, VP, BI, LT, CP / FM, WF, VP, BI, LT, CP, BC, HC, CS	BK, KE, RD, ST, BL, TU / PR, ST, SR, WJ, 7	SE, CR, 14, WH / ES, 19, 20, WB, IP, 5	DK, EL, UB / 27, DB, SQ, SP, 31, GR, 33, 35, 36, 38, KR, 47, AB, 23, HE	50 / BN, 52
CV, HU, NO, 57, SB, PL, CM, PF, SK, WA, 58, FR, FE, LE, HR, MY, IA, HL	AE, FM, CB, WY, WF, VP, BI, LT, AD, CP, HT, PY, BC, HC, 10, CS, WL	LA / BK, KE, 2, PR, LA, RD, ST, WJ, SC, BL, 7, TU	SE, ES, 18, 20, WH, WB	DK, 25, EL, 27, DB, 28, SQ, SP, GR, 35, 36, 38, CY, 39, MM, HB, KR, HN, KH, 41, LG, 43, 44, 45, CD, FC, 46, 47, AB, 23, HE	BN, HM, 50, 51, 53, 54, 56, HW
CV, FA, FR, LE	AE, FM	KE, PR, RD, SR, SC, BL		MF, 27, DB, SP, 38, 44, FC	BN
CV, HU, HR	WF, HT	KE, LA, RD, 7	14, WH, ML, IP	EL, SQ, UB, MM, HB, KR, HN, 42, 43, CD, FC, 67, AB	BN, 50, 51, 54, HW
			19, KG	23	HW
SK, 58, FR, FE, LE, IA	LA	7	14	HE / SP, 33; 35, HB, KR, HN, FC, 47	54
IA / HL			5	EL, 23	HW
HL	FM, CB, WF, VP, BI, PY, 10, CS	KE, PR, LA, RD, SR, WJ, 7	SE, ES, 14, 20, 22, KG, 5	DK, EL, 27, CE, DB, SQ, UB, 31, GR, 33, 38, MM, HB, KH, 41, 42, FC, 47, 23 FC	BN, 53
SB	WF / WY, VP, HC, CS	BK, ST	14, 19, 20, WH, KG / SE, ES, 14, 19, 22, WB, KG	36, CD, 23 / EL, 27, DB / DK, MF, 25, 27, DB, UB, SO, NA, 49, AB, HE	50 / BN, HW
HU, 57, SK	WY, HC, CS / HE, FM, CB, WY, WF, VP, BI, LT, AD, HT, BC, HC, 10, CS, WL	BK, 7, 12, TU, 68 / BK, BG, KE, PR, LA, RD, ST, BL, 7, 12, TU, 68	CR, 14, 20, 22, 5 / SE, CR, ES, 14, 18, 19, 20, WH, 22, ML, WB, KG, 5	23 / DK, 16, EN, MF, 24, 25, EL, 27, DB, SQ, UB, 31, 32, GR, CY, 39, NA, MM, HB, KR, FC, 48, 49, AB, HE	BN, 55 / BN, 55, HW
	WF / HC, CS / WF, AD, HT, BC, HL, CS	LA, RD, BL, 7, TU, 68	14, KG / KG / SE, ES, BF, 14, 19, 20, WH, 22, ML, 69, WB, KG, IP	HE / 67, HE / EL, 27, DB, UB, NA, MM, 48, HE	BN / BN, HM
CV, HU, HL	AE, CB, WY, LT, AD, CP, BC, 10, WF	7, TU	CR, BF, 14, 20, 21, 22, 69, WB, 5	DK, 17, MF, 24, 25, EL, 27, DB, 28, 29, SQ, SP, 31, 32, GR, CY, 39, NA, 40, MM, HN, 43, FC, 48, 23, BS	BN, HM, 52, 55
HU, 57, SK	AE, WY, WF, VP, BT, AD, BC, 10	PR, LA, RD, ST, BL, 7, 12, TU, 68	SE, CR, ES, 14, 18, 19, 20, WH, 21, 22, ML, WB, KG, 5	DK, 16, 17, 24, 25, EL, 27, DB, 28, SQ, 31, 32, GR, 33, CY, 39, 40, MM, 43, FC, 47, 67, AB, HE	BN, HM, 50, 52, 55, HW
	VP, CS	RD, BL, 7, 12, TU, 68	SE, 14, 15, 19, 20, WH, 22, ML, 69, WB, KG, 5	EL, SQ, 32, 39, AB, HE	BN
	FM, HC	ST / PR, LA	14, 18, 19, WH / ML	27, DB, HE / DK, 24, 25, EL, 29, SQ, GR, NA, HB, 48, 67, HE	55
	FM, CB, WY, WF, VP, BI, LT, CP, HT, BC, HC, BS / CB, WF	BK, PR, LA, RD, 7 / 12, 68	SE, CR, ES, 14, 19, WH, KG, 5 / 14, 20, IP	DK, 25, EL, 27, DB, SQ, UB, 37, HB, 46, 67, 23 / EL, GR, HE	BN, HM
HU, SK, HL	AE, CB, WY, WF, VP, BI, LT, AD, HT, BC, HC, CS	BK, KE, PR, LA, RD, 7, 12, TU	SE, CR, ES, 14, 18, 19, 20, WH, 21, 22, ML, 69, WB, KG, IP, 5	DK, 17, EN, EL, DB, 29, SQ, WB, SP, 32, GR, SO, BS, NA, 40, MM, HB, KR, HN, 43, FC, 46, 48, 49, AB, HE	BN, HM, 50, 52, 53, 54, 55, HW
HL	CB, WF, BC	BK, SR	<u>14</u>, 19, 20, WH, 21, 22, 69, WB, KG, IP / CR, 14, 20, 21, ML, KG / 14, ML, KG / 14, KG	27, DB, 29, 30, <u>GR, 40</u> / 27, DB, UB / EL, 27, DB, UB, GR / EL	BN, HW
	WF, HT				

89

CANADA – ALBERTA, BRITISH COLUMBIA, MANITOBA, PRINCE EDWARD'S ISLAND, QUEBEC, SASKATCHEWAN	CANADA – ONTARIO	NORTH DAKOTA, SOUTH DAKOTA, WISCONSIN, MINNESOTA	IDAHO, COLORADO	MICHIGAN	SHRUBS AND TREES AVAILABLE FOR YOUR GARDEN
BB	SH	65, GE	WM	LI, BU	ILEX verticillata
ED, BB	SH, WV			WR, LI, FB, HW	KALMIA latifolia
ED, PN, BB	RO, SH, PH, WP, HD, MA RO, SH, WP, NI, VN	LD			KERRIA japonica " 'Picta'
ED, PN, LW	RO, WE, SH, PH, NI, VN, ME, 3, WV			60, EM, WR, LI, FB	" 'Pleniflora'
ED, WX, BB	SH		NL, WM, CG, NZ, GB	WR, 62, LI, FB, BU	KOELREUTERIA paniculata
ED, WX, DD, PN, BB, LW	HB, RO, WE, SH, PH, MC, NI, HA, CA, VN, ME, DO, 3, BA, WV, HD, MA	GU, WD, LD, WT, JG, 65, GE, PK	NL, WM, CG, NZ	59, WR, LI, FB	KOLKWITZIA amabilis
BB					LABURNUM alpinum
ED					" 'Pendulum'
			NL, CG		anagyroides
					watereri
ED, LW	SH, PH, MC, NI, CA, VN, ME, MA		NL	EM, 62, LI, FB	" 'Vossii'
					LAUROCERASUS (see PRUNUS laurocerasus)
	RO		RO		LAVANDULA officinalis
ED					" 'Munstead'
					LAVENDER (see LAVANDULA)
					LESPEDEZA bicolor
					.. thunbergii
					LEUCOTHOE axillaris
ED, BB				BE, WR, LI, FB, HW	fontanesiana
ED				LI	" 'Girard's Rainbow'
DD, PN, BB, LW	RO, WE, SH, WP, MC, MD, NI, CA, VN, ME, BA, WV, HD, MA	GU, WD, LD, MK, WT, JG, WG, 64, 65, SA	KB	60, EM, 62, LI	LIGUSTRUM amurense
PN, BB	WE, SH, WP, MC, NI, HA, CA, 3, MA			BE, LI	ibolium
BB	SH, HA, 3, MA	GU, LD, MK, WT, JG	WM, NZ	60, LI	obtusifolium " regelianum
			NL		ovalifolium
ED, WX	SH, PH, WP, NI, CA, VN, ME, 3, WV, MA	LD, 65, GE	NL, WM, NZ, GB	BE, 62, LI, FB	vicaryi
	CA, VN, WV, MA		WM, CG, AL, NZ, GB, RB, KB		vulgare
PN	SH, WP, NI, HA, CA, ME, 3, WV, MA	LD	NL, WM, AL, NZ, GB, RB, KB	BE, LI	" 'Lodense'
		LD, MK, 65		LT, FB BE, LI	LINDERA benzoin LONICERA bella 'Candida' fragrantissima
AT, WX, PN, BB, LS, MT, PT, LW, GH, SM	SH, SD, PH, WP, MC, NI, CA, VN, 3, BA, WV, MA	LD DV, WD, LD, MK, WT, JG, WG, 64, RH, 65, SA, GE, SW, PK	KB NL, WM, CG, AL, NZ, GB, RB, KB	BE, 60, WR, LI, BU	korolkowii " 'Zabelii'
	SH				maackii " podocarpa

MISSOURI, KANSAS, NEBRASKA, IOWA	CONNECTICUT, MASSACHUSETTS, VERMONT	NEW YORK, NEW JERSEY (Note: Long Island and southern New Jersey nurseries are in Zone 7)	MARYLAND, VIRGINIA, DELAWARE Note: These states are in Zone 7.	WEST VIRGINIA, PENNSYLVANIA, OHIO, INDIANA, ILLINOIS	KENTUCKY, TENNESSEE Note: Southern Kentucky and most of Tennessee are in Zone 7.
HU, LE, HR	AE, FM, CB, WY, WF, VP, LT, CP, HT, BC, HC, CS, WL	BK, PR, LA, RD, WJ, SC, BL, 7, 12, 68	SE, ES, WH, ML, WB, KG	DK, 25, EL, 27, DB, UB, 33, CY, MM, KR, 41, CD, FC, 46, 47, AB, 23, HE	HM
	AE, EA, FM, CB, WY, WF, VP, BI, LT, AD, CP, HT, PY, BC, HC, CS, WL	BK, KE, 2, PR, LA, RD, SR, WJ, SC, BL, 7, 68	SE, 14, 18, 19, WH, ML, IP	EN, LB, EL, 27, DB, SQ, UB, GR, FC, AB, HE, BS	54, HW
	WF, HT, CS		14, WB	EL, UB, MM, FC, AB	
NO, 57, CM, SK, HL	WY, WF, VP, BI, LT, HT, BC, HC, 10	BG, KE, PR, LA, WJ, 26, 12	WH, KG	MF, 25, DB, SP, 38, KR, HN, LG, 23	
CV, HU, NO, 57, PL, SK, WA, IA, HL	AE, WY, WF, VP, BI, LT, AD, HT, CS	BK, KE, LA, RD, 7, 68	SE, ES, 14, 19, WH, WB, KG, IP, 5, ML	25, EL, 27, DB, UB, SP, 33, 35, MM, HB, KR, KH, 43, FC, 47, HE	BN, HM, 50, 51, 52, 54, 56, HW
CV, HU, NO, 57, PL, CM, SK, WA, 58, FR, FE, LE, HR, IA, HL	AE, FM, CB, WF, VP, LT, AD, CP, HT, PY, BC, HC, CS, WL	KE, PR, LA, RD, ST, SR, WJ, SC, 26, BL, 7, 12, TU	ES, 14, 20, ML, KG, 5	EN, 25, EL, 27, DB, SQ, UB, SP, 33, 35, 36, 37, 38, CY, NA, MM, KR, HN, KH, 41, 44, 45, CD, FC, 46, 47, AB, 23, HE	BN, HM, 50, 53, HW
			14	23	56
CV, WA, SK	WF BI LT	WJ, KE RD	14, 18	EL, 27, DB, FC, SP	56, HW
IA	AE, CB, WY, WF, VP, AD, CP, 10, CS,	BK, PR, ST, BG, LA, TU, 68, BL, 7	WB, KG, 5	27, DB, EL, SQ, 33, 38, HB, KR, 43, FC, 23, HE	BN, 50, 52
	FA, WF, HT HT, GS		CR		
HL, NO, WA, 57	WF, HT GS	7, 68	14, KG, IP	23 UB, SO	50, 56
HR	AE, FM, CB, WY, WF, VP, BI, LT, AD, CP, HT, PY, BC, HC, 10, CS, WL	BG, 2, PR, LA, RD, BL, 6, 7, 8, TU, 68	SE, CR, ES, 14, 18, 19, WH, ML, KG, 5	DK, 16, LB, 24, EL, 27, DB, 29, SQ, UB, SP, 31, 32, GR, 36, HB, FC, 49, AB, HE	
	BI		CR, 14	SP, 32, GR, SO, BS	BN
CV, HU, 57, SB, CM, SK, WA, 58, FR, LE, HR, MY, IA, HL	AE, WF, VP, LT, AD, PY, BC	KE, RD, ST, SR, WJ, SC, 26, 7	WH	DK, 25, EL, DB, 28, SQ, SP, 31, 36, 38, CY, 39, MM, HB, KR, HN, KH, 41, LG, 43, 44, 45, CD, FC, 46, 47, 23, HE	50, 51, 52, 53, 54, 56, HW
FA, 57, 58	AE, FM, CB, WF, VP, BI, LT, AD, CP, PY, CS	RD, 7		25, EL, SQ, SP, 31, 35, 38, CY, MM, HB, 43, 44, FC, 67	HM, 50, 51, 52, 53, 54, 56
	AE, VP	WJ, 7		SQ, FC, HE	
HU, SB, SK, WA, FR, LE, HR, HL	AE, WF, VP, BI, LT, CS, WL	BK, LA, ST, SC, 26, 7, TU	20, WB, 5	DK, 25, EL, SQ, UB, 31, 33, 35, 36, CY, MM, HB, HN, 41, LG, 42, 43, 44, 45, CD, FC, 46, 47, 67, HE	HM
HU, 57, SB, 58	WY, WF, VP, AD, BC, HC, 10, CS, WL	BK, LA, RD, ST, 26, BL, 7, TU, 68	SE, ES, 20, 5	DK, EN, EL, 27, DB, SQ, UB, 32, 36, 38, 39, HE	HM, 50, 51, 52, 54, 56
CV, FA, NO, SB, CM, SK, FR, LE, HR, IA, HL	AE, FM, BI, AD, CP, BC	KE, ST, SC, 7	14, 20, IP, 5	DK, EL, 27, DB, SP, 31, 32, GR, 33, 35, 36, 37, 39, MM, HB, HN, KH, 42, 44, FC, 46, 47, 23, BS	BN
HU		WJ		EL, NA, 44, 45, FC	
PL, LE, HR, HL				EL, HN, KH, 43, 44, FC, 46, 47	
	AE, WF, HT, CS	LA, BL, 7		EL, 27, DB, SQ, 33, FC, 43, 44, FC	50, 54
CV, HU, 57, SB, SK, WA, 58, HR, HL	WF, BI, LT, HT, HC, CS, WL	BK, ST, 7, TU	SE, ES, 20, WH, ML, 5	DK, EL, SP, 33, 35, CY, HB, HN, LG, 43, 44, FC, 46, 47, 67, AB, HE	BN, HM, 51, 54, HW
			14	EL, CY, 44, FC	
CV, HU, NO, 57, CM, PF, SK, WA, 58, FR, LE, HR, MY, IA, HL	AE, FM, WF, VP, BI, LT, AD, CP, CS, WL	BK, KE, ST, SC, 7	WB, 5	25, 27, DB, SQ, GR, 33, 35, 37, 38, CY, MM, HB, HN, KH, 41, LG, 42, 43, 44, 45, CD, FC, 46, 47, 67, HE	BN, HM, 51, 53, 54, 56
LE			14	CY, FC	
FA		7			

CANADA – ALBERTA, BRITISH COLUMBIA, MANITOBA, PRINCE EDWARD'S ISLAND, QUEBEC, SASKATCHEWAN	CANADA – ONTARIO	NORTH DAKOTA, SOUTH DAKOTA, WISCONSIN, MINNESOTA	IDAHO, COLORADO	MICHIGAN	SHRUBS AND TREES AVAILABLE FOR YOUR GARDEN
DD, PN, LW	RO, SH, MA	MK, 65, PK		LI	LONICERA morrowii
BT, DD, BB, GT, LS, SM, MT	HA, VN	GU, LD, RH			tatarica
PN, ST		GU, RH, 65			" 'Alba'
MT	SH	CH		62	" 'Arnold Red'
DD	RO, SH, PH, WV, MA				" 'Grandiflora'
LC, PN, GT, PT, LW	SD, WP, CA, 3	GU, MK, PK		60, EM	" 'Rosea'
		WD, 64, 65		60	" 'Sibirica'
PN, PT, GH	SH, SD, ME, 3	CH, DV, GU, WD, MK, WT, JG, WG, 64, RH, 65, SA, GE, SW, PK	NL, WM, GB	BE, LI, FB	xylosteoides 'Clavey's Dwarf'
					MACLURA pomifera
					MAGNOLIA
					MAGNOLIA kobus
ED, BB	WV, MA, MC		NL	EM, WR	liliflora 'Nigra'
ED, WX, DD, PN, BB, LW	RO, WE, SH, PH, WP, MC, NI, CA, VN, ME, 3, WV, MA	WD, LD	NL	BE, EM, WR, 62, LI, FB, BU, HW	loebneri 'Merrill'
					soulangiana
ED					" 'Alba Superba'
ED					" 'Alexandrina'
ED				HW	" 'Lennei'
					" 'Rubra'
ED, WX, DD, PN, BB	HD	LD	NL	62, LI, FB, HW	stellata
				LI	" 'Rosea'
					" 'Rubra'
				LI, HW	" 'Waterlily'
					virginiana
ED, PN	RO, WE, SH, PH, NI, HA, VN, ME, 3, WV, HD, MA, CA	LD	WM, CG, AL, NZ, GB, RB	BE, 59, EM, WR, 62, LI, FB, HW	MAHONIA aquifolium
ED					bealii
			WM, CG, NZ, GB, RB		repens
DD	RO, SH	LD	NL	BE, WR, 62, LI	MALUS sargentii
ED					MYRICA cerifera
	SH	LD, SA		59, LI, FB	pensylvanica
			GB		NANDINA domestica
					OSMANTHUS ilicifolius
				LI	OXYDENDRUM arboreum
	RO, WE, SH, NI, WV	GE, PK		LI, 63, FB	PACHISTIMA canbyi
				EM, 63	PAEONIA suffruticosa
					PARROTIA persica
ED	SH, VN			LI	PHILADELPHUS 'Atlas'
LC, DD, PN, BB, GH	SH, PH, HA, CA, 3', HD	CH, LD, MK, WT, 64, RH, 65, PK	NL, CG		coronarius
DD, PN, BB	RO, WE, SH, PH, WP, MC, MD, NI, HA, CA, VN, ME, 3, BA, WV, HD, MA	CH, GU, LD, WT, JG, WG, RH, 65, SA, GE, PK	KB	BE, 60, EM, WR, LI, FB	" 'Aureus'
ED		LD	NL	60, FB	'Belle Etoile'
	RO, SH, CA	LD, MK, WT	NL		'Bouquet Blanc'
					'Cole's Glorious'

MISSOURI, KANSAS, NEBRASKA, IOWA	CONNECTICUT, MASSACHUSETTS, VERMONT	NEW YORK, NEW JERSEY (Note: Long Island and southern New Jersey nurseries are in Zone 7)	MARYLAND, VIRGINIA, DELAWARE Note: These states are in Zone 7.	WEST VIRGINIA, PENNSYLVANIA, OHIO, INDIANA, ILLINOIS	KENTUCKY, TENNESSEE Note: Southern Kentucky and most of Tennessee are in Zone 7.
	AE, WF, VP	WJ, 7	WB	EL, SQ, 38, HN, 44, 45,	53, 56
				FC	
MY	FM, VP, BI, LT, HT, BC,	KE, WJ, BL	SE, ES	MF, HB, HN, 44, 46, AB	HM, 50, 51, 54
	CS, WL				
57, 58	WF, VP, AD	RD, 26, 7		45, FC	53, 56
	CB	KE		SP, 35, 37, 23	
		BK	CR, 5	33	
57	CB, AD, CP, PY	LA, RD, ST, SC, 26, 7	20, WB	EL, SQ, SP, 38, 43, 45, FC,	53, 56
				47, HE	
SB		26		FC, 47, 25, 43, 45	56
CM, PF, 58, FR, LE, HR,	AE, WF			25, SQ, 35, NA, MM, HB,	HM
IA				KR, HN, KH, 41, LG, 43,	
				44, 45, CD, FC, 46, 47	
PL					
		12	ML, KG	UB	
	WL		14, ML, KG	DK, EN, 25, EL, 27, SP,	50
	BC, AD	BK, BG, LA, 12, 68	18, 20, 5, 14, 19, KG, 5	GR, 35, 36, CY, MM, HB,	
				43, 67, 23, HE	
IA				FC, 23	
CV, HU, FA, NO, SB, CM,	AE, FM, CB, WY, WF, VP,	BK, BG, KE, PR, LA, RD,	SE, CR, BF, 14, 18, 19,	DK, EN, MF, 25, EL, 27,	BN, HM, 50, 52, 53, 55,
SK, WA, FR, LE, HR, IA,	BI, LT, AD, CP, HT,	ST, WJ, SC, BL, 7, 12,	20, WH, ML, WB, KG, 5	DB, SQ, UB, SP, GR, 33,	56, HW
HL	DC, IIC, 10, CS, WL	TU, 68		34, 35, 37, 38, CY, NA,	
				MM, HB, KR, HN, KH, LG,	
				42, 43, 44, 45, CD, FC,	
				BS, HE, 23, 67, 46, 47	
	VP	BK, LA	18, KG	DK, GR, 33, HB, FC, 46,	
		WJ, 7	18, KG	23	
	WF, HT, HC	BK, RD, BL, 7	CR, ML, KG	27, DB, CY, NA, KH, LG,	
				FC	
NO, HR	10, CS	DK, BG, LA, RD, BL, 7, 12,	ML, KG, 5	GR, 33, 36, CY	HM
CV, HU, SK, LE, HR	AE, CB, WY, WF, VP, BI,	TU, 68	SE, CR, ES, BF, 14, 18,	DK, 25, EL, 27, DB, SQ,	BN, HM, 56, HW
	LT, AD, CP, HC, 10, CS	7, 12	19, WH, 21, WB, KG	UB, 33, 34, 35, CY, NA	
	CS		KG	EL, HE	
				33, FC	
57	WY, CB, WF, LT, CS	7, 68	14, ML, KG	EL	HW
			SE, ES, 14, 20, WH, ML,	DK, EL, 27, DB, SQ, UB,	BN, HM, HW
			KG, IP	33, NA, HB, FC, 67, HE	
CV, SB, PL, CM, SK, HR,	AE, WF, VP, BI, AD, HT,	KE, LA, RD, ST, SR, WJ,	SE, CR, ES, 14, 19, 20,	24, 25, EL, 27, DB, 29,	BN, HW
HL	CS	BL, 7	KG, IP, 5	UB, SP, 32, 33, 34, 37,	
				NA, MM, HB, KR, HN, KH,	
				42, 43, 44, 45, CD, FC,	
				46, 47, 67, 23, BS, HE	
		68	SE, CR, ES, 14, 19, 20,	27, DB, UB, FC, AB, HE	HM, 50, 53, HW
			WH, ML, KG, IP, 5		
	HT	68	14	33, 40, 45, EN, EL, 27,	
LE, HL	AE, FM, WF, BI, LT, PY,	LA, RD, SC, 7	14, ML, KG	DB, SQ, 33, CY, NA, 40,	
	IIC, CS, WL			HB, HN, KH, 41, LG, 43,	
				44, 45, FC, 67, HE	
			IP, WH, 21		
LE, HR	AE, CB, WY, WF, VP, LT,	BK, RD, WJ, 7, TU, 68	ES, 14, 19, 20, IP, 5	EL, SQ, 33, 37, NA, MM,	HM
	CP, CS			HB, FC, 67	
57, SK, HL			WH, 21, 22, 20, WB, KG,	27, DB, UB, HE	BN, HM, 50, 52, 53, 55,
			ML		HW
			WH, 21, 20, WB, KG, ML	27, DB, UB	
HU, HR	AE, FM, WY, WF, VP, BI,	BK, PR, LA, RD, 7, 68,	SE, 14, 18, 20, ML, WB,	EL, 27, DB, SQ, UB, SP,	BN, 50, 51, 54, 56
	LT, HT, BC, HC, CS	12	KG, IP, 5	31, 33, MM, HN, LG, FC,	
				HE	
PF, LE, HR	EA, WF, VP, HT, GS		14, KG	EL, 31, 32, NA, MM, KR,	BN
				42, FC, 23	
FA, FR, HR, IA	FM, VP, HT	KE, SR	SE, CR, 14, ML	27, DB, UB, KR, KH, 23	
HR	HT		14, ML, KG	27, DB	
SK	WY, WF, VP, HT		KG, 5	CD, FC, HE	
HU, SB, LE, MY	AE, CB, WY, WF, UP, BI,	2, PR, LA, RD, ST, WJ,	14, 20, ML, WB, KG, 5	EL, 28, SQ, UB, GR, 37,	50, 51, 53, 56
	LT, CP, HT, PY, BC, HC,	SC, BL		38, CY, 39, NA, HB, HN,	
	CS, WL			KH, 41, 43, 44, 45, CD,	
				FC, 46, 47, AB	
CM, PF, FR, FE, LE, HR,	AE, WF, BI, LT	KE, MS, ST, SC, 26		32, GR, 33, 36, MM, HB,	
MY				KR, HN, KH, 42, 44, CD,	
				FC, 67, HE	
57	WF, HT		SE, CR, KG	37, FC, 23	
	VP	MS	KG, 5	SQ, 44, 45, FC, 67	
	WF		KG	33	

93

CANADA – ALBERTA, BRITISH COLUMBIA, MANITOBA, PRINCE EDWARD'S ISLAND QUEBEC, SASKATCHEWAN	CANADA – ONTARIO	NORTH DAKOTA, SOUTH DAKOTA, WISCONSIN, MINNESOTA	IDAHO, COLORADO	MICHIGAN	SHRUBS AND TREES AVAILABLE FOR YOUR GARDEN
LW		GE			PHILADELPHUS 'Enchantment'
ED		LD, WT, WG, 65, GE, SW, PK	NL		'Frosty Morn'
		GU, WT	WM, KB	WR, LI, FB	'Glacier'
		LD, MK		60, FB	'Innocence'
DO, PN		RH			inodorus grandiflorus
PN, BB	PH, WE	CH, LD, MK, WT, 64, RH, 65, GE, PK			lemoinei
PT, BT, AT, ED, LS, MT, SD, LW					lewisii 'Waterton'
ED	RO, SH, PH, VN	LD			'Manteau d'Hermine' 'Mont Blanc'
ED	SH	LD, 65		BE, 60, 62, FB	'Silberregen' ('Silver Showers')
GH		GE			'Silvia'
GH, SM	RO, WE, SH, SD, PH, MC, MD, NI, CA, VN, 3, BA	CH, DV, GU, WD, LD, MK, WT, 64, 65, SA, GE, SW	NL, AL, NZ, GB, RB	BE, 60, WR, 62, LI, FB	virginalis
ED, DD, PN, BB	RO, SH, PH, MC, NI, HA, CA, 3, MA	CH, WD, LD, WT, JG, WG, 64, 65, SW	NL, NZ, KB	BE, EM, LI, BU	ʺ 'Minnesota Snowflake'
				LI	PHOTINIA villosa
					PHYSOCARPUS monogynus
GT, GH	SH	LD, PK			
	SD	MK, WT, WG			opulifolius
LC, AT, PN, BB, GT, LW, GH	RO, WE, SH, SD, WP, NI, VN, ME, 3, MA	WD, LD, WG, 64, RH, 65, SA, GE, SW, PK	WM, CG, AL, KB		ʺ 'Luteus'
PN, BB	MC, 3	CH, GU, MK, WT, JG, 64, RH, 65, SA, GE, SW	WM, NZ, KB	LI	ʺ 'Nanus'
ED, BB	NI				PIERIS floribunda
ED, BB	SH, PH, WV	LD	NL	BE, 62, LI, FB, HW, WC	japonica
				WR	ʺ 'Compacta'
					ʺ 'Variegata'
					taiwanensis
SD	SH				POTENTILLA arbuscula
BT, GT, MT, SM			KB		davurica
PT, LC	RO, CA				ʺ 'Veitchii'
SM, MT, LC					friedrichsenii
LC	SD				ʺ 'Ochroleuca'
LC, BT, ED, WX, PN, BB, SM, LW, MT, LS, GT	HA, CA, HD, PF				fruticosa
DD, BB, PT, LC	SH, WV, RO				ʺ 'Manelys' ('Moonlight')
MT, LC		RH, GE			'Jackman's Variety'
					'Lemon Drop'
BB					'Mt. Everest'
PN					parvifolia
LC, AT, DD, BB, MT, PT, SM, GH, PN	RO, WE, SH, SD, PH, MD, NI, CA, VN, ME, BA, MA		AL, NZ, GB, KB		ʺ 'Farreri'
PT, SD		LD, 64, SA, PK	WM, RB, CG	LI, FR	ʺ 'Gold Drop'
SD, LW, LC	SH		KB		ʺ 'Katherine Dykes'
BB	VN, SH, CA, PH, 3, WV, RO				ʺ 'Klondike'
PN, SD	SH, SO, MC, PH, WE, CA, BA				ʺ 'Tangerine'
GT, LS, PT, GH, SM	SD				PRINSEPIA sinensis
MT	DO	LD, 64			PRUNUS besseyi
ED, WX	NI		NL	BE, WR, LI	blireiana
LC, WX	RO, WE, SH, NI, HA, 3, BA, WV, MA, HA				cerasifera 'Atropurpurea'
GT, LW		WD, LD, MK, WT, SA, GE, PK	WM, CG, NZ, GB, RB, KB	60, LI, FB	ʺ 'Newport'
ED, BB	WE, PH, CA, KN, MA		AL		ʺ 'Nigra'
WX	MC, CA, 3		NL, KB	BE, 60, WR, 62, LI, FB	ʺ 'Thundercloud'

MISSOURI, KANSAS, NEBRASKA, IOWA	CONNECTICUT, MASSACHUSETTS, VERMONT	NEW YORK, NEW JERSEY (Note: Long Island and southern New Jersey nurseries are in Zone 7)	MARYLAND, VIRGINIA, DELAWARE Note: These states are in Zone 7.	WEST VIRGINIA, PENNSYLVANIA, OHIO, INDIANA, ILLINOIS	KENTUCKY, TENNESSEE Note: Southern Kentucky and most of Tennessee are in Zone 7.
CM, PF, SK, LE	WF	KE	KG	27, DB, FC, 23 LG, 44	
CM, PF				EL	BN
	WF, VP		CR, WB, KG, 5	SP, 31, 45, CD, 23	
PF	WF, VP, LT		KG, WH	38, HB, 44, 45, FC, 47 PL, SQ, UB, 41, 44, 45, CD, FC, AB	HM, 54, 56 HM
SB	VP	BK		27	
FR	WF, GS, BC			FC 23, 31, 35	
LG				FE	
CV, HU, NO, 57, SB, CM, PF, SK, WA, 58, FR, FE	AE, FM, VP, LT, CP, BC, HC, 10, CS, WL, CB, AD	KE, PR, LA, RD, ST, SR, WJ, SC, 26, BL, 7, 12	SE, CR, ES, WH, WB, 5	DK, EL, GR, 35, 38, CY, KR, HN, KH, 42, 43, 44	BN, HM, 50, HW
CV, NO, 57, PL, PF, SK, WA, 58, HR, HL	WF, HT	BK, KE	ML	EL, 27, SP, 35, 36, 37, MM, HB, HN, KH, 44, CD, FC, 46, 47	HM
HR	AE, WF, VP, CS, WL	LA, RD, 7	SE, 15, ML, 5	DB, 33, MM, FC, AB 42, 44, 45, CD, FC, 23	HM, 50
LE		BK, 2, 7		41, 44, 45, CD, FC	54
PF, FR, LE, MY		ST, WJ		36, KR, 43, FC, 47	56
SB, PF, WA, 58, FR				EL, SQ, 33, 39, 41, 43, 46, 47	53, 56
	AE, EA, FM, CB, WY, WF, VP, BI, LT, CP, HT, PY, BC, CS, WL	2, LA, WJ, BL, 68	14, 18, KG, KE	16, LB, 24, EL, DB	
CV, HU	AE, FM, OD, WY, WF, VP, BI, LT, AD, CP, HT, BC, 10, CS, WL	BK, BC, KE, PR, LA, RD, SC, BL, 6, 7, 8, 9, 12, TU, 68	SE, CR, ES, 14, 15, WH, ML, 69, WB, KG, 5	DK, FN, MF, 24, 25, FI, DB, 28, SQ, UB, SP, 31, GR, 32, 36, 37, NA, HB, FC, 47, 48, AB, HE, BS	BN
	WF	BK, LA, 8	19	EL, FC	
	WF		14, ML, KG	UB, GR, BS	
	WF		14, KG	DB, GR, BS, GD 23	BN
	WF		KG		
PF	CP, LT	KE, RD, 7			BN
	WF		14		
LE, SK	WF	BK	14	23	
CM, HR			CR		
PF	CB		14		BN
	EA, CP				
58	WF		KG		
CM, PF, LG, SB	LI, BI, BC, GS, CS		14, KG	36, 23	BN
	CB, BI, WF	BK, ST	14		
	WF, CP, CB, BI	SR			
			KG		
58			14, BL	44, FC, 46	50
CV	AE, AD, HC	7	5	EL, 27, DB, MM, KH, FC, 23	HM, 50, 56
	HT	BG, LA, ST		CY, FC, 23	HW
PF, SK, WA, 58, FE, LE, HL	AE, VP, 10	KE, ST	5	25, EL, SQ, GR, 33, 35, NA, HB, KR, 41, LG, 42, 43, 44, 45, CD, FC, 46, 47	50, 51, 54, 55, 56
CV, HU, NO, 57, PL, CM	FM, CB, WF, LT, AD, BC, CS	BK, 2, RD, SC, 26, BL, 7	SE, ES, 18, 19, 20, WH, WB, 5	DK, 25, EL, 28, SP, 33, 38, CY, NA, 40, MM, HB, 43, 44, FC, 46, 47, 67, HE	BN, HM, 50, 52, 54, 56

CANADA – ALBERTA, BRITISH COLUMBIA, MANITOBA, PRINCE EDWARD'S ISLAND, QUEBEC, SASKATCHEWAN	CANADA – ONTARIO	NORTH DAKOTA, SOUTH DAKOTA, WISCONSIN, MINNESOTA	IDAHO, COLORADO	MICHIGAN	SHRUBS AND TREES AVAILABLE FOR YOUR GARDEN
BT, AT, WX, DD, PN, BB, LS, GH	HB, RO, WE, SH, SD, PH, WP, MD, NI, CA, VN, ME, 3, BA, WV, HD, MA	CH, DV, GU, LD, MK, WG. 64, RH, SA, GE, SW, PK	NL, WM, CG, AL, NZ, GB, RB, KB	BE, 60, WR, 62, LI, FB	PRUNUS cistena
LC					glandulosa
ED, BB				BE, 60, FB	" 'Albiplena'
ED, BB, DD	RO, SH, PH, WP, MC, NI, HA, ME, WV, HD, MA	GU, WD, LD, MK, WT, WG, 64, 65, SA, GE, SW, PK	CG, AL, NZ, GB, KB	BE, 60, EM, WR, 62, FB, BU	" 'Sinensis'
				WR, LI	'Hally Jolivette'
			NL		laurocerasus
	SH, WV		NL	LI	" 'Schipkaensis'
ED			NL	LI	" 'Zabeliana'
		LD		LI	maritima
WX			NL	WR, FB	persica cultivars
					serrulata
ED	SH			LI, FB	" 'Amanogawa'
					" 'Kwanzan'
					(see 'Sekiyama')
BB	SH, PH, NI, HA, VN, 3, WV, CA	LD	NL	BE, EM, WR, 62, LI, FB	" 'Sekiyama'
			NL	62, LI	" 'Sirotae'
			NL		subhirtella
ED	SH			LI	" 'Autumnalis'
	HD		NL	BE, EM, 62, LI	" 'Pendula'
GH, SM, PN	SD				tenella
LC, BT, AT, PN, BB, LS, MT, GH	SH, PH, NI, HD	LD, MK, WT, JG, GE, SW	NL, AL, GB, KB	LI, FB	tomentosa
WX, GH, SM, LC, BT, AT, DD, PN, BB, GT, LS, MT	WP, HD, RO, WE, SH, SD, PH, MC, MD, NI, CA, VN, DO, 3, BA, WV, MA, PT, LW	CH, DV, GU, WD, LD, MK, WT, JG, WG, 64, RH, SA, GE, SW, PK	NL, GB, KB	EN, WR, 62, LI, FB	triloba
LS, MT, PT	SD				virginiana
		LD			PTELEA trifoliata
ED	WE, CA		NL, NZ	60, EM, WR, 61, 62, LI, HW, WC	PYRACANTHA coccinea 'Lalandei'
ED, WX	CA, SH, NI, WV, MA	GU	WM, AL, GB	BE, 60, 61, 62, LI, FB	" , other cultivars
		MK, SW, PK			RHAMNUS cathartica
		MK, WT		LI	frangula
		SA		62, LI	" 'Columnaris'
					" 'Tallhedge'
					(see 'Columnaris')
				LI	utilis
ED, BB				HW, WC	RHODODENDRON
				WC	RHODODENDRON (AZALEA)
				LI	'Album Elegans'
	WE, SH, PH			WR, 62, LI	'America'
					arborescens
ED					calendulaceum
					canadense
	PH			LI	'Caractacus'
					carolinianum
					" album

MISSOURI, KANSAS, NEBRASKA, IOWA	CONNECTICUT, MASSACHUSETTS, VERMONT	NEW YORK, NEW JERSEY (Note: Long Island and southern New Jersey nurseries are in Zone 7)	MARYLAND, VIRGINIA, DELAWARE Note: These states are in Zone 7.	WEST VIRGINIA, PENNSYLVANIA, OHIO, INDIANA, ILLINOIS	KENTUCKY, TENNESSEE Note: Southern Kentucky and most of Tennessee are in Zone 7.
CV, CM, PF, SK, 58, FR, LE, HR, MY, HL	AD, BC, 10	SC, 26		EL, 33, 35, 36, 37, 40, MM, HN, KH, 41, LG, 42, 44, CD, FC, 46, 47, 67	BN
	AE, VP	LA, BL		42, 43, AB, CD	HM, 54
LE, IA	WF, LT, HT, PY, HC, CS, AE, VP	RD, 26, 7		FC, 23, HE	BN, 50, 56
CV, NO, 57, SB, PL, CM, PF, SK, WA, 58, FE, LE, HR, IA, MY, HL	FM, WY, WF, BI, LT, AD, CP, HT, PY, BC, HC, 10, CS, WL	KE, PR, RD, ST, WJ, SC, 26, 7, TU	SE, ES, 20, WH, WB, 5	DK, EN, 28, SP, GR, 33, 35, 36, 38, CY, NA, HB, CR, KH, 41, LG, 44, FC, 47, 67, 23, HE	BN, 50, 51, 53, 56, HW
	FM, WF, HT, CP	RD, 8, 12, 68	14, KG / SE, ES, WH	23, 27, 33, HE / HB	
	WF, HT	TU	SE, 14, 18, 19, 20, WH, ML, WB, 5	27, DB, UB, FC	BN, 52, HW
			CR, 14, 19, 20, 5, IP / 14	UB	HM
NO, 57, SB, PL, CM, SK, WA, 58, HL	AE, WF, VP, CS / AD	BK, RD, 7 / KE, LA, ST, 7	CR, ES, BF, 18, 20, WH, WB, 5	DK, EN, EL, 28, SQ, 32, FR, 38, CY, HB, KR, KH, 41, 44, FC, 46, 23, HE	BN, HM, 50, 51, 52, 54, 55, 56, HW
	WF, VP, CS / WF, BI, LT, AD, CS	RD, BL, 7, TU	14, KG / SE, KG, 5	33, FC, 46 / EL, 27, DB, FC, 23	50, 52
CV, HU, NO, SK	AE, FM, CB, WY, WF, VP, BI, LT, AD, BC, HC, 10, CS, WL	BK, BG, KE, PR, RD, ST, SR, BL, 7, 12, TU	SE, CR, ES, BF, 18, 19, 20, WH, 21, 22, ML, 69, WB, KG, 5	DK, EN, MF, 25, EL, 27, DB, 28, SQ, UB, 33, 35, 38, MM, HB, HN, KH, LG, FC, 47, 23, HE	BN, HM, 50, 52, HW
CV	CS, WF, BI, LT, AD / WY / WF, CS	7, 12, TU, BK, RD / 7 / RD, 7	BF, 18, 19, WH, KG / 14, 20 / 14	EL, 27, DD, FC, 23, HE / FL, 46 / 27, DB, 23	BN, HM, 52 / HM / HM, 52
CV, HU, SB, WA, 58	AE, FM, WF, VP, BI, LT, AD, BC, HC, CS	RD, 7	SE, ES, BF, 18, 19, 20, WH, 22, ML, 69, WB, KG, 5	DK, EL, 27, DB, SQ, UB, 32, 33, 35, 38, MM, HB, KR, KH, LG, FC, 67, 23, HE	BN, HM, 52, HW
CM, 58, HR	AE, WF, VP, CP, HT, PY, BC	WJ, 7	14, KG	35, HN, KH, 41, 43, 44, 45, CD, FC, 46, 47	
CV, CM, FR, FE, LE, HR, MY, HL, PF, 58	WF, VP, BI, LT, AD, HT, PY, 10, CS	KE, BL, 7		27, DB, UB, HB, KR, 42, 44, 45, 47	BN, HW, 52
HR				45, FC	
CV, FA, 57, SK, HR, HL	HT / AE, FM, CB, WF, VP, BI, LT, AD, HT, HC, 10, CS	BK, BG, KE, PR, LA, RD, ST, SR, WJ, BL, 7, 8, 12, TU	14 / SE, ES, BF, 14, 19, 20, WH, 21, 22, ML, WB, KG, IP, 5	41, FC / DK, EN, EL, 27, DB, SQ, SP, GR, 37, 39, NA, HB, HN, KH, 43, 44, FC, 46, 48, 49, AB, 23, BS, HE	50 / BN, HM
FE, IA	CB, WY, WF, VP, HT, PY, GS, BC, HC	SR, TU	CR, ES, 14, 21, WB, KG	EL, 31, GR, 35, 37, 67, HE	
	WF, VP, HT, CS	7	14	EL, 41, 43, 44, 45, CF, 46, 47	
HU	WF, HT, CS	7	14	EL, 33, CY, MM, 43, 44, 45, CD, FC, 46, 47	53
	WF	KE, 8		DK, EL, SP, 41, 42, 46, 47, 33, CY, MM, HN, LG, FC, 67	
				FC	
	WF, CP, CS		15	LB, 24, SQ, BS	
		LA, RD, MS, 12	KG, 14, 69		
HU	WF, VP, CP, HT, CS	LA, 8	WH, 5	24, BS	
	CB, WY, WF, CP, CS	BK, BG, LA, RD, 8	14, 69, KG, 5	24, EL, 28, SP, 32, GR, 34, FC, HE	
	CB, WY, WF, HT, PY	2, PR, LA, RD	18, KG	LB, SO	
	AE, FM, WF, VP, BI, LT, CP, HT, PY, HC, 10, CS	2, PR, LA, RD, SC	SE, 14, 18, KG	LB, MF, EL, 27, DB, SQ, UB, GR, LF	53, 54, HW
	WF, PY, 66		14		
	AE, WY, WF, VP, CP, HT, CS	BK, BG, 2, RD, 8	14, KG, 5	24, 25, EL, 29, SQ, 32, GR, FC	
	AE, FM, CB, WY, WF, VP, BI, LT, CF, HT, BC, HC, 10, CS, WL	BK, 2, PR, LA, RD, BL, 7, 9, 12, 68	SE, CR, 14, 18, ML, KG	EN, LB, EL, 27, DB, SQ, UB, GR, NA, AB	
	CB, WY, WF, BI, HT, BC	12	CR, 18, ML	LB	

CANADA – ALBERTA, BRITISH COLUMBIA, MANITOBA, PRINCE EDWARD'S ISLAND, QUEBEC, SASKATCHEWAN	CANADA – ONTARIO	NORTH DAKOTA, SOUTH DAKOTA, WISCONSIN, MINNESOTA	IDAHO, COLORADO	MICHIGAN	SHRUBS AND TREES AVAILABLE FOR YOUR GARDEN
ED	SH, PH, NI, WV, CA		NL	EM, WR, LI, HW, WC	RHODODENDRON catawbiense hybrids (other than those listed here)
				LI	catawbiense
	WE, PH			EM, WR, 62, WC	'' 'Album'
	WE, PH			EM, WR, 62	'English Roseum'
ED	SH, NI	LD		BE, WR	'Exbury hybrids'
ED			NL	BE, WR, LI	Gable hybrids
ED, BB	WE, SH			LI	gandavense (Ghent hybrids)
				WC	kaempferi
				LI	'' hybrids
ED	NI			LI	Knap Hill hybrids
ED	CA	SA, GE	NL	BE, LI, FB	kosterianum (Molle hybrids)
					laetevirens
	WE, PH				'Lee's Dark Purple'
				62, LI	maximum
	PN, NI	GU, LD, PK		EM, WR, 62, WC	molle
ED	SH	GE		LI, WC	mucronulatum
					nudiflorum
					obtusum 'Amoenum'
					'' arnoldianum
					P. J. M. hydrids
					'Purpureum Elegans'
					roseum
ED	SH			BE, LI, WK	'Roseum Elegans'
				LI	'Roseum Superbum'
ED, BB		LD		LI, WC	schlippenbachii
	SH				Shamarello hybrids
					vaseyi
					viscosum
ED				LI	Vuyk hybrids
				LI	yeodoense
		GE		62	'' poukhanense
	RO	LD, MK	NL	60, 62, LI	RHODOTYPOS scandens
	SH	LD, MK, WT, RH, 65, GE, PK	NZ	62, LI	RHUS aromatica
		LD			copallina
					cotinus (see COTINUS coggygria)
ED		LD, MK	NL, WM, GB, KB		glabra

MISSOURI, KANSAS, NEBRASKA, IOWA	CONNECTICUT, MASSACHUSETTS, VERMONT	NEW YORK, NEW JERSEY (Note: Long Island and southern New Jersey nurseries are in Zone 7)	MARYLAND, VIRGINIA, DELAWARE Note: These states are in Zone 7.	WEST VIRGINIA, PENNSYLVANIA, OHIO, INDIANA, ILLINOIS	KENTUCKY, TENNESSEE Note: Southern Kentucky and most of Tennessee are in Zone 7.
HR	AE, EA, FM, CB, WY, VP, BC, LT, CP, HC, 10, CS, WL	BK, BG, KE, 2, LA, RD, SR, BL, 6, 8, 9, 12, TU, 68	SE, CR, 14, ML, 69, WB, KG, IP, 5	DK, 16, EN, LB, MF, 25, EL, 27, DB, 29, UB, 30, SP, GR, KR, HN, KH, 47, 48, AB, BS	BN, HW
	AE, EA, FM, CB, WF, VP, BI, LT, CP, HT, PY, BC, HC, CS, 66	KE, 2, PR, LA, WJ, SC, BL, 68	SE, 18, WB	LB, 26, 28, SQ, UB, NA	
	FM, CB, WY, WF, VP, CP, HT, CS	BG, LA, RD, 6, 8,	14, WA, KG, 5	24, 25, EL, 28, 29, 30, 32, GR, FC, 47, BS, HE	
	FM, CB, CS	BK, LA, RD, 6, 8	14, 69, 5	24, 25, EL, 28, 29, 32, GR, FC, 47, BS	
		8, 68	CR, ES, 14	CE, GR, SO, KH, 23, HE, BS	
	CB, WF, AD, BC, CS	KE, RD, SR, MS, 6, 8, 12, TU, 68	SE, ES, 14, 20, WH, 22, 69, WB, KG, 5	17, MF, 24, 25, EL, 27, DB, SQ, 30, 31, 32, GR, SO, 34, 37, 39, 48, HE, BS	BN
	CB, WY, WF, VP, CP, HT, BC, HC	BK	ML	26, GR, AB, BS	BN
	AE, FM, CB, WY, WF, VP, DI, LT, CP, HT, BC, CS	BK, PR, LA, RD, BL, 7		27, DB, SQ, UB, 39, FC, AB, BS	
	WY, WF, HT, HC, CS	BK, BG, PR, RD, 7, 8, 9, 12	SE, 14	DK, 24, 25, EL, 32, GR, 39	BN
		68	CR, 14, KG	EL, 27, DB, GR, HE	
HR, IA	CB, WF, VP, LT, AD, GS, HC, 10, CS	SC, 68	CR, ML	EL, 27, DB, GR, KR, KH, 23, HE, BS	
	FA, FM, CB, WY, WF, VP, HT, BC	2, RD, 68	CR		
	WF, VP, CS	8	14, WH, 69, 5	24, EL, 28, 29, SQ, 32, GR, HE	
	AE, EA, FM, WY, WF, BI, LT, AD, CP, HT, PY, BC, HC, CS, WL, 66	BK, KE, 2, PR, LA, RD, WJ, SC, DL, 7, 12, TU, 68	SE, 14, 18, WH, ML, WB	DK, 16, EN, LB, 24, 27, DB, SQ, UB, NA, AB	54, HW
SK, HR	AE, WY, WE, VP, BI, LT, HT	BK, KE, LA, RD, ST, SR, WJ, BL	SE, ES, 14	DK, MF, SQ, UB, SP, 31, GR, 36, 41, LG, CD, FE, 47, HE, BS	53
LE	AE, FM, CB, WY, WF, VP, BI, LT, CP, CS	BK, PR, LA, RD, BL, 7, 12, 68	14, ML, KG	EL, 27, DB, SQ, UB, 31, GR, 36, KH, FC, 23	
	AE, LT, CP, PY, HC, CS	2, LA, RD	18, KG	16, LB, EL, UB	54
	WF, VP, BI, HT, CS	BK, PR, LA, MS, 6, 9, TU, 68	SE, 14, WH	EN, GR, HE	HW
	VP, HT, 10				
	FM, WF	8		23	
	CP	8		24, BS	
	WF, CP, HT	PR		16, LB	
HU	FM, WF, VP, AD, CP, HT, BC, CS	BG, 2, RD, WJ, 6, 7, 8, 68	14, 20, WH, 69, 5	24, 25, EL, 28, 29, SQ, 32, GR, 34, FC, 48, 67, BS, HE	
	WF, CS	6, 8	WH, 5	24, 28, 32, FC, 48, BS	
	FM, WF, BI, LT, CP, HT, HC, CS, WL	PR, LA, RD, 68	CR, 14, ML, KG	EL, 27, DB, LG, FC	BN
		8		32, SO	
	AE, EA, FM, WY, WF, BI, LT, CP, HT, PY, HC, 10, CS	2, PR, LA, RD, SC, 68	ES, 14, 18, KG	LB, 27, DB, SO	
	WF, BI, HT, PY, CS	RD, 12	14, KG	LB, UB	
	FM, CB, WY, WF, VP, CP, HT, BC, CS	PR, RD, 6, 8, 12, 68	SE, 14, 20, 22, ML, WB, KG, 5	DK, 24, 25, EL, 27, DB, SQ, 31, 32, GR, 39, 48, AB, 23, HE, BS	BN
	HT, 10, CS		KG	EL, 27, DB, HE	BN
NO, LE, HR	CB, WY, WF, VP, BI, LT, CP, HC, 10, CS	BK, BG, PR, RD, SC, 7, 9, 12, 68	SE, CR, 14, WH, KG, 5	24, EL, SQ, UB, FC, HE	HW
HU, FR, LE, HR	AE, VP, LT, HT, CS	LA, MS, WJ, BL, 8, TU	5	EL, SQ, GR, 33, 35, 38, 39, HB, 41, 43, 44, 45, CD, FC, 47	BN, HM, 50, HW
58, LE	AE, WF, LT, HT, VP	WJ, MS, 7		EL, 33, HB, HN, KH, 41, 43, 45, FC, 46, 47	HM, 50, 51, 54
		7		HB, FC	HM, 50, 53, 54, 56
LE	66	7		45, FC, 46, 47	50, 53, 54, 56

CANADA – ALBERTA, BRITISH COLUMBIA, MANITOBA, PRINCE EDWARD'S ISLAND, QUEBEC, SASKATCHEWAN	CANADA – ONTARIO	NORTH DAKOTA, SOUTH DAKOTA, WISCONSIN, MINNESOTA	IDAHO, COLORADO	MICHIGAN	SHRUBS AND TREES AVAILABLE FOR YOUR GARDEN
ED, PN, BB		LD, MK, WT, PK	WM		RHUS trilobata
ED, BB		GU, LD, SW, PK	KB		typhina
			NL, WM, CG, RB		" 'Laciniata'
LC, BT, AT, ED, DD, PN, BB, GH, SM	RO, WE, SH, SD, WP, MC, MD, NI, HA, CA, VN, ME, 3, BA, WV, HD, MA	CH, GU, WD, LO, MK, WT, JG, WG, 64, RH, 65, SA, GE, SW, PK	GB, KB	BE, 60, WR, LI, FB	RIBES alpinum
LC, PT, AT, DD, PN, BB, LS, MT, GH	RO, WE, SH, SD	CH, LD, 65, SW, PK		LI	aureum
BT, GT, MT, SM					diacanthum
					odoratum
ED, PN, BB	SH, NI, CA, HD			62	ROBINIA hispida
	CA				" , tree form
					ROSA
		MK			ROSA blanda
					centifolia 'Muscosa' (moss rose)
					eglanteria
BT, WX, BB, LW		WT, GE	NL, WM, NZ, GB		foetida 'Bicolor'
LC, BT, AT, ED, WK, GT, LS, MT, LW, GH	SD, MD, DO				foetida 'Persian Yellow'
LC, AT, MT, GH	RO, SH, CA		WM, NZ		glauca (rubrifolia)
ED, BB, GT	RO, SD, MC, BA, PA	GU, MK, RH, 65, SW	WM, NZ, GB		harisonii
BB	RO, MA	CH, MK, WT, WG, 65, PK			hugonis
				FB	moschata (musk) hybrids
		GU		EM	" 'Robin Hood'
BB	SH, PH, WP, MC, NI, CA, ME, DO, 3, BA, WV, MA	GU		EM, LI, BU	moyesii
	SH, MA				multiflora
BB					nitida
LC, BT, AT, GH, SM					pimpinellifolia (spinosissima)
LS, MT					" altaica
ED, BB					" hybrids
					(Kordes hybrids)
BB	RO, SH, PH, MD, NI, CA, 3	MK, WT, SW			rugosa
					" 'Alba'
LC, BT, AT, ED, WX, BB, GT, LS, MT, LW, GH	RO, SD, PH, MC, CA, ME, DO, BA, PA	CH, DV, GU, WD, LD, MK, WT, JG, WG, RH, 65, SA, GE, SW, PK	WM, CG, NZ	FB	" hybrids
		MK			setigera
		GU			'The Fairy'
		MK			virginiana (lucida)
	SH			LI	wichuraiana
					RUBUS odoratus
					SALIX
GT	WE, NI, SH, PH, DO, 3, WV, MA	GU, WD, LD, WT, JG, WG, 65	NL, CG, NZ, RB	BE, EM, WR, FB	caprea
LS		MK, PK			discolor
	SH, PH			BU	gracilistyla
SM	SD				purpurea
DD, PN, GT, LW, SM	WE, SH, SD, WP, MC, NI, ME, DO, 3, BA, WV, HD, MA	WD, LD, 64, 65		60, EM	" 'Gracilis'
	SH	LD			repens
LC, AT, PN, BB, GT, LS, MT, LW	RO, NI, CA, VN, 3	CH, GU, LD, WT, 64, RH, 65, GE, PK	WM, GB, RB, KB		SAMBUCUS canadensis
DD	RO, WE, SH, BA, WV, MA				" 'Aurea'
PN, LW					nigra 'Aurea'
PN, LS, PT, SM, GT, AT, LC, BT	SH, SD				" 'Laciniata'
LC, BT, AT, ED, PN, BB, PT, GH	SD, VN, ME				racemosa
				60	" 'Plumosa aurea'
LC, BT	SD	DV, MK, 65, SA, GE, SW, PK	NZ, KB		SHEPHERDIA argentea
					SORBARIA aitchisonii
BT, PN, PT, GH	RO, SH, SD, MA	CH, JG, 65, GE, SW, PK			sorbifolia
LC, BT, ED, GT	SD	LD, MK			SORBUS americana
SM	SH, WV				decora
				LI	tianshanica
	LC				SPIRAEA
BB, SM			NZ		albiflora

MISSOURI, KANSAS, NEBRASKA, IOWA	CONNECTICUT, MASSACHUSETTS, VERMONT	NEW YORK, NEW JERSEY (Note: Long Island and southern New Jersey nurseries are in Zone 7)	MARYLAND, VIRGINIA, DELAWARE Note: These states are in Zone 7.	WEST VIRGINIA, PENNSYLVANIA, OHIO, INDIANA, ILLINOIS	KENTUCKY, TENNESSEE Note: Southern Kentucky and most of Tennessee are in Zone 7.
HR				FC	
CM, WA, LE, RH	66			KH, 41, 45, FC, 46, 47	50, 53, 56
CM, LE, RH	HT			42, FC, 67	
FR, LE, HR	WF	ST, WJ		EL, SQ, 35, NA, MM, HB,	
				KR, HN, KH, 41, LG, 42,	
				43, 44, 45, FC, 47, 67	
				44, FC	
LE, HR				FC	
LE	VP, HT, PY	7		33, FC, AB	50, 51, 54
58				27, DB, 23	
		7		CE, WP, KA	
				45, FC	
				WP, KA	
	WF, PY			45, FC	
				KA	
			14	KA	
LE, HL	WF, BC	WJ	KG	WP, KA, FC, 23	
LE, HR, HL	AE, FM, CB, WF, VP, BI, LT, CP, HT, PY, HC, WL	KE, RD, ST, 7	SE, ML	KA, 37, FC, 47	BN, HM
				KA, 23	
CV, IA		BK, 7	CR	SP, 23, CE, HN	
				KA, 23	
FA, NO, 57, SK, WA, FR, MY, IA, HL	AE, FM, WF, BI, LT	KE, RD, SR, WJ, 7	BF, 20, WB	MF, CE, 28, 35, CY, KR, 43, 45, FC, 47	50, 51, 54, 56
		7		45	
	WF			KA, FC	
				KA, 23	
FA	AE, FM, CB, WY, WF, VP, BI, LT, CP, BC, HC	BK, KE, LA, RD, 7, TU	14, 20	33, KA, 42, 45	
	AE, CB, WF, VP, LT	7, 68	14	KA, FC	
PF, FR, LE, MY	WF, BI, LT, PY, BC	ST, SC		WP, KA, HN, 41, LG, FC, 47, 23	
		7		45, FC	
IA				CE, SP, 23	
	HT	7		45, FC	
	WF, PY, BC, WL	BL, LA, ST, 7	14, 20	SQ, KA, FC, 23	
	WF, HT, 66				
	HT				
CV, CM, SK, WA, FR, LE, HR, IA, HL	AE, WY, WF, VP, HT, BC, HC	KE, PR, 7	ES, 20, WB	GR, 35, MM, HB, 43, CD, FC, 47, 23	BN, HM, 52
PL, 58	AD, 10	SR, 26	WH	DK, 25, EL, 27, DB, SQ, 3, CY, KR, HN, KH, 41, 44, FC	50, 51, 52, 54, 56
	FM, HT, BC	RD, 26	14	43, FC	
	HT	7		HE	
SB, FR, IA	AE, WF, BI, LT, HT, 10	BK, KE, ST, WJ	14	25, EL, 27, DB, SP, 38, 39, HB, KR, 41, LG, 44, 45, CD, FC, 47, 23	
			CR, 14		
	HT, 66	7		45, FC, 47	53
FR, FE, HR, HL	WF			42, FC, 46	
	HT				
HR	HT		KG	FC	
	VP, HT			23	HW
LE	WF, HT			FC	
	AE, HT, 66			EL, 45, FC	
			14	25	
		ST	5	FC, 47, HE	

CANADA – ALBERTA, BRITISH COLUMBIA, MANITOBA, PRINCE EDWARD'S ISLAND, QUEBEC, SASKATCHEWAN	CANADA – ONTARIO	NORTH DAKOTA, SOUTH DAKOTA, WISCONSIN, MINNESOTA	IDAHO, COLORADO	MICHIGAN	SHRUBS AND TREES AVAILABLE FOR YOUR GARDEN
LC, BT, ED, DD, PN, BB, LW, GH	WE, SH, SD, NI, CA, VN, ME, WV, MA	GU, LD, MK, 64, RH, 65, PK	NL, CG		SPIRAEA arguta
		SA		62	" compacta
LC, BT, AT, PN, BB, LS, SM	SD, CA, ME, 3, WV, MA	GU, LD, 64, 65, GE, SW, PK		60, FB	billiardii
ED, WX, DD, PN, SM, LW, BB	RO, WE, SH, WP, MD, HA, VN, BA, WV, HD, MA	DV, GU, WD, LD, MK, WT, JG, WG, 64, RH, 65, SA, GE, SW, PK		WR, F.B	bumalda 'Anthony Waterer'
ED	SH, MA				" 'Crispa'
GH, LC, BT, AT, PN, BB, LS, MT, LW, PT	SH, SD, PH, WP, MD, NI, CA, ME, 3, WV, HD	CH, DV, GU, LD, MK, WT, WG, 64, RH, 65, GE, SW	NL, WM, CG, AL, NZ, GB, RB, KB	BE, 60, FB	" 'Froebelii'
	ME, 3	LD		EM, LI	japonica alpina " 'Atrosanguinea'
LC, GH	MC	JG		LI	lemoinei alpestris macrothyrsa
BT, LS, MT, SM, LC					media sericea
	SH	SA			nipponica opulifolius (see PHYSOCARPUS opulifolius)
LS, GH, SM, BT	SD				pikovensis
ED, BB, LW	RO, NI, VN, ME, HD	LD, WT, 65, SA, PK	NL, WM	BE, 60, WR, LI, FB	prunifolia
					sanssouciana sorbifolia (see SORBARIA sorbifolia)
PN	RO, NI, CA, VN, 3, HD	WT, RH, 65, SA, GE, SW, PK		BE	thunbergii
					tomentosa
LC, BT, BB, LS, SM, GH, LW, PT	RO, SH, SD				trichocarpa
WX, AT, ED, LC, BT, AT, PN, LS, PT	SD, PH	CH, JG			trilobata
PN	MC				" 'Swan Lake'
LC, ED, DD, PN, GH, LW, BB	RO, WE, SH, SD, PH, MC, WP, MD, NI, HA, CA, VN, ME, 3, BA, WV, HD, MA	CH, DV, GU, WD, LD, MK, WT, JG, WG, 64, RH, 65, SA, GE, SW, PK	NL, WM, CG, AL, NZ, GB, RB, KB	60, EM, WR, LI, FB	vanhouttei
	RO				STAPHYLEA trifolia STEPHANANDRA incisa
				FB	" 'Crispa'
ED					STEWARTIA ovata
ED					pseudo-camellia
					STYRAX japonica
ED					obassia
DD, PN, BB	RO, WE, SH, NI, HA, CA, ME, 3, MA, HB	CH, GU, LD, MK, RH, 65, GE, SW, PK	WM, AL, NZ, KB	60	SYMPHORICARPOS albus laevigatus
DD	SH, 3, MA	LD, MK, JG, 64, 65		60, 62, LI	chenaultii
	SH	LD, MK		60, 62, LI	" 'Hancock'
	CA			60	'Erect'
				BE	'Magic Berry'
ED	SH, PH			60	'Mother of Pearl'
PN	SH, NI, CA, ME	MK, RH, 65, GE, SW	WM, AL, NZ, KB	60, FB	orbiculatus
					'White Hedge'
BB, SM					SYMPLOCOS paniculata SYRINGA
LC, PN, BB, LS, PT, GH	SH, SD, NI, ME, MT, HB	LD, SA, GE, PK		LI	SYRINGA amurensis japonica
PN, BB, LW	RO, PH, WP, WV	GU, MK, WT, JG, WG, RH, 65, GE	NL, WM, CG, AL, NZ, GB, RB, KB	LI	chinensis
DD, PN, BB	WE, SH, SD, PH, CA, WV	DV, 64, SW		WR	" 'Saugeana'

MISSOURI, KANSAS, NEBRASKA, IOWA	CONNECTICUT, MASSACHUSETTS, VERMONT	NEW YORK, NEW JERSEY (Note: Long Island and southern New Jersey nurseries are in Zone 7)	MARYLAND, VIRGINIA, DELAWARE Note: These states are in Zone 7.	WEST VIRGINIA, PENNSYLVANIA, OHIO, INDIANA, ILLINOIS	KENTUCKY, TENNESSEE Note: Southern Kentucky and most of Tennessee are in Zone 7.
58, FR	AE, WF, VP		SE, ES	EL, DB, 35, KR, 44, 45, FC	HM
				23	BN
CV, SK, FE, MY		7, TU	ES, WB	25, 27, DB, 28, 38, FC, AB	50, 51, 52, 53, 54, 56, HW
HU, NO, 57, CM, PF, SK, FR, FE, LE, HR, MY, HL	AE, EA, FM, WY, WF, VP, BI, LT, AD, HT, PY, BC, HC, CS, WL	KE, PR, LA, RD, ST, MS, WJ, SC, 26, BL, 7, TU	SE, ES, 20, WH, WB, 5	EN, MF, 25, EL, 27, SQ, UB, SP, 38, CY, MM, HB, KR, HN, LG, 43, 44, 45, CD, FC, 46, 47, 49, AB 67	BN, HM, 50, 51, 53, 54, HW
CV, HU, 57, CM, PF, SK, WA, 58, FR, LE, MY, HL	AE, WY, BI, LT, HT, CS	2		EL, SQ, 38, MM, HB, HN, KH, 41, LG, 42, 43, 44, 45, CD, FC, 47, AB	50, 51, 53, 54, 56
CV			14, 20, IP, 5		
FA, CM, 58, FG, HR, IA	CB	ST	14	DK, EL, 27, DB, 33, 35, 36, KH, 43, CD, FC, 23	
		KF, SR		HE	BN
				33, FC, 47	
	CB, WF		CR, 5	35, 37, HB, FC, 23	55
CV, HU, CM, PF, SK, 58, FE, HR, HL	AE, EA, WY, WF, VP, BI, LT, AD, HT, PY, BC, HC, CS, WL	LA, RD, MS, SC, BL, 7, TU	SE, ES, WH, WB, 5	25, EL, 27, DB, GR, 35, HB, HN, KH, LG, 44, FC, AB, HE	BN, HM, 50, 51, 54, 56, HW
				23, HE	
NO, SK, WA, 58, LE, MY, HL	EA, FM, WF, VP, BI, LT, AD, HT, PY, BC, HC, CS, WL	PR, LA, RD, ST, SC, BL, 7, TU	WH, ML, WB, 5	27, DB, 28, UB, GR, HN, KH, 41, 44, 45, CD, FC, 47, AB, HE	BN, HM, 50, 51, 53, 54, 56, HW
	CS, 66	7			
	HT, WL			FC	
IA	WF, GS			36	
		26		23	
CV, HU, NO, 57, CM, PF, SK, WA, 58, FR, FE, LE, HR, MY, IA, HL	AE, FM, CB, WY, WF, VP, BI, LT, AD, CP, HT, PY, BC, HC, 10, CS, WL	BK, KE, PR, LA, RD, MS, ST, SR, WJ, SC, DL, 7, 12, TU	SE, ES, 20, WH, 22, ML, WB, 5	DK, EN, 25, EL, 27, DB, SQ, UB, SP, GR, 33, 34, 35, 36, 38, CY, 39, MM, HB, KR, HN, KH, 41, 42, 43, 44, 45, CD, FC, 46, 47, 49, 67, AB, HE	BN, HM, 50, 51, 53, 54, 56, HW
	HT		14	45	
	VP	WJ, LA, 7		EL	
FE, HR				33, 23	BN
	HT		14	27, DB, UB	
	CS	7	CR, 14, KG, IP	27, UB, 23, HE	
HU	WE, VP, HT, WL	LA, RD, BL, 7, 12, TU	14, ML, KG, IP	EL, 27, DB, UB, HB, AB, HE	50, 53
			14, ML, KG		
MY	AE, FM, WF, VP, BI, LT, CP, HT, BC	BK, KE, LA, ST, SC, 26, BL, 7	WB	25, EL, 27, DB, SQ, 38, HB, 41, 43, 45, FC	51
SB, LE	AE, WF, VP, HT	KE, ST, SC, 26, 7	SE	25, EL, 27, DB, SQ, 35, 36, 38, HB, HN, 43, FC, 46	HM, 51, 53
	HT, BC	7		25, 33, HB, LG, 43, FC, 47, 67	
			14	31	
			14	31, LG, 23	
	WF		14	31, HN	
LE, MY	AE, LT, BC	BK, LA, ST, WJ, 26, 7	5	EL, 33, 38, HB, KR, 41, 43, 45, FC, 46, HE	HM, 50, 51, 53, 54, 56
	WF			31, 35, HN, LG, CD	
	WF, HT, HC, CS, WL		14, KG	27, DB, UB, 23, HE	
HR			KG	CD, FC	
LE, HR, IA	AE, WY, WF, BT, HT, CS, WL	LA, SR	ML, KG, 5	EL, SP, MM, 41, LG, FC	HM
CV, HU, FA, NO, 57, SK, 58, FR, FE, LE, HR, MY, HL	FM, CB, WY, WF, VP, CP, BC	SR, SC, 7, TU	20	EL, SQ, 33, MM, KR, HN, KH, LG, 43, 44, 45, 47	BN, 50
CM		WJ	KG		

CANADA – ALBERTA, BRITISH COLUMBIA, MANITOBA, PRINCE EDWARD'S ISLAND, QUEBEC, SASKATCHEWAN	CANADA – ONTARIO	NORTH DAKOTA, SOUTH DAKOTA, WISCONSIN, MINNESOTA	IDAHO, COLORADO	MICHIGAN	SHRUBS AND TREES AVAILABLE FOR YOUR GARDEN
					SYRINGA French hybrids (see S. vulgaris hybrids)
PN, BB	HB	SA			josikaea
		LD	NL		laciniata
					microphylla
BB	WE, SH, PH, CA, VN			60, FB	" 'Superba'
LC, AT, PN, BB, PT, SM	SD, CA, VN, 3	CH, WD, LD, 65, PK		BE, EM, FB, BU	persica
					" 'Alba'
BB	MA				pubescens
				FB	reflexa
SM	WE, SH, NI			BE	swegiflexa
		GU, LD, MK, WT, 65, SW, PK	WM, NZ, KB		velutina
LC, PN, BB, LS, PT, AT, SM	SH, HB, WV, DO	GU, 65, GE, SW	NZ		villosa
					" hybrids (including Preston lilacs)
BT, DD, PN, BB, GH	WE, SH, SD, WP, MD, NI, HA, CA, VN, ME, 3, WV, MA	GU, DV, LD, MK, WT, WG, 64, RH, 65, PK	WM, CG, NZ, GB, RB, KB	59, 62, LI, FB	vulgaris
PN	SD	GU, LD, MK, WT, 64, 65, SA	GB, KB	WR, LI	" 'Alba'
LC, BT, AT, ED, GT, BB, PN, LW, PT, MT, LS, GH, SM, DD	RO, WE, SH, SD, PH, WP, MC, MD, NI, CA, VN, ME, DO, 3, WV, HD, MA	CH, DV, GU, WD, LD, MK, WT, WG, 64, RH, 65, GE, SW, PK	NL, CG, AL, NZ, GB, KB	BE, EM, WR, 62, LI	" hybrids
DD	SH, MA				" tree form
BB	WV, MA				TAMARIX africana
					gallica
		GU, MK, 64, 65, SA, SW	NL, WM, CG		hispida
ED, PN, BB	MA				odessana
BB	CA				parviflora
DD, PN, BB, LS, PT, MT, LW	RO, WE, SH, PH, NI, CA, VN, 3, BA, WV, HD, MA	PK			pentandra
	SH, MC, PH			LI	" 'Pink Cascade'
	CA	RH, 65, GE, LD, JG		WR, LI	" 'Rubra ('Summer Glow')
	RO		NL, WM		TEUCRIUM chamaedrys
BB					VACCINIUM corymbosum
ED	DO, BA			EM, WR, 61, BU	" hybrids
ED	SH	MK, LD		LI	VIBURNUM
		LD			VIBURNUM acerifolium
					bitchiuense
			NL, WM		bodnantense
ED, LW	RO, SH, NI, MA	LD	NL, WM, GB	60, WR, FB	burkwoodii
				62, LI	" 'Chenault'
ED, BB, DD, LW	RO, WE, SH, PH, MC, NI, CA, VN, ME, 3, WV, HD	LD, GE		BE, 62, LI, FB	carlcephalum
BB	CA				" , tree form
ED, WX, DD, PN, LW	RO, SH, PH, WP, NI, CA, VN, WV, MA	GU, LD, MK		BE, 59, 60, EM, 62, LI, FB, BU	carlesii
	SH	LD		LI	" 'Compactum'
BB	SH, CA				" , tree form
	SH				cassinoides

MISSOURI, KANSAS, NEBRASKA, IOWA	CONNECTICUT, MASSACHUSETTS, VERMONT	NEW YORK, NEW JERSEY (Note: Long Island and southern New Jersey nurseries are in Zone 7)	MARYLAND, VIRGINIA, DELAWARE Note: These states are in Zone 7.	WEST VIRGINIA, PENNSYLVANIA, OHIO, INDIANA, ILLINOIS	KENTUCKY, TENNESSEE Note: Southern Kentucky and most of Tennessee are in Zone 7.
	HT, WL		KG		
	CS		KG	44, FC	
			KG	33, 35	
			CR, 14, 5	LG, 46, 23	
SK			SE, KG, 5	EN, UB, GR, 34, 35, 38, HB, 41, 45, CD, FC, 46, 67, 23, HE	
PF	AE, WF, BI, LT, AD, HT	BK, LA, 7, 12			BN, HM, 51, 54, 56
			KG	FC	
			KG	27, DB	
			KG		
	WF		KG	23	
CV, SK, HR, IA, HL			14, KG	67, 23	BN
CV	AE, CB, WF	7		EL, SQ, 33, 41, LG, 43, 45, CD, FC	BN, HM, 53
LE	WF		KG	35, KR, CD	
CV, 57, SB, PF, 58, FE, MY, HL	AE, FM, CB, WY, WF, VP, BI, LT, CP, HT, PY, HC, 10, CS	BK, KE, PR, LA, RD, ST, WJ, SC, 7, TU, 68	SE, ES, 14, 20, WH, ML, WB, 5	DK, EN, EL, 28, SQ, UB, SP, 33, 35, 38, CY, NA, MM, HB, HN, 41, LG, 43, 44, 45, CD, FC, 46, 67	HM, 53, 54, 56
CV, HL	AE, FM, CB, VP, BI, LT, HT, PY	KE, RD, WJ, 7, 68	20, ML, 5	EL, 38, HR, 41, 43, 44, FC, 67	HW
CV, NO, 57, SB, PL, CM, PF, SK, WA, 58, FR, FE, LE, HR, MY, IA, HL	AE, FM, CB, WY, WF, VP, BI, LT, AD, CP, IIT, PY, BC, HC, 10, CS, WL	BK, KE, 2, PR, LA, RD, ST, SR, WJ, SC, 26, BL, 7, TU	SE, CR, ES, 18, 20, WH, ML, WB, KG, 5	DK, EN, 25, EL, 27, DB, SQ, UB, SP, GR, 34, 35, 36, 38, CY, NA, MM, HB, KR, HN, KH, 41, LG, 43, 44, 45, CD, FC, 47, 67, AB, 23, HE	BN, HM, 50, 51, HW
	VP	SR	ES, WB	CY	HM, 53, 56, HW
	HT	BK, ST			
CV, CM, SK, WA, 58, NO, SB		SR		EL, 27, DB, HB	BN
	BC				
		7	20	UB	
MY	HT, HC, BI	7	WH	41, 43, FC, 47	HM, 50
FE		KE, 7	IP, ES, ML	CE, HN, HE	HM
CM, 58, FR, FE, LE, IA, HL	WF	KF	KG	27, CE, DB, SP, 33, 42, 43, 23	
CM, HR	HC		14, 19, 5	27, DB, SP, 33, KR, HN, FC, 23	
	WF, VP, LT, CP, HT, HC, CS, WL	2, LA, RD		LB, 49	
NO, FE, IA	AE, FM, CB, VP, BI, PY, BC	BK, KE, ST, SR	BF, WB	DK, DB, SP, GR, HB, KR, LG, FC, 23	
HU	HC, CS	BL, 26	KG	HB, MM, SQ, 33, CY, NA, CF	
		7	KG	25, FC	
	CS		KG	CF, AB	
	CD, WF		14, KG		
CV, HU, HR, HL	WF, AD, HT, BC, 10, CS, WL	BK, BL, 7, 12, TU	SE, ES, 14, 18, WH, 21, 5	EL, UB, 31, 34, 36, 37, CY, NA, MM, HB, KR, HN, 41, LG, 43, 45, CD, FC, 67, AB, HE	BN, HM, 52, 55
FR	VP, 10, CS	7	CR, 14, 20, IP, 5	25, DB, SP, 35, CY, HB, 45, FC	HM, 55
SK, HR, HL	WF, BI	26, BL	SE	27, DB, SQ, 32, KG, 67, 23, HE	BN
CV, HU, SK, FR, FE, HR, IA	FM, CB, WY, WF, VP, BI, LT, AD, CP, HT, BC, HC, 10, CS, WL	KE, PR, LA, RD, ST, WJ, SC, 7, TU, 68	SE, CR, ES, 14, 19, WH, ML, WB, KG, 5	EL, 27, DB, SQ, UB, SP, 31, 32, GR, 33, 35, 36, 37, 38, CY, 39, NA, MM, HB, KR, KH, 41, 42, 43, 44, 45, CD, FC, 46, 47, 67, AB, HE	BN, HM, 50, HW
	AE, WF, CS	BL	CR, ML		
	CB, CS	2, BL, 7	KG	FC / SQ, FC, HE	

CANADA – ALBERTA, BRITISH COLUMBIA, MANITOBA, PRINCE EDWARD'S ISLAND, QUEBEC, SASKATCHEWAN	CANADA – ONTARIO	NORTH DAKOTA, SOUTH DAKOTA, WISCONSIN, MINNESOTA	IDAHO, COLORADO	MICHIGAN	SHRUBS AND TREES AVAILABLE FOR YOUR GARDEN
PN, PT, SM	ME	LD, MK, WT, 64, RH, 65, GE, PK	NL	59, LI, FB	VIBURNUM dentatum
	SH	LD		LI	dilatatum
					" xanthocarpum
	SH	LD			fragrans
BB	SH			WR, 62, LI, FB, WC	juddii
ED, DD, PN, LW	SH, SD, NI, ME	WD, LD, MK, WT, 64, RH, 65, SA, GE, SW, PK	NL, WM, CG, AL, NZ, GB, KB	59, LI, FB	lantana
					lantanaphyllum
PN, PT, LW, GH	SH, SD	WD, LD, MK, WT, SA, GE	NL	59, LI	lentago
		LD, MK			molle
BT, AT, DD, PN, BB	NI, RO, WE, SH, CA, VN, ME, DO, 3, BA, WV, HD, MA	CH, DV, LD, RH, SW, PK	CG, AL, MZ, KB	59	opulus
DD, PN, LW	RO, SH, SD, WP, ME, 3, WV	HG, GE	NL	BE	" 'Compactum'
		WD, LD, PK		WR, LI	" 'Nanum'
BT, ED, PN, BB, GT, PT, LW, GH, SM	WE, SH, WX, PH, WP, MC, NI, HA, CA, VN, ME, DO, 3, BA, WV, MA	CH, DV, GU, LD, MK, WG, 64, RH, 65, SW, PK	WM, CG, AL, NZ, GB, RB, KB	60, WR, 61, BU	" 'Roseum'
PN, BB	SH				" , tree form
		LD			" 'Xanthocarpum'
ED	SH, SD			LI	plicatum
WX					" 'Grandiflorum'
ED, BB		LD		62, LI, FB	" 'Mariesii'
	CA			LI	" 'Rotundifolium'
	RO, WE, SH, MD, NI, ME	LD	NL	59, LI	" tomentosum
		MK, PK		59, LI	prunifolium
					pubescens (see V. dentatum)
				LI	rhytidophylloides
ED			NL	WR, 61, 62, LI	rhytidophyllum
		LD, MK	WM, GB		sargentii
ED		LD		60, LI	setigerum
	SH			59, 60, LI, FB	sieboldii
GT, LS, MT, PT	SD	GU, WD, LD, MK, WT, JG, WG, 64, SA, GE	NL	59, WR, 62, LI	trilobum
	SH			EM, LI	wrightii
BB		LD		FB	VITEX agnus-castus 'Latifolia'
DD	WE, SH, WP, NI, VN				WEIGELA 'Abel Carriere'
					'Boskoop Glory'
EA, DD, PN, BB	RO, SH, PH, WP, MC, MD, NI, HA, CA, VN, ME, DO, 3, BA, MA	LD, MK, WT, 65		BE, 60, FB	'Bristol Ruby'

MISSOURI, KANSAS, NEBRASKA, IOWA	CONNECTICUT, MASSACHUSETTS, VERMONT	NEW YORK, NEW JERSEY (Note: Long Island and southern New Jersey nurseries are in Zone 7)	MARYLAND, VIRGINIA, DELAWARE Note: These states are in Zone 7.	WEST VIRGINIA, PENNSYLVANIA, OHIO, INDIANA, ILLINOIS	KENTUCKY, TENNESSEE Note: Southern Kentucky and most of Tennessee are in Zone 7.
HU, 57, CM, PF, 58, FR, LE, HR	AE, CB, WF, VP, LT, CP, HC, CS, WL	BK, 2, LA, RD, MS, WJ, 26, BL, 7, TU	SE, WB, KG	25, EL, SQ, 33, 34, 35, NA, MM, HB, HN, KH, 41, LG, 42, 43, 44, 45, CD, FC, 46, 47, 67, AB	
HU	FM, WF, VP, BI, LT, CP, CS, WL	BK, LA, RD, MS, WJ, BL, 7, 12, TU	SE, CR, 14, WH, KG, 5	EL, 27, DB, SQ, SP, 33, NA, MM, HB, FC, 67, AB	BN
			CR, 14, KG, 5		
	WF, GS, CS	68	KG, 5	UB, FC	
HU, NO, HR	HT, CS	BK	ES, 19, WB, KG	EL, 27, DB, 31, 33, 34, 35, 37, 39, HB, HN, 45, 67, 23	BN, HM, 52, 55
57, CM, PF, LE, HR	AE, HT, CS	2, LA, MS, WJ, 7	SE, 14, WB, KG	25, EL, SQ, 33, 35, 38, CY, 39, NA, MM, HB, KR, HN, KH, 41, LG, 42, 43, 44, 45, CD, FC, 46, 47, 67	HM
		12	KG	35, HE, BS	
LE, HR	AE, FM, HC, WL	BK, 2, WJ, 7, 68	KG	25, EL, 27, 33, CY, NA, MM, HB, 41, 42, 43, 44, 45, CD, FC, 46, 47, 67	
	WF	7	KG	EL, SQ, 43, 44, FC	
HU, 57, SB, PL, CM, PF, SK, 58, FE, MY, HL	AE, AD, HC	BK, KE, LA, MS, ST, 7	ES, 14, KG, 5	DK, 25, EL, 27, DB, SP, GR, 36, 37, CY, 39, NA, HB, HN, KH, 41, 43, 44, 45, 46, 47, HE	BN, HM
IA CM, FR			CR, 14	35, 37, MM, HB, 23, HE	
	AE, FM, WF, BI, LT, BC, 10, CS	DK, 2, LA, RD, ST, 7		DK, 25, EL, 27, DB, SQ, 33, 35, 36, NA, MM, HB, LG, 42, 44, FC, 23	
CV, NO, 57, PL, CM, PF, WA, 58, FR, FE, LE, HL	CB, VP, BI, LT, CP, HC	BK, 2, SC, 26, 7	CR, ES, WH, WB, KG, 5	SQ, SP, GR, 35, 36, 38, CY, 39, NA, MM, HB, KR, HN, KH, 41, 43, 44, FC, 47, 67	BN, 50, 51, 55, HW
	CS		KG	27, DB, FC, 23	
	WF, BI, AD, BC, CS	BL, 7, 12	SE, CR, ES, 19, 20, 5	DK, EL, 27, DB, SQ, SP, 36, CY, 39, MM, HB, HN, 44, FC, 23, HE	50, HW
				33, HE	
	WF, HT, CS		CR, 14, KG, 5	EL, DB, 33, 35, FC, 67, 23	BN
HU				33, FC, 47	
HU, NO, 57, PL, HR	WF, LT, AD, CP, HT, PY, BC, HC, CS, WL	BK, KE, 2, LA, RD, MS, ST, WJ, BL, 7, 12, TU	SE, 18, 19, 20, WH, ML, WB, KG, 5	DK, 25, EL, 27, DB, SQ, SP, 31, GR, 36, CY, NA, MM, HB, KR, HN, LG, 42, 43, 45, FC, 46, 67, AB, HE	BN, HM, 51, 55, 56, HW
LE, HR	WF, PY, HC, CS	2, LA, RD, BL, 7, 68	SE, 14, 18, 20, ML, KG	EL, SQ, 33, 35, MM, FC, 67	
HR				27, 67	
57, SK	WF, AD, CS	LA, MS, WJ, 7	SE, CR, ES, 18, 19, 20, WH, ML, WB, KG, 5	17, EL, 27, DB, SQ, UB, SP, NA, MM, HB, HN, FC, 67, AB, HE	BN, HM, 50
			14, KG	FC, 46	
HU, HL	WF, HC, 10, CS, WL	BK, LA, BL, 7, 12	SE, ES, 14, 20, WH, ML, KG, 5	DK, EL, 27, DB, SQ, SP, GR, KH, FC, 67, 23, HE	BN, HM, HW
HU, HR	FM, WF, BI, LT, CP, HC, CS, WL	LA, RD, WJ, SC, BL, 7	14, 20, ML, WB, KG, 5	EL, 27, DB, 35, NA, MM, HB, LG, 42, FC, 67	
CV, HU, FR, LE, HR	AE, CB, WY, WF, VP, BI, LT, PY, HC, CS	2, RD, SC, BL, 7, TU, 68	SE	EL, SQ, 33, 35, 38, CY, 39, MM, HB, KR, 41, LG, 42, 43, 44, 45, CD, FC, 47, 67	HM
HU, NO	FM, CB, WF, CP, HC, 10, CS	KE, MS, SC, 12	CR, ES, 14, 18, ML, KG	25, EL, DB, SQ, 35, CY, MM, HB, FC, 47, 23	
CV, HU, NO	BI, LT, HT, WF	BK, KE, LA, ST, BL, 7, TU	20, WH, WB, 5	EL, CE, SQ, UB, SP, NA, FC, 46, 49, 23, HE	BN, HM, HW
NO, 57, CM, HL	AE, WF, BI, PY	BK LA, ST, SC, BL	SE, CR, 5	GR, 36 EL, 27, DB, UB, 34, MM, HB, KR, KH, 43, CD, 23	BN

CANADA – ALBERTA, BRITISH COLUMBIA, MANITOBA, PRINCE EDWARD'S ISLAND, QUEBEC, SASKATCHEWAN	CANADA – ONTARIO	NORTH DAKOTA, SOUTH DAKOTA, WISCONSIN, MINNESOTA	IDAHO, COLORADO	MICHIGAN	SHRUBS AND TREES AVAILABLE FOR YOUR GARDEN
					WEIGELA 'Bristol Snowflake'
					'Candida' (see W. florida 'Alba')
DD, BB, LW	RO, SH, CA, 3, WV, HD, MA				'Eva Rathke'
BB				LI	'Feerie' ('Fairy')
					floribunda
BB	RO, PH, 3, MA, HB	WD, LD, MK, 64, SA, PK	NL	60, FB	florida
BB	VN				" 'Alba'
ED	VN, MA, WE, SH	LD			" 'Purpurea'
ED, DD, PN, BB	WE, SH, WP, NI, CA, VN, ME, 3, BA, WV, HD, MA	WT, 65, SA	NL, NZ	BE, FB	" 'Variegata'
	SH, CA				" 'Venusta'
DD	SH, CA			60	'Henderson'
					'Newport Red' (see W. 'Vanicek')
PN, BB	WG, SH, NI, VN, 3	WD, MK, WT, JG, WG, 64, RH, 65, SA, GE, SW, PK	DV, GU, NL, NZ	60, EM, WR, LI, BU	'Vanicek'

XANTHOCERAS sorbifolia
XANTHORHIZA simplicissima
ZENOBIA pulverulenta

KENTUCKY, TENNESSEE
Note: Southern Kentucky
and most of
Tennessee are in
Zone 7

MISSOURI, KANSAS, NEBRASKA, IOWA	CONNECTICUT, MASSACHUSETTS, VERMONT	NEW YORK, NEW JERSEY (Note: Long Island and southern New Jersey nurseries are in Zone 7)	MARYLAND, VIRGINIA, DELAWARE Note: These states are in Zone 7.	WEST VIRGINIA, PENNSYLVANIA, OHIO, INDIANA, ILLINOIS	KENTUCKY, TENNESSEE Note: Southern Kentucky and most of Tennessee are in Zone 7
FE, IA			CR		
CV	WF, LT, HT, HC, 10	KE, LA, ST, SR, 26, BL, 7, TU	ES, 20, ML, WB, KG, 5	EL, 27, DB, 43, 44, FC, 46	50, 54, 56, HW
	WF			31, 35, 23, HE	
FR		TU	SE, KG	CY, 44	50, 53
CV, HU, NO, SB, CM, SK, WA, 58, FE, HL	FM, AD, HC, CS, AE, CB, WY, WF, BI, LT, CP, HT, PY	BK, PR, LA, ST, WJ, SC, 26, BL, 7, 12, TU	ES, 18, WH, WB, 5	EN, EL, SQ, UB, 34, 38, NA, MM, HB, HN, KH, 43, 44, 45, CD, FC, 47, 49, AB, HE	BN, 50, 51, 54, 56
	WF, HT 10	BL, 7	KG, 5, 18 KG	27, DB, FC 31, 44, FC, 36	HM, 54
CV, SB, CM, LE	WF, BI	KE, LA, 5, ST, BL, 7	CR	DK, EL, 27, 31, GR, 34, 36, CY, KH, 43, 44, CD, FC	BN, 50, 51, 53, 54
	BC		KG	25, 27, SQ, CY, AB	
FA, NO, CM, PF, SK, WA, 58, FR, FE, LE, HR, MY, IA	AE, FM, CB, WY, WF, AD, CP, HT, BC, CS, WL	BK, KE, PR, BL, 7	SE, 20, WH, WB, 5	DK, EN, MF, 25, EL, SQ, UB, SP, 31, GR, 33, 35, 36, 37, 38, CY, NA, HB, KR, HN, 41, LG, 42, 43, CD, FC, 46, 47, 67, AB, HE	BN, HM, 50, 56
			KG		
	AE, FM, WF, HT HT	LA, 7	14	EL, FC, HE 27, DB	

CODE	NAME AND ADDRESS	LOCAL	GARDEN CENTER	MAIL ORDER
AD	Adams Nursery, Inc., Springfield Road, Westfield, Mass.	x	x	
AE	Adams–Brainard, Inc., 654 Enfield St., Thompsonville, Conn.	x		x
AL	Alameda Nursery, 3160 South Zuni, Englewood, Colo.	x	x	
AT	Alberta Nurseries & Seeds Ltd., Bowden, Alberta,	x		x
AB	Albrecht Nurseries, Narberth, Penna. (no current catalog)	x	x	
BG	Bagatelle Nursery, Inc., Box 196, Huntington Station, N.Y.			x
BT	Banff Trail Nurseries & Greenhouses, Banff Highway 1A & 32 Ave., NW, Calgary, Alberta	x		
BC	The Barnes Bros. Nursery Co., Box 337, Wallingford, Conn.	x		x
BE	The Begick Nursery, 5993 W.S. Saginaw Rd., Bay City, Mich.	x		
BI	Bigelow Nurseries, 455 W. Main St., Northboro, Mass.	x		
BL	Blair's Nurseries, Inc., 652 Centre St., Nutley 10, N.J.	x		
BN	Boone Gardiner Nurseries, 9409 Shelbyville Rd., Louisville, Ky. 40222 (retail and wholesale)	x		
BF	Bountiful Ridge Nurseries, Princess Anne, Md. 21853			x
BA	Brookdale Kingsway Nurseries, Bowmanville, Ontario			x
BK	Bulk's Nurseries, Inc., 610 W. Montauk Hwy, Babylon, N.Y. and Smithburg–Manalapan Rd., RD3, Freehold, N.J. (serves Metropolitan N.Y., Long Island, and N.J. area, retail and wholesale)	x		
BB	Bunbury Nursery, Box 70, Charlottetown, Prince Edward's Island (DOES NOT SHIP)	x		
BU	Burgess Seed & Plant Co., Galesburg, Mich. 49053			x
BS	Bosley Nurseries Inc., 9579 Mentor Ave., Mentor, Ohio 44060 (retail and wholesale)	x	x	
CM	Campbell's Nurseries & Garden Center, 2342 South 40th, Lincoln, Neb.	x	x	
CR	Carroll Gardens, Westminster, Md. (retail and wholesale)			x
CS	Peter Cascio Nursery Inc., 2600 Albany Avenue, West Hartford, Conn.	x		
CP	Cherry Hill Nurseries, West Newbury, Mass.	x		x
CH	Christianson Landscape Service, Fargo, N.D.	x		x
CD	Elmer Clavey, Inc., 290 Oakwood Rd., Vernon Hills, Mundelein, Ill. (retail and wholesale)			x
CV	Cloverset Nursery & Landscape Designers, 10550 Wornall Rd., Kansas City, Mo.	x		
CB	Corliss Bros., Inc., Reynard St., Gloucester, Mass.	x	x	x
CY	The Clyde Nursery, U.S. Highway 20, Clyde, Ohio	x		x
CG	Colorado Gardens & Nursery, 2406 Wood Ave., Colorado Springs, Colo.	x		
CE	The Conard–Pyle Co., West Grove, Penna.	x	x	x
CA	John Connon Nurseries, Ltd., P.O. Box 200, Waterdown, Ontario	x		x
DD	E. Daccord Ltd., 900 Montée de Liesse, St. Laurent, Quebec	x		
DB	Dauber's Nurseries, Box 1746, York, Penna. (retail and wholesale)	x		x
DK	Dieckmann's Nurseries, Wheeling, W. Va. 26002	x	x	
DO	Dominion Seed House, Georgetown, Ontario			x
DV	Dybvig Nursery, Colton, S.D.	x		
EA	Eastern Nurseries Inc., Holliston, Mass.	x		
ED	Eddie's Nursery (H.M. Eddie & Sons Ltd.), 4100 S.W. Marine Dr., Vancouver 13, B.C. (retail and wholesale)	x		x
EL	Eisler Nurseries, 219 E. Pearl St., Butler, Penna. 16001	x	x	x
EM	Emlong Nurseries, Stevensville, Mich. 49127	x		x
EN	Enterprise Nurseries, Wrightsville, RD 1, York County, Penna.	x		x
ES	Eastern Shore Nurseries Inc., P.O. Box 743, Easton, Md. 21601	x		x
FA	Forrest Keeling Nursery, Elsberry, Mo. 63343	x	x	x
FR	Earl Ferris Nursery, Hampton, Iowa			x
FE	Henry Field Seed & Nursery Co., Shenandoah, Iowa	x	x	x
FC	Charles Fiore Nurseries, Inc., Box 67, Prairie View, Ill. 60069 (retail and wholesale)	x		x
FM	The Framingham Landscape Co., 1224 Worcester Rd. (Rte 9), Framingham Center, Mass.	x	x	x
FB	Fruit Basket Gardens, Corner S. Belt Line & Clyde Park, Grand Rapids, Mich.	x	x	
GS	Gardenside Nurseries Inc., Shelburne, Vt.	x		x
GR	Girard Nurseries, Geneva, Ohio (retail and wholesale)	x		x
GH	Glenorchie Nursery, Box 23, Group 2, RR 1, Winnipeg, Manitoba	x		
GB	Green Bowers Nursery & Garden Center, 3915 E. Exposition, Denver 9, Colo.	x	x	
GT	Green Thumb Nursery, 10th & Cameron St., Regina, Saskatchewan	x		
GE	Greguson's Nursery & Garden Center, Hwy 169, Eden Prairie, Minn. Mailing address: Rte 1, Box 403, Hopkins, Minn.	x	x	
GU	Gurney Seed & Nursery Co., Yankton, S.D. 57078			x
HR	Heard Gardens, Rte 1, Box 134, 5355 Merle Hay Road, Des Moines, Iowa 50323 (does not issue catalog)	x		
HT	Heatherfells Nursery, Sunset Rock Rd., Andover, Mass.	x		x
HN	Henry Nurseries Inc., Henry, Ill.	x		x
HE	Hershey Gardens, Hershey, Penna.	x	x	
HM	Hillenmeyer Nurseries, Georgetown Rd., Lexington, Ky.	x	x	x
HD	Hillside Gardens, South River Rd., Elora, Ontario	x		
HL	Hillside Nursery, 2200 S. Hillside, Wichita, Kan.	x		
HB	C.M. Hobbs & Sons Inc. Bridgeport Nurseries, 9300 W. Washington St., Indianapolis, Ind. 46231	x		x
HA	Hollandia Gardens Ltd., RR 1, London, Ontario (Hwy 2)	x		
HU	Houlihan Nursery Co., 640 N. Mosley Rd., Creve Coeur 41, Mo.	x		
HW	Howell Nurseries, Boyd's Bridge Rd., Knoxville, Tenn.	x		x
HC	The Hoyt Nurseries, 46 Carter St., New Canaan, Conn. 06840	x		x
IP	Ingleside Plantation Nurseries, Mail Order Dept., Oak Grove, Va.			x
IA	Interstate Nurseries Inc., Hamburg, Iowa			x
JG	J.W. Jung Seed Co., Randolph, Wis.	x		x
KE	Kelly Bros. Nurseries, Inc., Dansville, N.Y.			x
KA	Joseph J. Kern Rose Nursery, Box 33, Mentor, Ohio 44060	x		x
KG	Kingsville Nurseries, Kingsville, Md. (no current catalog)	x		
KH	Klehm Nursery, Algonquin & Arlington Heights Rds., Arlington Heights, Ill.	x	x	
KR	The Krider Nurseries Inc., Middlebury, Ind.			x
KB	Kroh Bros. Nurseries, Box 536, Loveland, Colo.	x		x
LB	LaBar's Rhododendron Nursery, Stroudsburg, Penna.			x
LA	Lawrence Labriola Nurseries, 68 Gaylor Rd., Scarsdale, N.Y. (retail and wholesale)	x		
LC	Lacombe Nurseries Ltd., Lacombe, Alberta	x		x
LG	La Fayette Home Nursery Inc., La Fayette, Ill.	x		
LS	Lake Shore Nurseries, Sub P.O. 11, Saskatoon, Saskatchewan	x		
LI	Light's Landscape Nurserymen, Richland, Mich.	x		
LE	The Linn County Nurseries, Center Point (Hwy 15), Iowa	x	x	x
LD	Lied's Nursery Co., 6413 North Range Line Rd., Milwaukee, Wis.	x		
LT	Littlefield–Wyman Nurseries Inc., 217 Centre Ave., Abington, Mass.	x	x	x
LW	Lynnwood Nursery, 1537 Lakeview St., Kelowna, B.C.	x		
MM	Maschmeyer's Nursery, 244 W. Troy, Indianapolis, Ind.	x		
MA	Mayfarm Nurseries, Highway 97, Galt, Ontario (retail and wholesale)	x		
MC	The McConnell Nursery Co. Ltd., Port Burwell, Ontario			x
MD	McDonald's (Kenneth McDonald & Sons Ltd.), Box 375, Ottawa, Ontario	x	x	x

CODE	NAME AND ADDRESS	LOCAL	GARDEN CENTER	MAIL ORDER	CODE	NAME AND ADDRESS	LOCAL	GARDEN CENTER	MAIL ORDER
MK	McKay Nursery Co., Madison, Wis.	x			SH	Sheridan Nurseries Ltd., 100 Sherway Drive, Etobicoke, Ontario and 650 Montée de Liesse, St. Laurent, Montreal 9, Quebec	x	x	x
ME	Meadowlands Nursery Ltd., RR 3 (Streetsville Rd.), Streetsville, Ontario	x			SK	Skinner Nursery & Garden Store, P.O. Box 150, North Topeka, Kan.	x	x	
MY	Meyers Nursery, 1435 Independence Ave. (Hwy 281), Waterloo, Iowa	x			SM	Skinner's Nursery Ltd., Dropmore, Manitoba			x
ML	Millcreek Nursery Inc., Corner Ketch, Newark, Del. (retail and wholesale, DOES NOT SHIP)	x			SP	Spring Hill Nurseries, Tipp City, Ohio	x	x	x
MS	Alfred L. Moses, Lima, N.Y.	x			SQ	Squirrel Hill Nursery, 2945 Beechwood Blvd., Pittsburgh, Penna. 15217	x		x
MT	Mountain's Nursery, P.O. Box 522, Lloydminster, Saskatchewan	x		x	SB	Stark Brothers Nurseries & Orchards Co., Louisiana, Mo.	x		x
MF	Musser Forests Inc., Indiana, Penna. (retail and wholesale)	x	x	x	SR	Stern's Nurseries Inc., Geneva, N.Y.	x		x
NL	Nelson's Nurserymen, 2100 Block, Broadway, South Boise, Ida.	x			SE	Stock's Nursery (Stock Bros., Inc.), 6001 W. Montrose Rd., Rockville, Maryland	x		
NO	Neosho Nurseries, Neosho, Mo.			x	ST	C.W. Stuart & Co., Newark, N.Y.			x
NA	New Augusta Nursery Inc., New Augusta, Ind. 46268	x			SW	Swedberg Nursery, Battle Lake, Otter Tail County, Minn. 56515	x		x
NI	Robert Nielsen & Son Nurseries Ltd., Lakeshore Highway East, Oakville, Ontario	x			TU	Turner Bros. Nursery, Monmouth Rd., Rte 71, West Long Branch, N.Y.	x		
NZ	Nuzum Nurseries and Landscape Service, 96 Arapahoe, Boulder, Colo.	x			UP	Upper Bank Nurseries, Media, Penna.	x		
PA	Carl Pallek & Sons Nurseries, Box 137, Virgil, Ontario (retail and wholesale in Canada, retail mail order only to U.S.A.)	x		x	VN	Vaughan Nurseries, 3444 Sheppard Ave., East, Agincourt, Ontario	x		
PK	The Park Nurseries Inc., 1200 St. Clair Ave., St. Paul, Minn. 55105	x	x	x	VP	Marinus Van Der Pol, Washington St., Rte 6, Fairhaven, Mass. (retail and wholesale)	x	x	x
PT	Patmore Nurseries Ltd., Brandon, Manitoba			x	WA	The Wagoner Nursery, Hutchinson, RFD 4, Kan. and Lyons, Kan.	x		
PL	Paulsen's Nursery, Minden, Neb.	x			WD	Wald–Heim Nurseries, 4422 S. 12 St., Sheboygan, Wisc.	x		
PN	W.H. Perron & Co. Ltd., 515 Labelle Blvd., Chomedey, Quebec	x	x	x	WH	Watkins Nurseries Inc., Rte 60, Midlothian, Va.	x		
PH	Pinehaven Nurseries, 475 Upper Middle Rd., Cooksville, Ontario	x	x		WB	Waynesboro Nurseries, Waynesboro, Va.	x	x	x
PF	Plumfield's Garden Center, 735 West 23 St. (Hwy 30), Fremont, Neb.	x	x	x	WE	Weall & Cullen Nurseries Ltd., 784 Sheppard Ave. East, Willowdale, Ontario	x	x	x
PR	Poundridge Nurseries Inc., Pound Ridge, N.Y.	x			WR	Wedel's Garden Center, 1832 South Westnedge Ave., Kalamazoo, Mich.	x		
PY	Putney Nursery Inc., Putney, Vt.			x	WG	Wedge Nursery, Albert Lea, Minn.	x		
RB	Roberts Nurseries Inc., 7201 South Santa Fe Drive, P.O. Box 192, Littleton, Colo.	x	x		WC	Westcroft Gardens, 21803 West River Road, Grosse Ile, Mich.	x		
RD	Rosedale Nurseries Inc., Saw Mill River Parkway, Hawthorne, N.Y. (DOES NOT SHIP)	x			WF	Weston Nurseries Inc., E. Main St., Hopkinton, Mass. 01748	x	x	x
RH	Rose Hill Nursery, 2380 W. Larpenteur Ave., St. Paul 13, Minn. and E. Hennepin at Fulham, Box 495, Minneapolis 40, Minn.	x		x	WT	Wetli Landscape Service & Garden Store, Bellevue Rd., Green Bay, Wis.	x		
RO	Rowancraft Gardens, Meadowvale, Ontario	x		x	WJ	White Nurseries, Mecklenburg, Schuyler County, N.Y. 14863	x		
SA	Sargent's Red Wing Nursery, Hwy 61, Burnside, Red Wing, Minn.	x		x	WP	White Rose Nurseries Ltd., Unionville, Ontario	x	x	x
SC	Scoharie Nurseries, Schoharie, N.Y.			x	WX	Wilcox Nurseries, Oliver, British Columbia	x		
SO	A. Shammarello & Son, Nursery, 4590 Monticello Blvd., South Euclid 21, Ohio (retail and wholesale)	x		x	WM	W.W. Wilmore Nurseries Inc., West 38 Ave. at Wadsworth, P.O. Box 218, Wheat Ridge, Colo.	x	x	
SD	Shelmerdine Nurseries Ltd., 3612 Roblin Blvd., Charleswood 20, Manitoba	x	x		WV	Windover Nurseries, Petrolia, Ontario	x		
					WL	Woodcock Nurseries, Ridgefield, Conn.	x		
					WP	Melvin E. Wyant Rose Specialist Inc., Johnny Cake Ridge, Mentor, Ohio	x		x
					WY	Wyman's Framingham Nurseries Inc., Framingham, Mass.	x	x	

WHOLESALE NURSERY CODE NUMBERS USED IN BUYERS GUIDE
(AND THE RETAIL OUTLETS NAMED BY EACH WHOLESALER)

Note: These are retail nurseries which may ship plants or may not –
inquire before attempting to order by mail.

2–– Cedar Brook Landscape Nursery, 1070 Morris Turnpike, Short Hills, N.J.
The Kennedy Nursery, Clapboard Ridge Road, Greenwich, N.J.
Green Valley Nursery, Hawthorne, N.Y.
Pine Knoll Nursery, 45 North Airmont Rd., Suffern, N.Y.

3–– Did not furnish names.

4–– " " " "

5–– J.H. Burton & Sons Inc., 5950 Ager Rd., Box 596, Hyattsville, Md.
Carroll Gardens, Westminster, Md.
Gustin Gardens Inc., Old Georgetown & Montrose Rd., Rockville, Md.
Valley Landscape Co., Falls Rd., Mt. Washington, Baltimore, Md.

6–– Did not furnish names.

7–– " " " "

8–– James S. Wells Nursery Inc., 474 Nut Swamp Rd., Red Bank, N.J. 07701
James J. Kelley & Sons, New Canaan, Conn.
Harold Thomas Nursery, Livonia, Mich.
Thompson Nurseries, Rte 9, Kinderhook, N.Y.

9–– Garden World Inc., Flushing, N.Y.
M. Goldfarb Florist, 160 E. 57 St., New York, N.Y.

10–– Preston Nurseries, Uncasville, Conn.
The Garden Exchange, Trumbull, Conn.
Treeland Garden Shop, Huntington Ave., Bridgeport, Conn.
Patrissi Nursery, Rhingold St., Hartford, Conn.
Holdridge Nursery Farm, Ledyard, Conn.
Colonial Gardens, Danielson, Conn.

12–– F.D. Moore & Sons, Summit Rd., Narberth, Penna.
Doyle & McDonnel Inc., Berwyn, Penna.
Pebble Creek Nursery, Marlkress Rd., Cherry Hill, N.J.
Turner Bros., West Long Branch, N.J.
J. Franklin Meehan & Sons, Skippack Pike, RD 3, Norristown, Penna.
Albrecht's Nursery, Narberth, Penna.
Paul Stadler Nursery, Silver Springs, Md.
Huttars Nursery, Richmond Rd., Richmond, Staten Island, N.Y.
Hansen Bros. Inc., Narberth, Penna.

14-- Did not furnish names.
15-- Upaway Azalea Gardens, 7423 Dulaney Drive, Mclean, Va.
 L.A. Reynolds Co., 1100 W. First St., Winston-Salem, N.C.
 O.W. Houts & Son Inc., 120 N. Buckout St., State College, Penna.
 Gustin Gardens Inc., Rockville, Md.
 Pleasant Hill Gardens, 130 Pleasant Hill Rd., Owings Mills, Md.
 Smeltzer's Nursery & Garden Shop, 6431 Baltimore National Pike, Catonsville 28, Md.
16-- Did not supply names.
17-- " " " "
18-- Beaver Valley Nursery & Garden Center, 5601 Concord Pike, Wilmington, Del.
 Treeland on the Turnpike, 397 Tolland Turnpike, Manchester, Conn.
 Hicks' Nurseries, Jericho Turnpike, Westbury, L.I., N.Y.
 Green Valley Nursery, Old Saw Mill River Rd., Hawthorne, N.Y.
 Breck's Home & Garden Center, Morris Turnpike, Short Hills, N.J.
 Jones Ornamental Nursery, Hobbs Rd. at Estes Ave., Nashville, Tenn.
 Styer's Garden Center, U.S. 1, Concordville, Penna.
19-- Gresham's Garden Center, 6725 Midlothian Pike, Richmond, Va.
 L.A. Reynolds Co., 1100 West First St., Winston-Salem, N.C.
 Campbell & Ferrara, 7804 Duke St., Alexandria, Va.
 William G. Burton Landscaping, 6100 Ager Rd., Hyattsville, Md.
20-- Ingleside Plantation Nurseries, Mail Order Dept., Oak Grove, Va.
21-- Gustin Gardens Inc., Old Georgetown & Montrose Rd., Rockville, Md.
 Towson Nurseries Inc., Paper Mill Rd., Box 175, Cockeysville, Md.
 Millcreek Nursery Inc., Rte 3, Corner Ketch, Newark, Del.
 Valley Evergreen Nursery, Rte 2, Williamsport, Md.
22-- Atlantic Avenue Nurseries, 248 Atlantic Ave., Freeport, L.I., N.Y.
 Palmer's Nurseries, Oakland Beach Ave. & Post Rd., Rye, N.Y.
 Land O'Trees Nursery, 1042 Wehrle Drive, Williamsville, N.Y.
 Cahoon Nursery, 27630 Detroit Rd., Westlake, Ohio
 Lavalette Nursery & Garden Centre, 5th St. Hill, Huntington, W. Va.
 Lairds Nursery, 8900 W. Broad St., Richmond, Va.
 deKalb Nurseries, 2700 deKalb St., Norristown, Penna.
 South Mountain Nurseries, 120-230 Millburn Ave., Millburn, N.J.
24-- Did not supply names.
25-- Hall's Nursery, 24300 Harper Ave., St. Clair Shores, Mich.
 DeSloovere Nursery, 14954 E. Warren Ave., Detroit 14, Mich.
 D.A. Hoerr & Son, 5109 W. Memorial Drive, Peoria, Ill.
 Krantz Nursery, 1138 Millersport Hwy, Buffalo 26, N.Y.
 Ross Co. Nursery, 512 Buckeye St., Chillicothe, Ohio
28-- Pounds Nursery, RD 1, Newark, Ohio
 Possum Hollow Nurseries, 6909 Henly St., Philadelphia, Penna.
29-- Colonial Nursery, 123 Drake Rd., Bethel Park, Penna.
 Duncan Landscape Associates Inc., 2306 Logan Ave., Youngstown, Ohio
 Four Winds Nursery Inc., 2635 Millersport Highway, Getzville, N.Y.
 Russell's Nursery, 905 E. Jericho Turnpike, Huntington Station, L.I., N.Y.
30-- Did not supply names.
31-- Wayside Gardens, Mentor, Ohio
32-- Allen's, Plymouth Rd., Redford Township, Mich.
 Wm. Mihelich & Son, Warren, Mich.
 Sloan Nursery, 17184 Schaefer Rd., Detroit 35, Mich.
 Viaene's Nursery, St. Clair Shores, Mich.
33-- Chalet Nursery & Garden Shop Inc., 3132 Lake Ave., Wilmette, Ill.
 Tures Bros. Nursery, 726 Howard Ave., Des Plaines, Ill.
 Bunch Nurseries, 3500 Hulman Street, Terre Haute, Ind.
 Eagle Creek Nurseries Co. Inc., New Augusta, Ind.
 Hillsdale Company Inc., 7845 Johnson Rd., Indianapolis 50, Ind.
 Tri-State Nursery, 8001 Lincoln Ave., Evansville, Ind.
 Goldner-Walsh, 28185 Telegraph Rd., Southfield, Mich.
 Bachman's Inc., 6010 Lyndale Avenue S., Minneapolis 23, Minn.
 J.V. Bailey Nurseries, 1325 Bailey Rd., St. Paul 19, Minn.
 Summit Nursery Inc., Rte 4, Stillwater, Minn.
 Gravina's Nursery Inc., 4344 S. Salina St., Syracuse 8, N.Y.
 Land O'Trees Nursery, 1042 Wehrle Drive, Williamsville, N.Y.
 Lauweret Garden Store, 3280 Monroe Ave., Rochester 18, N.Y.
 Lincoln Park Landscaping Co. Inc., 319 Old Falls Boulevard, North Tonawanda, N.Y.
 Burwell Nursery Co., 4060 East Main St., Columbus, Ohio 43213
 Horton Nursery Sales Inc., 21605 Center Ridge Rd., Cleveland, Ohio
 Loose Nursery, Inc., 3300 Philadelphia Drive, Dayton, Ohio 45405
 The William A. Natorp Co., 4400 Reading Rd., Cincinnati, Ohio 45229
 Wickliffe Nursery, 28820 Euclid Ave., Wickliffe, Ohio
 Busch Nursery Inc., 7903 Thompson Run Rd., Pittsburgh 37, Penna.
 Colonial Nursery, 123 Drake Rd., Bethel Park, Allegheny Co., Penna.
 Brown Nursery, Box 53, Hartland, Wis.
 Evergreen Nursery Co., Rte 3, Sturgeon Bay, Wis.
 McKay Nursery Co., Waterloo, Wis.
 Webb & Son Nursery & Garden, Neenah, Wis.
34-- Bain Bros., 30615 Southfield Rd., Southfield, Mich.

Frank's Nursery, 14 Holland-Sylvania Rd., Toledo 7, Ohio
 Wm. Reinhold, 23206 Telegraph Rd., Flat Rock, Mich.
35-- Interstate Nursery, Hamburg, Iowa
 Earl Ferris Nursery, 811 Fourth St. NE, Hampton, Iowa
36-- Did not supply names.
37-- Harold Thomas Nursery, 14825 Middlebelt Rd., Livonia, Mich.
 C&S Landscape Co., 21724 Harper Ave., St. Clair Shores, Mich.
 Viaene Nursery Sales, 21807 Mack Ave., St. Clair Shores, Mich.
 Franklin Hills Nursery, 28774 Northwestern Hwy., Southfield, Mich.
 Regal Garden Store, 2690 Woodward Ave., Bloomfield Hills, Mich.
38-- Did not supply names.
39-- " " " "
40-- Outlets already listed under own catalogs (Interstate, Fiore)
41-- Did not supply names.
42-- D. Hill Nursery Co., Rts 55 &59, Warrenville, Ill.
         621 N. Main St., Mt. Prospect, Ill.
         Rts 72 and 31, Dundee, Ill.
 C & P Shopping Center, 108 Cottage Grove Rd., Madison, Wis.
 Hawks Nursery, 12217 Watertown Plank Rd., Wauwatosa 13, Wis.
 Bohling's Nursery, 822 Ridge Rd., Munster, Ind.
43-- Onarga Nursery Co., Inc., Onarga, Ill. 60955
44-- Did not supply names.
45-- F.D. Clavey Ravinia Nurseries Inc., 1615 Deerfield Rd., Deerfield, Ill.
46-- Egyptian Nursery & Landscape Co., Farina, Ill. 62838
47-- Worth's Kankakee Nursery, P.O. Box 288, Waldron Rd., Kankakee, Ill. 60901
48-- Did not supply names.
49-- Coles Nurseries, Rogers Rd., Furlong, Penna.
50-- Did not supply names.
51-- " " " "
52-- Franz Nursery, Napoleon, Ohio
 Natorp Garden Centers, Cincinnati, Ohio
 Colonial Garden Center, Evansville, Ind.
 Folker's Nursery, Cherry Hill & Middlebelt Rds., Garden City, Mich.
53-- Grounds Beautiful Inc., Rte 25A & Edgewood Ave., St. James, L.I., N.Y.
 J.F. Newman & Son Garden Center, Nashville, Tenn.
 Boone Gardiner, 9409 Shelbyville Rd., Louisville, Ky.
 McCarty Colonial Garden Center, 735 S. Green River Rd., Evansville, Ind.
 Walnut Ridge Nursery, Jeffersonville, Ind.
 Minor's Garden Center, 5835 W. Appleton Ave., Milwaukee, Wis.
54-- Kelsey Nursery Service, Highlands, N.J.
55-- Jones Ornamental Nursery, Hobbs Rd. at Estes Ave., Nashville 12, Tenn.
 Wm. A. Natorp Co., 4400 Reading Rd., Cincinnati 29, Ohio
56-- Savage Farm Nursery, McMinnville, Tenn.
 Vernon Barnes Nursery, Rte 2, McMinnville, Tenn.
 Garden Plants Inc., McMinnville, Tenn.
57-- Ben Asjes Raytown Nursery, 8005 Spring Valley Rd., Raytown, Mo.
 Blue Hills Nursery, 7601 Troost Ave., Kansas City, Mo.
 Gragg Bros. Nursery, 1212 Walnut, Nevada, Mo.
 Green Thumb Nursery, 8027 Troost Ave., Kansas City, Mo.
 Nashua Nurseries, Rte 29, Nashua, Mo.
58-- Blue Ridge Nurseries, 5348 Blue Ridge Blvd., Kansas City, Mo. 64100
 W.W. Wilmore Nurseries, Box 218, Wheat Ridge, Colorado 80033
 Bornholdt Seed & Garden Center, 1518 West 4th, Hutchinson, Kan. 67501
 Campbell Nursery, 3542 S. 40th, Lincoln, Nebraska 68500
59-- Krider Nurseries, Middlebury, Ind.
 Rocknoll Nurseries, Morrow, Ohio
60-- Did not supply names.
61-- " " " "
62-- Ewing Nursery & Landscape, Reckeweg Rd., Fort Wayne, Ind.
 Anderson Bros., Maumee, Ohio
 Richters Gardens, 4801 S. Cedar, Lansing, Mich.
 Zimmerman Nursery, Traverse City, Mich.
63-- Did not supply names.
64-- Baker Nursery Gardens, Rte 1, Fargo, N.D.
 Goldfine's Inc., 700 Garfield, Duluth, Minn.
 Medary Garden Center, Onalaska, Wis.
65-- Did not supply names.
66-- The Siebenthaler Co., 3001 Catalpa Drive, Dayton 5, Ohio
 Harold Thomas Nursery, 14825 Middlebelt, Livonia, Michigan
 Folker's Nursery, Cherry Hill & Middlebelt Rds., Garden City, Mich.
 The Garden Shop, Lincoln Park, Mich.
67-- The Siebenthaler Co., 3001 Catalpa Drive, Dayton 5, Ohio
68-- Light's Landscape Nursery, RR 1, Box 5, Richland, Mich.
 Howe Nurseries Inc., 304 Burd St., Pennington, N.J.
 The Burwell Nurseries Co., 4060 E. Main St., Columbus, Ohio
 Beaver Valley Nurseries, Inc., 5601 Concord Pike, Wilmington 3, Del.
69-- Did not supply names.

Chapter 12

HOW TO IMPORT SHRUBS

While importing shrubs is more complicated than buying them in your own country, it is not nearly as hard to do as the length of this chapter would indicate. However, importing does involve a number of "ifs, ands, and buts." Enough of these are discussed here so that you will know not only generalities, but sufficient details to judge in advance whether or not you wish to import or to transport between states and provinces.

In Chapter 11 there is a Buyer's Guide Chart which gives you U.S. and Canadian sources for 579 shrubs. Chapter 11 tells you of a good many other places in the U.S. where you may locate a source for a given shrub. If you have tried every one of these and still have been unable to find it in your own country, you may wish to import the shrub from another country.

Be Sure You Can Import

Importing involves *first,* finding the shrub listed in the "export" catalog of a foreign nurseryman. Some nurseries have two catalogs: one for local sales, one for foreign sales. Be sure you have the proper one.

Even the inclusion of the shrub in an "export" catalog does not mean that the nursery can, may, or will ship to you. Nurserymen shipping to other countries must conform to certain specifications of plant treatment, inspection, export certification, packing, etc. that may be more trouble to the nurseryman than a small order is worth. Or, the nursery may be willing to ship, but unable to because importation of that particular shrub from that particular area is forbidden.

So, *second,* after you have located the shrub and before you attempt to import it, ASK THE NURSERYMAN IF HE WILL SHIP that particular shrub to you.

And, *third,* before you order the shrub, make certain that your country will allow it to be imported.

Generalities

Both the United States and Canada, the two countries with which this book is concerned, have statutes covering the importation of plants and plant materials. These restrictions were written for the good of the country at large, to keep out pests which otherwise might destroy crops and plants of value. It would be a selfish gardener indeed who would try to circumvent the restrictions imposed just in order to have one particular shrub in his garden.

In general, these regulations exclude some shrubs entirely, either because the areas in which they grow are the homes of pests which are not yet in either of the two countries or because the shrubs in question are "alternate hosts" of some pest, or for some other equally valid reason.

An example of complete exclusion of certain species of a genus is barberry. Both countries prohibit importation of plants, including seeds, of all species, hybrids, and horticultural varieties in the genus, *except* the ones that have been determined to be immune to black stem-rust of wheat.

The prohibited barberries are "alternate hosts" of the black stem-rust which has, as its other host, wheat. Some plant diseases, black stem-rust included, are unable to complete their development on one type of plant: part of their life cycle is passed on one type and the other part on another type of plant. Thus the two plants are alternate hosts. By eliminating one host, the other host is saved from infection. Since wheat makes bread, often called "the staff of life", it is the host that a country will not purposely "eliminate"; rather laws are made to keep out those barberries which are not immune to black stem-rust of wheat.

Both countries, then, have some such specific exclusions (see Tables 2 and 4); both have also restricted importations (see Tables 3 and 6), which will be explained later in the chapter; and both allow some shrubs entry (see Table 1). As you can tell from the words above, the laws of both countries are similar and they also are similar to those of many other countries which guard their boundaries from the depredations of plant pests.

To avoid confusion, the regulations of each country will be given in sufficient detail so that you will know what to expect and what to do should you wish to import shrubs.

Application for Permit to Import

BEFORE YOU ORDER from any nursery in any country except your own, write for a permit to import. In the U.S. this permit may be secured, by residents of the U.S. only, from Plant Quarantine Division, Agricultural Research Service, 209 River St., Hoboken, New Jersey. In Canada, Canadian residents should write to Plant Protection Division, Production Service, Department of Agriculture, Ottawa, Ontario.

When you write for this permit in the U.S., name the kind of plant material you wish to import, giving the botanical (Latin) name, or a well-known common name for each item. State whether plants, cuttings, seeds, or other plant parts are desired. For items other than seeds, the applicant should state whether the plant material to be ordered represents true species or horticultural varieties (cultivars) that will not grow true from seed. This information may be in the catalog of the nursery from which you want to import. If not, you will have to ask the nurseryman for it.

If you are not certain of what you wish to import, as when you are going abroad, you may ask for a permit for "Admissible Plant Material," but when doing this, you must remember that any plant listed in the several plant quarantines as "prohibited" will necessarily be refused at the time you offer it for entry.

In addition to giving the information listed above, the applicant for a permit in the United States should name the country of origin (because entry from some countries may be prohibited), the U.S. port of ports at which plants will arrive, the method of shipment and the approximate date of arrival.

Canadian Application for Permit

A Canadian application for permit asks for the following information: quantity of plants, botani-cal or other well known name (but not the variety name), name and address of importer (this means you), name and address of exporter (the nursery from which you are buying), country and locality where plants were grown, probable date of arrival of shipment, ultimate destination of shipment, method of travel of shipment, how many packages will comprise the shipment, name and address to whom permit should be sent.

Ports of Entry

The applications for permits in both countries require information on ports of entry. Each country has only certain places equipped to handle (i.e. inspect and fumigate) incoming plants. In the U.S. these ports of entry are: New York, New York (including Kennedy International Airport and Hoboken, New Jersey); Miami, Florida; New Orleans, Louisiana; Brownsville and Laredo, Texas; San Francisco and San Pedro, California; and Seattle, Washington, for mainland destinations; Honolulu for destinations in Hawaii; San Juan for destinations in Puerto Rico and the Virgin Islands.

Ports of entry in Canada are: St. John's and Corner Brook, Newfoundland; Halifax, Nova Scotia; Saint John, New Brunswick; Quebec and Montreal, Quebec; Ottawa, Toronto, Niagara Falls, London, and Windsor, Ontario; Winnipeg, Manitoba; Estevan, Saskatchewan; Lethbridge and Edmonton, Alberta; Vancouver and Victoria, British Columbia. In addition to the above, mail shipments may arrive through Toronto and London, Ontario or Edmonton, Alberta.

Plants coming by mail from various parts of the world normally enter through one of these specified ports of entry. If there is one near you, it would be sensible to try to have the plants arrive there. Otherwise the one nearest the country from which the plants are coming probably will be the port used. If you intend to import by mail, ask for the estimated number of special mailing tags you will need to receive with your permit from either the U.S. or Canada.

When shipments move by means other than mail, the port of entry will be that at which or nearest to which the ship or plane arrives.

U.S.A. Permit to Import

Shortly after your application for permit has been received and approved, the permit will come to you with instructions to follow in making the importations. Permits to authorize entry of Canadian material are valid for one year from the date of issuance and authorize only one importation of admissible items. Permits for material from other countries cover any number of importations of items mentioned on the permit, during the period of validity shown on the permit, unless the permit specifically limits the number of importations.

Canadian Permit to Import

In Canada, the permit forms are serially numbered, multiple-copy, continuous forms. They are, of course, dated and are addressed to the Collector of Customs at the port of entry, telling him that permission has been granted you to import the nursery stock listed in accordance with the existing regulations under the Destructive Insect and Pest Act.

A new permit is required each time a gardener wishes to import into Canada. In most instances, Canadian import permits expire one year from date of issue.

Up to this point in the description of requirements, those of the two countries have been similar. From now on they are less so, therefore those for each country will be discussed separately.

Importing into the U.S.A.

By Mail

You may import material by any medium you wish. The easiest way to import is by mail because (1) the shipment does not require a bonded carrier to get the material to an inspection station, therefore you save the cost of one; (2) the special mail tag which should have been requested when you stated that you wished to import by mail (in your application for permit), routes the parcel directly to the approved inspection station (port of entry), where, after plant quarantine clearance, it is returned to the mails for forwarding to you under the original postage, and (3) if the value of the shipment is less than $250, the Customs duty, if any, is collected at your local post office.

If the shipment is valued at $250 or more, it goes to the Customs port nearest the destination post office and you must either appear yourself to make a formal entry and pay the duty or employ a Customs broker to do so for you. You will be notified by Customs of the arrival of the shipment and the port at which entry must be made.

A mail shipment may be by letter mail, parcel post, air parcel post, or any other class of mail, but air express and air freight should not be confused with air mail and air parcel post.

If you are importing by mail, remember that mail service differs in different countries, some offering air parcel post and some not. Furthermore, the character of air parcel post service may vary with the country. From some countries air parcel post moves by air only to the U.S. port of first arrival and from there by surface transportation to its destination; other countries provide air movement to the final destination; still other countries provide both types of air parcel post service, leaving you to select the type you wish. Ask the nurseryman from whom you expect to buy, which type of service his country offers.

It may be advantageous to you to send the shipment by letter-rate air mail where air parcel post is not available, since this carries the material through to its destination by air. Shipments sent at letter-rate air mail or first class mail should be marked "This parcel may be opened for inspection".

Should air parcel post not be available, leaving you only a choice between letter-rate air mail and air express, remember that air express (or air freight) is NOT CONSIDERED mail shipment and that added Customs brokerage and bonded carrier fees may make these last two methods of shipment quite as expensive as letter-rate air mail.

Shipments Other Than by Mail

When you import shrubs by any other way than mail, each shipment requires a Customs entry regardless of its value and must move in bond to an inspection station. You or your agent must make arrangements for this IN ADVANCE OF ARRIVAL OF SHIPMENT and also arrange for the shipment to continue to its final destination.

In case of shipments other than by mail, each container of the shipment must be clearly and plainly marked to show the general nature and quantity of the contents and the country where grown; it must bear distinguishing marks, be individually numbered, and be addressed to Collector of Customs at the port where the material is authorized to clear quarantine, "For delivery to Plant Quarantine Inspections Station, for account of (your name and address), Permit No. (your permit), from (name and address of foreign nursery)."

Information for the Shipper

Regardless of the manner of shipment, you are expected to tell the foreign shipper about a number of regulations. Those given below cover areas from which you might be importing shrubs for the area in the U.S. and Canada covered by this book. If you are importing from the tropics there are additional regulations which cover shipments.

1. Freedom from soil: All plant material must be free from sand, soil and earth. Leaf mold and other decayed vegetable molds are considered as soil. Plants arriving in or contaminated with sand, soil, or earth may be refused entry because soil is a potential carrier of plant pests.

2. Packing material: Only approved packing material should be used, because it, too, may harbor pests. Leaves, forest litter, woods moss, and any similar material taken from or out of the ground and dried grasses, weeds, hays, and straws are not approved. Among the commonly used packing materials which are approved are peat moss, sphagnum, pulp-free coconut or other vegetable fibers (excluding sugarcane and cotton), osmunda fiber, excelsior (woodwool), shavings, sawdust, ground cork, buckwheat hulls, and vermiculite. Willow withes should not be used to tie bundles.

Nursery stock that has been wrapped, coated, dipped, sprayed, or otherwise packaged in plastic, wax, or other impermeable material which renders adequate inspection and treatment unreasonably difficult or impracticable, may be refused entry if the objectionable condition is not corrected by the importer.

3. Woody seedlings: Only seed may be imported in the case of woody plants and palms which grow true from seed. Permits are issued only for varietal material which must be propagated by budding, grafting, cuttings, or other vegetative means. Exceptions are made only when the applicant can show in advance of importation that it is impossible or impracticable to import viable seed.

4. Size-Age Limitations: All restricted trees and shrubs to be imported shall be limited to the youngest and smallest, normal, clean, healthy plants which can be successfully freed from soil, transported to the U.S. and established. Only plants no more than two years of age when they have been grown from cuttings, or having no more than one year's growth after severance from the parent plant when produced by layers, or having no more than two seasons' growth from the bud or graft when they have been produced by budding or grafting are admissible, except that for rhododendron (including azalea) or other genera or species of similar slow growth habit, an additional year is allowed.

The size-age limitations do not apply to naturally dwarf or miniature forms of woody plants not exceeding 12 inches in height from the soil line nor to artificially dwarfed forms of the character popular in parts of the Orient. Exceptions are made only when an importer makes a showing in advance of importation that a larger plant is needed.

5. Labeling: All material must be plainly and legibly labeled as to genus, species and variety. Lack of labeling delays handling; hence, it is important that plants or bundles of plants be labeled, preferably with scientific names. If the latter are not available a good common name may suffice. When only a provincial common name is known, its scientific name should be determined from a competent horticultural authority near the source.

6. Invoices: The copies of invoices required for plant quarantine clearance are in addition to those required by Customs, the broker, and the importer. For cargo importations: a copy must accompany the U.S. Department of Agriculture "Notice of Arrival" at the time Customs entry is made. In addition a packing list must accompany each container of material or a copy of the invoice must be enclosed within container Number 1. For importations by mail: one copy of the invoice must be enclosed within the parcel or within one of the parcels in the event of a lot shipment.

7. Certification: Quarantine No. 37 requires that material be appropriately certified by the proper phytopathological official of the country of origin. For cargo importations: a copy of the certificate must be attached to the outside of each container and the original certificate must be submitted with the U.S. Department of Agriculture "Notice of Arrival" when Customs entry is made. For importations by mail: a copy of the certificate must be attached to the outside of each parcel, and the original certificate must be enclosed within the parcel or within one of the parcels in the event of a lot shipment.

8. Medium of Importation: As has already been stated, you may import material by any medium you wish but you should instruct the foreign shipper as to the means by which shipment is to be made.

Bringing the Shrubs Home with You from Countries Other Than Canada

Bringing shrubs into the country in your baggage may cost you more than sending them home by mail because it may be necessary to arrange for a bonded carrier to transport them to the nearest inspection station. After the shrubs have been inspected someone also will have to care for forwarding them to you and pay the costs of forwarding. Eventually you pay for all of this.

If, despite the possibility of these extra costs, you decide to bring them into the country with you, it will help you to know that inspection stations are generally open from 8:30 A.M. to 5:00 P.M, Monday through Friday, except on Federal holidays.

Importing from Canada into the U.S.

MOST shrubs, with the exception of those prohibited entry, may be brought in your luggage from Canada, may be mailed to you or otherwise shipped to you subject to the usual conditions and requirements already discussed. However, unless the inspector at the port of entry thinks that the condition of the shipment necessitates its treatment with chemicals, this requirement of entry is waived, provided the required plant health certificate is present.

Charges and Risks

In addition to paying for the shrubs—for their shipment to you and, if they arrive by any means other than mail, for bonded carrier and forwarding —you also pay for unpacking and repacking the plants at the inspection station, for fumigating them if necessary, for any special labor, chemicals, or supplies needed to handle the plants regardless of the manner of shipment. Add these costs together and figure just what the shrubs will actually cost you before you import. They may not be worth the price.

Of course you also assume all risk of the shrubs arriving in good condition and surviving any necessary treatment.

When Plants Do Not Qualify

If inspection shows plants are unsafe, they may be refused entry into the country. This may be because they are definitely on the prohibited list or because they are infested by pests and there is no practical way of eliminating the risk of bringing these into the country. Or it may be because the plants are in such poor condition that they cannot, in the opinion of the inspector, be treated without "substantial injury."

When plants are refused entry because regulations have not been complied with, the plants must be immediately removed from the country by the importer or abandoned by him. Meanwhile the shipment must be safeguarded against escape of plant pests in a manner prescribed by the inspector. All costs incidental to such safeguarding are borne by the importer and there is no recovery of the cost of any plants which are ordered destroyed.

Postentry Quarantine

Certain genera of shrubs which are restricted in their importation may be brought into the country despite this if you will sign an agreement to grow the plants under "postentry quarantine" (see Tables 1 & 3). This means just what it says—quarantine after entry. You agree to grow the plants on certain definite premises that you own, and to keep them there until they are released from this quarantine. You agree to permit inspectors access to this place during the day, agree to keep the plants labeled with their names and your permit number and to keep any increase from them labeled the same way. You also agree that you will not distribute any parts of these plants from this place during the duration of the quarantine and that you will follow the inspector's directions as to pest control, including possibly destroying the plants to prevent dissemination of a plant pest.

Permit for Postentry Quarantine

A permit to grow plants under postentry quarantine may be obtained only by the person who will grow the plants on land controlled by himself. This person will be held responsible for meeting the requirements of this type of quarantine and the dealings of the Plant Quarantine Division will be with him.

The application for a postentry quarantine permit should be made to the same address and in the manner described for ordinary permits, on page 114. When your request is received you will then be sent copies of the growing agreement for your completion and signature. When the request is approved the permit is issued and requires the importer to abide by the postentry quarantine growing conditions.

The actual length of time that plants are held under postentry quarantine usually will be two growing seasons but it may be longer if the material is such that inspection at a certain time (as at bloom time) is necessary.

A list of shrub genera covered in this book which must be grown under postentry quarantine is on page 126.

U.S. Customs Requirements

In order to avoid delay which may result in loss or deterioration of plants, MAKE ARRANGEMENTS IN ADVANCE for a Customs broker or other agent to attend to Customs formalities in connection with freight, air freight, express, or air express consignments. Unless these are under an

"In-Transit entry" (explained below), they cannot be forwarded to you until all Customs requirements have been completed. Plant quarantine inspectors ARE NOT Customs brokers and cannot act as such.

The Customs broker will need to know, IN ADVANCE, the expected time of arrival and the carrier on which the plants are expected to arrive. You should supply him with invoices, other necessary documents, your permit number and instructions for forwarding the plants—and tell him the type of Customs entry to be made. Your Customs broker can arrange, if necessary, for bonded transportation of plants to the inspection station and can supply labor and materials if needed. If you have never imported before and for some reason or other cannot import by mail and keep the cost of the shipment under $250 (in which case, as previously stated, a Customs broker would not be required), you had better ask your broker well ahead of time what is expected of you.

There are three kinds of Customs entries normally used for plants imported by means other than by mail.

1. Informal entry: When the port of arrival is the same as the authorized port of plant quarantine and the shipment is valued at less than $250, this type of entry may sometimes be advantageous. Duty must be paid in cash or certified check to a Customs inspector at the port of entry. Sometimes, even if allowable, an informal entry may not be practical or convenient for a broker or agent.

2. Duty Paid Entry: Payment of duty is guaranteed by the broker's bond or is paid at the customhouse. When the port of arrival is not the same as the authorized port of plant quarantine clearance, the shipment must move under a Customs Special Manifest to the port of plant quarantine clearance.

3. In-Transit Entry: Under this type of Customs entry, your broker or agent makes the entry and arranges for handling at the inspection station and for forwarding onward to you. He does not pay duty or clear the shipment with Customs. At your nearest Customs port, another broker (whom you employ) takes care of Customs formalities and pays the duty. Because of the employment of two brokers, this is a more costly type of entry.

Once again, your attention is called to the fact that you pay not only the duty, but also the cost of moving plants from one place to another, the labor of unpacking and repacking the shipment and of loading containers into and out of fumigation chambers at the inspection station, to say nothing of the brokerage. Also, you risk losing the plants either because of their loss of life in transit or because of their low vitality when fumigated.

Duty

All articles (plants included) are subject to duty on entry into the United States unless specifically exempt therefrom. Rates of duty vary according to the commodities. As far as shrubs, cuttings, seedlings, budded or grafted plants, and nursery or greenhouse stock are concerned, the duty is but a few cents on the quantity a gardener would be likely to buy. It is less when plants are imported from Canada than when they are brought in from other countries.

The only plants on the "free entry list" are those being imported by either the U.S. Department of Agriculture or the U.S. Botanic Garden.

Gardeners returning from abroad, may, if they wish, use part of their travel exemption to cover plants shipped from abroad or carried with them.

This exemption applies only if the gardener has been outside of the U.S. for at least 48 hours once within 31 days. If you have acquired shrubs in the Virgin Islands, your exemption is greater and if you return from there or from Mexico by a port along the California-Mexico border, there is no time limit as to your stay there, but you cannot (from the Virgin Islands) claim your exemption more often than once in a 31-day period.

A Customs declaration giving the amount paid for the plants must be made before you enter the country, whether or not you bring the plants back with you. The best and easiest way to prove what you paid for the plants is to get a bill for them from the nursery and bring it along with you, so you can show it to the Customs inspector at the port of entry. The inspector may make an adjustment according to current regulations.

When Plants Follow You

If you shipped plants home and the shipment is coming by mail, the post office will inform you when it has arrived. The Customs Service does not inform you of the arrival of a shipment which is mailed but has a value of over $250 or which comes into the country by any other means. You usually are notified by the carrier. You should make your own arrangements with the carrier to be sure you or your Customs broker or agent are informed immediately so your Customs entry may be filed and there will be no delay in forwarding the plants.

If your shipment is not entered through Customs within five days of its arrival, it is sent by the Collector of Customs to a bonded warehouse to be held as unclaimed. This is one good reason why your arrangements for the reception of the plants should be made well in advance of their arrival.

Movements Of Plants Between States Of The U.S.

Movements of plants between the states, whether they are parts of plants for propagation or the entire plants (and certain plant products) also is regulated—by both Federal and state quarantines or regulations. There are 12 Federal domestic plant quarantines that regulate interstate movement of specified insect and plant disease host plants and other materials that may carry such pests from place to place.

In order to move such material interstate from areas known to be infested with such insects or plant diseases, or areas which are quarantined on account of such a pest to other parts of the U.S.A., the shipper must obtain a Federal certificate.

The white-pine blister rust quarantine requires control-area permits which are obtained from state officials in the state of destination of the shipment, in order to move currant and gooseberry plants (which are the alternate hosts of the white-pine blister rust) into certain areas in which their planting is prohibited in order to protect white pine. However, the movement of such plants into some areas of some states is prohibited entirely.

Each state has its own specifications for the certification of plants, specified parts of plants for propagation, and for certain plant products. Certificates are issued by state inspectors following an inspection of the shipment just before it is sent, or after an examination of the plants growing during the growing season in field or greenhouse. In addition, many states have special quarantines regulating or prohibiting movement to them of specified plants because of certain insects or plant diseases that occur in other parts of the U.S.

In addition, regulations of the Post Office Department require that certificates of inspection from the state where the plants were grown, as well as any required Federal inspection certificates, accompany all shrubs, cuttings, grafts, scions, buds, and seeds of shrubs for propagation except field, vegetable, and flower seeds, bedding plants and other herbaceous plants, bulbs and roots. Many plants or plant parts for propagation, must be inspected upon arrival in some states at their destination by agricultural inspectors of those states before they may be delivered to the consignee.

Mail-order nurseries, of course, know of these prohibitions and regulations and, when buying from them, you need not be concerned with these rules except to avoid ordering an item when the catalog states that shipment into your state is prohibited.

But when you are bringing shrubs into your state, from the garden of a friend or a nursery outside the state, in your car or by mail, it certainly would be sensible to check first with the proper authorities in your State Department of Agriculture to make certain that you know the restrictions and do not run afoul of the law.

Importing Into Canada

As previously stated and discussed, the Canadian importer must apply for a permit in advance of each importation of nursery stock, the stock must enter the country by one of the ports of entry listed and he has the privilege of importing by any carrier he wishes.

Mail Importation

If the importation is to be by mail (the easiest way to import), the permit should be kept until it is needed to release the shipment from your local Customs office.

A mailing label should have been requested when the permit was requested and should have been sent you with the permit. This label must be sent by you to the nursery from which you buy the shrubs. With it you also forward the sheet of "Instructions to the Shipper" which will come with your permit.

This sheet, which is printed in English on one side, in French on the other, tells the nurseryman that the official mailing label (which is addressed to the Inspector of the Plant Protection Division at the port of importation) must be used for mail shipments and mail shipments ONLY. He is asked to destroy the label unless shipment is to be by mail. He is told that your permit number must be on the label; that, since the Inspector is the person addressed on the package, your address should be put inside the package; and that the inspector will re-address the parcel after inspecting the contents. It also tells him that a certificate of inspection (which is explained) MUST accompany each shipment and, in case of a mail shipment, should be inside the container.

Shipments By Means Other Than Mail

Shipments that move by any other carrier must have the original certificate of inspection and any necessary special certificates accompanying them, together with the waybill or bill of lading and these certificates shall be furnished to the inspector at the port of importation by the transportation company.

The certificate must state the country and locality where the stock was grown, as well as the date of inspection. The official seal of the authorized inspection service of the country of origin and the actual signature of the authorized official must be on the original copy; the seal must be on other copies, though the signature may be actual or reproduced on these.

Marking Of Containers

Each container must be marked with name and address of both consignor and consignee, permit number, and quantity and kind of nursery stock inside.

Certificate Of Inspection

Phytopathological Certificate
(Certificate A in Table 5)

Each shipment of nursery stock originating in a country maintaining an inspection service must be accompanied by a phytopathological certificate issued, dated, and signed by an authorized official of the country of origin, certifying that the nursery stock for which the certificate was issued was thoroughly examined *at time of packing* by that official or his authorized agent and was found, to the best of his knowledge, to be substantially free from injurious diseases and pests, and that the consignment is believed to conform to the current phytosanitary regulations of the importing country, both as stated in any additional declaration and otherwise.

Phytosanitary Certificate
(Certificate B in Table 5)

The phytosanitary certificate accompanying each shipment of nursery stock from countries other than the U.S. (except the state of Hawaii) where the golden nematode (potato root eelworm) or the potato wart disease (black wart) is known to occur shall include a declaration that the stock in the shipment was grown in soil where, by soil test or official soil surveys, neither of these pests has been recorded or is known to occur.

Special Certificates

Certain special certificates are required in order to import certain specific plants. You will find the plants listed in Table 5 and reference is made in the table to these special certificates as C, D, and E.

Special Certificate of Place of Growth
(Certificate C in Table 5)

Special certificates are required from the United States for the importation of stone fruit nursery stock. Each shipment must be accompanied by a certificate of inspection issued and signed by an authorized state or Federal official establishing that the material included in the shipment was grown in a nursery or other source which was duly inspected during the growing season and is believed to be free from the virus diseases listed in Table 5 under subject 5.

Special Certification of Freedom from Infestation
(Certificate D in Table 5)

Shipment must be accompanied by a certificate of inspection, issued and signed by an authorized officer of the U.S. Department of Agriculture or a State Department of Agriculture, establishing that the shipment was examined and found free from infestation by either the gypsy moth or brown-tail moth. This certification applies to Table 5, item 4.

Special Declarations Certifying Fumigation
(Certificate E in Table 5)

The special declarations required for shipments containing any or all of the hosts of the Oriental fruit moth, from any point in the U.S.A. to British Columbia, shall establish that the said hosts in each shipment were fumigated in accordance with set instructions. This declaration applies to Table 5, item 6.

These special declarations and certifications are available in form of mimeographed sheets. The sheet which is applicable to nursery stock you are ordering should be sent to the shipper, together with the instruction sheet because the shipment may be refused entry if the proper certificates do not accompany it.

In the case of shipments from the United States the certificates may be issued by either state or Federal officials. "Blanket certificates" based on growing season inspection only, are not acceptable for shipments of nursery stock consigned to Canada.

Inspection

It is the responsibility of the shipper to arrange for inspection in the country of origin and to ensure that the appropriate certificate accompanies each shipment and is available to the Inspector of the Plant Protection Division when the shipment reaches one of the designated ports of importation in Canada.

Plants With Sand, Soil, Or Earth Around Roots

FROM U.S.

Plants and plant parts with sand, soil or earth may be imported from the mainland of the U.S. (including Alaska) when shipped in accordance with the requirements of existing state or Federal quarantines.

FROM EUROPE

Plants and plant parts with sand, soil, or earth may be imported only from certain approved nurseries in Belgium, Denmark, England and Wales, the Netherlands, and the Provinces of Schleswig-Holstein and Oldenburg of the Federal Republic of Germany. The approved nurseries must have complied with certain conditions regarding cultural and sanitary practices and official soil sampling indicating freedom from the golden nematode and potato wart disease. The official certifying agency in each of these countries or provinces is responsible for approving nurseries and maintaining a list of those that have been approved.

FROM ALL OTHER COUNTRIES

Plants and plant parts from all other countries must be free of sand, soil or earth with certain exceptions which do not apply to shrubs.

Import Inspection

Unless otherwise directed by an inspector, nursery stock entering Canada shall be inspected at one of the ports of importation before being allowed to proceed to destination. It cannot be moved from this port until a certificate of inspection or of clearance has been issued by an inspector and, if allowed to proceed to its destination for inspection, shall not be unpacked before the arrival of an inspector.

Treatment Of Infested Or Infected Nursery Stock

Where, on inspection, any nursery stock is found infested or infected with any pest or disease, it shall be subjected to treatment or destroyed, to the extent deemed necessary by the inspector. Package and packing also may be destroyed. At the discretion of the inspector and where no apparent danger exists, condemned nursery stock may be returned to the shipper, but all details and costs relating to the return of the stock shall be arranged between the importer and the shipper.

Charges

All charges for storage, demurrage, cartage, labor, and delays incident to inspection and cost of treatment or destruction, other than the services of an inspector, and any risk or damage incurred through any such action, shall be borne by the importer.

Compensation

Compensation not exceeding two-thirds of the value, assessed by the inspector, of the plants or containers thereof, destroyed by the instructions of an inspector, may be granted by the Governor in Council upon the recommendation of the Minister, except in any case in which plants or containers are destroyed on the order or at the direction of the government of a province which does not grant compensation in such cases.

Delivery Of Shipment From Customs

Nursery stock may not be delivered to you unless you present your permit to import; a certificate of inspection or of clearance, signed by an inspector, has been filed with the Collector of Customs at the port of importation; and a copy of either certificate is on file at the port from which the nursery stock is to clear Customs.

Duty

All commercial shipments of nursery stock to Canada are subject to the ordinary provisions of the Canadian Customs tariff.

If a resident of Canada makes a casual trip to the U.S. and returns immediately with purchased nursery stock, it will be subject to duty. However, in such instances, the 11 percent sales tax as applied to other commodities would not apply.

If, however, a resident of Canada remains in the U.S. for more than 48 hours and has not used his tariff exemption for a period of four months before the date of his return, any nursery stock actually carried with him could be entered free of duty. However, a permit to import as well as a valid certificate of inspection must accompany the plants and, of course, they will be inspected at the port of importation.

Occasionally relatives and friends of Canadian residents ship a small shrub or tree to them in Canada, purely as a gift. If the value of this is not over $10, it will be allowed entry to Canada free of duty but, of course, subject to certification at origin and inspection on arrival. This category does NOT include plants or shrubs shipped by a commercial firm or nursery in the U.S. to a resident of Canada, as such a shipment would be subject to duty.

Movement Of Living Plant Material From One Point In The U.S. To A Second, Including Alaska, Via Canada

In order to ship plants from one point to another in the United States, especially to Alaska from "Outside", which is the Alaskan's name for the rest of the states, it is sometimes necessary that the shipment cross part of Canada.

In this case a plant health certificate in duplicate must be obtained by the person moving the plants. This certificate must be issued, dated, and signed by an authorized state or Federal inspector at or near the point where plants are grown or leave the U.S. and must be based on inspection of the plants just before departure. The number and kinds of plants should be entered on the certificate, which should also be marked "in transit via Canada."

One copy of the health certificate must be presented to the Canadian Customs at point of entry into Canada and the second copy of the certificate must be retained for presentation to the U.S. Customs at point of re-entry into the U.S. When the above requirements have been met, no permit is required from the Plant Protection Division of the Canadian Department of Agriculture: it being understood that neither the plants nor the packing will be disposed of in Canada. The reverse procedure applies when plants are moved from one point in Canada, via the United States, to another point in Canada: duplicate certificates issued by Canadian inspectors, must be obtained.

Restricted Movement Of Plants Within Canada (From Province To Province)

Movement Prohibited

The movement within Canada of the following genera of plants is prohibited:

Corylus (hazel, cob and filbert, except seeds) to British Columbia from any other province in Canada.

Plants, including seeds of *Berberis, Mahonia* and *Mahoberberis* except those species, hybrids, and horticultural varieties which have been determined to be immune to black stem-rust of wheat, from any province to any other province.

Plants, including seeds of buckthorns (*Rhamnus*) except such species determined to be immune to

crown rust of oats, from any province to any other province.

Plants (including trees, rootstock, cuttings, scions, budsticks, fresh fruits and seeds) of all species, hybrids, and horticultural varieties of peach and nectarine (*Prunus*) to British Columbia from Ontario.

Movement Restricted

The movement within Canada of the following plants is prohibited EXCEPT in accordance with certain regulations of inspection and certification or fumigation:

All species, hybrids, and horticultural varieties, including flowering forms of almond, apple, apricot, cherry, chokecherry, hawthorn (*Crataegus* species), pear, plum, and quince trees, plants and parts thereof, including fresh fruits and seeds thereof and any living stage of Oriental fruit moth from any province in Canada to British Columbia unless fumigated, and accompanied by a certificate of origin if from a province other than Ontario.

All species, hybrids, and horticultural varieties of cherry and chokecherry, including trees, rootstock, cuttings, scions, and budsticks from British Columbia to any other province, unless inspected during the growing season in a nursery or other source and believed free from virus diseases Little Cherry, Twisted Leaf and Lambert Mottle.

All species, hybrids and horticultural varieties of peach and nectarine, including trees, rootstock, cuttings, scions, budsticks, fresh fruit, and seeds from any province other than Ontario to British Columbia, unless a certificate of origin accompanies the shipment.

Conclusion

Don't let this chapter lead you to think that importing is fantastically complicated. It would be if all the "ifs, ands and buts" applied to the few shrubs you might want to import, but they won't. Many gardeners have imported and continue to import plants, including shrubs. Most of the time the plants are received in good condition. Sometimes they are not. This is the risk you take in importing plants and you should understand this.

If the plants that you wished to import were not approved for entry, do not start cussing the regulations. Most of them are sensible and reasonable and are intended to safeguard your country from pests of one kind or another that are not already found there.

No one who has seen the destruction that has been wrought in the United States by either the

Japanese beetle (I've seen every leaf eaten off grape vines and most of the grapes injured) or the Dutch elm disease (I've also seen streets in New England towns bare to the sun, with every stately elm cut down, a victim to this disease) can question the need of regulation or inspection.

Just remember that both of these pests "sneaked" into the United States and that the authorities are trying their best not to let others get in to cause similar destruction.

I could give statistics of the annual damage to the corn crop by the European corn borer, and so on, but I don't think it is necessary. If you are a good citizen and a thinking person (and most gardeners are both), you will be the first to appreciate the protection these regulations give your garden.

The fact that $14,000,000 worth of plants were imported into the United States in one year, recently, bears out my premise that this isn't too hard to do.

Photo courtesy of U.S. Department of Agriculture

The fungus disease called black stem-rust which infects wheat (and also oats, barley and rye) costs farmers several million bushels of grain annually. This pest spends one part of its life on common barberry (*Berberis vulgaris*). Shown here are the cup-like growths which develop on the undersides of barberry leaves from the fungus spores. When these cups mature and shoot spores into the air the wind will scatter them. Should they fall on grain plants they will cause infection of stems and another crop of lightweight, shriveled grain kernels will result.

No wonder that both the United States and Canada prohibit importation of plants of common barberry while permitting the harmless barberries (described in this book) to grow in gardens.

TABLE 1

SHRUBS INCLUDED IN THIS BOOK WHICH ARE <u>NOT</u> PROHIBITED ENTRY INTO THE U.S.A. OR ARE SUBJECT TO ENTRY UNDER POSTENTRY QUARANTINE

AS OF 9/2/61

The following shrub genera included in this book are allowed entry into the U.S. as of the date above. If the genus you wish to import is not listed, write to the Permit Section, Plant Quarantine Division, 209 River St., Hoboken, New Jersey, to find out its quarantine status BEFORE YOU ORDER THE PLANT. This will avoid having it rejected or delayed in transit.

Abelia	Caragana	Cotoneaster	Exochorda	Koelreuteria	Potentilla	Sambucus
Abeliophyllum	Ceanothus	Davidia	Forsythia	Leucothoë	Pyracantha	Spiraea
Amelanchier	Chaenomeles	Deutzia	Halesia	Lonicera	Rhamnus	Symphoricarpos
Aralia	Chionanthus	Diervilla	Hamamelis	Oxydendrum	Rhododendron (including Azalea)	Syringa
Buddleia	Clethra	Elaeagnus	Hypericum	Philadelphus	Rhodotypos	Tamarix
Callicarpa	Cornus	Enkianthus	Kalmia	Photinia	Rhus	Viburnum
Calluna	Cotinus	Erica	Kerria	Pieris	Robinia	Weigela

The following genera, whether plants or cuttings, from all sources except Canada, Europe, Asia Minor, and Mediterranean Africa, must be defoliated at the time of shipment if plants are entering at ports other than New York (including Hoboken, New Jersey) and Seattle: <u>Buxus</u>, <u>Crataegus</u> (except <u>C. monogyna</u> from Europe) <u>Cydonia</u>, and <u>Magnolia</u>. Defoliation is not required when entry is made through New York, Seattle or certain Canadian ports. The reason for the above regulation is that the citrus blackfly may be introduced on leaves.

TABLE 2

SHRUBS INCLUDED IN THIS BOOK WHICH ARE PROHIBITED FROM ENTERING THE U.S.A.

NAME OF SHRUB GENUS	FOREIGN COUNTRIES FROM WHICH ENTRY IS PROHIBITED	PEST WHICH MAKES IMPORTATION ILLEGAL
Aesculus, all species	Czechoslovakia, England, Germany	Horse-chestnut variegation virus
Berberis, all species NOT designated RESISTANT to black-stem rust of wheat	All foreign countries	Black-stem rust
Berberis, all species designated RESISTANT to black-stem rust	All foreign countries if destined to eradication states*	Black-stem rust
Seeds of all species of Berberis	All foreign countries	Black-stem rust
Corylus, all species	Canadian provinces east of Manitoba when destined to California, Oregon or Washington	Filbert blight
Daphne, all species	New Zealand	Daphne mosaic virus
Euonymus, all species	Germany	Euonymus mosaic virus
Hibiscus, all species	India Sudan, Nigeria Trinidad	Yellow mosaic of okra Cotton leaf curl virus Mosaic-disease virus of okra
Hydrangea, all species	Germany	Hydrangea-virescence virus
Ilex, all species	England, France	Ilex-variegation virus
Laburnum, all species	Bulgaria, England, Germany	Laburnum-mosaic virus
Ligustrum, all species	Germany	Ligustrum-mosaic virus
Mahonia, all species NOT designated RESISTANT to black-stem rust of wheat	All foreign countries	Black-stem rust
Mahonia, all species designated RESISTANT to black-stem rust	All foreign countries	Black-stem rust
Seeds of all species of Mahonia	All foreign countries	Black-stem rust
Malus, all species except vegetatively-produced understocks	Austria China Europe Japan Korea	Leaf, branch & fruit fungus Branch canker fungus Brown rot of fruit Brown rot of fruit and Branch canker fungus Leaf, branch & fruit fungus
Prunus, all species	Germany Switzerland	Pox disease virus of sweet cherry Rigi cherry disease virus
Prunus, all species except vegetatively produced understocks	Europe, Asia, Africa, Oceania (including Australia & New Zealand)	A diversity of plant diseases
Prunus, all species	All foreign countries, except Canada, when destined to Calif.	A diversity of plant diseases
Ribes nigrum	England, New Zealand	Black Currant eel worm
Ribes nigrum (both plants and seeds)	All foreign countries when destined to states designated as non-infected #	White-pine blister-rust
Rosa, all species	Australia, Italy, New Zealand	Rose wilt virus
Salix, all species	England, The Netherlands	Watermark disease
Seeds of all kinds when pulp adheres to them	All foreign countries	Fruitflies

* Eradication states include: Colorado, Illinois, Indiana, Iowa, Kansas, Michigan, Minnesota, Missouri, Montana, Nebraska, North Dakota, Ohio, Pennsylvania, South Dakota, Virginia, Washington, West Virginia, Wisconsin and Wyoming.

States designated as non-infected include: Arizona, Colorado, Nevada, New Mexico and part of California.

TABLE 3

SHRUBS MENTIONED IN THIS BOOK WHICH MUST BE GROWN UNDER POSTENTRY QUARANTINE IN U.S.A.

NAME OF SHRUB GENUS	COUNTRIES FROM WHICH IMPORTED
Acer, all species	All foreign countries except Bulgaria, Canada, England, France, Germany, Japan
Aesculus, all species	All foreign countries except Canada, Czechoslovakia, England, Germany
Berberis, all species RESISTANT TO black-stem rust of wheat	All foreign countries
Crataegus monogyna	Europe
Corylus, all species	The Canadian province of Manitoba and provinces west thereof, when destined to California, Oregon and Washington
Cytisus, all species	All foreign countries except Bulgaria, Canada, England, Germany
Daphne, all species	All foreign countries except Canada and New Zealand
Euonymus, all species	All foreign countries except Germany
Hibiscus, all species	All foreign countries except Sudan, Nigeria, India and Trinidad
Hydrangea, all species	All foreign countries except Germany
Ilex, all species	All foreign countries except Canada, England, France
Laburnum, all species	All foreign countries except Bulgaria, Canada, England and Germany
Ligustrum, all species	All foreign countries except Canada and Germany
Mahonia, all species RESISTANT TO black stem-rust of wheat	All foreign countries
Malus, all species	All foreign countries except Canada
Prunus, all species, including stocks, when not prohibited entry	All foreign countries except Canada, and from Canada when destined to California
Ribes nigrum	All foreign countries except British Isles, Canada and New Zealand (These may not be grown under postentry quarantine in states designated as non-infected #)
Rosa, all species	All foreign countries except Australia, Canada, Italy and New Zealand
Rubus, all species	All foreign countries
Salix, all species	All European countries except England and The Netherlands
Sorbus, all species	All foreign countries except Canada, China, Germany, Japan, Philippine Islands and those in Southeastern Asia and Oceania (including Australia and New Zealand)

For list of states designated as non-infected see the bottom of Table 2

TABLE 4

SHRUBS MENTIONED IN THIS BOOK PROHIBITED ENTRY INTO CANADA

NAME OF SHRUB OR GENUS	EXCEPTIONS	COUNTRIES FROM WHICH IMPORTING IS NOT ALLOWED
Ornamental plants and plant parts WITH SOIL, etc. around roots	See table 5, entry 2	All countries except U.S. (but not including Hawaii), Belgium, Denmark, England, Wales, The Netherlands, Germany (Schleswig-Holstein & Oldenburg only)
Plants and seeds of species, hybrids, horticultural varieties of Berberis / Mahonia / Mahoberberis / SUSCEPTIBLE TO BLACK-STEM RUST OF WHEAT	Those IMMUNE to Black-stem rust See table 5 and *	All foreign countries
Plants, grafts cuttings & seeds of Ribes americanum / R. bracteosum / R. hudsonianum / R. nigrum / R. petiolare / (all currants) and horticultural varieties of same (but not fresh fruit of these) #		All foreign countries
Plants and seeds of all species of buckthorn (Rhamnus) SUSCEPTIBLE TO CROWN RUST OF OATS*	See *	All foreign countries
Plants, roots, cuttings of all species, hybrids and horticultural varieties of willows (Salix)		Europe

* List of immune varieties of Berberis, Mahonia and Mahoberberis and Rhamnus available from Plant Protection Division, Canada Department of Agriculture, Ottawa, Ontario.

Ribes nigrum (European black currant) is the only one of these currants mentioned in this book.

TABLE 5

SHRUBS MENTIONED IN THIS BOOK PROHIBITED FROM IMPORTATION INTO CANADA EXCEPT WITH SPECIAL CERTIFICATION

NAME OF SHRUB OR TYPE OF PLANT	ENTRY PROHIBITED FROM:	BUT NOT INCLUDING	CERTIFICATE NEEDED*	PEST BEING CONTROLLED
1 – Ornamental plants and plant parts WITH SOIL, etc. around roots	Belgium, Denmark, England, Wales, The Netherlands, Schleswig-Holstein and Oldenburg in Germany		A, B	Golden nematode Potato wart disease
2 – Ornamental plants and plant parts WITHOUT SOIL, etc. around roots (but not scions, and budsticks) or plants grown in media other than soil	Any country where golden nematode & potato wart disease OCCUR	U.S. (except Hawaii)	A, B	Golden nematode Potato wart disease
3 – Ornamental plants and plant parts WITHOUT SOIL, etc. around roots	Any country where golden nematode & potato wart disease are NOT KNOWN TO OCCUR	U.S. (except Hawaii)	A, B	Golden nematode Potato wart disease
4 – All nursery stock from gypsy moth or brown-tail moth areas		plants grown in and shipped from greenhouses	A, D	Gypsy moth Brown-tail moth
5 – All species, hybrids & horticultural varieties of Prunus cerasus, besseyi, persica, amygdalus, including rootstocks, cuttings, scions, budsticks	U.S. if destined to British Columbia and other provinces		A, C, E	Albino cherry Cherry buckskin Pink fruit Little cherry Twisted leaf Phony peach Peach mosaic Peach yellows Little peach Yellow leaf roll Oriental fruit moth
6 – All species, hybrids & horticultural varieties (including flowering forms) of Almond, Apple, Apricot, Cherry, Choke-cherry, Hawthorn (Crataegus), Nectarine, Peach, Pear, Plum and Quince — plants & parts thereof, including fresh fruit & seeds	U.S. if destined to British Columbia		A, C, E	Albino cherry Cherry buckskin Pink fruit Little cherry Twisted leaf Phony peach Peach mosaic Peach yellows Little peach Yellow leaf roll Oriental fruit moth

* See section of this chapter titled "Certificate of Inspection" page 120

Chapter 13

OTHER WAYS OF
ACQUIRING SHRUBS:
PROPAGATION

Growing Your Own

The next best thing to finding the shrub you want in your local nursery or listed by a reliable mail order firm is to know a friend or neighbor who owns that shrub. For then, if the laws of your state permit moving a piece of a plant with roots on without requiring the plant first to be inspected, and if the plant is of the type that grows with numerous stems from the ground, your problem is solved.

Division

Assuming the owner of the shrub is amenable, for most shrubs you need only dig from the outer edge of the plant a group of stems or shoots, with roots attached, take them home and plant them, and that's that. This should be done in early spring or after the leaves drop in fall. You now own the shrub, unless it happens to be one of the few kinds that are grafted on an understock that is a different kind of plant.

This process is called, in nursery parlance, "division." You divided your friend's shrub and took a piece or portion or division of it home. Since your shrub is actually a part of the parent plant, it will produce growth and blooms exactly like the parent. Kerrias, spireas, mock oranges and lilacs are among the shrubs that are easily divided. Just be sure you take a division of such size that it need not be nursed along for years. If you want more plants of the same shrub, you'll soon be able to grow them from this division you have just acquired.

It would be convenient, since division is the easiest possible way of propagating shrubs, if all shrubs might be propagated by this method. But most of them do not send out many shoots from their bases, so to get a new shrub from these you must use other methods.

Layering

If the shrub that you want and someone else owns has supple stems which may be easily bent to the ground without breaking, then it probably is possible to "layer" it. This process is akin to division since you make the plant grow its own "offset" or new plant, then divide or remove that from the parent after it has grown its own roots.

With shrubs which root readily, like forsythias or rose daphne, layering may be done in spring or early summer and often the young plant will be sufficiently rooted to be cut from the parent and transplanted in fall. Shrubs which take longer to form roots still may be layered in spring and the young plant removed early in summer of the following year. Or they may be layered in fall and the young plant removed the following fall. A few shrubs are so slow to form roots that it will take two full seasons of growth before the young plant can be separated from its parent.

Layering is an excellent method for the home gardener to use because it is easy and requires no special equipment. The number of layers that may be made from one shrub is limited only by the number of supple branches around its perimeter. Layering is widely used in European nurseries and is used in America for plants that do not come true from seed and that are hard to propagate by other methods.

SIMPLE LAYERING

Select one slim, young stem or slender branch that is long enough to reach the ground and is on the outer edge of the plant for ease in handling. Bend it to the ground, noting exactly where it touches the soil. Using a clean, sharp knife, wound the stem at this spot, on the side of the stem next to the ground when it is bent down.

Stems may be wounded in one of four ways: (1) by removing a narrow strip of bark all around the stem; (2) by making a cut into the stem, almost half way through it and inserting a pebble in the cut to keep it open; (3) making a slashing cut upward in the stem, almost half way through it; (4) making a V-shaped notch in the stem, extending almost half way through it. This last method is the one I prefer.

After the cut has been made, dust into it a minute amount of root-inducing hormone powder such as Hormodin 3, or Rootone (available at any garden supply store). This promotes rooting of some shrubs. On others, it seems to have no effect, but since it costs only a few cents and often helps, its use should be routine. Remove the leaves for a few inches either side of the wound. Bend the branch to the ground again and anchor it in place, using a forked stick, a stone, or a U-shaped piece of wire turned upside down with ends thrust into the ground either side of the stem. The idea is to keep the rest of the branch, that portion between the wound and the tip, above ground: only the wounded area underground. Heap soil, preferably sandy soil or a mixture of soil, peat and sand, over the wounded area to a depth of 3 to 5

Simple layering: Bend stem to ground, wound underside where it touches ground. Bend to soil once more, anchor it in place, and heap soil over wounded stem. Keep soil moist and roots will grow from wound.

inches. If the soil under the wounded area is not light and does not have plenty of organic matter in it, it also will help root growth if you mix sand and peat with it.

The soil both above and below the wounded area should be kept moist, always. In time roots will grow from the cut into the soil. When these have grown sufficiently so that they can support the tops of a new plant, cut the branch between the parent plant and the youngster and move the latter wherever you want it to grow.

SERPENTINE LAYERING

When branches are especially long and pliable as on some shrub roses, and you want several more plants of the same shrub it is possible to wound a long branch in several places, always, of course, on the side of the branch that touches the soil when it is bent down. Wounds should be so spaced that there are several leaves or leaf buds between them. The wounded areas are bent to the ground and anchored as previously described. The portions of the branch between cuts are arched slightly and allowed to remain above ground. Since this means that the finished layer looks rather like a snake, the name of this type of layering becomes obvious. It is possible to sink pots into the ground under each wounded area so that the roots grow into the pots. This makes it even easier to transplant the young plants later, when cuts are made along the branch between each layer to allow the youngsters to be moved.

MOUND LAYERING

When shrubs have stiff branches like deutzias and mock oranges, that do not lend themselves to bending to the soil, another method of layering can be used to propagate them. This process starts one year and finishes two years later, the long time being the reason it is not more generally used.

The first year the plant to be mound layered is cut back severely to encourage it to grow many shoots from the base. The next year, in spring, soil is mounded around the base of the plant. New shoots, as they grow from the roots, will root in this soil mound, the additional roots forming at the "nodes" of the shoots. If you will look at a branch of any shrub, you will see that there are distinct places from which leaves or buds grow and areas between these places where no leaves or buds grow. Leaves or buds grow from a branch at a "node." The areas between nodes are called "internodes." Roots usually form most readily from nodes—a convenient fact, useful in any type of propagation.

AIR LAYERING

A fourth type of layering is called "air" layering because it is done up in the air instead of bringing stems in contact with the soil. This method is used to propagate plants with very tall, almost rigid stems or plants hard to reproduce by other means. The same type of wound is made as in simple or serpentine layering, wherever you wish roots to form, the hormone powder is dusted into the wound, and then a little damp sphagnum (pronounced sfág-num) moss is moulded around the wound and a handful is tied to the branch over the wounded area. A sheet of polyethylene plastic is placed over the moss and wrapped to overlap so that no moisture can evaporate from the moss in-

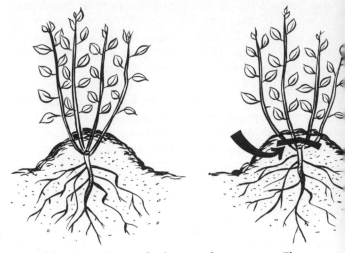

Mound layering: Prune shrub severely one year. The next year, mound soil around base. New shoots will grow from roots and form their own roots in soil mound.

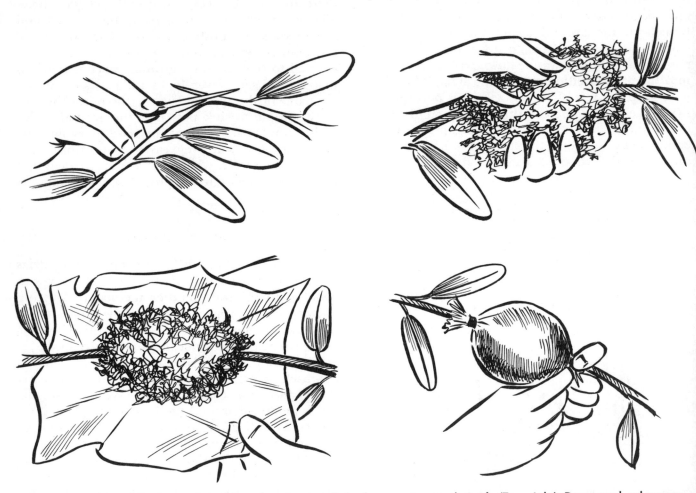

Air layering: (Top left) Stem of growing plant is wounded where roots are desired. (Top right) Dampened sphagnum moss is moulded around wound. (Lower left) Sheet of polyethylene plastic is wrapped around moss; (Lower right) and fastened firmly to branch or stem so no moisture will be lost from moss. Roots will form in time from wound and will grow in moss (can be seen through plastic).

side and no rain can penetrate to soak the moss. Sphagnum moss is available from bogs (if you have one handy), from greenhouses, florists, or nurseries. Garden supply stores sell a kit which contains all necessities for air layering, including sphagnum.

Bind the ends of the plastic with strips of plastic tape or electrician's tape to hold the plastic to the branch as well as to seal the covering over the moss. Thus, while the polyethylene permits passage of air, the moisture in the moss remains constant and very little after-care is required. Air layers have been known to need no care for a year when polyethylene has been correctly applied. If you are worried about the state of affairs, open the plastic occasionally to see if all is well, adding a little water if it is needed.

Air layering may be done during spring or summer, but is best done in spring as then roots usually will be formed by fall. Air layers made in summer usually do not root until the following spring, though much depends on the kind of plant being air layered. No additional protection of the layered area is necessary during winter.

In due course of time roots will grow from the wound into the moss. Sometimes you can see them through the plastic covering. Other times you must loosen the plastic to see if they have grown. When the moss ball is well filled with roots, cut the young plant from the parent, removing the plastic but leaving the moss in place. Plant the youngster with the moss still around its roots. Water well and give the usual care that you would give any shrub after planting.

All of these methods, as well as other methods of layering, will produce plants with characteristics identical with the parent plant because, as in division, the new plant is actually a part of the parent plant. A portion of the parent plant also is used for another method of propagation—by cuttings.

Cuttings

TYPES

There are several different kinds of cuttings, named for the part that is removed from the parent plant, as stem, root, or leaf cuttings. Shrubs are most frequently and usually most satisfactorily propagated by stem cuttings so this is the only type that will be considered in this book.

Stem cuttings, that is pieces of the stems of the parent plant, may be removed from the parent at various times of year, when the parent is in various stages of growth. Early in the season, when the new growth on the parent plant is still "soft" and easily manipulated with the hand, the cuttings are called "softwood" or "green" since they are taken from immature, "green" or succulent parts of the plant.

Later in the season, in July and August, when branches have "hardened" somewhat, the cuttings taken then are called "half-ripened" or "semi-hardwood." Still later, in the fall, when the season's growth is mature, "hardwood" cuttings may be taken from the parent plant.

The best time of year to take cuttings depends on the particular genus and species of the parent plant. In general, the harder the wood of the plant, the earlier in the season the cuttings should be taken. The lists at the end of this chapter indicate the season or seasons at which cuttings may be taken advantageously from various shrubs. Sometimes cuttings may be taken at several different seasons from the same kind of shrub.

There is no set length for a cutting, other than the irreducible minimum of one node for root formation, one node for top growth and, of course, the internode between them. A cutting this short may be made when only one small branch of the parent plant is available. But usually three to four or four to five nodes are used for a single cutting.

SOFTWOOD CUTTINGS

There are two requirements for a parent from which softwood cuttings are to be taken. The first is that the shrub be in vigorous growth and excellent health. The second is that the wood be at such a stage of growth that the top of a branch will snap off like a snap bean (break off cleanly all across) when bent over. If it bends rather than breaks, the wood is too old for softwood cuttings.

Assuming the parent plant meets both requirements, take pieces from tips of branches, from wood that grew during the current season and that has leaves unfolded and mature. Take the branch tips to a cool, shaded place and here make the cuttings, meanwhile keeping the branches covered with moistened burlap.

Cuttings will vary in length according to the length of the internodes of the plant you are propagating. Unless you are short of cutting wood, cuttings should have three or four nodes when finished. You can make one cutting from the tip of each branch or make several from one branch. Use a clean, sharp knife to make cuttings of any kind: sharp so it does not leave irregularities in the cut, clean so it does not transmit disease. Usually, with softwood cuttings, it is a good idea to cut just under a node but this is not absolutely necessary, except

Lower leaf is removed from cutting as it would decay in rooting medium. Here is cutting ready for insertion in medium. Note that leaf area has been reduced by cutting off part of each leaf.

with plants having hollow stems like philadelphus. Softwood cuttings usually root easily from almost any part placed underground. Make the cut at a 45 degree angle across the stem.

Remove all leaves from the lower third of the cutting so that they will not be in the rooting medium and decay there. If upper leaves are very large, reduce their size by cutting off part of each. Except for removing what is necessary, remember, at this time, that the more foliage you can leave (without having leaves wilt), the better. Any flower buds on a cutting should be removed. The best time to make cuttings is in early morning. After each is made, wrap it in damp paper or cloth or pop it into a polyethylene plastic bag so that it keeps fresh. Under no circumstances allow cuttings to dry out.

When you have made all the cuttings you wish, plus a few extra to make up for those that do not root, it is time to plant them. For this you need a special rooting medium and a special place. Both of these are discussed beginning in the column to the right.

SEMI-HARDWOOD OR HALF-RIPENED CUTTINGS

These are taken when wood is partly matured, during summer (July and August) and even sometimes into early September. The exact time will depend on the growth stage of the plant you are propagating. The wood should still be brittle enough to snap across when you bend it double. Cuttings from branch tips should be taken 4 to 6 inches long, with a clean cut made just below a node.

Because softwood or semi-hardwood cuttings of some species seem to root more readily when a bit of the branch is left attached to the cutting, such "heels" often are left. To take a cutting with a "heel," select a side shoot and pull it downward to separate it from the branch. As it comes off, a bit of the branch will adhere to it, both above and below. This adhering part of the branch is the "heel." The letter "H" following the name of the shrub in the lists at the end of this chapter indicates that a heel is a desirable addition to cuttings of that shrub.

Handling Softwood and Half-Ripened Cuttings

Rooting Mediums

Rooting mediums should have the following properties: be able to hold cuttings upright, be as sterile as possible so as not to support disease, be loose so that there is good aeration around the rooting cutting, yet hold moisture. These mediums (and some others) meet these requirements: sharp,

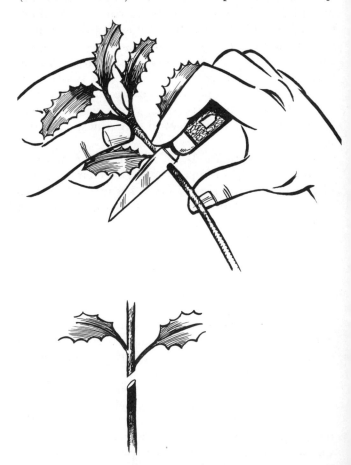

Cuttings: Stem of holly being made into tip cutting; cut is made directly under a leaf.

clean sand (mason's or builder's #2 grade); vermiculite (exploded mica); Perlite, a mixture of 50 percent vermiculite and 50 percent perlite, and sphagnum moss. In some cases sphagnum is used as it comes from the bale, merely shredded with the hands; in others it is milled (ground) before using.

A good rooting medium to use for broad-leaved evergreen shrubs which grow best in acid soil is composed of 75 percent peat moss and 25 percent granular styrofoam.

Probably the best place to put whichever rooting medium you decide to use is in a cold frame. In the case of half-ripened cuttings a cold frame is almost a necessity because of the time of year the cuttings are taken. They must be protected from the winter cold in some way, since it will take 5-15 weeks for them to root and sometimes more than that.

An inexpensive cold frame may be made from a window frame and sash bought at a second-hand lumber yard.

If you do not own a cold frame and wish to root just a few cuttings, try a "double flowerpot." For this propagator you need a 3-inch pot (measured across the top of the pot), and a larger, flattish pot, called a "pan." Plug the drainage hole in the bottom of the 3-inch pot with a small cork. Hold the small pot in the center of the larger one so that the

Pot-within-a-pot: Cuttings are inserted in rooting medium placed in large, flat flower pot (called bulb pan). Small pot is set in center of large one, drainage hole having been plugged with cork. Water is put into small pot, gradually seeps into growing medium, thus providing the proper amount of moisture.

rim of the little one is level with that of the big one. Fill the space below and around the little pot with whichever rooting medium you have selected.

The idea of the pot within a pot is that the small one is kept filled with water. Since the hole in the bottom is plugged with a cork, there will be only gradual seepage of water into the rooting medium. Thus it will be kept evenly moist yet never too wet.

The double pot must be set in a shaded place. A tent-like cover of polyethylene plastic may be set over it to keep moisture in. Make this by cutting several wire coat hangers and rebending them into U-shape, like croquet wickets. Stick the ends of these U's into the ground over the pot and drape the plastic over these supports, anchoring the ends with soil. If it gets too hot and humid under the plastic, slit it here and there for additional ventilation, and cover the plastic with burlap or newspaper between 11 A.M. and 2 P.M. You can buy a kit which includes a wooden framework large enough to hold two flats or several pans, wire to curve over, and a plastic cover complete with vents.

For more than a very few cuttings, you can make a propagating bed in a shady, sheltered place outdoors by simply digging out the soil to a depth of 4 inches and replacing it with vermiculite or another rooting medium. Plant the cuttings in this, spacing them half an inch apart, and put a plastic "tent" over them. Just before you insert the cuttings into the rooting medium, it is a good idea to treat the base ends with a root-inducing hormone powder.

Water the rooting medium just before inserting cuttings. Push a third of their length into the medium if rooting them where humidity is high; half of their length if rooting outdoors. Water again when they have been inserted. This second watering settles the medium around the cuttings. Don't forget to label cuttings with the name of the plant from which they were taken and the date on which you made them.

Aftercare

For the first ten days at least, the cuttings need to be shaded and the rooting medium should be kept always moist, never waterlogged. After this, though broad-leaved evergreen cuttings may continue rooting in the shade, those of deciduous shrubs will need a little sun. Adjust the light accordingly.

You can usually tell when roots are forming by the appearance of new top growth. It is also possible to investigate root growth by pushing a bit of the rooting medium aside with a finger and looking at the roots.

Softwood cuttings usually root quicker and easier than other types, though they do require more attention to prevent leaves wilting. They take from 2 to 12 weeks to root and will respond more to higher temperature than other types of cuttings taken later in the season.

When roots are at least an inch long, softwood cuttings may be potted into separate pots or planted in flats or cold frames. This must be done soon after rooting takes place since rooting mediums have little or no nourishment in them, depending on which medium you use. If a peat-styrofoam mixture is used, even softwood cuttings can be left in it over winter. Half-ripened cuttings are left in the frame during winter; transplanted in spring. Some may take that long to root. The more mature the wood from which these cuttings were taken, the longer it will take for roots to form.

If you have only a few cuttings, make a little bed in a protected corner of the garden and transplant cuttings to this, spacing them 6 to 8 inches apart. Or pot them and sink the pots to the rims in such a bed. Keep cuttings well shaded for at least two weeks after transplanting.

If roots are well established in late autumn, the cuttings may be left as they are for the winter and protected from heaving and thawing of the soil by a straw covering, placed after soil is frozen. In early spring you can move them to their permanent positions in the garden.

Rooting Cuttings under Mist

For about the past ten years, state universities and nurserymen have been experimenting with the use of a constant or an intermittent mist of water to keep leaves of cuttings (especially softwood cuttings) from wilting and to help rooting. With these systems no shading is necessary and plants may be rooted outdoors with great ease, even some kinds formerly thought difficult to root.

The gardener who wishes to try propagation under mist needs: (1) a mist nozzle, (2) a place where water is available so the nozzle may be used, (3) a propagating bed that is perfectly drained, (4) polyethylene plastic.

To make the propagating bed, level the area and put coarse drainage material (coarse gravel or crushed stone) over it to a depth of at least 2 inches. Over this put the rooting medium selected. Box the bed in with boards and peg them in place. Enclose the bed on three sides with polyethylene film supported on a wooden or metal framework. When enclosing the bed, consider the direction of the winds prevailing in your area, for wind can carry the mist away from the cuttings. A shield of plastic properly placed will prevent this.

Install the mist nozzle either in the bed or just outside it, so placed that the mist covers the bed area. The nozzle should use low pressure and may be connected by hose to the water supply. The nozzle is turned on only during the hot part of the day, during which time it may run either constantly or intermittently. Intermittent mist is even more satisfactory than constant mist but requires either a person willing to turn the water on and off or an electric time switch which will do the job.

Unless the nozzle has a very small opening and is carefully adjusted the propagating bed will be drenched and the cuttings will not thrive.

HARDWOOD CUTTINGS

These are taken from the plant when wood is mature or "hardened" after the leaves fall and up until mid-winter, but while the plant still is dormant or resting. A list of shrubs that may be propagated from hardwood cuttings is at the end of this chapter.

Select branches from wood of the current season's growth, that are about as thick as a lead pencil. Make cuttings with at least three to four nodes. Since the cuttings should be tied in little bundles and it is easy to confuse which end is up, make your top cuts straight across (square to) the stem, an inch or so above a node, and your bottom cuts just under a node and slanting across the stem. Thus the top and bottom of the cuttings will be marked in a way easily distinguished. Arrange cuttings of each kind of plant in your hand with tops up, level the bottoms against a table top or other surface, and tie the cuttings into bundles. Label each bundle with the name of the shrub from which the cuttings were taken.

The bundles now must be stored for the winter so that a "callus" will have time to form over the cut ends. This takes at least six to eight weeks, so cuttings must be made at least this long before planting time.

To store indoors one needs a dark cool cellar where temperature can either be controlled or will remain between 40 and 45 degrees F. If temperature can be controlled, store cuttings at 50 to 55 degrees the first month to promote quick callusing, then reduce temperature to between 40 and 45 degrees.

Lacking a cellar, the cuttings can be buried outdoors in a well drained place, in a hole dug to below the frost line.

When cuttings are to be stored indoors they should be buried in a box (preferably wooden) filled with sawdust, soil, sand, or peat, any of these materials being slightly moistened. When cuttings are buried outdoors, they are set into the hole either vertically or horizontally and slightly moistened sand, peat, sphagnum moss, sawdust, or light, sandy soil is packed around them.

As soon as ground can be worked in spring, take the cuttings from storage and plant them in rows in a place in full sun and near a water supply. Dig a V-shaped trench for the cuttings. If you wish them to remain in this place for several years, plant 9 inches to a foot apart and dig trenches 2 feet apart; if you intend to transplant them in fall or the following spring, plant 6 to 8 inches apart and dig trenches a foot apart. In any case, set cuttings so only the top bud or node is above ground, regardless of how many nodes the cutting has. Use sand or sandy soil to fill in around the cuttings. Firm the soil, leaving a slight depression at the top to hold water.

Except for watering as necessary (which will, of course, depend on the weather), no further care is necessary. By fall the cuttings should have sufficient roots to be transplanted where you wish them to grow. Or, you can, if you wish, leave them in the row over winter and transplant them in spring. And you also can leave them in the row for several years.

Grafting

There are still two other ways to increase shrubs by using a piece of the shrub you want to own. These are called "grafting" and "budding." They are similar to one another in that you apply a piece of the plant you want to a plant that is usually less desirable. They differ in plant parts used and in methods.

In grafting, the piece of the desired shrub is made to grow on another shrub by bringing together the growing layers of their stems and holding them together until they grow together.

The plant on which the graft is to be made usually is chosen because of its strong growth. It is called the "stock" or "understock" or "rootstock." This plant supplies roots and sometimes part of the stem of the new plant you are going to make. The piece of branch you take from the shrub you want is called a "scion" or "cion." This will become the top of the new plant.

It is essential that the understock and scion be closely related botanically; otherwise their growing layers will not knit together. Thus you graft holly on holly, rose on rose, and so on. If you wish to know the botanical relationship of shrubs you are considering grafting, go to the nearest library which owns the *Cyclopedia of American Horticulture*, edited by Liberty Hyde Bailey and Ethel Zoe Bailey, and look up the botanical relationships of the plants in the "Key to the Families and Genera" in Volume I. The more closely they are related, the more compatible they will be.

The plant to be the understock should be a strong seedling (which you probably will have to grow yourself since these are virtually unavailable) or a rooted cutting from one to three years old. It is best to decide which plants you will use for understocks in fall, since grafting is done in very early spring, just as the buds start to grow.

Scions are taken from the shrub you wish to multiply while that shrub is dormant (resting, minus leaves or flowers), either in very late fall or during winter or in earliest spring. Unless you are bringing scions from a distance, it is easier to cut a few scions in early spring and store them in a plastic bag in the refrigerator. However, if you must take them well ahead of time, tie them in small bundles, label them and bury them in sand or sawdust, using the same procedure as for hardwood cuttings.

In taking scion wood, select that which grew the previous season, because young wood unites more readily with the understock. Twigs that grew a foot or more during the past season are best. You can trace back from the tip of the twig to the first growth ring, readily visible on the twig, and thus measure how much growth was made during the season past.

There are numerous types of grafts, such as "splice," "whip," "side," "tongue," "cleft," "bridge," etc., but only two will be discussed here: "splice" grafting because it is most used with shrubs and is easiest; and "bridge" grafting because it sometimes offers the only way to save a shrub that has been girdled by rodents.

SPLICE GRAFTING

This is one of the easiest ways to graft and is used, usually, when stock and scion are about the same thickness. Both scion and understock are prepared by making, with a razor-sharp knife, diagonal cuts from an inch to two inches long, the stock being cut off at whatever height you wish to graft. The scion should have a "matching" cut made across the bottom. These cuts should be made as nearly alike in angle and in diameter as possible, the better to fit one to the other. The cut edges should be carefully fitted together so that the growing layers of stock and scion touch one another as far around the circumference of each part as possible.

The growing layer or cambium is the green layer, usually directly under the outer bark or skin of a branch. It grows between bark and wood. Cut across a branch and you'll see it plainly. This is the only part of a branch that grows and, in order to have the graft "take," the cambium of the scion must unite or grow together with that of the stock. This knitting together of stock and scion will take place *only when scion buds are dormant.*

It rarely is possible to have cambium layers touching all around the circumference of both stock and scion because the stock usually is thicker than the scion, but a substantial part of each *must touch.*

Once you have stock and scion correctly placed, bind them together so they stay in that position. Raffia, a dried grass from Italy, which comes in hanks and is available from nursery suppliers and seedmen who carry sundries, is the time-honored material to use. It is soft but not too soft, easy to handle, and will in time disintegrate by itself. Rubber bands or special grafting tape or waxed thin twine will do as well since they will break under pressure as the branch grows larger.

After stock and scion have been tied together, you may wish to cover the entire area of the graft with grafting wax obtained from a garden supply store, or ordinary paraffin from the kitchen. Either of these must be melted over hot water, allowed to cool so that it won't injure the plant but not so much that it begins to solidify, and then applied to

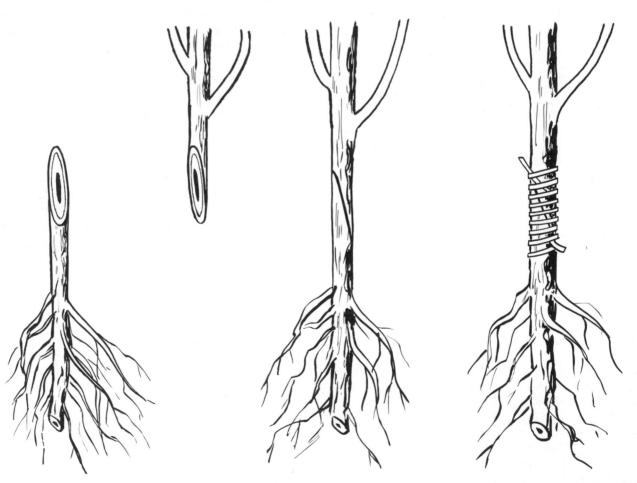

Splice grafting: (Left) Plant selected for rootstock has been cut off at an angle. (Second left) Scion of selected shrub is cut at the same angle. (Next sketch) The two are fitted together. The closer to the same diameter they are, the better, as then the cambium or growing layer of each will be easier to fit together. (Right-hand sketch) Scion has been fitted to rootstock and the two have been bound together. Grafting wax may be used to cover the area.

the area. This waxing seals the graft from air, infection, and mechanical injury—but it is not absolutely essential to the graft.

In due course of time, exact time depending on the species, the cambium layers of stock and scion will unite and growth of the scion will show when this has happened. Watch to see that the material used for binding stock and scion together does not stay intact and strangle the plant. After the scion has grown a foot or more you may loosen the ties if you wish. Otherwise no special aftercare is necessary, unless growth appears from the understock. As soon as you see it, remove it at the point of origin.

BRIDGE GRAFTING

When you discover, in early spring, that rabbits, mice, or what have you, have girdled (stripped and eaten bark all the way around) your favorite shrub, first aid is in order. If done as soon as you find the injury, bridge grafting may save the shrub.

In this type of grafting you actually bridge the gap where the bark no longer exists with several scions, splicing the cambium layer below the girdling with that above and thus allowing continued flow of nutrients and water within the plant. The number of scions used will depend on the circumference of the girdled plant. Use enough so that eventually they will grow together and replace the bark of the girdled portion. Even one scion used as a bridge may save the shrub. Two or even three may be used on a fair-sized shrub.

Scions should be taken while still dormant (though in an emergency they may be taken when buds have started to grow if these developing buds are immediately removed). Wood used should be from growth of the previous year which is from ¼ to ½ inch in diameter. Naturally the scions must be from a compatible or related species. Be sure, when making them, to mark which end of each scion is "up" by the same system as previously described under "Hardwood Cuttings."

Before grafting, prepare the injured area on your shrub by trimming off any loose or wounded bark until you have only healthy, undamaged tissue. Cut this back until there is a straight line of bark around the plant at both upper and lower edges of the girdled area.

Cut slots in the bark just above and just below the girdled area, each from 2 to 3 inches long and precisely the width of the scion to be inserted in each. Cut only through the bark, leaving a ½ to ¾-inch long flap of bark at each end of the slot and removing bark from the rest of the vertical

area you are preparing. Now, having tailored each slot to a specific scion, tailor scions to fit the slots, making each just long enough to fit into one pair of slots, plus enough extra length so the scion will be slightly bowed when inserted. This bowing is for two purposes: to allow for good contact between cambium layers of stock and scion, and to allow for necessary movement when the branch or trunk sways in the wind.

To tailor a scion, make long, smooth, slanting cuts on the same side of the scion, at both top and bottom of it, each cut the same length so the scion will fit smoothly when inserted into the slot. On the opposite side of the scion from these cuts, make ½-inch slanting cuts so that a scion actually will be wedge-shaped at either end. Trim off any buds on the scion, as these are not desirable.

Insert each scion in the slot made for it, pushing the top wedge of the scion under the flap of bark left for it at the top of the girdled area, with the long, slanting cut against branch or trunk. Then insert the bottom of the scion the same way. Check to make sure scions are right side up. Nail scions in place, using very small, flat-headed, wire nails. Use a nail through each flap of bark and more if necessary, so the scions will stay as you have placed them and not pull out of place. Cover the places where scions meet branch or trunk and the entire girdled area very carefully and thoroughly with grafting wax or paraffin. It is as important to keep air from the girdled area as from the places where scions touch branch because dried wood is not conducive to good growth of the shrub.

There is no reason to remove nails later, when scions have grown in place. But, if growth starts from buds on scions, be sure to remove these shoots.

Budding

Budding is a kind of grafting in which a single bud of a desired variety, with a bit of bark attached, is inserted into the stem of an understock. This operation is performed during late summer (late July to early September) when the bark "slips" easily—in other words may be readily separated or peeled from the wood of the stem or trunk.

Because of this timing, the bud scion material (called by the nurseryman "budstick") always is of the current year's growth. To make a budstick, first select a stem about the diameter of a pencil on the plant you want to propagate. Cut off all the leaves except a portion of the leaf stems (petioles) which you leave on to serve as "handles." Then cut a thin segment from this stem which includes the bark and the buds with their "handles" intact budders. This is your budstick.

Under normal circumstances you will cut a budstick from the plant you wish to own and then perform the budding operation. If, however, the plant you wish to own is at a distance and you are going to transport budsticks, put them in water or wrap them in polyethylene plastic bags to carry them. If you must store them, they will keep for several days in plastic bags, in a refrigerator at about 40 degrees.

The budding operation consists of cutting a single bud, with its attached bark above and below it (called a "shield") from the budstick, making a T-shaped cut in the BARK ONLY, not into the cambium of the stock, lifting the bark, and inserting the bud right side up UNDER the bark and ON TOP of the cambium layer of the stock. Since you can gently lift the bark with the tip of a budding knife and expose the cambium only when the bark slips easily, the reason for budding when this is possible (in late summer), becomes clear.

The bud, once it has been inserted in the T-shaped cut, must be gently pushed down until it fits snugly against the cambium. Some budders remove any wood in back of the bud before inserting it, to get a better fit. The bark is allowed to settle back in place and then the bud is tied into place, using rubber bands, special grafting rubbers, or grafting tape or raffia or similar materials. Rubber strips or tape may be cut in three weeks.

Early in the following spring, the top of the stock is cut off just above the bud you inserted, and the ties that held the bud in place are removed. By this time the bud should have grown firmly in place and the growth from it will become the top of the plant. If you wish to grow the plant in tree form, instead of as a shrub, cut off the top of the stock 6 inches above the bud and tie the stem that grows from the bud to this stub so it will grow vertically and straight. Watch budded plants to see if the understock tries to grow. If so, take off any growth at point of origin from the stock.

If, at this point, you wonder why anyone would graft or bud a plant when it is so much simpler to divide it, or to grow it by layering or from cuttings, the answer is that certain plants cannot be reproduced easily by those methods (and many

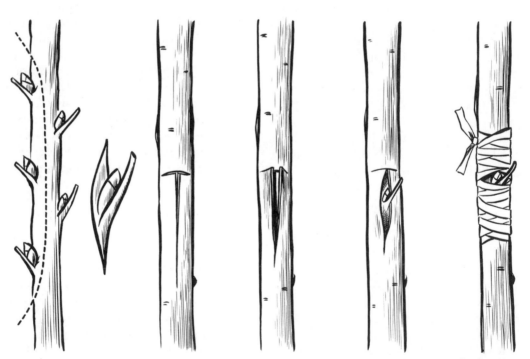

Budding: (Left) A "bud stick" is a piece of the desired shrub which has many buds on it (dotted line indicates "bud stick"). Leaves are removed but parts of their stems are left as "handles." One of the buds is selected (second left) and cut from the bud stick with a small bit of bark adhering above and below the bud and one leaf-stem handle. (Next sketch) A T-shaped cut is made through the *bark only* of the understock. (Next sketch) The bark is gently lifted; and (next sketch) the bud is inserted and pushed down until it fits snugly against the cambium layer under the bark. Bark is replaced over the bud. (Right-hand sketch) The bud is bound in place.

plants will not come "true" from seed) so the best way to propagate them is by grafting or budding. These two processes also are used when plants do not grow strongly on their own roots, or to make "weeping" forms of shrubs or trees.

Grafting or budding also may be used to solve the problem of pollination, as when a female holly plant is not producing berries and obviously needs pollen from male flowers. In such a case one or several branches of a male holly may be grafted or buds budded onto the female plant.

LARGER PLANTS SOONER

The nurseryman uses grafting or budding for another purpose which is important to those who buy shrubs. He uses it to make a saleable sized plant more rapidly than he could by any other method. Most of the time this is satisfactory to the purchaser of the shrub, though a grafted or budded plant always needs an extra bit of supervision lest the understock produce shoots. If the graft or bud is close to where the soil line was where the plant grew previously, setting the plant so that the union is several inches below the soil line will discourage the understock from growing shoots.

In some cases, however, as in the grafting or budding of lilac on privet, this practice by nurserymen is decidedly undesirable. For one thing a disease may develop. For another, privet is a stronger grower than lilac and even though privet leaves are very different in appearance from lilac leaves, the uninitiated gardener may not notice that the understock has grown until the privet has outgrown the lilac and he sees the undistinguished white flowers of privet where before he had large, beautiful lilac blooms.

This type of undesirable growth is not restricted to privet. At the moment I have two caraganas which must have been grafted or budded on *Caragana arborescens* for the shoots from the understock have leaves of that species, though the plants are of *C. arborescens* 'Lorbergii'. The only thing to do is cut off these *arborescens* shoots. Then, each year, I must watch to see that they do not grow again.

My *Viburnum carlesii*, since it was allowed to grow for picture purposes, is now a dual shrub— the lower part *Viburnum carlesii*, the upper and much larger part, *Viburnum lantana*. *Carlesii* was budded onto *lantana* because *lantana* is a strong-rooting shrub which *carlesii* is not. However, I would much prefer the less sturdy growth of *carlesii* on its own roots than the chore of hacking back and keeping back the *lantana* growth.

These examples are given to show you that more than one kind of shrub is grafted or budded on an understock by the nurseryman and that, in every case, the understock may become a problem to the gardener who owns the shrub. Thus the gardener must be ever watchful.

In the case of roses, the most popular outdoor plant in America today, this problem becomes acute, for roses are grown in innumerable localities where winters are sufficiently cold to kill the named variety top which has been budded onto a rootstock. In this case, unless plants are carefully protected, the gardener will be shocked to find that the big, beautifully colored flowers of the named variety he bought have been replaced by the smaller, definitely less desirable, flowers of the understock (see Chapter 7 for further discussion of this subject.)

Before leaving this interesting subject of growing a new plant from a piece of an existing one, an important point must be made. This is that cultivars of shrubs ALWAYS MUST be propagated by one of the methods previously described for any of these will produce a plant resembling the parent, whereas propagating by seed will not, as you will see when you read on.

Seedage

Shrubs may, of course, be grown from seed. Some that grow very easily in this way will present you with "volunteer" seedlings each year, under or near the female parent plant. If you grow these to flowering size, you will often find that their flowers do not exactly resemble those of the plant you found them under. This is because they probably had two parents, not just one as did the plants reproduced by the methods already described. Therefore they have inheritance that is far wider than the one-parent plants and often do not come "true" from seed, that is, resemble either parent. Of course the female parent is the only one of which you are certain, unless you yourself have applied the pollen that produced the seed and have kept away all other pollen and thus are familiar with the flowers of the plant from which it came.

It is precisely because of this wide variation in plants grown from seeds that nurseries or people interested in new varieties grow shrubs from seeds. Among thousands of seedlings there may be one that has foliage or flowers or form noticeably different from any shrub of that genus or species already in commerce. This seedling may be named by the nursery or person propagating it and, in time, become a popular new cultivar.

If you will examine closely the flower of almost any shrub, you will see first the conspicuous parts, the petals, which are usually white or brightly colored. Around the outsides of the petals at their bases are shorter, green or greenish or sometimes other colored parts called "sepals." These two groups of parts, the petals collectively called "corolla" and the sepals collectively called "calyx," are held in a thickened part of the flower stem, which is called the "receptacle." The flower stem itself is called the "peduncle." All these parts you will see at a glance.

But, in the center of the flower, usually surrounded by the petals, there are smaller, less readily visible parts. These are of two different kinds. Near the center there is usually one, but sometimes several thickened parts; and around this or these, are more slender parts which vary in number. The thickened part is called the "pistil" and is the female organ; the slender parts are the "stamens," the male organs.

The stamens produce the pollen which, when deep yellow and ripe, may be deposited on the tip of the pistil. This tip, when ready for pollination is sticky and thus holds the pollen deposited on it. The pollen grain then germinates, grows a pollen tube downward, through the "style" (stem part of the pistil) to the "ovary" below. Reaching the ovary, the pollen grain unites with one of the "ovules" in the ovary, and fertilizes it. From this fertilized ovule a seed gradually develops. The ripened ovary becomes the fruit.

Flowers of a few shrubs lack some of these flower parts: petals in *Neviusia* or snow wreath and *Fothergilla,* pistils in *Alnus* or alder. In flowers of other shrubs, parts are more or less united (sepals in *Cephalanthus* or buttonbush, petals in *Lonicera* or honeysuckle, stamens in *Baccharis,* pistils in *Rhododendron*). However, most of the shrubs you may wish to grow from seed will have all the flower parts clearly visible.

There are two types of flowers in flowering plants, called "perfect" and "imperfect". The perfect flowers have both stamens and pistil or pistils, that is both male and female organs, in the center of the flower. Most shrubs have this kind of flower. The imperfect flowers have either stamens or pistil but not both.

Imperfect flowers are borne sometimes on the same plant as perfect ones; sometimes male flowers are borne on one part or several branches of a plant, female flowers on another part or branches of the same plant; and again, male and female flowers may be borne on separate plants.

When they are on separate plants it is obvious that, in order to get seeds, the gardener must own plants of both sexes (or graft or bud a part of a plant of one sex onto that of another) since the female flowers produce fruit and therefore seeds but not without pollination by pollen from a male flower. Holly (*Ilex*) is an excellent example of this type of plant—male flowers are borne on one plant, females on another. The gardener who wonders why his holly does not bear red berries should examine the flowers when they appear in May and see if they are male or female. If he then purchases a plant of the opposite sex, it should be set within 40 feet of the first one to insure good pollination.

Under normal circumstances, the wind, the bees, butterflies, or sometimes simply gravity will carry pollen from one flower to another on the same plant or from a flower of one plant to a flower on another plant and so seed is set.

Plants with perfect flowers usually will fertilize themselves or each other but occasionally the pollen from flowers of one plant will not fertilize flowers of the same plant. Such is the case with many varieties of fruit trees. Pollen from another tree of another variety is necessary to fertilize flowers of the first tree and produce the fruits which contain the seeds.

CONTROLLING PARENTAGE

When you want to control the parentage of the seed you wish to grow, you can select both parent plants. Remove the stamens as soon as the flower or flowers open on the plant selected as female parent, so that they cannot ripen pollen, and cover the flower or flowers with small plastic bags to prevent natural agencies from depositing pollen on the pistil. When the pollen is ripe on the plant selected as male parent, use a soft brush to remove a bit from the "anther" (tip) of a stamen, remove the cover over the flower on the female parent, and deposit the pollen on the sticky apex of the pistil. Then replace the cover over the pollinated flower. Under normal circumstances this flower will produce seeds and you will know the immediate parentage of that seed.

This still does not necessarily mean that the seedlings will resemble either parent, because ancestors also contribute to their appearance. But a percentage will resemble one parent or the other.

Assuming that you have made a cross of pollen from one parent onto the pistil of a flower of another parent, you next must wait for the fruits to ripen. This you also must do if you wish to collect seeds from naturally fertilized plants.

Ripeness usually is told by the changing color of the fruit. Holly berries change from green to red (sometimes first to yellow or orange), pods of Siberian pea from green to yellowish to brown. Drying and splitting of seed coverings also is a sign of ripeness. When these signs show you it is time, gather the fruits and, if necessary, treat them to extract the seeds. This is a very simple matter with such shrubs as Siberian pea (*Caragana*) because you need only split open the pods and harvest the seeds.

It is a little harder with shrubs that bear fleshy seeds like currants (*Ribes*) or honeysuckles (*Lonicera*) because you have to remove the flesh in order to get the seed. By soaking these seeds in water you can reduce the flesh to a soft mass. Then, with your fingers, you can separate seeds from flesh. Sometimes fleshy fruits are merely dried, then the seeds with dried flesh attached are planted. The same thing may be done with seeds that have appendages adhering to them, as maple (*Acer*).

With the seeds ready for planting, recall to your mind those volunteer seedlings that grew so well under and near the mother plant. This recollection gives you the right idea as to the environment you should try to reproduce in order that the seeds germinate (sprout) and grow well. A great many amateurs simply plant the seeds under the parent plant, but care for them by giving water when needed until they have sprouted and grown. This works well with seeds that are ready to sprout soon after they are planted, like ornamental horsechestnuts (*Aesculus*). They can be either planted right after they are harvested or stored outdoors, in a container, for the winter, then planted in spring.

But there is a little matter of individuality with seeds. Many of them do not sprout readily. Some don't because they are not chemically ready to sprout, others because the conditions necessary for growth are not satisfactory. Still others have hard seed coats which resist the penetration of the air and moisture necessary for sprouting.

DORMANCY

Those seeds that are not yet ready to germinate are said to be "dormant," which means resting. There are a number of reasons for dormancy, the first being the hard seed coat which will not permit penetration of the necessary oxygen and water. For the same reason, the bud inside the seed may not be able to penetrate outward. The temperature outside the seed may not be right (some seeds sprout only at certain temperatures). Or the light may not be right (some seeds need light to sprout, others will not sprout in light). Then again, there are times when the conditions inside the seed itself are not right for germination to take place. When two of these factors affect the seed dormancy, it is said to be "doubly dormant."

BREAKING DORMANCY

Something has to be done to break the dormancy if the seed is to be sprouted and grown. If the seed has a hard coat, there are three commonly used methods of circumventing it: (1) Put it in water which has just stopped boiling and let it soak in that water as it gradually cools for about 12 hours. (2) Treat with concentrated sulphuric acid. Pour this over the seeds which have been placed on or in an acid-proof container and stir the seeds until each has been coated with acid. This method requires great caution and some special equipment. (3) Use a small file to open the seed coat in one place. This method requires patience and a delicate touch.

Which one of the three methods you use will depend on the hardness of the coat of the particular seed. Seeds which have the hardest coats will require method #3.

STRATIFICATION

When dormancy is caused by conditions within the seed, the seed may merely need a period of after-ripening during which it is supposed that chemical changes take place in the seed which allow it to germinate. This period of after-ripening may be speeded up by a process known as "cold stratification." While the word "cold" still belongs in the name, since seeds are exposed to low temperatures as well as given moisture and air, the "stratification" usually does not belong since seeds are routinely mixed with whatever medium is selected to hold them rather than placed in layers between layers of the medium, as used to be the practice. Yet cold stratification is the term still commonly used.

Select the medium you prefer to mix the seeds with from sand (best for seeds that have pulp remaining around them), granulated peat moss (acid peat if plants are those requiring acid soil like rhododendrons), or shredded sphagnum moss. Find a container that will hold some of the medium plus the seeds. This could be a glass jar, a plastic bag, or a tin can. Mix the seeds with the moist (but not saturated) medium, or put them in layers between layers of the medium if you wish. Cover the jar or can to keep moisture in so that seeds will not dry out, but not so tightly as to keep all air out. Closed polyethylene plastic bags permit passage of air while retaining moisture. Store the containers in the refrigerator. A temperature of 40 degrees is an ideal one during stratification, but most refrigerators are set at about 45 degrees, a deviation too slight to cause any trouble. Look at the seeds occasionally and, if any show signs of sprouting, take them out and plant them. If it is winter, plant them in pots indoors.

Some seeds, like American hollies' (*Ilex opaca*), do not seem to be mature enough to sprout until about two years after they have been harvested. Do not despair when seeds you have fussed over do not respond in what seems to you a reasonable length of time. Maybe they just aren't ready to grow yet. Be patient!

The seeds which are doubly dormant may need several of these treatments before they will sprout. Try this treatment for them: mix seeds with the medium, store in a polyethylene bag at room temperature for four months, then in the refrigerator for another four months.

PLANTING SEEDS

Select a half-shaded place in the garden where soil is good. Prepare a bed by removing stones, mixing peat or sand with the existing soil if necessary, and tilling the soil until the texture is fine. Make the bed narrow enough so you can weed it by reaching in from either side. Sow the seeds by broadcasting over the surface of the bed, or make rows and sow in those. Cover lightly with sand. Keep the soil evenly moist but not wet. If it dries rapidly, put a piece of burlap over the surface to keep moisture in. The burlap, however, must be removed at first signs of growth.

If you make the bed in spring, keep weeding and watering it as needed. In about 30 days quite a few seeds should have sprouted. These should be kept in this seedbed until large enough to transplant. If you make the bed in fall, plan to protect seedlings from rodents. Bend a piece of wire screening so it will cover the bed. After planting the seeds and covering them with sand, put on the screening cover and leave the bed alone for winter. By spring many of the seeds will have grown and you may be able to transplant some.

Very fine seeds like those of rhododendron are stored for the winter and are sown in spring over the surface of flats or pots filled with sieved, moist, acid peat moss. They are not covered, just watered with the finest possible mist spray. The flat or pot is covered with glass or plastic, set in a warm, semi-dark place where the temperature is 65° to 70° F, and moved to a light, airy one when sprouting starts. Young seedlings are then moved into flats filled with 50 percent granulated Dutch or German peat and 50 percent Michigan peat. After ten months, move into the nursery row.

TRANSPLANTING

When seedlings are large enough they may be transplanted to a nursery row, where they are spaced from 6 to 9 inches apart, and grown there for a year or two (depending on the size of the plant), after which it is time to move them wherever you want them to grow to full size.

Most shrubs may be moved to a nursery bed made in the same manner as the seedling bed, though the soil need not be as fine and the bed should be in full sun. The acid-soil loving plants, sprouted in peat, are transplanted into a mixture of 1 part sand, 2 parts each of very acid peat and mildly acid or neutral peat. In this they can be grown for almost a year, after which they are transplanted again to a cold frame or a bed raised above the surrounding soil level, into a mixture of half garden soil and half granulated acid peat.

WINTER PROTECTION

All small seedlings require some protection from winter's cold. Covering the seedling bed with granulated corn cobs or straw or some other light mulch material is sufficient protection, but this covering should not be placed until after the soil is frozen, otherwise rodents may make their winter homes in it. The covering is intended to keep the soil frozen and thus avoid the alternate freezing and thawing of soil which might heave the seedlings out of the soil entirely. Chicken wire around the bed will protect seedlings from rodents.

Summing Up

It is easy to grow some shrubs from seed; not so easy to grow others. With these it may be a long, fussy process. But growing shrubs from seed can be an interesting hobby. Those truly interested in this method of propagating shrubs may want to purchase the *Woody Plant Seed Manual*, prepared by the Forest Service, U.S. Department of Agriculture (Miscellaneous Publication #654) available from the U.S. Government Printing Office, Washington, D.C. 20025.

Many gardeners find the other methods of propagating shrubs equally interesting as a hobby and are thrilled to see—several years from the time cuttings, layers, or grafts were made—first blooms on a shrub they have grown from a bit of the parent plant. Occasionally, a shrub is propagated by one method or the other because of sheer necessity—it is absolutely the only way to acquire that particular variety of plant.

It should always be borne in mind that many woody ornamental plants are patented. These may not be vegetatively propagated (that is, increased by any method other than seeds, which may not reproduce the desired plant) without the permission of the owner of the patent.

And, should you be one of the lucky ones to produce a shrub different from all others (which should be carefully checked with authorities at your nearest state university before you jump to conclusions), please take the trouble to name it correctly and thus avoid thwarting botanists, nurserymen and many others. Write for a free copy of "How to Name a New Plant," produced by the Committee on Nomenclature and Plant Name Registration of the American Association of Nurserymen, Inc., and available from the organization, 835 Southern Bldg., Washington, D.C. 20005. It is an excellent little leaflet.

WAYS OF PROPAGATING SHRUBS AND SMALL TREES

Note That Many Shrubs May Be Propagated In Several Ways
(D) Indicates a Difficult Method for that Shrub.

DIVISION

Some shrubs naturally sucker, as noted below. Suckers may be removed to make new plants.

Amorpha
Aralia (suckers)
Aronia (suckers)
Berberis (some)
Buxus
Calycanthus (suckers)
Cornus, species (suckers)
Corylus, some species (suckers)
Erica, species
Euonymus (some)
Hypericum calycinum
Kerria
Kolkwitzia
Mahonia aquifolium
Philadelphus
Prunus glandulosa (and cultivars)
Ribes odorata
Robinia (suckers)
Rubus (suckers)
Spiraea japonica & other dwarf varieties
Symphoricarpos (suckers)

LAYERING

(L) means it takes a long time for roots to form. Month indicates best time to layer.

Aesculus parviflora
Amelanchier
Amorpha
Andromeda (Aug.)
Aronia
Azaleas (May-June)
Berberis (some) (Apr.)
Chaenomeles (own root plants only)
  (June or July)
Cornus (spring)
Corylus (fall)
Cotoneaster (spring)
Crataegus
Cytisus (spring)
Daphne cneorum
Daphne genkwa
Elaegnus angustifolia
Elaeagnus umbellatum
Enkianthus
Erica
Euonymus (early summer)
Exochorda
Fothergilla
Halesia (spring)
Hamamelis (L)
Ilex (fall) (L)
Kalmia
Magnolia (early spring)
Philadelphus (fall)
Photinia
Pieris (fall)
Potentilla
Pyracantha
Rhododendron
Rhus
Ribes
Rosa
Staphylea
Stephanandra
Stewartia
Styrax
Symplocos
Syringa (early spring)
Vaccinium (fall)
Viburnum opulus & other varieties (June)
Zenobia

Tip layer --Rubus species

Mound layer--Calycanthus
  Cotoneaster
  Hydrangea arborescens,
    paniculata,
    quercifolia

CUTTINGS

(H) means with heel
(L) means it takes a long time for roots to form

Acer palmatum
Aesculus parviflora
Amelanchier
Amorpha
Aronia
Azalea (evergreen)
Buxus
Callicarpa
Calluna vulgaris
Calycanthus
Caryopteris
Ceanothus
Cephalanthus
Chamaedaphne
Clethra
Comptonia
Cornus florida,
Cornus kousa
Corylopsis (H)
Cytisus (H)
Deutzia
Diervilla
Eleagnus multiflora
Elscholtzia
Enkianthus
Euonymus
Exochorda
Fontanesia
Forsythia
Hibiscus

Hippophaë
Hydrangea species,
  H. macrophylla
Hypericum (H)
Kalmia
Kerria
Lavandula (H)
Ligustrum
Lonicera
Magnolia species
Photinia
Physocarpus
Pieris
Potentilla
Prinsepia sinensis
Prunus maritima
Prunus tomentosa
Prunus triloba
Rhodotypos
Salix
Sambucus
Spiraea
Staphylea
Stephanandra
Stewartia
Styrax
Symphoricarpos
Symplocos
Syringa (H)
Tamarix
Vitex

SEMI-HARDWOOD CUTTINGS

Abelia (H)
Andromeda
Azalea (evergreen and deciduous)
Berberis (H)
Buddleia alternifolia
Buddleia davidii
Buxus (H)
Caryopteris
Ceanothus
Chaenomeles
Clethra
Colutea
Cornus
Cotoneaster (H)
Cytisus (H)
Daphne burkwoodii 'Somerset'
Daphne cneorum
Daphne mezereum
Deutzia
Erica carnea
Euonymus
Exochorda
Forsythia
Hibiscus (H)
Hydrangea
Hypericum (H)
Ilex (D)
Kolkwitzia
Lavandula (H)
Lonicera
Magnolia (H, L)
Mahonia bealei
Philadelphus
Pieris
Potentilla
Pyracantha
Rhododendron

Rhus
Ribes
Rosa
Spiraea
Syringa
Viburnum x burkwoodii
Viburnum carlesii
Viburnum fragrans and others
Weigela

HARDWOOD CUTTINGS

Acanthopanax sieboldianus
Amorpha
Berberis
Buddleia alternifolia
Buddleia davidii
Buxus
Caryopteris
Ceanothus (H)
Cephalanthus
Chaenomeles
Cornus alba & varieties
Cornus -- others but not florida
Cotoneaster (evergreen) (H)
Cytisus
Deutzia (H)
Diervilla
Eleagnus angustifolia
Erica
Forsythia
Hibiscus
Hydrangea
Hypericum
Ilex (L)
Kerria (H)
Kolkwitzia
Laburnum watereri 'Vossii'
Ligustrum vulgare & others
Lonicera
Philadelphus
Physocarpus
Potentilla
Pyracantha
Rhododendron
Rhus
Ribes
Rosa
Salix
Sambucus
Spiraea
Symphoricarpos albus
Symphoricarpos orbiculatus
Syringa persica
Tamarix
Weigela

SEED

(I) means plant immediately when ripe
(ES) means sow in early spring
(S) means stratify
(L) means long to germinate, possibly two years.

Acer species (I or S)
Aesculus (I)
Amelanchier (S, L)
Amorpha
Andromeda (early spring)
Aronia
Azalea
Berberis thunbergii & others (S, ES)
Buddleia alternifolia
Buxus (L)
Callicarpa
Calycanthus
Caragana
Caryopteris
Ceanothus americanus
Cephalanthus
Cercis species

Chaenomeles (ES)
Chamaedaphne
Chionanthus
Clethra
Colutea (ES)
Comptonia
Cornus florida (S, L and other species ES)
Corylopsis
Cotinus coggygria
Cotoneaster (S, L)
Crataegus (L, S for 18 months)
Cytisus (ES)
Daphne mezereum (I or S)
Deutzia (ES)
Eleagnus (S, L)
Elscholtzia
Enkianthus (ES)
Erica (ES)
Euonymus (ES)
Exochorda (ES)
Fothergilla
Hamamelis (ES, L)
Hibiscus (ES)
Hippophaë
Hypericum (ES)
Ilex (L, S for 18 months)
Kalmia (ES)
Laburnum anagyroides (ES)
Lespedeza
Leucothoë
Ligustrum (I or S)
Lonicera (I or S)
Magnolia (S)
Mahonia (S, L)
Malus species (S)
Myrica
Paeonia suffruticosa
Philadelphus
Photinia
Physocarpus
Pieris
Potentilla (ES)
Prunus species
Pyracantha
Rhamnus
Rhododendron (ES)
Rhodotypos
Rhus
Ribes
Robinia (ES)
Rosa (I)
Sambucus (ES)
Sorbus
Spiraea (ES)
Staphylea
Styrax
Symphoricarpos
Symplocos
Syringa species (ES)
Viburnum (S, L)
Vitex
Weigela (ES)
Zenobia

GRAFT
(all cultivars in species listed below are grafted or budded)

Cornus florida rubra on C. f.	Laburnum
	Malus
Crataegus (April)	Prunus
Cytisus (May)	Rhododendron
Ligustrum	(& azalea)
(variegated on common)	Syringa on S. vulgaris (NOT on Ligustrum)
Hamamelis	
Hibiscus	

BUD

Crataegus	Rosa
Ilex	Sorbus
Malus	Syringa
Prunus	

144

PART IV: SHRUBS AND TREES TO KNOW AND GROW

Chapter 14

SHRUBS TO KNOW AND GROW

Explanations

The purpose of this chapter is to tell you, in quite a bit of detail, about the shrubs that are available for your garden. The *descriptions* are of the shrubs as I know them, through presently growing over a thousand, through previously having grown hundreds more, through observations in countless nurseries and thousands of gardens, including all major botanical gardens, in many parts of the world.

The *heights* given are those of the largest shrubs of each kind I ever have seen or, if the shrub was immature when I saw it, the height to which the nurseryman or the director of the botanical garden (if he knew) said it grew. In the case of the comparatively few shrubs that I have neither grown nor seen growing, the height given is that shown in standard reference books.

Flower sizes, where they are indicated, were measured by me in my own garden, several times in several different years, using a transparent ruler. *Flower colors,* where these are given, follow the Nickerson color fan, which is the color authority for this book. This fan, which I find extremely easy to hold next to a flower, is illustrated on this page. It was devised by Miss Dorothy Nickerson of the United States Department of Agriculture as a result of the work of a commission of the American Horticultural Council (now merged with the American Horticultural Society under the latter name) headed by R. Milton Carleton. The fan is published by Munsell Color Co., Inc. and is available from the American Horticultural Society, 1600 Bladensburg Rd., N.E., Washington 2, D.C.

Although the fan furnishes a simple, easy way to designate the color of a flower, it has, partly because of its simplicity, certain limitations. For instance, it lacks sufficient gradations of some colors, notably the yellows and the dark blues, to precisely match all flower and fruit colors. However, it is surprising how many flower colors may be matched so precisely with such a small, handy reference.

The names on the color fan are not always those one might use in describing the color of a flower. For instance, all catalogs and most gardeners refer to the flower color of double-flowering almond (*Prunus glandulosa* 'Sinensis') as "pink" when, according to the color fan, it is "strong purplish pink," 5RP 7/9. In this case the description given by the color fan is far more accurate than "pink."

Sometimes a *flower form* is described as "pea-shaped." By this I do not mean that it is round like a pea, but is shaped like the flower of either a sweet pea or an edible pea.

Single flowers have one row of petals. *Semi-double* flowers have several rows of petals, while *double* flowers may have so many petals that their form is ball-like. The reason that double flowers do not produce fruits is that the pollen-producing stamens (seen in the centers of single and semi-double flowers) have developed into petals. With-

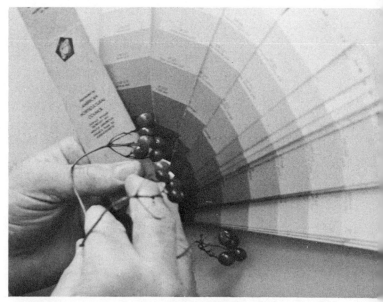

Nickerson color fan in use. Viburnum fruits held over fan to find matching color.

out pollen there can be no fruit or seed production. Thus double-flowered shrubs must be propagated by some vegetative means.

The *zones of hardiness*, or areas in which a given shrub will survive, are numbered according to those shown on the "Plant Hardiness Zone Map," Miscellaneous Publication Number 814, published by the Agricultural Research Service, United States Department of Agriculture, May, 1960 and available from the Superintendent of Documents, U.S. Government Printing Office, Washington, D.C. 20025, for 15 cents.

This map is reproduced on the insides of the covers of this book in the "adapted" version which is small and suitable for reproduction. A much larger map, with zones shown in colors, with finer gradations of zones into *a* (northerly) and *b* (southerly) and with all counties and large cities indicated, is part of Miscellaneous Publication Number 814. The larger version is the one you probably will wish to use to find the plant hardiness zone in which you live.

Both maps were compiled by a commission of the then American Horticultural Council with Dr. Henry Skinner, director of the National Arboretum, Washington, D.C., as chairman.

Degrees of shade which a plant will tolerate without ceasing to bloom are defined at the top of the list of shade tolerant plants in Chapter 3, page 21.

The *shrub listings* are alphabetical by *botanical names,* because the only way you can be sure of buying the shrub you want is by using these names. If you know only a common name, look first in the index where such names are given followed by the correct botanical name. Older botanical names, no longer correct, and incorrect catalog names are all listed as synonyms in parentheses following the currently correct botanical name. "Syn" has been used as an abbreviation for "synonymous with."

The "×" between genus and species names of a shrub (e.g. *Abelia* × *grandiflora*) indicates that it is a *hybrid* and its parents are those given in parentheses after the botanical name of the shrub (*A. chinensis* × *A. uniflora*). This information will be of value to nurserymen and gardeners hoping to propagate, for it means that seeds taken from the shrub are not at all likely to produce one identical with it.

Our cultivar designations do not have "×" in front of them to designate that they are hybrids but, in most cases, any binomial, that is a two-word name, of which the second name represents a cultivar is a hybrid.

I have followed the common practice of using only the initial of a generic name in discussions after the genus already has been named. Thus *Abelia grandiflora* is followed by *A. chinensis*.

In addition to as many synonyms as possible, I also have listed, following the botanical name of each shrub, as many *common names* as I have been able to find. Those used in standard reference books and in catalogs have been augmented by names of woody plants collected over a period of 30 years by R. Milton Carleton, compiler of "Index of Common Names of Herbaceous Plants."

As you will see, if you examine the common names listed for each shrub, these vary widely. In fact they may not be the same from state to state or from locality to locality, as explained in Chapter 2. Furthermore, if you will look at the variety of common names after, for instance, *Corylus avellana,* you will see why it is impossible and, in fact, downright silly to attempt to designate a shrub by a common name. Even if it has only one that is widely used, that one *cannot be depended upon* to be the only one. Step over the border into Canada or fly to London and the common name may change. The botanical name usually is identical in any country (the word "usually" is a disclaimer, to cover the times when the person from one country is using the currently correct name and the person from the other country is using an older name).

If you wish to know which plant is a variety and which a cultivar, with a view to determining a method of propagation, look at the way the name is written. All *cultivar names* are enclosed by *single quotation marks* and the first letter of the cultivar name is a capital. *Varietal* names are not set off and not capitalized. Names which are enclosed by *double quotation* marks are those not yet recognized by botanists—called "invalid." The shrub bearing such a name may vary from others and the nurseryman naming it realize this, but botanists simply haven't gotten around to recognizing it.

When I refer to "the species" in both Chapters 14 and 15, I mean the species to which the particular shrub belongs. For instance, *Kerria japonica* is the name of a species of shrubs. *Kerria japonica* 'Picta' differs from "the species," that is *K. japonica,* by having green and white leaves instead of plain green ones. It resembles "the species" in having single flowers. *Kerria japonica* 'Pleniflora' differs from "the species" because of its double flowers, although it resembles "the species" in growth habit and foliage color and form.

In order to make clear my descriptions of the *forms* of shrubs, I asked Clifton Wirth to walk around my shrub borders with me and pointed out

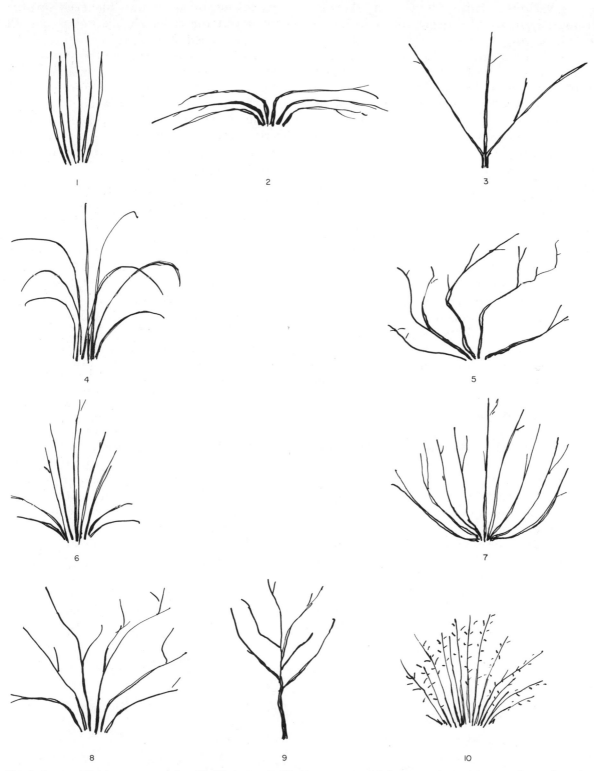

Shrub forms; (1) Narrow, upright, (2) Horizontal, (3) Few stems, widely spreading, (4) Upright and arching or "fountain" form, (5) Irregular, (6) Upright and spreading, (7) Upright with curving branches, (8) Upright, widely spreading, (9) "Tree" form or "standard" form with single stem, (10) Dense and compact.

to him the various forms. Then, from sketches made from the shrubs, he drew the outlines on the left. Thus, you always can refer to them if you wish to reconcile my words with your mental picture of what they mean. There are, of course, other shrub forms, but these are the most common therefore the ones you will meet and I shall describe most often.

The *natural habitat* of as many native shrubs as possible is given to serve as a guide as to whether a shrub will survive your climate. This information also should make you swell with pride that the northern part of the continent has so many natives worthy of cultivation in gardens.

Should you regard the planting of "native" plants with derision, may I remind you that all plants, except those known as "cultivars" are native to some part of the world.

Blooming times, given as early, mid-, or late in a certain month, are the times the shrubs bloom in my garden in hardiness Zone 5b. You can adjust the blooming time given to that in your garden by adding or subtracting a week for every 100 miles that you live north or south of me. This is on the theory that frost moves northward at the rate of 15 miles a day and that flower bloom depends on the time frost disappears—a theory that will not stand close analysis but which at least furnishes you a guide.

The black-and-white *pictures* in this and the following chapter were taken either by my husband or by me (mostly by him) of branches of shrubs growing in our garden. When we did not own the shrub or our shrub was small and either had not bloomed or would have been injured by cutting the blooming branch, we have been fortunate in "borrowing" branches from Mr. John Light, proprietor of Light's Tree Co., Richland, Michigan, whose nursery boasts the longest list of stock in Michigan. Whenever one or the other of us has made the across-the-state trip to his nursery, he has permitted us to cut branches of whichever shrubs were in bloom at the time. He maintains that the plants probably need pruning anyway.

These branches we have transported home with stems in water and then photographed as fast as possible (often continuing until midnight and later). A very few of the branches have been begged from owners of shrubs which have fruited a year when our own did not bear or for some similar reason and we are grateful to these people as well as to Mr. Light.

Because this book deals only with shrubs hardy from hardiness Zone 6 and northward, *shrubs listed in catalogs of· nurseries in Zone 7* which are *not hardy* in Zones 6 to 1 have been ignored.

In many cases a certain shrub is listed by only one nursery out of all those whose catalogs are the basis for this book. Because a disease or insect or act of God might easily wipe out the stock of a single nursery, I have in most cases also ignored these listings. Occasionally, when a shrub is particularly desirable for one reason or another, I have described it and listed it in the Buyer's Guide Chart *despite* its listing by only one or two nurseries. After all, even though the offerings of 214 nurseries are listed here, this still is only a sampling of nursery offerings in the United States and Canada.

In order that you get the most information from this chapter, I would suggest that you read the general discussion of a genus if there is one under the genus heading. This covers characteristics shared by members of the genus or, sometimes, ways in which they are used in the landscape.

Then go on to read the description of the particular species, variety or cultivar of shrub that interests you.

For more ready reference the main listing of each genus is capitalized in boldface type and is set off from other genera by a rule. Species of a genus are paragraphed. Varieties and cultivars of a species are arranged in alphabetical order.

Top left: Salix caprea; *top right:* Magnolia stellata; *center left:* Rhododendron mucronulatum; *center right:* Corylopsis glabrescens.

Ribes odoratum

Forsythia intermedia 'Primulina', left; F.i. 'Spectabilis', right.

Above: Malus sargentii (white, in foreground); *right:* Aesculus pavia.

Left: Crataegus oxyacantha 'Paul's Scarlet'.

Right: Prunus cistena; *below left:* Acer palmatum 'Atropurpureum' (center) and Philadelphus coronarius 'Aureus' (left and right); *below right:* Mahonia aquifolium.

Prunus subhirtella 'Pendula'.

Kerria japonica 'Pleniflora'.

Left: Cornus florida rubra

Left: Prunus serrulata 'Sekiyama' ('Kwanzan'); *below left:* Rhododendron Knap Hill hybrid, photographed at Knap Hill Nursery, England; *below right:* Syringa vulgaris hybrid.

Above: Daphne cneorum; *left:* Laburnum arbor photographed at the Royal Botanic Garden, Edinburgh, Scotland.

Above: Paeonia suffruticosa; *below:* Kalmia latifolia.

Above: Rhododendron 'America' (red), R. 'Roseum Elegans' (pink); *below:* Rosa foetida 'Persian Yellow'.

Above: Rosa setigera; *left:* Colutea arborescens.

Above: Hypericum calycinum; *below:* Spiraea bumalda 'Anthony Waterer'.

Above: Physocarpus opulifolius 'Luteus'; *below:*
Abelia grandiflora.

Vitex agnus-castus 'Latifolia'.

Viburnum lantana berries.

Above: Koelreuteria paniculata seed pods; *below:* Hibiscus syriacus 'Lucie'.

Koelreuteria paniculata flowers.

Nandina domestica, flowers (white) and berries (red).

Right: Berberis thunbergii 'Atropurpurea' (foreground), Cornus alba 'Argenteo-marginata' (background).

Top left: Hamamelis japonica; *top right:* Cotinus coggygria; *center left:* Pyracantha coccinea 'Lalandei' berries; *center right:* Chaenomeles japonica alpina fruits (quinces).

Above: Euonymus alata; *left:* Hamamelis virginiana in flower.

Cornus stolonifera 'Flaviramea'.

Viburnum trilobum berries.

Left: Red-twigged dogwoods (several of those mentioned in the text look like this in winter). *Right:* Rhamnus utilis berries.

Ilex crenata 'Convexa'.

Ilex verticillata berries.

ABELIA

Abelia 'Edward Goucher' (*A. grandiflora* ×
A. schumannii).

Not as vigorous in growth as *A. grandiflora* and
not as hardy (only to Zone 6), this semi-evergreen
hybrid looks much like *A. grandiflora* but has
larger flowers, more lavender or purplish pink in
color.

Abelia × *grandiflora* (syn *A. rupestris*) (*A.
chinensis* × *A. uniflora*) (Glossy abelia, Bush-ar-
butus or, sometimes, just Arbutus). Zone 5b; 6' in
the south, 3' in Zone 5. Illustrated on Color Page V.

This is a pretty and useful densely growing shrub
with small, glossy leaves that are evergreen further
south, but deciduous in Zone 5. Beginning in late
June it has pale pink tubular flowers, 3/4" long, in
clusters, which it continues to bear until frost.
After they have gone, the rose-colored calyxes (the
plant parts which surround the petals) remain on
the plant and are effective for weeks. The leaves
turn bronzy in autumn, deep bronzy-purple as winter approaches, and remain that color for as long as
they stay on the shrub, which depends on the
weather.

In Zone 5b this shrub needs a protected situation, for even in such a place it kills to the ground
in severe winters, but it grows again from the roots
each spring. Usually there is some winterkill even
when the winter isn't severe. This means a slight
pruning job in early spring, to cut out the dead
wood. In milder climates, as on Long Island, New
York (Zone 7), abelias are sometimes cut to the
ground each spring in order to keep them from
getting "leggy." This drastic pruning is possible
because the flowers are borne on wood of the current season's growth.

Abelia likes best a light, peaty soil but will grow
in any reasonably good soil with no special preparation needed.

Abelias are prettiest combined with broad-leaved
or needled evergreens because their glossy leaves
show best then. South of Zone 5 abelias are used
for pruned or unpruned hedges and are well
adapted to this use because of the many fine twigs.

A form with white flowers and one with rose
flowers are listed by one or two wholesale nurseries,
but are not generally on the retail market.

Abelia × *grandiflora* 'Prostrata' (Prostrate
glossy abelia). Zone 6 to southern part of Zone 5 (in
a protected place); 2'.

This plant is just what the Latin name says it is
—a prostrate or almost prostrate form of glossy

Abelia grandiflora, branch.

, closeup of flowers.

abelia. Flowers are white, growth is dense, and the
plant is an excellent ground cover where it is hardy.

Abelia × *grandiflora* U.S.D.A. 210092. Zone
6, possibly Zone 5b with protection; 3' to 4' in
Zone 7.

An introduction of the United States Department of Agriculture, this plant is described as "Very compact, covered with rose-pink flowers from late June to fall. Grows well in sun or partial shade in ordinary soil." The flowers are apparently much deeper pink than those of *grandiflora*.

Abelia grandiflora, pink sepals remaining after flowers have fallen.

Abeliophyllum distichum, branch.

ABELIOPHYLLUM

Abeliophyllum distichum (Korean abelia-leaf, Korean white forsythia). Zone 5b; to 5'.

An attractive, upright-growing shrub which blooms in mid-April at the same time as *Forsythia ovata*, it may be planted in the foreground of that shrub, perhaps with *Erica carnea* in front of it, for a very early spring picture.

Abeliophyllum will grow in any fairly good soil. It should be set in a protected place in Zone 5 because its purple flower buds, which are formed in autumn, are apt to winterkill in severe winters. This shrub is slow to reestablish itself after transplanting and this causes many people to complain that it does not grow well for them. Given a year to reestablish its roots, then fertilized lightly each spring, it grows very well.

The little flowers, opening pale pink, then turning to white, are borne in dense clusters all along the slender stems, which are first upright in growth and then arch downward. Because of the density of the blooms, even a small shrub becomes a conspicuous feature of the spring landscape.

, closeup of flowers.

ACANTHOPANAX

Acanthopanax pentaphyllus (see *A. sieboldianus*).

Acanthopanax sieboldianus (syn *Aralia pentaphylla*, *Acanthopanax pentaphyllus*) (Five-leaf aralia, Angelica shrub). Zone 5; 6'.

If you are looking for a shrub to use in a city garden where soil is poor and smoke and dust are plentiful, or a shrub for a shady spot or dry area where not too many shrubs will grow, choose acanthopanax. It has a graceful, upright growth habit. The deeply cut, shiny foliage is attractive and covers the branches to the ground. The leaves will look fresh and green when foliage on other nearby shrubs turns brown because acanthopanax tolerates even drought.

Flowers are greenish-white and so small that they often open unseen. Flowers of each sex are borne on different plants and apparently most nurseries sell only male plants, for, while I've seen flowers on many plants, it is only rarely that I've seen fruits. These, too, are small and have no landscape value.

Because of the prickles underneath each leaf, acanthopanax often is used for a hedge. It may be trimmed lightly or left to grow untrimmed. But acanthopanax also looks well as a specimen shrub. Occasionally, because it is so often planted in shade, a plant may get "leggy," in which case it is possible to renew growth by cutting the plant to the ground in early spring. It will grow again from the roots.

Acanthopanax sieboldianus flowers.

AESCULUS

Aesculus parviflora (Bottlebrush buckeye). Zone 5; 8'-10'.

The height of this shrub does not give a true idea of its size because, in time, it may grow twice as broad as it does high or even more.

This means that when planting it, space must be allowed for the shrub to spread. This it does by means of underground suckers.

The flowers appear in late July and August when few other shrubs bloom and, partly because of the long pink stamens of the white flowers (the clusters of which look not unlike candles) and partly because of the gray undersides of the leaves, the effect of a shrub in bloom is "feathery."

The seeds which follow the blooms are deep brown, enclosed in capsules ¾" long, ⅜" wide at the widest point, which first are bright yellow then turn brownish orange (5 YR 5/8). Stems with capsules on them are widely used in Japan in flower arrangements.

Foliage turns from green to yellow in autumn, giving a second season of interest.

Acanthopanax sieboldianus, fruits.

Aesculus parviflora, bloom spike, above; detail of long-stamened flowers below.

Aesculus parviflora will grow in any reasonably good soil. It tolerates slight shade but grows better in full sun. It is a handsome shrub when well grown. It is native from South Carolina to Alabama.

Aesculus pavia (syn *A. pavia rubra*) (Red buckeye). Zone 5. Illustrated on Color Page II.

In its native habitat, from Florida to Virginia and westward to Louisiana and West Virginia, this buckeye may grow either as a shrub or as a small tree. It may be as small as 4' or as tall as 20'.

It is similar to *A. parviflora* in its horsechestnut-like leaf and in the fact that is usually grows broader than it does high. Flower clusters are the same shape as those of *A. parviflora* but the flowers are bright reddish-rose and appear, not in late summer, but in May and June. Oddly, they rarely open fully.

A. pavia also is tolerant of many soil conditions, though it too responds to good soil. This plant rarely is listed by nurseries and the few that carry it may not always have it in stock when you want to buy it.

ALTHEA (see HIBISCUS)

AMELANCHIER (Shadbush, Shadblow, June-berry, Service-berry, Bilberry, Canadian medlar, Maycherry, Sugar-pear, Showy Mespilus)

The chief reason for growing any shadblow is the white flowers which open in late April or early May before the leaves fully expand. Should the weather at that time of year turn warm, these blooms will last only two or three days, but if the weather is first sufficiently warm to allow the flowers to open, then turns cool and stays cool, the blooms may be in good condition for as long as ten days.

All shadblows are suitable for woodlands or along the margins of streams or lakes, especially when there are taller trees back of them. The sight of a shadblow in flower against black water is one to remember.

After the flowers have finished blooming, there still is some interest to the gardener in amelanchiers in the coloration of the new leaves of some species, but after leaves are fully grown, an amelanchier is just another shrub until the fruits color. Most gardeners never see this stage for birds eat fruits as soon as the first bit of color (other than green) appears. In autumn, some amelanchiers have outstanding yellow foliage color.

Amelanchier alnifolia (Saskatoon). Zone 1; 10'.

Native in Canada from the Yukon southward to Ontario and in the United States from Oregon eastward to Iowa, this shrub is used in the north for its early white flowers, usually appearing in May. Edible, blue-purple to blue-black fruits ripen in July.

The common name of this shrub is that of a city in Saskatchewan, named for the shrub.

152

Amelanchier stolonifera (Creeping service berry). Zone 3; 4'.

This is one amelanchier that is not normally found in moist places. Instead, it grows in poor, dry soil and exposed areas, often in rocky sites. Upright growing, but creeping by underground stolons, this shrub forms patches of growth which will hold loose soil in place. For this reason, it is useful on banks or in wild areas where soil needs holding. It blooms in late May to early June and the almost black, juicy, edible fruits ripen in July to August. This is one of the best species for fruits. A "bloom" like that on plums, overlays the fruits.

AMORPHA (Indigo-bush, False-indigo, Bastard-indigo

Amorpha fruticosa (False indigo, Bastard indigo, Indigo-bush) Zone 4, possibly Zone 3; 12'.

This usually is seen as an awkward shrub because it has been allowed to grow without pruning. Fortunately, whenever it grows too widespread and open, it may be cut to the ground in early spring and will grow again from the roots. Since the flowers are borne on wood of the current season's growth, there will be no lost season of bloom.

Leaves of this amorpha are on the gray side of green, but not gray like those of *A. canescens*, a

Amorpha fruticosa flowers, the stamens golden with ripe pollen.

close relative. The flowers are tiny, borne in long spikes, opening in July. The false indigo rarely has a spike of blooms which are all open and perfect at the same time. A notable feature of the flowers, pretty when seen at close range, is their golden stamens against their violet-purple petals.

False indigo, because it grows wild along streams from Florida to Wisconsin, is said to prefer a moist soil. In both this garden and my former one, the plants have done well in dry, sandy soil. Seed pods of false indigo, which are purplish-brown, stay on all winter, giving winter interest.

ANDROMEDA

Andromeda calyculata (see *Chamaedaphne calyculata*). Andromeda also is a common name for *Pieris* and *Zenobia*.

ARALIA

Aralia pentaphylla (see *Acanthopanax sieboldianus*).

Aralia spinosa (Hercules' club, Devil's walking stick, Angelica-tree, Tearblanket, Monkeytree, Prickly ash). Zone 5; 20'-30'.

This tree-like shrub is exotic in appearance and might be suitable for use as an accent plant in an Oriental-style or perhaps a Mediterranean type landscape, but in the average landscape it sticks out like a sore thumb. Flowers are white; small, but grouped in large clusters; open in August. Leaves are very long, sometimes to three feet. Fruits, which ripen in September and are popular with birds, are small black berries on red stems. Branches are thick and spiny. This shrub tolerates almost any soil; will grow in the light shade of tall trees as well as in sun.

ARONIA (Chokeberry)

These hardy shrubs usually are recommended for use because of their colorful berries but I think the white flowers in late May are just as pretty as those of many other shrubs grown chiefly for flowers. The leaves of some aronias are shining and are attractive all season.

Aronias grow best in moist soil, but will tolerate dry places too. They do well in full sun or light shade. They may be used at the edge of a woodland or in a shrub border. All are upright and slightly spreading in growth, easy to move and to grow.

Aronia arbutifolia (Red chokeberry). Zone 5; 6'.

Native from Ontario and Nova Scotia to Michigan and Missouri and southward to Florida and Texas, this aronia has the showiest fruit of any—

bright red, but only ¼″ in diameter. It usually is produced in abundance. If the shrub is not in too-deep shade, the leaves turn red in fall and contrast beautifully with the berries.

Aronia arbutifolia 'Brilliantissima' has even more abundant, glossy, red berries. Apparently birds do not like them and they therefore hang on the shrub until late in winter.

Aronia arbutifolia 'Brilliantissima', flowers.

, fruits.

Aronia melanocarpa (Black chokeberry). Zone 4; 3′.

Adapting well to drier soils, this native is often found in thickets and on cliffs from Newfoundland to Ontario and Minnesota, south to Nova Scotia, New England, South Carolina, and Tennessee. It has narrower leaves than the red chokeberry and they are shiny. They turn purplish red in autumn. The berries are purplish black, gradually turning black—and they drop within a short time of ripening.

AZALEA (Azalea)

Botanists classify all azaleas as rhododendrons. A few progressive nurserymen follow the botanists but most nurseries continue to list these plants as azaleas in catalogs and call them azaleas in sales lots. In order to reconcile the names, I have listed below the name given in most catalogs for each azalea in this book and, in the second column, the proper botanical name.

In an effort to bridge the gap between the thinking of botanists and nurserymen, I am discussing the rhododendrons called azaleas under the heading of Azalea, but they are listed under their proper names (that is under Rhododendron) in the Buyer's Guide Chart and Bloom Time Chart.

Hybrid groups widely available in the catalogs are listed below the proper names of the plants.

Catalog name	Valid botanical name
Azalea amoena	Rhododendron obtusum 'Amoenum'
arborescens	arborescens
arnoldiana	obtusum arnoldianum
calendulacea	calendulaceum
kaempferi	kaempferi
mollis	molle
mucronulata	mucronulatum
nudiflora	nudiflorum
nudiflora roseum	roseum
poukhanensis	yedoense poukhanense
poukhanensis yedoensis	yedoense
schlippenbachi	schlippenbachii
vaseyi	vaseyi
viscosa	viscosum
yedoensis	yedoense
yedoensis poukhanensis	yedoense poukhanense
Yodogawa	yedoense

Hybrid groups: Exbury hybrids, Gable hybrids, Ghent hybrids, Kaempferi hybrids, Knap Hill hybrids, Mollis hybrids, Vuyk hybrids.

Azalea flowers are among the most brilliantly colored of any group of shrubs in existence. It is for these bright, gay, prettily formed flowers that these plants are grown. They also are the reason why gardeners in regions where azaleas are not native want so desperately to grow them, even if soil and climate are not precisely suitable.

For, to grow azaleas (and other rhododendrons), the first point you must consider is that most of them need acid soil in order to thrive. They prefer pH 4.5 to pH 5.5, and need this acidity not just at the soil surface but for a full foot of depth, if not a foot and a half.

If you live in an area where the soil is naturally acid, you will have little concern over this point—in fact you may wonder why it is stressed. The gardener who lives where soils are neutral (pH 7) or slightly alkaline (above pH 7) will know, for he must replace existing soil with a more suitable acid soil mixture in order to grow most azaleas.

This is not as difficult as it sounds, because all azaleas are shallow-rooted and even an extra-large, extra-deep hole need only be 18" deep to contain the root system and allow for root growth in acid soil.

Furthermore, a few kinds like Mollis hybrids and *R. schlippenbachii* will grow in neutral or slightly acid soil and may not need soil replacement in order to thrive.

Therefore, if you are not blessed (?) with acid soil and wish to grow azaleas, you have a choice of restricting the ones you grow to those that will thrive without soil replacement or of replacing soil for any that will grow in your hardiness zone.

Soil preparation and replacement for acid soil plants is discussed in Chapter 5.

There are two types of azaleas—evergreen and deciduous. Most evergreen azaleas are not hardy north of Zone 6. As you saw in Chapter 8, I am a firm believer in trying to grow plants generally considered hardy in the zone south of the one in which one lives—on the theory that perhaps, in certain microclimates in one's garden, one may be able to grow an especially beautiful or rare plant.

Therefore, some years ago, I started trying various evergreen azaleas, knowing perfectly well that my garden is in Zone 5b (the southerly part of Zone 5). A variety of evergreen azalea that shows no signs of injury, either to plant or to flower bud, despite temperatures of −12° F for three days and nights at a time, is Fedora. Some other evergreen azaleas have proven hardy below the line of snow which covers them some winters, though the part above that line will die. If you too are of an ad-

venturous spirit, try evergreen azaleas, one variety at a time, and see if you too can make them at home in your garden.

Although a well-drained sub-soil is essential, for azaleas cannot stand wet feet, dry soil should be avoided because the shallow roots of azaleas dry out easily. For this reason, a mixture of acid peat moss and soil is ideal for azaleas. Even when growing in this mixture, azaleas must be watered if the summer is dry. Soaking the plants once a week is plenty. If the water used, city or well water, is alkaline in reaction, as it often is, and much of it is needed to keep the plants alive, there is danger of changing soil reaction because of the alkaline water. Your community probably has an analysis of its water available from city hall. It might be well to provide yourself with a copy since the pH will be indicated.

Mulching often is recommended for azaleas to keep their roots cool and moist. However, recent advice from the United States Department of Agriculture, while advocating mulching for the rest of the year, warns that mulching delays the hardening of wood in autumn and thus makes the plants more sensitive to freezing in winter cold. Therefore, the gardener who mulches his azaleas is advised to remove the mulch in early autumn for three weeks to a month and then replace it for the winter.

Oak leaves have been recommended for a mulch for azaleas because, when they decompose, they are acid in reaction. Lacking oak leaves, pine needles or ground corn cobs provide a good mulch. Peat is a poor mulch because it absorbs so much water itself that the rain or watering must be extremely heavy in order to penetrate the mulch *and* get to the soil below to give the azalea roots needed water. In summer the surface of peat dries, cakes, and becomes impenetrable. Cocoa bean hulls also are a poor mulch for acid soil plants because potassium salts are leached from the hulls in too great quantity for the well-being of the plants.

Use your common sense in selecting a mulch material. Whatever you apply should be loose to admit water, yet cover the soil sufficiently to keep it cool and moist.

In addition to proper soil, the site chosen for an azalea should have conditions as much as possible like those in which it grows naturally. These will vary with the species. For instance, *R. viscosum,* the swamp azalea, grows naturally in low, damp places and will thrive in your garden if you can provide such conditions. If you can't, grow it anyway and give it extra water. The scent of its white flowers will repay you for the extra effort.

R. calendulaceum, on the other hand, delights in light shade on a dry ridge or high land, so, if you have such a place, light it up with this azalea.

If you haven't such a place, then select the northeast side of a tree or building, where there is morning sun but afternoon shade—enough sun to make flowering certain, but not sufficient to scorch—and grow azaleas like *R. calendulaceum* (the flame azalea) there.

The spot to avoid planting any azalea is a hot, dry corner in full sun, for no azalea will grow under this combination of adverse conditions.

The best time to plant azaleas is in late spring or early fall—late April or mid-September. They can be moved bare root if plants are very small, but otherwise should be purchased only with a ball of earth around their roots. They may be moved with no injury while in full bloom providing you water them weekly during the following summer. In fact, if you are selecting azaleas to carry out a specific color scheme, it is best to buy them in bloom so that you can see the flower colors.

Only the azaleas commonly listed in the catalogs and hardy from Zone 6 northward are described here. These are mostly species but several groups of hybrids also are included. It is impossible in this book to attempt to describe the numerous cultivars so, if you wish to know more about them, refer to *The Azalea Book* by Frederick P. Lee, published by D. Van Nostrand Company, Inc.

Rhododendron arborescens (syn *Azalea arborescens*) (Sweet or smooth azalea). Zone 5 and part of Zone 4; 6'-9'.

This species is native from New York and Pennsylvania to Georgia and Alabama; westward to Kentucky and Tennessee. It grows along mountain streams and in cool mountain meadows; is tall, upright, but becomes wider than it is high. It flowers in mid-June (one of the last azaleas to bloom).

Buds are pinkish and flowers, which smell like those of heliotrope and are 1½" to 2½" in diameter, vary in color according to the individual plant bearing them. Sometimes they are white, flushed pink or red; other times they are blotched yellow, with or without the flush. Always they have red stamens.

Because of the color variation and because many wild plants (sold as "collected stock" by some nurseries) are "straggly" in form, you should buy only plants you've seen growing in a good nursery.

Foliage is glossy, bright green, turning dark red in autumn. It is easy to tell this azalea from *R. viscosum* which usually blooms a bit later, because *viscosum* has hairy leaves and branches while in *arborescens* these are smooth.

Rhododendron calendulaceum (syn *Azalea calendulacea*) (Flame azalea). Zone 5 to part of Zone 4; 6'-8', sometimes taller.

This colorful azalea is native from Pennsylvania to Georgia; westward to Ohio and Kentucky. It grows in open woods on hills or mountains and, when it is in bloom, with flower colors ranging from yellows through oranges to scarlets, it is easy to see how it acquired its common name, for truly the woods seem aflame and stay that way for several weeks as the blooms are long-lasting.

Flowering time is early June; flowers of some plants are more fragrant than those of others. If you select your plants while they are in bloom, you can not only select those with more fragrant blooms, but also can best arrange them in your planting to show their colors to advantage. Plants with darker colored blooms will bloom slightly later than those with paler coloring, a point to consider in color scheming.

In autumn the foliage turns yellow to bronze.

Rhododendron canadense (syn *Rhodora canadensis, Azalea canadensis*) (Rhodora). Zone 3 to part of Zone 2; 3'.

Native from Newfoundland and Labrador to New York, Pennsylvania and New Jersey, rhodora grows well only where the soil is very acid and moist and the air is moist and cool. Rhodora has dull, bluish-green leaves, rose-purple flowers in mid-May, and is best used in a mass planting in a boggy place.

Exbury hybrids. Zone 6 and some probably in Zone 5. Some are being grown at the University of Minnesota Arboretum, which is in Zone 4.

The Exbury group is listed as one of four subgroups of Knap Hill hybrids (described subsequently), all named for the places in which they were developed. This particular group was developed at Exbury, Southhampton, England by the late Lionel de Rothschild, who started hybridizing shortly after World War I, using Knap Hill hybrids developed by the late Anthony Waterer in his nursery.

There are numerous selected cultivars and these hybrids also are sold in mixed colors. All are beautiful, but form and flower color vary with the cultivar so that it would be sensible to see in bloom what you're buying before you buy it.

Gable hybrids.

These were bred by Joseph B. Gable, Stewartstown, Pennsylvania and are intended to be a group of very hardy evergreen azaleas. The Korean azalea

(*R. yedoense poukhanense*), a very hardy evergreen azalea, which becomes deciduous but survives in Zone 5a, and the Kaempfer azalea (*R. kaempferi*) were used as parents for many of this group, though a wider range of parentage is found.

There are a number of cultivars ranging widely in form and in flower color. Most of them are hardy in Zone 6; a few in Zone 5b. If you live in these zones or south of Zone 6, it will pay you to try these hybrids.

Rhododendron × *gandavense* (Ghent hybrids, Pontic or Pontica hybrids). Zone 4; heights vary according to the cultivar—generally 6′ to 10′ at maturity.

This group of azaleas has an extremely mixed parentage, including the species *calendulaceum*, *luteum* (syn *A. pontica*), *molle*, *nudiflorum* and *viscosum*. It is, therefore, only to be expected that these hybrids will vary greatly, which leads to a lengthy list of cultivars to be found in the catalogs of nurseries designated in the Buyer's Guide Chart (in Chapter 11).

Flowers of the Ghent hybrids may be single or double; white, pink to red, yellow or orange and often are combinations of two colors as in the cultivar 'Daviesi', which is white with a yellow blotch.

The most important single fact about these azaleas, as far as the gardener is concerned, is their hardiness. This, coupled with the wide color range in the group, gives the gardener in the north a chance to combine them with various species for a first rate azalea garden. The Ghents seem to grow best in light shade.

Ghent hybrids (see *R. gandavense*, above)

Rhododendron kaempferi (syn *R. obtusum kaempferi*, *Azalea kaempferi*) (Torch azalea, Kaempfer azalea). Zone 5; to 7′ and sometimes more, broadening with age.

Like the flame azalea, this one got its common name of torch azalea because of the brilliance of its flower colors. These range from salmon through orange-red to brick red and the plants do not necessarily bloom all at the same time—some, regardless of color, will bloom much earlier than others. They are upright growing, bear single, semi-double or double flowers from 1¾″ to 2½″ in diameter. Plants are deciduous in the north, evergreen in the south.

In Japan, where it is native, this azalea grows all over the mountains and makes a blazing mass of color when in bloom. It does the same in the Arnold Arboretum which has large plantings on hillsides. In order to maintain the flower color at its brightest, this azalea should be planted in shade.

It will tolerate deep shade and still flower.

Kaempferi hybrids

This group is not for very cold climates. Most cultivars are hardy in Zone 6, a few in Zone 5b. Plants usually are tall and upright, some cultivars eventually becoming 6′ and more high. Blooms of most are single, range from 1″ to 1½″ in diameter and range in color from white through rose and red and orange red to red violet and purple.

Knap Hill hybrids. Zone 5a, but some are being grown at the University of Minnesota Arboretum in Zone 4. Illustrated on Color Page III.

This is a group of azaleas which started with hybridizing by Anthony Waterer in England and was continued after his death by Knap Hill Nursery, which he had owned. Parents of the group were *Rhododendrons molle, calendulaceum, occidentale,* and *arborescens*.

The resulting hybrids were not widely disseminated until after World War II and, at the present time, the nursery has one list of cultivars which it will export to the United States and other countries and a much longer list of cultivars for sale only in Great Britain.

There are so many gorgeous azaleas in this group that it would be a chore to decide which to buy first. I spent a long morning walking and photographing at Knap Hill and came away with a mile-long list of azaleas I must own.

The present Mr. Waterer told me that he has bred cultivars which bloom in July but that the flower colors are pale and he now is breeding for deeper colors with the same late blooming habit.

Knap Hill hybrids are characterized by flowers of huge size, 2″ to 3″ across, mostly wide and flat in form, most single, but a few with double blooms. In addition to the huge flowers, many cultivars bear them in enormous trusses. I counted 28 flowers in a single cluster and I do not doubt that there were larger groups on some plants. Some of the plants bear flowers in rounded clusters, others in wider, flatter clusters. Flower color range from creamy whites and creams through many pinks, roses, reds as well as yellow, salmon, and orange.

Most of the plants grow upright in form but some are wider than high and, apparently, are dwarf. Most of the cultivars bloom in late May or early June.

As already explained, the Exbury hybrids come under the classification of Knap Hill hybrids since they started with Anthony Waterer's older hybrids. A nursery near Knap Hill, Goldsworth Old Nursery, owned by Walter Slocock, also has hybrids which derive from the original Knap Hill's and I saw some beauties among them. A fourth group deriving from the Knap Hill hybrids has been developed in New Zealand, but these are mostly unnamed and apparently unavailable in this country.

Rhododendron × kosterianum (*R. molle × R. japonicum* and, more recently, other species) (Mollis hybrids). Zone 5; though some are being grown in Zone 4; 3' to 5'.

R. molle, with yellow flowers, and *R. japonicum*, which occasionally has yellow flowers but usually has blooms of orange or red, have given these hybrids a color range from pale yellow through gold and orange-yellow to salmon, orange, and many shades of red. Many sales lots offer plants grown from seeds, some of them practically "pure" *R. molle*, and nurseries offer these plus numerous cultivars, so it is best to buy plants while in flower. If you must buy in fall, it is possible to tell which plants will have light-colored blooms simply by observing the bud color, which is pale in those plants and dark in plants which will have darker colored flowers.

Mollis hybrids bloom in late May with the late tulips and beautiful color combinations may be devised using these two together. Bloom clusters are usually 5" or more in width. Flower sizes of the hybrids vary with the cultivar but many are 2" to 3" or more in diameter. The commonest "orange" flowered sort has 3¼" blooms of strong reddish orange (7.5 R 5/13); the commonest yellow flowered is colored closest to 7.5 YR 9/4, pale orange yellow, but yellower.

Mollis hybrids are not as hardy as Ghent hybrids and they are not, generally speaking, long-lived. They will, however, thrive in circumneutral rather than acid soil and in full sun.

Rhododendron molle (syn *R. sinense, A. mollis*) (Chinese azalea). Zone 5; 3'-4'.

Blooming in late April to early May, *R. molle* has golden-yellow flowers blotched with deeper color (sometimes green), and 3½" in diameter. They are borne on upright plants. However, most of the plants sold in the United States under this name probably are hybrids since the species rarely is found in the trade.

Rhododendron mucronulatum (syn *A. mucronulata*) (Korean rhododendron). Zone 4 to part of Zone 3; 4'-5'. Illustrated on Color Page I.

One of the few deciduous rhododendrons, this plant blooms with the later forsythias, with single, light pinkish-lavender or rosy-lavender single-flowers in mid-April to late-April before the leaves appear. It has one weakness—because it blooms so very early its buds and sometimes its flowers may be nipped by a late frost. A plant in full bloom may be frosted and ruined in a single cold night. Though this happens only about once in five years, it would be wise to set the plant where too much sun does not make the buds open even earlier than they would normally.

Rhododendron kosterianum (Mollis hybrid), flowers.

Rhododendron mucronulatum, flowers.

Rhododendron nudiflorum (syn *A. nudi-flora*) (Pinxterbloom, Pinxterflower azalea, Honeysuckle, Honeysuckle azalea). Zone 4 with protection; Zone 5 without; 4'-5'.

A deciduous shrub, this azalea is native from Massachusetts to North Carolina and westward to Tennessee and Ohio. It has 10 RP 8/5, moderate pink or white flowers, 1½″ in diameter, in May, before the leaves start to grow. It grows in open woods and along streams and is one of the azaleas that will grow in full sun. It also is native in Germany and, when I was a youngster, following a European custom which sets aside a special Sunday for picking these flowers, my father and I used to walk to the woods in northern New York state and come home with armsful of blooms.

Rhododendron nudiflorum, flower cluster.

Rhododendron obtusum 'Amoenum' (Amoena azalea). Zone 6; 4'-5'. This has magenta flowers of the hose-in-hose type, blooming in mid-May. The plant is spreading, usually becoming wider than high, and is dense in form.

Rhododendron obtusum × *arnoldianum* (*R. amoenum* × *R. kaempferi*). Zone 6 to Zone 5b. Hardier than *amoenum* and slightly taller grow-

Rhododendron schlippenbachii, showing width and flat form of flower. →

159

ing, this has 1¼″ wide flowers colored 7.5 RP 6/12, deep purplish pink.

Rhododendron roseum (Roseshell azalea). Zone 4 to part of Zone 3; 4'-5', but may become taller.

Native from New England to the high mountains of Virginia and westward to northern Ohio and northern Indiana, this azalea often is confused with a similar native species, *R. nudiflorum*, which it resembles so much that it formerly was considered a form of *nudiflorum*. Its bright pink flowers are fragrant while those of pinxter-bloom are not. Individual flowers are about 1½″ in diameter and they appear in late May. Leaves are bluish green.

Rhododendron schlippenbachii (syn *A. schlippenbachi*) (Royal azalea). Zone 4; 10' or even more.

This is a beautiful azalea in both spring and fall, for in mid-May it has 3″ wide, single, flattish, purplish pink (5 RP 8/5) or sometimes white, fragrant flowers with brown dots in the throats. Blooms appear just as the leaves are unfolding and in autumn these leaves turn yellow, orange and crimson. The plants grow upright, yet eventually spread to be wider than they are high. There is sufficient variation in flower color among plants of this species to make it sensible to see in bloom the plant you intend to buy. This is one of the few azaleas that does not demand highly acid soil.

Rhododendron vaseyi (syn *A. vaseyi*) (Pink shell azalea). Zone 4; 8'-10'.

Native in the mountains of western North Carolina, this lovely azalea forms tall, upright plants, blooms in mid-May before its leaves unfold, with single flowers which may be white (in variety *album*), or pale pink. They are graceful and give an airy effect; are particularly pretty when seen reflected in water. The plant will grow in either moist or dry soils and in full sun as well as in light shade. The leaves turn red in autumn, giving it another season of color.

Rhododendron vaseyi, flowers.

Rhododendron viscosum (syn *A. viscosa*) (Swamp azalea). Zone 3; to 15'.

Because this azalea grows in swamps and along streams from Maine to South Carolina and Tennessee, it is a prime choice for that damp spot in your garden. It is the last of the azaleas to flower, blooming usually just after *R. arborescens* (though sometimes opening while *arborescens* still is in flower) in early to mid-July.

The flowers are single, white to cream, 1" to 1½" wide and extremely fragrant. How many blooms appear on your plant depends on the care with which the nursery which propagated it se-

lected the parent stock and the particular season. Some years a plant will be laden with flowers and others produce only a few blooms.

Rhododendron viscosum, flowering branch.

Vuyk hybrids (listed in many catalogs as *A. vuykiana*).

Introductions of Vuyk vanNes Nursery, Boskoop, Holland, these have several hybrids in their ancestry. As a group they were bred for hardiness and larger blooms in evergreen azaleas. Flowers, which range from 2" to 2½" in diameter, are single, with a color range from white to rose and rose-red, through red to red-violet and purple. The most popular cultivar is Wilhelmina Vuyk (syn Pale-

Rhododendron viscosum, closeup to show viscous or sticky surfaces of buds and flower tubes.

strina) with single, white, 2″ diameter flowers blotched with chartreuse green and borne on a medium-high plant.

The series of cultivars named for musical composers belongs here and these are listed in some catalogs. Some of these cultivars were in bloom when I visited the Vuyk vanNes Nursery in The Netherlands in mid-May. It is a shame they are not hardier, but Zone 6 is about their northern limit though some may grow in protected places in Zone 5b.

Rhododendron yedoense (syn *R. poukhanense yedoense*, *R. poukhanense* 'Yodogawa', *R.* 'Yodogawa', *Azalea poukhanensis yedoensis*) (Yodogawa azalea). Zone 4; 3′ to 4′.

This double-flowered form was found first in gardens and given the specific name of *R. yedoense*. Later, when the single-flowered form was found in the wild, it was given a varietal name, *R. yedoense poukhanense*. This is confusing, to put it mildly, but a few other plants also are named "backwards." Blossoms are 2¼″ in diameter, closest to strong reddish purple (2.5 RP 5/10) in color.

Rhododendron yedoense.

161

Form is low and spreading, the leaves evergreen in the south, the plant becoming deciduous in the north.

Rhododendron yedoense poukhanense (syn *R. poukhanense, Azalea poukhanensis*) (Korean azalea). Zone 5 to part of Zone 4; 3', but growing taller in shade. This is a low, spreading evergreen azalea in the south, though deciduous in the north. It has fragrant, single, 2½" wide, strong reddish purple (2.5 RP 5/10) flowers with red markings. It blooms reliably in mid-May which its double-flowered variety often does not. It seems to me well adapted to semi-shaded situations as it grows so well for me in such a place. I cannot say the same for the double-flowered form.

Rhododendron yedoense poukhanense, flowers.

BENZOIN

Benzoin aestivalis or *aestivale* (see *Lindera benzoin*).

BERBERIS (Barberry)

People tend to regard barberries solely as hedge plants. While it is true that many species make excellent hedges, it also is true that there are species worthy of planting as specimens. The difficulty is that most gardeners, when they think of barberries, think only of *Berberis thunbergii,* the Japanese bar-

berry. This is an attractive and extremely useful plant but it is not by any means the only barberry to grow.

In addition to having foliage that blends well with that of other plants and that often furnishes beautiful fall color, barberries produce attractive yellow flowers, especially pretty when viewed at close range, and handsome berries which may be red, purplish or black. Some barberries are evergreen, certainly in Zone 6 and most winters in Zone 5b.

All barberries will grow in practically any kind of soil and in full sun or light shade, though they will not have as brilliant foliage color in autumn when growing in shade. They all are easy to move, so it is quite possible to transplant a full-size plant or a full-size hedge. Diseases and insects trouble them but little.

Some barberries, however, notably *B. vulgaris,* are alternate hosts to a disease of wheat called black stem-rust. In the interests of healthy wheat, such barberries are not permitted in states which grow wheat, nor are they permitted to be imported into either the United States or Canada. See Chapters 9 and 12 for further discussions of this matter.

Berberis candidula, flowers.

Berberis candidula (Paleleaf barberry). Zone 5; 2'-3'.

A dwarf, densely branching, evergreen barberry, which makes a beautiful small specimen on top of a wall, in a rock garden, or in a raised bed. It has bright yellow 5/8″ diameter flowers in May, followed by purplish berries in autumn. The 1½″ long leaves are white on their undersides and the twigs are thorny.

Berberis erecta (see *B. thunbergii* 'Erecta').

Berberis julianae (Wintergreen barberry). Zone 5; 5′ to 6′.

As hardy an evergreen barberry as can be found, *julianae* is sturdy and strong, erect in growth, with handsome, dark green leaves and long, sharp spines growing from them. The twigs, too, have thorns, and one of the funniest stories told in the local nursery industry is of the nurseryman who, enamored of the beautiful evergreen leaves of this plant, set one on each side of a narrow doorway, with a resulting enormous bill for constant replacement of the nylon stockings of the lady of the house.

This barberry has clusters of yellow flowers, each ⅓″ in diameter in mid-May, and blue-black berries in autumn. It may be used as a specimen or in a house planting (not near the doors) or in a shrub border, but it should be borne in mind that weeding near it is no joy unless the hands are covered with leather gloves. Those spiny leaves and branchlets blow off in winter, and spring cleanup time finds them on the ground.

Berberis julianae 'Nana' (Dwarf wintergreen barberry). Zone 5; 3′, sometimes 4′. The dwarf form of *julianae* which is, except for the smaller size, identical with it.

Berberis julianae 'Pyramidalis'. The pyramidal form of *julianae*, this differs only in shape.

Berberis koreana (Korean barberry). Zone 4; 5′ or 6′.

This is, to my way of thinking, the most beautiful of the barberries that can be grown in the north. It is deciduous, growing erect while young, later spreading more, with upper branches arching gracefully. The twigs are thorny, the leaves bright green in spring, becoming veined with red later in the season and deep orange-red in autumn. Vivid yellow. (2.5 Y 8/12) ¼″ diameter flowers in mid-May become berries hanging in drooping clusters 1¾″ long. These 3/16″ long fruits are first greenish yellow (10 Y 7/9), later bright scarlet-red. They remain in good condition for some time.

Korean barberry may be used as a hedge, clipped or unclipped, but is prettier when unclipped. It also has a place in a shrub border or may be used as a specimen or in a house planting. It should be placed where it may be enjoyed all year.

Berberis julianae, flowers.

Berberis koreana, closeup of flowers

(other pictures on next page).

Berberis koreana, branch of fruits left, flowers right (description on previous page).

Berberis × *mentorensis* (*B. julianae* × *B. thunbergii*) (Mentor barberry). Zone 5 to part of Zone 4; to 7'.

An excellent barberry because it is evergreen in mild winters and holds its leaves well into cold weather even in severe winters, while it also tolerates hot summer weather probably better than any other barberry. If the climate in which you live is too rigorous for evergreen barberries, try this semi-evergreen sort. It just might grow for you as it has withstood 15 degrees below zero, F in my garden with no injury and I understand that it survives even colder weather.

This is an upright-growing barberry, excellent for hedges, but pretty enough for specimen use too. The twigs are thorny, the leaves have spines; flowers are yellow, ¼" in diameter, open in May. The berries are dark red, against yellow to red autumn foliage color.

Berberis minor (*see B. thunbergii* 'Minor').

Berberis thunbergii (Japanese barberry). Zone 5 to part of Zone 4; 6'-7'.

The most adaptable of the barberries, this is the one most often seen in hedges. It will thrive in any type of soil, will grow in semi-shade as well as in sun, and tolerates dry conditions with no apparent difficulty.

Berberis thunbergii, flowers.

It grows upright, is densely branched, thorny, has yellow flowers, tinged reddish on the outsides, to ½″ in diameter, the middle of May. Oval, brilliant red berries follow and these, against the scarlet autumn color of the deciduous leaves, make the plant especially attractive at that time of year. Birds dislike the berries so they stay on the plant all winter to become red contrasts for the next spring's yellow flowers. This barberry is a good specimen plant, a first-rate hedge, and is acceptable in the planting around a building or in the front row of a shrub border.

Berberis thunbergii 'Atropurpurea' (Red Japanese barberry, Purple-leaf Japanese barberry). Zone 5 to part of Zone 4; 5′-6′. Illustrated on Color Page VI. This red-foliaged form is not quite as hardy as the species but compensates for that with younger leaves of 7.5 R 3/6 and older ones of 10 R 3/4, both reddish-brown, but different in degree. While a hedge entirely of this barberry is bright enough to knock one's eyes out, the plant combines well with green barberry and may be used to accent the corners where a hedge turns or the ends of a hedge of green barberry. It also is a good specimen and may be used in the foreground of narrow-leaved evergreens. Plant it only in sun as in shade it loses its bright foliage color and leaves are green.

Berberis thunbergii 'Atropurpurea Nana' (syn *B. thunbergii* 'Crimson Pigmy'). Zone 5 to part of Zone 4; 2′. Dark red (5 R 3/7) leaves and a dwarf, very compact habit of growth are characteristics of this little shrub. It may be used as a low hedge (providing the leaf color is not objectionable), as a specimen in a rock garden, as a "facing down" plant for taller shrubs or evergreens.

Berberis thunbergii 'Erecta' (syn *B. t. pluriflora erecta*) (Upright Japanese barberry, True-hedge columnberry). Zone 5 to part of Zone 4; 4′. Should you desire a hedge that is thorny but that needs little or no pruning or other care, choose this barberry. Plants grow straight upright, are dense without having sideways branches: therefore, except for pruning at the top if a formal effect is desired, no pruning is necessary. Flowers are yellow, 3/16″ in diameter.

Berberis thunbergii 'Erecta', center, B. thunbergii, right. Compare size and shape of berries.

Berberis thunbergii 'Atropurpurea', flowers.

Berberis thunbergii 'Minor' (Box barberry). Zone 5 to part of Zone 4; Usually about 1½′ though it may grow taller. In the far north, where boxwood will not grow well, this little barberry makes an excellent substitute in summer, though not in winter since it is not evergreen. Its little, bright green leaves look not unlike those of boxwood and its compact, slow growth is similar, though box barberry needs more pruning than boxwood if it is to be used for a formal or clipped hedge. In addition to hedge use, this may be used in plantings of larger shrubs or evergreens to bring these big fellows down to earth.

Berberis thunbergii nana 'Crimson Pigmy' (see *B. thunbergii* 'Atropurpurea Nana').

Berberis thunbergii 'Sheridan Red'. An introduction of Sheridan Nurseries Limited of Ontario, this barberry is described by the nursery as "vigorous grower with deep, dark red foliage. Makes an excellent tall hedge."

Berberis thunbergii 'Thornless' (Thornless Japanese barberry). This differs from the Japanese barberry only in lacking the thorns. It is listed also as *B. t. inermis* which means "thornless."

Berberis triacanthophora (Threespine barberry). Zone 6 to southern part of Zone 5; 4′.

This barberry differs from many other barberries because its flowers are not yellow. Instead, they are whitish, tinged with red and about a quarter inch in diameter. They open in May and are followed by blue-black berries, coloring in autumn.

Foliage is evergreen and the leaves may measure 2″ in length. As the botanical name tells, the plant is thorny. This species is regarded as among the hardiest of the evergreen barberries.

Berberis verruculosa (Warty barberry). Zone 6 to part of Zone 5; 3′-4′.

Glossy, dark green, evergreen leaves, white underneath, turning bronze in autumn; ½″ diameter golden-yellow flowers late in May, followed by deep violet-black berries; plus a neat, compact growth habit and spreading form are the characteristics of this barberry. The twigs are thorny and warty, hence the common name. Where it can be grown, this makes a beautiful specimen shrub.

BUDDLEIA (Butterfly bush)

Buddleias or butterfly bushes are grown for their spikes of flowers which, in the most popular *B. davidii* cultivars, are borne throughout the summer months when not too many other shrubs are in bloom. The only "hardy" buddleia is *B. alternifolia* and the word "hardy" is not too accurate in describing it. Even in Zone 5b the shrub occasionally dies to the ground, not necessarily in a severe winter. That is, it may survive several severe winters only to die to the earth during a winter which does not have particularly low temperatures but during which some other factor or factors kill this buddleia. *Buddleia davidii* cultivars all die to the ground each winter or should be pruned at ground level in spring if they do not winterkill entirely to the ground. Since they all bloom on wood of the current season, this annual dying back makes no difference. Even *B. alternifolia* will grow again from the roots, though a season's flowers will be lost since it blooms only on wood produced the previous year. Soil may be hilled around the roots of all buddleias in autumn for protection from severe cold and this sometimes will save a bush from complete death. But buddleias, at best, are not long-lived plants.

Perfect drainage and a protected spot often help keep buddleia roots alive even without protection. These shrubs need full sun and will grow and bloom better when soil is rich.

Berberis verruculosa, flower.   →

Buddleia alternifolia (Fountain butterfly bush, Hardy butterfly bush). Zone 5 and occasionally, with some die-back each winter, in Zone 4; 10'-12'.

Shaped just as one of its common names implies and spreading wide so that it must be allowed plenty of room in the garden, this butterfly bush is a beautiful sight when in flower. Long spikes of fragrant, ⅛" wide florets, light purple (5 P 7/7) in color, arranged in ¾" wide clusters appear in mid-May to June and their very numbers make this shrub a bouquet of bloom.

Leaves are small and gray-green and keep the shrub attractive when it is not in flower.

Buddleia alternifolia, branch of blooms, left; effect of branch with seed pods pictured above; closeup of flowers, below.

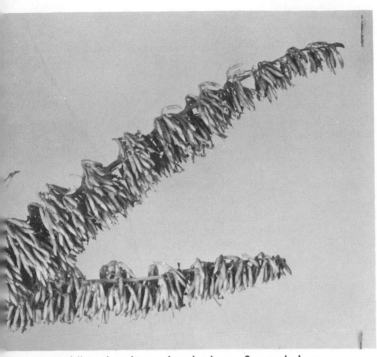

Buddleia davidii, seed pods above; flowers below.

Buddleia davidii (Orange-eye butterfly bush). Zone 5, occasionally in Zone 4; 6'-12'.

Lilac-purple flowers with a not-too-conspicuous orange eye distinguish this shrub; it is rarely seen in comparison with its cultivars, which are widely grown.

These cultivars are commonly called "summer lilacs" because the flower colors of most are similar to those of lilac blooms.

There are many cultivars available in a color range from white (as in 'White Bouquet'), through pink (as in 'Charming' or 'Fascinating') through lilac, lavender, deep purple, and reddish violet. All cultivars have fragrant blooms which are attractive, so you can allow your taste to dictate the flower color you want to buy. Blooms continue to appear until frost on most cultivars.

Buddleia davidii magnifica. Blooming from the middle of August onward, this variety is stronger-growing than *davidii*; has rose-purple or violet-purple flowers with dark orange eyes and the outer edges of the petals are rolled or reflexed. Blooms are larger than those of *davidii* and borne in dense clusters.

Buddleia × *farquhari* (*B. asiatica* × *B. officinalis*). Zone 6 to Zone 5b; 5'.

Fragrant, lavender flowers in drooping clusters start to open on this plant in mid-July and con-

Buddleia farquhari, flowers.

Buddleia farquhari, seed pods.

tinue until frost. They seem rarely to open fully and therefore are not nearly as conspicuous as those of *B. davidii* cultivars. The plant on which they are borne also is much smaller than the other buddleias.

BUXUS (Box, Boxwood)

Boxwoods are the glory of southern gardens, where tiny plants are used to edge rose beds and where enormous older plants form handsome specimens put to numerous uses in the landscape. In the northern states only a few boxwoods thrive and huge plants are practically unknown.

Boxwoods are grown for their foliage and their form, not for their inconspicuous flowers. All are evergreen and, in the warmth of a sunny day, their foliage gives off an unusual and unforgettable aroma—not precisely a fragrance. If you visit the boxwood garden at Mt. Vernon or any other estate where there are boxwood plantings on a warm, sunny day, stand still near the plants and treat yourself to a sniff. Ever afterward, the unmistakable scent will tell you if you are near boxwoods.

Boxwood plants should preferably be moved in early spring and, if of any size, should always be purchased with a ball of earth around the roots. Plants should be set where drainage is good and the soil texture is open. Where soil is reasonably good, no special preparation is required; nor need holes be especially deep, for the plants are shallow-rooted. A hole a foot wider on each side than the earth ball will, however, be appreciated.

Plants should be set at precisely the same depth as they grew in the nursery (look for a dark line around the stems of the plant, which marks this place)—never deeper. On the other hand, they should not be set shallower than they grew in the nursery lest the roots be exposed to air.

Boxwood thrives in either full sun or light shade. In northern climates it is best to set the plants where they will be sheltered from drying winter winds, as well as hot sun in late winter and early spring. As far as low temperatures are concerned, if you choose the kind of box that will survive in your climate and don't attempt to grow the kinds that won't, winterkill will not be one of your worries. There is nothing but extra work in store for the gardener who ignores hardiness and therefore must build shelters of burlap and wood to help his box plants survive the winter.

Boxwood needs additional water if the summer should be dry, but do not wait until there is a drought to give water as boxwood is slow to show the effects of lack of moisture. Never mound soil up around boxwood plants, for then water will run away from the roots. Deep mulching is inadvisable because it excludes air from the roots. Cultivation on top of the root area should be avoided because of the possibility of injuring the shallow roots.

If boxwood is planted for a low hedge, plants should be set 10″ apart. If the hedge is to be formal, it must be pruned as needed to keep it shapely. Once a year any dead twigs should be cut out from the plants. A good time to do this is late spring, before new growth begins, but after you can see which parts are dead.

There are two species of boxwood that will survive winters in the north; *microphylla* and *sempervirens*. Of the two, *microphylla* is the hardier; so make your choice depending on how far north you live.

Buxus microphylla (Littleleaf box). Zone 6 to Zone 5b; 3'-4'.

Littleleaf box, as previously stated, will withstand lower temperatures than will *B. sempervirens,* which may have tips of branches injured by cold even in Zone 7.

Littleleaf box has leaves to an inch long, is compact in form, low and slow-growing. Unfortunately leaves sometimes turn brown in winter and for this reason some of the cultivars may be preferable to the species.

Buxus microphylla 'Compacta' (syn *Buxus microphylla nana compacta,* syn Kingsville dwarf box). Zone 5; 1' but many times wider than high. A very dense, naturally low-growing form, this has good, green leaves.

Buxus microphylla koreana (Korean box), also listed in some catalogs as *koraensis.* Zone 5 to part of Zone 4. 2'-3', but occasionally to 5'. The hardiest box, this forms a nice looking plant, broader than high, even though it has not the billowing form or the height of the beautiful southern boxwoods. It has withstood 18 degrees below zero, F in my garden with absolutely no injury while two cultivars of *B. sempervirens,* not 30' away, in the same general part of the garden but in a slightly more protected place, have browned to the snow line.

The only criticism that can be made of Korean box is that the foliage often turns tannish or yellowish or brownish-green during winter so as to refute the description of "evergreen." The "browned" leaves are alive and well and will turn green again in spring. A cultivar named 'Wintergreen' is now starting to appear in the nursery lists. It is said to remain green all winter. I have not yet seen it.

Buxus sempervirens (syn *B. s. arborescens*) (Common box). Zone 6 and protected places in Zone 5b; 6'-8'.

The shiny, dark green leaves grow to 1¼" long, the form of the plant is dense and "billowy," and specimen plants or hedges have a charm all their own. This is the boxwood commonly used throughout the south, where it grows to 25' high and almost treelike.

Most of the varieties of *B. sempervirens* need winter protection, which is most easily given by sticking evergreen branches into the soil near the plants on the windward side and the side from which the hottest sun comes. Wooden and burlap screens also may be built on this or these sides to keep off wind and hot sun.

Buxus sempervirens arborescens (see *B. sempervirens*).

Buxus sempervirens 'Grand Rapids'. Zone 5b; 3'. A selection that is hardier than the species, it is listed only by nurseries near the Michigan city for which it is named.

Buxus sempervirens 'Inglis'. Zone 5b; 3'. Some years ago the late Mrs. James Inglis of Ann Arbor, Michigan told me about a really hardy boxwood she had growing on the grounds of her estate. This plant, she said, showed no signs of winter injury even when the temperature dropped to 20 degrees below zero, F. She said that she had given cuttings of the plant to several Michigan nurserymen and hoped that at least one would propagate and introduce it. As you can see from the Buyer's Guide Chart in Chapter 11, one of them did. If you garden where temperatures are severe, this and the Korean box, as well as 'Vardar Valley' and 'Welleri' are boxes worth trying.

'Inglis' is pyramidal in form, very dense and bushy in growth and the leaves stay green all winter.

Buxus sempervirens 'Newport Blue'. Zone 6 to Zone 5b. Bluish-green leaves which are small and round, slow growth and the ability to stand shearing to shape are characteristics of this cultivar.

Buxus sempervirens 'Suffruticosa' (sometimes listed in the catalogs as *B. suffruticosa*) (Edging box). Zone 5b; 2'-2½'. The smallest boxwood, a true dwarf, this is the kind to use to edge flower beds or garden paths. It has roundish leaves about ¾" long, is very slow-growing and has a dense,

←   Buxus microphylla koreana, flowers.

compact form. Foliage is more fragrant than those of other boxwoods.

Buxus sempervirens 'Vardar Valley'. Zone 5a, 2'-3'. The Vardar Valley is in the Balkan Mountains and the original plant of this cultivar was found growing there. Plants are flattish on top, may grow twice as wide as they grow high.

Buxus sempervirens 'Welleri' (Weller's box). Zone 5b, possibly Zone 5a, sometimes survives in Zone 4; to 3', growing eventually wider than high. An introduction of the Weller Nursery, Holland, Michigan, this is a hardy form which grows very well in my garden and in other gardens in our state. I have had 60 plants for nine years, some in a curving hedge, some used to edge either side of a short flight of steps. The only fault that I can find with this cultivar is that in severe winters it browns above the snow line, but when none of the plants are snow-covered, there is little browning.

CALLICARPA (Beauty berry, Jewel berry)

Callicarpas are deciduous and are "die-back-to-the-ground" shrubs in Zone 5, although the tops often survive the winter in Zone 6 and southward. Where tops do winter, they should be pruned severely in early spring for vigorous growth and many fruits later in the season, since flowers and fruits are borne on wood of the current season's growth.

Callicarpas grow in any soil; prefer full sun but tolerate light shade. They are all upright growing, have inconspicuous flowers, and are grown only for their colorful fruits. These are berries which are borne at the tips of the new wood and, while they are perfectly beautiful in color, they remain on the plants for only 2 or 3 weeks after the leaves have turned yellow and then fallen.

Callicarpa dichotoma (syn *C. purpurea*, syn *C. koreana*) (Korean jewel berry). Zone 6 to part of Zone 5; 4'.

Upright in growth, this shrub has inconspicuous pink flowers, but the berries are lilac-violet, coloring in September, October, and November.

Callicarpa japonica (Japanese beauty berry, Japanese jewel berry). Zone 5; 4'.

White or pink inconspicuous flowers in early June are followed by 3/16" diameter violet colored berries in October to November. These show off well against the leaves, which turn pale yellow.

Callicarpa japonica 'Leucocarpa' is a form with white berries.

Callicarpa purpurea (see *C. dichotoma*).

Callicarpa dichotoma, closeup of buds and blooms.

, buds, flowers and berries

171

Callicarpa dichotoma, berries.

CALLUNA (Scotch heather, Heather)

In Europe, covering thousands upon thousands of acres of poor land where apparently nothing else will grow, you can see heather plants, and when they are in bloom they look like a sea of color. I have seen and photographed them singly and in vast numbers in Scotland, Holland, and Greece and these acres of color are a joy to remember.

These same heather plants can be grown in the garden provided they are supplied with the same perfect drainage, poor, acid soil and sunshine that they have in their native habitats. These conditions are not hard to duplicate. Choose a slope or the top of a wall for your heather planting, replace the existing soil with half sand and half acid peat, adding a handful of sulphur to each bushel of soil as you mix it, and plant heathers in this. If they have good soil the plants will grow vigorously, become "leggy," will flower sparsely or won't bloom at all. They just cannot stand luxury.

The soil should not be allowed to dry completely during the summer heat and the easiest way to accomplish this is to mulch over the soil and under the plants after they have had time to reestablish their roots. Buckwheat hulls make a satisfactory mulch.

To keep plants compact and to force plenty of new growth, which means plenty of bloom, heather plants may be pruned as needed or even sheared if necessary, but this must be done in early spring or not at all.

Because the plants must be in full sun to bloom, their evergreen foliage may become burned in late winter and very early spring. For this reason, save boughs from your Christmas tree and lay them over the tops of the heather plants, leaving them in place until the cold weather is past.

Calluna vulgaris, flowers.

172

Heathers may be used to cover banks, as ground covers in sunny areas, in rock gardens and on tops of walls. They vary in height, most hugging the ground in mats, but the tallest growing to several feet in height.

Calluna vulgaris (Scotch heather, Heather). Zone 5 to part of Zone 4; 1½'-2½'.

Scotch heather is an evergreen shrub with tiny, needle-like leaves and small spikes of bell-shaped purplish-pink flowers. There are many cultivars of Scotch heather with different flower colors, foliage colors and growth habits. Given below are short descriptions of the cultivars most frequently found in the catalogs.

Calluna vulgaris 'Alba' is just like the species but has white flowers.

Calluna vulgaris 'Alba Erecta' has a more upright form and white flowers.

Calluna vulgaris 'Alportii (see *C.v.* 'Atrorubens').

Calluna vulgaris 'Atrorubens' (syn *C.v.* 'Alportii') (Red heather). Crimson flowers against grayish foliage are the distinguishing features of this dense, erect-growing heather.

Calluna vulgaris 'Aurea' sports pink flowers against golden yellow foliage.

Calluna vulgaris 'Cuprea' has purple flowers against golden yellow leaves.

CALYCANTHUS

Calycanthus floridus (Strawberry shrub, Sweet shrub, Carolina allspice, Bubbly blossoms, Sweet Bubbie, Peat shrub, Peat tree, Sweet Betsy), Zone 5 to parts of Zone 4; usually 4', but may grow to 6' or 7'.

Although this shrub is native from Virginia to Florida, it is hardy in the north. In an especially severe winter it may die to the ground but it will grow again from the roots. The form of the shrub varies from dense to open and straggly depending on the soil in which it grows. In clay soils the shrub tends to grow more open in form.

The branchlets give off an odor like camphor. The shiny green leaves are aromatic when crushed. They turn yellowish in autumn and the large seed pods turn brown about the same time. Pods are borne, usually, only once in several years.

This shrub, however, is really grown for its 1¼" to 1¾" diameter reddish-brown (10 R 3/4) flowers which open from June to July. These have an unusual fragrance, at first rather like a spicy strawberry but, when older, more like that of a spicy, ripe apple.

Calycanthus floridus, branch in bloom, closeup of flowers, and fruit, below.

173

For generations, children have tied these flowers in the corners of their handkerchiefs or held them cupped in their hands, smelling them from time to time. They have been used in bureau drawers as substitutes for sachet and carried to church to "perfume" the owner. The fragrance is most noticeable on a warm, sunny day or when your hand has warmed a flower.

Sad to say, the fewest of strawberry shrubs on the market now have fragrant flowers. Propagation should be from fragrant plants only, but unfortunately this is not the case. Search out a nursery that sells plants with fragrant flowers if you want to grow this shrub for its chief attraction.

Strawberry shrub grows in any soil, in sun or light shade, but thrives best in a rich, moist soil, in part shade and a protected place.

CARAGANA (Pea tree, Pea shrub)

Very hardy, deciduous shrubs or small trees, these are natives of Russia and China which will grow in any soil, even almost pure sand. All of them prefer sunny places and start to flower when very young. They are inclined to be straggly in growth, so should be heavily pruned every few years. If necessary, any of them may be cut to the ground and will grow anew from the roots.

Caragana arborescens (Siberian pea tree). Zone 3 to part of Zone 2; 20'.

This often is used in shelter-belt plantings on the Great Plains. It is a native of Manchuria and Siberia; an excellent plant for a tall hedge, when planted 18" apart, or may be used to give height to a shrub border. Growth is upright, bark gray and young twigs yellow-green. The flowers, which open in May, are vivid yellow (5 Y 8/12), and shaped like those of peas. The pods, which contain the seeds, also are shaped much like those of peas but are flatter. They are 2" long, ⅛" wide, and are strong yellow green (2.5 GY 6/8) before they turn tan.

There are half a dozen cultivars of Siberian pea tree available in Canada, all apparently having the same hardiness and resistance to drought as the species.

Caragana arborescens 'Lorbergii' (Lorberg's pea tree). Zone 3; 8'-10'. A graceful, fountain-form plant with slender leaves that make an airy impression, this has flowers larger than those on the Siberian pea tree and fewer of them. They are vivid yellow (5 Y 8/12), ½" long and ⅜" wide across the top two petals. They are shaped like

Caragana arborescens, flowers above; seed pods, below.

Caragana arborescens 'Lorbergii', branch in bloom, above; flower and foliage detail, below.

those of peas. This shrub is best used as a specimen and should be set where it has at least 6′ of space around it.

Caragana arborescens 'Pendula' (Weeping pea tree). Zone 4. This pendulous form usually is grafted on a tall trunk of the Siberian pea tree and thus forms a "weeping" plant. Its height, therefore, depends on the length of the trunk used. It is otherwise like the Siberian pea tree. Because of its form, it should be used only as a specimen or special accent.

Caragana frutex (Shrubby pea tree). Zone 4; 6′-9′.

This caragana is not often found in gardens. It is native from southern Russia to northern China. It is erect in growth, has bright green leaflets, four to a group, aranged like fingers on a hand. Flowers are bright yellow, ¾″ to 1″ long, and borne singly.

Caragana pygmaea (Dwarf Russian pea tree). Zone 4, probably to parts of Zone 3; 2′-2½′.

Slender, arching branches give this low, spiny shrub its character. The young twigs are colored red-brown, the older ones dark gray and the bark shreds more or less. Flowers are two-toned, the lower petals brilliant yellow (2.5 Y 9/9), flushed vivid yellow (2.5 Y 8/12) which is the color of the top petals. Blooms are ⅞″ long and 9/16″ wide across the top petals (widest part of the flower). They are borne singly and are marked reddish on the outsides. This shrub may be used as a specimen in a rock garden or where a small accent is needed or in the front of a shrub border. It often is grown in "tree" form, especially in Canada, and is effective as a specimen when so grown.

Caragana pygmaea flowers, below.

CARYOPTERIS

Caryopteris × *clandonensis* (syn *Spiraea caryopteris*) (*C. incana* × *C. mongholica*) (Bluebeard, Blue spirea, Chinese beardwort, Verbena shrub). Zone 6 to Zone 5b; 2'-3'.

Grown for its blue or bluish flowers in late August and early September, this is a delicate little shrub with slender branches and gray leaves. The following cultivars, each with a different shade of blue flowers are listed in the catalogs: 'Azure', 'Blue Mist', 'Dark Knight', 'Heavenly Blue'. I understand that the U.S. Department of Agriculture has introduced a cultivar with deep blue flowers and darker foliage than 'Blue Mist'.

Of the cultivars listed above, I have grown two, the two most widely available: 'Blue Mist' and 'Heavenly Blue'. 'Heavenly Blue', which has strong violet (10 PB 4/10) flowers, never lives through even a mild winter with me, though I've tried growing it half a dozen times. 'Blue Mist', with flowers of light violet (2.5 P 5/8) grows well, surviving even severe winters without protection.

Set these plants only where they have good drainage and full sun. If they die to the ground during winter, they usually will grow again from the roots in spring. In milder climates they should be pruned to the ground each spring to encourage new growth and shapeliness.

A single shrub is not particularly effective in the garden unless planted with another shrub having flowers of a contrasting color or placed in a perennial border next to perennials of contrasting hue that bloom at the same time. However, a group of three or more of the same cultivar, planted 3' apart, will give an airy gray and blue effect at a time of year when it is needed.

Caryopteris incana (syn *C. mastacanthus*). Zone 7 to part of Zone 6; to 5'.

Dull green leaves, violet-blue (and occasionally white) flowers, which appear in October to November are the characteristics of this species.

Caryopteris mastacanthus (*see C. incana*).

Caryopteris clandonensis 'Blue Mist', branches and flower details, above; seed pods, below.

CEANOTHUS

Ceanothus americanus (New Jersey tea, Mountainsweet, Redroot). Zone 4; 3'.

Native from Canada to South Carolina and Texas, this little shrub is a poor substitute for the gorgeous, blue-flowered ceanothuses that grow so well in California and states with similar climates. However, since this is the only one I can grow, I grow it, though it frequently dies to the ground

176

Ceanothus americanus, blooms above; seed pods, below.

in winter. It always comes up again in spring and, since it blooms on wood of the current season's growth, no flowers are lost.

This shrub has tiny white flowers in dense clusters at the tips of the branches, produced most heavily in July but with a few appearing now and then during the rest of the growing season. The reddish fruits in September are interesting in shape and of some garden interest.

In a spot where the soil is too poor for other shrubs, this one will thrive with no care at all. It has formed large colonies along the roadside near our lakeside cabin where it is in the poorest possible soil and is covered with dust from the road all summer.

CEPHALANTHUS

Cephalanthus occidentalis (Buttonbush, Honeyballs). Zone 4; 12'-15'.

If the shrub described above is one to grow in poor soil, buttonbush is one to grow in wet soil. It grows naturally in swamps, along the shores of lakes and by the sides of streams from New Brunswick to Cuba. It does not mind having its feet in water several feet deep during spring floods.

From late July through August the white or cream-white, fragrant flowers open in round heads and with pinkish pistils. The common name is said to be for a fancied resemblance of the round flower heads to buttons, but I think they look more like pincushions. The fragrance of the blooms attracts many insects.

This shrub need only be planted in a wet place in sun or light shade and left strictly alone. Once in a long time, in the interests of appearance, it is a good idea to cut out any dead branches.

Cephalanthus occidentalis, flowering branch.

Cephalanthus occidentalis, flower detail, above. Note that it has no petals. Seed head is pictured below.

CHAENOMELES (Flowering quince, Japanese flowering quince, Japonica)

The flowering quinces furnish brilliant color in the garden in early spring. In addition to their bright flowers, they have shiny, dark green leaves, bronze or reddish on some varieties and cultivars when first open. The flowers appear with the leaves or after the leaves unfold. Growth habit of the different varieties and cultivars varies; some grow upright and dense, others low and dense and in still others growth is so open as to be straggly.

This is one genus in which most catalogs are years behind in proper nomenclature. This is due, in part at least, to the number of times that botanists have changed its name. First it was *Pyrus,* then *Cydonia* and now is *Chaenomeles.*

One reason for all these changes is that originally a botanist gave an incorrect description of the fruit which temporarily confounded later botanists. Another is that the dried herbarium specimens made by early botanists are incomplete and were collected at the wrong time of year for correct identification.

In the genus *Chaenomeles* (still called *Cydonia* in most catalogs) there are two species which account for the flowering quinces grown in northern gardens. Of these *C. japonica* is from Japan and is a low-growing shrub, usually to about 3′ in height. The second species, *C. speciosa* (formerly *C. lagenaria*), is from China and is a big shrub, to about 6′ high and sometimes more.

Because they flower so early in spring, flowering quinces should be transplanted or moved in autumn. They move easily, are undemanding as to soil, but should have full sun to bloom their best. Most varieties have thorns, so should be placed elsewhere than along a narrow path. Occasional pruning is required but only for renewal of growth or for better form.

Chaenomeles japonica (Japanese quince, Firebush). Zone 5; occasionally to Zone 4 where usually it is not flower-bud-hardy; 3′.

If you will notice the height to which this shrub grows you will immediately recognize its usefulness. Here is a plant with excellent foliage (though lacking autumn color) which requires little care and has brilliant orange-red, single flowers 1¼″ in diameter in late April or early May. It may be used under many windows without any worry about its growing so tall as to obscure them, or anywhere else where a low shrub is required. The quince-like fruits are excellent for jelly.

Chaenomeles japonica alpina (Dwarf Japanese quince). Zone 5; 1'-1½', usually the lower figure. Illustrated on Color Page VII. An even dwarfer form of the species, this can be used in house plantings where windows come practically to the ground, or as a ground cover for a bank or level area, or to "face down" higher shrubs. It spreads widely. My aunt used to have one of these shrubs in her garden that was fully 8' in diameter. Flowers are strong reddish orange (10 R 6/12) 1¼" in diameter. New foliage is bronze to reddish bronze.

Chaenomeles 'Appleblossom', left, C. japonica alpina, right. Note variation in flower size.

Chaenomeles lagenaria (see *C. speciosa*).
Chaenomeles 'Maulei'. Zone 5; 2'-2½'.

A small plant, therefore useful in many places, this has single, salmon-pink, but sometimes orange, flowers against dark green leaves. Usually each plant bears an abundant crop of fruits.

Chaenomeles speciosa (syn *Chaenomeles lagenaria*, syn *Cydonia japonica* of the catalogs) (Flowering quince). Zone 5; occasionally to Zone 4; 6'.

Tall, generally upright growing plants with dark green leaves, sometimes glossy, which unfold with or before the scarlet flowers, these have large quinces which turn from green to yellow when ripe and make excellent jelly. If you will combine these quinces with apples, half and half, the jelly is not so heavily flavored and, in my opinion is more delicious. Several plants are needed for cross pollination in order that fruit be produced.

Chaenomeles cultivars:

In *Arnoldia* Volume 23, No. 3, dated April 5, 1963, and titled "Cultivars In The Genus Chaenomeles" by Claude Weber, there are six pages of names of all known cultivars with roughly 100 names to the page. This explains why I am not going to attempt to describe even those commonly listed in the catalogs. *Arnoldia* is published by the Arnold Arboretum, Jamaica Plain, Massachusetts, and if you are interested, you should buy a copy of this booklet.

All I am going to say about these cultivars is that they have larger flowers than the species in a wide range of colors which may be grouped as: (1)—white, (2) pink and white, (3) pink, in varying shades, (4) red, in varying shades and (5) orange, in varying shades. Salmon and near apricot would be included under either pink or orange, whichever they most closely resembled.

I own about 35 cultivars in addition to the species and variety already described. If I were to start collecting them over again, I would stop with the 2 species, the variety and the following cultivars: 'Snow', white; 'Appleblossom', first white, then flushed deep yellowish pink (5 R 6/11) and gradually becoming that color all over; 'Charming', which is nearest to 5 P 6/11, deep yellowish pink but deeper and has no match on the color fan; 'Coral Beauty', deep yellowish pink (5 R 6/11); 'Blood Red', strong red (5 R 4/12) and 'Stanford Red', vivid red (5 R 5/12). All have flowers at least 1¼" in diameter, most to 2" across, and most of the color range is found in the few quinces listed above.

In addition to all the cultivars now on the market, new ones are coming. The University of Illinois is introducing six selections, one of which, named 'Arthur Colby', if planted with other flowering quinces blooming at the same time, will not only produce an abundance of flowers but a par-

ticularly heavy set of fruits which are larger than those usually found on *C. speciosa*. The idea is to provide usable quinces in small space.

Furthermore, new cultivars are being produced in Europe as well as in the United States. To cite one instance, Mr. Ruys, owner of Royal Moerheim Nursery in the north of Holland showed me a large bed of seedlings, indicating a few that he thought worthy of naming and introducing.

So, since we can look forward to more and more flowering quinces, careful selection is required to insure the height, form and flower color desired.

Chaenomeles 'Appleblossom', branch of blooms, above; close view of buds and flowers, below.

Chaenomeles fruit (quince) typical of both species described. Only the size varies from one species to the other. Excellent jelly can be made from these fruits.

CHAMAEDAPHNE

Chamaedaphne calyculata (also spelled *caliculata*) (syn *Andromeda calyculata*) (Leatherleaf). Zone 4 at least; usually about 1½' but sometimes to 3'.

Native from Newfoundland to Alaska, southward to Georgia, westward to Ohio, northern Indiana, Illinois, Wisconsin, northern Iowa, Alberta, and British Columbia, this little evergreen grows best in a spot resembling its native haunts which are swamps, bogs, and edges of ponds.

However, it will grow, though not as well, in drier soil. Its leaves are small, dull green and rusty on the undersides. Flowers are ¼″ long and white. The only reason for growing this shrub in a cultivated garden is its early flowering time—late April. Otherwise it is best reserved for a wild garden, where it can have a soil mixture of peat and sand and the dampness that will insure its thriftiness. It should be moved only with a ball of earth around its roots.

Clethra alnifolia, flowers.

Chamaedaphne calyculata, flowers.

CLETHRA

Clethra alnifolia (syn *C. paniculata* of the catalogs) (Summersweet, Sweet pepper bush). Zone 4 to part of Zone 3; 3′-8′.

White, sweet-scented flowers in erect clusters appearing in July and August when few other shrubs are blooming are certainly the outstanding characteristic of this genus. The shrub itself also is attractive with its shining green leaves. Its height depends on how well it likes its environment. It grows naturally in wet woods or swamps, though sometimes in drier places, usually along the eastern coast from Maine to Mississippi. The closer you can duplicate its accustomed habitat, the taller it will grow. Even in dry places it will be about 4′ high. It does equally well in full sun or semi-shade, but in full sun the foliage takes on a deeper yellow

Clethra alnifolia 'Rosea', flowers and seed pods.

to orange coloring in autumn. It is tolerant of many soils though it grows best in acid, peaty soil. Increasing by underground stems, it soon forms clumps; so adequate space for these should be allowed when it is planted. This shrub may be used in a border, by a pool or stream, or in a wild garden, and is most effective in groups of three or more plants.

Clethra alnifolia 'Rosea'. The pink-flowered form of *C. alnifolia*, this starts to bloom about a week later than the species, and the flower spikes are a bit heavier (see photographs) than those of the species. Nurserymen have complained to me that the plants they bought for resale as pink-flowered had pinkish buds but white flowers. Our plants have deep purplish pink buds (7.5 P 6/12) and flowers pale purplish pink (7.5 RP 9/2) inside and light purplish pink (7.5 RP 8/5) on the outsides of the petals. Forewarned is forearmed, so they say; evidently the plants you buy should be seen when in flower.

Clethra paniculata (see *C. alnifolia*).

Clethra paniculata rubra (see *C. alnifolia* 'Rosea').

COLUTEA

Colutea arborescens (syn *C. arborea* of the catalogs) (Bladder senna). Zone 5 to some parts of Zone 4; usually about 6′, sometimes to 10′. Illustrated on Color Page V.

Thriving in poor, sandy soil, growing best in full sun, bladder senna bears 1″ long, ¾″ wide brilliant yellow (2.5 Y 9/9) flowers in 1½″ clusters from May throughout the summer months. The burst of bloom is in May, but there usually are a few blooms on a plant all during the summer. The flowers are shaped like those of peas and their yellow color is veined and tinged reddish. After the flowers fade, an unusually shaped fruit forms—shaped like a bladder or inflated pod. A single fruit may be 3″ long and turns pinkish green to tan.

Because of the long blooming season, both flowers and bladders are on the plant at the same time. Children love to pop the bladders and usually there are so many on a plant that there is no reason why they should not have their fun.

The shrub grows broad, sometimes broader than high, and is not easy to transplant. It is best moved in early spring, though it may be moved with bare roots. In some situations many seedlings will sprout around a mother plant. These should be ruthlessly weeded out.

Colutea arborescens, flowers, below.

Clethra alnifolia 'Rosea', closeup of flowers.

Colutea arborescens, branch of bladder-like seed pods, above, closeup of seed pods, below.

COMPTONIA

Comptonia asplenifolia (see *C. peregrina*).

Comptonia peregrina (syn *C. asplenifolia*) (Sweet fern). Zone 2; 4'.

Even though this grows naturally in an acid peat or dry acid sand, it will grow well in any acid soil where nothing else will thrive. It is native from New Brunswick to Manitoba, southward to Virginia, westward to northern Indiana and northeastern Illinois.

Its merits are the graceful habit of growth, the form and the aromatic fragrance of its leaves which are fern-like, quite different from those usually found on woody plants. This plant is said to be difficult to transplant, though many people say they do not find it so. If you intend to try moving it from the wild, wait until it is dormant in fall, take a good-sized piece of the sod in which its roots are contained, and move the entire piece of sod to a place where the soil is poor and acid.

Sweet fern may be used in a wild garden or as a ground cover for banks where soil is poor.

CORNUS (Dogwood)

This large genus contains plants which are trees, others which are shrubs and even one species (*C. canadensis*) which is a low-growing ground cover. The tree forms commonly used with shrubs are described in Chapter 15. It is these trees which are most spectacular when in flower. The shrubby dogwoods usually are grown more for the color of their twigs and branches or their fruit or even their bright leaves in autumn than for their flowers. These blooms, while not spectacular individually, usually are borne in such large quantities that a shrub is conspicuous while in blossom.

The dogwoods grown primarily for their twig color should be pruned heavily every year or two, whether they otherwise need it or not, because the younger twigs have the brighter colors. Some professional gardeners cut these particular dogwoods to the ground about every 5 years in order that new and more colorful growth start from the roots.

There is one dogwood, grown as a shrub or sometimes as a tree which is spectacular in bloom— *Cornus kousa*, the Korean dogwood. Read the description below and admire the shrub in the frontispiece.

Cornus alba (Tatarian dogwood, Siberian dogwood). Zone 2; 3'-9'.

While the young twigs are greenish early in the season, they are bright red by the end of it and, with branches of the same color, this shrub is grown because of their brightness. It is particularly lovely in winter against snow. Leaves are yellow-green, flowers white, borne in flat clusters in May. Fruits are white, grayish-white or bluish-white. The shrub is upright in growth habit.

Cornus alba 'Argenteo-marginata' (syn *C. elegantissima* of the catalogs). Zone 2; 6'-7'. Illustrated on Color Page VI. This form is a less vigorous-growing shrub than *C. alba*. It has red branches and the leaves, which may grow to 5" long, are edged with white. Flowers are white, arranged in 2" diameter clusters. Because of the foliage a planting of these shrubs gives a striking green and white effect, impossible to reproduce adequately in a photograph. This shrub is especially effective when used in a border in combination with green-leaved shrub or tree dogwoods.

Cornus alba 'Argenteo-marginata', flowers and variegated foliage.

Cornus alba aurea (see *C. alba* 'Spaethii').

Cornus alba elegantissima (see *C. alba* 'Argenteo-marginata').

Cornus alba 'Gouchaultii' (also spelled Gouchalti and Gouchatti in the catalogs) (Gouchault dogwood). The foliage of this dogwood is yellowish and pink or red or yellowish white and pink or red, in streaks. It makes a good specimen where such a color combination is desired or may

be combined with green-leaved dogwoods or shrubs.

Cornus alba 'Kesselringii'. The characteristic which distinguishes this dogwood from others is the branch color—very dark purple, nearly black. The unfolding leaves are red.

Cornus alba 'Sibirica' (Siberian dogwood, Coral dogwood). Zone 2; 9'. Because of its coral-red twigs, this is an even more colorful dogwood than *C. alba* to use when winter color is the aim. Flowers are creamy-white, small, and arranged in the usual flat clusters. They are effective in May and are followed by berries which usually are white but may be blue-white. Fall foliage color is red. One possible advantage of this dogwood is that it is not as rampant in growth as the species.

Cornus alba 'Spaethii' (Yellowedge dogwood, Spaeth dogwood). The leaves of this cultivar, which grow to 5" in length are yellow green (closest to moderate yellow green (5 GY 5/6) bordered with brilliant greenish yellow (7.5 Y 9/8), a most effective combination.

Cornus amomum (Silky dogwood, Redbrush, Squawbush, Swamp dogwood, Blueberried dogwood). Zone 4; 9'.

Native from Massachusetts to Georgia and westward to New York and Tennessee, this dogwood has reddish winter twigs but they are duller red than those of 'Sibirica', so for winter color 'Sibirica' is superior. However, *amomum* has a point in its favor which is that the blooms appear later than those of most red-twigged dogwoods—mid-June. Plants of this dogwood tend to grow more tree-like than those of other dogwoods with red twigs. This plant needs room to spread and grows particularly

Cornus amomum flowers.

well in damp soils. Fruit is blue, but shades vary, so that it may be pale blue, deeper blue and sometimes is almost white. Leaves turn red in autumn. It is easy to distinguish this species from others. Just break off a stem and look at the pith in the center. It is dark in this dogwood.

Cornus elegantissima (see *C. alba* 'Argenteomarginata').

Cornus flaviramea (see *C. stolonifera* 'Flaviramea').

Cornus kousa (Japanese dogwood, Kousa dogwood). Zone 5; 20′.

As you can see in the frontispiece, *Cornus kousa* is the shrub I have chosen to plant next to our front door.

Slow growing when small, and with rather upright growth when young, the branches become more horizontal with age. The bracts are white, pointed at the tips, unlike those of *C. florida,* and minus the notches of *florida* (see Chapter 15). Green at first, the bracts begin to change to white in early June after the leaves have grown and gradually enlarge until the diameter of a group of bracts is 1¾″. After several weeks pink or rose spots dot the bracts. These spots spread and the rose color gradually suffuses the bracts until the effect is of pink bracts. Unless the weather turns hot, the bracts remain in good condition for a full month. *Kousa* flowers about three weeks later than *C. florida* (see Chapter 15).

The true flowers are greenish yellow, appear in the center of the bracts, and are inconspicuous. The fruits that follow them look like pink or rose raspberries. Birds love them so they do not last long. The foliage color in autumn is dull red.

Cornus kousa chinensis (Chinese dogwood, sometimes called Korean dogwood by nurserymen). Zone 5; 20′. The differences between this variety and *kousa* are three. The bracts are larger than those of *kousa* and they are shaped differently. They are longer, start to narrow when halfway to the tip and are sharply pointed at the tip. This variety does not bloom reliably in my garden while *kousa,* except when an unusually severe winter kills the flower buds, blooms every year. However, I have seen, in a sheltered situation between two houses in Ithaca, New York a plant of *chinensis* so laden with bracts that the leaves scarcely were visible. Evidently this is how *chinensis* can perform when sufficiently protected.

Cornus kousa and *C.k. chinensis* flowers are pictured on the next page.

Cornus kousa, fruits.

Cornus mas (also written *mascula*) (Cornelian cherry). Zone 5; 20′ or sometimes a little taller.

Blooming before the forsythias, usually in early April, this dogwood shows off the true flowers since it has no bracts. Each yellow flower (5 Y 9/9, brilliant yellow) is tiny, only ⅛-inch in diameter, but the clusters of blooms may be 1 inch in diameter and often are so profusely borne that the entire shrub appears yellow since it has no leaves as yet.

The shrub is rounded in form, dense in habit, with shining green leaves. The ½″ long, ¼″ wide, plum-shaped fruits turn from 5 R 4/12, strong red, to 2.5 R 3/7, dark red, but, since they are hidden by the leaves, are not effective in the landscape. They are edible and excellent jelly may be made from them.

Cornus mas will grow in any soil and in light shade or full sun. It blends well with many other shrubs and is a good border plant or a specimen at the end of a border.

Cornus officinalis (Japanese cornel). Zone 5; 30′.

Similar to *Cornus mas,* this dogwood blooms a week earlier; also has yellow flowers borne before the leaves unfold. Flower petals are narrower and more pointed than those of *C. mas* and there are other minor differences, but the effect of the two plants is much the same. The fruits, scarlet in color,

185

Cornus kousa chinensis, left, with the last flower of Cornus kousa, right. While this shows difference in size between bracts, the C. kousa bract is not typical in form. Most bracts are more tapered and pointed (see Frontispiece).

borne from August to September, are thinner than those of *C. mas* and more nearly oblong in shape. Leaves are shiny green, turning red in autumn. Older plants have interesting bark that hangs in thin strips.

Cornus paniculata (see *C. racemosa*).

Cornus racemosa (syn *C. paniculata*) (Gray dogwood, Panicled dogwood). Zone 4; 3'-15'.

A native dogwood that grows from central Maine to Ontario, Minnesota, and Manitoba, south to Delaware, West Virginia, Kentucky, Missouri, and Oklahoma, this is a good plant to use for a screen planting. It can be sheared or allowed to grow naturally with equal success. It grows easily, is upright in form with many branches, and has long, narrow leaves. Small creamy-white flowers in the usual flat clusters, in this case 1½" wide, are followed by little white berries in early summer, borne on bright red stems which remain on the shrub after the birds have eaten the berries, thus making it colorful late in the season. It is because these berries appear before those of most other shrub dogwoods that they are so popular with the birds. Foliage color is purplish when autumn arrives, twig color is gray, so the plant is not particularly effective in winter.

Cornus mas, flowers, above; fruits, below.

Cornus racemosa, flowers.

187

Cornus racemosa, fruits.

Cornus sanguinea (Bloodtwig dogwood, Red dogwood). Zone 4; 12′.

While the common and botanical names of this dogwood would lead one to believe that it has the brightest red twigs and branches of any shrub dogwood, such is not the case. Their color is duller than that of the same parts of *C. alba* 'Sibirica'. The growth of this shrub is more upright than that of the Siberian dogwood, however, and the leaves are hairy on both sides. The flowers are the usual small, white florets arranged in flat clusters, but the white in this case is tinged greenish. Blooms appear in late May or early June; fruits that follow are black, ripening in September. The foliage is a dark, blood-red in autumn.

Cornus stolonifera (Red osier dogwood). Zone 2; 3′-9′.

This shrub grows in swamps, along the shores of lakes and in moist thickets from Labrador to the Yukon, south through New England to West Virginia and west to Ohio, Illinois, Iowa, Nebraska, and New Mexico. Kinnikinnik, which is one of the common names sometimes applied to either *C. amomum* or this dogwood, is given because the Indians used the bark of *C. stolonifera* to make the kinnikinnik which they smoked.

The characteristic which a gardener must remember about this dogwood or its varieties is that they all spread by means of stolons or underground stems (which is just what the botanical name indicates they do). Therefore they should be planted only where they have room to expand, otherwise there will be a constant pruning problem. Since the red osier grows especially well in moist situa-

tions, it is sensible to use it in these, though it will tolerate drier soils. Its place is definitely in a naturalistic planting.

The branches often are prostrate, rooting where they touch the ground, though most of them grow upright. Their color is blood red or purplish red and the winter twigs are bright red. Leaves are dark green on the tops, whitish underneath. The small flowers are dull white, borne in rather loose clusters starting in late May, but continuing to appear intermittently for several months. Fruits, borne in summer, are white; autumn foliage color is reddish.

This dogwood may be distinguished from *C. alba* because the disks in its flowers are red and conspicuous while those of *C. alba* are yellow.

Cornus stolonifera baileyi (Bailey's dogwood). Zone 3; to 9′. North of Lake Superior, this variety is the one most commonly found in wet places, rather than the red osier dogwood which dominates in these areas further south. The Bailey

Cornus stolonifera baileyi, flowers above; fruits below.

dogwood (named for Liberty Hyde Bailey, late dean of American horticulturists), is an erect-growing shrub which also has dark red branches, red winter twigs, 2″ wide clusters of white flowers which appear almost all summer, and white fruits, which are eaten by the birds almost as soon as they ripen.

The distinguishing feature of this dogwood is its generally "grayish" effect, which is due to the upward curling of the leaves, thus exposing their lower sides which are white and "woolly." Even the flower clusters have a woolly appearance. The foliage turns a beautiful red in autumn and, coupled with the red branches and the red winter twigs, make this a really handsome shrub dogwood.

Cornus stolonifera coloradensis. Zone 2; 6′. Native from the Yukon and Manitoba to New Mexico and California, this dogwood has strongly recurved branches, brownish red in color, smaller leaves than the red osier dogwood, the usual white flowers in clusters and bluish-white fruits. It is an extremely hardy variety.

Cornus stolonifera 'Flaviramea' (syn *C. stolonifera lutea*) (Goldentwig dogwood). Zone 2; 5′. Lower growing than the red osier dogwood, this also spreads by means of underground stems. The branches are yellowish and the twigs bright yellow. Flowers are white in 1¼″ clusters and fruits also are white but are not effective for any length of time as the birds eat them as soon as they whiten. It may be used wherever the yellow color of its branches and twigs is desired.

Cornus stolonifera 'Flaviramea', closeup of flowers, above; flowering branch below, on left.

Cornus stolonifera 'Kelsey' (syn *C. s. nana*) (sometimes listed as Kelsey dwarf or Kelsey's dwarf). Zone 4 to part of Zone 3; 2′-2½′. A densely branched, dwarf dogwood, this also has red stems and makes an excellent dwarf hedge.

Cornus stolonifera lutea (see *C. stolonifera* 'Flaviramea').

CORONILLA

Coronilla eremurus (Scorpion senna). Zone 5b; 3′-5′.

Evergreen in the south, this is deciduous in the north. It is an upright growing, dense shrub with small, glossy green leaves and bright yellow flowers shaped like those of peas. Some flowers have petals tipped with red. They start to appear in May and continue until the end of the summer.

Coronilla eremurus, flowers.

I do not understand why this shrub is not more widely available because it is so easy to grow, asks for nothing but a sunny spot, and flowers for such a long time. When there are many blooms on a plant it is showy; in any case the foliage is fine and pretty. Rabbits dote on this plant and start to eat the branches even before cold weather starts. It simply must have a protective wire placed around it if it is to attain any size. But, even if eaten to the ground, it will grow from the roots the following spring, and will bloom that summer.

CORYLOPSIS (Winterhazel)

Relatives of the witch hazels, these shrubs have clusters of yellow blooms in mid-April and these early flowers are the reason for growing them. They are not as husky or as hardy as witch hazels. *C. glabrescens* is considered the hardiest and will bloom fairly often in Zone 5b, regularly in Zone 6.

Winterhazels prefer to grow in sun but will do well in light shade. Moist, but well drained, peaty or sandy soil is best for them. They should be pruned in summer if it is necessary to make them grow more compact.

Corylopsis glabrescens (Fragrant winterhazel). Zone 6 to Zone 5b; 15′. Illustrated on Color Page I.

A compact, rounded shrub with fragrant, pale yellow flowers in drooping clusters before the leaves unfold, this is a native of Japan.

Corylopsis pauciflora (Buttercup winter hazel). Zone 6 to Zone 5b; 4′-5′.

This spreading shrub has fragrant, primrose yellow flowers, in nodding clusters before the leaves appear. Each spike of flowers has only a few blooms, two to four, and there is a large bract at the base of each group. This species has the smallest leaves of the commonly grown winterhazels; bluish green in color.

Corylopsis sinensis. Zone 6 to Zone 5b; 10′ or more.

In late March and early April the pale yellow, fragrant flowers are borne in the same type of pendulous spike described under previous species.

Corylopsis spicata (Spike winterhazel). Zone 6 to Zone 5b; 4′-5′.

Handsomer and hardier than either *pauciflora* or *sinensis,* this species is not quite as hardy as *C. glabrescens.* It has showier flowers than the three species just mentioned and more of them. They also are fragrant, are bright yellow and have purple anthers.

CORYLUS (Hazel, Filbert)

Ranging in height from 9′ to 30′, depending on the precise species or varieties, hazels are grown for their interesting catkins early in spring and for the bright colored foliage of certain varieties, the unusual form of others. All those named below are easy to grow in any fairly good soil and require practically no care.

Corylus americana (American hazelnut or hazel). Zone 4; 3′-8′.

Found growing from Maine to Saskatchewan, southward to Florida and Georgia, westward to the Dakotas, this shrub usually grows in hillside pastures and thickets. The catkins appear in April and May and the edible fruits ripen in August and September.

Corylus atropurpurea (see *C. maxima* 'Purpurea').

Corylus avellana (European hazelnut). Zone 5 to parts of Zone 4; 15′.

A large shrub, rounded in form, with big, coarse-appearing, roundish leaves, this grows in full sun, light shade, or even quite deep shade, in almost any soil short of clear sand.

The male catkins expand before the leaves open in early spring, but since they have been noticeable all fall and winter, they also give interest at those seasons. This shrub suckers badly, so must be placed where it has room to spread or the suckers kept cut. It makes a good clipped hedge where suckers do not matter or can be controlled. Otherwise it is best used in a naturalistic planting. Many cultivars of this hazel are used for commercial crops of nuts.

Corylus avellana atropurpurea (see *C. a.* 'Fusco rubra').

Corylus avellana 'Aurea' (syn *C. maxima aurea*) (Golden filbert). Yellow leaves early in the season and yellowish branches distinguish this variety and are the reasons for growing it. Some selections have far better yellow coloring than others, so buy this from a good nursery and see it before buying.

Corylus avellana 'Contorta' (Contorted hazel, Harry Lauder's walking stick). In the United States I never have seen this plant growing taller than 6′, but in Europe, in the north of Holland, it was a small tree with a single trunk and about 20′ high.

The only reason for growing this shrub is for its curiously contorted branches. These form a pattern

Corylus avellana, branch of catkins, right.

Corylus avellana 'Contorta, below, showing catkins and contorted branches.

Corylus avellana 'Fusco-rubra' catkins, below on right.

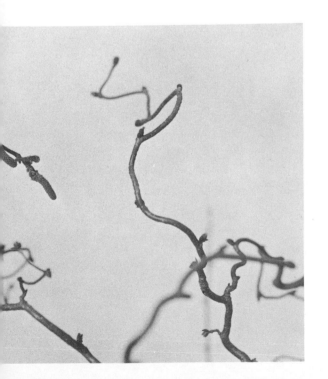

against a wall, particularly effective in winter. It has the usual catkins early in spring and the foliage, while not as large as on some hazels, looks like that of the others.

This shrub usually has the top of the contorted hazel grafted or budded onto an understock of the European hazel. As a result it must be watched so that the understock does not outgrow the less vigorous contorted variety. See Chapter 7 for a discussion of this situation.

Corylus avellana 'Fusco-rubra' (syn *C. avellana atropurpurea*). The foliage of this hazel is brownish-red to dull purple and the leaves are hairy underneath and rounded in shape. The leaf color is brightest in spring, becoming duller and more greenish as the season advances. Since the shrub is grown only for this foliage color, it should be used where the hue is desirable.

Corylus maxima atropurpurea (see *C. maxima* 'Purpurea').

Corylus maxima aurea (see *C. avellana* 'Aurea').

Corylus maxima 'Purpurea' (syn *C. maxima atropurpurea*). Zone 5; 10'. This cultivar is the best of the purple-leaved hazels and should be purchased in preference to others. The foliage color will be deepest if the plant is grown in full sun. Leaves are rounded, flowers the usual catkins, and nuts (if any form) have a red or pinkish husk and are edible.

COTINUS

Cotinus coggygria (syn *Rhus cotinus*) (Smoke tree, Smoke bush). Zone 4, though sometimes dies back in winter in this zone; usually 10'-12', but may reach 15'. Illustrated on Color Page VII.

While this shrub has been used for enough years to call it "old-fashioned," it still is extremely popular today. It is entirely different in effect from any other plant while it is in bloom because the fruiting panicles, which most plants bear in quantity, look like fluffy smoke. In this species the smoke is pinkish or grayish at first, later the pinkish smoke turns brown while the grayish smoke remains much the same color as it was at the start. The seeds are found in the midst of the smoke.

The flowers of the two sexes are found on different plants. It therefore becomes important to buy a female plant since the male plants do not produce the smoke. Also, because plants grown from seeds vary greatly in their production of the

Cotinus coggygria, flowering branch, above; closeup of flower formation ("smoke"), below.

Cotinus coggygria, seeds among the "smoke."

fruiting panicles, they should be seen before purchasing. The smoky effect lasts for many weeks.

The leaves of smoke trees are unusual in shape and handsome in their brilliant yellow and orange autumn colors.

Cotinus coggygria 'Purpureus' (syn *C. rubrifolius*) (Purple-leaved or Red-leaved smoke tree). Zone 5 to parts of Zone 4, though it may die back in the winter in this zone. If anything, this variety is almost more beautiful than the species, for in it the young foliage is purple and the smoke gives the same color effect. The leaves remain purplish green all season.

There are several selected types of the purple-leaved smoketree. 'Notcutt', a British selection, is said to be hardy and to grow 10' to 12' high, with leaves of a deep bronzy-purple and dark purple fruiting panicles. 'Royal Purple' is said to grow 6' to 8' high with dark, shiny red to purple leaves, turning to green, edged pink all summer. Dark maroon smoke is said to appear in June and July.

Cotinus coggygria rubrifolius (see *C. coggyria* 'Purpureus').

COTONEASTER (Rockspray, Quinceberry) (pronounced ko-toe-nee-a'ster, not cotton-easter)

This is a large genus of shrubs and occasionally trees, some evergreen, some half-evergreen, others deciduous. They are grown for their glossy green foliage, their various interesting growth habits or their beautiful fruits. Sometimes they are grown for their flowers, but only occasionally, as in most species these are small, even though numerous. Most cotoneasters are easy to transplant, though the evergreen forms should be purchased with balls of earth around their roots. Cotoneasters grow well in full sun, tolerate light shade, but do not thrive in deep shade. They are happy in any fairly good soil, but need good drainage and dislike moist places or moist soils.

Cotoneaster acutifolia (Peking cotoneaster). Zone 4; 12'.

A dense, upright-growing shrub with slender branches spreading as they grow upward, this is widely used for hedges in the far north and makes handsome ones. It also may be used in shrub borders or wherever its glossy leaves and upright habit are needed.

Not only are the leaves shiny, but they have a firm texture. They are 1" to 1½" long. Flowers are almost white, only very faintly purplish or pinkish, and 3/16" in diameter. The fruits which follow them are black.

Cotoneaster acutifolia, fruits.

193

Cotoneaster apiculata, flowers, above; fruits, below.

Cotoneaster adpressa (Creeping cotoneaster). Zone 4; 6".

A prostrate shrub that presses itself to the soil and often roots where it touches earth. It is irregularly branched. The leaves are glossy green, slightly undulating or wavy at the margins, the flowers are small and pink, the fruits bright red. The plant is at its best when fruits are on it and one can see the contrast in color between them and the shining leaves.

This is a shrub to be used in very special places, perhaps in a rock garden or on top of a wall or anywhere else where the long branches can trail downward.

Cotoneaster adpressa praecox (syn *C. praecox*). Zone 4; 15"-2'. Forming a low mound with a dome-like shape, this variety is useful in front of taller shrubs, as a specimen in a rock garden, or wherever its unusual shape will make it useful. It has dark green, shiny leaves, 3/16" wide, pale pink flowers flushed deep purplish red (10 RP 3/10), followed by bright red fruits.

Cotoneaster apiculata (Cranberry cotoneaster). Zone 4; 3'-4'.

This shrub has horizontally spreading branches that, when they reach a suitable place, will fan out flat to the ground or a wall, much in the manner of those of *C. adpressa*. For this reason it may be planted on top of a wall where it first will grow upright, then send out the branches which droop and finally grow flat on wall or ground. We have one plant set at the top of a wall that has first spread itself across the wall and then across a flight of several steps. Two other plants, set at the side and top of another short flight of steps, have billowed onto the steps, then fanned out across them. This unusual growth habit can be used to advantage in landscaping certain areas, sometimes as a ground cover.

The foliage of this cotoneaster is glossy, dark green; flowers are 1/4" in diameter, deep purplish pink (7.5 RP 6/12) flushed strong purplish red (7.5 RP 4/11). The berries are larger than those of many other cotoneasters and look like cranberries, hence the common name of the plant. They are 1/2" long, 3/8" in diameter, shining and strong reddish orange (7.5 R 5/12) in color. Chipmunks dote on them and soon strip the bushes.

Cotoneaster apiculata praecox (this listing in the catalogs is an error. The plant meant is *C. adpressa praecox*).

Cotoneaster dammeri (syn *C. humifusa*) (Bearberry cotoneaster). Zone 5 to part of Zone 4; 1'.

A prostrate, evergreen shrub with long, trailing branches which frequently root where they touch the soil, this differs from many other cotoneasters because of the odd habit of growth. It is a good plant for use as a ground cover or possibly in a rock garden to trail over rocks.

Flowers are small and white, appearing in early June. The berries, ripening in fall, are bright red against glossy, dark green leaves.

Cotonéaster dielsiana (Diels cotoneaster). Zone 5; 5'-6'.

A graceful, deciduous shrub with arching branches, this will eventually spread to become slightly wider than it is high. Small leaves are hairy and yellowish or grayish on the undersides. Pinkish flowers opening in June produce a profusion of scarlet berries in September. By the time these are fully colored, the leaves have turned orange-red, making this cotoneaster a striking sight.

Cotoneaster divaricata (Spreading cotoneaster). Zone 5 to parts of Zone 4; 6'.

The growth of this shrub is upright, but with widely arching branches, not as gracefully arching as those of Diels cotoneaster. The 3/4" to 1" long leaves are glossy green above, lighter underneath. Their autumn color is red. Light purplish pink (7.5 RP 8/5) flowers, each 1/8" wide, borne in clusters of three, are on the plant in late May to early June and numerous bright red, small fruits cover the

branches in August to September. If left alone, these remain beautiful for several weeks, but we have one large plant of spreading cotoneaster under one of my office windows that is stripped bare of berries as soon as each ripens by two little chipmunks which run along a branch eating one fruit after the other.

Cotoneaster dielsiana, fruits.

Cotoneaster divaricata, flowers, above; fruits below.

Cotoneaster foveolata (Glossy cotoneaster). Zone 4; 8′-9′.

Upright growing and deciduous, this cotoneaster has shiny, dark green leaves which turn orange and scarlet in autumn and shiny black berries which are handsome against them. The flowers are pinkish, arranged in clusters of from 3 to 6 and open in June.

The bright green leaves are ½″ long; turn red and orange in autumn. Flowers are small, pink and appear in mid-June. The bright red fruits are small and there are rarely many of them, at least on my plants. Apparently a milder climate is needed for heavy berrying, for I have seen plants laden with fruits in Zone 7.

Cotoneaster foveolata, fruits.

Cotoneaster horizontalis in flower. Note flat branching habit.

Cotoneaster horizontalis (Rockspray cotoneaster, Rock cotoneaster, Quinceberry, Plumed cotoneaster). Zone 6 to Zone 5b; 2½′.

In the north this is deciduous, in the south it is evergreen, but in Zone 5b it is semi-evergreen, the leaves remaining on the plant until winter is well along. The outstanding feature of this shrub is its horizontal branching habit which is beautiful and useful.

The plant may be used as a ground cover on sloping or level ground or on top of a wide, double wall with earth between the two walls, or even as an espalier by inducing the horizontal branches to grow vertically against a wall.

Cotoneaster horizontalis perpusilla. More depressed in growth than the species, this variety has more small branches and many more, larger berries than the rockspray cotoneaster.

Cotoneaster humifusa (see *C. dammeri*).

Cotoneaster integerrima. Zone 4; 4′-6′.

Upright in growth, with slender, arching branches, this deciduous shrub has leaves that are dark green on the upper sides, lighter and woolly on the undersides, pale pink flowers in small clusters opening in late May and early June and bright red, globular berries in August.

Cotoneaster microphylla (Small-leaved cotoneaster, Wall cotoneaster, Rockspray). Zone 6; 3′.

This plant grows into a sort of tangled mound if left untrained. In that form, it is useful only in between rocks in a rock garden or place in which there naturally are rocks. However, with a little training and pruning it forms a mat instead of a mound. It is dense in growth, has glossy, dark

green leaves, more evergreen than those of the Rock cotoneaster, small white flowers in June and scarlet berries in fall. Its leaves are the smallest of any cotoneaster.

Cotoneaster multiflora. Zone 5 to parts of Zone 4; 8'.

This shrub and its variety *calocarpa* are exceptions to the general rule with cotoneasters for they definitely are grown for their flowers as well as their fruits. The plants flower profusely in May, with upright clusters of white blooms borne all along the branches. These are followed by equally profuse, large, red fruits in autumn. The forms of the plants are spreading and 10' to 12' must be allowed for either shrub to reach its full size. Branches are slender and arching, leaves oval, bluish-green and deciduous. Both *C. multiflora* and *C. m. calocarpa,* either in bloom or in berry, are gorgeous shrubs by any standards.

Cotoneaster multiflora, flowers, below; fruiting branch, right above, and closeup of fruits, right.

Cotoneaster multiflora calocarpa. Slightly larger flowers and fruits distinguish this variety from the species.

Cotoneaster praecox (see *C. adpressa praecox*).

Cotoneaster racemiflora soongorica (Sungari rockspray). Zone 4; 6'-8'.

This plant has gray-green leaves which make it different from other cotoneasters. Its gracefully arching branches may droop to the ground. Small clusters of small white flowers in June and many oval, 5/16" long, strong red (2.5 R 5/12) berries in autumn, combined with the foliage color, make this an outstanding member of the genus.

Cotoneaster racemiflora soongorica, flowers above; fruits, below.

CYDONIA (see CHAENOMELES)

CYRILLA

Cyrilla racemiflora (American cyrilla, Leatherwood, Black ji-ti). Zone 6 to Zone 5; to 25′ and 30′ in the south, but rarely more than 15′ in the north.

A native of the southern states, this shrub or small tree is semi-evergreen with shiny, bright green leaves, drooping clusters of small, white flowers in June to July, borne on wood of the current season's growth, and brilliant orange and scarlet foliage color in autumn. It needs a moist, sandy soil with plenty of peat mixed with it, and a well-drained situation, preferably in semi-shade.

CYTISUS (Broom, a common name applied also to the genus *Genista*)

These slender-branched, sometimes almost leafless shrubs have value in the garden for their bright colored flowers and for the fact that the branches stay bright green during the entire winter. However, even in Zone 5, where many of them are supposedly hardy, they sometimes die to the ground in a severe winter, growing again from the roots the following spring.

They like full sun, most of them dote on poor, sandy soil, and all must have perfect drainage. They are not easy to transplant even when young and rarely can be moved when mature. The best way to buy them is grown in pots or, if this form is unavailable, then with earth balls around the roots. It is best to move them in spring.

Flowers of all are shaped like those of peas (they belong to the same plant group) and, in the hardy brooms, almost all are some shade of yellow.

Cytisus andreanus (see *C. scoparius* 'Andreanus').

Cytisus battandieri. Zone 6; 3′.

This shrub is grown for its silvery gray leaves and cone-shaped heads of fragrant, bright yellow flowers which appear in clusters in July to August.

Cytisus × *praecox* (*C. multiflorus* × *C. purgans*) (Warminster broom) (Some catalogs list other brooms as Warminster broom). Zone 6 to part of Zone 5; 4′ to 5′.

Blooming from mid-May to early June, this is the earliest broom to flower. The 3/8″ to 1/2″ wide blossoms are borne all along the arching branches and are two-toned, the 2 lower petals brilliant greenish yellow (7.5 Y 9/8) and the 2 upper petals such pale yellow that they are almost white. A plant in bloom is literally covered with flowers.

Cytisus × praecox 'Albus'. The same as the Warminster broom, except for white flowers instead of yellow.

Cytisus × praecox 'Hollandia' (Warminster broom). Zone 6 to part of Zone 5; 6'. This is a cultivar of *praecox* with a red eye in the yellow flowers the same shade as the species.

Cytisus purgans (Provence broom). Zone 6 to part of Zone 5: 3'.

A dwarf shrub with a dense habit of growth and stiff, upright branches, this has brilliant, deep yellow flowers in mid-May.

Cytisus scoparius (Scotch broom). Zone 5; 4'-6'.

Upright-growing, this shrub is laden with comparatively large, to 1" long, bright yellow flowers in mid-May. These are usually borne singly or in pairs in the axils of the leaves.

Cytisus scoparius 'Andreanus'. Zone 5b. More erect growing than the Scotch broom, this variety has yellow flowers with crimson "wings" and is well worth trying to grow for the bright flower colors.

Cytisus praecox, flowering branch and closeup of flowers, above; seed pods, below.

DAPHNE

Daphnes are considered "cantankerous" shrubs to grow. This is because their requirements so often are not met and they simply will not grow unless conditions suit them. Perfect drainage is requirement number one. Loose, sandy soil is requirement number two, and full sun is requirement number three. A cool "root run" is the fourth and last requirement. No protection is needed in winter if temperatures do not go below 10 degrees below zero, F. If they do, then throw straw or a few evergreen branches over the daphnes after the ground is frozen. These plants should be watered in summer only if the soil has been dry for 10 days or more, as they do not like wet soils. They should be purchased with balls of earth around their roots and are best moved in spring. They are worth any additional trouble it takes to grow them for the scent of their flowers if nothing else—and I say that about very few shrubs.

Daphne × burkwoodii 'Somerset' (*D. caucasica × D. cneorum*). Zone 4; 5' to 6'.

For all garden purposes this daphne is identical with the species, *burkwoodii*. If the two are not the same plant, they certainly have the same parentage and are treated as one in this book.

Originating in England, this daphne is an upright-growing shrub which, in May and early June,

has star-shaped, fragrant, pale pink (2.5 R 9/3) to white flowers in great quantities. Individual florets measure ⅜″ across and the clusters in which they are arranged are 1½″ in diameter. The plant is almost evergreen in Zone 5b, dropping its leaves for only a few weeks in spring. It is effective when planted at the front of a shrub border or may be used as a specimen near a sitting-out area. It should be purchased as a potted plant for ease in transplanting and also because larger sizes are expensive.

Daphne burkwoodii 'Somerset', flowers.

Daphne cneorum (Rose daphne, Garland flower). Zone 4 in well-drained soil; 6″ to 8″. Illustrated on Color Page IV.

When this shrub is in flower its fragrance pervades the area near it, so that visitors search for the source. It has evergreen, gray-green foliage, makes a low, flat mound in the garden, so is best used on top of a wall, in a rock garden or as a ground cover.

When it is in bloom, in late May or early June, this mound of foliage is almost obscured by the

¾″ wide clusters of strong purplish pink (7.5 RP 7/10) flowers. Since large plants of this daphne may be a yard across, a plant in bloom is quite a sight. Plants that are happily situated will bloom a little now and then during the summer, but particularly about September. The plant has sufficient foliage to furnish coolness for its own roots, but many gardeners mulch under the leaves and over the soil with stones in an effort to insure a cool area for the roots.

Daphne cneorum, flowers.

Daphne genkwa (Lilac daphne). Zone 6 to Zone 5b in a protected place; 3′.

Upright-growing and deciduous, this shrub gives the impression of fragility. The flowers are set all along the arching branches, are lilac color, appear in early April and are scentless. This is a beautiful early-flowering shrub and would make a welcome addition to those blooming in April, but the plant is not reliably hardy, freezing to the ground some winters even in Zone 6. If it does this, it must be cut to the ground immediately, as otherwise it will not grow again from the roots.

Daphne mezereum (February daphne). Zone 4; 3′.

This is a small, upright-growing, deciduous shrub planted for its extra-early rosy pink flowers which are intensely fragrant. These are borne in clusters along the branches and appear before the dark green leaves unfold. Whoever gave this shrub its common name must have lived in a milder climate than I do, for I can depend on flowers on April 10 to April 14 from the pair of these daphnes in a protected place under one of the west windows of my office. Vivid red (closest to 5 R 5/12), oval, ⅜″ long berries follow the flowers, clustered along the stems. Although these are attractive, they are poisonous.

Daphne mezereum should be moved only when very small, as it is difficult to move when larger; should always be purchased with a ball of earth around its roots and should not be set in a prominent position for it has a disconcerting habit of dying with no apparent cause. When two or three plants are set side by side and all appear to be growing equally well, one may be dead in spring while the others are in full bloom. There seems to be no sensible explanation for this behavior.

Daphne mezereum 'Alba'. This is the white-flowered variety of the plant described above and is identical with it except for more vigorous growth, the flower color, and the color of the berries, which are yellow. Regardless of color, they still are poisonous.

Daphne mezereum, flowers, right. Berries (deadly poison to eat), below.

DESMODIUM *penduliflora* (see *Lespedeza thunbergii*)

DEUTZIA (Deutzia)

A group of shrubs grown for flowers which in most are white or white tinged with pink, rose, or purple. Only one, *D. gracilis,* has particularly pretty foliage. None have any autumn coloration and none have fruit of any significance (see picture).

Furthermore, since they bloom on branches grown the preceding year and start growth with the first warm weather, they lose some twigs every year and these brown areas must be removed or the shrubs look unsightly.

On the other side of the balance sheet are the facts that deutzias will grow in any soil, like full sun the best but will tolerate light shade, and when they flower, some are so laden with blooms that the branches hardly can be seen. They have little or no trouble from insects or diseases. All deutzias can be moved with bare roots but, because some of them have a tendency towards tenderness, are best moved in spring.

201

Deutzia crenata (see *D. scabra*).

Deutzia crenata rosea, rosea plena, or *D. rosea floriplena* (see *D. scabra* 'Plena').

Deutzia gracilis (Slender deutzia). Zone 5; 3'-4'.

A slender-branched, graceful, delicate-looking shrub, with narrow leaves of pale green, this is the first deutzia to flower. It bears a wealth of white, scentless, ½" to ¾" wide blooms in upright clusters 2" to 4" long in late May. If you can have but one deutzia, this is the species to grow. It may be used at the front of a shrub border, for edging a walk or makes an interesting unclipped hedge. If a small specimen shrub is needed, it even can be considered for that use. It will grow well in light shade.

Deutzia gracilis rosea (see *D. × rosea*).

Deutzia × kalmiaeflora (*D. purpurascens × D. parviflora*) Zone 6 to Zone 5b; 2'-3'.

A bushy plant with slender, slightly arching branches, this has single, cup-shaped, ¾" flowers in 3"-wide clusters. The blooms are strong purplish pink (5 RP 7/9) on the outsides of the petals and pale purplish pink (2.5 RP 9/2) on the insides of the petals. This is one of the most beautiful of the deutzias. It will grow in sun or in light shade and is best placed in the front of a shrub border.

Deutzia gracilis, branch of blooms above, closeup of flowers, below.

Deutzia × *lemoinei* (*D. parviflora* × *D. gracilis*) (Lemoine deutzia). Zone 5 to part of Zone 4; 5′.

In late May this shrub bears white flowers in upright clusters. It is a good, compact plant, a parent of a group of hardier hybrid deutzias.

Deutzia × *lemoinei* 'Compacta'. Even hardier than *D.* × *lemoinei*, this is a smaller plant with even more compact form.

Deutzia × *rosea* (*D. gracilis* × *D. purpurascens*) (syn *D. gracilis rosea*) (Rose-panicle deutzia). Zone 6 to Zone 5b; 4′-5′.

The flowers of this shrub are differently formed from those of most deutzias. They are bell-shaped and white, tinged pink on the outsides of the petals. They appear in late May to early June.

Deutzia × *rosea* 'Pink Pompon'. Zone 6 to Zone 5b; 3′-4′. If you are looking for a pink deutzia and live where this one is hardy, buy this first. The flowers are double, 5/8″ in diameter, borne in tight clusters 1½″ in diameter and almost that in depth. The overall effect of the blooms is of light purplish pink (5 RP 8/5) but the outsides of the petals and the buds are striped with deep purplish pink (5 RP 6/10). The petals are not white, they are definitely pale pink, on the lavender side. The flower color fades as the blooms age, the first effect being more pink than the effect a week later which is more lavender. Blooms appear in early to mid-June. The shrub needs a place in full sun for best color.

Deutzia lemoinei, branch of flowers, left, above; details of blooms, left, below. Deutzia rosea, flowers, below.

Deutzia seed receptacles, often seen on single-flowered deutzias, above; Deutzia scabra 'Plena', flowering branch, below.

Deutzia scabra 'Pride of Rochester,' closeup of flowers showing flush of color on outsides of florets.

Deutzia scabra (syn *D. scabra crenata,* syn *D. crenata*). Zone 6 to Zone 5b; 8'.

In late June this handsome deutzia bears single, white flowers, sometimes tinged purplish on the outsides. It is better known for its double-flowered varieties.

Deutzia scabra crenata (see *D. scabra*).

Deutzia scabra 'Plena' (syn *D. scabra roseaplena*). Zone 5b; 8'-9'. The double, ¾" wide, white flowers, tinged moderate purplish red (5 RP 5/10) on the outsides of the petals, are borne in 4½" long spikes. They appear after the middle and usually towards the end of June.

Deutzia scabra 'Pride of Rochester'. Zone 5b; 8'. Blooming just before *D. scabra* 'Plena', 'Pride of Rochester' still is one of the latest blooming of the deutzias. It has double, ¾" to 1" wide, white flowers flushed moderate purplish red (5 RP 5/10) on the outsides of the petals. The spikes in which these are borne are 4" long.

DIERVILLA

Diervilla lonicera (syn *D. trifida*) (Dwarf bush-honeysuckle). Zone 4 to parts of Zone 3; 3'.

Native from Newfoundland to Manitoba, south to New England and west to Indiana, southeastern Minnesota, and Iowa, this shrub is useful for holding soil on steep banks and also looks well in a wild garden. If it didn't sucker so badly that it overruns nearby plants, it also would be pretty in a cultivated part of the garden. The very characteristic which makes it a prime choice for covering banks is a disadvantage in a cultivated area.

This shrub will grow in shade but prefers full sun. It is easy to grow and, as has been stated above, spreads by means of underground stems. The funnel-shaped flowers, 3/8" wide at the mouth, bloom in June to July, are brilliant greenish yellow (7.5 Y 9/8) and borne in clusters. They turn gradually to deeper yellow and then to various shades of red. The leaves are pretty, especially in autumn when they become reddish. This species is hardier than the one described below.

Diervilla sessilifolia (Southern bush-honeysuckle). Zone 5; 4½'.

From North Carolina to Georgia and Alabama, this shrub takes the place of *D. lonicera* in the southern wilderness. It has the same uses, is possibly more ornamental with its deep yellow, trumpet-shaped blooms in late June and July. The foliage turns reddish in autumn.

Diervilla trifida (see *D. lonicera*).

Diervilla lonicera, flowering branches.

Diervilla lonicera, closeup of flower clusters.

ELAEAGNUS

Some members of this genus are small trees, others are shrubs. *E. angustifolia,* the Russian olive, is described in Chapter 15. None of the members of this genus has outstanding flowers, so they are grown chiefly for their fruits or, in several cases, for their foliage color.

Elaeagnus argentea (see *E. commutata*).

Elaeagnus commutata (syn *E. argentea*) (Silverberry, Wolfwillow, Missouri silvertree). Zone 1; 3½'-14'.

The range of this shrub in the wild is from Alaska to Quebec and southward to Minnesota, Utah, and South Dakota. It grows on dry, alkaline soils, has many branches but no thorns and the branches are covered with scales that become silvery. The leaves, too, are silvery on both sides. The flowers, appearing in May, are fragrant, yellow inside, silvery outside, but not particularly conspicuous. That is, you smell them rather than see them as you approach the shrub. The fruit, which is ripe from July through September, is silvery in color, globe-shaped, dry and mealy inside. This is one of the hardiest shrubs. However, if the summer is dry, it will suffer from the drought.

Elaeagnus longipes (see *E. multiflora*).
Elaeagnus multiflora (syn *E. longipes*). Zone 5; 9'.

Succeeding in sandy soils, this plant is grown for the two-toned effect of its foliage which is dark green on the tops of the leaves, silvery below; and for the decorative fruits which look much like oval cherries, and are ½″ to ¾″ in diameter, orange to red, partly covered with a silvery scale. These fruits are edible and ripen in June. The flowers, borne in May, are plentiful but still not conspicuous. They are small, ⅞″ long, ¼″ wide, closest to 5 Y 9/9, brilliant yellow, fragrant and drooping. The shrub is vigorous in growth.

Elaeagnus umbellata (Autumn elaeagnus). Zone 4 to part of Zone 3; 12'

Somewhat like the Russian olive (*E. angustifolia*) in appearance, but smaller and more spreading, this has branches that are yellow-brown with a silvery overlay. They may be spiny. The young leaves are silver underneath, smooth and dark green above and are crimped at the edges. Flowers in mid-May are small, fragrant, and dull yellow or white. The fruits that follow them are scaly and brown at first, changing to salmon-red when mature in October.

Elaeagnus multiflora, flowering branch, above; closeup of flower and details of leaves, below.

Elaeagnus multiflora, fruits.

Elaeagnus umbellata flowers (see description on left).

Elsholtzia stauntonii, flowering branch, above. Closeup of flower spike, showing long stamens, below.

ELSHOLTZIA

Elsholtzia stauntonii (Mint shrub, Staunton elsholtzia). Zone 5; 3′.

If you see this shrub without its flowers, it is just another shrub and not a very pretty one at that, even though its leaves are aromatic, smelling like mint. But, in late August and early September, when the strong reddish purple (10 P 5/10) flowers appear in loose spikes, to 6″ wide and 7″ long, you realize that this shrub is useful for its late and effective bloom.

It dies to the ground during winter in Zone 5b and is pruned to the ground in early spring, after which new shoots grow from the roots. Flowers are borne on branches that grow during the current season, so this dying back makes no difference in the amount of bloom.

To flower profusely the plant needs sun; extra water when the weather is dry. Except for these two things and the severe pruning in spring, it requires no care. It may be used in front of other shrubs in a grouping or wherever the late flowers, which stay in good condition for several weeks, are needed.

207

Erica carnea, spray of flowers, above; closeup of blooms, below.

ENKIANTHUS

Enkianthus campanulatus (Redvein enkianthus, Necklace shrub, Bell-flower tree). Zone 5 to parts of Zone 4; 8′ or 10′ in the north, to 20′ in the south.

While in general this shrub needs the same soil and environment as do azaleas and rhododendrons, it will grow in soil that is less acid and in a drier situation than most of them, though it grows more compact under these circumstances than it normally would. It will grow either in full sun or quite deep shade. Its growth is unusual because of its lateral branches which are arranged in whorls. This is not particularly noticeable as long as the tufts of leaves are green, but comes into view when they turn brilliant scarlet in autumn. The flowers appear in mid-May, before the leaves unfold, looking like little bells in long-stalked clusters. They are yellowish or orangish in color; are pretty but not exactly showy. The capsules which follow them are inconspicuous.

ERICA (Heath)

These plants are related to *Calluna* (heather) and require the same general conditions of growth. See *Calluna,* page 172 for directions for growing them.

Erica carnea (Spring heath). Zone 6 to Zone 5b; 6″ to 1′, depending on growing conditions.

The rose-colored flowers in early April against the fine, evergreen foliage are the chief reason for growing this plant. It is compact if pruned occasionally, is pretty even without the flowers, and the buds which form in mid-summer to open the following spring are light green and interesting much of the year. There are numerous cultivars of this heath in the catalogs, far too many to list here.

Erica carnea 'Vivellii' (Purple heath). This blooms in March to April; has purple foliage and purple flowers.

Erica × darleyensis (parentage uncertain) Darley heath; Zone 6; 3′.

The advantage of this hybrid over other heaths is twofold: its vigorous growth and its ability to survive poor conditions—even to thriving in a soil which contains lime (that is, is not acid in reaction). It flowers from late autumn, about November, through the winter providing it is in a sheltered place.

The foliage is evergreen and fine in texture, the flowers are lavender-pink and small.

208

Erica vagans (Cornish heath). Zone 6 to part of Zone 5; 1' to 1½'.

Pink or pinkish-purple flowers from August to October, dark green, needlelike foliage and a spreading form distinguish this shrub. There are several varieties and cultivars available with flowers of different colors.

Erica vagans 'Alba' (White Cornish heath) has white flowers; is otherwise like the species.

EUONYMUS (also spelled EVONYMUS, an older spelling) (Spindle tree)

The botanical name, so often mis-pronounced, is U-on'-uh-muss with the accent on the second syllable. The genus *Euonymus* is a large one with many species, varieties and many forms. Some of this group are vines, some are prostrate and best used as ground covers, others are shrubs many of which become vines if support is near them. Some may be grown either as vines or as shrubs, depending on how they are pruned. Some are evergreen or nearly so. None have showy flowers; all are grown either for their foliage color in autumn, their interesting bark or shape, or their bright fruits. So, if you are looking for a flowering shrub you can skip this genus entirely.

Euonymus tolerates almost any soil, though it grows best in good soil. All kinds will grow in sun and a good many will tolerate light to quite heavy shade.

An important pest which attacks most often the evergreen vining types is euonymus scale which can ruin a plant. See Chapter 9 for a discussion of scale insects. This scale is more of a pest in some parts of the country than in others. There are localities in which it hardly is known.

Euonymus alata (Winged spindle tree). Zone 4 to part of Zone 3; 8' or 9' and eventually about as wide as high. Illustrated on Color Page VII.

An extremely useful shrub because of the autumn coloring of its leaves, which turn first pink, then scarlet. Best color is obtained when the plant is in full sun but, since a plant in shade will have different and deeper coloring than one in sun, the gardener interested in foliage for flower arrangements should grow at least one plant in each situation.

The shrub form is dense, rounded at the top; the branching stiff with the branches spreading horizontally. Branches and twigs have from two to four broad, corky "wings" attached (see picture). Flowers are ⅜" across and are insignificant because they are not only small but strong yellow green

Euonymus alata flowers, above; fruits below (see next page also).

Euonymus alata, closeup of fruits and corky appendages to branches.

Euonymus americana (Strawberry bush, Hearts-a-bustin'-with-love, Bursting heart, Fish wood, Brook euonymus, American spindletree, American burningbush). Zone 6 to Zone 5b, though it will kill to the ground line in a severe winter in Zone 5b; 5' to 6'.

Upright in growth with slender branches, this has delicate, pale pink flowers with dark purplish red stamens, beautiful especially when seen at close range. These are followed by fruits which are pinkish-red and warty, quite different from those of other species. While these are on the plant, the foliage is dark red. Strawberry bush will tolerate shade and grows especially well in damp spots, though it also will thrive in dry soil.

Euonymus americana, fruits (see also opposite page).

(2.5 GY 7/10 to strong greenish yellow 10 Y 8/11) in color so hardly are visible. The fruits are small and red; often lost against the bright autumn foliage. Winter silhouette is interesting because of the branching habit and the wings.

This shrub may be used in a border, as a specimen or for a hedge.

Euonymus alata 'Compacta'. Zone 5 to parts of Zone 4 where it is a "borderline" shrub; 4'-5'. A dwarf form of the species described above, this is even more useful because it is smaller. It is rounded in form, has the same bright autumn foliage coloration as the species, but often lacks entirely the corky appendages to the branches. These always are smaller than those in *alata* and, as stated above, often are non-existent, especially in mature plants.

This plant is useful in many ways—as an unclipped or lightly clipped hedge (it is so compact that it needs clipping but rarely), as a specimen shrub where bright fall color is needed in a landscape design, or as a foreground shrub in a border.

Euonymus alata 'Gracilis'. Zone 4; 3'. The branches of this variety first grow upright to about 3' and then curve downward. Because of the generally stiff form of the plant this curving looks extremely odd to me.

Euonymus aldenhamensis (see *E. europaea* 'Aldenhamensis', Chapter 15).

Euonymus atropurpurea (See Chapter 15).
Euonymus europaea (see Chapter 15).
Euonymus fortunei (Wintercreeper). Zone 5.
This species is a clinging vine which sends out little protrusions that look like roots but actually hold the vine to its support. This *vine* is listed in

Euonymus americana, closeup of distinctive fruit surface when fruits are closed.

Closeup of fruits opened, disclosing bright orange seeds.

this book about *shrubs* because it is the most variable of any species of woody plants and, before its assorted shrubby varieties and cultivars are discussed, an explanation is needed.

First of all, it must be borne in mind by every gardener who reads this that *E. fortunei* is the hardiest of evergreen vines. If you were a nurseryman, you too would be on the lookout for any evergreen vine (or its shrub forms) hardy in the north because these would be excellent plants to offer your customers, who have not too many hardy plants from which to choose. (This is the reason why nurserymen have selected far too many forms.)

Next, it must be recognized that the variability of the varieties of this species because of "sporting" (see explanation in Chapter 7, page 49) is so great that only the varieties of *Euonymus kiautchovica* (a species formerly called *E. patens* and still so listed in many catalogs) comes near to rivaling it in variability.

And, finally, these varieties of *E. fortunei* vary depending on whether the plants are mature or juvenile in form. As an example of these two forms and what happens to make one cultivar change from one form to the other, I shall use a vining type of euonymus, *Euonymus fortunei* 'Colorata'. This vine normally is used as a ground cover and is a splendid plant for this use. Its cultivar name comes from the color of the leaves in late autumn and all winter—a purplish red.

Now as long as 'Colorata' is grown as a ground cover vine, it will remain juvenile in form. Just let it reach and climb a support and it will become mature in form. When the nurseryman (or you) takes cuttings (see Chapter 13, page 131 for propagation by cuttings) from a juvenile form of 'Colorata' the plants grown from these cuttings will retain the juvenile, *vining* form. If cuttings are taken from the mature form, *shrubby* plants will result. These are referred to in nursery catalogs as E. fortunei colorata erecta and, in this book as E. f. 'C', erect form.

The variability does not end here, for both large and small-leaved types of the erect form are listed in nursery catalogs and I own plants of both types, purchased at the same time, in the same lot of plants. These erect forms of 'Colorata' are easily distinguished from other erect forms of euonymus by that reddish-purple winter foliage color.

There is one more point to be made in this discussion and that is that the mature form of 'Colorata', like the mature form of *E. fortunei* 'Vegeta', will eventually bear fruits, while the juvenile forms of both of these plants never fruit.

211

Euonymus fortunei 'Carrierei' (syn *E. radi-cans carrierei*). 4'. This euonymus normally is a shrub but if supported it will revert to the vining form and become *E. fortunei*. You see, this cultivar is a selection from *fortunei* that is one of the first "sports" to appear on a mature plant of *fortunei*. It is one of the two cultivars (the other being 'Vegeta') that can be depended upon to bear fruits at a reasonably early age.

The leaves are glossy, dark green and semi-evergreen in Zone 5. Fruits, which are bright orange, remain on the plant for a long time.

Euonymus fortunei 'Colorata', erect form. 3'. You already know all about this form from the discussion under *E. fortunei* above. Both large and small-leaved types are useful plants for "facing down" taller shrubs or as a planting all by themselves in a place where minimum upkeep is desired and winter color would be an asset.

Euonymus fortunei, Emerald (or Corliss) selections. Corliss Bros., Inc. of Gloucester and Ipswich, Mass. have introduced a number of shrub forms of *E. fortunei*. All are hardy in Zone 5. All of their names start with the word "Emerald" and, while all are evergreen, their heights and widths vary according to the particular selection. All are patented.

Those listed in the current catalog of the nursery are: Emerald Beauty, 5'-6' tall, 8'-10' wide, with orange berries; Emerald Charm, bushy and compact, upright, columnar form to 4'-5' with an 18" spread; Emerald Cushion, very dwarf, dense, compact, 15"-18" high with 3' spread (recommended for "facing down" taller shrubs); Emerald Gaiety, 4'-5' high, 3' spread, drought resistant, pronounced white margins on the leaves; Emerald Leader, 4'-5' tall, 2½' spread, bushy, with orange berries; Emerald Pride, 4' tall, 3½' spread, recommended for a low hedge.

I have described these selections as the catalog describes them but without any superlatives. I have not yet grown any of them. I have, however, seen them growing in many nurseries. They are becoming increasingly popular as they are more widely used, which speaks well for them.

Euonymus fortunei, erect form. There are so many, many selections which could be described by this name that it is impossible to tell what a nursery offers under this listing. Some nurseries give this erect form as synonymous with the selection 'Sarcoxie' described below. At any rate, if you are interested in buying an erect form of *fortunei*, it probably would be sensible to see first what you are buying.

Euonymus fortunei radicans, erect form. *Euonymus fortunei radicans* is a vining euonymus with semi-evergreen leaves about an inch long, usually with pointed tips and slightly heavier or thicker texture than those of *fortunei*. They often are not glossy. The erect form carries these characteristics into a shrub.

Euonymus fortunei radicans vegetus or *vegeta* (see *E. f.* 'Vegeta').

Euonymus fortunei 'Sarcoxie'. Zone 6 to part of Zone 5; 4'. Introduced by the Sarcoxie Nurseries, Sarcoxie, Mo., this has shiny green leaves about an inch to an inch and a half long. Even if planted in full sun, this selection holds its foliage far into the winter. It will grow in partial or even quite heavy shade as well as in sun and is easy to shear to any desired form. However, it kills to the ground in a severe winter and does not grow again from the roots.

Euonymus fortunei 'Vegeta' (Evergreen bittersweet). Zone 5 to parts of Zone 4; 4'. A semi-evergreen cultivar in Zone 5 and northward, this plant will grow as a vine if set next to a support, but will be an irregularly shaped shrub if not given a place to climb. It "piles up" its branches since each branch grows more or less horizontally. It may be trained to any desired shape, although I

Euonymus fortunei 'Sarcoxie', fruits.

212

Euonymus fortunei 'Vegeta', branch of fruits above; closeup of opened and partly opened fruits below. Note leaf bud formation at top, right.

think its natural form is "artistic." It sometimes is used as a clipped hedge.

Leaves are rounded, thick-textured, often described as "leathery," and range from 1″ to 1½″ in diameter. The bright orange fruits have earned it its common name. These remain in good condition for months until the birds finally eat them, sometimes as late as early spring. The plant is easy to grow, easy to transplant.

Euonymus kiautschovica (syn *E. patens*). Zone 6 to Zone 5b, where it kills completely in a severe winter, but may live for years if set in a sufficiently protected place; 7′ or slightly more and spreading almost as wide.

This shrub is semi-evergreen in the north, evergreen in the south. While the general growth habit is upright, some stems run along the ground, rooting where they touch, then turning upward. In this manner large clumps often are formed.

Leaves are deep green, narrow, and leathery in texture. Flowers, which are the usual yellowish-green or greenish-white, appear in early September and, since the plant is literally covered with them, they give it a light, airy appearance. Pinkish or red fruits follow these blooms but only where the growing season is sufficiently long, which is not usually the case in Zone 5b. In that zone fruits ripen only about once in ten years.

This is a beautiful, almost evergreen shrub which combines well with broad-leaved evergreens or narrow-leaved evergreens. It also may be used as a clipped or unclipped hedge.

There are several cultivars of this species in the catalogs, some said to be improvements on it, others much lower-growing and therefore well worth investigating.

Euonymus kiautschovica 'Dupont'. 4′. The Willis Nursery Co., Ottawa, Kansas, which introduced this selection considers it a form of *kiautschovica* and it is on this basis that I am listing it here. It is semi-evergreen in Zone 5b and has leaves about 2″ or a bit more in length.

Euonymus kiautschovica 'Manhattan'. An introduction of Kansas State College, this is a hybrid euonymus with dark green, shining, 2½″ long, almost evergreen leaves. This seems to be hardier than the species, although a severe winter might tell a different tale.

Euonymus kiautschovica 'Newport'. Referred to as the "spreading euonymus" in one catalog, this is said to have glossy, evergreen foliage, a medium sized leaf and orange berries in fall.

Euonymus nana turkestanica (syn *E. nanus koopmannii*) (Fernleaf euonymus). Zone 5 to part of Zone 4; 4'-6'.

The species, *E. nana*, is half-evergreen and low growing, only to 2', and procumbent in form. This has the common name of Dwarf euonymus. The variety, *turkestanica*, is more vigorous in growth, and taller, 4' to 6'. It has narrow leaves that turn bronze-purple in autumn and stay on all winter in Zone 6, much of the winter in Zone 5b. Fruits are bright orange-red in late summer.

Euonymus patens (see *E. kiautschovica*).

Euonymus planipes (see *E. sachalinensis*).

Euonymus radicans (see *E. fortunei radicans*).

Euonymus vegeta (see *E. fortunei* 'Vegeta').

Euonymus yedoensis (Yeddo euonymus). Zone 4; 10' or more.

A big shrub with stiff, upright form, flattish or slightly rounded at the tip, this has leaves often 5" long. They turn bright red in autumn when the plentiful dull pink or pinkish-purple fruits appear in great profusion. These remain on the plant for a long time after the leaves have fallen.

Euonymus sachalinensis buds, at left; open flowers, above; fruits closed, below. Note odd shaped open fruit, at bottom, showing seeds.

Euonymus sachalinensis (syn *E. planipes*). Zone 5 to parts of Zone 4; 7' to 8'.

It is the pendant fruits of good size which make this euonymus different from the others. They are bright red, handsome, and most years there are plenty of them. The new leaves are bright red, turning bright green as they unfold.

214

EXOCHORDA (Pearl bush)

The two species of pearl bush most frequently grown are large shrubs, erect and broad when older, inclined to be "leggy" when young, therefore occasionally needing hard pruning directly after flowering. They are grown for their beautiful strings of white, pearl-like buds and the flowers which open from them in late April to early May.

Pearl bushes grow easily in any soil; prefer a sunny spot. Both may be used in the back row of a shrub border. Neither of the large species needs to be grown in a small garden since 'The Bride' takes up so much less space, while still contributing the same pearl-like buds and white flowers.

Exochorda giraldii wilsonii (Wilson pearl bush). Zone 5 to parts of Zone 4; 8'-10'.

This variety has slightly larger flowers (1½" in diameter) than *E. racemosa* and usually is a larger, more shapely plant. Leaves are more gray-green than those of *E. racemosa* and the plant flowers about a week earlier.

Exochorda giraldii wilsonii, buds and flowers.

Exochorda racemosa, pearl-like buds and flowers.

215

Exochorda racemosa, seed capsules.

Exochorda grandiflora (see *E. racemosa*).

Exochorda × *macrantha* (*E. korolkowi* × *E. racemosa*) 'The Bride'. Zone 6 to parts of Zone 5; 3'-4'.

A dwarf pearl bush of much more compact form than the two larger ones, it has the same strings of white buds and flowers but blooms are larger, sometimes to 2" in diameter. This is a valuable addition to the group since it takes up comparatively little space. It may be used in the front of a shrub border or in a grouping of low-growing shrubs or even as a specimen.

Exochorda racemosa (syn *E. grandiflora*) (Pearl bush). Zone 5 to parts of Zone 4; 8'-10'.

This is said to be hardier than either of the other two pearl bushes described above, but since I've never had any trouble with any of them, even after a severe winter, I cannot say whether this is true or not. The flowers of *E. racemosa* are slightly smaller than those of the Wilson pearl bush (to 1¼" wide), but not enough to make any real difference in the garden picture. They are white, centered with green. The plants definitely are "leggier" than those of the Wilson pearl bush.

FONTANESIA

Fontanesia fortunei. Zone 5—it is a "borderline" shrub in Zone 4 where it may kill to the ground in winter but grows from the roots in spring; 15'.

It seems a shame that this shrub is available from so few nurseries for it is drought resistant, grows well in any soil in full sun or light shade and is a real "toughy."

Growth is upright, vigorous and graceful. Foliage is much like that of a willow but very shiny. The ⅛" diameter, greenish-white flowers are arranged in 3"-long pendant clusters and appear in June to July. This shrub has very small (about ¼ inch-long), flat, oval fruits; creamy-tan in color, borne in clusters. These have no ornamental value.

This fontanesia is an excellent hedge plant, clipped or unclipped and should make a welcome change from the more common privet since fontanesia is more graceful. It may be used also at the back of a border with lower growing shrubs in front.

Fontanesia fortunei, flowers.

FORSYTHIA (Golden bell)

In most gardens forsythias signal the arrival of spring, though in our garden they are among the second-round of shrub bloom, the witch hazels and other extra-early shrubs having already finished flowering.

Widely planted for their bright yellow, scentless flowers, forsythias are a welcome note in the garden after a dreary winter. For this reason, if for no other, every garden ought to boast at least one forsythia. Their flowering season starts, depending on the year, usually in late March or very early April and continues for three full weeks if proper selection of species and varieties is made.

Forsythias are easy to transplant, easy to grow, tolerate almost any soil (though a long, severe drought in summer will have a deleterious effect on a plant in dry soil), and thrive in sun or light shade. The plants will grow in deep shade, but will not bloom to any extent.

Books on plant pests say that forsythias may be attacked by several, but in all the years I've been growing forsythias I've never seen any sign of disease nor have I noticed any evidence of insects—a fact worth remembering.

There are several different forms of forsythias—dwarf and compact; upright and spreading, but still fairly compact; and widely spreading, usually arching. Due consideration should be given to the ultimate size of a forsythia since the larger-growing sorts need plenty of room. If crowded, they will require constant pruning.

Forsythias bloom on wood grown the previous year. For this reason the proper time to prune them is immediately after flowering. However, as long as the flower buds already are formed, it seems to me more sensible to do any necessary pruning a month to six weeks before flowering time and use the pruned branches for forcing indoors. By doing this, pruning is accomplished without loss of a year's bloom and the forced branches provide indoor beauty long before blossoms are possible outdoors.

Forsythias never should be given a "crew hair-cut" as they so often are in parkways or around public buildings. Their natural form is gracefully arching or stiffly erect and whichever it happens to be, it should be followed and not modified in pruning. Cutting one of the older branches to the ground every year is good practice as new shoots will grow from the roots and renew the shrub.

The only forsythia which will bloom reliably in the north (Zone 4) is *F. ovata*. Several others will grow well, but since flower buds are killed each winter, rarely if ever will bloom. 'Arnold Dwarf' may be used as a ground cover in Zone 4 and makes an excellent one since no flowering is involved.

Forsythia 'Beatrix Farrand'. Zone 4; 6'-8'.

Plentiful golden yellow flowers, darker than those of *F. intermedia* 'Spectabilis' and 2" to 2½" in diameter, plus extremely vigorous growth are the hallmarks of this triploid forsythia. Originated at the Arnold Arboretum, Jamaica Plain, Mass., it is named for the late well-known landscape architect.

Forsythia 'Beatrix Farrand', flowers.

Forsythia × *intermedia* (*F. suspensa* × *F. viridissima*) (Border forsythia). Zone 5; 8' to 9'.

This plant shows signs of its hybrid nature by displaying, on occasion, traits from both parents. Some plants will be found which have purplish red and gold autumn color, inherited from *F. viridissima* and also, on some plants the generally upright growth habit of the border forsythia will be modified by arching branches, like those of *F. suspensa*.

Border forsythia is a vigorous-growing shrub which, when older, may grow as broad as it is high. It is best known in gardens for its cultivars.

217

Forsythia intermedia 'Spectabilis', blooming branch above; closeup of flowers, below.

Forsythia × *intermedia* 'Arnold Dwarf'. Zone 5 to parts of Zone 4; 2'-3'. Growing at least as wide and often twice as wide as it is high, with branches that droop and root where they touch the ground, this plant is a fine ground cover. Its disadvantage is its almost complete lack of flowers. If flowers are desired on a low-growing plant, use *F. viridissima* 'Bronxensis' instead of 'Arnold Dwarf'.

Forsythia × *intermedia* 'Arnold Giant'. Zone 5; 8'. A tetraploid forsythia with an upright growth habit, thickish leaves and large, dark yellow flowers, this cultivar does not seem to me as good a plant as many others.

Forsythia × *intermedia* 'Lynwood' (syn 'Lynwood Gold'). Zone 4; 5'-7'. A branch sport of *F. intermedia* 'Spectabilis' found in Ireland, this cultivar has deep yellow flowers almost evenly spaced along the straight, erect stems. I have been told by southern nurserymen that it will grow and bloom better if cut to the ground directly after flowering. I have hesitated to copy them for where I live I do not believe there would be sufficient growth during the remainder of the growing season to produce flowers the next spring. The blooms are slightly lighter in color than those of the species and of good size.

Forsythia × *intermedia* 'Primulina' (syn *F. primulina*). Illustrated on Color Page I. This shrub differs from the species in its flower color which, despite the name "brilliant yellow" (5 Y 9/9) of the color fan is pale yellow. This softer bloom color makes the shrub more generally useful in the garden as it can be more successfully combined with other flower colors.

Forsythia × *intermedia* 'Spectabilis' (syn *F. spectabilis*) (Showy border forsythia). Zone 4; 5'-6'. Illustrated on Color Page I. The most floriferous of any forsythia, this has vivid yellow (2.5 T 8/12) blooms, from 1¼" to 1¾" in diameter. A plant in bloom is like a living bouquet. Although I own plants of all of the species listed here and all the newer cultivars, I would rather grow this forsythia than any of the rest. People who do not like bold flower colors should grow 'Primulina', for 'Spectabilis' is certainly bold and brassy in bloom.

Forsythia × *intermedia* 'Spring Glory'. Zone 4; 6'-8'. A bud sport of *F. intermedia* 'Primulina' found in Ohio, this shrub has the paler yellow flowers of its parent but they are larger, to 2" in diameter, and they are more evenly spaced along the upright branches. A well-grown plant usually

Forsythia intermedia 'Spectabilis', seed capsules.

Forsythia intermedia 'Spring Glory', branch laden with bloom, above; closeup of flowers, below. Note difference in petal width between this cultivar and F. i. 'Spectabilis'.

has more flowers than one of its parent growing in similar soil and light.

Forsythia 'Karl Sax'. Zone 4; 6'-8'.

A tetraploid forsythia, this is more graceful in growth habit than 'Arnold Giant'. It bears a profusion of inch-wide, deep yellow flowers, darker than those of 'Beatrix Farrand'. It is said to be hardier than that cultivar.

Forsythia ovata (Early forsythia, Korean golden bell). Zone 3; 6'-8'.

If you live in the north and want to grow a forsythia, try this species first. If it will not flower for you, no forsythia will. The flower buds are the most winter-hardy of any forsythia.

People often compare the early forsythia with the showy border forsythia and say that the early sort is not as beautiful. I do not agree with this at all. In the first place the showy border forsythia is not in bloom until the early one is almost finished flowering, so there is no direct comparison in the garden. In the second place, I find the early forsythia quite as lovely in its own way. It is true that its blooms are individually smaller than those of some other forsythias and that it does not have quite as many blossoms as many others, but it still is an excellent garden plant and delightful in flower. For these reasons I commend it to gardeners who love forsythias and wish to extend their blooming season.

F. ovata is upright and spreading in form, more compact than many other forsythias and, for that reason, often more desirable. Flowers are ½″ to ⅜″ in diameter and 5 Y 9/9, brilliant yellow, in color.

Forsythia primulina (see *F. intermedia* 'Primulina').

Forsythia spectabilis (see *F. intermedia* 'Spectabilis').

Forsythia suspensa (Weeping forsythia, Weeping golden bell). Zone 5, flower buds winter kill in Zone 4, although the plant survives; 6′-7′.

A graceful forsythia, this has slender, arching or drooping branches that touch the ground and root where they touch. It has golden yellow flowers. It may be used to cover banks, be planted on top of a wall to droop over it, or be espaliered against a fence or wall because its branches are so flexible.

Forsythia suspensa fortunei (syn *F. fortunei*) (Fortune forsythia). Zone 4; 8′.

The growth habit of this variety differs markedly from that of the species. Branches first grow erect to almost the full height of the shrub, then those around the outer edges droop downward. Flower color is the same as that of the species.

Forsythia suspensa sieboldii (Siebold forsythia, Siebold's weeping golden bell). Zone 5; from 3′ up. A low-growing, spreading shrub, this is a first class ground cover for sunny banks, or anywhere that a downward-growing shrub is needed. It grows upright to a few feet in height, then the branches, which are almost procumbent, arch over to touch the ground, rooting where they touch. Flowers are darker yellow than those of *F. suspensa* and therefore contrast with them. Thus, where a long bank needs to be covered, the two may be used together for variety in yellows. The Siebold forsythia also may be used almost as a vine, to grow flat against a fence or wall or be trained and pruned to form patterns against any solid surface.

Forsythia viridissima (Greenstem golden bell). Zone 6 to Zone 5b in protected places; 9′.

Upright in growth, then with branches arching, this forsythia is distinguished from the others by its olive-green branchlets. Flowers, too, are tinged greenish and are darker yellow than those of some forsythias. They start to show color just as those of the Siebold forsythia are passing their prime. Because of this later flowering habit, this species may be used to extend the forsythia season in a large garden; but a more important reason for

Forsythia ovata,
flowers.

Forsythia suspensa, flowering branch. Note drooping growth habit (see description on opposite page).

Forsythia suspensa, above left; F. 'Beatrix Farrand', above right. Compare flower sizes.

growing this plant is for the purplish-red color of its leaves in autumn. It is the one forsythia with dependable fall color, though leaves of some others turn gold or purple and gold some autumns.

Forsythia viridissima 'Bronxensis' (also listed as 'Bronx'). Zone 5; 2'.

This plant grows into a low mound, more than twice as broad as it is high. Because of this growth habit it may be used for a low accent or in front of a shrub border as a "facing down" shrub. This is the only dwarf forsythia that flowers.

Forsythia, tree forms.

Some nurseries train forsythias to a single, long, straight stem, allowing the plants to branch only at the top. Thus the shrub is made into a "tree." This "tree-form" is usable on either side of a flight of steps or an entranceway, but you had better see it to make certain that you like it before you buy.

FOTHERGILLA (Witch alder)

Fothergillas are relatives of the witch hazels, with similar fruit capsules, but entirely different flowers. They are all native to the southern Appalachian Mountains, mainly to Virginia and Georgia, and are useful in the garden because they have two seasons of interest. In spring, as the leaves are unfolding, the odd, thimble-form, petalless, white flowers appear; and in autumn, providing the plants are not in deep shade, the leaves turn yellow, orange or scarlet. Flower buds are formed in autumn, so plants should be pruned (if this is necessary, which it is only rarely) after flowering.

All fothergillas are slow growing, preferring light shade and moist, but well drained soil. However,

Fothergilla monticola, flowers, below. Notice that they have no petals.

221

they will grow in full sun and dry soil if watered well during dry weather. Fothergillas are pretty when planted in woodlands, but even prettier in house plantings or when placed in front of or with evergreens.

Two species are available: two additional species only rarely appear in nursery catalogs.

Fothergilla major (Large fothergilla). Zone 5; 8′.

Stiff in branching, upright in growth, becoming a rather large plant, pyramidal in shape, this has flowers in late April to mid-May. Clusters may be 2″ long, midway in size between those of *F. gardeni* and those of *F. monticola*.

Fothergilla monticola (Alabama fothergilla). Zone 5; 5′-6′, sometimes taller.

Growth habit is more spreading than that of *F. major* and branches are less rigid. The flower spikes also are longer, 2½″.

Fothergilla monticola, seed capsules. Compare with those of witch hazel (Hamamelis).

GENISTA (Whin, Woadwaxen, Broom)

Genistas should come to mind when the place in which you want to plant has poor, dry, sandy soil. This genus loves these conditions and all members prefer full sun. All genistas are hard to transplant so should be purchased grown in pots if at all possible.

Genista tinctoria (Dyer's greenweed). Zone 2; 3′.

The common name of this shrub indicates its former use in dying cloth. It has erect, angled branches, blooms in early June and is the hardiest member of this genus. There are single and double-flowered forms, both with bright yellow flowers. In winter the twigs remain bright green. Where soil and exposure are suitable, this genista may be used for holding dry banks or in a rock garden.

HALIMODENDRON

Halimodendron halodendron (Salt tree). Zone 5; 6′.

The common name of this shrub refers to its ability to thrive in salty soils—in fact it is native to places having such soils. It is upright and wide spreading, with slim branches and gray-green leaves which when young are covered with fine, silky hairs. It is pretty when not in bloom, but in late June to early July it bears small, pea-shaped flowers, 2.5 RP 6/10, deep purplish pink, according to the color fan.

This is not a shrub that is carried by every nursery. It is listed here because of its usefulness for gardeners who live by the sea and a source is given in the Buyer's Guide Chart.

HAMAMELIS (Witch hazel)

Witch hazels have the distinction of being the last shrubs (or small trees) to bloom in autumn and, with the possible exception of pussy willow, the first to bloom in spring in the north. It is because they thus prolong the flowering season at both ends that they are grown in gardens.

They are natives, growing along streams, in low land or on banks, from Wisconsin east to Quebec and south to northern Georgia and Missouri. The bold leaves have large, rounded teeth and turn gold in autumn. The flowers of all witch hazels have long, slim petals. Blooms appear while the brown, wood-like seed capsules from the year before still are on the plants.

Witch hazels are useful both in wooded areas and in city gardens, for they tolerate the smoke, dust and dry air in cities better than most shrubs. They are upright and spreading in form.

There are several new and beautiful cultivars of witch hazels listed in the catalogs of a few nurseries. These I believe to be importations from Europe because the only new witch hazels I have seen were there. The flowers of these are orange or orange-red and larger than those of the witch hazels usually grown in this country. A shrub in bloom is positively striking in appearance—a description seldom, if ever, previously applied to a witch hazel. Look in the catalogs you own for names like 'Ruby Glow' and 'Orange Glow'. Then try to see the shrubs in bloom before you consider buying them.

Hamamelis japonica (Japanese witch hazel). Zone 5; usually a shrub, 10'-12', but may be a tree to 20'. Illustrated on Color Page VII.

One of the early-spring-flowering witch hazels, this prefers a drier, sunnier situation than the other species. Small leaves, at most 4" long, turn bright orange-yellow in fall. The flowers have bright yellow petals with purplish sepals and are not as fragrant as those of other witch hazels.

Hamamelis japonica flavo-purpurascens (Red Japanese witch hazel). The difference between this variety and the species is that in this the flower petals are red or reddish, sometimes entirely so and sometimes only at the base. Sepals are deep purple.

Hamamelis japonica rubra (see *H. j. flavo-purpurascens*).

Hamamelis mollis (Chinese witch hazel). Zone 6 and the southern part of Zone 5; usually a shrub to 12', but may be a tree to 25'.

With the largest and most fragrant blooms of any witch hazel, this should be more widely grown than

it is. The plant has a neat, compactly rounded form, hairy branches and top leaf surfaces. The lower leaf surfaces are covered with gray "wool." Leaves turn bright yellow in late autumn.

Flowers are golden-yellow, the bases of the petals often red. Petals are an inch and a half long and slender. Blooms are fragrant. If you have space for but one witch hazel, choose this one.

Hamamelis mollis 'Brevipetala'. A fast-growing, vigorous cultivar with flowers of orange-yellow in early spring and the shorter petals suggested by the cultivar name.

Hamamelis vernalis (Vernal witch hazel, Spring witch hazel). Zone 6 to southern part of Zone 5; 6', but sometimes to 10'.

Usually the first shrub to bloom in spring, this witch hazel is native from Missouri and Arkansas southward to Louisiana. In a protected spot, like a corner between house walls, this shrub is quite likely to have flowers in January or even earlier. In an unprotected place it will bloom, depending on the weather, in late February or early March. Because weather usually is cool to cold at that time of year and witch hazel flowers close on a cold day to reopen again when weather warms, they remain in good shape for weeks.

Blooms of the spring witch hazel are not nearly as large as those of *H. mollis*, being only ½" in diameter, but there are many of them on a shrub

Hamamelis japonica flavo-purpurascens, branch showing curious flowers, left; closeup of flowers, right. Notice long, slender petals.

Hamamelis vernalis, closeup of flowers and last year's seed capsules, open, empty, but still on the plant in spring.

Handsome foliage and closed seed capsules of Hamamelis.

———————

———————

Hamamelis virginiana, flower details.

After petals of Hamamelis fall, these sepals remain, resembling tiny flowers.

Early-blooming Hamamelis vernalis, above; late-flowering H. virginiana, below.

and they are fragrant. Color range is from yellow to two-toned reddish and yellow.

Because it sprouts from the base and spreads by means of suckers, this witch hazel makes a dense clump in time. Leaves turn yellow in autumn.

Hamamelis virginiana (Virginian witch hazel, Common witch hazel, American witch hazel, Monkey faces, Pistachio, Tobacco-wood, Winterbloom). Zone 5 to part of Zone 4; 15'. Illustrated on Color Page VII.

The witch hazel with which men anoint their faces after shaving is made from the branches of this shrub distilled and mixed with alcohol. Its branches also have been used for centuries and still are used by water dowsers as divining rods.

Native to the woods from Quebec westward to Minnesota and southward to Georgia and Tennessee, this hardiest witch hazel blooms from late September onward. I have seen it still in bloom in Michigan, in a sheltered spot in the woods, on Christmas day. It is the last shrub to bloom in the north.

Growth habit is open, rather straggly; leaves are large for a witch hazel and turn bright yellow in autumn. This shrub does not sucker, but often is found in colonies in the woods because its seed capsules, when they are dry and ripe, pop open with a sharp sound and shoot the black seeds out for several to many feet. The record shot seems to be 36'. This habit is disconcerting when it happens with pods on a branch which has been brought indoors.

Flowers are bright yellow; sepals brownish. The shrub will grow in light shade but blooms more freely in full sun. It is an excellent plant, not only for the edge of a woodland, but also in the background of a shrub border.

HIBISCUS (Shrub althea, Rose-of-Sharon)

Hibiscuses are narrow-growing shrubs with almost vertical branches. Their chief use in gardens is for their late summer bloom. In August and September, when few other shrubs flower, their bright blossoms are most welcome. Their secondary use is in seaside gardens for they will tolerate growing conditions by the seashore.

Foliage is not outstanding and leaf buds do not unfold until late in spring. Because of this, many gardeners are certain that their plants are dead. Patience usually will prove otherwise. Hibiscus plants are not easy to establish. They should be moved only in spring and the soil over their roots mulched for the first two winters. Once they are

225

well established they should need no protection.

Hibiscuses grow well in many soils but prefer one with plenty of organic matter, that holds moisture. They wilt easily when summers are dry and should be watered during drought. They survive city conditions, tolerate some shade (but bloom better in full sun) and are useful in narrow places where wider-growing shrubs would need constant pruning. They sometimes are used for unclipped hedges.

Heavy pruning in spring results in larger flowers but an unsightly shrub. Unless there is a reason for wanting these larger blooms, it is simpler to let nature take its course, which means a plant will produce many more, but smaller, blossoms.

Hibiscus syriacus (Shrub althea, Shrubby althea). Zone 5; 6′-8′. Illustrated on Color Page VI.

This plant is known in gardens through its cultivars, many of which are listed in nursery catalogs and available in nursery sales lots. The flowers of some are mediocre, of others beautiful. If I could choose but one cultivar it would be 'Blue Bird', with clear blue blooms centered with a dark "eye."

You will find that there are three flower forms in hibiscus: single, semi-double and double. Most cultivars have flowers with dark centers or centers of rose or rose-red, but a few have unmarked blooms.

To mention a very few of the handsome, newer cultivars, there are: 'William R. Smith', with flat, white flowers, blooming earlier than most other cultivars, sometimes starting in late June;

Hibiscus syriacus, single-flowered form, above; double-flowered form, below.

Hibiscus syriacus seed capsules which follow single flowers.

'Hamabo', with rose-red markings and center on a pale pink flower and 'Woodbridge', with rose pink blooms.

"Tree" forms are available, trained to a single stem with branching allowed only on top of this, as are also hibiscuses with variegated green and white leaves and hibiscuses sold as "Tricolor" with branches of three different cultivars grafted onto a single plant.

HOLLY (see ILEX)

HOLODISCUS

Holodiscus ariaefolius (see *H. discolor*).

Holodiscus discolor (Rockspirea, Cream bush, Ocean spray) (syn *H. d. ariaefolius H. ariaefolius*). Zone 6 to southern part of Zone 5; 12'.

Holodiscus is a west-coast native, useful in eastern or midwestern gardens in zones where it is hardy, for its July-flowering habit. It has slim, arching branches laden with many drooping clusters of creamy-white flowers. Foliage is white and woolly underneath; green on top.

Ocean spray may be grown in a shrub border or at the background of a perennial border. It is handsome enough for use as a specimen (anywhere but in a western garden because it is a native and therefore considered a weed) and is particularly pretty against evergreens. The shrub may be used in groups on a steep bank and not only holds the soil well, but transforms the bank into a mass of feathery snow when it flowers.

Holodiscus is tolerant of many soil types, but prefers full sun.

HYDRANGEA (Hydrangea)

Hydrangeas are particularly useful in the garden because they bloom during summer. Most of the species are easy to grow but the more "tender" kinds often are difficult to "flower." After a mild winter, plants may be loaded with blooms but often after a severe winter there will be no flowers.

Hydrangeas are not particular about the soil in which they grow. Some of them, notably the oak-leaved hydrangea (*H. quercifolia*), will thrive in shade.

Most hydrangeas have white flowers. On some species these turn green or greenish as they age and merge with the foliage. On others they turn from white to pink or rose as they grow older, thus prolonging their effectiveness in the garden. The more tender hydrangeas have handsome pink, rose, blue,

Hibiscus syriacus trained to "standard" or "tree" form.

or lavender flowers, depending on the acidity or alkalinity of the soil in which they are growing. (See page 50 for an explanation of this phenomenon.)

Hydrangea flowers have three distinct forms which vary with the species. One is conical, as in *H. paniculata* 'Grandiflora'; another is practically flat, as in the "lacecap" varieties and cultivars; and the third is a globe, as in *H. arborescens grandiflora*. You will see these different shapes most readily if you look at the pictures of these hydrangeas.

There also are two different flower cluster forms, one composed of small fertile flowers in the center with large, showy sterile flowers around the outside and the other of practically all sterile blooms. The "lace" design in the "lacecap" hydrangeas is due to the placement of fertile and sterile flowers in the flower cluster.

Hydrangea arborescens (Wild hydrangea, Seven bark, Bissum, High geranium). Zone 5 to part of Zone 4; 9'.

Native from southern New York, Indiana, and Illinois south to Florida, Missouri, and Oklahoma, this hydrangea is not as showy nor is it as widely seen in gardens as its variety, *grandiflora*.

For garden purposes, the difference between them is that almost all of the flower head of *grandiflora* is of large, sterile flowers whereas that of *arborescens* often is composed of all small, fertile

227

Hydrangea arborescens, flower cluster. Note sterile flowers outside, fertile flowers in center.

flowers, therefore it is not nearly so effective in the landscape. For this reason, *arborescens* might be used in a wooded area, while *grandiflora* would be more likely to be used in a cultivated garden. Flowers of both are white, turning greenish with age.

Hydrangea arborescens 'Annabelle'. Zone 6; 3'-4'. A selection of Prof. J. C. McDaniel at the University of Illinois, this has larger heads than the Snowhill hydrangea, up to 8" across and even larger. These are effective in June and continue to color until August. Like the Snowhill hydrangea, this will grow well in part shade or on the north side of the house. It does not thrive in the southern part of the country.

Hydrangea arborescens grandiflora (Hills of Snow or Snowhill hydrangea). Zone 5 to part of Zone 4; 3'. The dwarfness of this variety, the large creamy-white blooms, plus the fact that it flowers in early July, make this an extremely popular shrub. It flowers so profusely, most years, that it seems truly a small "hill of snow." Form is upright and usually quite dense. The heart-shaped leaves are attractive but do not turn color in autumn. The white blooms turn greenish, then brown as they get old.

This shrub is not absolutely hardy in some of the northern parts of Zone 5 and in Zone 4. If winters are severe it may kill to the snow line but, since it flowers on new growth, no blossoms will be lost. The plant simply grows smaller than it would elsewhere.

Snowhill hydrangea grows in almost any soil, prefers full sun and is easy to transplant and grow.

It is widely used in foundation plantings, in rows to mark the property line and in shrub borders.

Hydrangea bretschneideri (see *H. heteromalla*).

Hydrangea domotoi (see *H. macrophylla* 'Domotoi').

Hydrangea heteromalla (syn *H. bretschneideri*) (Shaggy hydrangea). Zone 5; 8'.

The common name of this hydrangea was given it because of its appearance when the bark of the past year peels off the branches. It has vertical clusters of white, sterile flowers in July, leaves that are whitish and woolly on the undersides, and grows upright and spreading. It should not be pruned as severely as *H. arborescens* or *H. paniculata*.

Hydrangea hortensis (see *H. macrophylla hortensis*).

Hydrangea macrophylla (syn *H. hortensis*, *H. opuloides*, *Hortensia opuloides*) and

H. macrophylla hortensis (Hortensia, French hydrangea, Blue hydrangea, Florists' hydrangea). Zone 6 to protected places in the southern part of Zone 5; About 3' in Zone 5b.

These two hydrangeas, *H. macrophylla* and *H. macrophylla hortensis* are listed here together because the catalog nomenclature is so hopelessly confused that it is impossible to guess which one is meant by the catalog listing. Catalog names used for this group or members of it include: *H. domotoi, H. hortensis, H. otaksa* and *H. mariesi* and,

Hydrangea arborescens grandiflora, flower cluster. Notice that all flowers are sterile.

Hydrangea macrophylla 'Mariesii', a "lacecap" type, above.

229

in addition to these, just the word "Hydrangea" in front of any cultivar name.

To a gardener this confusion of names should mean that he should see either the plant he wishes to purchase while it is in bloom or a good picture of it. This is the only way he can be certain of getting what he wants.

None of the hydrangeas in this group is hardy in the far north. A few cultivars, notably 'Nikko Blue', will live and bloom annually if they are set in protected places in Zone 5b. 'Nikko Blue' flowers on wood of the current year's growth so that any dieback during winter does not lessen the amount of flowering.

The "lacecaps" and many others of the cultivars bloom from buds at the tips of branches grown the previous year, so that there are no buds left to bloom if these branches winterkill.

If these hydrangeas demand sheltered places and winter protection, is it worth while to grow them? I think so, because their bright blooms certainly help the garden picture to be beautiful in July and August.

The best way to protect plants of the tender hydrangeas is to bend their branches downward as far as they will grow without breaking and to heap soil over them. Some gardeners top this mound with a bushel basket turned upside down. This holds all underneath it firmly in place. It also is possible to lift the plants and move them into a cool basement for the winter, but to me this does not seem worth the effort.

Flower color of these hydrangeas depends on the reaction of the soil in which they are growing. If they are in acid soil, the plants will produce blue flowers; in alkaline soil the blooms will be pink or rose. It is possible to control flower color by adding lime to the soil to make flowers pink or sulphur or iron sulphate to the soil to make flowers blue. I do not advocate the use of aluminum sulphate as an acidifier because, sooner or later, a residue of free aluminum will be left in the soil (it shows as a white coating on top of the soil) and this may kill the plants.

I would advise anyone who wants to grow these hydrangeas to try one or two plants to see how well they bloom before buying more. Start with 'Nikko Blue' and, if you live in Zone 5b, set it in a protected corner. (In Zone 6 you need not bother.) If this thrives, it does not mean that another, less hardy cultivar will do the same. Try another and see what happens under your conditions.

Varieties and cultivars in the catalogs include: 'Blue Boy', 'Blue Prince', 'Blue Wave', 'Bouquet Rose', 'Domotoi', 'Mariesii', 'Nikko Blue', 'Otaksa', 'Parsival', 'Pink Monarch', 'Royal Blue', 'Veitchii', and *Hydrangea serrata* 'Grayswood'. Most have globe-shaped flower heads and single blooms.

'Parsival' and 'Domotoi' have double flowers. 'Blue Wave', 'Mariesii', 'Veitchii', and 'Grayswood' are all "lacecaps." A variegated, green and white-leaved form of 'Mariesii' also is offered.

Hydrangea paniculata (syn *H. p. praecox, H. p. tardiva*). Zone 4: 12' to 15' as a shrub, to 30' as a tree in Japan. May be kept to any size by drastic pruning early each spring.

Hardiest of all the hydrangea species, this rarely is seen in species form. The people who would prefer a smaller flower head than the peegee hydrangea has, should grow the species instead. It has a dense, rounded form, is tolerant of many soil conditions and light shade. However, it grows best in full sun and in good, rather moist soil. It has escaped from cultivation in some places in Massachusetts.

The panicles are composed mostly of sterile flowers plus a few fertile ones. They are creamy-white and change to pink and rose as the season advances. Flowering starts in August. The plant may be used as a specimen or at the back of a shrub border.

Hydrangea paniculata, flowers just opening. Some will be fertile, some sterile.

Hydrangea paniculata 'Grandiflora' (Peegee hydrangea, P. G. hydrangea, for the initials of its specific and varietal names, but not, as one catalog says, obviously due to a printer's error, Gee Gee hydrangea). Zone 4; 20′-25′, but may be kept a more reasonable height by severe pruning in early spring.

The chief difference between this variety and the species is the flower form. Bloom clusters are larger in the peegee hydrangea and practically all the flowers are sterile. A well-grown shrub may have panicles a foot and a half long and a foot "through." The flowers, which are first green, turn white and then, as they age, pink, rose, or sometimes purplish. They remain on the plant well into the winter. They may be cut and dried at any of their color stages and often are used for winter bouquets.

Blooming time, like that of the species, is August and the flowers remain in good condition for weeks, if not months.

This hydrangea often is seen trained to "tree" form, that is to a single main stem or trunk. When nurseries list "tree form," they mean a plant so trained. There are, occasionally, places in a large garden where such a plant is well situated, but this does not happen often.

Hydrangea paniculata praecox (scc *H. paniculata*).

Hydrangea paniculata tardiva (see *H. paniculata*).

Hydrangea quercifolia (Oak-leaved hydrangea). Zone 6 to Zone 5b, worth trying further north in a protected place; 5′ or 6′.

Hydrangea paniculata 'Grandiflora' trained to a single stem and grown as a "tree", above; flower cluster below, showing all sterile flowers.

Hydrangea quercifolia showing flower cluster and oak-shaped leaves.

Growing wild in Georgia, Florida, and Mississippi, this plant is as much at home in the garden as in its native habitat. Its handsome leaves are reason enough for growing it, but its autumn foliage color and lovely flowers, as well as its ability to thrive in dense shade, are additional reasons.

As the botanical name (and, for once, also the common name) implies, the leaves are shaped rather like those of an oak. They are, however, of softer texture than those of oaks. Medium green on top, leaves are white underneath, effective when the breeze blows and the undersides show. They turn dark red and reddish-purple in autumn.

Shrub form is upright and dense. Flower panicles also are upright, with white florets turning purplish as they age.

Florets are 1¼″ in diameter, the clusters 6″ long and 4″ across.

HYPERICUM (St. Johnswort, Touch and heal)

Hypericums are of various sizes. Some may be classed as ground covers; others range in height from 2′ to 4′. All are able to thrive and grow in hot, dry places and poor, sandy soil. Most also will grow well in light shade.

A few are extremely hardy; others will grow only in Zone 6 and southward. Any which are doubtfully hardy in your area should be moved in spring only and preferably purchased with an earth ball around the roots.

All have yellow flowers, most with prominent yellow stamens in their centers. The taller-growing varieties make good additions to shrub borders because they bloom during summer when there are not many other shrubs in flower. The lower-growing ones are excellent ground covers, spreading rapidly. One or two even might be used in a border among perennial flowers.

Hypericum aureum (see *H. frondosum*).

Hypericum calycinum (Aaron's beard, Rose of Sharon (in England), Aaron's beard St. Johnswort). Zone 6 to southern part of Zone 5; 1′. Illustrated on Color Page V.

Set 18″ apart, plants of this species make a fine ground cover for a hot, sandy, sunny, steep bank. This plant, spreading by means of underground stolons, fills in between the plants rapidly, and discourages weed growth by its denseness. What more could you ask in a ground cover except that it also thrive in semi-shade, which this one does?

It is hardy certainly as far north as Ithaca, New York and in my garden. However, it is not ever-green in either place. In more southerly climes it is evergreen. Leaves are leathery in texture, gray underneath. The four-angled stems are reddish in color.

2½″ blooms appear in late July or early August and usually continue to open at least until mid-September. Bright yellow, they are borne at the tips of the stems and are centered with several anthers which, until pollen is shed, are bright red.

Hypericum frondosum (syn *H. aureum*) (Golden St. Johnswort). Zone 5; 3′.

Native to South Carolina and Tennessee, Georgia and Texas, this St. Johnswort can be grown successfully further north. It is upright-growing, dense, and has heavy branches for so small a shrub. Sometimes there is but a single stem. Foliage is bluish-green. The 2″, single, bright yellow flowers, borne singly or 2 or 3 together, start to appear the middle of July and continue through most of August.

Hypericum kalmianum (Kalm St. Johnswort). Zone 5 to part of Zone 4; 2½′.

One of the hardiest St. Johnsworts, this grows wild over a wide area of Ontario and Quebec, Michigan, and Illinois. It does not have as good a growth habit as some of the other species, for it is a rather straggly bush with many branches. Leaves are bluish-green with grayish undersides. The flowers are smaller than those of many other hypericums, from ½″ to 1″ across, arranged in clusters. There usually are a good many of them on the plant, so that it presents an attractive picture.

Hypericum patulum henryi (Henry St. Johnswort). Zone 6; 3′. In the southern states this plant is evergreen. It is semi-evergreen in Zone 6 but becomes deciduous in Zone 5b. It also dies to the ground in severe winters in Zone 5 but grows again from the roots in spring.

It is a pretty plant with very long leaves, sometimes 3 inches long. Flowers appear in July and are single, yellow and 2″ to 2½″ across.

Hypericum patulum 'Hidcote'. Zone 6 to southern part of Zone 5; 18″ and about the same in width. This cultivar is from the Hidcote estate in England. While it freezes to the ground every winter in Zone 5b, it comes up from the roots in spring. Since flowers are produced on new wood, this freezing back does not mean that bloom is lost.

The 2″, fragrant, bright yellow, cup-shaped flowers start opening in late June and there are some on the plant until frost. Where it can be grown, this is a shrub well worth growing.

Hypericum prolificum (Shrubby St. Johnswort). Zone 5 to parts of Zone 4; 4'.

Native from Ontario to Iowa and southward to Georgia, upright and dense in growth, this shrub becomes mounded in shape. Branches are thick with peeling, light brown bark. Leaves are narrow; shining dark green. Flowers, which appear from July through September, are only ¾" in diameter; bright yellow and single. They are borne in clusters of a few flowers each.

Hypericum 'Sun Gold'. Zone 6 to southern part of Zone 5; 2', may be more than that in diameter.

This cultivar winterkills to the ground in Zone 5b but grows again from the roots in spring. However, it blooms on wood of the current season's growth so flowers are produced despite the freezing back.

Leaves are medium green. Blooms are 2½" in diameter, in 4" wide clusters, vivid yellow (2.5 Y 8/12) and are produced from July through August and part of September. This is a handsome hypericum which should be grown where it is hardy.

Many species of Hypericum have flowers similar to those shown in top picture on right. Center picture shows H. 'Sungold', much improved, with large flowers. Lower picture shows 'Sungold', right, with the same species depicted above, for size comparison.

ILEX (Holly)

The most beautiful hollies are evergreen trees. Their berry-filled branches frequently are used for Christmas decorations. The hardy tree hollies are described briefly in Chapter 15. In Chapter 14 both deciduous and evergreen shrub hollies are described if they are hardy from Zone 6 northward and are listed in nursery catalogs used in this book.

All evergreen hollies are best moved in spring. Sometimes, when transplanted in fall, they drop all their leaves. Usually these grow again in spring, but sometimes the plants simply die during winter. Evergreen hollies should always be purchased with earth balls around their roots, never "bare root." On the other hand, deciduous hollies may be moved in either spring or fall and with bare roots.

233

Good garden soil, preferably one retaining moisture and acid in reaction, will grow good hollies. The situation in which hollies are planted MUST be well drained, except for those which often grow wild in swamps, noted in their descriptions below.

It is important for the gardener who wishes to grow hollies to realize that, with few exceptions, male and female flowers are borne on separate plants. Of course the female plants bear the berries, but a male plant is needed within about 40′ to pollinate the flowers of the female plant.

Many people who grow hollies set plants of both sexes in the same hole to insure pollination. Then they keep the male plant pruned so that it is small compared with the female but produces enough flowers so that their pollen, when carried by bees or wind, will pollinate the female flowers and berries are produced. Since foliage of male and female plants of the same species is identical, the two plants can be pruned to appear as one to the casual observer.

Ilex crenata (Japanese holly). Zone 7 and therefore not described in this book. However, some of its varieties and cultivars are hardier than the species, so are listed below.

Ilex crenata bullata (see *I. crenata* 'Convexa').

Ilex crenata 'Compacta'. Zone 6; a particularly compact form of *I. crenata*, this has the same small, deep green leaves, dense growth habit and black berries as the species.

Ilex crenata 'Convexa' (syn *I. bullata, I. convexa, I. crenata bullata, I. convexa bullata, I buxifolia* of the catalogs) (Convex-leaved holly, Box-leaved Japanese holly). Zone 6 to southern part of Zone 5: 3′ but may grow twice as wide. Illustrated on Color Page VIII. An evergreen holly with small leaves, convex on top, which makes them concave below, this is an extremely useful holly. It makes an excellent low hedge; may be used in place of boxwood where box is hard to grow. It is pretty with needled evergreens or deciduous shrubs in house plantings and may be used as a specimen where a low, wide, evergreen plant is desired.

It will grow in part shade as well as in full sun. It should *not* be given a protected spot. I know this sounds odd, but in a planting of 22 of these hollies, my only losses were among the plants more protected than others. When I complained to Paul Bosley, Sr. from whom I had bought the plants, he said he had noticed the same thing—that plants in the open field survived winters during which plants in more sheltered locations succumbed.

This holly is grown for its foliage. The blooms, like those of all hollies, are inconspicuous and the black berries are borne some years and not others; are not particularly beautiful in any case.

Ilex crenata 'Glass'.

A compact, upright habit of growth and shiny, dark green leaves, only ¼ to ½″ long and about half as wide characterize this clone of *I. crenata* 'Microphylla'. All plants are male.

Ilex crenata 'Green Island'. A dwarf form that is flat topped, spreading, and almost horizontally branched. It has little twigs and light green foliage, sometimes tinged purplish-brown. It has a solid appearance, rather like a cushion. As for size, the pair of plants Frank Styer, the originator, gave me years ago when he first selected this holly, grew only 7″ high but over 2′ wide in the six years I owned them.

Ilex crenata helleri. Zone 6 to southern part of Zone 5; 3½′. Because it is so compact and slow-growing, this holly might be used as a specimen in a rock garden. It is an evergreen dwarf with tiny leaves, very dark green. So thickly do these leaves cover the plant that you hardly can put your finger between them.

Ilex crenata 'Hetzi'. Zone 5; 3′. Another dwarf holly with the convex leaves described under *I. crenata* 'Convexa', this holly seems to be even hardier.

Ilex crenata 'Latifolia' (syn *I. crenata rotundifolia*) (Round-leaved Japanese holly). Zone 6. This is a form of holly distinguished by its large, round, shining leaves, which are evergreen.

Ilex crenata 'Microphylla' (Little-leaf Japanese holly). Zone 6. Excellent for a low hedge because it is compact and "twiggy," responding well to pruning, this holly has black fruits and the tiny leaves indicated by its botanical name.

Ilex crenata 'Repandens'. Zone 6. As its botanical name suggests, this plant grows flat, very compact, and slowly. It has narrow, pale green leaves.

Ilex crenata 'Stokes' (also listed as 'Stokes Dwarf'). Zone 6, about 1′. A tiny, compact holly useful for edging rose beds or for tiny hedges.

There are many other varieties and cultivars of *I. crenata,* but these are most widely listed in the catalogs.

Ilex glabra (Inkberry, Gallberry). Zone 5; 6′ or more.

Useful as a hedge plant or near the house, this holly may be evergreen or it may drop its leaves, depending on the severity of the winter. Leaves may be 2″ long, are usually light, but sometimes dark green and also sometimes have glossy surfaces. Fruits are black, and ⅜″ in diameter. They follow tiny white ¼″ wide flowers which are greenish yellow in the center, the color turning to brown as the flowers age.

While this holly is not nearly as handsome as many of the Japanese holly varieties and cultivars, it is much hardier. It is native from Nova Scotia to Florida and westward to Missouri, growing in low, damp places. It will, however, succeed in dry soil in the garden. It spreads by means of stolons and forms a dense clump. Growth habit is upright.

Ilex glabra 'Compacta'. Growing only 3′ high, this has dark green, glossy foliage which may not be as pleasing in color when the plants, which are all female, bear their abundant fruits.

Ilex pedunculosa (Long-stalk holly). Zone 6 and protected places in the southern part of Zone 5; to 15′.

The berries hang on inch-long stems, hence the botanical name of this holly. Fruits are bright red and ¼″ in diameter. Leaves are smooth, dark green and glossy. This is one of the hardiest of the evergreen hollies.

Ilex glabra, berries.

Ilex serrata (Japanese winterberry). Zone 5; 6′-7′.

The saw-toothed edges of the leaves are responsible for the botanical name of this deciduous holly. The flowers are 3/16″ in diameter in ⅜″ wide clusters and are pale pink, nearest to 2.5 R 9/3 but slightly more yellow. The red berries stay in good condition for some time.

Ilex glabra, flowering branch.

closeup of flowers showing coloration.

Above: Ilex serrata, branch with flowers and the toothed or serrated leaves, indicated by the botanical name.

Below: Male flowers, stamens with ripe pollen.

Ilex serrata, berries.

Ilex verticillata (Michigan holly, Virginia winterberry, Swamp holly, Winterberry, Coonberry, Black alder, because leaves turn black after the first frost). Zone 4 to part of Zone 3; 10' but sometimes 18'. Illustrated on Color Page VIII.

This deciduous, widely spreading holly grows in swamps from Newfoundland to Minnesota, southward to Missouri and Georgia. However, it also will grow, but never as tall, in dry soil, so may be used in any ordinary garden situation.

Its smooth, gray branches are conspicuous in winter; the dark green leaves are virtually lost in the summer landscape, but the shrub is outstanding in autumn when the bright red, quarter-inch berries ripen while the leaves still are in evidence. After the leaves fall the berries remain on the plants and often are cut for Christmas decorations by commercial florists.

This holly should be purchased in a small size as large plants are difficult to move. There is a yellow-berried form, rarely purchasable.

Ilex verticillata polycarpa. The red berries of this variety are larger than those of the species and the twigs are brownish.

Ilex verticillata, flowering branch.

Ilex verticillata, berried branch, above; closeup of berries, below.

KALMIA (Laurel, American laurel)

Laurels are evergreen shrubs which need acid soil to thrive. One is outstanding in flower—mountain laurel (*K. latifolia*).

The foliage of several species, including the one named here, is poisonous to cattle when eaten in quantity. It also would be poisonous to humans but, since it is thick and leathery in the species most often planted, it hardly is likely that humans would try to eat it.

Laurels are pretty when combined with narrow-leaved evergreens or with rhododendrons and azaleas.

All laurels should be purchased with earth balls around the roots and preferably moved in spring.

Kalmia latifolia (Mountain laurel, Calico bush, Big-leaf ivy, Bush ivy, Poison ivy, Spoonwood, Wicopy, Clamoun). Zone 5; 25′ in the wild, but about 6′ under cultivation. Illustrated on Color Page IV.

This is one of the loveliest of American natives and when it flowers the middle of June the woods from New York and New England south to Florida, westward to Louisiana, Ohio and Indiana become a glory.

Flower color varies from plant to plant. Blooms on some are pure white, on others varying shades of pink, mostly moderate pink (10 RP 8/5). The inch-wide florets are borne in 5″ diameter or larger clusters and are most beautifully detailed inside each floret (see photograph). The buds, too, are exceptionally pretty. Both buds and blooms appear against dark, glossy, evergreen foliage. Growth habit is upright and spreading.

Mountain laurel is found at the edges of woods in which soil is gravelly or in clearings. Sometimes

237

it is found growing in swamps which indicates the wide range of soil conditions in which it will grow. However, the soils in which it is found always are acid and, in order for it to thrive in gardens, soil which is not naturally acid must be acidified for it (see Chapter 5, page 36 for directions).

After the flowers have faded, the evergreen leaves remain for interest the rest of the year. The seed pods are not pretty nor are they interesting. Furthermore, in the interests of more flowers another year, they should not be allowed to develop but should be removed from the plant as soon as they form.

If you are buying mountain laurel, be sure to ask if the plants are nursery grown or "collected." Those "collected" have been dug from the wild and are not as likely to survive transplanting as those grown in nurseries.

Mountain laurel often is used in plantings near the house or at the edges of woodlands and on banks. It also may be used in front of evergreens in a position not too far from the house, so its flowers may be enjoyed, or with other broad-leaved evergreens. It looks particularly effective when massed.

Kalmia latifolia, flowering branch, above. Below: closeup of blooms showing curious and beautiful details of buds and blossoms.

KERRIA (Kerria, Kerrybush, Corchorus, Jews-mallow)

Kerrias are upright-growing shrubs with many small twigs which often winterkill, necessitating some pruning each spring. Branches are slender, leaves attractive and the double flowers on one variety particularly so. The kerrias described below bloom in mid-May.

Kerria japonica (Japanese kerria). Zone 5; 4'-6'. Can be kept to the lesser height by pruning one or two old branches to the ground each year.

This is a rather temperamental plant because while it may be alive in autumn it quite often is dead by spring. This single-flowered form is far more often winterkilled than the double-flowered. But the single-flowered has one great advantage—it will thrive and flower in quite heavy shade.

The plant is upright-growing, with thin branches which remain bright green all winter, many fine twigs, medium green leaves with prominent veins and coarse teeth. The flowers are 1½ to 1¾" in diameter and there is no match for them on the color fan. They are more yellow than strong orange-yellow (7.5 YR 7/11) and more gold than medium orange-yellow (10 YR 8/10). Unfortunately the flowers do not remain on the plant for more than five days to one week, while those of the double-flowered form are in good condition for two to three weeks. There may, however, be occasional blooms during summer and usually a fair show of them in early fall. This plant is best used in a shrub border.

Kerria japonica floriplena (see *K. j.* 'Pleniflora').

Kerria japonica 'Picta' (Silver kerria, Variegated kerria). Zone 5; 2½'. This is not only a much lower-growing kerria but, on the same bright green, slender branches as the species, it has green leaves edged with white and single, ¾" to 1" diameter flowers, closest to strong orange yellow (7.5 YR 7/11).

Care must be taken to suppress ruthlessly any shoots growing from the ground that have all-green leaves or these will outgrow the branches with variegated leaves.

The plant is particularly suitable for use as a specimen.

Kerria japonica 'Pleniflora' (Globeflower, Japanese rose). Zone 5; 6'. Illustrated on Color Page III. This shrub looks the same in form and everything else except bloom as the species previously described. It is different in hardiness, surviving winters during which the single-flowered species is killed. Because of the double, rose-like flowers, the blooms are far more effective in the garden than the single-flowered form. These little "roses" are 1½" to 1¾" in diameter, are so full of petals that they are practically ball-shaped and are sufficiently conspicuous to have both common names refer to them. Use this Kerria as a specimen or in a border.

Kerria japonica 'Picta', above, showing flowers and variegated foliage.

Kerria japonica, below, detail of leaves and flowers. Note masses of stamens in centers of blooms.

Kerria japonica, branch with flowers.

KOLKWITZIA

Kolkwitzia amabilis (Beauty bush). Zone 5 to part of Zone 4; 12' high and spreads to 8' in width.

This big shrub has upright branches that arch over all around the outside of the plant, creating a fountain-like effect. The leaves are small and not remarkable except in autumn when they turn reddish. The thousands of small tubular, ½" wide flowers are the reason for the shrub's common name.

These occasionally are white and equally occasionally deep pink, but usually the 2 upper petals are light purplish pink (7.5 RP 8/5), while the paler throats are veined and marked with strong orange (5 YR 7/11).

These flowers remain in good condition for at least 2 weeks if the weather is cool in early June. They are followed by gray, feathery seed heads which are interesting for additional weeks.

Of easiest culture, this shrub needs only a well-drained, sunny situation with plenty of room around it. It is indifferent to soil types and takes care of itself.

It is best used as a specimen, but is also a fine choice for the corner of a large house or the back of a shrub border.

Kerria japonica 'Pleniflora', flowering branch, above; closeup of double flowers, below.

Kolkwitzia amabilis, branch with seed heads.

Kolkwitzia amabilis, flowers, above; seed heads and sepals left after blooms and seeds fall, below.

LAUROCERASUS (see *Prunus laurocerasus*)

LAVANDULA (Lavender)

Lavandula officinalis (syn *L. spica, L. vera*) (True lavender). Zone 6 to southern part of Zone 5; 2′.

When and where winters are mild, this little shrub is evergreen; during cold winters the leaves drop to appear again in spring. These gray-green leaves, more gray than green, and the lavender flowers are the parts of the plant which are dried for sachets to place among linens. They also are used in making perfume and oil.

The flowers appear late in June and blend with the leaves so that they do not spoil the overall effect of gray. Two strains are listed in the catalogs:

'Hidcote', also listed as 'Hidcote Blue', is hardier than the species. It grows 15″ high and the flower spikes may add another 15″. Foliage is silvery; purplish-blue flowers open from early July until frost.

'Munstead' (also listed as 'Munstead Dwarf') grows only 1′ high and, because of its compactness, makes an unusual hedge around herb or rose beds. Flowers are deep heliotrope in color.

Lavenders are used as hedges in herb gardens and in perennial borders, but wherever they are used they will profit by pruning to just above the growth of the previous year. This should be done in early spring. While lavenders may be moved in either spring or fall, spring is best especially in cold climates. They prefer a warm, sunny place, in a dry, not-too-heavy soil.

Lavandula spica (see *L. officinalis*).

Lavandula vera (see *L. officinalis*).

LESPEDEZA (Desmodium, Bush-clover)

The chief reason for growing these shrubs is that they flower in late summer and early autumn. Their slender, arching stems die to the ground in winter but grow again in spring and bear myriad three-parted leaves, much like those of clover, and even more pea-shaped flowers.

Bush-clovers thrive in full sun in any soil. They will profit by being cut to the ground each spring should any of the tops survive the winter.

Lespedeza bicolor (Shrub bush-clover). Zone 5; 6′, occasionally to 9′.

The enormous quantities of rose-purple flowers, borne in clusters at the branch tips in August and September are reason enough for growing it.

Lespedeza formosa (see *L. thunbergii*).

Lespedeza penduliflora (see *L. thunbergii*).

Lespedeza thunbergii (syn *L. formosa, L. penduliflora, Desmodium penduliflora*) (Purple bush-clover). Zone 6 to southern part of Zone 5; 6′.

Long, arching branches, laden with small strong purplish red (closest to 7/5 RP 4/11) flowers in 3″ long clusters drooping from the branch tips enliven the garden picture in August and September. The blooms are not good for cutting, since they wilt the second they are picked, but, what a lift they give the garden in late summer!

There is a lower-growing form of the purple bush-clover occasionally listed in the catalogs as *L. t. nana*.

Lespedeza thunbergii, flowering branch.

LEUCOTHOË

The name of this genus has a diaeresis over the final e and is therefore pronounced loo-coh′-thoh-ee.

The leucothoës described below are broad-leaved evergreen shrubs grown for their attractive forms and foliage and for their white, wax-like flowers. They need an acid soil and prefer one that has plenty of peat mixed with it and thus holds moisture. They should be purchased with earth balls around the roots and moved only in spring.

Leucothoë axillaris (Coast leucothoë). Zone 6 to part of Zone 5; 2′.

This is a useful leucothoë where it is hardy. As you see from the height given above, it is low, its form is dense, it has arching stems, the usual dark green, shiny leaves and tiny bell-shaped flowers in May. It prefers to be placed in semi-shade.

In an area where soil is acid, this plant makes a splendid groundcover, if a 2′ high one is desired, and it also may be used as a "facing down" shrub in front of mountain laurel, rhododendron (the lower growing sorts) or pieris.

Leucothoë catesbaei (see *L. fontanesiana*).

Leucothoë fontanesiana (syn *L. catesbaei*) (Drooping leucothoë, Fetter bush, Dog laurel, Dog hobble). Zone 5b; 2′ to 3′.

Although this shrub grows wild from Virginia to Georgia and Tennessee, usually in the mountains, it is hardy in the southern part of Zone 5. It is a graceful plant with spreading and arching stems and thick, shiny, dark green leaves, lighter green underneath. These turn bronze in autumn and remain that color during a mild winter, though in a severe winter they drop. The flowers are bell-shaped, ¼″ long and 1/16″ wide, creamy-white and fragrant. They hang in little clusters from the undersides of the stems, often along almost the entire length of the stems.

This plant spreads by means of underground stems and, if in an ideal location, will prove that it is satisfied by gradually forming a clump. Because of this growth habit it is hard to use drooping leucothoë as a specimen plant—one never can tell how large it will get eventually. However, along a woodland path or at the edge of a rhododendron planting, the edge of woods, or with narrow-leaved evergreens in a house planting, leucothoë is quite at home and blends perfectly.

Leucothoë fontanesiana 'Girard's Rainbow' (also listed as 'Rainbow' and called that by nurserymen). Originated at the Girard Nursery, Geneva, Ohio, this leucothoë with variegated leaves colored white to cream, pink to rose and green is not yet fully tested as to hardiness. While several plants in my garden have survived two winters, one Michigan nurseryman lost a large planting the first winter after setting them out. So, unless you live in Zone 6 or southward, try one plant on the north side of a building before you buy more. Except for a more upright growth, 'Girard's Rainbow' appears to be similar to *L. fontanesiana*. I have yet to see a plant over a foot high.

LIGUSTRUM (Privet)

Privets are used, if used at all, for hedges although many of them make outstanding specimen plants. Grown primarily for their foliage, some of them also have attractive flowers if the plants are not clipped to hedge form.

The leaves may be evergreen (on privets grown in the south) or deciduous; they may be variegated light green, yellow or white. The flowers of all privets are white, of a few species fragrant and most sorts bloom in June or July. Florets are small but the clusters are, in some privets, large and showy. Privet berries, usually black or blue-black and shiny, often are handsome. Of course they mature only on plants that have not been pruned.

Leucothoë fontanesiana: flowering branch, left, and seed capsules, right.

Privets are fast, strong growers or they would not make good hedge plants. Except for the European or common privet they are exceptionally free of pests. They are extremely tolerant of soil variations and of city growing conditions.

Ligustrum amurense (Amur privet, Amur River privet). Zone 4; 15′.

A dependable privet for the north, this species is semi-evergreen when grown sufficiently far south but deciduous in the north. If left unpruned it forms a pyramidal-shaped plant. Leaves grow 1″ long and are glossy on the tops. Blooms appear about the middle of June and are followed by small, dull black berries. This is not as good-looking as either *L. ovalifolium* or *L. × ibolium* but is much hardier than either.

There are two distinct types of Amur privet listed in the catalogs. These are designated as "Amur north" and "Amur south." By "Amur south" nurserymen mean *L. sinense,* which is not hardy in the north.

Ligustrum californicum or California privet (see *L. ovalifolium*).

English privet or European privet (see *L. vulgare*).

Ligustrum × ibolium (*L. ovalifolium × L. obtusifolium*) (Ibolium privet). Zone 5; 6′-8′.

California privet, described below, probably is the prettiest of the privets grown in the north. The Ibolium privet most closely resembles the California and should be used instead of it in the north because California privet is not reliably hardy under northern conditions. In zones where Ibolium privet is not hardy, Amur privet should be tried.

Ibolium privet is an upright-growing, deciduous shrub. The foliage is dark green and glossy. Flowers open in mid-June and black berries, which remain on the plants well into winter (unless the birds strip them from the shrub) follow the flowers.

Ligustrum ibota (see *L. obtusifolium*).

Ligustrum ibota vicaryi (see *L. vicaryi*).

Ligustrum lodense (see *L. vulgare* 'Lodense').

Ligustrum obtusifolium (syn *L. ibota,* which is the name usually listed in the catalogs) (Border privet). Zone 5 to parts of Zone 4; 6′-8′, possibly 10′.

Arching branches make this privet a graceful shrub and a good looking specimen plant. A further characteristic which makes it interesting is the autumn color of its leaves which may be purplish to purplish-brown. The flower clusters are nodding, blooms open from mid-June to July and, for privet flowers, are showy. Berries are dull blue-black to black.

Ligustrum obtusifolium regelianum (Regel's privet). Zone 5 to parts of Zone 4; 4′-5′. This privet has many good qualities. In the first place it never grows tall. In the second, it has a distinctive horizontal branching habit. This form, plus the oppositely placed leaves make the plant unusual in appearance. And, if it needs any more recommendation, another good point is that it will thrive in as deep shade as any shrub. All of these characteristics make it a popular shrub.

The ⅜″ diameter, white blooms are arranged in ¾″ long spikes. They open in mid-June to July and the berries, like those of the species, are dull blue-black to black.

Ligustrum obtusifolium regelianum, flowers.

Ligustrum obtusifolium regelianum, berries.

Ligustrum ovalifolium (syn *L. californicum*) (California privet). Zone 6 and southward.

As you can tell from the hardiness zone stated above, this privet barely comes within the scope of this book. However, it is widely sold in more northerly hardiness zones where *it should not be sold* because it is not reliably hardy there. Sometimes it winterkills even in the northern part of Zone 6.

What usually happens to the unwary gardener is that just when his hedge is high and tight and he is proud of its appearance, a severe winter will cut it to the ground. If you wonder how often this happens, exact records show that both the hedge belonging to our next-door-neighbors (in our former home) and that across the road from us were killed to the ground three times in the 21 years we lived in that house. Each time years were required for the plants to grow from the roots to useful height.

California privet is handsome, so it appeals to people looking for a hedge plant. Where it is hardy it probably is the perfect choice. But it is not a sensible buy for gardeners in the north, especially since there are hardier privets that can be depended on to live through severe winters.

California privet is half-evergreen and upright-growing. Its glossy green leaves are its most important characteristic. The cream-white blooms in mid-June and the black berries which follow them are no more effective than those of many other privets.

Numerous varieties of this privet are listed in the catalogs but will not be described here because none of them is hardier than the species.

Ligustrum regelianum (see *L. obtusifolium regelianum*).

Ligustrum × *vicaryi* (*L. ovalifolium* 'Aureum' × *L. vulgare*) (syn *L. ibota vicaryi*) (Vicary privet, Golden privet, Golden Vicari privet). Zone 5; 2'-3'.

Because of its vivid greenish yellow (7.5 Y 8/12) foliage color and its comparatively slow growth (for a privet) this has become an extremely popular plant. It may be used for an accent with evergreens or other shrubs in a house planting, as a low hedge or edging for a driveway or for edging a large flower bed in a formal garden. In fact, it is useful wherever its foliage color is desirable.

Ligustrum vulgare (European privet, Common privet, English privet, Prim, Prim-print, Primwort, Print, Skedge, Skedgewith). Zone 5; 10'-12'.

Because in certain localities this privet is subject to a blight which makes it a poor choice, ask to see some hedges of it already growing in your neighborhood before you buy plants of common privet.

It is a wide-growing plant, deciduous, or sometimes semi-evergreen. Although its chief use is for hedges, it also makes a handsome specimen. When grown in this manner the 1/4" white flowers in 2" long clusters in mid-June to July and the shining black berries, both against 2½" long leaves, make it attractive over a long period. When the birds leave them alone, the berries hang on well into the winter.

Ligustrum vulgare 'Lodense' (syn *L. lodense, L. lodense nana, L. densifolium nana*) is a dwarf, compact form of Common privet, useful where a lower, thick hedge is needed.

Ligustrum vulgare flowers. Note similarity to lilac blooms.

245

Lindera benzoin, flowering branch, above; closeup of blooms, below.

LINDERA

Lindera benzoin (syn *Benzoin aestivale*) (Spice bush, Wild allspice, Fever bush, Snap-weed, Snap-wood, Spice-wood). Zone 4; 12′ or slightly more.

Walk in early spring near almost any lake or pond with wooded shores and you're almost certain to see the vivid yellow (2.5 Y 8/12) ¼″ to ⅜″ diameter flowers on a spice bush. This large shrub or small tree grows upright and, in the wild, branches widely. In gardens it is more compact in form. It is deciduous and its light green leaves turn golden yellow in autumn before they fall.

The flowers are small clusters of tiny florets and look showier than they actually are because of their color contrast with the almost black bark of the shrub. After the flowers fade, small berries form, ripening to red in August. These remain on the shrub after the leaves have fallen.

Flowers of the two sexes are borne on separate plants, so that a plant with blooms of each sex is necessary in order that berries be produced on the female plant.

This shrub is native from Maine and Ontario westward to Kansas and south to Florida and Texas. It is best used in a site that resembles its natural habitat—alongside a stream or other body of water. It also may be used where soil is moist even if there is no body of water. The flowers are too delicate in effect to be shown in competition with those of other more showy shrubs in bloom at the same time.

LONICERA (Honeysuckle)

There are both shrub and vine forms of honeysuckles, but only the shrubs are considered in this book. They are upright in growth, are easy to move and to grow in almost any soil. Most prefer to be placed in full sun but many will tolerate a great deal of shade and still flower and fruit. All are vigorous in growth.

Even the evergreen forms of honeysuckles have undistinguished small leaves which do not change color in autumn. Small fragrant flowers are produced in abundance and may be white, yellow, lavender, pink, rose, or red in color. They are followed by equally large masses of berries, beloved by birds. These usually are red, orange-red, or orange, though some honeysuckles have blue or black fruits which are not as conpicuous.

Honeysuckles are of the easiest possible culture. They need no special care, for the shrub forms have no insects or diseases which attack them. They may be used for unclipped hedges, in shrub borders and some kinds make beautiful specimen plants. Many honeysuckles unfold their leaves so early in spring that it is almost impossible to transplant them while still dormant. For this reason it is better to order them for fall delivery. They may be moved with bare roots.

Lonicera alba (see *L. tatarica alba*).

Lonicera bella albida (see *Lonicera bella* 'Candida').

Lonicera bella 'Candida' (syn *L. b. albida*) (White Gotha honeysuckle). Zone 4; 6'-8'. This is a large, graceful bush which is covered with large, white flowers in late May. The red fruits ripen in July.

Lonicera 'Clavey's Dwarf' (see *L. xylosteoides* 'Clavey's Dwarf').

Lonicera fragrantissima (Fragrant honeysuckle. Winter honeysuckle). Zone 6 to southern part of Zone 5; 7'.

For many years in our former garden we had a plant of this honeysuckle in a corner made by house wall and porch. In this situation it often bloomed in late February and also often was evergreen. When we moved the plant with us to our present larger, more exposed garden, it changed its habits; it is now deciduous and blooms in early April.

The plant grows upright, then the stiff branches spread outward and arch. Leaves are thick and dark green. Flowers are tiny, creamy-white and so fragrant that even a small spray of them brought indoors will perfume a room. Berries are red but, since they color early, birds eat them as fast as they ripen.

This is a wide spreading shrub which needs room to grow its full size. If not given plenty of space, it will require constant pruning. It blooms on wood grown the previous year so should not be pruned in late autumn or early spring or the flower buds will be cut off.

Lonicera korolkowii (Blue-leaf honeysuckle). Zone 5 to southern part of Zone 4; 10' or a little more and 8' in width.

The reasons for growing this honeysuckle are its blue-green leaves and its bright rose-colored flowers the third week in May. Berries which follow, ripening in July and August, are bright orange-red.

Blue-leaf honeysuckle may be used as a specimen, in the shrub border or for an unclipped hedge. It should be placed only where the unusual color of its foliage is suitable. It is difficult to transplant so

Lonicera fragrantissima, flowering branches.

should be moved only in spring and purchased with a ball of earth around its roots.

Lonicera korolkowii 'Zabelii' (Zabel's honeysuckle). Zone 4; 5'-6'. The same blue-green leaves as the species described above adorn this plant but the flowers are darker (nearest to 7.5 RP 4/11, strong purplish red, but more rosy) and the plant is smaller and neater. Berries are ¼" in diameter, and strong red (5 R 4/12). Zabel's honeysuckle also is difficult to transplant. (See last sentence of description of species.)

247

Lonicera korolkowii 'Zabelii', branch with flowers, above; with berries, below.

Lonicera maackii (Amur honeysuckle). Zone 2 to part of Zone 1; 12'-15' and spreading about as wide, making it one of the largest honeysuckles.

A full-grown plant of Amur honeysuckle is a gorgeous sight, particularly when in berry. It is pretty when in flower but the fragrant blooms are white, yellowing as they age, so even though there are many of them it is not as showy as some of the honeysuckles with brightly colored flowers.

It blooms in late May and the berries do not color until September in Zone 5b. The leaves remain on the plant until late fall or early winter and so do the berries (if the birds do not eat them). Sprays of this honeysuckle make beautiful table decorations for Thanksgiving.

Lonicera maackii podocarpa (Late honeysuckle). Zone 5 to part of Zone 4; 8'-10'. This plant is nearly evergreen in Zone 6 and some winters in Zone 5b. It is one of the last honeysuckles to bloom and retains its fruits later than the others—often to late October and November. Its form is even more widespread than that of the species described above and the leaves are even darker green. This shrub, too, may be grown for berried sprays to use on holiday tables.

Lonicera morrowii (Morrow honeysuckle). Zone 4; 6'.

Wide-spreading, dense growth, gray-green leaves, quantities of creamy-white flowers in late May and early June, yellowing as they age, and followed by blood red berries in July are the characteristics of this popular honeysuckle. It thrives in any soil, forms a handsome specimen plant, though it probably is best used in groups of three or more plants in a large area.

Lonicera rosea (see *L. tatarica rosea*).

Lonicera tatarica (Tatarian honeysuckle) Zone 4 to parts of Zone 3; 8'-10'.

An extremely hardy honeysuckle, this probably is the most popular species. It is upright-growing, tending to become "leggy," especially if planted in deep shade. Depending on the variety grown, flowers may be white, pink, or rose. They open in mid-May, are fragrant, and are followed by orange-red or yellow fruits. The white flowers in this group do *not* change to yellow as they get older as is the case with many other honeysuckles.

Plants are tolerant of almost any soil, grow strongly, do not have any pests bother them, are trim in appearance and laden with both fruits and flowers in their proper seasons.

Tatarian honeysuckle may be used as a hedge, (better looking when unclipped), as a specimen, near the back of a shrub border, or to accent a house corner in a more intimate planting.

Lonicera tatarica alba has pure white blooms.

Lonicera tatarica 'Arnold Red' has flowers of a darker red than those of any other honeysuckle

Lonicera xylosteoides 'Clavey's Dwarf', flowers.

(deep purplish red, 10 RP 3/11). The fruits are large and red.

Lonicera tatarica grandiflora has white blossoms, twice as large as those of the species and also has larger leaves.

Lonicera tatarica rosea has two-toned blooms—pale pink inside, rose color outside.

Lonicera tatarica rubra (see *L. tatarica* 'Sibirica').

Lonicera tatarica 'Sibirica' (syn *L. t. rubra*) has blooms with white margins and stripes of very deep pink down the center of each petal. The leaves are larger than those of the species.

Lonicera tatarica zabelii (see *L. korolkowii* 'Zabelii').

Lonicera xylosteoides 'Clavey's Dwarf' (also listed as 'Clavey' or *claveyi*). Zone 4; 6'.

An origination of F. D. Clavey Ravinia Nurseries, Inc., Deerfield, Illinois, this is an excellent plant for hedges. It may be kept clipped or left unclipped with equal success. Flowers are not particularly noticeable, being brilliant greenish yellow (7.5 Y 9/8), nor are the red berries. This plant is grown primarily for its dense habit and the many gray-green leaves.

Details of typical honeysuckle flowers, above.

Lonicera tatarica, berried branch, below.

, and berries.

Mahonia aquifolium, flower cluster, above; grape-like fruits, below.

MAGNOLIA

The tree forms of magnolias are discussed in Chapter 15. Here, only one shrub form is described.

Magnolia liliflora 'Nigra' (syn *M. nigra, M. soulangiana nigra*) (Lily-flowered magnolia, Purple lily magnolia). Zone 7 to part of Zone 6; 8′.

A late-blooming, exceptionally long-flowering, very darkly colored magnolia, this has 5″ long purple flowers, darker on the outsides of the petals, lighter, almost white, on the insides. These color in mid-May and are followed in early fall by red fruits shaped like a large-size pod. In the north it is difficult to grow this magnolia to any great height. It kills to the ground in Zone 5b during a severe winter.

Magnolia nigra (see *M. liliflora* 'Nigra').

Magnolia stellata and *Magnolia soulangiana*. Descriptions of both of these magnolias are in Chapter 15. This is merely a note to say that both of these may be grown with many stems from the ground as shrubs instead of with one stem as trees.

MAHONIA (Hollygrape)

Mahonias are evergreen shrubs with handsome, holly-like leaves and yellow flowers followed by blue or blue-black berries. Unfortunately, in northern climates the foliage browns in spots during winter so that by spring there are many unsightly areas on the leaves. To at least partially avoid this mottling, it is best to place mahonias where they are sheltered from winter sun and wind. These old leaves drop in early spring and new, unmarked ones appear shortly thereafter.

Mahonia aquifolium (Oregon hollygrape, Oregon grape, Holly barberry). Zone 5 to southern parts of Zone 4; 3½′. Illustrated on Color Page I.

The state flower of Oregon, this mahonia is a native of the West Coast. Its first-listed common name refers to the dark blue (10 B 3/5) berries in grape-like clusters and to the holly-like leaves, shining green and spiny-toothed.

This evergreen is not hard to grow. It prefers some shade; tolerates many soils but does best in one that is moist. It spreads by means of underground stolons and, if it is in the proper location, soon forms large clumps. For this reason it is an excellent ground cover where one several feet high can be used.

Vivid greenish-yellow (7.5 Y 8/12) flowers in late April and early May are borne in dense groups at the branch tips. These are followed by the fruits which turn color in July.

The plants vary in leaf size, glossiness, and fall color because nurseries grow them from seeds. Thus it is possible to collect varying forms of the same plant.

Oregon hollygrape responds to pruning, so may be kept lower than it normally grows if this seems desirable. It will not be evergreen if placed where hot sun beats down on it in winter. It may be used in front of taller broad-leaved or narrow-leaved evergreens and is a handsome plant for use near a house.

Mahonia bealii (Leatherleaf mahonia, Southern hollygrape). Zone 6 and protected places in Zone 5b; 12′ in the south, 3′ in the north.

Zone 7 is where this shrub shines, but it is not reliably hardy even in the northern part of Zone 6. In Zone 5b, even though it kills back some in severe winters and the flower buds are blasted, it still grows in a northern exposure.

Tall, upright stems; long, stiff leaves which grow horizontally from the stems and are dark blue-green on top, grayish underneath are characteristics of this shrub. In southern climates the individual leaves may measure 15″ long. They are leathery in texture.

The flowers are paler yellow than those of the Oregon hollygrape and are borne in pyramidal clusters. They are followed by dark, blue-black berries. The plant thrives in semi-shade. Its leaves do not change color in autumn.

Mahonia repens (Creeping hollygrape, Creeping mahonia, Ash barberry). Zone 6 to protected places in Zone 5b; 1′ or less.

In places where the Oregon hollygrape is too tall for a ground cover, this lower-growing species may be used instead. It spreads in the same manner, by underground stolons, but does not have as shiny leaves as the Oregon hollygrape. They are dull and bluish-green instead of glossy, dark green. The flowers are similar, but like the rest of the plant, are smaller than the Oregon species. Berries are black; have a bloom on them like plums have.

MALUS (Apple)

Malus sargentii (Sargent crabapple). Zone 5; to 8′, usually less. Illustrated on Color Page II.

This is the only crabapple that I will admit is a shrub. It grows wider than high, sometimes twice as wide, and is densely branched in almost horizontal fashion. The flowers are single, 1″ to 1¼″ in diameter, white with golden stamens, and appear in mid-May. They are followed by ⅝″ diameter fruits in small clusters, that first are greenish yellow with a red "check," later turn completely red. Birds love them.

Sargent crab, like most other crabs, is easy to transplant and to grow. Tolerant of almost any soil, it prefers a position in full sun. This is one crabapple that may be planted without any fear that it will act as a host of the cedar-apple rust (see Chapter 9). It is not a native American crabapple, but an Oriental crabapple, which makes all the difference.

Malus sargentii, blooming branch, below. See also branch with fruits on next page.

Malus sargentii, fruits.

The plants grow upright and have stiff, straight branches. Leaves are gray-green and aromatic. The flowers of the two sexes are on different plants so both male and female plants must be set near together to produce berries. The blooms are greenish and interesting when seen close, but not effective in the landscape. The berries, used to scent bayberry candles since Colonial times, are first green, then gray and remain on the plants all winter and until the Baltimore orioles and catbirds arrive in the north in spring. Within a few days after that they are all gone.

Myrica pensylvanica, flowering branch.

MYRICA

Shrubs with aromatic foliage and berries, these grow well in full sun and sandy soil; are widely used in seashore gardens, especially if they do not grow wild in the vicinity, in which case they usually are scorned. However, they will grow well also in heavier soils.

Myrica carolinensis (see *M. pensylvanica*).

Myrica cerifera (Wax myrtle, Southern bayberry). Zone 6; 30'.

Evergreen in Zone 7 and in parts of Zone 6,.this shrub has dark green, aromatic foliage and aromatic gray berries as does the bayberry, described below. The berries remain on the plants during winter, thus insuring a food supply for certain species of birds.

Since male flowers are borne on different plants from female flowers, plants of both sexes must be set out to insure fruit formation.

Partly because of its size, partly because it spreads widely, this plant is particularly suited for naturalistic plantings.

Myrica pensylvanica (syn *M. carolinensis*) (Bayberry, Candleberry). Zone 1; 8'-9'.

There is a low, blue-gray stone house in Cleveland Heights, Ohio which is landscaped entirely with bayberries. They are clipped to form a hedge along the sidewalk and are used in varying heights for the house planting. The effect is unusual and exquisite.

Although you may not wish to copy this idea, a bayberry or two in the garden will provide plenty of gray berries for use indoors in winter.

Myrica pensylvanica, berried branch, above; closeup of berries, below. Note their texture.

NANDINA

Nandina domestica (Heavenly bamboo) Zone 6; 8'. Illustrated on Color Page VI.

Upright in growth this plant has beautiful, fine foliage which turns from green to red and bronze in autumn. In July the white flowers appear and are followed by clusters of berries which turn

bright red in fall. If the birds do not eat them they stay on the plant until early the following year.

This is one of the few plants I want to grow but find impossible to winter. Three different times I have purchased three plants each time, setting them in different sheltered locations, only to lose them during the first winter that was not extremely mild.

Nandina does not require any particular soil but grows best in full sun. It is widely used in house plantings where it is hardy.

OSMANTHUS

Osmanthus ilicifolius (Sweet holly, Holly osmanthus) Zone 6; 15'.

Suitable for use in house plantings or for clipped hedges, this evergreen plant has shining dark green leaves which are shaped like those of hollies, as the botanical name says. In late summer osmanthus bears tiny greenish-white, very fragrant flowers which are followed by blue-black fruits turning color in autumn.

This shrub does equally well in sun or shade, which increases its usefulness.

PACHISTIMA

Pachistima canbyi (Canby pachistima, Mountain-lover, Cliff-green, Rat stripper). Zone 5 to sheltered locations in Zone 4; 1'-1½'.

Semi-shade and a moist, acid soil are all this low-growing plant needs to make it happy. It has narrow (½" to 1"), dark green leaves which turn

Pachistima canbyi, closeup of tiny blooms.

253

bronze in autumn. The flowers are tiny and inconspicuous but interesting if you happen to notice them. These are presumably followed by fruits, but I have never seen one either on my plants or on those in other gardens.

This plant is a fine ground cover, thriving in shade. It also may be used to edge a path or as a border for taller shrubs.

PAEONIA (Peony)

The peonies most people know and love are herbaceous—meaning that their tops die to the ground each winter and new ones grow from the roots each spring. The peonies described below are not herbaceous—they are deciduous shrubs. While the leaves fall in autumn, the tops do *not* die during winter. Instead, new leaves grow each spring from the branches as with other shrubs. These shrubby peonies are no harder to grow than herbaceous peonies, no matter what you may have read to the contrary. And, borne on them are certainly some of the most beautiful flowers in the world. The foliage, too, is exceptionally attractive.

Paeonia arborea (see *P. suffruticosa*).

Paeonia moutan (see *P. suffruticosa*).

Paeonia suffruticosa (Tree peony). Zone 5 to parts of Zone 4; 6′ and may spread twice as wide. Illustrated on Color Page IV.

Someone should long since have given this peony a more realistic name, for it certainly is not a tree, but a shrub. The largest plant I ever have seen is in front of a house outside London, Ontario and it is 6′ high and more than 12′ across. This, however, is an unusually large plant as I have seen plenty of mature specimens elsewhere that were not nearly so large.

In addition to not being able to fathom the common name of this shrub, I also do not understand why gardeners everywhere are not growing these plants. When young, they are small enough for the tiniest backyard garden, beautiful enough to suit any connoisseur and as easy to grow as any herbaceous peony. They flower before the herbaceous peonies and are far handsomer with their beautifully shaped gray-green leaves and enormous blooms. The flowers are borne singly instead of in groups as in herbaceous peonies, and may be 6″ to 8″ in diameter, single, semi-double or double in form. Their buds open in late May.

If you have never seen tree peonies, a verbal description or even the accompanying picture cannot possibly describe their beauty to you. I would suggest that you visit one of several collections and see for yourself what you've been missing by not growing these plants. There are collections at Swarthmore College, Swarthmore, Pennsylvania, in Rochester, New York parks (I have seen only that in Highland Park), at the Montreal, Quebec Botanical Garden, in the Cornell Plantations at Cornell University, Ithaca, New York and commercial collections at William Gratwick's, Pavilion, New York and Miss Sylvia Saunders', Clinton, New York. There also are other collections, but these are the ones I have seen and with which I am therefore familiar. Specialists in these shrubs are noted in the Buyer's Guide Chart, Chapter 11.

After you have seen tree peonies there will be no stopping you from buying as many as your pocketbook will permit. They are not cheap. Because there is little written about tree peonies, I am going to go into more detail about growing them than I have about most shrubs.

See the plants you want to buy in bloom and order them for delivery in mid- to late October. In September ready the soil by digging out your existing soil (unless it is that gardener's dream soil—a good loam) and replacing it to a depth of 2′ with ¾ compost and ¼ granulated peat. If drainage is poor, put 4″ or 5″ of gravel at the bottom of the hole or bed. Just remember that these plants will be in your garden for your lifetime and that the only time you can give them the best growing conditions is before you plant them.

Space tree peonies widely—6′ apart is rather close, 8′ or 10′ is better, although it will take them many years to spread more than the 6′ first suggested. Plant tulips or some other bulbs between the peonies and annuals over the bulbs for the first years until the peonies fill the space between plants. Be sure to set the peonies at the depth marked by the nursery, for the graft (where the cultivated peony, which is the top of the plant, meets the rootstock of the species peony) must be well below ground level.

Protect the plants from heaving out of the soil by placing straw over the ground around the plants for the first winter. Protect from rabbit damage by chicken wire screens, also for the first winter. After that neither type of protection is necessary.

We keep our plants mulched with buckwheat hulls several inches deep and our "care" consists in pulling any weeds that appear, pruning any dead branch tips in early spring, and fertilizing after blooming time with 10-6-4 fertilizer, with ureaform, intended for lawns but just as good for tree peonies.

Paeonia suffruticosa, plant in bloom. See also Color Page IV.

If you wish to read about tree peonies, there is one book devoted to these plants, *The Moutan or Tree Peony,* by Michael Haworth-Booth, a British nurseryman, and a section of another book tells about them, *The Peonies,* published by the American Horticultural Society.

There are many cultivars of tree peonies, some originated in France, some in Japan and some in the United States. The hybrid forms are interesting and different and must be seen to be believed, for some of them have deep yellow flowers, the least usual bloom color in herbaceous peonies.

PARROTIA

Parrotia persica (Persian parrotia, Persian ironwood, Irontree). Zone 5 and occasionally in Zone 4; 15'.

Parrotia may be called a small tree or a large shrub. It looks rather like a witch hazel, with the same wide-spreading branches and coarse leaves. Indeed, these two shrubs may be planted together for the combined autumn color effect of the golden witch hazel leaves and the scarlet, orange, and yellow parrotia leaves.

Parrotia flowers, which bloom in April before the leaves appear, are unusual in that they have no petals. Instead, like flowering dogwood, the small, closely packed flowers, with hanging red to purple stamens, are surrounded by a purplish-brown bract. While the blossoms are inconspicuous to the casual passerby, they are interesting to the close observer.

Parrotia may be used as a background shrub in a border or at the edge of woodland. It is tolerant of almost any well-drained soil but grows best in full sun.

Pavia rubra (see *Aesculus pavia*).

PHILADELPHUS (Mock orange, Orange-flower bush, Syringa)

A large group of shrubs which hybridize easily with one another both in the wild and in cultivation, the members are grown for their white or creamy-white flowers, in many cases intensely fragrant. Sometimes mock oranges are grown for their compact form or their foliage color.

Mock oranges will grow in almost any soil but a wet one; do well in semi-shade and in full sun. Once planted, they need little or no care except for occasional pruning of dead wood, unless, of course, a large-growing member of the group is planted where space is limited.

The tall mock oranges may be used for unclipped hedges or screen plantings and sometimes are used for specimens. The low forms may be used in the front of a shrub border or as specimens.

The foliage of most mock oranges is not outstanding, though some, notably the *lemoinei* hybrids, have small leaves and a neat appearance. Leaves of some turn yellowish in autumn and one has yellow leaves during spring and early summer.

Mock oranges range in height from 3' to 20' and include all sizes between these two figures. Their flowers may be single, semi-double or double in form. All are white or creamy-white, a few have colored blotches or are purplish or are pinkish when first open, but soon fade to white. The fruits which follow them are brown capsules.

The name "Syringa," used for mock oranges all over eastern United States, was formerly the botanical name of the group but now belongs to lilacs.

Many of the cultivars are the work of one nurseryman, Victor Lemoine of Nancy, France. Some of them have one parent which would not be hardy in the southernmost zone covered in this book—Zone 6—so it should not be taken for granted that all mock oranges are hardy, because many are not.

Two cultivars, 'Frosty Morn' and 'Minnesota Snowflake', are said to live through temperatures as low as —30 degrees F. These are both well-formed plants and double-flowered. The hardiest single-flowered forms described in this book are *P. coronarius* and *P. × lemoinei* 'Mont Blanc'.

The forms of some mock oranges are far superior to those of others. For example, the widely grown *P. virginalis,* for all the pleasing sight and scent of its blooms, is a "leggy" shrub that needs frequent pruning.

Philadelphus 'Atlas', flower.

Philadelphus 'Atlas'. Zone 5; 6′ to 8′.

This cultivar has single, 2″ to 3″ diameter fragrant flowers.

Philadelphus aureus (see *P. coronarius* 'Aureus').

Philadelphus 'Belle Etoile' (meaning Beautiful Star). Zone 6 and protected places in Zones 4 and 5; 6′.

This exceptionally beautiful mock orange was hybridized by Victor Lemoine. It differs from other mock oranges in its flower form (see picture) and from most mock oranges by having a rose or purplish blotch in the center of the bloom.

Flowers are fragrant, 2¼″ in diameter, single, with pointed petals, borne on plants with a gracefully arching habit.

Plants will survive many winters if in a protected place in both Zones 4 and 5, but may be killed to the ground should the winter be severe. Usually they come up from the roots in spring.

Philadelphus 'Bouquet Blanc'. Zones 5 to parts of Zone 4; 4′ high, 5′ wide.

The plant forms a symmetrical mound evenly covered in June with single, 1″ diameter flowers.

Philadelphus 'Cole's Glorious'. Zone 6 to Zone 5b; 6′.

This hybrid has very fragrant, single, 2″ diameter flowers.

Philadelphus coronarius (Fragrant mock orange, sweet mock orange, False syringa). Zone 5 to parts of Zone 4; 10′.

This is the plant most people have in mind when they say "mock orange." It is upright growing, vigorous in growth, will tolerate drier soil conditions than most shrubs, has ordinary foliage, and single flowers in early June, 1½″ in diameter, which have the delightful fragrance suggested by the common name.

Philadelphus coronarius 'Aureus' (Golden mock orange). Zone 5 to parts of Zone 4; to 6′. Illustrated on Color Page II. Usually much lower growing than *coronarius,* this cultivar has yellow leaves (10 Y 8/11 or 10 Y 7/9, both strong greenish yellow) in spring which, if the plant is growing in a sunny place, turn yellowish green later in the season. This color change can be delayed and sometimes warded off altogether, by placing the plant where it gets light shade. Otherwise this plant is like the species but its flowers are not so conspicuous against the foliage because it too nearly resembles their color.

Philadelphus 'Belle Etoile', above. Notice blotch at base of blooms. Blotch is purplish.

Philadelphus coronarius, below.

257

The varying forms and sizes of Philadelphus flowers: 'Innocence', left; 'Beauclerk', center; 'Enchantment', right.

Philadelphus 'Enchantment'. Zone 4; 6'.

This is a graceful shrub bearing double, 1" diameter flowers in loose clusters. Flowers have fringed petals.

Philadelphus 'Frosty Morn' (Plant patent #1174). Zone 4; 3' high, 3½' wide.

Patented by Guy D. Bush, Minneapolis, Minnesota (Zone 4a), in 1953, this dwarf mock orange with fragrant, double flowers is especially recommended for its hardiness. It is said to survive —30 degrees F.

Philadelphus 'Glacier'. Zone 5 to Zone 4b; 4' to 5'.

Double, fragrant, 1½" diameter flowers and small leaves characterize this mock orange.

Philadelphus grandiflorus (see *P. inodorus grandiflorus*).

Philadelphus 'Innocence'. Zone 5 to parts of Zone 4; 6' high and 5' wide.

One of the most fragrant of mock oranges, this has single, 1¾" blooms borne in clusters of from seven to nine. Innocence does not bloom well every year but sports a real bouquet of flowers every second or third year. Apparently it needs fertilizer to help it produce sufficient new growth for better and more frequent bloom.

Philadelphus inodorus grandiflorus (syn *P. grandiflorus*) (Big scentless mock orange). Zone 4; 10'.

Although the botanical name stresses the size of the flowers of this variety, the botanist who named it could not have made adequate comparisons for the blooms are only 1¾" in diameter, not by any means the largest of any mock orange. As the species name states, they are not fragrant. The plant is upright, handsome, and well covered with flowers, but the gardener who sniffs one gets no reward.

Philadelphus × *lemoinei* (*P. microphyllus* × *P. coronarius*). Zone 4; 3'-4'.

A dense, mound-shaped plant which has small leaves and single, very fragrant flowers from ¾"

Philadelphus 'Glacier', closeup of flowers.

to 1½″ in diameter, this mock orange will tolerate light shade and bloom as well there as in full sun.

Philadelphus lewisii 'Waterton'. Zone 2b; 4′.

Nurseries situated in Zones 3a and 2b say that this is the only mock orange hardy in their climate. It is valuable for this feature alone. But it also is said to have masses of single, fragrant blooms.

Philadelphus 'Manteau d'Hermine'. Zone 4; 3′ tall and 4′ wide.

This is an excellent dwarf mock orange with cream-white flowers, semi-double or single, which blend so well with the small leaves that they are not too conspicuous.

Philadelphus 'Mont Blanc'. Zone 4; 4′.

Single, 1¼″ flowers which are fragrant usually are borne in great numbers. However, because they droop slightly and have widely spaced petals, they sometimes disappoint gardeners. The plant has a mounded form.

Philadelphus 'Silberregen' (syn 'Silver Showers'). Zone 5 to part of Zone 4; 3′.

This dwarf mock orange is upright and narrow in form, usually is laden with single flowers which are extremely fragrant. It is a good plant for a small place.

Philadelphus 'Silvia' (also listed as 'Sylvia'). Zone 4; 5′.

Double flowers, 1½″ in diameter, borne in clusters of eight to nine appear on a shapely plant with drooping branches.

Philadelphus × *virginalis* (syn *P. virginalis* 'Virginal', *P. virginal*) (*P. lemoinei* × *P. nivalis* 'Plenus'). Zone 5 to part of Zone 4; 5′ to 6′.

Semi-double and double, 2″ diameter, intensely fragrant blooms are borne on this upright "leggy" plant and transform it into a bouquet. This is a coarse shrub which becomes bare of leaves at the bottom and needs frequent pruning to keep it not only looking its best but also within bounds. If such pruning is not possible, then plant a lower growing shrub in front of this mock orange to hide the bare base.

The blooms are so beautifully placed on the branches of this mock orange that they are valuable for cutting.

Philadelphus virginalis 'Minnesota Snowflake' (Plant Patent #538) (sometimes listed as "Snowflake"). Zone 4; 6′ high and 4′ wide. Double, fragrant, 1½″ to 2″ diameter flowers are borne in clusters of eight to ten on a handsome plant which

Philadelphus lemoinei, above.

Philadelphus 'Silberregen' ('Silver Showers'), below. Note distinctive narrow, vertical growth and compact flower placement.

259

unfortunately becomes bare of leaves at the bottom as it grows older. This mock orange is recommended for its hardiness. Introduced by the same man as was 'Frosty Morn', this plant is said to survive temperatures to —30 degrees F.

Seed capsules of Philadelphus.

Philadelphus virginalis, above, showing single, semi-double and double flowers.

'Minnesota Snowflake', below.

PHOTINIA (Christmas berry, Chinese hawthorn, Photinia)

Photinia villosa (Oriental photinia). Zone 5 to parts of Zone 4; 6' in the north, 15' in the south.

An upright-growing shrub with dark green leaves and little white flowers borne in flat clusters in late May, this later has bright red berries, coloring in October. It is not widely grown but makes a pleasant change from the more commonly seen shrubs. It is prettiest when in berry for by that time its leaves have turned reddish or bronze or a combination of the two colors, and the berries are particularly effective against the leaves.

PHYSOCARPUS (Ninebark, Neillian spiraea, Opulaster)

Physocarpus monogynus (Mountain ninebark). Zone 4; 3½'.

A western native, found wild in the states of South Dakota and Wyoming to Texas and New Mexico, this little shrub is upright-growing, compact and dense. It bears white, sometimes pinkish,

Photinia villosa, blooms above; berries below.

Found wild from Quebec to Virginia, westward to Michigan, this is a larger version of *P. monogynus*. It is upright and spreading, with arching branches; vigorous and quick-growing, tolerant of almost any soil and thriving in semi-shade as well as in sun.

Flowers are small, white to pinkish with purple stamens, are arranged in clusters, but more to a cluster than in *P. monogynus*. They appear in early June. The same interesting seed pods form after the flowers have gone, but in this species they turn reddish during the process of maturing, before they turn brown. In the brown stage they remain on the plant all winter, adding interest to the garden. Apparently, birds care nothing for them.

These seed pods are excellent material for use in flower arrangements from July, when they redden, through winter when they are brown.

The shrub is best used in the background of a shrub border or for an unclipped hedge, though in a large garden it also makes a handsome specimen.

Physocarpus opulifolius aureus (see *P. o.* 'Luteus').

Physocarpus opulifolius 'Luteus' (Golden ninebark, Goldleaf ninebark). Zone 1; 9'-10'. Illustrated on Color Page V. Yellow foliage, brighter

Physocarpus opulifolius 'Luteus'.

flowers centered with yellow, ¼" in diameter, in 1¼" clusters in early June. After these fade, the interesting seed pods appear, first green, then tan, then brown. While they are still tan they look almost like flowers when seen from a distance.

This shrub may be used for a low hedge or in the front of a shrub border.

Physocarpus opulifolius (Common ninebark, Eastern ninebark). Zone 1; 9'.

261

Physocarpus opulifolius 'Luteus', closeup of flower cluster
Long stamens make flowers look "fluffy."

Physocarpus opulifolius 'Nanus.'

Physocarpus opulifolius 'Luteus', seed capsules.

in spring and duller later in the season, differentiates this cultivar from the species. The coloring will be brightest when the shrub is in full sun; remain yellow longer if the shrub is in semi-shade. Because of the bright foliage, this shrub usually is considered for a specimen.

Physocarpus opulifolius 'Nanus' (Dwarf ninebark). A smaller version of the common ninebark, this grows from 4' to 5' tall and has smaller leaves of the same dark green, also smaller flowers and fruits.

PIERIS (Andromeda, Lily-of-the-valley shrub, Portuna)

Andromedas are broad-leaved evergreen shrubs, upright in form, with arching branches, glossy leaves and in April fragrant, white flowers in clusters. The flower buds form in autumn, therefore are prominent all winter. After the flowers fade, new foliage grows which is pale bronze, contrasting beautifully with the older, green foliage.

Andromedas prefer light shade and a location sheltered from winter winds. They need a soil that is at least slightly acid and prefer one which is loose and moist, but well-drained.

These shrubs are choice ones for use as specimens or in house planting or in groupings with other broad-leaved or needled evergreens near the house. They should never be crowded as then their beauty is lost.

Pieris floribunda (Mountain andromeda, Mountain fetterbush). Zone 5; 4'-5'.

Upright in growth, this plant often grows wider than high. It has thick, dark green leaves and clusters of fragrant, waxy, white, bell-shaped flowers which grow either upright or nodding. Blooms open in late April, about a week later than those of the Japanese andromeda.

Pieris japonica (Japanese andromeda). Zone 6 to part of Zone 5; 7'.

Taller than the species described above, this also is more tender to winter cold. It should be accorded a situation near a house wall where warmth from inside tempers the cold or a place protected from winter wind.

It may be planted with the mountain andromeda or with its own variegated form in the foreground. It also looks well against needled evergreens. It shows off best when not crowded.

The leaves are dark, glossy and evergreen. Flowers are creamy-white, fragrant, and borne in drooping clusters. Fruits are brown capsules. A well-grown specimen of Japanese andromeda typifies, to me at least, the perfect broad-leaved evergreen.

Pieris floribunda flowers, above; those of P. japonica, below.

263

Pieris japonica in late autumn with flower buds, left, and seed capsules, right. Buds remain on plant all winter.

Pieris japonica 'Compacta'. Growing 6' high, but compact and dense, this has leaves only half the size of those of the species.

Pieris japonica 'Variegata' (syn *P. j.* 'Variegata Nana', *P. j.* 'Albo Marginata'). The leaves of this cultivar have narrow, white edges. The plant is dwarf, grows very slowly, and mine never has bloomed during the five years I've owned it. Since the other andromedas next to and in back of it bloom every year and I have seen flowers on other variegated plants, mine must be lacking in some regard.

Pieris taiwanensis. Zone 6; 6'

If you live in Zone 6 or south of that zone, this is a lovely pieris to grow. Seemingly more compact in growth than *japonica,* it starts to flower when young and holds its upright clusters well above the leaves.

Other Pieris: There are several pink-flowered forms of *Pieris japonica* available and various cultivars are being introduced which have larger flowers or longer bloom clusters or similar variations.

POTENTILLA (Cinquefoil, Buttercup shrub, Five finger blossom, Five finger grass)

A visiting nurseryman, looking at some of my potentillas, remarked, "An English nurseryman told me that if we'd change the name we'd sell more of them." Isn't it too bad that a name can cheat gardeners everywhere from knowing and growing these shrubs? If the name meant was "potentilla," that comes from the Latin word "potens" which means "powerful" (just like our English word "potent") and refers to the powerful medicine of some species used for medicinal purposes. If the name meant was "cinquefoil," that comes from the French words "cinq" meaning five and "feuilles" meaning leaves and refers to the five leaflets of most potentillas. Are these names really so dreadful that they scare you off? If so, you're missing some carefree shrubs.

Potentillas will grow in any soil but a wet one, tolerate light shade but bloom best when in full sun. They bloom for weeks during summer when not too many other shrubs flower. They have no pests to bother them. They need no pruning, no spraying. What more could you ask?

Potentillas are happy shrubs with varying shades of yellow or sometimes white single blossoms against small leaves that look somewhat like those of strawberries. Blooms are followed by brown capsules that remain on the plants until hidden by the following spring's growth. The plants are all dwarf or of medium height. The foliage of some is gray-green rather than green and, occasionally, silvery.

All are of the easiest possible culture, asking only a sunny place where drainage is good. They may be used for hedges (planted 18" apart), for specimens, or in the front of a shrub border.

Before I start listing and describing the potentillas in the catalogs that make up this book, I should explain that the nomenclature follows a monograph in *Baileya* by Mr. Hubert L. J. Rhodes, until recently with the Canada Department of Agriculture, and has been brought up to the present date by correspondence and telephone conversation with Mr. Rhodes.

Potentilla arbuscula. Zone 5.

Prostrate growth habit, large yellow flowers.

Potentilla davurica (also spelled *dahurica*) (Dahurian cinquefoil). Zone 3; 2'.

From northern Manchuria comes this hardy little shrub. Flowers are creamy-white, look like single roses, and are borne all summer.

Potentilla davurica 'Veitchii'. Zone 5; 4½'.

Upright, compact growth, and white flowers distinguish this cultivar.

Potentilla × *friedrichsenii* (*P. fruticosa* × *P. davurica*). Zone 4, possibly to Zone 3; 3'.

Sturdy growth, light yellow flowers and continual

bloom from mid-June on make this a popular cinquefoil.

Potentilla × *friedrichsenii* ·'Ochroleuca'. Zone 5.

Creamy-white flowers from June to September are borne on this dwarf, rounded shrub.

Potentilla fruticosa (Shrubby cinquefoil, Bush cinquefoil). Zone 1; 3½'.

This species is native to most areas of the northern hemisphere but is not appreciated by gardeners. Once planted in dry soil and full sun it will be a joy every year from June until frost. There is a burst of bloom in June, then fewer but some flowers always on the bush until September when there is another, but lesser, burst of bloom. After that occasional flowers may be found until frost. Blooms are single, yellow and 1" in diameter.

Potentilla fruticosa 'Moonlight' (syn 'Manelys'). Zone 5; 3'.

This cultivar was bred in Sweden where Manelys means Moonlight. It has dark, blue-green leaves and pale yellow flowers, 1⅛" across. It blooms from June intermittently until frost.

Potentilla 'Jackman's Variety' (also listed as Jackmani). Zone 5; 3' to 4'.

Upright in form and compact in growth, this shrub is an excellent choice for a low hedge. Flowers are bright yellow, almost 1½" in diameter, largest of any of the yellow-flowered potentillas.

Potentilla 'Lemon Drop'. Zone 5; 2'.

A continuous bloomer from June until frost, 'Lemon Drop' has sulphur yellow flowers.

Potentilla 'Mt. Everest'. Zone 5; 3'.

Upright and vigorous in growth, this cultivar has dark green leaves and white, 1" diameter flowers.

Potentilla parvifolia. Zone 5.

An excellent rock garden subject, this cinquefoil is a dwarf, with the small leaves its botanical name suggests and, surprisingly, seven leaflets instead of the usual five. The new growth hides the seed capsules. Blooms are lemon-yellow.

Potentilla parvifolia 'Farreri'. Zone 3; 1½' to 2'. Spreading eventually wider than its height, this shrub has tiny leaves to ½" long, but flowers ¾" wide, deep yellow in color.

Potentilla parvifolia 'Gold Drop'. Zone 3; 3' has very bright yellow flowers over the usual long blooming period. This is given as synonymous with 'Farreri' by many nurseries.

Potentilla parvifolia 'Katherine Dykes'. Zone 5. Usually taller growing than the shrubby cinquefoil, this has primrose-yellow blooms.

Potentilla fruticosa, flowers.

Potentilla parvifolia 'Klondike'. Zone 5: 2'. A dwarf, compact shrub, this has large, deep yellow flowers. There seems to be a great deal of variation in the plants offered as some people find their shrubs bearing very few flowers, while others speak of the floriferousness of their plants.

Potentilla parvifolia 'Tangerine'. Zone 4; 3'. A new cultivar with flowers which open a tangerine-orange color, changing, with age, to golden yellow.

, seed capsules.

PRINSEPIA

Prinsepia sinensis (Cherry prinsepia). Zone 5; 5'.

A comparatively little known shrub useful for interesting-looking and impenetrable hedges, especially on the prairies. The upright habit of the plant plus its thorns are both assets as far as forming a hedge is concerned. The light, bright green leaves appear exceptionally early in spring. Blooms are small, inconspicuous, greenish-white to yellowish-white. They are followed, in July, by little red or reddish-purple fruits. These are edible but hardly palatable.

Princepia sinensis, flowers.

PRUNUS (Plum, Cherry, Peach, Almond, Apricot, Nectarine)

The genus *Prunus* is an extremely large one and includes plums, cherries, peaches, almonds, apricots and nectarines. In general, members of this genus are tolerant of most soils and, unless they are susceptible to attacks by insects or diseases, are easy to grow. All of the members of this genus prefer full sun. They vary so greatly in growth habit, size, foliage, flowers and fruits that these characteristics cannot be generally described, so are discussed under each species. Tree forms are discussed in Chapter 15.

Prunus besseyi (Western sand cherry). Zone 4 to parts of Zone 3; 6'-7'.

On sandy hills or rocky slopes, even the shores of lakes in the provinces and states from Manitoba to Minnesota, south and west to Wyoming, Nebraska, and Kansas, is found a bushy shrub known as the Western sand cherry, which has nearly black fruit, tiny, but sweet to the taste.

This shrub has ½" diameter, single, white flowers in mid-May.

From this species, by the process of selection, Prof. N. W. Hansen, Brookings, South Dakota, produced what is known as Hansen's bush cherry, which is *Prunus besseyi* with larger fruits and many more of them. If you wish to grow this shrub for its fruits, be certain you are getting Hansen's form as it is hard to tell from the catalog descriptions whether the species or the improved form is meant.

The fruits of either make delicious pies and preserves. In rigorous climates where regular cherries will not grow, these are substitutes.

Prunus × cistena (*P. cerasifera* 'Atropurpurea' × *P. pumila*) (Purple-leaved sand cherry). Zone 1; 8'. Illustrated on Color Page II.

The same Professor Hansen who selected fine fruiting forms of the Western sand cherry originated this large shrub. It has so-called "purple" leaves which actually, according to the color fan, are moderate reddish brown (7.5 R 3/6) on the upper sides and dark red (5 R 3/7) underneath, and retain this color all summer. White or pink, single, ½" diameter flowers with prominent stamens the same color as the foliage open in mid-May and are followed by small cherries almost the same color as the leaves so that they are hard to find without a search. These are edible and, when borne in sufficient quantity, may be used for preserves.

The shrub form is upright and quite widely branching. The plant is useful for the back of a border, in a house planting or as a specimen, always provided that its bright foliage color will look well where it is placed.

Prunus glandulosa (Dwarf flowering almond, Flowering cherry). Zone 5 if plants are grafted or budded; Zone 4 if on their own roots; 5', but usually nearer 3'.

Dwarf flowering almond bears single, pink or white flowers in late April or early May at a time when bright flowers are needed in the garden. Red, ½" diameter cherries follow. This shrub, however, rarely is seen in gardens. Instead, its double-flowered forms are the choice of gardeners everywhere.

Prunus bosseyi, flowers, above; fruits, below.

Prunus cistena, branch in bloom, above; closeup of flowers, below.

Prunus glandulosa 'Albiplena' (White double-flowering almond). Slender, straight branches growing from the ground bear faintly pink buds which open to almost ball-shaped, many-petaled, ¾″ diameter flowers and the shrub is so covered with them that the leaves, which then are just starting to grow, are barely visible.

This is a beautiful plant when in bloom, though it seems not nearly so well known as the double-flowered "pink" form. Double-flowered forms do not bear fruit. They are grown only for their early flowers.

Prunus glandulosa rosea (see *P. glandulosa*).

Prunus glandulosa roseoplena or *rosea plena* (see *P. g.* 'Sinensis').

Prunus glandulosa 'Sinensis' (*syn P. g. roseoplena* or *rosea plena*). (Pink double-flowering almond). Zone 4; 5′, usually nearer 3′. The most popular dwarf flowering almond, this plant is seen in thousands of gardens. Although it does not bear fruit, it has attractive foliage, as have the rest of the dwarf flowering almonds. The flowers, which literally cover the shrub in late April to early May are ⅝″ to ⅞″ in diameter and deep purplish red (5 RP 7/9) in color. The shrub is best used in the front of a shrub border or in a low planting elsewhere.

Prunus glandulosa 'Sinensis' above, left; P. g. 'Albiplena', right, showing difference in form.

Prunus glandulosa 'Sinensis', below.

Prunus glandulosa 'Aibiplena' in bloom.

Prunus laurocerasus schipkaensis (Schipka cherry laurel). Zone 6 to protected places in Zone 5b; 18′ in the south, 6′ or less in the north.

A broad-leaved evergreen extremely popular in the south, this is grown for its horizontal branching form and the beautiful, shining leaves. In Zone 5b it needs the protection of evergreen boughs in winter to keep it from "burning." It looks well at the base of a taller-growing broad-leaved evergreen like a rhododendron or with narrow-leaved evergreens and is sufficiently choice that it may be used in a house planting or other intimate setting.

Prunus laurocerasus 'Zabeliana'. Zone 6 to protected places in Zone 5b; to 5′ in the south, 3′ in the north. Smaller in all ways than the Schipka cherry laurel, it is otherwise similar and should be protected for winter in the same manner.

Prunus maritima (Beach plum, Black plum). Zone 4 to parts of Zone 3; 6′.

Along the Atlantic seashore and near it, especially in the New England states, this plant grows wild. The first settlers must have found its small but delicious fruits a blessing. Nowadays selections have been made which bear fruits at least an inch in diameter and these are being propagated for sale. The fruits make excellent jam.

The chief value of this shrub is for planting in seaside gardens. It bears white, single or sometimes double flowers early in May and the dull purple, or occasionally crimson, ½″ to 1″ diameter fruits follow these. It will grow inland too, if you'd like to try it, but there are many other more ornamental shrubs for inland gardens.

There is a yellow-fruited variety that I saw once in Ohio and it is possible that some nursery is propagating it. There also is a selected form named 'Autumn'.

Prunus tenella (syn *Amygdalus nana,* syn *Prunus nana*) (Dwarf Russian almond). Zone 2; 3′-4′.

Single, rose-red, ½″ to ¾″ flowers bloom on this hardy shrub in late April or early May just as the leaves are unfolding. These are followed by ½″ diameter red fruits in late July. There are many handsomer shrubs for moderate climates, but this may be grown far north.

Prunus tomentosa (Nankin cherry, Nanking cherry, Manchu cherry). Zone 1; 9′ in the south, 5′ in the north.

Upright and spreading in form, this is one of the welcome, early-flowering shrubs. Blossoms appear before the leaves in late April, are pink in bud, and pale pink to white when open, but are surrounded by red calyxes and centered with red stamens so that the overall effect is quite different from that of most white flowers.

Edible, strong red (5 R 4/12), ⅜″ diameter fruits ripen in late June and early July. They may be eaten as they are, since they are small cherries and very good to the taste, or they may be made into jelly or jam.

Prunus maritima.

Prunus tomentosa.

Prunus triloba.

Prunus tomentosa, flowers, above; fruits, below.

Some friends of ours have a long hedge of plants of this shrub and, either in bloom or in fruit it is a lovely sight. The plant also may be used in a border or as a specimen.

Prunus triloba (syn *P. triloba plena* of the catalogs, *P. t.* 'Multiplex') (Rose tree of China). Zone 5 to parts of Zone 4; 15'.

The double-flowered form of this shrub was discovered before the single-flowered form. Botanists, therefore, not knowing there was a single-flowered form, gave it the specific name, *P. triloba*. This means that *P. triloba plena,* of innumerable nursery catalogs, is a name without scientific standing. The shrub that is meant is properly called *P. triloba*.

The many-petaled, double flowers look so much like little roses that it is easy to see why the common name was given this shrub. Blooms are 1" in diameter, bright pink, and borne before the leaves appear in late April. This shrub is useful in a border.

PYRACANTHA (Firethorn)

These handsome shrubs are evergreen in the south, almost evergreen in the north, with shining green leaves, white flowers in late May to early June and brilliant orange, red-orange, scarlet, or yellow berries in late September to October.

They should be planted in full sun for most flowers and therefore most fruits. Because they are not easy to transplant, they should always be purchased with balls of earth around their roots and, in the north, moved only in spring.

Pyracantha coccinea 'Lalandei' (also spelled 'Lalandii') (Laland's firethorn). Zone 5b; 6'-7'. Illustrated on Color Page VII.

Pyracantha coccinea 'Lalandei', blooms, and berries. Closeup of berries, below.

This cultivar is hardier than the species, *P. coccinea,* and also more vigorous in growth. It may be used for a hedge, espaliered against a wall or planted with needled evergreens in a house planting.

Its white flowers are as pretty as those of many other shrubs grown exclusively for their flowers and its berries are bright, gay, and showy—brilliant orange-red.

Pyracantha coccinea cultivars (other than 'Lalandei'): There are at least a dozen other cultivars listed in the catalogs, all varying somewhat from one another, usually in berry color, but sometimes in ultimate height or in density of form. All are desirable, but, if hardiness is a prime consideration, 'Kasan' is the hardiest. It is more upright in form than 'Lalandei' and has orange-scarlet berries.

RHAMNUS (Buckthorn)

Because several buckthorns grow wild from Quebec to Minnesota, and southward to Nova Scotia, New England, Virginia, Ohio, Indiana, Illinois and Missouri, they are widely regarded as worthless for the garden. Such is not the case. For

271

one thing, considering buckthorns as shrubs and not as weeds, they are attractive in form, foliage, and fruit. For another, there are improved forms, even more useful than the wild ones. And for a third point, there also are buckthorns which are not native to this country (but doubtless are considered weeds where they grow wild) and therefore are different from those we know.

In gardens, the chief features of buckthorns are their foliage and their fruits. The flowers are inconspicuous. Several buckthorns are useful for hedges. They grow best in full sun, but tolerate light shade and almost any soil, even a moist one.

Rhamnus cathartica (Common buckthorn, Hart's thorn, Hell purge, Rain-berry thorn, Rhineberry, Sap-green tree, Shrubby trefoil, Swamp dogwood, Way-thorn, Three-leaved hop tree, Wing seed). Zone 1; 12′, but sometimes more.

Stiff, upright and irregular in form, with spine-tipped branches bearing dark green leaves and inconspicuous greenish flowers, this shrub is widely used for hedges. Its blue-black berries are powerful laxatives (as the common name, Hell purge, attests), so should be kept away from children and pets.

Rhamnus chadwickii (see *R. utilis*).

Rhamnus cathartica, closeup of flowers, above; branch with fruits, below.

Rhamnus cathartica, flowering branch.

Rhamnus frangula (Alder buckthorn, Persian berry, Glossy buckthorn, Berryalder, Black dogwood). Zone 1; 18′, usually less.

Erect in form when young, this plant becomes more spreading with age. The foliage is dark green and shining. The flowers, produced during the summer, are light yellow and are followed by ¼″ diameter berries which first are yellowish green, then dark red orange, then dark red, and finally black. For some weeks berries in all different color stages are on this shrub at one time, making an attractive sight; probably the shrub's chief merit.

Rhamnus frangula 'Columnaris' (syn *R. f.* 'Columnar', 'Colc's Columnar' and 'Tallhedge'). A thornless, columnar form of buckthorn which is extremely dense, stands shearing well and therefore is excellent for hedge use, this plant has been widely advertised under the name Tallhedge (Plant patent 1388). It is listed by this name in many catalogs.

Rhamnus utilis (syn *R. chadwickii* of the catalogs) (Chadwick buckthorn). Zone 5b; 9'. Illustrated on Color Page VIII.

The time to see and appreciate this shrub is in winter when its stiff, upright branches still are laden with black berries. It is outstanding for winter effect.

At other times of year it is an upright, stiffly branching shrub with yellowish-green foliage, inconspicuous yellowish-green flowers in late April to early May and fruits which start to change from green to black in late September or early October. It is undemanding as to soil or exposure, but grows best in full sun.

Very few nurseries list this shrub and it is hard for me to understand why more do not offer it because of its winter beauty.

I got my plant by accident. It was on the steps of the office of a nurseryman friend—Arnold Folker, and I asked him what its name was. He replied that someone had left it with him to try, and that person had said it was a callicarpa. One look at the leaves told me otherwise and I told Mr. Folker this. But, since I could not identify it, he urged me to take it home, grow it, and let him know what it was.

One evening last autumn I told him its name and showed him, by flashlight, the shrub in full berry. When he saw the beautiful plant he exclaimed, "Do you mean to tell me I *gave* you that?" He took away a berried branch, and no doubt will grow plants from the seeds so that other gardeners will be able to enjoy this little-seen buckthorn.

RHODODENDRON (Rhododendron, Azalea)

Both rhododendrons and azaleas are members of the same genus, the genus Rhododendron. Because the nursery catalogs list the two separately, I have attempted to bridge the gap between what the nurseries call the plants and what the botanists call the same plants by describing the rhododendrons known as azaleas under the heading "AZALEA" on pages 154 to 162, I have, however, given them their correct botanical names as Rhododendrons.

Rhododendrons (as distinguished from azaleas) are mostly broad-leaved evergreens which may be

273

Rhamnus frangula, blooms above; fruits below.

tall or short, so that they may be selected to suit the landscape.

Their form is generally upright and spreading with comparatively few, sturdy branches. The leaves of the hardy sorts are dark green, thick and leathery in texture. The flower colors vary widely and the blooms include some of the most spectacular in the entire roster of shrubs.

While many more rhododendrons than are listed here grow well in Zone 6, those that will survive from Zone 6 northward are limited to species, varieties and cultivars of unquestioned hardiness. Even though the flowers of these are exquisite in both form and color, it is not fair to judge the entire rhododendron clan by those hardy in the north. Once one has seen hillsides of rhododendrons in Italian gardens or the collection of species in the experimental garden in Boskoop, Holland, one cannot help but be impressed by the enormous range of height, flower color, and blooming time encompassed by this genus. The Pacific Northwest is fast becoming as good a place to see rhododendrons in all their variations as is the south of England: there, the collection at Wisley, the test garden of the Royal Horticultural Society, is outstanding.

Rhododendrons MUST have an acid soil to survive. Furthermore, the underlying subsoil must NOT be of heavy clay, for the water that then would collect around their roots would kill them. They like a loose, sandy, peaty soil mixture with plenty of air in it (because their roots are shallow) but still able to retain moisture. These plants require perfect drainage.

Because of these needs, the best place to plant them is on a slope or in a raised bed and, where the soil is not naturally acid, soil must be mixed especially for them. The preparation of acid soil mixtures is explained in Chapter 5, page 36. Fortunately, because of the shallow-rooting habit, replacing soil is not too great a task although deep preparation means better growth. The rhododendrons will repay the gardener many times over with their blooms for making growing conditions suitable for them.

Also because of the shallow root system, it is advisable always to keep a mulch over the soil around rhododendrons. Best materials for this purpose are oak leaves or pine needles, both of which have an acid reaction as they decay. (See the section on mulching in Chapter 6.)

In the north, rhododendrons should be transplanted only in spring. They should be purchased with their roots in earth balls and should be placed in their new positions so that the soil is level with the tops of these earth balls. If the weather is dry during summer, even established rhododendrons need copious watering once in ten days. The mulch, of course, helps keep the sun from drying the soil under it, but will not add moisture to the soil.

When rhododendrons have finished flowering it is a good idea to cut off the faded flowers. Not only does this improve the appearance of the plants, but it avoids the use of nutriment to form seeds and allows the use of these substances for next year's flower bud formation. Rhododendron buds are formed in late summer and early autumn, remain on the plants all winter and open in spring, precise time depending on the kind of rhododendron. For this reason, all pruning should be done right after blooming time, except for broken branches which might as well be cut off when they are noticed. However, pruning rarely is necessary when rhododendrons are grown in the north. They don't grow that fast or that much.

Rhododendrons may be used in house plantings, as unclipped hedges, as specimens, in a border with other broad-leaved or needled evergreens, or in a woodland. They are beautiful in any situation, especially, of course, when in flower.

Most of the ultra-hardy rhododendrons listed in the catalogs and sold in nurseries today are either North American species like *R. catawbiense* or *R. maximum* or hybrids, largely bred in England during the last century by Anthony Waterer, Sr., also responsible for many azalea hybrids. The same careful and extensive breeding work probably would be impossible today because of present high labor costs; probable reason why these hybrids continue to stand at the top of the list of "iron clad" hardy varieties for the north. Most of them are hybrids between *R. catawbiense* and various Asiatic azaleas brought into England during the last half of the nineteenth century. All of them are beautiful and well worth growing. Those most frequently listed in the catalogs are described below.

Rhododendron 'Album Elegans'.

One of Waterer's *R. maximum* hybrids, which grows tall, blooms late and has light mauve flowers which fade to white.

Rhododendron 'America'.

This plant has beautiful clear dark red flowers, but has a poor habit of growth—rather open and spreading with branches that are inclined to droop.

Rhododendron arborescens (see page 156).

Rhododendron calendulaceum (see page 156).

Rhododendron canadense (see page 156).

Rhododendron 'Caractacus'.

Another Waterer hybrid of *R. catawbiense* with an excellent form, but flowers which are dull purplish-red and not easy to combine with other rhododendron flower colors, except white of course.

Rhododendron carolinianum (Carolina rhododendron). Zone 5 to part of Zone 4; 5'-6', usually less.

An evergreen rhododendron, this blooms in mid-May. It is an exceptionally dainty species with 3" diameter flower clusters which may be white or between pale, purplish pink (10 P 8/5) and light purplish pink (2.5 RP 8/5). The variation in color represents the normal variation in seedling plants. The leaves are narrow compared with those of most rhododendrons and are dotted with brown underneath. The new leaves unfold about the time the flowers are opening. The form of the plant is rounded and compact.

Rhododendron carolinianum album is the white-flowered form of the species just described. It, like the species, is found native in the North Carolina mountains. It has either white flowers or blooms of such pale pink that they are practically white.

Rhododendron catawbiense (Catawba rhododendron, Mountain rosebay). Zone 5 to part of Zone 4; Usually to 6', taller in the south.

Native to the Allegheny Mountains, chiefly in the states of Georgia and Virginia, this evergreen rhododendron will survive without severe injury a winter temperature of −25 degrees F. It will grow better, however, if protected from such severe cold. It is hardier than any of its hybrids.

Its form is upright and spreading. The flowers appear before the new leaves have opened, so are particularly effective. They are freely borne; are red-purple or sometimes lavender-purple (some people call them magenta), spotted with dull yellow-green.

If you live in the far north and would like to try growing rhododendrons, start with this one.

Rhododendron 'Catawbiense Album'.

This is *not* the white-flowered variety of *R. catawbiense* but a Waterer hybrid which is probably the best hardy white which blooms in the middle of the rhododendron flowering season.

Flower clusters of Rhododendron 'America', above; R. carolinianum, below.

Rhododendron 'English Roseum'.

This hybrid has the same general color of flowers as 'Roseum Elegans' but is definitely inferior to the true 'Roseum Elegans'. Try not to buy this one, but the real thing.

Exbury hybrids—(see page 156).

Gable hybrids—(see page 156).

Rhododendron gandavense (Ghent hybrids) (see page 157).

Rhododendron kaempferi (see page 157).

Kaempferi hybrids (see page 157).

Knap Hill hybrids (see page 157).

Rhododendron kosterianum (see page 158).

Rhododendron × *laetevirens* (*R. carolinianum* × *R. ferrugineum*) (syn *R. wilsonii*) (Wilson rhododendron). Zone 5; 3½'.

Differing from many other rhododendrons in its light green leaves, this evergreen plant is compact in growth with 1" diameter flowers, pink to purplish-pink, in mid-June. Because of the excellent growth habit it may be used as a specimen, on top of a wall or in a house planting.

Rhododendron 'Lee's Dark Purple'.

This is not as hardy as two other purple-flowered hybrids 'Purpureum Elegans' and 'Purpureum Grandiflorum'. It seems, however, to be more widely available. It has dark green, wavy leaves and large trusses of purple blooms.

Rhododendron maximum (Rosebay, Rosebay rhododendron, Cow-plant, Spoon-hutch). Zone 4 to parts of Zone 3; 12', up to 30' in the south.

Found in the wild from Nova Scotia and Ontario, down the east coast to Georgia and Alabama and west as far as Ohio, this rhododendron grows as a large shrub (or, sometimes, a small tree). It is the tallest rhododendron hardy in the north.

The leaves are long and the new ones are well grown before the flowers open. This is definitely a disadvantage because the flowers thus are partly hidden by the foliage.

They usually are rose-colored, but may be purplish-pink and are spotted with dull yellow-green to orange. They open in late June and look particularly beautiful when seen on a mass of plants. In fact, massing is the best possible use for this plant; along the edge of a wood or a waterway or at the back of a shrub border. The rosebay also is an excellent subject for a hedge.

This rhododendron requires a situation in semi-shade. It is folly to try to grow it elsewhere.

Rhododendron molle hybrids (called *molle* or *mollis hybrids*) (see page 158).

Rhododendron mucronulatum (see page 158).

Rhododendron nudiflorum (see page 158).

Rhododendron obtusum 'Amoenum' (see page 159).

Rhododendron obtusum arnoldianum (see page 159).

P. J. M. hybrids (also listed as P. J. Mezzitt). Named for the owner of the Weston Nursery, Hop-kinton, Mass., these hybrids are comparatively new. They are reported hardy in the northeastern states and Professor Clarence Lewis says they do well in East Lansing, Michigan. I have not yet grown them or seen them so know nothing about them.

Rhododendron 'Purpureum Elegans'.

This is one of Waterer's hardy hybrids. It has 3" wide, blue-violet or lilac-purple flowers with purple centers. These are marked with orange-brown. The plant is compact and has a good growth habit.

Rhododendron roseum (see page 159).

Rhododendron 'Roseum Elegans'. Illustrated on Color Page IV.

One of the hardiest hybrids, dependable in Zone 4, this has mauve-rose flowers with greenish markings almost 3" in diameter and bears them every spring. The plant has an excellent growth habit and is vigorous.

Unfortunately there are several different plants offered in the trade under this name. So buy it from a reliable nursery and get the true 'Roseum Elegans'.

Rhododendron 'Roseum Superbum'.

One again, this is a Waterer hybrid of *R. catawbiense* which has purplish-rose or purplish-pink flowers. It is not considered as good a flowering shrub as the true 'Roseum Elegans' but, nevertheform when older.

less, is hardy, vigorous in growth, with a plant that requires a little pruning in its youth for a good

Rhododendron schlippenbachii (see page 159).

Shammarello hybrids.

Bred by A. M. Shammarello, South Euclid, Ohio (near Cleveland), these plants are, of course, hardy in that area which is in hardiness Zone 6. The lowest winter temperature expected in this zone is —18 degrees F. Some of them are bud hardy to a few degrees lower than this.

Mr. Shammarello has bred for "large-leaved, early-blooming plants in pink and red; for later blooming plants in dwarf pinks and dwarf reds; and tall growers exhibiting good plant characteristics in clear pink, red and white."

These hybrids furnish a continuity of bloom from early to late May and are listed in three groups: for early May, mid-May and late May flowering. They certainly should be tried by people living in Zone 6 and some of them probably are hardy in Zone 5, at least the southern part of the zone.

Mr. Shammarello grows the plants in the open field and is one of the comparatively few people

Rhododendron 'Roseum Elegans', above.

with soil too acid for best growth of rhododendrons. He told me he often has to use lime to make the soil more alkaline than it is naturally, so the plants will thrive.

> *Rhododendron vaseyi* (see page 160).
>
> *Rhododendron viscosum* (see page 160).
>
> Vuyk hybrids (see page 160).
>
> *Rhododendron wilsoni* (see *R. laetevirens*).
>
> *Rhododendron yedoense* (see page 161).
>
> *Rhododendron yedoense poukhanense* (see page 162).
>
> *Rhodora canadensis* (see *Rhododendron canadense*, page 156).

RHODOTYPOS

> *Rhodotypos kerrioides* (see *R. scandens*).
>
> *Rhodotypos scandens* (syn *R. kerrioides*, *R. tetrapetala*) (Jetbead, White kerria). Zone 5; 5'-6'.

Jetbead is an upright, spreading plant with single, white, 1¼" wide flowers starting to open in mid-May and continuing intermittently all summer. They are followed by shiny jet-black fruits

Rhodotypos scandens, below.

277

Rhodotypos scandens, closeup of flowers, above; berried branch, below.

which stay on all winter. The leaves are dark green, remain that color all season, and are on the plant until late autumn, long after the leaves of most other shrubs have fallen.

This is not an outstanding shrub, but it is reliable and makes an attractive addition to any shrub border. The common name, "white kerria," refers to a similarity between jetbead and the kerrias. The differences between them are, however, marked. Kerria leaves are alternately placed up and down the branches, while those of jetbead grow from the branches opposite one another. Kerria has green twigs, effective all winter, while those of

jetbead are black. Kerria's brown fruits are not at all like the black "beads" of jetbead. And, of course, the flower colors differ; those of kerria being golden yellow. These details are given to show that common names cannot be depended upon at all.

Rhodotypos tetrapetala (see *R. scandens*).

RHUS (Sumac)

Many people recoil in horror at the mere mention of the name "sumac," because they think only of the scarlet or upland sumac (*Rhus glabra*) which grows along roadsides, in fields and spreads widely where it is allowed to grow as it will. Because of its rapid spread, it frequently becomes a pest in areas where such growth is not desirable.

However, there are other sumacs, and even the scarlet sumac is welcome where a screen is needed or around a summer cottage.

Sumacs vary greatly in height, but all are weak-wooded, so break easily; all thrive in poor, dry, sandy soil and in sunny situations (points in their favor); and all spread by means of underground stems. In autumn their leaves turn bright red and many of them have red fruits, provided plants with flowers of both sexes or plants of each sex have been planted. Otherwise, of course, there will be no fruits.

Sumacs are at home in wild places or semi-wild gardens, although the little fragrant sumac (*Rhus aromatica*) makes an excellent specimen if grown for its foliage and is ideal for covering and holding a steep bank. The shining sumac (*Rhus copallina*) also is good for a specimen because of its beautiful foliage. Other sumacs are grown for their finely divided leaves.

Still other sumacs should be avoided because they are poisonous to touch, especially poison ivy and poison oak. However, the poisonous species can be told from the non-poisonous easily since the poisonous kinds bear yellow, yellowish-white or white fruits while the non-poisonous forms bear red fruits.

Rhus aromatica (syn *R. canadense*) (Fragrant sumac, Sweet-scented sumac). Zone 4 to parts of Zone 3; 3'.

Growing wild from Quebec to the northern parts of Florida, Alabama, Mississippi, and Louisiana and westward to Texas, this is a first choice for planting on dry banks to hold soil in place. It also may merit a place near the front of a shrub border, provided it has plenty of room to spread, which it will do.

Upright in form, wider than high, with hairy leaves and small yellow flowers in clusters, opening before the leaves unfold in early May, this little shrub has hairy, 1/4" diameter, red fruits in early summer. The foliage turns orange and scarlet in autumn.

Rhus copallina (Shining sumac, Dwarf sumac). Zone 5 to parts of Zone 4; 3'-8'.

Shining, dark green foliage which turns scarlet in autumn, greenish yellow, small flowers in August, and red, hairy fruits characterize this sumac which may be used for a specimen plant in poor dry soil. It grows wild from New York to Florida and is treelike in growth in the southern part of its range.

Rhus cotinus (see *Cotinus coggygria*).

Rhus glabra (Smooth sumac, Scarlet sumac, Upland sumac). Zone 1; 8'-15'.

This is the common sumac of the fields and roadsides, growing wild over much of the United States and Canada. It is useful in gardens only for holding dry, sandy banks or for screen plantings at summer cottages. Despite the fact that it is common and spreads to become a pest, it is a pretty plant in autumn when its leaves are bright red and its fruits scarlet. The flowers preceding the fruits are greenish yellow and borne in early July.

Rhus aromatica, flowers above; fruits, below.

Rhus glabra, cluster of fruits.

279

Rhus rubrifolia (*see Cotinus coggygria* 'Purpureus').

Rhus trilobata (Ill-scented sumac, Lemonade shrub, Skunk bush, Squaw bush). Zone 5 to part of Zone 4; 3'-4'.

Somewhat resembling the fragrant sumac, but with more upright growth, this shrub is native to the west coast, eastward to Illinois. It rarely is grown in gardens. The flowers are not as conspicuous as those of the fragrant sumac, and, though leaves and fruits are both red in autumn, this is a shrub only for the wild garden.

Rhus typhina (Staghorn sumac, Vinegar tree). Zone 4 to parts of Zone 3; 30'.

The largest of the sumacs that grow wild in North America, this can be found from Quebec and Ontario southward to Georgia and westward to Iowa. It may be either a shrub or a small tree and, in either case, is upright in form. The twigs are hairy when young, like the new horns of the stag, hence the common name. The leaves turn red in autumn when the greenish-yellow June flowers have matured into crimson fruits. It is for this autumn coloration that the plant is grown. It is best used where it has plenty of room to spread into large clumps. Several of the plants, set to form a group, then growing together as they spread, are a handsome sight in autumn.

Rhus typhina 'Laciniata' (Cut-leaved staghorn sumac) differs from *typhina* by having the leaflets deeply toothed or divided. An unusual plant in appearance, this should be seen before it is purchased and used in a garden only where the cut leaves will show off to advantage, usually as a specimen. This cultivar should not be confused with 'Dissecta', which has leaves even more finely divided than those of 'Laciniata' and is too often incorrectly called 'Laciniata'.

RIBES (Currant)

The currants most people know best are those grown for their fruits which make delicious jelly. There are several species bearing useful fruits. However, the currants discussed here are those grown as ornamentals, either for their compact form or for their flowers, rather than their fruits.

Many currants, because they are alternate hosts for a plant disease called white pine blister rust, are not permitted entry into the United States or Canada, into many of the states, nor even permitted to be moved from one place to another within some of the states. The subject of alternate hosts is discussed in Chapter 9, page 54 and the prohibitions of plant entry are given in Chapter 12, page 119.

Ribes alpinum (Alpine currant). Zone 1; 6' but usually about 3' and slow-growing.

The best use for this shrub is as a hedge plant because it is extremely compact in form, making almost a solid mass of fine foliage that does not turn color in fall. Leaves are small, opening very early in spring. Flowers are 1/8" in diameter, borne in 1¼" long clusters, brilliant greenish yellow (10 Y 9/9) in color and therefore hardly show among the leaves. Should you observe them in early May, you will find them interesting in form. If the plants you own have female flowers, scarlet berries will follow the blooms. However, it is not a good idea to grow female plants as it is the males which have been found not to serve as hosts for white pine blister rust. For this reason, nurseries are propagating the male or pistillate plants almost exclusively.

Ribes aureum (Slender golden currant, Golden currant). Zone 1; 6'.

Upright in form, this currant is grown for its flowers, which bloom as the leaves unfold and are golden yellow and fragrant, though not as fragrant as those of *R. odoratum*, described below. They also are smaller than those of the clove currant, but there are more of them. Purplish-brown or black fruits follow the flowers.

Ribes diacanthum (Siberian currant). Zone 1; 5'.

Resembling the alpine currant described above, but more upright in form, this currant has prickles on the branchlets, glossy leaves, greenish-yellow, inconspicuous flowers, followed by small, scarlet fruits. It, too, forms an excellent hedge.

Ribes odoratum (Clove currant, Fragrant currant, Golden currant, Buffalo currant, Buffalo berry). Zone 5; 6'. Illustrated on Color Page II.

If you have smelled the fragrance of the blossoms of this currant you will not rest until you own a plant. Place it where its habit of suckering will not overrun any plant of value and where you can drink in the scent as you pass back and forth in your garden.

Clove currant is upright and irregular in form. It soon forms clumps because of its suckering habit. These are never dense, but rather sparse. However, the leaves are prettily shaped and the clumps never unsightly. The vivid greenish yellow (7.5 Y 8/12) tubular flowers, centered strong red (2.5 R 5/12) cover the plant in early May. Black, edible berries, but not many of them, ripen in late summer pro-

Ribes alpinum, flowering branch, above; closeup of flower cluster, below.

Ribes odoratum, bloom-laden branch, above; dainty blossoms and interesting leaves, below.

Ribes odoratum, ripe and unripe berries.

Robinia hispida flowers, below.

vided plants of both sexes are planted. The foliage, which opens with or after the flowers, turns scarlet in autumn.

This currant may be found wild from Minnesota and Arkansas west to South Dakota and Texas.

ROBINIA (Locust)

Most robinias are large trees, but several shrub and small tree forms are described in this book—a tree form in Chapter 15 and one shrub form here. All have compound leaves, with many leaflets and large, drooping clusters of flowers. The blooms are shaped like those of peas or sweet peas.

Robinia hispida (Rose acacia, Pink locust, Moss locust). Zone 6 to southern part of Zone 5; 3′.

If this shrub did not have a bad habit of suckering, sometimes near its base and at other times several feet away, it would doubtless be more widely grown because it is tolerant of poor soils. The form is upright and irregular. Long, red bristles cover the branches, accounting for the common name of "moss" locust. Great clusters of deep, purplish pink (5 RP 6/10) florets are borne in late May and early June. These resemble the clusters of laburnums or wisterias though they are not as long as either (usually 2¼ to 2½″ long) and the individual florets are larger than those of laburnum. It is for these flowers that the shrub is grown. Odd-looking pods, shaped like pea pods, but covered with red to purple bristles develop in late summer and remain on the plants for some time.

This shrub is wild in the states of Virginia and Kentucky, south to Georgia and Alabama.

Robinia hispida, hairy seed pods.

ROSA (Rose)

The roses most frequently grown in gardens nowadays are hybrid tea, floribunda, or grandiflora types which, while technically shrubs, require pruning, spraying and fertilizing to keep them producing flowers. In these days of high-priced garden help and therefore a trend to do-it-yourself gardening, the easy-upkeep plants are coming into their own. High among these are the really shrubby roses for they require comparatively little care. These are the only roses included in this book.

Shrub roses may be one-time bloomers, bearing flowers usually in June, or "remontant" which means you can expect a crop of flowers in June and occasional blooms during summer and autumn. They vary greatly in height and size, as well as in bloom production. The rose species described below all thrive in poor soil and most need full sun, but a few, which are indicated, will flower in light shade. Species roses should not be fertilized and, while the Austrian Cooper rose (*R. foetida* 'Bicolor') certainly needs spraying to control black spot, the remainder of the older roses named do not. The newer shrub roses also are trouble free, if not quite to the extent of the species. Most of them profit from light fertilization, few need spraying. In general, shrub rose pruning is confined to removing any dead canes in spring and any canes that are in the way of other plants or traffic.

Shrub roses are sturdy plants. As indicated above, many of them are rose species, found wild somewhere in the world, on this continent or another. Some are varieties or cultivars of these species and have flowers as handsome as those of any rose you care to name.

In this section I have tried to tell you a little about the most widely available of the older shrub roses and indicate some of the modern kinds. If you are seriously interested in the old shrub roses, there are several books and 2 catalogs which you should have. The books are: *The Old Shrub Roses* and *Shrub Roses of Today* both by Graham Stuart Thomas, the first published by Phoenix House, Ltd. of London, England and the second by St. Martin's Press, New York. Both of these are British books and both describe many, many roses which are not available in North America. An American book is *Old Roses for Modern Gardens* by Richard Thomson, published by D. Van Nostrand Co., Inc. The catalogs are those of Joseph J. Kern Rose Nursery, Box 33, Mentor, Ohio and Will Tillotson's Roses, Brown Valley Rd., Watsonville, California.

The only book I know of that tells anything at all about the modern shrub roses is an exceptionally fine book, *Roses* by Wilhelm Kordes. Originally published in Germany in 1962, it now is available in English, published by Reinhold Publishing Corp., New York. The difficulty with reading this book is the same as that encountered with the British books mentioned above—all these lovely roses are described and most of them can't be bought in either the United States or Canada for love nor money.

I would like to add a few words about modern shrub roses. Some of them, to my mind, rival azaleas when they are in flower—and that is certainly a challenging statement. A full grown plant of 'Nevada', for instance, is as beautiful as any shrub that blooms in the garden all season. 'Golden Wings' is hardy into Canada and a simply gorgeous dwarf shrub when it is laden with its single, golden-yellow flowers with their even more golden stamens.

'Betty Prior', while not listed as a shrub, is a good one with flowers throughout the summer and autumn as well as in June. 'The Fairy' (*not* Sweet Fairy) is, to my mind, in a class by itself. You will find a brief description later in the text.

Because most of these roses are not widely available, I have indicated them according to hybrid groups both in this chapter and in the Buyer's Guide Chart. You can search the catalogs to find the varieties in these groups as I have done. It's fun to find one you've been wanting to acquire.

A few years ago there were only 2 or 3 nurseries in the United States and Canada that listed shrub roses. The number is increasing each year because of the demand for roses that do not require endless care. Some nurseries specializing in shrub roses have much longer lists than others which grow not only shrub roses but other shrubs as well. Only roses listed in several to many of the 200-odd catalogs on which this book is based are described below.

Rosa altaica (see *R. pimpinellifolia altaica*).

Rosa blanda (Smooth wild rose, Labrador rose). Zone 1; 6'.

The first common name of this rose refers to the smoothness of the upper parts of the older canes; on the lower parts there are a few thorns or prickles.

This wild rose grows from Labrador and Quebec to Manitoba, southward to New Brunswick, through New England and Pennsylvania, north and west to Ohio, Indiana, Illinois, Missouri, and Nebraska.

Above: Bud of Rosa centifolia 'Muscosa' (moss rose) showing mossy growth. Fully open flower, below, hides "moss".

Rosa foetida 'Bicolor' (Austrian Copper rose), below.

The rose is many-branched and spreads into a large clump by means of suckers. Single, rosy-pink flowers, 2½″ in diameter, are found singly or in groups of up to 8 blooms. Round or oval fruits color scarlet in autumn.

Rosa centifolia 'Muscosa' (Moss roses).

These are all old-time roses which have a green growth resembling moss on the outsides of the sepals which surround bud and flower. This is most noticeable, of course, before the flower is fully opened, for when it unfolds, the flower spread hides the moss. This class of roses has been loved by gardeners for generations. The moss roses now available may be found in the catalogs of specialists in old roses.

Rosa eglanteria (syn *R. rubiginosa*) (Sweet brier, Eglantine). Zone 4, 8′.

This is the rose with apple-scented foliage that is mentioned in old garden books and in some novels. Its form is arching, it is extremely prickly and, if plants are set 3′ apart, will form an impenetrable hedge, almost as wide as it is high. Eglantine has single, small pink flowers in mid-June sometimes borne in clusters, sometimes solitary. It passes on the apple scent of the leaves to its progeny, for I own one named 'Lady Penzance', which while entirely different in form and flower color, is delightful to sniff during a warm, moist spell.

Such modern shrub roses as 'Herbstfeuer' (Autumn Fire) and 'Goldbusch' (Gold Bush) are hybrids of *R. eglanteria* (although more frequently listed under the former name as "*R. rubiginosa* hybrids").

Rosa foetida 'Bicolor' (Austrian Copper brier). Zone 5; 9′.

Certainly one of the most beautifully and brightly-colored roses, this has single flowers, 2¼″ in diameter, their centers vivid yellow (5 Y 8/12) and the outer parts of the petals nearest to vivid red (5 R 5/12) though there is no precise match on the color fan. The very edges of the petals are even deeper in tone, but the same general hue. The reverse or undersides of the petals are the same vivid yellow.

Austrian Copper blooms in early June on a tall, upright plant. The hips which follow the blooms are red and most effective in autumn.

The trouble with growing this rose is that it can be depended on to be attacked by black spot, a rose disease which will defoliate the plant unless the disease is controlled by spraying or dusting with Phaltan. The plant will get this disease every single year and will infect other roses around it.

Although it will survive for many years regardless of the defoliation, in due course of time it is likely to succumb to the periodic weakening through loss of foliage.

Rosa foetida 'Persian Yellow' (Persian Yellow rose). Illustrated on Color Page IV. This rose looks especially well when grown with Austrian Copper as the two are similar in height and form. This rose has deep yellow, double flowers which have the unpleasant odor suggested by the specific name. Persian Yellow forms a large bush, eventually, and is handsome in flower. It is best, however, to place it away from a porch or other outdoor living room. It is a handsome specimen plant or may be used in a border.

Rosa glauca (syn *Rosa rubrifolia*) (Red-leaved rose, Red-leaf rose). Zone 2; 8' and as wide as high.

If you live way up north and want to grow a handsome shrub, try this one. Not only is it extremely hardy, but it also is attractive from spring to fall with its upright growth and bluish-green foliage with purplish-red undertones and tinges. In early June it produces single, 1½" diameter deep purplish pink blooms (nearest to 5 RP 6/10 but much paler) tinged in their centers with moderate purplish pink (5 RP 5/10). It is these same tones that tinge the foliage.

The centers of the flowers are almost white and the light yellow stamens set them off beautifully. The flowering continues over several weeks, although there are rarely masses of flowers on the plant at any one time. The hips are an unusual strong red orange (10 R 5/11).

The coloring of this rose is best when it is growing in full sun. In shade the leaves "gray off" and are not as bright. Because of the height and the foliage color, this rose may be used at the back of a border or as a specimen where its leaves will aid the garden picture.

For the sake of those who wish to garden easily, I might add that my largest bush of this rose is now about 30 years old. It was moved 13 years ago from our former garden with a ball of earth around its roots. It was not cut back at that time to aid it in reestablishing itself and it kept right on growing and blooming. It never has been fertilized or sprayed, nor has it had any more pruning than the occasional removal of a broken or dead branchlet.

Rosa harisonii (R. *foetida* × R. *pimpinellifolia*) (Harison's Yellow rose). Zone 5 to part of Zone 4; 6'.

Paler yellow flowers than Persian Yellow (closest

Rosa glauca (rubrifolia) flowers, above; "hips", below.

285

Rosa harisonii

Rosa hugonis

to brilliant greenish yellow, 7.5 Y 9/8), 2″ wide and not as double, but fragrant (unlike those of Persian Yellow), and nearly black hips characterize this rose. It blooms just before the *R. foetida* trio of *R. foetida*, *R. f.* 'Bicolor' and *R. f.* 'Persian Yellow' about the end of May and a bushful of blooms can be counted on every year. Fine for use in a shrub border or as a specimen.

Rosa hugonis (Father Hugo rose, Golden rose of China). Zone 5 to parts of Zone 4; 3½′-4′.

There is no more delicately beautiful rose bud than that of this rose. Add to the exquisite buds finely cut, dainty foliage and brilliant greenish-yellow (7.5 Y 9/8), single 1¾″ to 2″ diameter flowers blooming with the late tulips in May and you have a rose that everyone who loves beautiful plants should be growing. This rose does not often fruit, but when it does the hips are dark red, almost black-red. The plants are upright and spread to form clumps.

Rosa lucida (see *R. virginiana*).

R. moschata hybrids (musk hybrids). 4′-5′. These are listed here because among them are some lovely shrubs, available in a few nurseries. 'Belinda', 'Elmshorn' and 'Cornelia' are just a few of their names. The one most widely listed is 'Robin Hood', especially recommended for hedge use. Its growth is dense and compact and the plant is hardy to below zero. It can be kept to any height over 3′ (it naturally grows a bit taller than this). It has cherry red flowers, small, but borne in fair-sized clusters, in June and occasionally during summer and fall.

Rosa moyesii (Moyes rose). Zone 6 to parts of Zone 5; 9′, sometimes more.

The growth habit of this shrub is positively "gaunt," if that word can be applied to plant growth. A few stout, tall stems support branches near their tops. The leaves are small and the flowers are single, 2″ in diameter, and blood red in color. They appear in mid-June. The fruits which follow them are unusual in shape; rather like small flasks, broad at the base, then narrowing to a "waist" and then widening again. They are orange-red and begin to color in August and September.

Cultivars of this rose are found in several catalogs and are indicated in the Buyer's Guide Chart in Chapter 11.

Rosa moyesii hybrids. Here, too are found beautiful, hardy shrub roses, such as 'Nevada', with large, semi-double, creamy white flowers set off by yellow stamens and 'Marguerite Hilling', its pink sport.

Rosa multiflora (Japanese rose). Zone 5; 12′ and as wide as high.

Contrary to many advertisements you may have seen, this is *not* a rose for small gardens. It makes a wonderful hedge to keep cattle confined or to mark the boundaries of a large piece of property and also is an excellent tall ground cover for steep banks along railroad rights of way where no one wishes children to climb or where soil needs to be held in place. It is an extremely vigorous, fast-growing shrub, beautiful when in flower or fruit, but *much, much* too large to be planted on a 50-foot lot.

Habit of growth is upright with widely arching branches. The leaves are small and the plants very spiny or thorny. Little white flowers, 1″ in diameter, are borne in tremendous quantities in mid-June, literally covering the bushes with bloom. These are followed by little red hips in the same large quantities. They are lovely to look at in autumn and usually stay on the plant during most of the winter, thus are available for use in Christmas decorations.

Rosa multiflora, closeup of flowers.

Rosa multiflora, flowers above; fruits below.

This rose is useful in the front of a shrub border or as a specimen in a rock garden, but in either situation room must be allowed for it to sucker and spread.

Rosa palustris (Swamp rose). Zone 5; 6′.

Upright in form, with slender stems, this shrub grows from Nova Scotia to Minnesota, southward to Florida and Mississippi. Its blooms are single and pink, opening in June. The fruits are red in autumn. The only reason for growing this shrub is that it will thrive in wet places, so is useful where these are found. It also will thrive in dry areas but far handsomer species are available for such situations.

Rosa pimpinellifolia (syn *R. spinosissima*) (Burnet rose, Scotch brier, Scotch rose). Zone 4; 3′.

Not only is this a low-growing shrub, but it also has a dense, mounded form, which makes it useful in many locations. In early June it bears 1″ to 2″ diameter, single, fragrant white flowers in profusion. These are followed, some years, by black or brownish fruits which are not particularly beautiful.

The former name of the plant was given because the stems are literally loaded with different sizes of thorns and spines.

Rosa pimpinellifolia altaica (syn *R. spinosissima altaica*). Zone 4; 4′-5′. With larger leaves than the species, fewer thorns, and a strong, upright growth habit, this is a lovely rose when its branches are drooping under their load of blooms. These are cream-white or ivory-white, about 3″ in diameter, and appear but once in early June. The fruits which follow them are reddish-black and unusual in appearance.

Rosa pimpinellifolia altaica.

Rosa nitida (Shining rose). Zone 2; 1½′-2′.

A wild rose, found from Newfoundland to Connecticut, often in low-lying, marshy areas, this is a very "twiggy" rose, with many thin prickles or thorns up the reddish stems. It spreads rapidly by means of suckers. The leaflets are narrow, pointed at the tips, glossy green on the upper sides and turning to bright scarlet in fall. It is this autumn coloring which is the shrub's greatest asset. Flowers are single, rose-red in color and, despite the low stature of the plant, are a full 2″ across. The hips are red, covered with bristles, and small, ⅜″ in diameter. They are not long-lasting.

Rosa pimpinellifolia hybrids. These are better known under the former name of *spinosissima* hybrids. They are mostly the production of Wilhelm Kordes of Germany and are handsome shrubs, larger than the species. These are not as yet widely available in this country. Look for them in the catalogs. Many of them have names beginning with the word "Frühling" which is German for "spring." Thus 'Frühlingsmorgen' translates to Spring's Morning and 'Frühlingsgold' to Spring's Gold and so on. These are hardy to temperatures ranging to at least —10 degrees F.

Most of these hybrids have disease-resistant foliage, bloom only once in May, and need minimum care.

Rosa rubiginosa (see *R. eglanteria*).

Rosa rugosa (Rugosa rose, Sea tomato, Eatin' rose). Zone 1; 6'.

This is another fine rose for the north. It also is well suited to seaside gardens because it will tolerate salt spray. Add to these advantages a tough constitution, handsome dark green leaves turning almost orange in fall, 2" wide flowers, carmine-violet according to my ideas, strong purplish red (7.5 RP 4/11) according to the color fan, and tomato-red fruits and you have the reasons why this rose is widely grown. Its faults are that it is very thorny and that both flowers and fruits often are on the plant at the same time, as flowering continues for months and fruits color early. This dual coloration is not an ideal color scheme. However, both colors are tempered by the green of the leaves.

The rugosa rose is useful for clipped or unclipped hedges, for covering banks, or for a place in a shrub border where it has room to spread. There are other flower colors available in its varieties and cultivars which eliminate one of the objections voiced above.

Rosa rugosa 'Alba' is a white-flowered cultivar. It is more upright in growth than the species and the remark about the color-clash between flowers and fruits does not, of course, apply.

Rosa rugosa cultivars.

The following cultivars of *R. rugosa* are those most frequently found in the catalogs:
'Agnes'. Double, pale amber, fragrant flowers. Once-blooming, 6', vigorous and hardy.
'Belle Poitevine'. Large, semi-double, rose-pink to magenta-pink flowers 3½" to 4" in diameter. Recurrent bloom. Vigorous growth.
'Blanc Double de Coubert'. Double, white flowers.

Rosa rugosa, flowers and tomato-like fruits, above; closer view of flowers and "rugose" leaves, below.

289

Rosa rugosa hybrids: 'F. G. Grootendorst; left, 'Pink Grootendorst', right.

'Pink Grootendorst'; closeup view of carnation-like blooms with feathered edges.

'Hansa'. Large, double, clove-rose scented, reddish-violet flowers. Repeat bloomer. Grows well on the western prairies.

'F. G. Grootendorst'. Small, double, slightly fragrant, bright red flowers with fringed petal edges. Recurrent bloom. Vigorous growth.

'Frau Dagmar Hastrup'. Single, silvery-pink flowers. Recurrent bloom.

'Grootendorst Supreme'. Deeper crimson-red than Grootendorst.

'Pink Grootendorst'. Fringed, clear pink flowers in clusters, otherwise like 'F. G. Grootendorst'. Recurrent bloom.

'Sir Thos. Lipton'. Double, fragrant, white flowers. Recurrent bloom.

Rosa setigera (Prairie rose). Zone 5 to part of Zone 4; 15'. Illustrated on Color Page V.

Native from Nebraska, Wisconsin and southern Ontario to the Gulf states, this rose may kill to the ground in winter in the far north but will grow again from the roots in spring, if protected with straw, and make great long canes in one season.

Whether the entire growth is made in one season or not, the canes of this rose are always long and weak. Thus, when the rose is not supported, they arch widely or, if a tree is nearby, they grow up into it and greatly enhance the appearance of the tree when they are flowering. Sometimes the canes lie on the ground and sprawl. Doubtless pruning would give the plant a better form but, if allowed plenty of room, it needs none. It definitely is not a rose for a small garden.

In early to mid-July, when most other rose species have finished flowering, the prairie rose bears single, 2½" diameter blooms in clusters which may be 5" across and 4" in depth. There is no match for the flowers on the color fan. They are between deep purplish pink (7.5 RP 6/12) and strong purplish pink (7.5 RP 5/12), but more rose color. They are fragrant, though many people will tell you that they are not. The foliage turns reddish in autumn and the fruits also are red.

Rosa setigera.

The Detroit Zoological Garden uses this rose as a specimen, next to large buildings, allowed to grow to its full size and kept upright by pruning. If anyone wished to train it flat, it undoubtedly could be used as a climber against a wall or fence.

Rosa spinosissima (see *R. pimpinellifolia*).

'The Fairy.' Zone 5; 3'

Because I made such a point of mentioning this rose earlier in this discussion of roses, I shall describe it briefly here. It is a low shrub that needs only the dead wood cut off in spring, no spraying at all, little fertilization, yet produces flowers all summer long. It blooms in spurts—that is, there is plentiful bloom in late June in my garden. Then the bushes rest, then form a new set of buds and become laden with flowers once more, and so on throughout the summer and early autumn.

This rose is a sport of one named 'Lady Godiva' which, in turn, is a sport of the well-known rambler rose, 'Dorothy Perkins'. The flowers of 'The Fairy' are the same pink as those of the pink-flowered 'Dorothy' and the same small size but borne in large clusters. In the twelve years that I have owned a dozen plants of 'The Fairy', I have seen black spot on it once, in a very wet season. Would that I could say the same of the hybrid teas, etc. that I also grow.

Rosa virginiana (syn *R. lucida*). Zone 4 to part of Zone 3; 6'.

Found from Newfoundland, southward to Alabama and westward to Missouri, this rose is vigorous in growth, spreading by means of underground stems. It thrives in sandy soil and forms a beautiful, unclipped hedge.

This is a handsome rose at any season of the year. In spring the shining leaves open and are attractive. In mid- to late June the cerise-pink, single flowers open, paler at the centers and with yellow stamens showing. The glossy leaves remain in good condition all summer, and in autumn turn first beet red, then orange with sometimes a little yellow added to make the appearance of the plant even more marked. The fruits are red and rounded, ½" in diameter. They ripen late in the season and are effective against the red-brown winter color of the twigs.

This rose grows too large for a small garden unless restrained by pruning. It is a fine hedge rose if lightly pruned.

Rosa wichuraiana (Memorial rose). Zone 5; procumbent.

With tiny, semi-evergreen, glossy leaves, this is a rose for covering the ground, especially banks, where it soon will grow so thickly that no weeds can penetrate. It has single, white, 2" diameter flowers the middle of July and the fruits which follow them are red.

RUBUS (Raspberry)

Gardeners usually think of raspberries as being grown solely for their fruits. There are, however, several which have such lovely blooms that they are grown as ornamentals. They are as easy to grow as any raspberry, needing little or no care except pruning of old canes at the end of the flowering season because, like all raspberries, the old canes do not flower or fruit a second year.

Rubus odoratus (Flowering raspberry). Zone 4 to part of Zone 3; Usually about 6'.

Found wild from Nova Scotia westward to Michigan and southward to Tennessee and Georgia, this is an upright-growing shrub with arching branches and large, hairy leaves. Fragrant, rose-purple, 2" diameter flowers open early in July, followed by flat, pale red berries which can be eaten. Both flowers and berries often are found on the plant at the same time.

While this shrub grows best in shade, it will grow in sun if it is set in a moist situation or gets sufficient moisture otherwise. It is not a shrub for a small garden as it suckers and spreads. It is best used in a wild garden, to hold a shady bank in place, or in a shady spot in the cultivated garden where there is plenty of room and not many other shrubs would thrive.

SALIX (Willow)

All willows are easy to grow unless and until they are troubled by borers. Most prefer moist soil but many will grow as well in drier areas. Some have colorful stems or contorted or weeping form; others have beautiful foliage and still others are grown for their ornamental buds and opening catkins. In willows the flowers of each sex are borne on separate plants. The male flowers are the more ornamental and these are the reasons for growing the shrubby willows described below. There are, of course, many other shrub willows listed by specialists in the genus.

Salix caprea (see Chapter 15).

Salix discolor (Pussy willow, American pussy willow, Glaucous willow). Zone 4 to part of Zone 3; 6' to 20'.

Our native pussy willow is found wild from Labrador to Alberta, south to Nova Scotia, New England, Maryland, west to Kentucky, Missouri

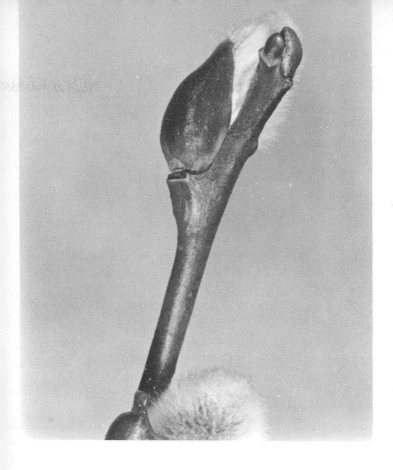

and South Dakota. It usually grows along streams or in swampy locations, but will grow well in drier locations in the garden. It is hardier than goat willow (*S. caprea*) described in Chapter 15.

The leaves of this species are bluish-green on the undersides, which gives the shrub the effect of gray foliage when viewed from a distance. Catkins are gray, the male ones producing bright yellow stamens in March to April. Unless the plants are heavily fertilized and well watered, catkins are smaller than those of goat willow and Korean rosegold pussy willow. They appear just as those of the latter are dropping.

Branch with catkins in three stages of maturity.

Salix discolor; above is a bud starting to open; below is a male catkin, its stamens laden with ripe pollen.

Salix gracilistyla (Korean rose-gold pussy willow, but often listed as "Rose-Gold"). Zone 5; 6'-7'.

Part of the common name of this pussy willow, the "Rose-Gold" part, was bestowed on the plant by a nurseryman who had a number of these willows on hand and wanted to sell them. It refers to the distinct reddish or rosy undertone in the coloring of the catkins which, when the stamens are pollen-laden, thus become rose and gold. "Korean" refers to the country of origin, though this willow is more commonly found in Japan and Manchuria.

Much lower growing than either of the other two pussy willows described in this book, this also matures its catkins slightly earlier. They are more elongated in shape than those of the other pussy willows.

Salix purpurea (Purple osier, Basket willow), Zone 5 to part of Zone 4; 10'.

On low ground, from Newfoundland to Ontario and Wisconsin, southward to Nova Scotia, New England, Virginia, West Virginia, Ohio, Illinois and Iowa, you'll find this willow growing.

When the Indians weave baskets, the supple stems often are their choice. The twigs are purple in winter, which accounts for both the botanical and first common name.

Plants are dense yet graceful, the foliage fine, the catkins very small and gray, appearing in March. This willow is not sufficiently attractive for use in the cultivated part of a garden, but is excellent in a damp place where a practically carefree, but still good-looking shrub is desired.

Salix purpurea 'Gracilis' (syn *S. p. nana* and also sometimes listed as "purpurea dwarf") (Dwarf purple osier, Dwarf Arctic willow). Zone 5 to part of Zone 4; 3'-4'. Narrow, blue-green leaves and many slender branches are the important characteristics of this delicate-appearing willow. It is used chiefly for low hedges where dainty appearance is important. Actually the plants are tough and easy to grow.

Salix purpurea nana (see *Salix purpurea* 'Gracilis').

Salix repens (Creeping willow). Zone 4; 3'.

That low, damp place in your garden where nothing much will grow and you don't want a shrub that will grow tall is the perfect spot to use this low-growing willow. It tolerates poor soil, moisture and even a little shade.

Salix gracilistyla, left, with stamens showing ripe pollen while those of S. discolor, right, are not yet mature. Note difference in shape of "pussies."

SAMBUCUS (Elder)

If you have a small garden, there is no reason for you to read about elders. They are too large, too vigorous in growth, for a limited area. They are at their best in wild gardens, especially in moist soil. They tend to grow straggly as time goes on, but can be cut to the ground if too unsightly and will grow again from the roots. Their leaves are large and, while some people consider them coarse in appearance, I think they are beautiful. All elders have tiny white florets arranged in large, delicately designed clusters, and edible fruits. From these some people make wine, some make pies and still others a tart jelly, delicious when served with meat. Birds love the berries so birds and humans often race to see who gets them first.

All elders are easy to transplant if moved when small but hard to reestablish if moved when large. They are not particular as to soil conditions but if moist soil is available they will grow better in it. They require no special care.

Sambucus canadensis, detail of flower cluster, above; flowers below left, fruits (elderberries), below right.

Sambucus canadensis (American elder, Common elder, Elderberry, Bore tree). Zone 4 to part of Zone 3; 12'.

Flower clusters of this elder may be 8" in diameter and are at their height of bloom in late June or early July. The blue-black berries are borne in just as large clusters as the flowers and make the plants prominent in the landscape in September. Selected forms now are being propagated for finest fruits.

This elder is native from British Columbia to Manitoba and south to New England, Georgia, Louisiana, west to Oklahoma.

Sambucus canadensis 'Aurea' (Golden elder) has brilliant golden-yellow leaves which retain their color all season and is a good choice where such a bright-foliaged plant is needed.

Sambucus nigra 'Aurea' (Golden European elder). Zone 5; 30'.

This elder may grow as a tree or as a large shrub. It is the yellow-leaved form of the European elder and is not in any way superior to the yellow-leaved form of the American elder. All yellow-foliaged plants should be used with care so that their foliage color does not conflict with nearby surroundings.

Sambucus nigra 'Laciniata' (Cut-leaved European elder). The leaves of this elder are deeply and regularly divided. The plant is grown for this characteristic.

Sambucus plumosa aurea (see *S. racemosa* 'Plumosa Aurea').

Sambucus racemosa (European red elder). Zone 5; 12'.

Earlier to bloom than the native elder, this has creamy-white flowers early in May. These are followed by scarlet berries in July and August.

Sambucus racemosa aurea (see *S. r.* 'Plumosa Aurea').

Sambucus racemosa 'Plumosa Aurea' (syn *S. plumosa aurea, S. racemosa aurea*) has leaves deeply cut, golden yellow in color. This does not change during the season, so this plant, often listed as "Golden Plume" in the catalogs, should be considered where a large, yellow-leaved plant is desired.

SHEPHERDIA

Shepherdia argentea (Silver leaf, Buffalo berry, Rabbit berry, Beef-suet tree, Wild oleaster). Zone 2; 3'-18'.

Growing wild from Manitoba to Alberta and south to Iowa, Kansas, Colorado, and New Mexico, usually on hillsides or along streambeds, this plant may be a shrub or a small tree. In either size it has rather thorny branches. Its outstanding characteristic is the silvery appearance of both its leaves (silvery on both sides) and its young branches.

Its flowers are yellowish, very small and inconspicuous even though they are arranged in clusters. They blossom in May and June. The berries, however, are red and borne in large clusters, so are conspicuous when they ripen in August and September. A good, rather tart jelly may be made from them.

This is a good shrub to grow where soil is poor and many others will not survive. Several plants must be set out to insure berries, for the flowers of the two sexes are borne on separate plants. Silver leaf is well suited for use in hedges.

SORBARIA (False spirea)

These plants often are confused with spireas which they resemble in several respects. They have interesting leaves with many leaflets and "plumes" made up of tiny white florets. These appear in July and August when there are not many other shrubs in bloom. A single plant is attractive by itself, but once you have seen a whole bank planted with false spireas, you will realize that they are far lovelier when planted in a large mass.

False spireas are easy to grow, thriving even in a poor soil. While they appreciate a little shade, they also will thrive in full sun. They need heavy pruning every few years.

Sorbaria aitchisonii (Kashmir false spirea). Zone 5 to part of Zone 4; 6'-7'.

In late July or early August this bears compact white flower clusters at the tips of the branches. These may be a foot long. The leaves are bright green and narrow. Young twigs are red. It is best to remove the spent flower clusters as they are not at all attractive and no decorative fruits will follow them.

Sorbaria sorbifolia (syn *Spiraea sorbifolia*) (Ural false spirea). Zone 1; 6'.

Stout branches grow straight up, bearing leaves before most other shrubs in spring. These light green leaves have many leaflets and are attractive. The flowers are borne in 4" to 12" long upright clusters, like plumes, beginning in June and continuing intermittently until late August.

The difficulty with this shrub is that it suckers so freely that a large clump soon forms around one plant. This is satisfactory if planned for when the shrub was placed, but otherwise these suckers can

Flower spike of Sorbaria sorbifolia.

summer-blooming spireas are either flat-topped clusters or elongated plumy clusters and, in both cases, are borne at the tips of the branches. In all cases, the individual florets are tiny—the clusters are the noticeable parts, not individual blooms, although they are attractive.

Spireas, as might be expected in so large a genus, vary greatly in height, form, and flowering time. However, practically all of them have undistinguished leaves, only a few have colored foliage in autumn, and none of them have decorative fruits.

Sorbus tianshanica; flowers above; berries below.

become pests. However, the clump will be a beautiful sight when in bloom.

SORBUS

Sorbus americana and Sorbus decora, both small trees, are described in Chapter 15.

Sorbus tianshanica (Turkistian sorbus). Zone 5; 15'.

Red-brown, upright branches and dark green, shining leaves make this a handsome plant all season. The florets are among the largest of the mountain ashes, nearly ¾" in diameter, and arranged in 4½" wide clusters. Fruits are bright red, ⅜" in diameter, and freely borne. This shrub forms clumps, so should be placed where it has room to grow.

SPIRAEA (Spirea)

There are many, many spireas available to the gardener. They fall into two groups for garden purposes—spring-blooming and summer-blooming. Within these two groups, they might be classified by their flower forms, because the spring-blooming spireas usually are borne in umbels (clusters in which all flower stems start from one point and are about the same length) growing close to the branch or on short, leafy stems. They also may be arranged in looser, flat-topped clusters quite regularly spaced along the branches. Flowers of the

Because of these facts, the gardener should realize that he is giving most of them space solely for their flowers (or, occasionally, their branching form). All spireas are easy to move and to grow. They need no special soil and have no particular pests. They thrive in sun and many will grow as well in light shade, though their flowers will be fewer. If a spirea should become unsightly through neglect, it may be cut to the ground in early spring and will grow again from the roots.

Spiraea albiflora (syn *S. callosa alba*, *S. japonica alba*) (Japanese white spirea). Zone 5; 1½'.

One of the summer-flowering spireas, this blooms in July. Flowers are white, as the botanical name tells. It is an excellent low shrub which may be used as a specimen if bloom at that time is required for effect, but is better in the front of a shrub border, perhaps combined with other summer-flowering spireas which have pink flowers.

Spiraea × arguta (*S. multiflora × S. thunbergii*) (Garland spirea). Zone 5 to part of Zone 4; 5'-6'.

This shrub resembles the widely-planted Vanhoutte spirea which blooms the end of May, but the garland spirea blooms at the beginning of that month. By planting both species, it is possible to have the same beautifully arched branches laden with flat clusters of white flowers for a longer period of time. The garland spirea may be used as a specimen or in the border. There also is a compact form of this plant, called in the catalogs *Spiraea arguta compacta*, which is extremely useful and very pretty. I am using it for a low hedge.

Spiraea × billiardii (*S. douglasii × S. salicifolia*) (Billiard's spirea, Billiard spirea). Zone 5 to part of Zone 4; 6'.

In late June, and intermittently during the next month or more, the 6" long, 2" wide spikes of this spirea enhance the garden picture. They are deep purplish pink (5 RP 6/10) according to the color fan and furnish a welcome change from the earlier white spirea flowers. Billiard spirea should be placed where there is room for it to form clumps, for this it will do. It is a good border shrub and excellent for massing wherever summer bloom is desired.

Spiraea × bumalda (*S. japonica × S. albiflora*). This plant is listed only occasionally in the catalogs. It is known through the cultivars described below.

Spiraea × bumalda 'Anthony Waterer'. Zone 4; 2'-3'. Illustrated on Color Page V.

Bloom spike of Spiraea billiardii, above.

Spiraea bumalda 'Anthony Waterer', left; S. b. 'Crispa', right, with similar flower clusters, different leaves.

Individual florets of Spiraea bumalda 'Anthony Waterer' are beautiful as this close view shows.

Spiraea bumalda 'Crispa', below, is noted for its handsome foliage.

This plant is named for the same Anthony Waterer mentioned in the discussions of Azaleas and Rhododendrons. Considering his contributions to the gardens of the world, it is rewarding to know that his memory is kept green by one of the most popular and widely-grown of summer-flowering shrubs.

Starting in late June and continuing intermittently throughout the summer, the strong purplish red (7.5 RP 5/12) flowers open. If the dead blooms are kept cut, flowering will be increased and will continue later in the season. Not only is there handsome flower color, but the young leaves are pink or pinkish, some years only in spring, other years continuing later in the season. The form of the plant is upright and quite compact. It occasionally needs some pruning because one or two branches will grow half a foot above all the others.

Spiraea × bumalda 'Crispa' (*S. japonica × S. albiflora*). Zone 5 to part of Zone 4; 2'-2½'. Crinkled leaves and flowers the same color as 'Anthony Waterer' in flat clusters 3" wide distinguish this little plant. It starts flowering in late June and, especially if flowers of the first blooming are cut off, will continue to produce additional blooms. Since these are so nearly like those of 'Anthony Waterer', the two shrubs may be used together for their contrasting foliages. 'Crispa' (usually called Crispy by nurserymen) does not form as large a plant as 'Anthony Waterer' so may be substituted for it when space is at a premium.

Spiraea × bumalda 'Froebelii' (*S. japonica × S. albiflora*) (Froebel spirea). Zone 5 to part of Zone 4; 3'-3½'. Taller-growing than 'Anthony Waterer', with flowers the same color, this spirea has the habit of making sufficient new growth to hide the dead flowers after they finish blooming the end of June or the beginning of July. For this reason it often looks neater than 'Anthony Waterer' and may be substituted for it.

All three of the *bumaldas* may be used as specimens or in the front of shrub borders.

Spiraea callosa alba (see *S. albiflora*).

Spiraea caryopteris (see *Caryopteris clandonensis*).

Spiraea froebelii (see *S. bumalda* 'Froebelii').

Spiraea japonica alba (see *S. albiflora*).

Spiraea japonica alpina. Zone 5, possibly Zone 4; 1' or a little less. A fine ground cover for a sunny spot, tolerant of any soil, this little plant grows 10"-12" high and, if plants are set 18" apart, soon will carpet the ground. Little light pink flowers appear in May and occasionally throughout the summer.

Spiraea japonica 'Atrosanguinea' (syn *S. j. coccinea*). Zone 6 to southern part of Zone 5; 4'.

In spring the new foliage of this spirea is red. In late June to early July, and usually intermittently for a month or more after that, the flowers bloom, strong purplish red (7.5 RP 4/11) in color and in large (to 5″ diameter) clusters which are flat.

The plant is taller and more open in growth than 'Anthony Waterer'; and new growth covers dead flowers, a decided asset.

Spiraea lemoinei alpestris. Zone 5; 6″. Like *S. japonica alpina*, this spirea is an excellent ground cover, but a lower one, hugging the ground. Plants set a foot apart soon grow together to form a mat-like mass—conducive to smothering weeds. Like all spireas this is tolerant of almost any soil. It prefers full sun but will grow in slight shade. Light pink, tiny blooms in May plus one or two at intervals during the rest of the season may be expected.

Spiraea × *macrothyrsa* (*S. douglasii* × *S. latifolia*). Zone 5; 6'.

This spirea and *S. billiardii* are so similar that it takes an expert to tell them apart. One difference, fairly easy to see, is the practically horizontal branching of this species. Both spireas bloom from late June through July, both have long spikes of flowers at the branch tips and the blooms of both are similar in coloring. *Macrothyrsa* has flowers of 7.5 RP 6/12, deep, purplish pink, but, because of the fuzziness caused by the stamens being longer than the petals, the effect is lighter.

Spiraea media sericea (Oriental spirea). Zone 4; possibly to Zone 3; 4'. Upright in growth, with arching branches this produces abundant creamy-white flowers in late May, much in the same manner as *S. vanhouttei*. It is hardier than the Vanhoutte spirea, a point in its favor.

Spiraea × *multiflora* (*S. crenata* × *S. hypericifolia* (Snowgarland). Zone 4; 5'.

Blooming in May, this has ¼ to 5/16″ diameter flowers in clusters several inches across, on branches that arch only slightly. This spirea grows particularly well in the northern part of the Middle West.

Spiraea nipponica tosaensis (Snowmound, Boxwood spirea). Zone 5; 2½'. Foliage like that of the species, dark green on top of the leaves, but bluish green on the undersides, white flowers in smaller clusters than those of the species, and a moundlike form characterize this pretty and useful spirea. Blooms appear in June.

Spiraea japonica 'Atrosanguinea' flower clusters.

Spiraea macrothyrsa, below. Compare this with S. billiardii.

299

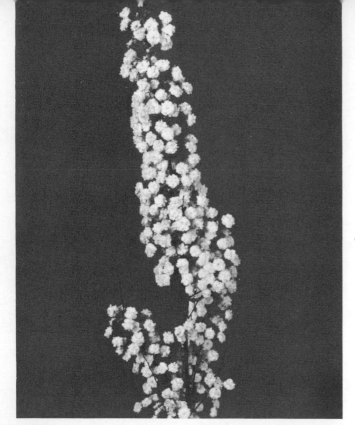

Spiraea prunifolia, blooming branch, above; closeup of button-like flowers, below.

Spiraea opulifolia and *S. opulifolia* 'Nana' (see *Physocarpus opulifolius* and *P. opulifolius* 'Nanus').

Spiraea × *pikoviensis* (*S. crenata* × *S. media*) (Pikov spirea). Zone 4; 4'.

More upright in form than the Oriental spirea,

with stiffer branches, this too has white to greenish-white flowers in May.

Spiraea prunifolia (syn *S. p. plena,* which is the listing commonly given in the catalogs) (Bridal wreath). Zone 5; to part of Zone 4; 6'-7'.

Botanists gave the double-flowered form of this plant the specific name because it was found first. Later, when the single-flowered form was discovered, it was given the varietal name of *simpliciflora.* This single-flowered form rarely is listed in any catalog. The double-flowered is the one meant, regardless of name.

Round ⅜" diameter buttons are what the blooms of this spirea resemble. A plant usually is loaded with them in mid-May. Growth habit is narrow and upright and the foliage, glossy green in spring and summer, turns bright orange in autumn, unusual in a spirea.

Spiraea × *sanssouciana* (*S. douglasii* × *S. japonica*). Zone 5; 4½'.

This is one of the summer-flowering spireas but it is earlier to start blooming than Billiard's spirea or *macrothyrsa,* sometimes starting in late June. This is its particular advantage because it has rose-colored flowers in pyramidal spikes at the branch tips and is easily mistaken for either of the other similar spireas. The accompanying photographs will show you that bloom clusters differ in shape.

Spiraea sorbifolia (see *Sorbaria sorbifolia*).

Spiraea thunbergii (Thunberg spirea, Thunberg's spirea). Zone 4; 5'.

Most years this has the distinction of being the first spirea to flower. It does this in early May, before its leaves have grown. The growth habit is upright and arching, the branches slender, the foliage light green (turning yellow in autumn) and

Spiraea sanssouciana, flower clusters.

300

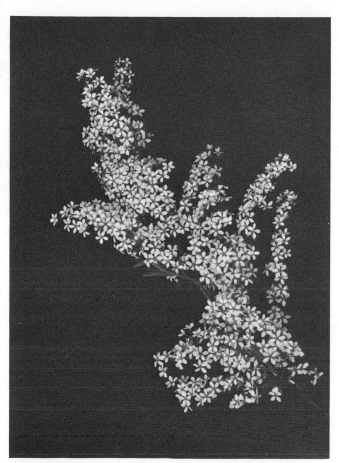

Spiraea tomentosa, flower spikes, above; flowers with their long stamens, below.

Flowering branch of Spiraea thunbergii, above; Spiraea trichocarpa, below.

Spiraea trilobata above; Spiraea vanhouttei, below.

finely textured. Unfortunately, a cold winter will cause some of the branches to die back, necessitating spring pruning. Florets are only ⅜" in diameter, but are borne in clusters of from two to five.

Spiraea tomentosa (Hardhack, Hardhack spirea, Steeple bush, Canada tea). Zone 5 to parts of Zone 4; 4'-5'.

From late June to September you will see this plant blooming in damp places from Prince Edwards Island to Quebec and Ontario, southward along the Atlantic coast to North Carolina. It is upright in form, spreads into large clumps, has deep rose or rosy-purple flowers set close together in short, upright spikes, pyramidal in shape. It is good to use in the wild garden or for planting by the sides of streams or lakes, but is much too spreading and not sufficiently showy for the cultivated garden.

Spiraea trichocarpa (Korean spirea). Zone 5 to part of Zone 4; 6'.

Blooming in June, right after the Vanhoutte spirea, is this shrub. It has spreading branches rather than arching ones, and the bloom clusters are larger than those of the Vanhoutte spirea—to 2¼" in diameter, composed of ¼" wide white florets with yellow centers.

Spiraea trilobata (Threelobe spirea). Zone 5 to part of Zone 4; 3'-4'.

The common name and the botanical name refer to the three lobes of the leaf, which make this spirea easy to tell from others. It has slender, arching branches and the flowers, white and formed into large clusters, are spaced all along them in late May to early June. There is a selection named "Swan Lake," which is available from a few nurseries.

Spiraea × vanhouttei (*S. cantoniensis × S. trilobata*) (Vanhoutte spirea) Zone 5 to part of Zone 4; 6'.

Once upon a time some traveling nursery salesman must have gone up and down every street in the middle west and sold every householder half a dozen plants of this spirea. This is the only way in which I can account for the vast numbers of Vanhoutte spirea one sees everywhere in this part of the country. It is this overplanting that makes some gardeners shy away from this plant.

If, instead of being influenced by its seeming commonness, you will take a good look at an individual plant, you will see that it is handsome when in flower. The myriad little ⅜" florets in the flat, 1½" diameter clusters in late May, borne along the gracefully arching branches, make this one of the best spireas. In some autumns the leaves turn red or orange, giving color at another time of year. The plant is as easy to grow as are all spireas, another good reason why so many gardeners possess one.

Try using this spirea as a specimen or placed in a conspicuous spot in a shrub border.

STAPHYLEA (Bladdernut)

Staphyleas may be large shrubs or sometimes small trees. They are grown for their smooth, striped bark, bright green foliage, drooping flower clusters, and inflated seed pods.

Staphylea trifolia (American bladdernut). Zone 4 to parts of Zone 3; 15'.

Found wild from Quebec and Ontario to Minnesota and south to Georgia, west to Missouri, Wisconsin, Iowa, Arkansas, and Oklahoma, this plant arouses interest when seen in the woods because, whether in flower or in fruit, it is out of the ordinary. It usually, but not always, is found in moist situations and therefore is useful for moist places in the garden, especially in shade.

Growth is upright, the bark grayish, the branches striped and green. The leaves, as the botanical name tells, are three-parted. In May the slender, drooping clusters of flowers appear. The petals of these are white; the sepals, which are almost as long as the petals, are greenish white and this variation gives an overall effect of pale green-white.

The fruits are three-lobed, inflated pods, first green then tan. They mature in October and last a long time when cut. Although the plant is an American native, these pods add an exotic touch to late autumn flower arrangements.

Staphylea trifolia, branch above; closeup of flowers, below.

Staphylea trifolia, bladder-like fruits.

Stephanandra incisa 'Crispa' above and below.

STEPHANANDRA

Stephanandras are grown for their graceful forms, beautiful, finely cut leaves and white flowers. They are easy to move, easy to grow, undemanding as to soil and require little or no care other than occasionally cutting out dead wood. They prefer a position in full sun but will grow in light shade.

Stephanandra flexuosa (see *S. incisa*).

Stephanandra incisa (Cutleaf stephanandra). Zone 5; 6', usually less.

Slender stems, arching branches, beautiful bright green, finely cut leaves that turn red in autumn, and tiny white flowers in small clusters in June all distinguish this shrub from others. It gives a dainty appearance because of the fine texture of its foliage. The flowers are merely an added touch. The zig-zag branches are interesting in winter.

This shrub is an excellent choice for a shrub border or as a specimen where fine texture is desired. In an extremely cold winter, some branches will die and should be cut out in spring.

Stephanandra incisa 'Crispa'. Zone 5; 2', usually less. One of the best of the low-growing shrubs, this has the same characteristics as *incisa* but is a much smaller and more spreading plant. It usually grows 3' to 4' wide or even wider, while only 2' or less high. Just think where this form, plus the dainty appearance, would fit into your garden picture. Under that low window, in front of taller shrubs, to provide a low planting on top of a wall, or as a ground cover this plant is a perfect choice. It will grow well in semi-shade. Plants may be spaced a foot apart for a very low hedge. Florets are ⅛" in diameter, borne in ¾" wide clusters.

STEWARTIA (sometimes spelled
Stuartia) (Stewartia)

Stewartia ovata (syn *S. pentagyna*) (Mountain stewartia, Mountain camellia). Zone 6 to protected places in Zone 5b; 15'.

If you want a beautiful summer-flowering shrub, try this one but move it in spring only; buy it "container-grown" (see Chapter 10), or with a large earth ball around its roots, and set it where it will get sun but is protected. My plants are on the east side of an evergreen windbreak and I never have had any winterkill, despite temperatures to —20 degrees F.

The growth habit of this shrub is upright, the foliage dark green, turning orange to scarlet in autumn. This particular species has larger leaves than the others, sometimes to 5″ long. The flowers, which open in July, are cup-shaped, white, with purple stamens. Bark on large branches is said to flake off, exposing lighter areas underneath, thus adding winter interest.

A tree form of *Stewartia* is described in Chapter 15.

Stewartia pentagyna (see *S. ovata*).

SYMPHORICARPOS (Snowberry or Coralberry, depending on the color of the fruits; Wolfberry)

Popular shrubs because of their pretty berries and the fact that they transplant easily and grow without care, these may be used for hedges (best unclipped) and for massed plantings on banks to hold soil in place.

Symphoricarpos albus (syn *S. racemosus*) (Snowberry, Waxberry). Zone 4 to parts of Zone 3; 3′.

While many of the nursery catalogs list this shrub, it is not what they are growing and selling under this name. This shrub is low-growing. The nurseries sell a taller shrub which has smaller leaves than the species, the variety *laevigatus*, described below.

Symphoricarpos albus laevigatus (Snowberry, Waxberry). Zone 4 to parts of Zone 3; 6′. Although the cultivated form of this shrub came from the west coast, where it is native to British Columbia and Washington, this variety of snowberry grows wild from the Gulf of St. Lawrence to the Virginia mountains in the east.

It is upright growing with arching branches which may bend to the ground when weighted with fruits. The flowers are tiny, pink and white, and not at all conspicuous. They appear in mid-June and the berries are fully colored in late August. These, as both botanical and common names imply, are white and waxy in appearance, unusual among shrub fruits. The leaves are small, bright green on the upper surfaces, paler green underneath.

This shrub thrives in dry soil where many others will not grow. It is used in gardens as a specimen, in shrub borders, on banks (to hang over them) or as an unclipped hedge.

Symphoricarpos × *chenaultii* (*S. microphyllus* × *S. orbiculatus*) (Chenault coralberry, Chenault's coralberry). Zone 6 to Zone 5b; 3′.

The difference between this shrub and *S. orbiculatus*, described below, is that this hybrid has a neater growth habit, the berries are larger and they

Symphoricarpos albus laevigatus, flowers.

are red only on the top sides. The undersides are white. Often each area is spotted with the color of the other. This is a handsome shrub when in berry and may be used wherever soil is not damp. It is pretty in the foreground of a shrub border or used as a ground cover on a bank, but is not sufficiently outstanding for use as a specimen.

Symphoricarpos chenaultii 'Hancock' (sometimes listed as 'Hancocki') originated in the Woodland Nurseries, Cooksville, Ontario and is a prostrate coralberry for use as a lower groundcover than *S.* × *chenaultii*.

Symphoricarpos 'Erect'.

This is simply a more upright-growing form of *chenaultii*. Its branches are vertical, its form narrow and it is an excellent plant for a low hedge—no clipping needed.

Symphoricarpos 'Magic Berry'.

Dwarf and compact, to about 3′ high, this selection has coral-red berries but, because the tips of the branches droop slightly, the fruits are held away from the body of the plant and therefore are not hidden by the leaves.

Symphoricarpos 'Mother of Pearl'.

This hybrid has creamy-pink berries.

Symphoricarpos orbiculatus (syn *S. vulgaris*, the name under which most catalogs list this shrub) (Indian currant, Coralberry, Buckbush, Snapberry,

Turkeyberry). Zone 2 to parts of Zone 1; 3'-4', sometimes to 6'.

In open woods and on stream banks, this shrub grows from South Dakota to Indiana and Illinois, Pennsylvania, and Ohio, south to Florida and Texas. It suckers, forming clumps as it spreads, so should be planted only where it need not be restrained. State highway departments often plant this shrub by the hundreds on steep banks to prevent soil erosion.

Its growth habit is upright, the leaves dull green and not particularly pretty. Inconspicuous flowers, borne in July and August in small clusters, may be yellowish-white but often are purplish. Fruits are coral-red, ripening in September and October.

Symphoricarpos racemosus (see *S. albus*).

Symphoricarpos vulgaris (see *S. orbiculatus*).

Symphoricarpos 'White Hedge'.

This is an upright-growing form with extra large white berries.

Symphoricarpos albus laevigatus, berried branch.

Symphoricarpos chenaultii 'Hancock', berries.

SYMPLOCOS

Symplocos paniculata (Sapphireberry, Sweetleaf, Asiatic symplocos). Zone 5; 15'.

Wide-spreading and yet dense in form, this is grown for its fragrant white flowers in late May or early June and the bright blue berries which follow them. It is too large a shrub for a small garden, thus its usefulness is restricted.

Even if it is considered for the large garden, one should realize that the flowers do not last long; that birds love the berries and will eat them as fast as they ripen. Even if the birds do not get them, they are on the plant in full color for only a week or so.

SYRINGA (Lilac)

Have you ever driven along a country road in May and seen a huge old lilac in full bloom by the foundation of what was once a home? Such survivors show not only the toughness and longevity of lilacs but also the regard in which they always have been held. If nothing else in the line of plants went along in that covered wagon, a few lilac suckers did.

Lilacs prefer slightly alkaline or neutral soil. They are grown for their beautiful, fragrant blooms. Most grow upright and are vigorous, producing large shrubs. Except in certain species, their foliage is not outstanding. Except for one species, they have no bright autumn foliage coloration and their brown seed pods certainly are not attractive. Furthermore, two pests attack almost any lilac in due course of time: lilac scale and borers, both discussed in Chapter 9.

I have written these discouraging words knowing perfectly well that they will deter no one who wants lilacs from owning one or many, but just for the record, so that a new gardener will know, at least, what he or she is up against.

When you are buying lilacs it is most important that you inquire whether they are grafted on common lilac (*S. vulgaris*) or on privet (*Ligustrum*). If they are, don't buy them at any price. Buy only lilacs grown on their own roots, that is from cuttings of the parent plants. This subject is discussed in more detail in Chapter 6 and it will pay you to read that discussion.

Even though they are gorgeous when in bloom, the hybrid lilacs which are most popular are not really plants for the small garden because of their suckering habit of growth. One of these hybrids may grow as wide as high, increasing in girth yearly by sending up new shoots around the outside of the plant. These may be allowed to grow if you want to propagate from the plants, but otherwise are a nuisance. The easiest way I know of to control suckers is this:

Dig the soil out around the base of the suckers until you can see where they grow from the main part of the plant. Cut them off at these points. Fit a piece of heavy linoleum around the part of the plant you wish to leave growing, right over the places from which the suckers grew and well beyond that area. Fit it tightly to the plant. Then replace the soil you removed and it will hold the linoleum in place.

One advantage of growing lilac species rather than the more popular so-called "French" hybrids,

is that most do not sucker. However, many of them still grow to be huge shrubs.

Before leaving the subject of lilac suckers, there is one more point to remember. A few suckers should be allowed to grow each year so that they may be used as replacements for the older stems, and the shrub constantly is renewed. The method of pruning old shrubs to renew them is described in Chapter 6.

If you keep the suckers under control and also cut the seed clusters from your lilacs as soon as they form, or better yet prune off the dying flowers, the bloom clusters the next year will be larger. This is fact, not fiction.

Lilacs, properly selected, will provide a blooming season of six weeks or more. Should you have room for several plants, bear this in mind and select species and cultivars accordingly.

Syringa amurensis japonica (syn *S. japonica* of the catalogs) is described in Chapter 15.

Syringa × chinensis (parentage not certain) (Chinese lilac, Rouen lilac). Zone 5 to part of Zone 4; 12'.

Both the botanical name and the first common name of this lilac are misleading. According to them one would think that the plant came from China. Actually, it was found in the botanic garden at Rouen, France, late in the eighteenth century as a chance hybrid.

Syringa chinensis, flower cluster.

307

The plant grows upright and spreading to form a dense shrub. It has slender branches which arch, especially when weighted with blooms in late May. The leaves are smaller than those of the common lilac (*S. vulgaris*) and daintier. Flowers are small, ½″ in diameter, borne in clusters to 6″ long and 4″ to 4½″ across. They are strong reddish purple (2.5 RP 5/10) in color and intensely fragrant.

This lilac is beautiful as a specimen plant. It also is a valuable addition to a shrub border of sufficient length so that it does not dwarf the border. It might also be used at house corners if the house were sufficiently large and high for such a big plant.

Syringa chinensis 'Alba' is the white-flowered form, rarely listed in catalogs, which is a pity.

Syringa chinensis rubra (see *S. chinensis* 'Saugeana').

Syringa chinensis 'Saugeana' (syn *S. c. rubra*) has red-lilac or lilac-red flowers and, probably because of their color, often is listed in catalogs as "sanguinea" instead of "saugeana."

Syringa, cut-leaved (see *S. laciniata*).

Syringa, French hybrids (see *S. vulgaris* hybrids).

Syringa japonica (see *S. amurensis japonica* in Chapter 15).

Syringa josikaea (Hungarian lilac). Zone 1; 12′.

Late flowering compared with other lilacs, usually blooming the first or second week in June, this often is confused with *S. villosa,* the late lilac, which blooms at about the same time. The leaves of the Hungarian lilac resemble those of the late lilac in shape, but are much glossier. The flower color is lilac-violet. Growth habit is upright and slightly spreading.

This species and *S. villosa* have produced a hybrid named *Syringa × henryi* and a selection from this cross is the cultivar 'Lutece', offered sometimes under that name but more often as "Henry Lutece" or "Henri Lutece." This has ¼″ diameter florets in clusters 6″ long and 3¾″ wide, colored light reddish purple (10 P 6/9).

There also has been hybridization of the Hungarian lilac with *S. reflexa.* Catalogs of lilac specialists offer the result of this cross as *S. × josiflexa* and at least one cultivar has been selected.

Syringa laciniata (syn *S. persica laciniata*) (Cutleaf or Cutleaved lilac). Zone 4; 6′.

Distinguished by its finely divided leaves on slender branches, this lilac often is planted as a

Syringa laciniata, flower clusters and finely cut foliage.

specimen. It blooms in May with ⅜″ diameter florets in clusters to 3½″ long, colored light purple (7.5 P 6/8).

Syringa microphylla (Littleleaf lilac, Everblooming lilac). Zone 5; 6′.

The first of the two common names given for this lilac is accurate, since the leaves are among the smallest grown by lilacs. The second common name, used by too many nurserymen, is far from accurate since it makes the gardener envision constant bloom. It is true that this lilac, in addition to its normal flowering in late May, has a few flowers in late summer and early fall, but these hardly justify the word "everblooming."

The shrub is upright, with arching branches, eventually grows much wider than high, blooms in late May and has pale lilac flowers. It is useful where the wide form and the small leaves are desirable—as a specimen, in a house planting or a border.

Syringa microphylla 'Superba' has single flowers, pale pink (2.5 R 9.3) in the bud and even paler when open. It is a delightful plant when in bloom, both for its flower color and its fragrance. Nurserymen often call it "daphne" lilac, but whether for its flower color or its fragrance I do not know. It blooms late in May, with smaller, tighter flower clusters than those of many other lilacs.

Syringa palibiniana (see *S. velutina*).

Syringa × persica (probably *S. afghanica × S. laciniata*) (Persian lilac, Persian elder, Persian jasmine). Zone 5 to part of Zone 4; 6′, often less.

There is an enormous amount of confusion in the nursery trade between this lilac and the Rouen (or Chinese) lilac. Most of the lilacs listed and sold as Persian actually are the Rouen. If you will ex-

Syringa microphylla 'Superba', above.

———————————

Syringa persica 'Alba', below. Notice the tiny leaves and compare with those of S. chinensis.

Syringa microphylla, flower detail. For leaf size see S. m. 'Superba' right, above.

amine the pictures of these two lilacs and notice both leaf shape and flower cluster form, you will know which is which at a glance when you see a plant in the nursery, even if it is not in bloom. To make certain that you actually get the lilac you want, either see the plant before you buy or read carefully the description of the plant in a catalog. If it is not sufficiently specific, write the nursery and ask for a sample of the foliage. This will tell you without a doubt which lilac is being sold.

The Persian lilac is, with the Korean dwarf lilac, the smallest of lilacs. Its growth habit is upright, the branches are slender, the flowers pale lilac, borne in small clusters in late May at the same time as those of the common lilac open. The most sensible use of this plant is as a specimen because it would be lost in a shrub border or even a smaller grouping of shrubs.

Syringa × *persica* 'Alba' is the white flowered form of the plant described above. The floret is ½" wide, the flower cluster to 8" long and 4"

Syringa 'Coral'. Notice cluster form and floret shape, both different from those of most lilacs.

across. Both the tube of the flower and its center are very pale purple (7.5 P 8/5).

Syringa × *persica laciniata* (see *Syringa laciniata*).

Syringa × *prestoniae* also spelled *"prestonae"* (*S. reflexa* × *S. villosa*) (Preston lilac). Zone 1; 10′.

The botanical name given above refers to a group of hybrid lilacs originated by Miss Isabella Preston when she was horticulturist of the Canadian Experimental Station, Ottawa, Ontario, Canada. This cross also has been made by other breeders, therefore I have listed the plants under *S. villosa* hybrids in the Buyer's Guide Chart. Far too many cultivars have been named in this group, for a great many, although sold under different cultivar names, are almost identical when they bloom.

These hybrids have two great assets—late flowering and extreme hardiness. Most of them flower in mid-June, which is several weeks after the common lilac and most of its hybrids are past bloom. All Preston lilacs are upright and dense in growth habit, vary somewhat in bulk or size, and have foliage similar to that of the late lilac (*S. villosa*). Their bloom spikes are large, too, comparing favorably with the largest clusters of the common lilac cultivars. The Preston lilacs are not, however,

really fragrant, though most of them lack the malodorousness of the blooms of the late lilac and a few are mildly fragrant.

These shrubs are so large and so dense that they even may be used as windbreaks to protect lower-growing shrubs or other plants. They also may be used in hedges or, where space is ample, as specimens.

My favorite of this group is 'Coral' which really has coral-pink buds although the color fan calls them strong pink (2.5 R 7/8) and pale pink (2.5 R 9/3) flowers. If you wish to buy one or more of these hybrids, you really ought to see them in bloom so you can select the flower color you like best.

Syringa pubescens (Hairy lilac). Zone 4; to 15′ but usually not more than 10′.

The outstanding characteristic of this lilac, as far as the gardener is concerned, is its fragrance, which is spicy. Its small pale lilac or pale pinkish blooms are borne in small clusters but there usually are many clusters on a shrub and, since they are borne in "pairs" they appear larger than they are.

The hairy lilac blooms with the first of the common lilacs and is also of value for this rather early flowering time.

Syringa reflexa 'Alba' with its pendant flower cluster.

Syringa reflexa (Nodding lilac). Zone 5; 12'.

Upright growing, with sturdy branches, this lilac differs from the others in the fact that the flower clusters are narrow and droop or nod from the branches. They grow to 5" long, with ¼" wide florets. Buds are bright pink, the flowers open pink on the outsides and white inside. This is a late-blooming lilac, usually blossoming the first or second week in June, with the Hungarian lilac. There is a white-flowered form, *S. r.* 'Alba.'

Syringa rothomagensis (see *S. chinensis*).

Syringa saugeana (see *S. chinensis* 'Saugeana').

Syringa × *swegiflexa* (*S. sweginzowii* × *S. reflexa*) (Pink pearl lilac). Zone 5 to part of Zone 4; 8'.

Blooming in early to mid-June, this lilac has red buds which open to pale pink (2.5 R 9/3) flowers borne in 6" long clusters. It is a fine addition to the group of late-blooming lilacs.

Syringa velutina (syn *S. palibiniana*) (Dwarf Korean lilac). Zone 5 to part of Zone 4; 6' to 8', but usually about 3'.

Here is a lilac that will fit into any garden. A small, neat plant with small leaves turning red in autumn and 6" long clusters of light purplish pink (2.5 RP 8/5) flowers with slightly darker tubes, (thus giving an overall impression of deeper flower color), this lilac blooms in early June.

At Wisley, the trial grounds of the Royal Horticultural Society of England, this lilac is used as a specimen plant in the large rock garden. It is small enough (and can easily be maintained that size by a slight amount of pruning) to be used in a house planting. It is well-placed near the front of a shrub border or might be used as a dense, compact specimen wherever such a plant is needed. It is available in "tree" or "standard" form for use in a formal garden.

Syringa villosa (Late lilac). Zone 1; 9', sometimes taller.

The big drawback to this lilac is that its flowers smell more like those of privet (to which lilacs are related) than they do like lilacs—and most people do not like their odor.

Aside from this, it is an extremely hardy lilac, upright and dense in form, blooming in early June to mid-June. Flower colors of this lilac vary because plants usually are grown from seeds (see discussion in Chapter 13, page 138). They may be any shade from white to rosy-lilac. My oldest plant of this lilac has moderate pink buds (2.5 R 8/5) and pale

Syringa swegiflexa, above.

Syringa velutina, below, with its small leaves and flower clusters.

 .

Syringa vulgaris 'Alba', left; Syringa vulgaris, right.

Syringa vulgaris right, with one of its hybrids, left. Compare sizes of florets and flower clusters.

pink (2.5 R 9/3 florets ¼" in diameter, grouped in clusters to 10" long and 9" across.

Plants produce many blooms so that a blossoming plant is a good landscape subject if only it is not placed where people constantly get the odor of the blooms. This lilac may be used for a wind-break or a heavy screen planting, also makes a fine unclipped hedge and can be used as a specimen.

Syringa villosa hybrids (see discussion under *S. prestoniae*).

Syringa vulgaris (Common lilac, English lilac, Blue ash, Blue-pipe privet, Pipe privet, Pipt tree, Roman willow, Celache). Zone 3; 15'.

This old-time, well-loved, fragrant lilac is as popular today as it ever was. Upright in form, with straight, heavy stems, this bears flowers in mid-May. Florets are ½" in diameter, clusters to 4" long and 3" wide. Bloom color is light purple (7.5 P 6/8).

This lilac is extremely hardy and thrives with little care, even growing wild in some parts of the country, though it has escaped from cultivation since there are no native wild lilacs in either the United States or Canada.

Syringa vulgaris 'Alba' is the white-flowered form of common lilac, also intensely fragrant.

Syringa vulgaris hybrids. Illustrated on Color Page III.

Practically every nursery in the country lists these as "French" hybrids. Actually, *Syringa vulgaris* is native to much of eastern Europe but the term "French" comes from the fact that a great many of these hybrids (cultivars) grown today are the products of one hybridizer—Victor Lemoine—who also gave gardeners many fine deutzias and mock oranges. His nursery in France was the birthplace of these hybrids.

However, many other hybridizers in other European countries and in North America also have hybridized the common lilac so the hybrids should not continue to be called "French."

There are hundreds of these cultivars. The best collection of them in the United States probably is that in Highland Park, Rochester, New York and a visit there at lilac time will provide a real thrill if you love lilacs. The Arnold Arboretum, Jamaica Plain, Massachusetts, also has a fine collection of lilacs and there are others on the continent.

Should you be confused by the numbers of cultivars sold, and wish recommendations as to which ones experts consider best, there is a booklet, "Lilacs for America," which lists those selected by a committee of the American Association of Botanical Gardens and Arboretums. It was published by the Association and is available from it. There are, of course, many people who disagree violently with the committee regarding, for instance, the best double-flowered white lilac, and so on, but you always can visit a collection of the plants in bloom and make your own choice.

Syringa vulgaris hybrids; double-flowered on left; single-flowered (with a few semi-double blooms) on right.

Syringa vulgaris, tree form. Some nurseries grow this lilac with a single main stem like a tree. Should you wish to buy a plant of this form, you will find the nurseries listed in the Buyer's Guide Chart.

TAMARIX (Tamarix, Tamarisk)

Tall, sometimes "leggy" shrubs with graceful, feathery foliage and large, fluffy clusters of tiny florets, usually borne at the tips of the branches, tamarix plants are grown mostly for their light, airy appearance, so different from that of most shrubs. They usually grow well in dry soil and will tolerate seaside conditions and even salt water spray.

The tall-growing species need to be pruned occasionally so that they do not grow too tall. The lower parts of the branches become bare of foliage if the plants are not pruned and so are unsightly.

Tamarix africana.

This shrub is listed in many northern catalogs but, since it is a native of the Mediterranian region and hardy only in the south, it is obvious that this name is incorrectly used. Usually the shrub sold under this name is *Tamarix tetrandra*.

Tamarix amurensis (see *T. pentandra*).

Tamarix gallica (French tamarix) Zone 4; 7'-25'.

This may grow as a shrub or as a small tree. It has slender, arching, wide-spread, brown branches with dull green or bluish-green leaves and white to rose-pink flowers in compact clusters in July and August. This shrub has escaped from cultivation and may be found growing wild in the south and as far north as Indiana and Massachusetts.

Tamarix hispida (Kashgar tamarix). Zone 4, even the northern part if planted in a sheltered spot; 4'.

Slender, upright branches, bluish-green foliage and pink flowers in large clusters at the ends of the branches all make this shrub desirable. The fact that it blooms in August and September makes it more so.

Tamarix hispida aestivalis (see *T. pentandra*).

Tamarix odessana (Odessa tamarix, Caspian tamarix). Zone 4; 6'-7'.

Upright in form, with slender branches, this has tiny leaves and little, pink, fluffy flowers in large, loose clusters in mid-July. This species flowers on wood of the same season's growth, so should be pruned in early spring, when necessary.

Tamarix parviflora (Small-flowered tamarix). Zone 5 to part of Zone 4; 15'.

313

Blooming in late May, this species makes it possible to have the airy, pink flowers of tamarix in spring as well as summer. As both botanical and common names suggest, the flowers are tiny. The branches are slender, arching and dark purple.

Prune this tamarix, if and when pruning is necessary, directly after it finishes blooming as it flowers on wood grown the previous year and pruning it in spring would eliminate the flower buds for that year.

Tamarix pentandra (Five stamen tamarix). Zone 2, possibly parts of Zone 1; 15'.

Purple branchlets, tiny, pale green leaves which give the usual feathery effect, and small pink flowers in mid-July are the characteristics of this shrub. As you see, from the hardiness zone given above, this is the hardiest tamarix. It does have a tendency to "legginess" and therefore needs hard pruning occasionally.

Tamarix pentandra 'Pink Cascade' (Plant patent #1275) Zone 5; 6'. Blue-green, feathery foliage and pink, feathery flower clusters borne well above the foliage and from July to September make this shrub a good choice for long-season bloom. Best results are said to be obtained if the shrub is pruned severely each spring.

Tamarix pentandra 'Rubra' (syn *Tamarix* 'Summer Glow') Zone 5; 6'. Tiny, blue-green leaves and tiny florets ⅛" in diameter, in spikes 9" long and 5" wide, colored deep purplish pink (7.5 RP 6/12) will ornament your garden if you decide to grow this shrub. Flowers appear from the beginning of July for a month or more.

Tamarix 'Summer Glow' (see *T. pentandra* 'Rubra').

TEUCRIUM

Teucrium chamaedrys (Germander, Chamaedrys germander). Zone 6 to southern part of Zone 5; 8"-10".

A neat little gray-leaved, almost evergreen shrublet, this has rose or purplish-rose flowers in thin spikes during most of the summer. It can be clipped to form a very low hedge for use as an edging for herb or rose beds. It also may be allowed to grow unclipped in a rock garden or at the front of a perennial border.

VACCINIUM (Blueberry, Huckleberry).

This genus includes the wild huckleberries and the cultivated blueberries. It is listed here because the low bush blueberry is a good ground cover in dry soil and the highbush blueberry is an excellent

Tamarix parviflora, flowering branch, above;

closeup of flower clusters, below.

314

Flowers of Tamarix pentandra 'Rubra' (Summer Glow).

Teucrium chamaedrys, flowering stem.

ornamental, even if most people think of it only as a fruit-bearing plant.

Vaccinium corymbosum (Highbush blueberry, Swamp blueberry, Whortleberry). Zone 4 to part of Zone 3; Usually about 6', but may grow taller in favorable situations.

Found growing wild in swamps and low areas, but sometimes in drier places, from Nova Scotia to southern Quebec and Maine, westward to Wisconsin and Minnesota, southward to Florida and Louisiana, this plant is the forerunner of our cultivated blueberries. The first cultivars were selected from wild plants for their extra-large fruits.

Highbush blueberries are used in gardens both for foliage and fruits, though their flowers are as pretty as those of many another ornamental and prettier than some. These shrubs may be used for unusual and beautiful unclipped hedges. The autumn color of the foliage, which is yellow, orange and red, is so vivid that they even are occasionally used in house plantings.

Growth habit is upright, foliage (any time but autumn) is glossy green, and the flowers are white and waxy, borne in dense clusters in late May. The

315

Blooms of a Vaccinium corymbosum hybrid.

berries, as you know, are blue to blue-black and arrive at edible stage from the end of June to early September, partly because not all the fruits in a cluster ripen at one time and partly because different cultivars bear fruits at different times.

The *Vaccinium corymbosum* cultivars are the blueberries which are grown commercially and may be grown by any home gardener who possesses acid soil or is willing to acidify it (as explained in Chapter 5, page 36).

VIBURNUM (Viburnum)

This is a large genus with many members useful to the gardener. Almost all viburnums are easy to grow, tolerant of almost any soil, and many will flower and fruit in semi-shade. Some are evergreen; most of these hardy only in the south. Others are semi-evergreen in the north, evergreen in the south. And more are deciduous in any climate.

Some are grown primarily for their handsome foliage which, in many, turns beautiful colors in autumn. Others are primarily interesting for their flowers or fruits and finally, some are grown for their branching habit.

If you will glance through the photographs which illustrate the next few pages, you will see how wide a range of foliage form, flower form and fruit colors are available to the gardener in this single genus.

Not only that, but flowering times vary greatly and so do the months during which the fruit ripens. There is usually some viburnum in bloom in my garden from late April until mid-July.

All viburnums have florets arranged in groups, but the forms of these groupings vary, though all

Closeup of luscious blueberries. Note form and "bloom."

Cluster of blueberries scaled to blooms, above, left.

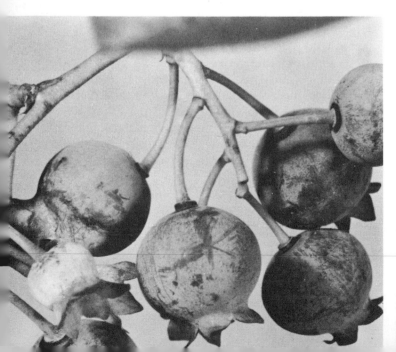

are borne at the tips of stems. Some clusters are flat, others almost half-round, still others almost completely ball-shaped. There also may be two different types of flowers: small, fertile blooms and large, sterile flowers, both borne in the same flower cluster in some viburnums.

When fruits mature they may be red, blue, black, or even yellow, and many of the species have fruits which change from one color to another during the ripening process. When fruits of several colors are on the plant at one time they present an interesting effect.

It must be remembered that fruits may not be produced every year on every plant, for fruits are "set" only when weather conditions encourage insects to fly and pollinate the flowers. It is best to plant viburnums in groups, to insure pollination as often as possible.

The usual use for viburnums in the garden is in a shrub border, but some are best suited to woodland planting and others are sufficiently handsome for use as specimen plants. Because there are tree-like viburnums (described in Chapter 15), medium-sized and small viburnums, the specific uses will be indicated in the descriptions below.

Only viburnums listed in several to many of the catalogs are described here. You will find others available from specialists in this genus, as indicated in the Buyer's Guide Chart.

Viburnum acerifolium (Mapleleaf viburnum, Dockmanie, Arrow-wood). Zone 4; 6'.

Found in dry woods from southwest Quebec to Minnesota, south to New England, Georgia, and Tennessee, this viburnum is best used in a wild garden or in the woods; there it will grow beautifully in deep shade where few other woody plants would grow at all. It will not, however, flower frequently under these conditions. It needs a little sun in order to bloom. The leaves are so prettily shaped that if flowers are not a prime consideration, they make this a satisfactory shrub for any shaded location. Leaves turn pinkish to purplish in autumn. Flowers are creamy-white and appear in late May to June, sometimes continuing to open occasionally until late July. The sparse fruits on upright stems are first crimson, later turning purplish-black.

Viburnum americanum (see *V. trilobum*).

Viburnum bitchiuense (Bitchiu viburnum, Yeddo viburnum). Zone 5 to part of Zone 4; 10'.

Flowering in early May, at the same time as the Koreanspice viburnum (*V. carlesii*), with white to pinkish blooms, the Bitchiu viburnum often has been confused with the Koreanspice.

Both are useful, but the Bitchiu has a more open form because its branches are smaller and thinner. The foliage and flower clusters also are smaller and the cluster form is less compact. Blooms of both species are equally fragrant and it would be hard to choose between the two if one could have only a single species in the garden. If this were the case, the fact that the Bitchiu viburnum is slightly hardier might be the deciding factor. Foliage color of the Bitchiu viburnum is bluish-green, turning dull red in autumn.

Viburnum × *bodnantense* (*V. fragrans* × *V. grandiflorum*). Zone 6 to southern part of Zone 5; 10'.

This hybrid is hardier than *V. grandiflorum*, but still not sufficiently hardy to be used in the far north. In flower, leaf, and growth habit, it is intermediate between its parents. It has dark, rose-colored buds, but the loose flower clusters, opening in April, are only faintly pink. Fruits are black, ripening in early August. Although this hybrid was produced in the 1930's, it still is not widely listed by North American nurseries.

Viburnum × *burkwoodii* (*V. carlesii* × *V. utile*). Zone 5 to part of Zone 4; 6'-8'.

Glossy, dark green foliage which is evergreen in the south and in mild winters may be semi-evergreen in the north, changes to orange or bright red in autumn. Fragrant, pinkish white flowers in early to mid-May much like those of the Koreanspice) and black fruits maturing in early August characterize this hybrid. Some nurseries describe it as "an improved *carlesii*," but I still prefer the Koreanspice viburnum to any of its hybrids and I own most of them.

Viburnum × *burkwoodii* 'Chenault' (*V. carlesii* × *V. utile*) (syn *V. chenaultii*). Zone 5; 6'.

This viburnum tends to be semi-evergreen in the south, but is deciduous in the north. It has finer-textured leaves and a more compact growth habit than *V. burkwoodii*, but not as compact as the Koreanspice viburnum (*V. carlesii*). It has pink florets, 3/8" in diameter, in 2" to 2¼" clusters, is fragrant, but not as much so as either the Koreanspice or Judd viburnums. It blooms after the Judd viburnum.

Viburnum × *carlcephalum* (parentage uncertain) (Fragrant snowball). Zone 6 to southern part of Zone 5; 6'.

This is a widely-spreading, openly-branched shrub with larger, coarser, and more shiny foliage

Viburnum burkwoodii 'Chenault'.

Viburnum carlcephalum.

Viburnum carlesii.

Comparative flower sizes of Viburnum carlcephalum, top, and V. carlesii, bottom.

The fruits, in the infrequent times when they appear, are black and seldom seen because they are hidden under the foliage and the birds find and eat them as soon as they ripen. At that time in summer the birds can find few other fruits to eat.

Unfortunately, nurserymen too often graft or bud this lovely viburnum on vigorously-growing understocks like *V. lantana,* the wayfaring tree. They do this to save time in getting a plant of saleable size, which is fine for them but not for the gardener who buys the plant. The understock too frequently sends out its own branches and if not cut back immediately they are seen, these soon will outgrow the more desirable Koreanspice portion, either reducing it to a subsidiary plant or killing it altogether by shading it unduly. You will find further discussion of this subject on page 138. You also will find that the common use of an understock makes the Koreanspice viburnum subject to a graft blight and so it often is considered a short-lived plant.

Occasionally a nursery grows—and lists—this viburnum on its own roots. In this case, of course, there will be no difficulty with constant pruning of an understock or with graft blight.

than the Koreanspice and ball-shaped, 4″ to 5″ diameter flower clusters (see photograph comparing the bloom sizes of the two viburnums). These flowers are pinkish to white and clove-scented, open as those of the Koreanspice are fading in early to mid-May, with the flowers of *V. burkwoodii.* The foliage colors brilliant red in autumn.

Because of the growth habit and the large flowers, this shrub needs to be used as a specimen in a very special place where these characteristics will help the landscape plan. The plant does not blend well in a shrub border and, except in bloom, is not particularly helped by an evergreen background.

The fragrant snowball is hard to transplant and reestablish. It may take several tries before you can coax one to grow, but once it has reestablished its roots it will cause you no further trouble.

Viburnum carlesii (Koreanspice viburnum, Fragrant viburnum). Zone 5 to part of Zone 4; 5′.

It is necessary only to pass within 30′ of this viburnum or one of its hybrids when it is in bloom to notice the fragrance of the flowers. These, in the case of this viburnum, are produced on a compact, spherically shaped plant which has dull green leaves, grayish on the undersides and turning reddish purple in fall. The florets are pale pink, fading to white, 9/16″ in diameter, and arranged in 3½″ to 4″ diameter clusters, rounded at the tops. They open in early May.

Viburnum carlesii, left and Viburnum juddii, right. Note difference in flower cluster forms.

319

This shrub is ideal for use in an intimate setting such as a planting around an outdoor living area or near a house door. There you can enjoy its fragrance each year without any effort.

As with other shrubs like forsythias, some nurseries offer the Koreanspice viburnum grown to a single stem, as a standard or "tree" form.

Viburnum carlesii 'Compactum' is a dwarf form with an extremely compact growth habit. Its blooms also are fragrant, but the foliage is darker green than that of the species. This form should be even more useful in the small garden than its parent. It is not a hybrid but a seedling discovered by happy chance.

Viburnum cassinoides (Withe rod, Swamp viburnum, Swamp black-haw, False Paraguay tea, Wild raisin, Appalachian tea, Teaberry). Zone 4; 4'-6', sometimes taller.

While the flowers of this viburnum do not compare with those of many others for beauty, they still are attractive. The tiny, creamy-white, fertile florets are arranged in clusters 3" to 4" in diameter and slightly rounded at the tops. Blooms usually appear the second week in June. They are set off by the glossy, yellow-green leaves and are followed by berries which put on a real color show. They first are green, then yellowish-white, then pink, bright blue, dark blue and finally almost black. At some times all of these berry colors are present in one cluster at one time. The only difficulty is that birds love these berries and eat them as soon as each one ripens—in August and September.

In a cultivated garden the form of this shrub is upright and compact, though in the woods, where the plants often lack sufficient light, they grow tall and straggly. This plant is found in thickets and near the edges of woods, as well as in swamps, from Newfoundland to Ontario, south to Nova Scotia, New England, Long Island, Delaware and Maryland, to upland Alabama, westward to Tennessee, Ohio, Indiana and Wisconsin.

The common name "withe rod" comes from the former use of its branches for switches by old-time school masters.

Viburnum chenaultii (see *V. burkwoodii* 'Chenault').

Viburnum dentatum (syn *V. pubescens*) (Arrow wood, Southern arrow wood). Zone 3; 15'.

In moist areas this viburnum may be found forming thickets, which it rarely does in dry, sandy soil. It is native from Rhode Island southward along the coast to New Jersey and Florida, west-

Viburnum cassinoides.

ward to Pennsylvania, West Virginia, Tennessee and Texas.

It flowers in early to mid-June, bearing creamy-white, flat flower clusters to 2" in diameter, followed by abundant, dark blue berries ripening in September. The leaves, sharply toothed at the edges, are glossy, dark green, and turn to rust-red in autumn.

The plant grows rapidly and vigorously, usually with many upright stems from the ground. It should be used in a large shrub border or in a wild garden but certainly never where space is limited. It grows in any soil in full sun or fairly heavy shade.

Viburnum dilatatum (Linden viburnum, Japanese cranberry bush). Zone 6 to southern part of Zone 5; 8'.

The bright scarlet berries in clusters that may be 5" across, coloring in September, combined with the purplish-red autumn color of its leaves, make this a handsome plant for any but the smallest garden. During the remainder of the season, the leaves are green and hairy on both sides, vary greatly in size and shape, and resemble those of the linden tree in general form. Flowers are cream-

white, mildly fragrant, borne in 1″ diameter clusters in late May or early June. At that time a plant is covered with them. Growth habit is upright, rounded and compact.

One advantage in growing this viburnum is that the fruit stays on it for several weeks or more. More fruit is formed when several plants known to be grown from seeds are planted fairly close together.

There also is a yellow-fruited form, *V. dilatatum* 'Xanthocarpum', and a cultivar named 'Moraine', selected for its larger and more abundant fruits.

Viburnum fragrans (Fragrant viburnum). Zone 6 to southern part of Zone 5; 9′.

Blooming before the forsythias in early April, this is the first viburnum to flower. Buds are deep pink to red, the flowers blush pink turning white and, of course, they are fragrant. They may be forced to bloom indoors even earlier since the flower buds were formed the previous autumn. In fact, forcing blooms is a good idea, for outdoors the flowers may last only two or three days. Except for their earliness and fragrance, the flowers are not outstanding. In severe winters in the north flower buds are killed, so that a plant should be set in a protected place.

The shrub grows upright, sometimes spreading by means of suckers. Leaves are 2″ to 3″ long, with a bronzy undertone to their green. They become

Viburnum dentatum, flowers above; berries below. Note "toothed" or "dentate" leaf margins indicated in the plant's botanical name.

Viburnum dilatatum, fruit cluster.

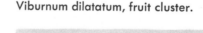

Viburnum lantana, flowers above; fruits below, showing varying degrees of ripeness.

even more bronze in color in summer and turn reddish-maroon in autumn. While the fruits are red, turning black, and mature in early summer, they are not effective in the garden for two reasons: there are not many of them and they are almost hidden by the leaves. They also are beloved of birds, so they soon disappear.

Viburnum × juddii (*V. carlesii × V. bitchiuense*). Zone 6 to southern part of Zone 5; 6'.

More spreading in form and more bushy than *V. carlesii,* this has flowers and leaves which might be described as midway between those of its parents. The flower buds are pink, but flowers are white. They bloom in early May, with the Koreanspice viburnum, before the Chenault viburnum. They are almost as fragrant as those of the Koreanspice viburnum.

As usual with these hybrids, the black fruits, if formed, go unnoticed under the leaves or disappear down the gullets of birds. Nurserymen advertise this plant as "an improved *carlesii*" and many people consider it superior to that species. I cannot agree with them. I feel that each shrub has its points and neither one is superior to the other.

Viburnum lantana (Wayfaring tree). Zone 4; 10' or more. Illustrated on Color Page VI.

Tall and upright, dense and rounded in outline, the wayfaring tree has round, gray-green leaves turning red in autumn and abundant clusters of creamy-white sterile flowers in late May to early June. The oval, 1¼" long fruits are first green, then greenish yellow underneath and vivid red on top, then red, later turning black. Often all color stages appear on the shrub at the same time. The bright color of the fruits lasts only about a week, however, before they turn black. During winter they wrinkle like dried raisins and birds gradually eat them all.

The usefulness of this large, almost tree-like shrub, lies in its ease of growth and its adaptability to almost any soil, including one that is dry. It also is hardy. It may be used at the back of a shrub border or at the edge of the woods. Where there is plenty of room, it also might be used as a specimen plant.

Viburnum × lantanaphyllum (*V. lantana × V. rhytidophyllum*). Zone 6 to southern part of Zone 5; 8'.

Larger and better looking leaves than the leather leaf viburnum, *V. rhytidophyllum,* and red berries turning blackish are the characteristics of this hybrid.

Viburnum lentago (see Chapter 15).

Viburnum molle (Possum-haw, Silky viburnum, Kentucky viburnum). Zone 6; 12'.

Found on bluffs and in woods from Indiana to Missouri, south to Kentucky and Arkansas, this viburnum has light gray branches and shiny, dark green leaves that are paler green and hairy on the under sides. The older bark flakes off the branches, thus giving the shrub winter interest. The flowers, appearing in late May, are cream-white to white, the clusters attached to an exceptionally long stem. Fruits are blue-black and ripen in late August to early September.

Viburnum opulus (European cranberry bush, Highbush cranberry, May rose, Ople-tree, Pincushion tree). Zone 4 to southern part of Zone 3; 12'.

Strong, dense growth; three-lobed leaves, turning orange to red in autumn; flowers in late May which are creamy-white and in flat clusters composed of fertile flowers in the center and sterile flowers around the outside; and vivid red (5 R 5/12) berries which hang on the plant all winter, becoming translucent with age, are all reasons for growing this plant.

Another reason is that this plant is tolerant of dry situations and of heat. It may be massed for colorful effect when it is in bloom or in fruit, or used in a shrub border. One or two plants set along the edge of water are lovely in winter while their berries still hang and are reflected in the water. There is no sense in trying to use these fruits for jelly as they are much too bitter.

Viburnum opulus 'Compactum' is a dwarf form with many more berries than the larger-growing species.

Viburnum opulus 'Nanum' rarely, if ever, flowers or fruits. It is used solely for its dense, 2'-high growth, well covered with foliage. It may be used for a low hedge and, even if planted in a quite formal area, rarely needs pruning. The most interesting use for it that I have seen is at the Cooley Rose Garden in Lansing, Michigan, where it has been clipped to form a low balustrade on either side of a short flight of broad steps leading from one level of the garden to another.

Viburnum opulus 'Roseum' (syn *V. o. sterile*) (European snowball, Common snowball, Guelder rose, Elder rose). Zone 4 to southern part of Zone 3; 12'. The hardiest of the snowballs, those viburnums with fully-rounded clusters of all sterile flowers, this can be a gorgeous sight when in flower, but usually is marred by having its leaves contorted

Viburnum opulus, fertile flowers in center, sterile blooms around outer edge of cluster.

Fruits, showing color changes as they mature.

323

by aphid infestations. Sometimes the stems also become oddly twisted. The new systemic insecticides will completely control this trouble if you wish to use them.

The blooms, which may be 3″ in diameter, open in mid-May, are at first the same color as lime sherbet, gradually turning white as they enlarge in size. In some plants these white blooms gradually become tinged with pink to rose as they age.

Since the blooms are composed solely of sterile flowers, no fruits follow them. The foliage looks much the same as that of the species but does not turn red in autumn.

Viburnum opulus sterile (see *V. o.* 'Roseum').

Viburnum opulus, tree form.

Some nurseries grow this viburnum as a standard or "tree," trained with a single stem.

Viburnum opulus 'Xanthocarpum' is the yellow-fruited form of *V. opulus.* Its ¼″ fruits are borne in clusters to 4″ in diameter and are brilliant yellow (2.5 Y 9/9) in color.

Viburnum plicatum (syn *V. tomentosum sterile, V. t. plicatum*) (Japanese snowball). Zone 6 to southern part of Zone 5; 9′, and as wide as it is high.

With wide-spreading, horizontal branches arranged in tiers, this is a handsome shrub. The flower clusters are arranged along the top sides of these branches. They are composed entirely of

Viburnum opulus 'Xanthocarpum' with yellow berries.

Viburnum opulus 'Roseum' with all sterile flowers in "snowball" form.

large, sterile white flowers and are at their best in late May, about a week later than *V. plicatum tomentosum*. Of course there are no fruits to follow later since the blooms are sterile.

The leaves of this plant are oval and quite long, dull green, smooth on top and slightly hairy underneath. They turn red to bronzy-purple in autumn.

Viburnum plicatum 'Grandiflorum' (syn *V. tomentosum* 'Grandiflorum') has slightly larger flowers than the species.

Viburnum plicatum 'Mariesii' (syn *V. tomentosum mariesii*) (Maries doublefile viburnum). This is a selection with larger sterile flowers, to 1″ in diameter, borne in larger clusters than those of the species. It is so beautiful in bloom that it has to be seen to be believed.

Viburnum plicatum 'Rotundifolium' (Roundleaf doublefile viburnum). Zone 5; 8′.

This has broader leaves than the variety and blooms several weeks earlier. The foliage turns red in autumn; the flowers are of the fully rounded "snowball" type.

Viburnum plicatum tomentosum (syn *V. tomentosum*) (Doublefile viburnum). Zone 5; 8′-10′.

The common name of this plant refers to the placing of the flower clusters in a double file along the top sides of the branches which may extend for 10′ to 12′ wide or even more on a fully-grown plant. The horizontal branching habit plus the length of the branches give this shrub a pyramidal form.

Viburnum plicatum 'Mariesii', closeup of cluster.

Viburnum plicatum 'Mariesii', group of flower clusters.

Viburnum plicatum tomentosum, below.

The leaves are dull yellowish-green with a few hairs scattered on the undersides. They are from 3″ to 6″ long. In autumn they change color to a dull, purplish-red. The flowers appear in mid-to-late May and the large clusters are composed of sterile flowers around the outsides with a group of small, fertile flowers in the center. Sterile flowers are white; fertile flowers cream-white.

In July the upright clusters of small, oval fruits ripen, first becoming red, then turning blue-black. They may be on the shrub for two full weeks before the birds devour them.

Viburnum prunifolium (see Chapter 15).

Viburnum pubescens (see *V. dentatum*).

Viburnum × *rhytidophylloides* (*V. rhytidophyllum* × *V. lantana*). Zone 6 to southern part of Zone 5; 8′ to 10′ in the south, lower in the north.

Hardier than its evergreen parent, *V. rhytidophyllum*, this plant looks much like it but has broader leaves, not quite so wrinkled; and staying on the plant longer in late autumn. In late May small clusters of creamy-white fertile flowers open, to be followed by small clusters of fruits which first are red and later change to black.

The difference in appearance between this plant and the leatherleaf viburnum is not marked, so it might just as well be substituted for the less hardy viburnum.

Viburnum rhytidophylloides fruits. Note buds already formed for next year's flowers.

Viburnum rhytidophyllum (Leatherleaf viburnum). Zone 6; 10′.

This shrub has heavy branches growing upright and may be round-topped to pyramidal in form. Its semi-evergreen (in Zone 6) to evergreen (south of that zone) foliage is very dark green, leathery in texture, curling like the leaves of rhododendron in cold weather.

The plant should be set where it is sheltered from the wind, and it will grow well only in good soil. The flower buds form in autumn, remain on the plant all winter, to open in mid-May into large, yellow-white or cream-white flower clusters. Scarlet fruits, which turn black as they age, appear in September. This plant is used as a specimen and is particularly effective against a building. It does not blend well with other shrubs but looks better with needled evergreens.

Viburnum sargentii (Sargent cranberry bush, Sargent viburnum, Manchurian cranberry bush). Zone 5 to part of Zone 4; 12′.

Resembling the European cranberry bush in form, flower and fruit, but slightly larger and more vigorous, this shrub may be substituted for the European cranberry bush and vice versa. The Sargent cranberry bush has darker branchlets which are more corky and a little more color in the foliage. The cream-white flowers are arranged in flat clusters with the small, fertile blooms in the center, ringed with the large, sterile flowers. Fruits are round or oval, red, highly acid to taste, and stay on the shrub for months. There never are as many fruits on this viburnum as on *V. opulus*.

Viburnum setigerum (syn *V. theiferum*) (Tea viburnum). Zone 6 to southern part of Zone 5; 10′, sometimes a little more.

Narrowly upright in form, sometimes "leggy," this shrub has arching branches, large, shiny, dark green leaves (to 4″ long) which turn yellow-orange and red in autumn. The flower buds are faintly pinkish-yellow. The fragrant flowers are borne in flat, 1½″ diameter clusters in early June and all are fertile. The berries are oval, ⅜″ long, ¼″ wide, and strong reddish orange (7.5 R 5/12) in color. With the first frost (provided the birds have left them on that long) they turn translucent and then brown. There is an orange-fruited form which is much handsomer when in berry than the species.

The common name refers to the use of the leaves for making a tea drunk by monks in the parts of China where this shrub grows wild.

Viburnum sieboldii (see Chapter 15).

Viburnum setigerum, flowers left, fruits right.

Viburnum theiferum (see *V. setigerum*).

Viburnum tomentosum (see *V. plicatum tomentosum*).

Viburnum tomentosum plicatum (see *V. plicatum*).

Viburnum tomentosum grandiflorum (see *V. plicatum* 'Grandiflorum').

Viburnum tomentosum mariesi (see *V. plicatum* 'Mariesii').

Viburnum tomentosum sterile (see *V. plicatum*).

Viburnum trilobum (syn *V. americanum*) (American cranberry bush, Cranberry bush, Highbush cranberry, High cranberry, Highbush, Pimbina, Cherry wood, Dow-rowan-tree, Water elder, Marsh elder, Gadrise, Gaiter tree, Gattan tree, Grouse berry, Love roses). Zone 2; 12'. Illustrated on Color Page VIII.

If you want to make delicious home-grown cranberry jelly, this is the shrub to choose. Its form, foliage, flowering and fruiting habits are quite similar to those of both the European cranberry bush and the Sargent cranberry bush, but, being a native shrub, it is hardier than either of them.

It grows wild in cool woods and slopes, as well as shores of bodies of water from Newfoundland to British Columbia and south to Nova Scotia, New England and Pennsylvania; is found in Ohio, Michigan, northern Indiana and Illinois and northeast Iowa, the Black Hills of South Dakota, Wyoming and Washington.

Though similar to the European form, this cranberry bush grows more widely spread and is generally more openly branched than its European counterpart. The foliage is smooth on the undersides while the leaves of *V. opulus* are sometimes quite hairy. The fruits, if you do not cook them, stay bright and cheery all winter.

Viburnum trilobum, flower clusters.

327

Viburnum trilobum, berries.

Flowers, too, are similar—flat clusters of both sterile and fertile flowers, the one around the outside of the other. The large (5/16″ long), oval berries are first brilliant yellow (2.5 Y 9/9) on one side, vivid red (5 R 5/12) on the other, and then gradually turn to red. If not picked and used for jelly, they will stay on the plant all winter on their drooping stems, making a plant a real asset in the garden. The berries are particularly effective when seen against snow or the dark color of water in winter.

Viburnum wrightii (Wright viburnum). Zone 6 to southern part of Zone 5; 7′-8′.

This shrub is narrowly upright in form with oval to rounded leaves which turn crimson in autumn. The berries are showy, bright scarlet. They are produced in more quantity and are larger than those of *V. dilatatum* so that this species is preferable for garden purposes. The berries also begin to color early in August and still are on the plant several months later. Flowers are creamy-white, in clusters and all are fertile.

If you wish to buy this viburnum, remember that most nurserymen grow it from seeds and therefore offer for sale a variable group of plants. Actually it should be grown only from cuttings taken from a plant known to fruit well. Because it is confused with *V. dilatatum* by nurserymen, and also because of the variation in plants from seeds, I would advise you to see the plant you buy in fruit before you purchase it. Since the shrub can be moved satisfactorily in autumn as well as in spring, you could mark your plant and transplant it later in the season.

VITEX (Chaste tree)

Vitex agnus-castus 'Latifolia' (syn *V. macrophylla*) (Chaste tree, Hemp tree, Monks' pepper tree). Zone 6 to southern part of Zone 5; 3′. Illustrated on Color Page VI.

Grown for its beautiful, cut-leaved foliage and its light violet (10 PB 6/8) flowers which start to bloom in mid-August and continue through September, vitex is worth a place in your garden.

Vitex is a southern shrub. In the north it dies back to the ground in even a fairly mild winter. This makes no difference as far as the bloom is concerned for the shrub bears flowers on wood of the current season. In spring the dead branches should be cut to the ground and new ones will grow from the roots, forming a whole new shrub the flowers of which will be welcome in late summer.

Because of this lack of hardiness, the shrub never grows much higher than 3′ in Zone 5b. In the south, of course, it is much taller, to 15′.

The leaves are gray and aromatic. They contrast beautifully with the soft light violet flowers.

Except for the necessary drastic pruning in spring, this shrub is easy to grow and presents no problems. It is upright in growth, with almost vertical branches.

Vitex macrophylla (see *V. agnus-castus* 'Latifolia').

Vitex agnus-castus 'Latifolia' flowers.

Vitex agnus-castus 'Latifolia', closeup of blooms.

WEIGELA (Weigela) (Formerly classified as Diervilla and still called that by some gardeners and some nurserymen)

Please note the spelling of the name of this genus. It is not W-e-i-g-e-l-*i*-a, but W-e-i-g-e-l-a; not wy-gee' le-uh, but wy-gee'-luh. It is so frequently misspelled in nursery catalogs and on nursery tags that, in the interests of accuracy, your attention is called to this here.

Weigelas are a group of shrubs grown for their beautiful, trumpet-shaped flowers and, in several cases, for bronze or variegated leaves. They are easy to transplant and grow, mature rapidly, and bloom with the late lilacs, the early deutzias and mock oranges, and the last of the spring-flowering spireas. In addition to this blooming period, they are likely to bear occasional flowers during summer.

Weigela 'Abel Carriere' grows 5' high, has deep pink flowers.

Weigela amabilis (see *W. florida*).

Weigela 'Boskoop Glory' is grown for its large, salmon-pink blooms.

Weigela 'Bristol Ruby' is patented by Bristol Nursery, Bristol, Connecticut. It grows 2½' high, has strong purplish red (7.5 RP 4/11) flowers, 1¼" in diameter with ½" long tubes. There is a burst of bloom in June and occasional flowers during summer.

Weigela 'Bristol Snowflake' (sometimes listed as 'Snowflake') is a white-flowered counterpart of 'Bristol Ruby'.

Weigela candida (see *W. florida* 'Alba').

Weigela 'Eva Rathke' has strong purplish red (10 RP 4/12) flowers, slightly lighter inside. Plant grows to 5'.

Weigela 'Feerie' (sometimes listed as 'Fairy') has light pink flowers and is May-June blooming.

Weigela floribunda (Crimson weigela). Zone 5 to part of Zone 4; 6'-7'.

Dark crimson flowers and hairy branches distinguish this weigela. It is best known for its popular cultivars, some of which are described above.

Weigela florida (syn *W. amabilis, W. rosea*) (Rose weigela). Zone 5 to part of Zone 4; 6'-9'.

Growth habit is upright and spreading, sometimes with branches slightly arched. The leaves are long and pointed, dark green, smooth on top but hairy at the veins underneath. Flowers are ¾" in diameter at the opening of the tube which is ¾" long and flared like a trumpet. New flowers are white, tinged deep purplish pink (5 RP 6/10) on

Weigela 'Bristol Snowflake'.

329

Weigela 'Eva Rathke', above.

———————

Weigela florida, below.

Weigela florida 'Variegata', below.

the outsides. Older flowers are moderate purplish pink (5 RP 5/10). Thus the effect is of two-toned blooms. The blossoms open in early to mid-June.

Weigela florida 'Alba' (syn *W. candida*) (White weigela). This is the white-flowered form of the species. It does not always grow into as large a plant as does the species.

Weigela florida 'Purpurea' (syn *W. purpurea, W. foliis purpureus, W.* 'Java Red') is a bronze-leaved form. Some nurseries call this foliage "purple," but it is not at all like the color of the "purple-leaved plums" or similar plants.

Weigela florida 'Variegata' (Variegated weigela). Zone 5; 4'. This shrub has leaves edged and variegated brilliant yellow green (2.5 GY 8/9). Despite the coloring, it blends well with other shrubs, which many variegated shrubs do not.

New flowers are white, tinged on the outer sides of the petals and in the throats with light purplish pink (5 RP 5/8). Older blooms are 1" in diameter and are strong, purplish pink (7.5 RP 7/10) in color.

Weigela florida 'Venusta'. Zone 4. This is the hardiest of the weigelas. It has rose-pink flowers in May, several weeks before those of most weigelas. It has smaller leaves than those of the rose weigela and the flowers are borne in dense clusters. It is considered the most graceful of all weigelas.

Weigela foliis purpureus (see *W. florida* 'Purpurea').

Weigela 'Henderson' is a strong-growing plant with deep rose blooms.

Weigela 'Java Red' (see *W. florida* 'Purpurea').

Weigela 'Newport Red' (see *W.* 'Vanicek').

Weigela purpurea (see *W. florida* 'Purpurea').

Weigela rosea (see *W. florida*).

Weigela 'Vanicek' (also listed as *vanicecki,* syn *W.* 'Newport Red') Zone 5; 6'-8'.

A satisfactory weigela where a large plant is desirable. Flowers are 1¼" in diameter, strong purplish red in two different tones—7.5 RP 4/10 and 7.5 RP 5/12 with a yellow line down the tube to guide bees to the nectary.

Weigela variegata (see *W. florida* 'Variegata').

Weigela 'Vanicek', above.

Weigela seed capsules, below.

XANTHORHIZA

Xanthorhiza apiifolia (see *Xanthorhiza simplicissima*).

Xanthorhiza simplicissima (syn *Xanthorhiza apiifolia*) (Yellowroot, Shrub yellowroot). Zone 5; 2'.

This shrub is excellent for underneath trees, covering moist shady or sunny banks, or for edging a shrub border. It also makes a good ground cover as it is not only low-growing but its plants are uniform in height. It spreads rapidly by underground stolons. The leaves resemble those of celery and are yellow-green. Flowers are purplish and borne in clusters but are infinitesimal so that most people are certain that this shrub has none. Fruits also are inconspicuous. Both bark and roots are yellow and bitter to the taste. A dye is made from the roots.

Yellowroot is found in damp woods and along streams from New York to West Virginia and south to Florida and Alabama.

ZENOBIA

Zenobia pulverulenta (Andromeda). Zone 6 to southern part of Zone 5; usually 2'-3', but may reach 6'-9'.

Found wild in peaty or damp, sandy places in southeastern Virginia to northeastern South Carolina, this shrub is upright in form with branches which sometimes arch. The leaves and twigs are covered with a white "bloom," which is what the specific name suggests. A member of the heather group, this plant needs damp, acid soil to thrive.

The flowers are white, bell-shaped, found in clusters and appear in late May to early June.

There are several forms of this plant which do not have the "bloom" on twigs and leaves. They have glossy, green leaves, and therefore do not appear as unusual as this form which has a generally grayish appearance.

Chapter 15

"SMALL" TREES TO PLANT WITH SHRUBS

Small-size trees go with shrubs just as butter goes with bread. They lend a difference in flavor, a difference in texture, and a difference in form to what might otherwise be a monotonous picture.

They may be combined with shrubs or used as an accent for shrubs in many ways, for instance:

in the back of a shrub border to lend height and also, perhaps, to screen an unsightly object that is sufficiently narrow so one or two trees will do the job;

as the back row for a windbreak, when the other row or rows are of shrubs;

near the front of a shrub border, at the end furthest from the house, to mark "finis" to the border;

as a transition between an evergreen windbreak and a shrub border where there is plenty of room and the planting is 25 or 30 feet wide;

as the center of a grouping of low shrubs, possibly to mark the outer corners of a property;

in a house planting, to add needed height at the house corners, to balance a shrub planting on one side of the entrance way, or to add height and silhouette to a long line planting of shrubs along one house wall;

to shade a terrace that is hedged or bounded by shrubs;

to add their fall color and winter silhouettes as a strong contrast to a shrub planting and to break the skyline;

as specimens, with shrubs framing the picture.

As you can tell, from reading the foregoing list, most of the situations described apply to small trees used with shrubs in a cultivated area. However, some also apply to small trees used with shrubs in a wild area. Therefore, in choosing the small trees to be included in this chapter I have selected some suitable for the wild garden as well as many to use with shrubs in the cared-for garden area.

The hardiness zone references, height figures and color descriptions are from the same sources as already are given in Chapter 14, page 144 so are not repeated here.

Please remember that many small trees may be cut to the ground when young and permitted to produce many stems from the ground. This would classify them as shrubs according to the very broad definition given in Chapter 2, page 2. The reverse also is true. Many plants which usually are called shrubs because they grow with many stems from the ground can be called trees, by that same broad definition, if only one of their many stems is permitted to grow.

The line of demarcation between tree and shrub is fine—and often, particularly in the matter of "large shrub" or "small tree" is a matter of personal opinion and therefore not worth quibbling about.

Now, let's consider the small trees available for use with shrubs. Alphabetically, according to botanical name, we have:

ACER (Maple)

Of the many maples that might be considered small trees, only two species are included in this book, because they often are planted with shrubs. They might be considered shrubs too, since they often are grown with many stems from the ground. In fact, nurseries may offer both "tree" and "shrub" forms.

Maples, as you undoubtedly know, are considered satisfactory trees to grow. Their leaves are attractive, with their several lobes; their flowers are not particularly conspicuous, but are followed by winged seeds, called samaras, which may be colorful. Many maples have leaves which turn color in autumn and are at the height of their glory at that time.

Acer ginnala (Amur maple). Zone 3 to part of Zone 2; 20'.

A very hardy maple, this has a densely branching, rounded form. The leaves, shiny, dark green, are small, about 3" long; have three lobes, the middle one much longer than the others.

The yellowish-white flowers, appearing in May, are not conspicuous but are fragrant, so that you smell them when near a tree in bloom and thus look for them. The numerous clusters, to 4" long and 1" wide, of two-winged samaras are handsome in late August to September as they turn bright red. They often are so numerous that a tree may exhaust itself by producing too many seeds each year. Amur maple foliage turns brilliant scarlet in autumn, and if you know where there is a hedge of this tree, or even a specimen, be sure to visit it to enjoy the exquisite coloring.

Amur maple may be used as a hedge, either clipped or unclipped, as a windbreak or as a specimen tree. With shrubs, it is best used in the background of a border. It thrives in almost any situation with little care.

Acer palmatum (Greenleaf Japanese maple). Zone 5; 20'-25'.

The heights given here rarely are reached by these trees in the northern states, but in the south and in Japan they are not unusual. This tree grows in rounded form and often a plant looks like a mound of foliage. Leaves are about 4" wide with from five to nine lobes. In the varieties and cultivars of *A. palmatum* leaves may be deeply divided or cut, but not in *palmatum* itself. The flowers, which are purple, appear in mid-May to early June. The fruits are the usual two-winged samaras, but it is unusual to see them on a tree, since most trees never fruit. Varieties and cultivars of *Acer palmatum* commonly found in the catalogs are:

Acer palmatum 'Atropurpureum' (Bloodleaf Japanese maple). Zone 5. Illustrated on Color Page II. If you like red-foliaged plants, this is one of the best. According to the color fan the foliage is closest to 5 R 3/7, though older leaves are even darker, but the same general tone. They remain the same color all season. Leaves are about 2¼" long, 2¾" wide.

The bloodleaf Japanese maple is best used as a specimen in a green lawn area or as an accent in a planting of lower growing shrubs with green leaves. It should never, never be planted near a red brick house.

Acer palmatum 'Dissectum' (Threadleaf Japanese maple). Zone 5. This maple has green

Acer ginnala, buds and open flowers, above;

,two-winged "samaras", which contain and transport maple seeds, below.

leaves, each divided so deeply that a segment is almost threadlike—hence the common name. This characteristic is lost when a plant is used in a border, but becomes an asset when the maple is used as the dominating plant with a few lower growing, glossy-leaved shrubs.

Acer palmatum 'Dissectum Atropurpureum' (see *A. p.* 'Ornatum', below).

Acer palmatum 'Ornatum' (Spiderleaf Japanese maple). From spring through the early summer months the leaves of this cultivar are red. Later they turn bronze with undertones of green. Leaves are delicately and very deeply cut so that the effect is "spiderlike." The branches tend to droop in "weeping" form, which gives the tree a graceful effect.

AMELANCHIER (Shadbush, Shadblow, Juneberry, Service berry, Bilberry, Showy Mespilus, Canadian Medlar)

Amelanchiers are at their best when situated at the edges of wooded areas, by the sides of streams or ponds where their white flowers reflect in water. They blend well with all other native shrubs. Though they seldom are used in cultivated areas, they look very much at home in such situations, in groupings with a few shrubs or as specimens at the ends of shrub borders.

Blossom time is late April or very early May and blooms may be fleeting. If the weather turns warm flowers may last only two or three days, while in cool weather they may last a week or longer. The berries which follow the flowers usually stay for only a short time, but for a different reason: birds love them. The smooth gray bark and bright autumn foliage colors make amelanchiers attractive anywhere.

Amelanchier × *grandiflora* (*A. arborea* × *A. laevis*) (Apple shadbush or Apple serviceberry). Usually about 10' but may grow to 25'.

Pale gray bark, dense foliage and narrow, upright growth characterize this tree. The newly opened leaves are purplish, the flower buds pinkish, but the flowers, though they may open faintly pink in color, soon fade to white. Flowers of this shadbush are larger than those of the others and are usually in bloom in early May. Edible fruits in early summer turn first red, then gradually black. Leaves turn yellow or orange in autumn.

Amelanchier laevis (Allegany or Alleghany serviceberry, Allegany or Alleghany shadbush or shadblow). Zone 5; Usually 15' or 20' but may grow to 35'.

Amelanchier, so at home by the water's edge in the wild, is equally effective in cultivated areas.

Upright growth with spreading branches and clusters of white flowers in late April are this tree's assets. The young leaves are pink, and the bracts which set off the flowers are red. In late June or early July the fruits color—bluish-purple to blackish-purple. Leaves turn yellow to red in autumn.

CERCIS (Redbud, Judas tree)

Small trees or large shrubs, the redbuds are dainty, delicate-looking plants with open form and very dark bark. They are native in the woods to Zone 5. They bloom in mid-May—at the same time as the flowering dogwoods, *Cornus florida*; and may be planted with them for a colorful effect. Do not, however, plant the pink-flowering dogwood with redbud as the flower colors clash. Seed pods of redbuds are shaped like those of edible peas, though narrower. They are at first pink, then turn tannish, then brown as they dry. Leaves are heart-shaped, turn from green to yellow in the fall.

In cold climates redbuds should be transplanted only in spring and purchased only with roots balled and burlapped.

Cercis canadensis (Eastern redbud, American redbud, Junebud, Salad tree). Zone 4; 30′.

The flowers are shaped like those of edible peas, appear to grow directly from the branches (though actually they are on little spurs that grew when the branch had leaves in the same places where the flowers now appear) and usually are produced on older wood. They are ⅞″ long, the same in width at the widest part, and 2.5 RP 5/10 (strong reddish purple) according to the color fan.

Cercis canadensis alba (White redbud, Whitebud). Identical with *C. canadensis* except for white flowers and a closer habit of growth. This variety is said to be not quite as hardy as *C. canadensis*. I have found just the opposite to be true as some of the plants of *canadensis* that I own die to the ground in severe winters but the white-flowered form never has done this.

Cercis canadensis 'Withers' Pink Charm', also listed as 'Pink Charm', has flowers colored 7.5 RP 5/12, strong purplish red. Otherwise it is identical with *C. canadensis*.

Cercis chinensis (Chinese redbud). Zone 5; usually about 20′ tall.

The Chinese redbud is not as hardy as the Eastern redbud—note the difference in northernmost hardiness zones as listed. It is tip-tender, that is the tips of the branches tend to be injured if the winter is severe, on the Michigan State University

Amelanchier laevis, flowers above; fruits below.

campus in East Lansing, which is in Zone 5b (that is the more southerly division of Zone 5). I live in the same part of the same zone and have had no difficulty wintering several small plants.

However, just to be on the safe side, it is better to grow this redbud as a shrub, with several stems, so that if one or two kill to the ground in winter

335

Cercis canadensis alba in flower. Notice heart-shaped leaves.

the others will be left to grow. Flower color is 2.5 RP 4/10, strong reddish purple, on the color fan. Blooms appear in mid-May.

CHIONANTHUS (Fringe tree, Old man's beard, Grancy graybeard, Grandfather graybeard, Graybeard tree)

Fringe trees are handsome small trees with quite large leaves that turn yellow in autumn. They are grown, however, for their fringe-like white flowers which appear about the beginning of June. Similar in appearance are the male and female flowers, though the male flowers are slightly larger. These blooms are borne on separate trees, according to sex. Female plants bear dark blue berries on long, thin drooping stems after the flowers are gone.

Fringe trees may be used in wide shrub borders, as specimens, or planted against large, high buildings. It should be remembered, however, that the leaves appear late in spring, unfolding just before the flowers, so that the early spring effect is of bare branches. Gardeners not acquainted with these trees should be warned against thinking they are dead because leaves have not yet appeared though those on most other trees and shrubs are partly grown.

Chionanthus retusus (Chinese fringe tree). Zone 5; 20', but usually less.

Leaves and flower clusters are shorter than in the native fringe tree discussed below, the petals of the individual florets ¾" long, the clusters 3" long. Leaves are more oval in form. The flowers appear a few days later than those of *virginicus* and the tree gives a more delicate effect in the landscape. It seems not to be quite as hardy as *virginicus*.

Chionanthus virginicus (White fringe tree, Native fringe tree, Flowering ash, Poison ash, Shavings, Snowflower-tree, White-ash, plus the common names given for fringe trees in general). Zone 5; 20'-25', though often less.

Native from New Jersey to Florida, this tree has large leaves turning yellow in fall, very fragrant white, fringe-like flowers with petals of each floret 1" long and a cluster of florets 4" long.

CLETHRA (White alder)

Clethra barbinervis (Japanese clethra). Zone 6 to Zone 5b; 30'.

Chionanthus retusus, fringe-like flowers.

A spreading, irregularly formed tree which often has several trunks, this also has brown, shredding bark. The flowers are white and fragrant, appearing in late July, thus making it the first clethra to flower. They are produced in clusters which are held on the tree in an unusual way—horizontally.

CORNUS (Dogwood)

The dogwoods are among the very best trees for use on home grounds. A glance at the list which follows will show that there are many worth-while dogwoods besides the well-known flowering dogwood.

Dogwoods grow small enough to use on a city lot, yet are equally effective on a large acreage. Branching habit is horizontal in most tree dogwoods, thus they have interesting silhouettes in winter. Foliage is dark green in most of them. Flowers are yellow, inconspicuous in the kinds that have ornamental bracts, which may be white, pink or reddish. Colorful fruits usually follow the flowers and autumn foliage color is outstanding in most tree dogwoods.

In cold climates tree forms of dogwood should be moved in spring only and purchased with roots balled and burlapped.

Cornus alternifolia (Pagoda dogwood, Umbrella tree, Alternate-leaved dogwood, Green-osier, Pigeonberry). Zone 5; 20′.

Chionanthus virginicus, flowers left, fruits right.

This tree grows naturally along the edges of woods and is prettiest when used with suitable shrubs in such a situation. The branches, greenish in color, are arranged in horizontal tiers and in irregular whorls, which gives the tree the shape of a pagoda. The winter pattern of these branches is particularly lovely. Leaves turn purplish in autumn. Flowers are greenish in clusters about 2 inches in diameter opening in late May and are followed by blue fruits borne on red stems. Damp soil and semi-shade are the chief requirements of this plant.

Cornus florida (Flowering dogwood, Arrow wood, Boxwood, False boxwood, Nature's mistake). Zone 5; 15'-25'.

This dogwood is one of the most popular of flowering trees because of its beauty and its adaptability. It is at home in any situation, from the edge of a woodland (which is where it grows wild from Massachusetts to Florida and westward) to a place of honor on the lawn or to part of the house planting on a 40' wide city lot.

The general effect of this dogwood is low and wide, because, under good growing conditions, a tree may spread to about 18'. If you compare this figure with the ultimate height figures given above you'll have a mental picture of the shape, so will realize that room should be allowed for this spread. Branches are arranged in tiers; grow horizontally.

Foliage is dark green, turning scarlet in autumn. What usually are called "flowers" are in reality white bracts coloring in mid-May around the inconspicuous yellow flowers in the center of the bracts. Bracts are notched, with the notched area usually pinkish or brownish (a result of cold injury during winter when the bract served as a bud scale). Bright red berries, borne in tight clusters, follow the flowers. Even brighter than the autumn color of the leaves, they contrast brilliantly with the foliage.

In winter the horizontal branches make a beautiful pattern against the sky (or a wall), while the flower buds, like little conical buttons, are prominent at the tips of the twigs. Birds frequently eat these buds so that there is little or no bloom the following spring.

Cornus florida 'Cherokee Chief' (Plant patent #1710). Although this cultivar is described in several catalogs as having "ruby red" bracts, the color fan shows them as 7.5 RP 6/12, deep purplish pink. They are slightly larger than those on most plants of *C. florida rubra.* This is a very nice pink dogwood with reddish coloring in the new foliage.

Although this cultivar and its white counterpart, listed below, are said to bloom when young, the word "young" is evidently subject to interpretation for my plant took 5 years from the time it was planted (2' to 3' high) to produce its first bloom and then presented me with a fine crop.

Cornus florida 'Cherokee Princess'. Like 'Cherokee Chief' this cultivar has larger bracts than the species but they are white. It also is patented.

Cornus florida 'Cloud 9' (Plant patent #2112). Definitely shrubby in form, without a leader (main shoot or trunk such as a tree has) this plant probably should be described in Chapter 14 but is listed here because it is a cultivar of *C. florida*. The bracts are white, much more rounded in form and borne more horizontally than those of *florida*. This plant is said to flower at an early age. I have seen only fair sized specimen stock so cannot vouch for the validity of this claim.

Cornus florida multibracteata (see *C. f.* 'Pluribracteata', described below).

Cornus florida 'Pendula' (Weeping dogwood). A "different" form of *florida*, this has branches which bend downward or "weep." It is best used as a specimen for an accent in a garden, with only low, ground-hugging shrubs around it. It looks very well drooping over a statue or a bird bath. I have seen it used in both situations. Do not depend on this dogwood for annual bloom. It is a shy bloomer at best.

Cornus florida plena (see *C. f.* 'Pluribracteata', below).

Cornus florida 'Pluribracteata' (syn *C. f. multibracteata, C. f. plena*) (Double-flowering dogwood). The bracts in this dogwood number from six to eight arranged in two rows, whereas *florida* has but four bracts in a single row. This tends to make the "double" form more showy than the single.

Cornus florida 'Prosser Red'. This cultivar is identical with *rubra* but has flowers deeper in color and more nearly true red.

Cornus florida rubra (Red-flowering dogwood). The bracts of this dogwood are not really red, but rose-colored. Otherwise the tree is identical with *florida* and exceptionally effective when planted with it.

Cornus florida 'Salicifolia' (Willow-leaved dogwood). The foliage of this cultivar is narrow, like that of a willow (*Salix*), hence the name 'Salicifolia'. Furthermore the whole tree is smaller than *florida*, with shorter branches, more twigs and a

Branch of Cornus florida in bloom. Flowers are tiny and may be seen in the center of the white bracts. For details of flowers see picture of Cornus mas in Chapter 14.

Cornus florida fruits.

more compact habit of growth. It does not grow as fast as *florida* either. The bracts are white; the fall foliage color is brilliant red.

Cornus florida 'Welchii'. A variegated form of *florida,* this has leaves which combine creamy white, green, and pink. The tree makes a handsome focal point in a garden because of the foliage colors. Flowers are sparse at best and the plant should not be grown for them. Foliage color becomes deeper in the fall. This plant is best set in light shade because the coloring may fade or the leaves "burn" when it is planted in a hot, sunny place.

Cornus florida xanthocarpa. This is the yellow-berried form of *Cornus florida,* like the species in every other way except berry color.

CRATAEGUS (Hawthorn, Haw, Thorn apple)

A group of small trees most of which are native over a large part of America; down the east coast from Quebec to North Carolina, westward to Michigan. Their form is dense, they are "twiggy"; branching habit is horizontal and shape "picturesque." Because of their shiny green leaves, close clusters of white (or pink or rose) flowers followed by red, scarlet, or crimson fruits, many hawthorns are excellent for garden use. Their thorns, which in some cases are an inch long, make them valuable for use as impenetrable hedges. They are useful in a border with shrubs, as tall plants in a house planting, or as specimens.

Crataegus 'Autumn Glory'. Zone 5; 15'-18'.
This tree is described as having a shapely head and deep green foliage, large clusters of white blooms in spring and immense clusters of brilliant red, giant berries in early autumn which remain on the tree well into winter.

Crataegus carrierei (see *C. lavallei*).
Crataegus coccinea (see *C. intricata*).
Crataegus cordata (see *C. phaenopyrum*).
Crataegus crus-galli (Cockspur Thorn, Pin-thorn, Newcastle Thorn). Zone 5; 40'.

A low, broad native tree (20'-30' spread) with flat top and horizontal branches, this flowers in late May. The glossy green foliage turns orange to scarlet in autumn, thus making this one of the comparatively few hawthorns with good fall color. Fruits, first green, then bright red, color in late October and stay on for most of the winter. They are hard, taste tart, and are inedible.

Because of its dense branching habit, this tree makes a good clipped hedge which will be impenetrable because of the long thorns.

Crataegus intricata (syn *C. coccinea*) (Red Haw, Scarlet Thorn). Zone 6, 12'-20' with the same spread.

This is a shrubby, rounded tree with a short trunk, up-curving branches, and yellow-green leaves in spring. These turn bright green in summer, tan in autumn and buff in winter. Flowers are white, appear in May and are followed in October by deep crimson, sweet, edible fruits.

Crataegus × *lavallei* (*C. crus-galli* × *C. pubescens*) (syn *C. carrierei*) (Lavalle hawthorn). Zone 5, 20'.

A spreading habit, clusters of white flowers in late May, leaves that remain on the tree longer than those of most hawthorns and turn bronze red in fall, and orange-red or brick red fruits in October distinguish this hawthorn from others. Fruits stay on all winter until February.

Crataegus mollis (Downy hawthorn). Zone 5; 30'.

Native from southern Ontario to Minnesota and South Dakota, southward to Alabama, Arkansas, and Oklahoma, this hawthorn has spreading branches which form a broad-topped crown. Leaves are dark yellow-green; flowers opening in early to mid-May are white with red disks; and fruit, which is larger than that of most hawthorns (an inch in diameter) and pear-shaped, is scarlet with thick yellow flesh, sweet to taste, ripe in August to September.

Crataegus monogyna (English hawthorn, Single-seed hawthorn, Haw bush, Hagthorn, Hag bush or tree, May bush, May bread, May bread and cheese tree or bush, Aglet tree, Fairy thorn, Glastonbury thorn, Hipperty Haw tree, Holy Innocents, Heg Peg bush, Moon flower, Peggall bush, Pixie pear, Quick thorn, Scrab, Scrab-bush, Shiggy). Zone 5; 30'.

This hawthorn is a shrub or tree with ascending branches and a rounded head. Its twiggy habit of growth and numerous thorns are the reasons it is so widely used for hedging purposes in England. Single white flowers in late May, red fruit in fall, are further characteristics. Fruits have only one seed, from which comes the botanical name "monogyna," which actually means "one woman," referring to the single carpel. The foliage of this hawthorn does not turn color in fall.

C. monogyna often is confused with *C. oxyacantha,* described below, but it is easy to tell them apart either in bloom or in fruit. When in bloom, *monogyna* has only one style in the center of the flower while *oxyacantha* has two; and when the trees are in fruit, *monogyna* has only one seed while *oxyacantha* has two.

Crataegus monogyna 'Stricta'. Zone 5; 30'. A columnar form of hawthorn, upright growing and extremely dense in habit, therefore useful in certain places in the garden. Unfortunately this cultivar seems to be quite subject to fireblight, a plant disease.

Crataegus × mordenensis 'Toba' (*C. succulenta × C. oxyacantha* 'Paul's Scarlet'). Zone 3; 20'.

This hybrid was introduced by the Dominion Experiment Station, Morden, Manitoba. It is hardier than *C. oxyacantha* 'Paul's Scarlet', the parent it resembles. Foliage is glossy; flowers are double, bright pink or deep rose, and fragrant. Fruits are half an inch in diameter and bright red.

Crataegus nitida (Glossy hawthorn). Zone 5 to part of Zone 4; 30'.

Rounded in form, densely branched, with glossy dark green leaves that are lighter on the undersides, white flowers in late May, and dull red 3/8" wide fruits coloring in October, this is a handsome hawthorn. Its leaves turn orange and scarlet in autumn and the fruits, while not bright in color, still are attractive against the snow for they remain on the tree throughout the winter and until early March (sometimes late March) of the following year.

This hawthorn is native from Ohio to Missouri and Arkansas.

Crataegus oxyacantha (English hawthorn, May, Quick, Quick-set-thorn). Zone 5; 15'.

A densely headed tree, rounded in form, with spreading branches which often touch the ground and leaves which do not turn color in autumn. White flowers are followed by small scarlet fruits in September to October. This species is planted all over England and is called "May tree" or simply "May" because it flowers late in that month. In the United States the varieties or cultivars of this species are more popular because many of them have double white flowers or pink or red blooms.

Crataegus oxyacantha 'Paul's Scarlet' (Paul's Scarlet Hawthorn). Illustrated on Color Page II. One of the most popular hawthorns because of its double florets, each 1/4" in diameter, borne in 1½" clusters and colored 7.5 RP 5/12, which the color fan describes as strong purplish red. In late May a tree in bloom is a lovely sight. When this hawthorn is used as a street tree, as it sometimes is in Europe, the entire street becomes colorful when the trees are in bloom.

Crataegus oxyacantha 'Paul's Scarlet', closeup of flowers.

Crataegus oxyacantha 'Paul's Scarlet', branch laden with blooms.

Crataegus oxyacantha 'Rosea Plena' has pale rose flowers, double in form.

Crataegus phaenopyrum (syn *C. cordata* of the catalogs) (Washington thorn). Zone 5, 30'.

Native from Virginia southward to Alabama and west to Missouri, this hawthorn blooms later than the others and certainly is one of the best. It has at least one interesting feature during each season of the year: in winter the dense, upright silhouette; in mid-June the white flowers borne in 4" diameter clusters, each floret 5/8" in diameter with green center; in summer the shining, densely packed green leaves; and in autumn both the orange-scarlet leaves and the small, bright scarlet fruits with which the tree usually is heavily laden in September and October.

Crataegus viridis (syn *C.* 'Winter King') Zone 5; 20'.

An introduction of Simpson Orchard Co. of Vincennes, Indiana this is described in the catalog of the company as follows: "A hawthorn with rather small, glossy leaves, silvery younger bark, only moderately thorny, white blossoms opening a few days later than Washington hawthorn, followed by masses of 3/8 inch orange-red fruits which normally persist throughout the winter. It is characterized by relatively disease-resistant foliage, freedom from blight, attractive silvery bark, and masses of orange-red fruits that do not soften or discolor from cold. This selection fruits well at an early age, and has not been difficult to transplant."

Crataegus 'Winter King' (see *C. viridis*).

Crataegus phaenopyrum, branch in bloom, above; closeup of flowers, below. Note long stamens.

Crataegus phaenopyrum, fruits.

DAVIDIA

Davidia involucrata (Dove tree). Zone 6; usually about 20′ high in that zone, though taller further south.

The handsome large, bright green leaves overlap one another and make this tree beautiful even without a flower on it. This is fortunate for, in many cases, gardeners have been disappointed in the lack of bloom or sparseness of bloom. While certain specimens are known to bloom every year, more do not flower until quite old and then have only a few flowers at irregular intervals.

When this pyramidal-shaped tree does bloom it is beautiful beyond words. In mid-May the flower bracts appear. There are two of these, one 6″ to 7″ long and the other less than half that length, both white. It is these, waving in the breeze, that give the tree its common name. Between the two bracts is the true flower, a ball-shaped, creamy-yellow, inch-wide mass of stamens. If any fruit forms it is pear shaped, green with purple "bloom" like a plum.

ELAEAGNUS

Small trees and large shrubs with interesting, sometimes handsome, foliage and fruits. Flowers are inconspicuous and this genus definitely is grown for either foliage or fruits or both and not for flowers.

Elaeagnus angustifolia (Russian olive, Oleaster). Zone 3; 20′.

The grayish-green foliage makes this little tree outstanding in any landscape. Flowers are tiny (3/16″ in diameter), 2.5 Y 9/9, brilliant yellow, according to the color fan, fragrant, so that you smell them from some distance away when, in early June, they perfume the air. Edible fruit, widely sold in Persian markets, also is yellowish, but covered with scales that appear silvery. This tree is very hardy, easily grown, adaptable to many soils and situations. One of my favorite foliage combinations is Russian olive planted with any of the purple-leaved plums.

EUONYMUS (Spindletree, Dagwood, Dogwood)

There are vine, shrub, and tree forms of euonymus. The taller shrubs may be grown trained to only one stem and called trees. The "tree" forms may be cut back to force several stems into growth and thus may be grown as shrubs. Several of the larger "tree-like" species are listed here with the

Elaeagnus angustifolia, flowers above; "olives" below. For closer view see next page.

Elaeagnus angustifolia, detail of flowers and leaves with silvery overlay.

close view of fruits.

small trees, for, whether grown in tree or shrub form, they are large enough to be used, as or in place of small trees. These plants are grown for foliage and fruit, not for flowers, because, in most species, these are inconspicuous.

Euonymus atropurpurea (Wahoo, Burning bush, Bitter ash, Indian arrow). Zone 5 to part of Zone 4; 25'.

The flowers are purple and appear in June, fruits are crimson and are showy in October when the leaves also are brilliant so that they appear "burning." This plant is native from northeastern America southward to Florida, westward to Montana, and usually is found growing along the banks of streams.

Euonymus europaea (European burning bush, Spindletree, Arrow-bean, Bitch-wood, Louse berry, Butchers-Prick-tree, Cardinal's cap, Death alder, Dog Timber, Dogbane, Dog tooth berry, European dogwood, Flower-ivy, Foul rush, Gaiter tree, Gattan tree, Hot cross buns, Ivy flower, Peg wood, Pincushion shrub, Pop corns, Prick timber, Prick wood, Skewer wood, Skiver). Zone 4; 20'.

The green, four-sided branches make this plant interesting even in winter. The flowers in mid-June are yellow-green and unpleasant to smell. Autumn foliage color is almost purple while the fruits, coloring pink on the outside in September and October, open to show the bright orange berries.

Euonymus europaea 'Aldenhamensis' (Aldenham spindle tree). Zone 4; 8' or more. Even more colorful than *E. europaea*, the dark green foliage turns reddish in autumn; the fruits are brilliant pink outside, opening to show bright orange berries. Fruits are borne on long stems and hang downward.

Euonymus europaea, fruits closed, partly open and open, disclosing seeds.

Halesia carolina, blossoms above; seed pods, below.

FRANKLINIA

Franklinia alatamaha (syn *Gordonia alatamaha*) (Franklinia). Zone 5; to about 6' in that zone, but to 30' further south.

In Zone 5 this tree lives, dying to the ground in severe winters but growing again from the roots the following spring. It does not flower because it never seems to make sufficient growth in a year to bloom. It flowers in Zone 6, though not as profusely as in Zone 7. It is desirable for its rarity, for the fact that its white flowers with conspicuous yellow stamens appear in September to October, and for the bright red and orange autumn coloring of its large leaves. Plant in full sun for the best autumn foliage color.

GORDONIA

Gordonia alatamaha (see Franklinia alatamaha).

HALESIA (Silverbell, Snowdrop tree, Bell-olive tree, Wild olive tree, Possum-wood, Tiss-wood)

Silverbells are native trees from West Virginia to Florida and westward to Texas. The common name refers to the flowers which are white, drooping, and bell-shaped, opening in mid-May on trees with an irregular habit of growth. This genus has no serious pests, a point in its favor. Silverbells should be planted close to the house or outdoor living room so their bells may be enjoyed. Blooms are not bulky enough to be effective at a distance. Seed pods are interesting, though not beautiful, much of the winter as they turn gradually from tan to brown. Foliage turns yellow in fall.

Halesia carolina (syn *H. tetraptera*) (Carolina silverbell). Zone 5; 30', but usually about 20'.

Flower buds are pinkish, "bells" are 3/4" long, 3/4" in diameter at the widest point, white with prominent deep yellow stamens. The fruit is a pod with from two to four wings. The leaves turn light yellow in autumn.

Halesia monticola (Mountain silverbell). Zone 6 to part of Zone 5; said to grow to 90' but usually seen as a small tree to about 30'.

This species has longer flowers, to an inch long, and fruits the same shape as *H. carolina*, but slightly larger. The tree is larger in every way than *H. carolina*, but has the same general form and the leaves also turn yellow in autumn.

Halesia tetraptera (see *H. carolina*, above).

HIPPOPHAË

Hippophaë rhamnoides (Sea-buckthorn). Zone 4 to part of Zone 3; 30', but usually about 12'.

Rarely seen in the United States, this small tree or large shrub is widely used in Europe, especially in park plantings. The first time I saw it, the cut branches laden with brilliant orange berries were being sold in the flower market in Aalsmeer, Holland in September. If not cut, berries remain on the plant until March.

The little tree has a rounded form, with branches quite widely separated. The leaves are gray-green on the upper surfaces, silvery below and shaped like those of the willow rather than our buckthorn (*Rhamnus*). Twigs are spiny. Male and female flowers are borne on separate plants, therefore plants of both sexes must be grown to insure berries. The blooms, which are inconspicuous, appear before the leaves in early April. The male plants grow more upright, the females more spreading in form. One male plant to half a dozen females is a good ratio to plant. The big clusters of 1/4" round bright orange berries which are fully colored on the female plants in September and remain for months are the prime reason for growing this plant.

ILEX (Holly)

Hollies grow in both tree and shrub forms and the genus includes both evergreen and deciduous species. Some hollies are hardy in the north, and these are the ones included in this book. The inconspicuous white flowers of the two sexes are borne on different plants so that a male plant should be set in the same hole as a female plant (and kept pruned to minimum size) or a male plant should be set out for every four to eight females. This male plant should be within about 40' of the female plants to insure pollination. In the north it is best to move hollies only in the spring and the evergreen sorts always should have earth balls around the roots. Evergreen hollies are beautiful in the background of either deciduous or other broad-leaved evergreen shrubs or as specimens.

Ilex opaca (American holly). Zone 5; 40', but not in Zone 5, where it usually grows only to about 15'.

From Massachusetts southward and west to southern Ohio and Illinois, Missouri and Oklahoma, this is the native holly. It is evergreen and is the holly you think of when you think of Christmas.

Ilex opaca, branch of female flowers, above; closeup of female flowers, below. Note pistils.

347

Ilex opaca, male flowers above. Note stamens in center. Berries, below.

American holly has light gray bark, a dense, horizontal branching habit, and large trees are pyramidal in form. The leaves have sharp, saw-toothed edges and the female plants bear tiny white flowers in early June followed by bright red berries in October, which will remain in good condition until the following April. There are many cultivars of this holly, some better than others for a given locality. If you wish to buy American hollies you should go to a nursery specializing in them and see them in berry the autumn before buying them.

American holly needs well drained, fertile soil and, in the north, a place protected from wind and the hottest winter sun so that the leaves are not "winter-burned." Good drainage is essential to hardiness of evergreen hollies in the north.

Ilex opaca cultivars:

There are many of these cultivars in the catalogs, most of them in those of the nurseries in Zone 7 and not hardy in the north. The holly expert I know best is Paul Bosley, Sr. of Bosley Nurseries, Inc., Mentor, Ohio. He has collected hollies in the wild for many years and he grows vast numbers of them in the nursery. Here is his recommended list (for his climate in Zone 6a):

Female cultivars: '1-B', 'Arden', 'Big Red', 'Christmas Carol'*, 'Cumberland', 'Farage', 'Hedgeholly'*, 'Jingle Bells', 'Menantico', 'Miss Helen', 'Old Heavy Berry', 'Red Velvet', 'Yule'*.

Male cultivars: 'Kentucky Gentleman', 'Santa Claus'*, 'Young Flowering Male'*.

(The cultivars marked with asterisks are his idea of the very best for his area.)

In his latest letter he calls my attention to something interesting: "The New Jersey experiment station has had many hollies in the orchard and at the present time say that if they had to choose one variety for our rugged climate it would have to be Hedgeholly. This is a very dense, self-branching type of plant and therefore its name, although we have found that the public have misconstrued the name. They feel that if they want a single specimen this is not the plant for them, where in reality we wished to convey the idea that it was dense growing and suggest that it would make a hedge."

Mr. Bosley has forgotten that he sold me a plant of Hedgeholly about ten years ago. As you know, I live in Zone 5b, but that plant is now a fine specimen about 10' high.

Ilex opaca xanthocarpa has yellow berries instead of red ones. It is particularly pretty when used with any of the red-fruited hollies as the berry colors contrast beautifully.

348

Koelreuteria paniculata, seed pods.

KOELREUTERIA

Koelreuteria paniculata (Goldenrain tree, Varnish tree, Pride of India, China tree). Zone 5, 20'-30'. Illustrated on Color Page VI.

This is one of the few flowering trees with yellow flowers. They are small, bright yellow with an orange-red blotch at the base of each, and are borne in early summer (mid-July) in large, upright clusters. The fruits which follow are bladder-like pods, yellowish or tannish in color. The tree has spreading branches and is flat-topped. It is not considered long-lived, but is worth planting anyhow. From observation of many full-grown trees in assorted northern states where hardiness is a factor, I think that the supposed lack of longevity is one of those myths started in "the year one" and copied by uninformed writers ever since.

LABURNUM (Golden-chain)

Laburnums belong to the pea family and have yellow flowers shaped like those of edible peas borne in long clusters, much like those of wisteria vines. These blooms open in late May or early June and last about two weeks. Growth habit is upright and narrow; leaves are gray-green and graceful. In both England and Scotland I have seen long arbors made of laburnums pruned to shape—an idea which might be used in gardens here. One is illustrated on Color Page IV. Laburnums do not change foliage color in autumn. All parts of laburnums are poisonous to eat.

Laburnum alpinum (Scotch laburnum). Zone 4; 30'.

This is hardier than the more commonly listed *L. anagyroides*. It also is taller, more upright in form, has larger, darker leaves and longer flower clusters which appear a little later. Fruits are pods, like pea pods but larger. Flowers, fruits and seeds are poisonous. Gardeners living in Zone 4 should buy this species and this one only.

Laburnum alpinum 'Pendulum' (Weeping golden-chain). A grafted, pendulous form of *L. alpinum*, this is useful where a weeping laburnum is desired—usually as a specimen tree.

Laburnum anagyroides (syn *L. vulgare*) (Golden-chain, Common laburnum, Bean tree). Zone 5; 20'.

All the comparative remarks made above about the Scotch laburnum apply in reverse, to this species. Only if you cannot obtain either of the other laburnum species described here should you grow this one.

Laburnum vossii (see *L. watereri* 'Vossii', below).

Laburnum vulgare (see *L. anagyroides*, above).

Laburnum × watereri (*L. alpinum × L. anagyroides*) (Waterer laburnum). Zone 5, 30'.

This hybrid has larger flowers (¾" long, ½" diameter, in clusters 8" long) of a deeper color (7.5 Y 8/12, vivid greenish yellow) and has a denser habit of growth than *anagyroides*. It is a better

Laburnum watereri 'Vossii', pendant flower clusters.

Laburnum watereri 'Vossii', seed pods.

MAGNOLIA

Magnolias are grown primarily for their flowers in the northern states, while in the south many species are grown as well for their evergreen foliage. Blooms are large, may be white, various shades of pink and pinkish-lavender, or reddish to red-purple. Flowers are followed by oddly-shaped fruits (see illustrations) which, when they split open to show the bright red seeds inside them, are conspicuous for a week or two. Magnolias have no autumn foliage color, but the velvety buds which become apparent during winter are interesting to watch then, when so many other shrubs show no signs of having made preparations to bloom another year.

Magnolias have fleshy roots, easily broken and bruised. For this reason buy only balled and burlapped plants and move them in spring, preferably when in bloom, for two reasons: so you can tell the flower color and because they move more readily at that time. When roots are dormant and plants are moved, the roots often decay and the decay may spread to the rest of the plant. So, pay no attention to the neighbors who accuse you of being cruel to move a plant in bloom.

Magnolia alexandrina (see *M. soulangiana* 'Alexandrina').

Magnolia glauca (see *M. virginiana*).

Magnolia kobus. Zone 6; 30'.

Although this plant is a tree, it is more often seen growing with several stems from the ground. Dark, glossy, green leaves are lighter on the undersides. White, 5" diameter blooms have a faint purple line on the outsides of the petals, near the base

plant in many ways. This probably is the reason it is more widely listed in the catalogs. Seed pods are borne in clusters 4½" long, are each 2" long and ⅜" wide. They are colored 10 Y 7/9, strong greenish yellow, at first, turning gradually to tan.

Laburnum watereri 'Vossii' (syn *L. vossii*) (Voss laburnum). Usually listed as an "improved" form of *L. watereri,* this has longer flower clusters, to 18"-20" in length. It is otherwise similar to the species, except for denser growth.

MACLURA

Maclura pomifera (Osage-orange, Bois d'arc, Bow-wood, Hedge tree). Zone 4; 60', but usually seen as a pruned hedge to about 20'.

This tree has a vigorous, dense growth and many twigs, plus heavy thorns. All of these characteristics make it admirable for hedging purposes or as a hedge background for lower-growing shrubs. Leaves are glossy and change to yellow in autumn. Fruits, at their best in September, look like big, dull green oranges with very rough surfaces. They have an unusual and delightful aroma. They are used for ornament and also are excellent moth repellents. Since male and female flowers are borne in June on separate plants, it is imperative that plants of both sexes be planted in order to insure fruits.

Maclura pomifera, fruit.

of the flowers and are fragrant. They appear in late April to early May, early in the magnolia parade. The fruits are the usual odd-shaped pods which split to show the red seeds inside in early autumn.

There is a hardier variety of this plant, *Magnolia kobus borealis,* which can be grown in Zone 5.

Both of these plants take years to flower, sometimes as many as twenty. For this reason, a hybrid magnolia, *M.* × *loebneri* 'Merrill' is described below.

Magnolia lennei (see *M. soulangiana* 'Lennei').

Magnolia × *loebneri* 'Merrill' (*M. stellata* × *M. kobus*) (syn *M. stellata* 'Dr. Merrill' of the catalogs). Zone 5 to southern part of Zone 4; 20'.

This hybrid is one of the "newer" magnolias and apparently it is going to fill a very definite need. It is listed here because it blooms early yet grows rapidly and blooms when young, offering a substitute for *M. kobus* and its variety, listed above.

'Merrill' has blooms slightly larger than those of the star magnolia and, like *M. kobus,* is fragrant, only not as much so as its one parent.

Magnolia rubra (see *M. soulangiana* 'Rubra').

Magnolia rustica rubra (see *M. soulangiana* 'Rubra').

Magnolia × *soulangiana* (*M. denudata* × *M. liliflora*) (Saucer magnolia). Zone 5; 25'.

Fragrant, 3¾" wide flowers open in early May before the leaves unfold. These are cup-shaped or saucer-shaped, as you prefer, and are usually white suffused with pinkish or purplish (7.5 RP 4/11). Depending on the weather at the time of bloom, flowers may last only four or five days or they may be in good condition for two weeks.

Following the blooms, slender pods grow to be rather like short cucumbers in shape. These gradually turn brown and then split to reveal bright red seeds inside. When the pods have split open and there are many of them on a tree, the effect is of a second, short season of beauty in early fall.

Growth habit may be either that of a tree or shrub depending on early training. When grown with several trunks, a plant may be as wide as it is high. Leaves are quite large—to 8" long.

Magnolia × *soulangiana* 'Alba' (syn *M. s. amabilis*) has especially large, fragrant white flowers.

Magnolia × *soulangiana* 'Alba Superba' (syn *M. s.* 'Superba') is another cultivar with larger flowers than the parent.

Magnolia soulangiana, above; single flower and buds, below.

351

Magnolia ×· *soulangiana* 'Alexandrina'. Earlier to bloom than the saucer magnolia, this cultivar has 6″ diameter blooms, white inside, flushed with rosy-purple on the outside.

Magnolia × *soulangiana* 'Lennei'. This cultivar has the deepest colored flowers of any of the saucer magnolias—they are white inside but deep, deep rosy-purple outside and are borne in late May, almost at the end of the magnolia season of bloom.

Magnolia × *soulangiana* 'Rubra' (syn *M. rustica* and *M. rustica rubra*). Flowers of this variety look much like those of 'Lennei', but are lighter in color. They may be 6″ in diameter and appear earlier than those of 'Lennei'.

Magnolia × *soulangiana* 'Superba' (see *M. s.* 'Alba Superba').

Magnolia stellata (Star magnolia). Zone 5; 20′. Illustrated on Color Page I.

When grown in a sheltered place, this will be one of the first magnolias to flower. It blooms when just a few feet high. It is a tree with a dense, rounded growth habit but often is grown with

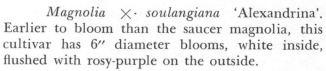

Magnolia soulangiana, closed seed pod. Resemblance to chick is purely coincidental. Compare with open pod of M. stellata, left.

Magnolia stellata, flower above; open seed pod with seeds displayed, below.

several stems like a shrub. Buds are 7/5 RP 9/2, pale purplish pink according to the color fan. The flowers are white, double, star-shaped and fragrant, the outsides of the petals tinged with the same color as the buds. Blossoms grow to 5″ in diameter when fully open. They appear before the leaves, about the middle to the end of April.

Leaves are small compared with those of other magnolias and rather narrow. Following the flowers come the twisted, 2″ long fruits, rather like small cucumbers. When ripe, these split open disclosing bright red seeds.

Leaves of this magnolia change color in fall, becoming yellow or bronze.

Magnolia stellata 'Rosea' (Pink star magnolia). Buds are pink and flowers are flushed pale pink on the outsides of the petals. They fade to white, however, as they age.

Magnolia stellata 'Rubra'. Flowers of this variety are a deep, purplish pink and this deeper color makes the plant more effective in the landscape than the paler 'Rosea'.

Magnolia stellata 'Waterlily'. Larger flowers and faster growth are the distinguishing characteristics of this cultivar.

Magnolia virginiana (syn *M. glauca* and generally listed this way in the catalogs) (Sweetbay, Swampbay, Indian bark, Swamp laurel, White bay). Southern part of Zone 5; 60′ in the south, but only about 25′ and shrublike in the north.

In late May this magnolia has fragrant, white flowers to about 3″ in diameter and these continue to appear sometimes until August.

Evergreen in the south, this magnolia is deciduous in the north. Leaves are glossy on top and have a grayish "fleece" beneath. As one of the common names implies, this tree grows and thrives in the wild in swampy locations and in moist soil. However, it does not absolutely need such conditions.

It will grow in drier soil, but if you plant it in such a situation, it is a good idea to leave a large, cup-shaped depression around the plant when setting it out. Thus you can easily give it extra water in this cup.

MALUS

Malus includes apples and crabapples. For the purposes of this book, we consider only the crabapples grown for their flowers. There are dozens of varieties and cultivars of flowering crabapples, one lovelier in bloom than the other. I consider only one of them, described in Chapter 14, a shrub. The rest are trees of varying heights and, since it

has taken a whole book to describe them (*Flowering Crabapples* by Arie F. Den Boer, published by the American Association of Nurserymen and available from the Association), it is obviously impossible to describe them adequately in this chapter, especially since this is a book primarily about shrubs.

Just because I have not described them, do not neglect flowering crabapples when you are planning groupings of small trees with shrubs. It is best to see flowering crabapples in bloom before purchasing any with flower colors other than white, because some of the colors do not combine well with the flowers of many shrubs.

OXYDENDRUM

Oxydendrum arboreum (Sourwood, Sorrel tree, Elk tree). Zone 5; may grow 75′ high, but usually is only 20′-25′ high in the north.

This plant forms a narrow pyramid; has lustrous, leathery leaves turning brilliant scarlet-red in fall. This bright color is its outstanding characteristic. Flowers are not pure white, but whitish; appear from the middle of July through October. They are small, shaped like miniature urns, and are borne in slightly drooping clusters.

Oxydendrum grows naturally in regions with acid soil. Therefore, unless your soil is acid, it is well to replace it when planting this tree.

PRUNUS

This genus includes peaches, plums, cherries, almonds, and apricots. In addition to those species grown primarily for their fruits, there are many others grown primarily for their flowers. These are the ones listed below. In height these species vary from medium-sized trees to small trees down to shrubs, which are described in Chapter 14. Many of the *Prunus* species are spectacular when in bloom.

Prunus × *blireiana* (*P. cerasifera* 'Atropurpurea' × *P. mume*) (Blireiana plum). Zone 6 to part of Zone 5; 25′.

This rounded, densely branched tree blooms in early May. Flowers are light pink, double, and an inch in diameter, against red-purple leaves. Small, edible fruits which are the same color as the leaves and therefore not conspicuous, are borne later in the season. This hybrid stays in flower longer than many of the other flowering plums.

Prunus cerasifera (Cherry plum). Zone 4 to part of Zone 3; 20′.

A small tree, this sometimes grows as a shrub with several stems from the ground. It is dense and

Prunus cerasifera 'Newport', flowers against dark foliage.

twiggy; sometimes has thorns. The leaves are light green, flowers are white or pale pink, appearing in late April, fruits are yellow or red, about an inch in diameter and delicious to eat. This species is not nearly as well known or as often used in gardens as its purple-leaved forms described below.

Prunus cerasifera 'Atropurpurea' (syn *P. pissardii, P. cerasifera pissardii*) (Pissard plum). Zone 4 to part of Zone 3; 15′ to 25′. Little pink flowers in late April, ¾″ in diameter, are followed usually by a few tiny edible plums which are the same color as and often hidden by the leaves. This is one of the satisfactory, colorful plants for use where such foliage color is needed. I am particularly fond of this plum, or one of the others with similar leaf color, planted with Russian olive, which has gray leaves.

Prunus cerasifera blireiana (see *P. blireiana*).

Prunus cerasifera 'Newport'. Slightly lighter leaf color than the Pissard plum and slightly greater hardiness are characteristics of this tree. It grows 10′-12′ high and has white to flesh pink flowers. It is a hybrid, developed at the State Fruit Breeding Farm, Zumbra Heights, Minnesota and is hardy there.

Prunus cerasifera 'Nigra'. This has very dark purple leaves, which have earned it the common name of Black Myrobalan plum. The flowers

Flowering branch of Prunus cerasifera 'Atropurpurea', below.

are pale pink, single, and about ½" in diameter.

Prunus cerasifera pissardii (see *P.c.* 'Atro-purpurea').

Prunus cerasifera 'Thundercloud' (Ruby tree). Growing a little taller and a little broader than 'Newport', this cultivar reaches 12'-15' in height. It has white to pink, single flowers and few fruits.

Prunus 'Hally Jolivette'. Zone 5; Ultimate height is probably about 12', but the tallest specimen I have seen was 8' high.

This densely branched, rounded little tree has pink buds, double white flowers 1¼" across over a long period of time, sometimes from mid-April to mid-May. This, of course, is a decided asset, as is also the fact that it starts to flower when very young.

Prunus persica (Peach). Zone 5; 25'.

Almost everyone knows the common peach with its pink, single flowers in late April and its yellow or red fruits.

The cultivars listed in the catalogs as "flowering" or "ornamental" peaches have been bred and are grown for flowers rather than fruits. They may have white, varying shades of pink, carmine, or bright red flowers, which may be single or double in form, depending on the precise name of the cultivar. These are beautiful when in bloom and many a new gardener (and an experienced one as well) has exclaimed over them. However, they are not the most desirable of flowering trees for they are subject to all of the diseases which make the common peach the subject of frequent and regular spraying by orchardists. The flowering peaches also are not "strong growers."

If you are willing to spray as necessary to control pests, and to prune the trees well, right after the flowers drop, to force as much new growth as possible, then the flowering peaches will delight you with their blooms. They grow as small trees or large shrubs and are best placed in the back of the border as they do not look well for some time after pruning is finished.

Prunus pissardii or *pissardii nigra* (see *P. cerasifera* 'Atropurpurea').

Prunus serrulata (Oriental cherry). Zone 6; 30'. Illustrated on Color Page III.

A wide-spreading tree which usually grows with the main trunk divided into several trunks just a few feet above ground level, this has handsome red bark and single white flowers appearing in early May. Its cultivars are hardy in Zone 6 and the southernmost part of Zone 5, but there only in protected places. There are many cultivars, one of the most popular of which is called 'Kwanzan' in the catalogs but is properly named 'Sekiyama'. This is one of the varieties used around the Tidal Basin in Washington, D.C. It grows to 18' in height and is upright in form. Young leaves are copper-red. Flowers are deep pink and double, 2½" in diameter.

Prunus serrulata 'Amanogawa'. Zone 6; 20'. The important character of this cherry, as far as the garden is concerned, is its tall, narrow growth, called "fastigiate." It has semi-double, light pink flowers. It is best placed in a spot where ice and snow will not collect on it in winter and gradually spoil its shape.

Prunus serrulata 'Shirotae' (also written Sirotae') (Mt. Fuji cherry). Zone 6; 30'. This lovely cherry is grown for its double white flowers which are fragrant. It is considered the finest of the cherries with either semi-double or double blooms.

Prunus subhirtella (Higan cherry, Rosebud cherry, Equinox cherry). Zone 6 to part of Zone 5; 25'-30'.

This is one of the earliest of the Oriental-type cherries to bloom, since the flowers appear in late April. They are light pink and single, about 1½" in diameter, and are borne before the leaves appear. They are so profuse that they practically hide the branches of the tree.

Prunus subhirtella 'Autumnalis' (Autumn Higan cherry). If this cherry were a rose or a raspberry it probably would be advertised as "ever-blooming" for it not only has flowers in spring, but occasionally blooms during summer and usually, but not always, has a few blossoms in autumn. These are semi-double, pale pink to white, ¾" in diameter.

Prunus subhirtella 'Pendula' (Japanese weeping cherry, Weeping Higan cherry). Illustrated on Color Page III. Long, slender leaves that stay green far into the fall, and the low, broad form with pendulous branches make this a picturesque tree during the entire year. However, it is no tree for a small yard as it will eventually grow 25' wide as well as 25' high. The form usually seen has single, mauve-pink flowers which appear before the leaves. When in bloom it looks like a flowering fountain. There is also a double-flowered form, usually listed in the catalogs as *Prunus subhirtella* "roseaplena" but properly named 'Plena Rosea'.

Prunus subhirtella 'Pendula', showing weeping form.

Prunus virginiana 'Shubert' (Shubert choke cherry). Zone 3; 30'.

An introduction of the Oscar H. Will Nurseries, Bismarck, North Dakota, this differs from the species by the changing color of its leaves as they age. When they unfold they are green. About the beginning of June they change and become deep reddish-purple and remain this color the rest of the summer and early autumn. The flowers are white, in clusters; the fruits are red, turning to reddish-purple.

PTELEA

Ptelea trifoliata (Hop tree, Wafer-ash, Shrubby trefoil). Zone 5 to part of Zone 4; 20'.

Native from Ontario and New York to Florida and westward to Minnesota, this tree will grow in a moist, shady location, though it usually is found on rocky slopes or in areas with gravelly soil.

It has small, greenish flowers in large, drooping clusters in May and early June. Because these appear after the leaves, they are not conspicuous. The fruits, which are small, round flat disks, similar to those of elms, are also in clusters. These stay on the tree all summer.

Leaves, if held to the light, will show dots. They are borne in groups of three, as the specific name of the tree implies. Both leaves and fruits have a strong, disagreeable odor when crushed. Some people say the smell is like that of hops, as one common name of the tree suggests. Both bark and fruits are bitter to taste.

ROBINIA

Robinia hispida 'Monument' (Upright rose-acacia). Zone 4 to part of Zone 3; 10'-12'.

The same foliage, flowers, and "moss"-covered seed pods as *Robinia hispida,* a shrub, are characteristic of this tree form. It is adapted to any type of soil, is pretty in the shrub border or used as a specimen and is covered with pendant clusters of flowers colored 5 RP 6/10, deep purplish pink, according to the color fan. These appear in late May to early June and are shaped like the blooms of edible or sweet peas. They are followed by pea-shaped pods which are hairy or mossy outside.

SALIX (Willow)

Salix caprea (Goat willow, because goats are said to be fond of the catkins, Sally, Sally withy tree, Great sallow, Palmer, Palm willow, Palm tree, Sallow, Black sally, Geese and goslings, Geese and gullies, Goose chicks, Gosling). Zone 5; 25'. Illustrated on Color Page I.

The handsomest of the pussy willows because the male plants have the largest catkins, this tree must be given plenty of room as it is vigorous in growth. The finest largest pussies for forcing in water indoors are the result of cutting this tree to the ground every few years or of pruning it drastically every year.

Like all willows, it will grow in swampy as well as dry areas.

SORBUS

The genus *Sorbus* includes two small trees that may be used with shrubs:

Sorbus americana (syn *Pyrus americana*) (American mountain-ash, Dogberry, Quickbeem). Zone 3; 30'.

Native from Labrador to Manitoba and southward to the Great Lakes area and the mountains of North Carolina, this little tree has a rounded head, compound leaves which turn orange and red in autumn, white flowers in late May, and clusters of orange-red fruits in October. It grows naturally in partly-shaded situations where the soil is moist. Since it is weak-wooded, it should be set where winds will not break the branches.

Sorbus decora (syn *Pyrus decora*) (Showy mountain-ash). Zone 2; 30'.

Sorbus americana, berries.

Stewartia pseudocamellia flowers, above.

This native of southeastern Canada and north-eastern United States used to be considered a variety of *S. americana* and is much like it but with larger and more showy fruits. Small white flowers appear in late May and clusters of half-inch fruits turn bright red in early fall. Foliage, like that of *S. americana*, turns to brilliant hues in autumn.

STEWARTIA (Stuartia, Malachodendron)

Stewartia pseudo-camellia (Japanese stewartia). Zone 5; 30′.

This species is not quite as hardy as *S. ovata* listed in Chapter 14 among the shrubs. Its white flowers are slightly smaller, to 2½″ in diameter, look like single camellias; but more cup-like in form. Unlike camellias, they are slightly fragrant. Because they appear in early July, when few other trees are blooming, they make this tree particularly desirable.

The tree itself is pyramidal in shape, with bright green leaves appearing early in spring and turning a dull purplish in autumn. Additional seasonal interest is provided by the red, flaking bark on older plant parts.

STYRAX (Storax, Snowbell)

Styrax japonica (Japanese snowbell). Zone 5; 10′-30′.

Styrax japonica blooms, below.

357

Sometimes this grows as a tree or sometimes as a wide-spread shrub with a flat top. Room must be allowed for the width, which may be twice the height when the plant is mature.

In early June the white, ¾"-diameter "bells," which are the flowers, appear, hanging conspicuously from the undersides of the branches, underneath the dark green leaves which are on the upper sides of the same branches.

This species prefers a moist but well drained soil in partial shade in a protected place. It is prettiest when planted so that one can look upward into the flowers.

Styrax obassia (Fragrant snowbell). Zone 6 to part of Zone 5; 10' to 30'.

Ascending branches rather than the horizontal ones of *S. japonica*, and early June-blooming fragrant, white flowers which grow erect or almost erect in clusters make this species different from the preceding one. The flowers often are hidden by the extra-large leaves. This species is said to be less hardy than *S. japonica* but I have not found it so.

SYRINGA (Lilac)

Syringa amurensis japonica (syn *S. japonica* of the catalogs) (Amur lilac, Japanese tree lilac). Zone 5; 25'-30'.

While this lilac usually is seen growing with one trunk as a small tree, it also may be grown with several stems as a large shrub. It is particularly useful in the garden because it blooms from mid-June to early July, after all the other lilacs have finished flowering.

It has creamy-white flowers in large heads or groups of clusters, to 8" or 9" in diameter, a single cluster being 6" long and 3½" across. The individual florets are only ⅛" in diameter and smell like those of privet rather than those of other lilacs.

VIBURNUM

Some of the species of this large genus grow into very large shrubs or small trees. They are therefore included in this chapter rather than in Chapter 14, with the shrubs.

Viburnum lentago (Black-haw, Nannyberry, Sheepberry, Black thorn, Nanny plum, Sheep paw, Sheep haw, Sweet berry). Zone 2; sometimes to 30' but usually nearer to 20'.

Blooming white in late May and early June, growing usually in moist woods or along the banks of streams, this is a native viburnum that is vigorous in growth. Left to itself it is a shrub, with branches first growing erect, then arching over to touch the ground, where they sometimes take root. However, it can be trained to a single stem (tree form) if so desired.

The flowers are borne in flat clusters and are followed by edible, blue-black fruits in August. Foliage is shining green, turning to purplish red in autumn. The fruits are ¼" in diameter, in drooping clusters to 2½" or 3" in diameter. They will be eaten by the birds in winter if not sooner.

Syringa amurensis japonica in flower.

Viburnum lentago, bloom cluster.

Viburnum prunifolium (Northern black-haw). Zone 4 to part of Zone 3; 15'.

This grows naturally in the same types of places as *V. lentago* but adapts better than it to drier soils. It has perfect white flowers in flat clusters, 3½" to 4" in diameter in late May, followed by edible blue-black berries on red stalks in September to October. The leaves are dark green, turning wine red in fall. It too is normally a shrub but also may be trained to a single trunk to grow in tree form.

Viburnum sieboldii berries. These are eaten by birds as fast as they ripen.

Viburnum prunifolium, blooming branch, above; details of fertile flowers, below.

Viburnum sieboldii (Siebold viburnum). Zone 5; usually about 20', but sometimes to 30'.

If it were not for the unpleasant odor of the leaves of this viburnum, given off sometimes in the fall, it could be recommended for use near a house. As it is, it should be used only at a distance and, because of its size, usually as a specimen to begin or end a border.

It has an interesting branching habit; rich green leaves to 5" and 6" long, turning red in autumn. Creamy white flowers borne in large, flat clusters to 5½" in diameter in late May to early June, are followed in summer by fruit clusters of the same diameter. The fruits turn progressively from 2.5 Y 9/9, brilliant yellow to 5 R 3/7, dark red, to blue black, darker than any blue on the color fan, starting in late July and becoming their final color in September. The little stalks on which the individual fruits are borne are red. A cluster in the process of changing color may consist of fruits of all three colors at once and is both beautiful and interesting to see.

359

Xanthoceras sorbifolia, young plant flowering.

XANTHOCERAS

Xanthoceras sorbifolia (Chinese flowering chestnut, Shinyleaf, Yellowhorn). Zone 6 to part of Zone 5; 25′.

This little tree is not easy to transplant, but it is worth while trying to grow. It likes an open loamy soil and full sun. The form is upright.

The white clusters of "feathery" flowers are borne in somewhat the same manner as those of wisteria vines. They appear in late April to early May just as the leaves are unfolding. The petals have blotches at their bases, first yellow, later red. The flowers are followed in August to September by green burs that look like those of horse chestnuts, but with shiny, black seeds inside instead of nuts. The leaves, which are shiny and dark green, do not change color in autumn, though they remain on the tree until late in fall.

Chapter 16

QUESTIONS MOST FREQUENTLY ASKED ABOUT SHRUBS

The questions that people can manage to ask about shrubs are so many and so varied that a book could be written about them alone. But there are certain questions which are asked over and over again with such regularity that, even though the answers may be elsewhere in this book, it seems sensible to give them here.

THE question is **Where can I buy _____?** And you can insert after the word "buy" the name of any shrub you please. Usually this question addressed to me is prompted by an article I have written, but it also may be because of an article that someone else has written or because of a shrub seen somewhere. The name of the shrub may or may not be correct and often identification is necessary before a source can be given.

THE question has accounted for one third of all my reader inquiries and is the reason for the inclusion of the Buyer's Guide Chart in this book (see Chapter 11) and for the listing, in Chapter 11. of possible ways to find shrub sources.

Now I know from experience that you would much rather have me give you a source for a shrub than find one for yourself but I am, at least for the time being, out of the question-answering business. For almost 20 years, as garden editor of *The Detroit Times,* I answered reader inquiries. After the *Times* ceased publication I answered questions for 15 months from the readers of *Flower Grower, the Home Garden Magazine.* This is obviously more question-answering than most people do in their lifetimes and certainly qualifies me for retirement from that phase of the horticultural field. So, DON'T write and ask me questions, for I have no intention of answering them.

Instead read those in this chapter and read this book. You'll probably find your shrub question answered in the appropriate chapter. I would like to use the word "undoubtedly" instead of "probably" but I know that there is, in the office of one large company dealing in horticultural products, a whole filing cabinet filled with questions that are not answered in any horticultural literature. So, maybe I missed answering one or two—

After "Where Can I buy _____?" the next most frequently asked question is **Why doesn't my shrub BLOOM?** And, once again, you can substitute the name of any shrub for the word "shrub" in this sentence. The first time I read this question I wondered how I could, unacquainted with the particular specimen of shrub, and at far too great a distance from it to go and see it, know why it didn't bloom. However, time and repetition of the same question, with or without descriptions of circumstances, have taught me that YOUR shrub doesn't BLOOM because:

(1) You haven't given it time to reestablish its roots. You *expect* flowers the first season after planting and this is just plain ridiculous. If the shrub *does* bloom in spring after fall planting or in fall after spring planting, consider these flowers a bonus. Most shrubs don't bloom so soon. Some take two years or even more to grow enough roots to absorb enough chemicals to produce enough leaves to manufacture enough food to produce flowers. So be patient! And, if you just can't wait, give the shrub a handful of superphosphate spring and fall for a year or two; perhaps supplying this chemical most closely associated with flowering will do the trick. It often does.

(2) Or, the shrub doesn't get enough sunlight to bloom. Time and time again, the description of the location of the shrub reveals this.

(3) Or, the shrub has been moved from place

to place too frequently for it to have time to reestablish its roots, etc. (see number 1). One reader had, in the interests (so she thought) of inducing flowering, actually moved a shrub five times in five years!!

(4) Or, you've pruned the shrub at the wrong time so that the flower buds have been pruned off. This requires some explanation. Some shrubs begin to form next year's buds (for next year's flowers) within a month from the time they bloom. Thus, by autumn the buds for many of the early-spring-flowering shrubs are all ready to open when the weather permits. If you prune these shrubs *in autumn* you are pruning off the buds for the following spring's flowers, so how can the shrubs bloom? These same shrubs which flower on wood grown the previous year, if pruned *in early spring,* will not bloom because flower buds are gone.

The gardeners who don't recognize flower buds when they see them and remove them from the plant because they think the buds aren't doing their job or are something else probably should be mentioned here. One reader removed all the buds on her rhododendron in late April because she said they hadn't opened so why leave them on. The rhododendron, of course, would have bloomed six weeks later, right on its regular schedule. Another bright woman cut off the stems of flower buds on her small palm (grown as a house plant) because she thought they were insects. The fact that they were obviously growing from a stem which was growing from the plant didn't penetrate at all.

(5) Or, there were heavy frosts in your area in late spring and these nipped the flower buds on your shrub even though the rest of the plant was uninjured. This happens most often with shrubs like *Abeliophyllym distichum* or *Rhododendron mucronulatum* or forsythias which flower very early.

Number 3 in the list of questions most frequently asked is **Which shrub should I plant to have flowers all season?** The answer to this question is "none." There is no shrub that will survive in northern gardens that blooms from early spring to frost. There are, however, three shrubs that I can recommend as having extra-long seasons of flowering. These are: *Potentilla fruticosa, Abelia grandiflora* (glossy abelia) and a polyantha rose named The Fairy.

You will find more detailed descriptions of these shrubs in Chapter 14, but the potentilla blooms from June until frost, with various shades of yellow or white flowers, the abelia from mid-June to frost with small pink flowers, and the rose, which also has small pink flowers, but in fair-sized clusters, from early to mid-June on.

The potentilla has most flowers in June and a good crop again in September with some always on the shrub during the rest of the season. The abelia really has no peak of bloom—it just has some flowers all during its blooming time. The rose blooms in "bursts." It covers itself with flowers which last a week or more, then forms new buds (meanwhile producing no flowers) then bursts into bloom again and so on during the summer. The first killing frost in my garden always catches my dozen bushes laden with buds ready to open, which, in a milder climate, they would have a chance to do.

Which shrub will bloom in a dark corner never reached by light? None. All plants with green leaves need some light to live. If, instead of "light" the word "sunlight" is meant, that changes the answer. For there are shrubs that grow without sunlight if only they have sufficient light. The two shrubs I have found most tolerant of subdued light are *Ligustrum obtusifolium regelianum* (Regel's privet) and *Hydrangea quercifolia* (oak-leaved hydrangea). If you cannot grow one or the other of these under your conditions of light you cannot grow any shrub. Better cover the soil with interesting stones or with gravel (with heavy building paper underneath) and install some sort of garden feature—statue, little fountain—and make the area attractive without any plants.

Which shrubs need no pruning? If you plant the right shrubs in the right places none of them need pruning except for occasional removal of a dead branch or pruning for renewal—that is to make the shrub young again. But if people persist in being too lazy to think before they plant and plant tall-growing shrubs where they should plant low-growing ones and wide-growing shrubs where they should plant narrow-growing ones and so on, innumerable shrubs will need pruning.

When is the best time to prune shrubs? Assuming that pruning is necessary (because, unless there is a sound reason to prune, a shrub is best left alone) right after the shrub flowers is the best time to prune it.

My husband gives all our shrubs a "butch" haircut every spring. This makes them look terrible all year. What can I do to stop him? (1) Hide the pruning shears and forget where they are when he wants them. (2) Read him page 42, Chapter 6 or, better yet, get him to read it himself.

How often should I fertilize my shrubs? If they are growing well and flowering each year, don't bother to fertilize at all. If you want a shrub to grow larger more quickly (remembering that every shrub will grow only to the limits of its kind and no more), fertilize in late February or early March using a double handful of any 10-6-4 fertilizer. Scatter this around on top of the ground underneath the spread of the shrub branches but not touching any shrub part. If the soil is workable, scratch the fertilizer lightly into the upper half inch. If it isn't, just scatter the fertilizer anyway. Spring rains will wash it into the soil where shrub roots can reach it. If you wish, you can repeat this fertilization in mid-May.

What soil preparation is needed for shrubs? Unless your soil is clear sand or heavy clay or you intend to plant shrubs which require a soil reaction different from that of your soil, the only preparation necessary is digging a hole large enough to contain the shrub roots (spread out as they naturally grow if they are bare or large enough for the earth ball if they are balled) plus room to allow the roots to start new growth in loose soil. Most shrubs grow in a wide variety of soils and need no special soil preparation.

What kind of fertilizer and how much shall I mix with the soil when planting a shrub? No fertilizer at all should be added to the soil at planting time. Add any kind of organic matter you have at hand (compost, granulated peat moss, rotted manure, etc.) and mix it thoroughly with the top soil removed when you dug the hole. This mixture then is used under and around the plant roots as you plant the shrub. Do not add any fertilizer to this mixture.

My shrub has bugs on it. I sprayed it with (here insert the name of any fungicide) and nothing happened. What is wrong? Or, reversing the same problem: My shrub had spots on its leaves and I sprayed (or dusted) it with (here insert the name of any insecticide) and nothing happened. What is wrong? What is really wrong in both cases is that the owner of the shrub didn't bother to read the label on the substance used to find out which shrub troubles it would control. A material formulated to control fungi which cause plant diseases will not kill insects nor will one intended to kill insects control plant diseases.

There are, of course, mixtures of insecticides and fungicides intended to control both and there are a few materials which control some pests in either category. But, generally speaking, the gardener who does not take the time and trouble to READ THE LABEL CAREFULLY and FOLLOW THE DIRECTIONS ON IT EQUALLY CAREFULLY has no one but himself to blame when the material does not do what he expects it to.

It is simply amazing how many people, at any sign of any trouble on any plant, simply grab the first material at hand without a glance at the label and think they've done something when they douse the plant with it. Depending on the particular material, they may have done more harm to the plant than good.

Why do you always use those awful Latin names when you write about shrubs? In the first place I don't think they're awful. Awful means full of awe and I am not awed by anything as simple to conquer as Latin names.

If you will look through any phone book you will find family names of a length and pronunciation to put Latin names of plants to shame. I don't think it is any harder, for either you or me, to memorize the plant names than the names of our friends and the people with whom we deal even if they happen to be long and, perhaps, hard to pronounce.

Perhaps you don't realize it, but you already *are* using and know a good many Latin names of shrubs. Did you ever hear a magnolia called anything but a magnolia? No. Well, that's its Latin name. Hydrangeas are hydrangeas in either Latin or English. So are rhododendrons. And so on. So, you see you know more Latin that you think you do and you aren't awed by those names, are you?

If I didn't use the Latin name you would never be sure which shrub I was naming or be able to buy it—for the same shrub may have a dozen common (English) names in as many parts of the country, but it has only *one correct* Latin name the world over (though sometimes it is difficult to determine which one is correct at the moment and occasionally botanists change a Latin name which has been in existence for hundreds of years). So, you see, I use the Latin names for *your* benefit.

Do I have to learn the Latin names of plants? It is very hard for me to do so. How do you learn them?

You don't have to learn anything if you don't want to. Certainly no one ever will force you to learn Latin names of plants. It is, however, helpful to know them when you wish to buy the plants and when you are talking about plants with other people, especially those in the profession of horticulture.

As to finding it "hard," I am going to tell you what I have told the members of every landscaping class I ever have taught. If I told you you were stupid, too stupid to learn Latin names, you'd resent it. So, I tell you you are not stupid, you are smart and can learn anything you decide you want to learn.

How do I learn the names? If I buy a plant I've never seen before I write the name of it on a wooden plant label and after the plant is set out I stick the label in the ground in front of the plant (it also has a permanent metal label hidden among its branches). As I weed or work around the plant during the season I read and spell the name out loud to myself, meanwhile taking a good look at the plant's form, foliage, etc., so I'll know it when I see it elsewhere. By the end of the season I know the name and the plant to which it belongs.

These are the baker's dozen of questions most frequently asked about shrubs. In addition there are three personal questions that I have answered so often it seems as if they must be among those most frequently asked so I will once more answer them here.

1. Which is your favorite shrub and flowering tree? As to favorite shrub the answer depends on whether you mean an evergreen or a deciduous shrub. My favorite evergreen shrub is Japanese andromeda (*Pieris japonica*) because it is interesting all year: in spring with fragrant white flowers, in early summer with the bronze new leaves, in late summer with brown seed pods and in winter with the flower buds already formed against its dark green leaves.

My favorite deciduous shrub is *Kolkwitzia amabilis* (beauty bush) because it is trouble free, has such masses of tiny pink flowers that its sight is a joy, and has continued interest in the fluffy gray seed heads.

My favorite flowering tree is a tropical one—Jacaranda, almost any Jacaranda with blue flowers, but particularly *Jacaranda mimosifolia* with its beautiful fine leaves.

Actually, as each tree or shrub blooms it is my favorite for the moment at least.

2. Do you grow all the shrubs you write about? (This question usually reads "plants" instead of "shrubs," but the answer is the same in either case.) Most of them I either am growing or have grown. The others I have observed in the gardens of friends or studied in botanical gardens, nurseries or other commercial establishments. I find it difficult to write about any plant I have not at least seen: you will be able to tell with no difficulty, I believe, which ones I do not know first hand because I write "is said to have—" or "is said to be—" instead of "has" or "is" when I describe it.

3. How large is your garden? How many shrubs do you grow? (The second part of this question sometimes reads "evergreens," sometimes "plants," but one way or the other is asked again and again.)

Six acres, but I just bought a 70-acre farm!

The last time I counted shrubs was the year before last and then, counting 60 Weller's box as one plant and a whole group of Oregon holly grape as one, and so on, I arrived at a figure slightly over 1000. But there also are over 400 evergreens on the place, most of them in windbreaks, and thousands of bulbs, perennials and so on. In other words I have plenty of work to do.

From the variety of even these few representative questions (and there were over 26,000 addressed to the garden department of *The Detroit Times* the last full year of its publication) you probably realize that readers are humans with wide interests and great curiosity. I have lived with readers for a good many years, rejoiced with them ("It is wonderful that you have been able to bring your Jacobinia into bloom for the fourth time. My limit so far is two years. What did you do that I should know about?"), commiserated with them ("Too bad that your lilac succumbed to scale insects. Cut it to the ground, fertilize and water well and perhaps new shoots will grow from the roots."), asked their advice ("Has any reader ever attempted to move an entire garden? If so, how did you go about it?"), questioned their sanity (a man from Canada sent an eight-page, handwritten letter telling me how to fertilize vegetables with discarded tomato soup cans), and gotten mad at them ("How could you and your husband be so stupid as to burn all the grass raked from 2 acres when you might have composted it?") and time and time again been amused by them. But I've never been bored by any reader's inquiry.

The readers, in turn, have told me their garden troubles and sometimes personal troubles, have sent me Christmas cards and "get well" cards, seeds, plants, insects for identification and have criticized what I have written or omitted. They have addressed me as "Dear Sir," though I am female, "Gentlemen," though I am singular, "Dear Isabel," though we never have met, "Chère Madame," (French-speaking, Canadian readers), "Deah Editah" (an Alabama reader), and misspelled my last name in countless ways. I am always amazed to see so many new misspellings.

However, the salutation I like best, used by a few readers the first time they have written me but by many more after we have corresponded, sometimes for years, is "Dear Garden Friend."

INDEX

Minor references to shrubs and trees are not indexed. This index refers to the main listings and includes both botanical and common names as well as general topics.

"f" following a page reference means that text or pictures continue on following page or pages. Other symbols and conventions are explained on pp. 4, 5, 8, and 146.

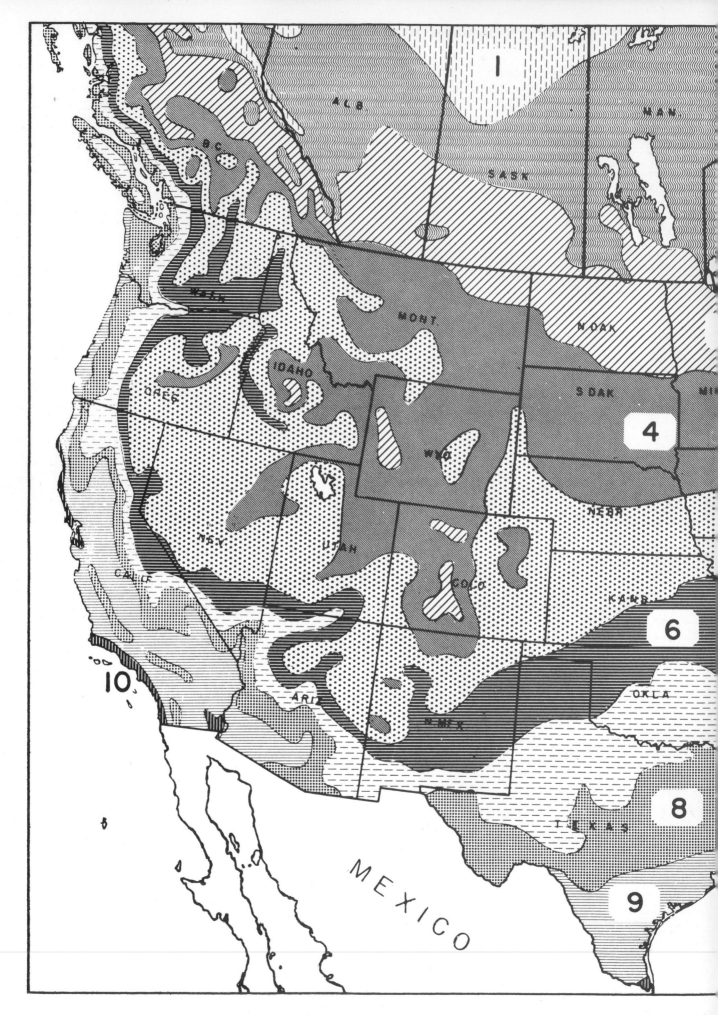

PLANT HARDINESS ZONE MAP